AT SEA
AGAINST THE SOVIET FLEET

AT SEA AGAINST THE SOVIET FLEET

The Evolution of U.S. Navy Operational Intelligence in the Cold War

BRYAN H. LEESE

NAVAL INSTITUTE PRESS
Annapolis, Maryland

Naval Institute Press
291 Wood Road
Annapolis, MD 21402

© 2025 by the U.S. Naval Institute
All rights reserved. No part of this book may be reproduced or utilized in any form or by any means, electronic or mechanical, including photocopying and recording, or by any information-storage and -retrieval system, without permission in writing from the publisher.

Library of Congress Cataloging-in-Publication Data

Names: Leese, Bryan H. author
Title: At sea against the Soviet fleet: the evolution of U.S. Navy operational intelligence in the Cold War / Bryan H. Leese.
Description: Annapolis, Maryland: Naval Institute Press, 2025. | Includes bibliographical references and index.
Identifiers: LCCN 2025011837 (print) | LCCN 2025011838 (ebook) | ISBN 9781682472026 hardcover | ISBN 9781591147015 ebook
Subjects: LCSH: United States. Navy—History—20th century | Soviet Union. Voenno-Morskoĭ Flot | Military intelligence—United States—History—20th century | Cold War—Military intelligence | Vietnam War, 1961-1975—Military intelligence
Classification: LCC VB231.U54 L44 2025 (print) | LCC VB231.U54 (ebook)
LC record available at https://lccn.loc.gov/2025011837
LC ebook record available at https://lccn.loc.gov/2025011838

♾ Print editions meet the requirements of ANSI/NISO z39.48-1992 (Permanence of Paper).
Printed in the United States of America.

9 8 7 6 5 4 3 2 1

All maps created by Chris Robinson.

The views expressed in this book are those of the author and do not reflect the official policy or position of the Department of the Navy, the Department of Defense, or the U.S. government.

To Betsy, Hannah, and Maris:
whose love, acceptance, resilience, and encouragement
are a gift beyond what I deserve

and

for the Navy Intelligence professionals toiling behind
the scenes to deliver the message

CONTENTS

List of Illustrations   ix
Foreword   xi
Preface   xv
List of Acronyms   xxi

Prologue   1

I. **THE VIETNAM WAR: INSTITUTIONALIZING SHIPBOARD OPERATIONAL INTELLIGENCE**   17
    1. The Integrated Operational Intelligence Center   19
    2. Adapting the Intel Center   43
    3. Air Combat and New Thinking about Targeting   61
    4. Learning and Adapting   78

II. **THE VIETNAM WAR: ADAPTING TO NAVAL WAR**   97
    5. A Close Blockade   99
    6. A Distant Blockade, in All but Name   120

III. **DECENTRALIZING**   153
    7. To Not Be Surprised   155
    8. OSIS Revolution to Opintel Evolution   172
    9. OSIS and Ship Opintel Evolve   187

IV. **FORMALIZING**   201
    10. Shipboard Tactical-Decision Support   203
    11. Formal "Two Squares" Effort   216
    12. A Period of Evolution   233
    13. "Selling" Opintel: Reinforcing and Embedding Mechanisms   249
    14. Observations   263

Epilogue: Afloat, at Last 282

Conclusion 297
Notes 305
Selected Bibliography 389
Index 431

ILLUSTRATIONS

Figure

1.1 CVA Integrated Operational Intelligence System (IOIC) spaces   20

Maps

1 Southeast Asia, theater orientation   31
2 A comparison of U.S. versus DRV radar coverage, 1968   65
3 Southeast Asia theater, Market Time surface-barrier patrol areas, 1966   101
4 The Mekong River delta   110
5 The northern Pacific operating area, 1975   130
6 The Mediterranean theater, 1968   154
7 The North Atlantic and Norwegian Sea area of operations   211

Photographs

1.1 Camouflaged RA-5C Vigilante of Reconnaissance Attack Squadron 13 (RVAH-13)   21
1.2 Checking the Vigilante's Camera System   22
1.3 Two-station stereo comparison viewer (SCV)   26
1.4 Sailors in USS *Saratoga*'s EDP   27
1.5 North Vietnamese SAM crew   38
2.1 U.S. Air Force Ryan AQM-34L Firebee drone "Tom Cat"   50
2.2 PH3 Robin "Lobster" Hartford "goes dark"   52
2.3 Mission planning, CVIC, OZ Division, *Saratoga*   54
2.4 Squadron AI delivers the mission event brief   56
3.1 Mikoyan-Gurevich MiG-21PF "Fishbed-D"   66
3.2 U.S. Navy A-4E Skyhawks   75

5.1 U.S. Navy River Patrol Boat (PBR) crew conducting an inspection   106
5.2 Vice Admiral Zumwalt with members of his NAVFORV staff   107
5.3 Captain Rectanus and his Da Nang First Coastal Zone officers   108
5.4 Operation Sea Float ammunition pontoons   111
5.5 Commander Jack Graf, USN   113
5.6 USCGC *Point League*, after forcing ashore a North Vietnamese trawler   119
6.1 YP3V-1 Orion buzzes a submarine   123
6.2 P-3 Orion sensor operators   127
6.3 Soviet missile-range instrumentation ship (SMRIS) *Marshal Nedelin*   137
7.1 Vice Admiral Richardson with Chief of Naval Operations Admiral Thomas Moorer on board the USS *Little Rock*   162
7.2 Fleet Ocean Surveillance Information Facility (FOSIF) Rota's Watch Floor   169
8.1 Soviet Tupolev TU-95 "Bear" reconnaissance plane   185
11.1 Naval Intelligence Command change of command   217
11.2 "SheShark," Commander Laurel Hargan-Wessman   230

FOREWORD

In this masterful book Capt. Bryan Leese explores the untold story of how people, machines, and ideas helped solve major operational and strategic problems for the world's most powerful navy, just as the Cold War threatened to go hot . . . and the United States became embroiled in a major regional conflict. This was a largely unseen revolution in naval warfare, one that harnessed the emergence of high-grade intelligence capabilities in the fleet at sea and critically for the aircraft carriers of the Cold War. It is based on some remarkable, highly adept research, combining personal experience with extensive archival research, a critical assessment of existing literature, and above all, a wealth of firsthand testimony gathered from key practitioners. These contacts were critical to developing a rounded understanding of complex events long shrouded in secrecy. Like all the best history, it speaks to the present and offers rich rewards to those who have to think through the implications of the latest dramatic shifts in the age-old balance between attack and defense at sea and the role of maritime power in national policy and strategy.

The shift from a centralized national intelligence to gathering and processing on board carriers was driven by the increased pace of naval warfare in the supersonic age, with rising threats from Soviet bloc submarines, aircraft, and surface combatants armed with large, ship-killing guided missiles, along with the emergence of new equipment that expanded the ability of ship-based intelligence operators to master the threat environment and senior officers who demanded more information. Intelligence specialists quickly developed these capabilities, feeding the admiral's appetite for more and better information.

A new type of intelligence specialist evolved as technical capabilities expanded. This would be taken further in the digital era, as processes became faster and equipment significantly smaller.

Not only did these developments make a major contribution to the preservation of peace between the superpowers, but they enabled the West to dominate the world ocean, exploiting the reality that it was only at sea that the United States/NATO alliance had clear superiority over the Soviet Union and its allies. Onboard intelligence enabled the U.S. Navy to operate significantly further forward, to challenge the defensive bastions where the Soviet Union hid its submarine-based nuclear second-strike capability, exposing the inferiority of their systems. Onboard intelligence gave admirals the confidence to enter regions where Soviet submarines and land-based air and missile systems were effective, harnessing the potential of the then-new Tomahawk cruise-missile system to neutralize tactical targets.

This book is not confined to "historical" methods; it reaches into the strategic studies and the wider war-studies repertoire to address institutional and international dimensions to analyze complex interlinked processes. The discussion of Navy "culture" across the various domains—one in which constant competition enriched the development of systems, ideas, and careers—ensured a war-fighting service remained engaged and evolving through the more peaceful 1970s, laying the groundwork for success. The Soviet Union could not compete with this dynamic development, and rigid command systems, predigital technologies, and economic stress brought the Cold War to a peaceful end. Maintaining that edge going forward will require similarly pioneering efforts to integrate intelligence as process and product, ever more closely into the decision-making at all levels. The same might be said of scholars working on earlier eras. In the nineteenth century a rush of new technology transformed the oceanic battlespace and the ability of navies to impact events on land, as steamships, undersea telegraph cables, and then radio compressed the seas and linked commanders afloat to headquarters ashore in time for the cataclysm of

1914. Historians of war have always needed to master technology, while practitioners need a better grounding in the past experience of their profession—as a reservoir of wisdom. This superb book offers a timely answer to those needs.

ANDREW LAMBERT FKC, FRHistS
Laughton Professor of Naval History,
King's College London

PREFACE

It might also be said that amateurs study strategy, professionals study logistics, and those who really know study intelligence.

—MICHAEL HANDEL, *Intelligence and Operations*

A February 2017 sunrise in the eastern Mediterranean Sea began this account of the U.S. Navy's afloat operational-intelligence evolution. On the gray horizon, closer than one wants, rode the 1960s-era Russian Federation Navy (RFN) *Kashin*-class guided-missile destroyer RFN *Smetlivy*. She had spent the night jockeying for position, USS *Philippine Sea* blocking her as she tried to penetrate the defensive screen of the aircraft carrier USS *George H. W. Bush*. Despite her forty-eight-year age, armed with eight SS-N-25 Switchblade (range seventy nautical miles) anti-ship cruise missiles, *Smetlivy* was still a tiger, a fast ship designed to go into harm's way against the U.S. Navy. She required constant surveillance; a dedicated team of intelligence professionals working in several of *Bush*'s intelligence spaces tracked her. The operational intelligence provided from those spaces created a common intelligence picture supporting operations across the six ships of the *Bush* strike group, the Sixth Fleet, and the U.S. Navy's global naval operations.

I leaned against the weather-deck railing, watching *Smetlivy*. I reflected on an early December 2016 conversation with Commodore Andrew Betton, commander of the Royal Navy's newly formed HMS *Queen Elizabeth* carrier strike group. He had been observing part of a wargame from *Bush*'s intelligence spaces. Betton had asked why the U.S. Navy created a decentralized shipboard operational-intelligence process. It seemed less efficient, he opined, than a centralized shore-based process that broadcasted intelligence to afloat units. My answer had been unsatisfactory, forgoing the *why* for the *how*, delving into the technicalities of how we conduct operational intelligence—what the U.S. Navy calls "Opintel." I could not explain why we had spent seventy years developing the Opintel process the way we did.

Nevertheless, here we were in the twenty-first century, conducting power-projection and intelligence operations similar to those conducted when I'd enlisted twenty years earlier. These were the same operations the Navy had performed since the 1970s and the Cold War. Despite almost fifty years of career guidance that Navy intelligence officers must master, I still did not understand how my vocation has come to be this way.[1] Mastering Opintel's systems and tradecraft did not equate to understanding its role. Part of the poor understanding comes from a lack of knowledge about how afloat Opintel evolved within the Navy.

The understanding could not be found only in exploring the technology; my rambling answer to Betton showed the inadequacy in that approach. No, the answer lay in how Navy Intelligence, the shore and afloat intelligence organizations, evolved within an environment of constant change fueled by computer technology. Opintel, to the Navy, is not just an acronym for operational intelligence; it represents the evolution of practices and priorities as well as an organizational philosophy and purpose for Navy Intelligence. As I pondered the past, I began to consider the future: Naval warfare is changing, and Opintel must change with it. Without understanding how we have arrived at the Opintel organization of today, how can we best plan for organizational change in the future? It was there, on the weather deck of *Bush*, that this book began.

A few volumes look at U.S. Navy Intelligence. Two in particular provide insight into Navy-intelligence organization, though much of shipboard Opintel historiography is missing from both. After thirty years of research, in 1996 U.S. Navy captain Wyman Packard published his 498-page book, *A Century of U.S. Naval Intelligence*. The late Packard's excellent reference remains a valuable resource, but it lacks any substantive analysis of shipboard Opintel evolution.[2]

The second title I reference, *The Admirals' Advantage*, has been the most thorough study of Navy Opintel since its publication in

2005, having been sponsored by three consecutive directors of Naval Intelligence (ONI).[3] Authors Christopher Ford and David Rosenberg relied on ONI's 1998 Opintel Lessons Learned Symposium as a primary source for their exploration of several recurring themes important to our present study: The application of technology, increased fusion of all intelligence sources, direct support to the commander, and the importance of high-quality personnel successfully frame their discussion of an evolving, problem-solving intelligence organization valuable to the decision-maker.[4] *The Admirals' Advantage* focuses on the strategic aspects of Navy Intelligence—tracking Soviet SSBNs (submarines with ship-submersible ballistic nuclear missiles), the operational success of the shore-based Ocean Surveillance Information System (OSIS), and support of the Reagan-era maritime strategy, the Maritime Strategy. *Admirals' Advantage* lightly touches on shipboard Opintel processes and organizational structures, pointing out that Navy intelligence grew in credibility after operating at sea "elbow to elbow" with the Navy's warfighters.

I was further aided by a number of other monographs and source materials. Norman Friedman's *Network-centric Warfare* (2009) does an excellent job filling in any information gaps regarding technology developments. Other works examining the relationship between technology and U.S. Navy organizational change include Trent Hone's excellent *Learning War* (2018), which shows the evolution of fighting doctrine during the World War II, incorporating observations Thomas Hone, his father, had made in his *History of the Office of the Chief of Naval Operations* (with Curtis A. Utz, 2020) and *Power and Change* (1989).[5] Another unique source of shipboard organizational and cultural insight is drawn from digital copies of ship "cruise books"—a type of yearbook commemoration of the deployment assembled and published by the ship's crew as a memento. My study has benefited immeasurably from each of these sources.

I have chosen to focus *At Sea against the Soviet Fleet* on the Cold War period spanning 1960 to 1980 because interviews conducted with retired U.S. Navy intelligence officers and enlisted personnel showed this to be a significant evolutionary period for Opintel. The 1960s and 1970s saw the introduction of revolutionary computer innovations into the Navy and the Navy's intelligence-gathering practices. These technological revolutions were followed by periods of evolution, when resulting informal organization changes were consolidated within the organization. The Vietnam War and the rise of the Soviet Navy during this dynamic period meant change was "hot and fast," as each side struggled for comparative advantage over the other. The rapid innovation and organizational adjustment driven by state-on-state competition provide a framework for this book.

In collating my research, I found the challenge to be achieving a well-balanced account of the recent past. Only thirty years have passed since the end of the Cold War, and most of the archives required for exploring shipboard Opintel are still classified. Additionally, information security classifications posed a challenge. To safeguard the origin of critical information, I discuss intelligence collection and products in general terms. For example, signals intelligence (SIGINT)— comprised of electronic intelligence (ELINT), communications intelligence (COMINT), and foreign-instrument signals intelligence (FISINT)—is referred to as "signals intelligence" or SIGINT with no specificity.[6] In this historical narrative I refer only to the declassified documents' general intelligence-collection domain (space-based, for example) or the actual collection sensor (the Corona satellite system, for example). This book avoids naming intelligence sources, methods, and product details, focusing instead on processes, people, and organizational changes.

Many who participated firsthand in the Navy's Cold War Opintel evolution are still alive. Having the ability to interview over thirty of them was amazing. For context, interviewees read sections of my doctoral thesis, on which this book is based.[7] To write this book I made use of several private archives as well as U.S. Navy and national archives. I extend my deepest gratitude to Rear Adm. Thomas Brooks, USN (Ret.), Capt. "Nels" Litsinger, USN (Ret.), and Vice Adm. Jake Jacoby, USN (Ret.). During the course of my four-year study several invaluable participants passed away: the loss of Capt. Robert Tolle, USN (1936–2019), and photographer's mate third class (PH3) Robin Hartford, USN (1953–2021), underscores the urgency of capturing the Cold War generation's remembrances.

Inspiration for this book came in many forms and from many people. I express my deepest thanks to Capt. Peter Swartz, USN (Ret.), Cdr. David Winkler, USN (Ret.), PhD, Col. Daniel Burghart, USA (Ret.), PhD, and Col. James Marchio, USAF (Ret.), PhD, for their sage advice and constant support. I appreciate Laura Waayers and the staff of the Naval History and Heritage Command's Operational Archive for their assistance. I also thank Professor Andrew Lambert, Dr. Huw Dylan, Dr. Tim Benbow, and Dr. Tom Hone, each of whom took the time to examine my work.

ACRONYMS

Acronym (pronunciation)	Definition
1350 (thirteen-fifty)	unrestricted line air intelligence officer
1630 (sixteen-thirty)	restricted line intelligence officer
ASCM (ass-cam)	anti-ship cruise missile
BuPer (beau-pers)	Navy Bureau of Personnel
C2 (see-two)	command and control
C2W (see-two-w)	command-and-control warfare
C3 (see-three)	command, control, and communications
CAGAI (cag-a-eye)	carrier air group air intelligence officer
CARDIV (car-div)	aircraft carrier division
CIA (see-eye-a)	Central Intelligence Agency
CIC (see-eye-see)	Combat Information Center
CINC (sink)	commander in chief
CINCPAC (sink pak)	commander in chief, Pacific
CIP (sip)	common intelligence plot
CNO (see-n-o)	Chief of Naval Operations
CO (see-oh)	commanding officer
COMINT (com-int)	communication intelligence
COMSEC (com-sec)	communications security
COP (kop)	common operational picture
CRUDESGRU (crew-des-gru)	cruiser destroyer group
CSG (see-s-gee)	cryptologic security group or aircraft carrier strike group (in 1990s)
CTF (see-t-f)	commander task force
CV (see-vee)	aircraft carrier, fixed wing

CVIC *(civick)*	Aircraft Carrier Intelligence Center
CWC *(see-w-see)*	composite warfare commander concept
DIA *(d-eye-a)*	Defense Intelligence Agency
DISUM *(die-sum)*	daily intelligence summary
DNI *(d-n-eye)*	director of Naval Intelligence
DRV *(dee-r-vee)*	Democratic Republic of Vietnam or North Vietnam
ECLIPS *(e-clips)*	Enhanced Calculator Link Processing System
ELINT *(ee-lint)*	electronic intelligence
FICFACPAC *(fick-fac-pack)*	Fleet Intelligence Center Pacific Facility (Subic Bay, PI)
FICPAC *(fick-pack)*	Fleet Intelligence Center Pacific (Hawaiʻi)
FOSIC *(foe-sick)*	Fleet Ocean Surveillance Information Center
FOSIF *(foe-sif)*	Fleet Ocean Surveillance Information Facility
GCI *(gee-see-eye)*	ground control intercept
HAM *(ham)*	individuals high in achievement motivation
HUMINT *(hume-int)*	human intelligence
IADS *(eye-ads)*	integrated air defense system
IDC *(eye-d-c)*	Information Dominance Corps (later IWC)
IFF *(eye-f-f)*	identification friend or foe
IMINT *(im-int)*	imagery intelligence
IOIC *(eye-oh-eye-see)*	Integrated Operational Intelligence Center
IS *(eye-s)*	enlisted intelligence specialist
IWC *(eye-w-c)*	information warfare community

IWCmdr *(eye-w-commander)*	information operations warfare commander
JICPAC *(jick-pack)*	Joint Intelligence Center Pacific
JOTS *(jots)*	Joint Operations Tactical System
LAM *(lamb)*	individuals low in achievement motivation
LRA *(l-r-ay)*	long-range aviation
LTJG *(lieutenant-jay-gee)*	lieutenant, junior grade
MPRA *(m-pea -r-eh)*	maritime patrol and reconnaissance aircraft
N2 *(n-two)*	intelligence officer position on a Navy staff
NIPS *(nips)*	Naval Intelligence Processing System
NILO *(nigh-low)*	Naval Intelligence liaison officer
NOSIC *(no-sick)*	Navy Ocean Surveillance Information Center
NRTSC *(nert-ska)*	Naval Reconnaissance and Technical Support Center
NRO *(n-r-oh)*	national reconnaissance office
NSA *(n-s-a)*	National Security Agency
NSG *(n-s-gee)*	Naval Security Group
NTDS *(n-tee-d-s)*	Navy Tactical Data System
ONI *(oh-n-eye)*	Office of Naval Intelligence
Opintel *(op-intel)*	Navy-specific operational intelligence
OpNav *(op-nav)*	Chief of Naval Operations staff
OpsComm *(ops-com)*	operations communication circuit
OSIS *(oh-sis)*	ocean surveillance information system
OTH-T *(oh-tee-h-tee)*	over-the-horizon-targeting
PH *(pea-h)*	photographer's mate
PT *(pea-tee)*	photographic intelligencemen (later an IS rate)
RL *(r-l)*	restricted line officer, special duty

SCI *(s-see-eye)*	special compartmented information
SEAD *(seed or see-ad)*	suppression of enemy air defenses
SI *(s-eye)*	special intelligence (usually SIGINT)
SIGINT *(sig-int)*	signals intelligence
SIO *(sigh-oh)*	ship's intelligence officer
SNOOPIE *(snoopy)*	ship's nautical or otherwise photographic intelligence exploitation
SOSUS *(so-suss)*	sound surveillance system
SpintCom *(spint-com)*	special intelligence communications space
SSES *(sess)*	ship's signals exploitation space
SSO *(s-s-oh)*	special security officer
SSSC *(triple S-see)*	surface, subsurface surveillance coordination
SupPlot *(sup-plot)*	supplemental plot
SupRad *(sup-rad)*	supplemental radio
SURFLANT *(surf-lant)*	Surface Forces Atlantic
SWO *(swoh)*	surface warfare officer
TAO *(tea-a-oh)*	tactical action officer
TASM *(taz-um)*	Tomahawk anti-ship cruise missile
TECINT *(tec-int)*	technical intelligence
TFCC *(tea-f-see-see)*	Tactical Flag Command Center
TSC *(tea-S-see)*	Tactical Support Center
UN *(you-en)*	United Nations
URL *(you-r-l)*	unrestricted line officer, referred to as "line"
VA *(vee-ay)*	fixed wing, attack squadron
VF *(vee-f)*	fixed wing, fighter squadron
VP *(vee-pea)*	fixed wing, patrol squadron
VQ *(vee-q)*	fixed wing, reconnaissance (SIGINT) squadron

PROLOGUE

The hot and humid Korean summer was beginning. As the sun rose on Sunday, June 25, 1950, seven infantry divisions and one armored brigade of the North Korean People's Army (KPA) drove south across the 38th parallel. No one was prepared for the invasion, though there had been some warning. A Central Intelligence Agency (CIA) report from February 1949 had assessed that withdrawing U.S. forces from Korea would, in time, lead to an attack. Sixteen months later, on June 19, the CIA noted that North Korean troops had gathered at the 38th parallel; an attack seemed imminent. Any aggression backed by the Soviet Union, the report continued, looked to unify the "Korean peninsula under Communist domination."[1] Washington believed that amid the Cold War developing with the Soviets, the security of Western Europe, not the Korean Peninsula, was the strategic priority.

The Republic of Korea troops were pushed south, almost into the sea. The U.S. forces of the Far East Command sent from Japan were down to 62 percent strength with only 14 percent of authorized tank firepower. They were just strong enough to stop the North Korean advance at the southern port town of Busan. The Far East Command had been weakened as a result of President Truman's belief that in the post–World War II environment it was more efficient to maintain a large reserve force than a large standing force; the United States could send its reserves where needed, using its globally postured navy if a fight were to break out. With the KPA's incursion, Truman quickly authorized more troops for the Far East Command, but critical time was lost as troops received mission-specific training and during the move into the operational theater.[2]

Until more troops and supplies arrived, Gen. Douglas MacArthur, commander of Far East Command, would have to make do. Most of the limited combat power at his disposal lay in ground and air forces, but they had little interoperability training. A United Nations (UN) Security Council resolution came on June 30, Truman authorized MacArthur to bomb north of the 38th parallel and establish a naval blockade.[3] The U.S. Navy had about a third of its overall strength in the Pacific, most of which was a thousand nautical miles south in the Philippines. Due to military force reductions following the close of World War II, only one of the mandated two aircraft carrier divisions operated in the Pacific, Carrier Division 3, with USS *Valley Forge* and her escorts.[4] The Navy's intelligence organizations scrambled to provide support as *Valley Forge* steamed north. The aviation squadrons in *Valley Forge* each had an air intelligence ground officer (135x officer designator). Only one of the newly designated special duty intelligence officers (163x officer designator)[5] was assigned to the staff of the Japan-based Seventh Fleet Flag. Sixteen special duty intelligence officers were "rounded up from the fleet in Pearl Harbor" to augment Seventh Fleet's operational forces.[6]

The special duty intelligence officer was created when the Navy realized that, while it had reduced its force, its global-presence requirement had not. The Navy required intelligence to act as a force multiplier, providing analysis that improved decision-making regarding where placing its dwindling fleet assets mattered most to national security. During World War II, the Navy trained some line officers in specialized areas like intelligence. A line officer was a warfare officer designated by law to hold command at sea. The subspecialist intelligence line officers helped break Japanese codes, providing the intelligence that allowed for victory at Midway in June 1942. A cadre of highly trained enlisted Sailors supported these subspecialist intelligence line officers. Enlisted Sailor ratings, like photographers mate (PH), radio man (RM), and yeoman (YN), supported line subspecialist intelligence and air intelligence officers (135x) with communication, information management, analysis, and watch standing. As the Navy incorporated more microelectronics and computers, the responsibility for maintaining the advanced systems fell to the enlisted Sailor ratings, like the machine accountant (MA)—later changed to data processing technician (DP) and data system technician (DS). Enlisted Sailors were a vital part of the Navy's intelligence enterprise, deserving of a book. Sadly this work only briefly discusses their contributions.⁷

By 1948 the postwar Navy needed to retain some educated and experienced subspecialist intelligence line officers. It selected a few and redesignated them as restricted line special duty intelligence officers (163x). These officers were "restricted" because they were prevented from having command at sea; they only worked as intelligence specialists. Other categories of restricted line officers provided specialists in cryptology, public affairs, and engineering. Special duty intelligence officers provided intelligence to senior line officers in command of operational forces. Line officers subspecialized in intelligence, like the aviation line community's air intelligence ground officers (135x) still existed. The air intelligence officers were in the line and not the restricted line, specializing in aviation-focused intelligence support to carrier aviation squadrons, creating other problems Navy Intelligence would deal with after the Korean War. Only forty Navy intelligence officers (163x) were on active duty when the Korean War ended.⁸

Being "in the line" versus the restrict line created a new category of officers, adding to an already-divisive warfare-community-focused U.S. Navy. The suborganizations within the Navy—warfare communities of surface ships, aviation, and subsurface submarines—had learned to cooperate during World War II. Without the adhesion war provided, the Navy's organizations, like the entire U.S. military service structure, returned to a resource-driven competition for organizational primacy. For Navy intelligence, the organization of intelligence by the separate warfare communities created a problem, and the Korean War highlighted it. Two separate intelligence organizations, air intelligence (135x) and special duty (163x), plus the line officer subspecialist, did not allow for efficient education, training, and placement (called "detailing") of intelligence personnel into fleet commands.

The only consistency in the Navy's intelligence organizations was that there was only one Office of Naval Intelligence (ONI) to support all three. Established in 1882, ONI was at the heart of Navy Intelligence. Chartered to collect information advancing the understanding of the naval sciences, its success soon drew it into supporting the formulation of national-security and naval strategies. ONI and the Naval War College, created in 1884, began a close relationship focused on naval-strategy formulation.[9] ONI shifted to intelligence production, supporting naval combat operations when the United States entered the First World War. Cdr. Dudley Knox, USN, employed new technologies and organizational practices he'd seen the British naval intelligence use during the First World War to create an effective operational intelligence organization for the U.S. Navy. Thanks to Knox and others, operational intelligence and ONI emerged from the war with credibility with the U.S. Navy Fleet.[10] Though important, credibility alone could not sway Navy leadership to create a specialized intelligence officer cadre. To the "battleship"-focused senior surface line officers, intelligence was still a collateral duty handled by subspecialized line officers until after World War II.[11]

By 1950 ONI was overwhelmed; it had too many customers. Photographic interpretation, for example, required that ONI not only train the aviation community's air intelligence officers (135x) in photographic interpretation but also provide the Navy and other national-security decision-makers with photographic interpretation and technical-collection analysts. The career path of a subspecialist intelligence line officer included some postgraduate education provided at Naval Postgraduate School's Naval Intelligence School.[12] Because the subspecialists were doing intelligence as collateral duty, taking a second or third subspecialty intelligence tour could jeopardize a line officer's career. At first the new special duty intelligence officers (163x) were taken up from the subspecialty intelligence line officers. As new 163xs came into service from the civilian world, training and education demands began to grow for the Navy and ONI. The Navy's system of operational intelligence support was too complicated. Having three intelligence communities was an organizational problem that impacted how operational intelligence was viewed and officer-career progression.[13]

Defining the Navy's perspective of operational intelligence is challenging. The 1948 *Operational Intelligence Manual* provides a partial definition, noting, "There is no sharp line of demarcation between operational and strategic intelligence; one flows into the other."[14] The primary distinction of operational intelligence is its direct concern with supporting operating forces, using all sources of information, and a focus on solving a specific operational problem. Retired Vice Admiral Lowell Jacoby, USN, a former Director of Naval Intelligence (DNI), provides a better definition, writing that Opintel is the "art of providing near-real-time information concerning the location, activity, and likely intentions of potential adversaries."[15] The process forces a synthesis of different information sources supporting various levels of war.

Here the perspectives of the three intelligence organizations become important. In his definition Jacoby refers to operational intelligence as "Opintel." The term became associated with the all-source fusion analysis of highly classified special intelligence material, meaning that Opintel could not be conducted everywhere, only where highly classified material existed. For the special duty intelligence officer (163x, from here onward referred to as an intelligence officer) and some of the subspecialist intelligence line officers, Opintel could only be conducted ashore where the special intelligence material resided. Therefore Opintel supported shore-based senior flag officers controlling forces at the strategic, theater, and operational levels of war. Intelligence officers rarely went to sea because there was no access to special intelligence material there.

For the air intelligence officer (135x), operational intelligence was air wing strike mission–focused, answering the questions, *What is the target, where is it, and how is it defended?* The character of air wing support intelligence was threat presentation and target analysis for shipboard commanders at the tactical level of war. Air intelligence officers spent much time at sea and rarely handled special intelligence material. The term "Opintel" was selective; only intelligence officers did Opintel. "Air intelligence" was conducted by airmen in the line, air intelligence officers (135x), providing strike-specific intelligence to other airmen in the line, the aviators at sea. The use of the term "Opintel" as all-encompassing Navy intelligence from operational to tactical levels of war did not occur until later in the Cold War. Jacoby makes an important point when he writes that there is an "emphasis upon timely warfighter support" of Opintel. The desire to move Opintel to sea and combine it with air intelligence required that the intelligence officer be collocated, cheek-by-jowl, with the commander at sea; it drove the revolutionary application of technology and the resulting organizational evolution.[16] It was not until communications and computers had advanced that special intelligence material could be used at sea and use of the term "Opintel" became ubiquitous.

Organizational Culture and the Fight for Primacy

The divide between line and restricted line officers was just one organizational divide within the Navy. The Navy's ability to respond in Korea was impacted by resource problems that emerged with downsizing after World War II, but those problems were exacerbated by the Navy's own culture. After World War II, the United States had naval supremacy; its inventory contained around 800 ships. There were over 28 fleet carriers, enough amphibious lift for over 400,000 troops, 250 submarines, and many other combatants. The Navy was too large; it needed to make cuts. Three Navy-imposed planning factors guided what was to be kept and what was to be mothballed or broken up: the desire to (1) have a balanced force, (2) maintain a constant forward presence, and (3) maintain a navy second to none.[17]

The challenge was that all the U.S. military services had similar postwar objectives without the funding to support them. The Defense Reorganization Act of 1947 complicated the budgetary issue by establishing the Air Force as an independent service. The atomic bomb's power had brought the need for conventional forces and the current strategic thinking into question. To many, achieving national security only required long-range strategic bombing with atomic weapons—the U.S. Air Force. Funding a large navy seemed unnecessary, and cutting it was a quick way to achieve a peace dividend. The postwar Navy struggled to cohere a solid intellectual argument for its existence. But the Korean War put a sharp point on the argument: conventional war was still viable, and the United States needed a navy.

Interservice rivalry and infighting over military roles, responsibilities, and importance were a backdrop to the Navy's organizational struggles. Given the Navy's organizational and suborganizational evolution, understanding Navy intelligence requires first an understanding of the organizational culture. The study of organizations and the idea that culture influences them developed as part of the economic landscape of the Cold War era. Since the Industrial Revolution industry has looked for ways to create a competitive advantage, and one way is to optimize management practices. One of the first studies looking at organizations and management was conducted between 1948 and 1950 by Jaques Elliott. He showed that within a business, social activity is linked to the company's organizational structure; the company's social structure, culture, and personality are factors in individual and group behavior and the "authority-responsibility relationship" between them.[18] In *The Organization Man* (1956) William H. Whyte paints a picture of organizations and their competition culture in the 1950s, illuminating discussion on the Navy's organization and promotion mechanisms. More recently works like Edgar H. Schein's *Organizational Culture and Leadership* (1985), John P. Kotter's *Leading Change* (2012), and Mats Alvesson's *Understanding Organizational Culture* (2002) have become foundational in the field of organizational change.

The study of organizational culture dominates the business world, but it is possible that some of these organizational ideas came from the battlefield. Examining warfare and describing military organization as a factor of battlefield advantage is a practice dating back to antiquity and undoubtedly inform modern study of war. Books exploring military culture, however, are a recent phenomenon, and most focus on why states choose war and how units conduct themselves in combat. In the 2019 RAND study "Movement and Maneuver: Culture and the Competition for Influence among the U.S. Military Services," Rebecca Zimmerman et al. look at military-bureaucratic cultures—mainly those service-based cultures focused on institutional and strategic decision-making. The RAND study offers insight into how and why each U.S. military service competes against the others for resources.[19] In *The Culture of Military Organizations* (2019) Peter Mansoor and Williamson Murray consider the role organizational culture has in developing military effectiveness, finding that three external factors shape military culture: "geography, history, and the nature in which navies, armies, and air forces exist."[20] How a military thinks about, prepares for, and conducts war is shaped by the geography and physical domains (land, sea, and air) they operate within. U.S. Navy Rear Adm. J. C. Wylie (1911–1993) offered in the 1950s that Sailors see future war through the lens of control of the sea, giving them a unique perspective on strategy.[21] Each military organization defines its role and its effectiveness through a domain-centric lens; how it describes itself, its identity, and the resulting culture produces synergy within its ranks to achieve battlefield effectiveness and win wars.

Assessing military culture is complicated, and there is no one single way to go about it—likely because, as American anthropologist Clifford Geertz noted in 1973, culture is too abstract and symbolic.[22] U.S. Army War College professors Leonard Wong and Stephen J. Gerras turned to Dutch social psychologist Geert Hofstede and American MIT professor Edgar Schein when making their groundbreaking attempt to understand military culture factors.[23] Organizational culture, Schein believes, is represented by artifacts, beliefs and values, and underlying basic assumptions. Wong and Gerras note that artifacts are observables; "they reflect the culture, not define it."[24] Beliefs and values, often seen in mission statements or command philosophies, reveal the motivations and rationale of the organizational culture, but only if what is said matches what is done by the organization. Wong and Gerras found Schein's model foundationally reliable but too abstract for analyzing military culture. They felt a better model was offered by Professor Robert J. House's extension of Geert Hofstede's work, the Global Leadership and Organizational Behavior Effectiveness (GLOBE) Research Program.[25] The GLOBE methodology uses nine cultural dimensions: performance orientation, future orientation, assertiveness, institutional collectivism, in-group collectivism, power distance, humane orientation, uncertainty avoidance, and gender egalitarianism. Elements of Wong and Gerras' modified GLOBE model are seen throughout this book, particularly performance orientation, collectivism, and power distance.[26]

Describing an organization's evolution is also tricky because evolution is a gradual development from a simple to a more complex form. Five dimensions affect organizational evolution: age, size, stage of evolution, stage of revolution, and industry growth rate.[27] As organizations age, they undergo an evolutionary period characterized by steady growth with only minor adaptations required. Turbulent times, as during a war, are periods of technological revolution for a military organization and are thought of as organizational change opportunities. Revolution can be good or bad, depending on how the organization handles the opportunity presented. Thus organizations change through these evolutionary and revolutionary periods over time. Often evolution is in linear phases of creativity, direction, delegation, coordination, and collaboration that consolidate changes made by a technological revolution. Of course, knowing where one is within the dimensions and phases of revolution and evolution is difficult, but understanding that one must assess the dimensions and phases is a start to managing change.[28]

While the Korean War solved the argument about whether the United States needed a navy, services found themselves in near disarray under the new Department of Defense structure, perceiving their cultures and identities to be under threat by the defense-reorganization efforts. The Navy was particularly against the reorganization, correctly perceiving U.S. Air Force and Army threats to its budget and independence of action. When Rear Adm. Arleigh Burke was made Chief of Naval Operations (CNO) in 1955, he went about ensuring the Navy was a significant part of President Eisenhower's new strategy while advancing his stance that the Navy supported "the principle of decentralization operations under authoritative policy direction."[29] The services' disparate perspectives on new technology created evolution/revolution drivers that in turn led to additional competition over resources. Obsolescence was a critical factor in the competition. Technology has outdated some of the services' thinking about how war should be conducted. Within the Navy, new technologies had made the battleship obsolete. This is not a new story; the development and application of new technology replacing old is a constant theme for all navies. The success of naval aviation and aircraft carriers during World War II created an organizational shift, and the battleship admirals lost control of the Navy. This highlights technology's power to reshape organizations and the uncomfortable realization that it leaves redundant machines and people in its wake.

The new technologies fascinated the post–World War II Navy, which saw them as an organizational cure-all for strategic-thinking ills. A navy's love affair with innovation is inherent to its nature: winning battles at sea is achieved when new ideas are identified, developed, and practically applied more quickly than the adversary can. "Technology is more to mariners than life," observes Roger Barnett; "it is [their] home."[30] Sailors live and fight from ships, creating a love-hate relationship with technology, which thus drives a navy's organizational structure. Chasing innovation to modernize was not a phenomenon born after World War II; rather, it is a constant for all navies.

Trent Hone writes that the Navy's modernization story began in the post–Civil War period "with an insurgency" bent on incorporating modern technologies that would revolutionize the way the Navy conducted warfare. An antiquated bureaucracy was dismantled, Hone writes, as the Navy struggled over what a modern American naval officer should be, how the Navy should promote and develop officers, and what the relationship between the military and its civilian leadership should be. The decades during which these questions were examined and answers were suggested and implemented, Hone offers, modernized the Navy.[31] Redesigning and professionalizing the Navy's officer corps was not a universal remedy; yet revolution and evolution rarely are. The problems of the old model that were solved were balanced by the problems inherent in the new system.

For example, the revolutionary introduction of steam power to the Navy divided the officer corps into two groups: thus was the divide between the "warrior-strategist" and the "engineers" codified in U.S. law and naval tradition. Only officers "in the line," the warriors, had command at sea, which in the age of sail equated to the ship's maneuver. The commanding officer was seen as the most experienced Sailor aboard; his expertise created maneuver, the purpose of his command. With the age of steam, the engineer, a specialist in the staff corps, not the line, provided maneuver; an incongruency between command and maneuver undermined authority within the ship. Not many of the "warrior" class understood steam technology, and to know modern naval tactics was to know steam technology, which the "engineers" did. Ultimately naval tactics are linked to the strategy directing them; thus engineers should be "in the line" with opportunities to hold command. The Naval Reform Act of 1899 ended the decades-long debate. Engineering officers were moved from the staff corps and brought into the line as equals. The engineers learned about strategy, through a technology lens, and the traditional sailing line officers learned about engineering.[32]

By the early 1900s, the "engineers'" view of strategy through technology won out over the history-infused view of the "warrior-strategists" group. Two decades later, at the end of the First World War, the engineers, now the "battleship" group, found themselves similarly fractured in the face of the aviation revolution. The Navy's recent successes reinforced aviation's vital role in sea control, sea denial, and power projection, propelling aviators over the battleship tribe. Aviation's success and future potential reinforced technology's allure as a panacea for all strategy ills. The postwar Navy had an "ahistorical culture," writes John Kuehn, "preferring technological solutions for the emerging problems of the Cold War."[33]

Promotion based on longevity, or seniority, was seen as a problem for those in the professionalism insurgency, who argued that sustained superior performance, or merit, was a more important promotion criterion than longevity. Finally, in 1916, the seniority system was replaced with a competitive selection system based on merit. Yet again the evolution brought with it a new problem: Either one was promoted or one was forced from service—up or out—which created intense competition across the officer corps.[34]

The competition extended beyond individual officer merit, and different suborganizations within the Navy found themselves pitted against one another. Each warfare-centric suborganization—the surface line (battleships), the submarine line, and aviation—saw their domain as primary to the Navy's mission. These subcultures reacted to technological changes in different ways. At the close of the First World War, the Navy was led by the "battleship admirals," who held high-level commands, including the position of Chief of Naval Operations—created in 1915. They saw aviation and submarine technology as only helpful as defensive or scouting tools in support of surface operations.

Over time, however, aviation technology challenged that perception—especially with the acceleration in engine capabilities seen in the late 1930s.[35] Even with the catastrophic losses at Pearl Harbor in 1941, seven of eight battleships sunk, the shift from a battleship-centric navy to an aviation focus was not automatic, and the Navy faced organizational struggles through the war. "Very often, members of the Navy [factions] were fighting not only the Japanese and Germans but one another," writes Roger Thompson.[36] By the mid-1950s the Navy was dominated by carrier-based aviation, which had proven successful in the Pacific campaigns; 40 percent of all Navy flag officers were aviators.[37]

By the time Dwight D. Eisenhower took the oath of office in January 1953, the United States could no longer maintain the conventional military buildup required to engage in the Korean War. The new president needed to cut defense spending and maintain national security through the containment policy established by President Truman before him. Eisenhower's "New Look" approach leveraged atomic weapons, to replace a force design based on quantity with one of quality. It was to be deterrence in the form of mutually assured destruction (MAD) with atomic weapons delivered by strategic airpower. The approach seemed absurd because it was unlikely to be used in a limited fashion. Lacking nuclear parity, the Soviets might become adventurous in limited-objective wars in contested areas, a form of asymmetry.[38] Thus the United States still required a smaller yet varied arsenal of sophisticated, beyond-the-horizon nuclear and conventional air, sea, and land weapons it could selectively use. New Look evolved in the mid-1950s toward developing long-range aviation and forward-deployed naval assets that would counter the Soviet use of asymmetry.[39] As a result, "no period of the Cold War saw the Navy develop technology with more urgency;" under CNO Burke, the Navy needed to quickly evolve strategic and operational "generic flexibility" to remain politically relevant within the national-security framework.[40]

By the 1960s the airpower Navy had mostly won the suborganizational fight on the back of the New Look strategy and would go on to dominate the service for the next three decades. Upward of 50 percent of the Navy's budget during the 1950s and 1960s went to aircraft and aircraft carriers. Between 1960 and 1970 the Navy commissioned five new supercarriers, one nuclear-powered (a second was under construction). In 1961, with the war escalating in Vietnam and rising geopolitical tensions that would soon lead to the Cuban Missile Crisis, an aviator ascended as CNO. And an aviator would go on to hold the position for all but four of the next twenty-one years.[41]

The naval aviation community had ascended, but the submarine community was just behind them. Like the airplane, the submarine had significantly contributed to winning World War II. The complexities of underwater operations delayed submarine technology progression after the war. Nuclear propulsion in the 1950s, led by the brilliant and irascible Adm. Hyman G. Rickover, was revolutionary, increasing submarine size, endurance, and lethality.[42] The submarine was further elevated within U.S. strategic security with surface line officer CNO Arleigh Burke's staunch support of the Polaris submarine-launched ballistic missile. After 1962 the Navy's primary contribution to the U.S. military's Single Integrated Operational Plan (SIOP) for nuclear war was not the carrier-based aircraft but the ballistic missile submarine and its Polaris missile—the third support in the nuclear deterrence triad. Through the 1950s and '60s, 25 percent of the Navy's budget went to Vice Admiral Rickover's nuclear submarine program.[43]

For Navy Intelligence, the service's evolution and revolutions had morphed the organization into "three separate navies"—aviation, surface, and submarine. With the aviation tribe controlling the Navy and a possible ground war brewing in Indochina, the air intelligence component of operational intelligence was essential to the fleet. Equally important to the Navy's senior operational commanders and decision-makers, however, was the highly classified all-source fusion

Opintel occurring at shore-based flag staffs and within the Pentagon. Navy Intelligence was in its evolution cycle, trying to match the demands of the technologically changing warfighting communities. Thus the modern iteration of Navy Intelligence started with several technological revolutions involving microelectronics and computers. Innovations at sea would refocus the entire Navy Intelligence organization toward support of operations at sea.

This change was made possible by what Trent Hone identifies as emergent potential and evolvability mechanisms.[44] The emergent potential stemmed from the forced cooperation of three separate intelligence organizations within one Navy. The only guidance provided on how the air intelligence, intelligence officer, and subspecialist intelligence line officers came from the customer, the warfare line officer, or senior decision-maker, being directly supported. At sea there was freedom to develop and informally reorganize personnel and modify processes to meet customer demands, meaning there was almost endless potential to adapt and test an organization, then change those less-successful elements and adapt again. The lack of top-down constraints—outside those of the customer—created a willingness to experiment and find ways to adapt informally to changing operational environments; in short, it made great evolvability.

The shipboard operational intelligence environment between the Korean War and 1960 showed emergent potential and evolvability. The revolutionary spark of organizational change came in the early 1960s with the development and installation of the Integrated Operational Intelligence Center (IOIC) and its successful use during the Vietnam War. A return to evolution occurred in the late 1960s, followed by another revolutionary period with the development of the shore-based Ocean Surveillance Information System (OSIS) in 1970. OSIS decentralized highly classified national intelligence, allowing forward-theater fleet commanders access to long-term analysis and timely indications and warning of Soviet naval activity. The cycles of change and adaptation accelerated in the 1970s, and a revolution period occurred in 1976 with the Outlaw Shark program that demonstrated the at-sea tactical use of satellite-collected national intelligence.[45]

In the following we will explore how new technology links a period of upheaval to periods of organizational growth, considering how the change mechanisms of performance orientation, collectivism, and other institutionalization mechanisms embed and then reinforce those changes. The result of this evolution is still seen in the Navy's afloat Opintel organization today.

The evolution of the Navy's shipboard operational intelligence was fostered by leaders who recognized the importance of timely, credible intelligence and of reliable and trustworthy intelligence officers who could deliver that intelligence to the operational leader at sea. The elbow-to-elbow working relationship at sea between operational commanders and their intelligence officers had far-reaching impacts. The successful U.S. maritime strategy of the 1980s was just one result of the operator-to-intelligence officer relationship. The following chapters describe how modern shipboard Opintel evolved during the Cold War.

PART I
The Vietnam War: Institutionalizing Shipboard Operational Intelligence

The submarine Navy never doubted the importance of their Polaris missile program; since 1957 they had been selling it as a system more invulnerable to surprise attack than the U.S. Air Force's strategic bombing and land-based ballistic missile approach.[1] President Kennedy wasn't in office two months before clarifying his SIOP weapons preference, telling Congress, "I strongly recommend that the Polaris program be greatly expanded and accelerated."[2] Secretary of Defense McNamara reinforced the president's direction, modifying defense research and development (R & D) and acquisition direction toward ballistic missiles. "Let's face it," he said, "the fighter-bomber aircraft is becoming vulnerable; therefore, we must have medium range ballistic missiles."[3] The change in atomic bomb delivery approach scuppered the aircraft carrier–centric Navy's long-range bombing strategy.

The Navy was out of the airborne-strategic-nuclear-strike-mission business, though a tactical atomic-strike capability remained. Their new strategic nuclear bomber was without its primary mission, yet the A-5 Vigilante, costly and relentlessly advertised as an altitude- and speed-record-setting aircraft, was about to enter the fleet in late 1962. At $168.5 million (about $1.6 billion today), the Navy could not afford to shelve the Vigilante project.[4] Determining what to do with the Vigilante would be a pivotal decision for the Navy and Navy intelligence.

CHAPTER 1
The Integrated Operational Intelligence Center

A man learns nothing from winning. The act of losing, however, can elicit great wisdom—not least of which is how much more enjoyable it is to win. It's inevitable to lose now and again. The trick is not to make a habit of it.

—UNCLE ALBERT, *A Good Year*[1]

The executive officer of the super-aircraft carrier USS *Forrestal* was nonplussed. "Rock, what d'you *mean* you need more space?"

Fresh out of the IOIC's Supervisor Course, Lt. Cdr. William "Rock" Ore, USN, knew that his request sounded absurd. At approximately 45 by 70 feet—3,185 square feet, 296 meters squared—the space allotted to the new Intel Center was already almost two and half times that of the previous Air Intelligence Office.[2] But Rock was overseeing installation, and he wanted more space. He'd figured out that converting the adjoining officer stateroom would enable him to expand the IOIC's mission-planning bay, meaning the new Intel Center could then accommodate a map-reproduction system. Rock may have been new to his post, but he knew what he was doing: his experience as a squadron air intelligence officer (1350) and shared wisdom from other IOIC supervisors who had served in the center, supporting combat missions into North Vietnam, spurred his "unorthodox" request.[3]

Built in the early sixties by North American Aviation (NAA) with ONI collaboration, the Integrated Operational Intelligence System (IOIS) was designed for use on aircraft carriers (CVAs) and was already active on seven warships by 1967. IOIS was first installed in *Saratoga*, in 1962.[4] Rock Ore was overseeing the eighth installation, on his ship, *Forrestal*.

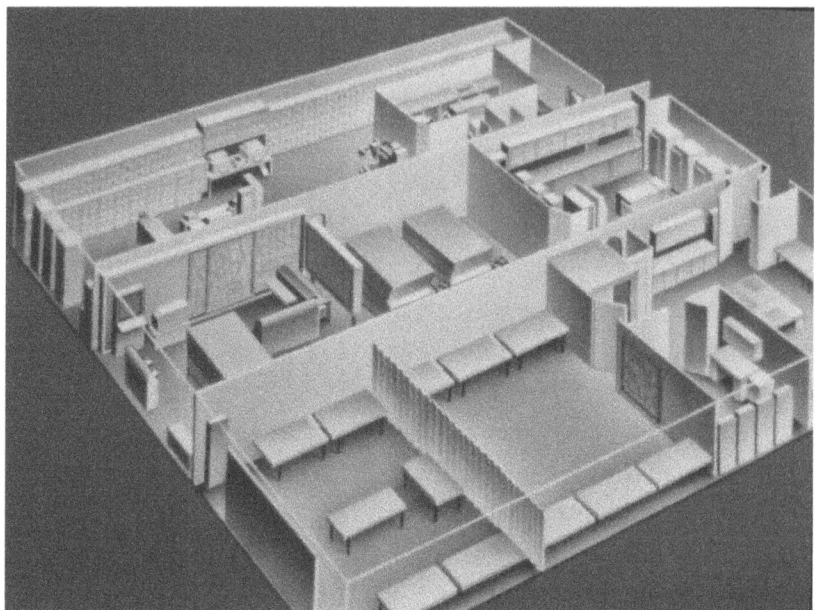

FIGURE 1.1
The Integrated Operational Intelligence System (IOIS) was designed for installation on aircraft carriers (CVAs). Its spaces (pictured) were athwart ship with the entrance from the starboard side main passageway. The first bay (bottom) contained the mission analysis and briefing spaces. The second bay held the Electronic Data Processing (EDP) and the imagery stereo comparison viewer (SCVs). The third bay held the darkroom, photo-processing equipment, and the storage-and-retrieval work center. IMAGE FROM THE NAVY'S 1967 TRAINING FILM, *IOIS: PHOTO INTERPRETATION STATION*

The IOIS had two components: the RA-5C Vigilante reconnaissance aircraft and the Integrated Operational Intelligence Center (IOIC). The entire system, both plane and IOIC, was owned by the aviation community—OpNav OP-05—through the Bureau of Naval Weapons. Vigilante's airborne sensors were an essential component. They had been developing since the late 1950s, but for other platforms, not the Vigilante.[5]

The A3-J Vigilante (later redesignated the A-5) was the Navy's long-range bomber, yet no long-range bombing missions remained.[6] To save the Vigilante, the Navy pivoted the program toward airborne reconnaissance. Growing conventional warfare–planning requirements reminded the Navy that it needed timely reconnaissance. The planning for a combined-arms assault on Cuba during the 1962 Missile Crisis reinforced the reality of modern strike warfare into integrated air defense systems firing high-speed missiles. Fighting this type of war required locating and suppressing enemy surface-to-air missile systems. That mission required a fast reconnaissance aircraft collecting high-resolution imagery simultaneously cross-cued with signals intelligence.

As it happened, the Navy had a bomber that could outrun the sound of its engines, and it was sitting idle. A reconnaissance version of the A-5 Vigilante began development as early as 1959. In 1962 efforts to save the Vigilante reworked it into a reconnaissance aircraft.[7] The resulting Vigilante RA-5C came with an advanced shipboard processing, exploitation, and dissemination system—the IOIC. The plane and IOIC improved the Navy's ability to project power in a missile environment.

PHOTO 1.1
Covered with "war paint," a camouflaged RA-5C Vigilante of Reconnaissance Attack Squadron 13 (RVAH-13) taxis for position on the flight deck of USS *Kitty Hawk* (CVA 63) during operations in the South China Sea, April 13, 1966. NARA

Airborne reconnaissance system development was where some interservice cooperations occurred, but only to a point. The Navy and the Air Force wanted to collaborate on a reconnaissance platform with photographic and electronic intelligence sensors. However, there was no common ground between the two services on a sensor package and reconnaissance platform. The "Navy, but not the Air Force, saw tactical electronic intelligence (ELINT) and communications intelligence (COMINT) as essential complements to other sensor outputs" like imagery.[8] The Navy's desire for a side-looking airborne radar (SLAR) system on the platform complicated the negotiations. The Air Force wanted high-altitude reconnaissance. The Navy wanted speed and the ability to operate from an aircraft carrier. The photographic, electronic-collection, and radar-sensor packages weighed so much that only a bomber could carry them. The two services could not agree and went their separate ways.

PHOTO 1.2
Photographer's Mate First Class Arthur R. Jorgensen checks over an RA-5C Vigilante aircraft camera system on USS *Independence* (CVA 62) while operating in the Mediterranean Sea, January 1971. NARA

Assembled at North American Aviation's plant in Columbus, Ohio, the Vigilante and its photographic system were day- and night-capable and could take images at varying altitudes and speeds. Three photographic sensor stations were integrated into a ventral "belly" canoe and loaded into the linear bomb bay.[9] The camera packages were mixed and matched to suit the mission's collection requirements. For example, a left- and-right oblique serial-frame camera could occupy the forward camera station, and a three-inch panoramic, or pan, camera could be in the aft. The addition of an 18-inch and a 3-inch pan camera allowed a broad panoramic search collection. The camera package loaded into the bomb bay was massive; all the cameras were mounted in the removable module. The module, assembled beforehand in the Aircraft Systems Support Center (ASSC) on the 02 level of the aircraft carrier, also part of the IOIS install, weighed upward of 1,000 pounds (450 kg). Moving the package required a hydraulic dolly and the ship's aircraft elevator. The Vigilante's bomb hoist, hand-cranked by the enlisted PHs, lifted the module into the bomb bay.[10]

Six more sensor stations were located on the Vigilante for the passive electronic countermeasures (PECM) system. The PECM had scanning receivers at different locations on the fuselage, collecting frequencies across twelve bands. The receivers covered the frequency range of 30 megahertz (MHz) to 14 gigahertz (GHz), with a scan rate of 15.5 seconds.[11] The PECM detected signals across the high, very-high, and ultra-high, and extremely high (HF, VHF, UHF, and EHF) frequency ranges and part of the super- high (SHF) frequency ranges. The collected frequency range contained the operating frequencies of the most dangerous Soviet-built surface-to- air (SAM) and surface-to-surface (SS) missile systems, such as the SA-2 Guideline, the SA-3 Goa, and the deadly anti-ship cruise missile SS-N-2 Styx. The system recorded the signal details onto magnetic tape for analysis by the electronic evaluator, using the Electronic Data Processing station inside the IOIC.[12]

The aft part of the ventral canoe held the side-looking airborne radar (SLAR) and the infrared mapping system. The linear bomb bay also held a digital data system providing flight data to the photographic, PECM, SLAR, and mapping systems. The AN/AYA-1 computer placed the collection sensors into a spatial relationship, such as location, altitude, speed, and aircraft angle of the sensors to the earth. The spatial data were digitally imprinted onto the film using a machine-readable code-matrix block. The AYA-1 simultaneously supplied data to all sensors, creating critical synchronization that allowed cross-cueing of all collections, a feature that was handy during postmission analysis.[13]

The Vigilante was a technological marvel and could produce a flood of information. The five photographic cameras, SLAR, and mapping package could expose thousands of feet of film during a mission. The PECM could record signals for 112 minutes. Thus the IOIC had to be equal to or better than the collection platform to be valuable. It had to be automated and staffed by highly trained personnel who could quickly process, exploit, and disseminate the information. The IOIC also needed analysts who could fuse the information and make assessments that affected future collection or strike missions.[14]

The Intel Center

The IOIC replaced the *Essex*- and *Forestall*-class aircraft carriers' old Air Intelligence Office. On *Forrestal* that office was about "one bay," approximately eighteen feet wide and seventy feet long. At approximately 1,260 square feet (117 m^2), the space, Rock Ore recalled, packed with cabinets and safes, was cramped.[15] The Air Intelligence Office on Rock's first ship, the smaller *Essex*-class aircraft carrier USS *Shangri-La*, was even smaller than *Forrestal*'s. It contained a long table for Single Integrated Operations Plan (SIOP) mission planning and a small office for the ship's air intelligence officer, a lieutenant commander (1350). The best thing about the Air Intelligence Office was that it was air-conditioned. Squadron air intelligence officers (135x, referred to as an AI), ensign or lieutenant junior grade in rank, sometimes slept on the deck underneath the planning table. The hot Pacific Ocean or Mediterranean Sea waters produced a suffocating humidity that made the ship a sweatbox. "Boys Town," as Rock referred to the junior officer berthing, had no air-conditioning, like the rest of the ship, and it "could get really hot up there."[16] Creative junior AIs found ways to beat the heat.

The young men in Boys Town were part of the approximately nine hundred squadron air intelligence officers (AI, 135x) working across the aviation community. Most AIs were at the lieutenant pay grade and below. There might be two AIs with each squadron in the air wing. The air wing staff AI and the carrier's AI were both lieutenant commanders.

The new *Forrestal* and *Kitty Hawk*–class super aircraft carriers and their aircraft were big. The Vigilante was almost seventy-seven feet (23.5 meters) long, nineteen feet (5.8 meters) tall, with a fifty-three-foot (16.2 meters) wingspan. The AD-3 Skywarrior, an older long-range bomber also converted to reconnaissance work, was about four feet taller. The fighters and attack bombers were smaller. For example, the F-4 Phantom fighter bomber was about two-thirds the size of the Vigilante, and the A-4 Skyhawk attack bomber one-half. The Vigilante and its IOIC required significant installation modifications to the aircraft carrier. A ship's alteration, or ShipAlt, increased the capacity of *Forrestal*-class ships' freshwater distilling plants to support the cooling of the Intel Center. A second ShipAlt was directed to install the IOIC on the 03 level (called the gallery deck) and an Aircraft System Support Center (ASSC) on the 02 level. Part of the installation increased air-conditioning capacity, adding sixty-ton and ten-ton air-conditioning plants.[17] The executive officer and ship's chief engineer's exasperation with Ore's request for more space came from the perspective that *Forrestal* already operated at a freshwater deficiency. Fresh water was used as chilling water, primarily cooling the electronic equipment and, by association, the compartment where the equipment resided. Now that the ship was finally getting more freshwater capacity, it would be for an additional intelligence requirement, not correcting the water deficiency.

The ship would never overcome its freshwater deficit. On top of that, the mechanical spaces for the Intel Center's air-conditioning plants, its valves, and pumps for the fresh chill-water cooling the air were located outside, expanding the footprint further. Adding the Intel Center took away officer staterooms, forcing the displaced officers to double up in the remaining staterooms. The loss of staterooms, among other issues, left some officers questioning the value proposition; some derisively referred to the IOIC as the place with a "Hundred and One (101) Clowns."[18]

The IOIC's computers and equipment for processing and exploiting the Vigilante's collection came from North American Aviation's plant in Columbus, Ohio. The equipment filled the three processing work centers (Electronics Data Processing, Storage and Retrieval, and Photographic Processing) and two exploitation work centers (Multi-sensor Interpretation and Electronic Evaluation) within the Intel Center.[19] The shipyard, controlled by the Navy's Bureau of Ships, configured the ship's spaces. With help from the ship's crew, NAA technicians installed the equipment.[20] From 1965 through 1970 North American Aviation, renamed North American Rockwell (NAR), was given $72.19 million ($651.2 million in today's money)[21] to convert the already-built A-5 to RA-5Cs. More money was provided to build replacement Vigilantes. The specific cost to develop and build the IOICs is challenging to determine because of the many contract vehicles used. After the IOICs were built, NAR received at least $12.11 million ($109.3 million today) to produce IOIC equipment and maintenance.[22] After the IOIC was installed and certified operational,

PHOTO 1.3
The two-station stereo comparison viewer (SCV) was in every IOIC, and photographic interpretation personnel often found them difficult to use and maintain. IMAGE FROM THE NAVY'S 1967 TRAINING FILM, *IOIS: PHOTOGRAPHIC INTERPRETATION STATION*

NAR contractors remained onboard, even during deployment, to help maintain the equipment.[23]

With *Forrestal*'s Intel Center's spaces configured, equipment installation began. The haze-gray-painted stereometric comparison viewers (SCVs), the photographic interpretation workstation, was hoisted up through a removable patch on the Multi-sensor Interpretation work center's deck. The two SCVs were the last major equipment hoisted; the computers and magnetic tape units were already installed. The SCVs were large— approximately five feet wide, seven feet tall, and eight feet deep. Bulky but relatively light, the two SCVs were metal frames covered in sheet metal and housed photographic film viewers. Each SCV had a separate AN/UYK-1 computer, called the K-1 or "yuck-one" by some Sailors, running the photographic interpretation programs.[24] The UYK-1s stood in the Electronic Data Processing (EDP) center next to the Multi-sensor Interpretation work center. The SCV had two side-by-side stations, allowing two photographic films to be loaded and compared by two photographic interpreters (PIs) working in coordination.

PHOTO 1.4
Photographer's Mate Third Class Robin Hartford (*seated, right*) with three Sailors in USS *Saratoga*'s EDP, 1976. Two Q-20 computers are seen against the wall to Hartford's right, and two magnetic tape units (MTUs) are against the far wall. A teletype printer (in front of the MTU) is seen with its cover lifted. SELF-PORTRAIT BY R. HARTFORD

A separate teletype printer and digital plotter were the SCV's UYK-1 output devices.[25]

EDP was the brains of the Intel Center—or at least the AN/USQ-20 was. UNIVAC built the USQ-20, the magnetic tape units (MTUs), and the high-speed paper-tape reader/punch. The equipment was the product of a separate Navy program, the Naval Tactical Data System (NTDS) anti-air battle management program. "Battle-hardened" electronic equipment designed for shipboard use, the USQ-20, or Q-20, was the workhorse of NTDS as well.[26] The UYK-1s supported the photographic-interpretation programs only. The Q-20 did much more for the IOIC; it processed the electronic emitter data collected by Vigilante's sophisticated PECM system. The Q-20 stored and retrieved data from three MTUs.[27]

More than anything else associated with the IOIC, the automated Storage and Retrieval system revolutionized shipboard intelligence. The Q-20 provided the ability to take large amounts of source data and process it into information—data with context. By the 1960s, because of the explosion of new collection sensors, Naval Intelligence was drowning in data; what it needed, however, was intelligence. In 1963 ONI was flooded by "approximately 5 million [data] subjects and approximately 20 million pages [of data], with a growth rate of 700,000 pages per year." Several automated data processing (ADP) initiatives were underway at ONI. However, there was no master ADP plan.[28] "Very few things," Wyman Packard quotes from an August 1961 Navy report, "could be more disastrous for naval intelligence than to introduce ADP equipment . . . without any overall concept of how they should be tied together."[29] ONI needed an ADP concept that coordinated hardware and databases. The IOIC-automated intelligence processing and rapid storage and retrieval system could solve Navy Intelligence's ADP problem. In 1964 the Naval Intelligence Processing System Support Activity (NIPSSA) was established to manage ADP support and research-and-development efforts. That same year the director of Naval Intelligence took control of the Naval Reconnaissance and Technical Support Center (NRTSC). The NRTSC controlled maintenance efforts for the fielded IOICs and the development of the master databases the system used. NIPSSA incorporated new information-management tools into systems and helped create new information-management business practices.[30] Navy Intelligence began its master ADP plan with the Storage and Retrieval system as an inspiration.

The Intel Center's Storage and Retrieval work center (S&R) was an intelligence library housing hundreds of reports and publications in miniature form. Gray metal, floor-to-ceiling multidrawer cabinets filled with data punch cards, 16- and 35-mm microfilm aperture cards, miniature transparencies (MITRANs), and stacks of magnetic tape all contained thousands of pieces of data, information, and some finished intelligence products. The cabinets lined the approximately thirteen-by-twenty-five-foot compartment. Teletypes and punch card readers in S&R communicated with the Q-20 in EDP. The rest of S&R contained microfiche viewers and teletype printers.[31]

The library, or database, was supplied by ONI and NRTSC; it included images from the Naval Photographic Interpretation Center (Anacostia, Maryland), the Fleet Intelligence Centers, the Defense Intelligence Agency, and the Central Intelligence Agency. The database given to each ship was curated to their expected operating area, Atlantic or Pacific theater. It took ONI over five weeks to prepare the database.[32] Once a carrier deployed, database updates for specific theater operations came from the Fleet Intelligence Center in the theater. For example, combat operations in Vietnam required updated enemy order-of-battle and target data. The updates, usually punch cards or magnetic tape reels, were flown out to the aircraft carrier on station and installed by EDP. Other database updates came from record messages and the ship's intelligence-collection missions.[33]

In late 1964 ONI's ADP plan wanted to link ship and shore automated intelligence systems. ONI approved the development of the Naval Intelligence Processing System (NIPS) to achieve the ADP goal. NIPS and the IOIC's Storage and Retrieval system were separate. The NIPS concept was born from those proven successful by the IOIC; the two systems became, though separate systems, synonymous.[34] The NIPS database improved the processes and automation established by the Storage and Retrieval work center of the IOIC. Even ships that did not have the IOIC might receive a Storage and Retrieval system, now in NIPS. By 1968 there were seventeen NIPS and eleven IOIC S&R database holders. ADP innovations matched computing and communication advancements, improving all-source fusion analysis. NTRSC's improvements had cut ONI's database build time from five weeks to just two, providing more timely information for analysis at sea.[35]

During World War II, Navy Intelligence learned a valuable lesson: signals intelligence was a critical advantage in war at sea. The 1957 creation of the Navy Field Operational Intelligence Office (NFOIO) advanced the fusion of signals collection with analysis.[36] As guided missiles became a threat to the aviation community, airborne electronic signal intelligence (ELINT) became necessary. The Vigilante provided much-needed tactical and operational ELINT. The collection system in the plane is complex, a labyrinth of wires and sensors. What matters is that the collection, recorded on 16-track magnetic tape, provided detailed information, like flight data, signal arrival times, signal strength, and the frequency of a signal collected. The airborne tape recorded 122 minutes of signals. It could record more, but the aircraft lacked space for more tape. As it was, the spool of tape was so large that it was cut into two spools for processing by the shipboard system (Q-20 computer). The processing system sorted and correlated the airborne tape's data and placed the information on a final emitter tape for analysis. "The processing took a great deal of time—two to three hours," noted Capt. Wayne Perras, USN (Ret.), electronic evaluator in 1973 for RVAH-6 in USS *America*.[37]

The printout of signals collected from a processed tape "could be 100 pages long with many radars [emitters] reported," Perras noted. "But by the time we did the correlations/matches, typically we had a dozen radars or less [emitters] to report." He emphasized, "This [signals] analysis was more an art than a science!" The report showed the emitter's location and details about the signal. The electronic evaluator compared the collected signals with those held in the electronic order-of-battle database. Imagery taken of the area might verify a radar or SAM system associated with a signal. The electronic evaluator would assess whether or not an emitter, meaning a SAM system, had moved, which is vital information for aircrew flying into the area. After the analysis, a report was sent via message to the theater intelligence center and the other carriers operating in the area. A plot of the corrected electronic order of battle for the area was also printed on the Electronic Evaluation work center's plotter and given to the Mission Brief work center to be briefed to aircrews before their missions.[38]

What the Intel Center brought to the Vietnam airpower fight, and why the experience institutionalized the concept within Navy carrier aviation, was the computerization of the processing and exploitation of the vast amounts of air-defense and target-focused collection the Vigilante produced. Space and skilled personnel were needed to operate the computers, which improved the analysis and synthesis of vast amounts of information. The Intel Center created, through access to well-organized and searchable records of information, better assessments of enemy activity more quickly. The improved understanding allowed for tracking and targeting enemy personnel and equipment—especially the growing numbers of lethal SAMs and anti-aircraft artillery. From the early days of U.S. involvement in the Southeast Asia conflict, the Intel Center's air intelligence personnel recognized that its focus was shifting toward providing detailed operational intelligence to defeat an evolving, modern, integrated air defense system. Not everyone came to that understanding as quickly as had those in the Intel Center.

Stumbling into Modern Air Defenses

> *"The White House anticipates a buildup and wants a victory over cavemen in black pajamas."*
> *"We wouldn't be there if they hadn't already beaten the French Army."*
> *"French Army? What's that?"*
> —MAJ. GEN. KINNARD, *We Were Soldiers Once, and Young* (2002)[39]

At the beginning of the air war in Southeast Asia, at least for those planning the U.S. bombing campaign, the threat Communist forces posed to modern U.S. jet aircraft was viewed with indifference. That opinion

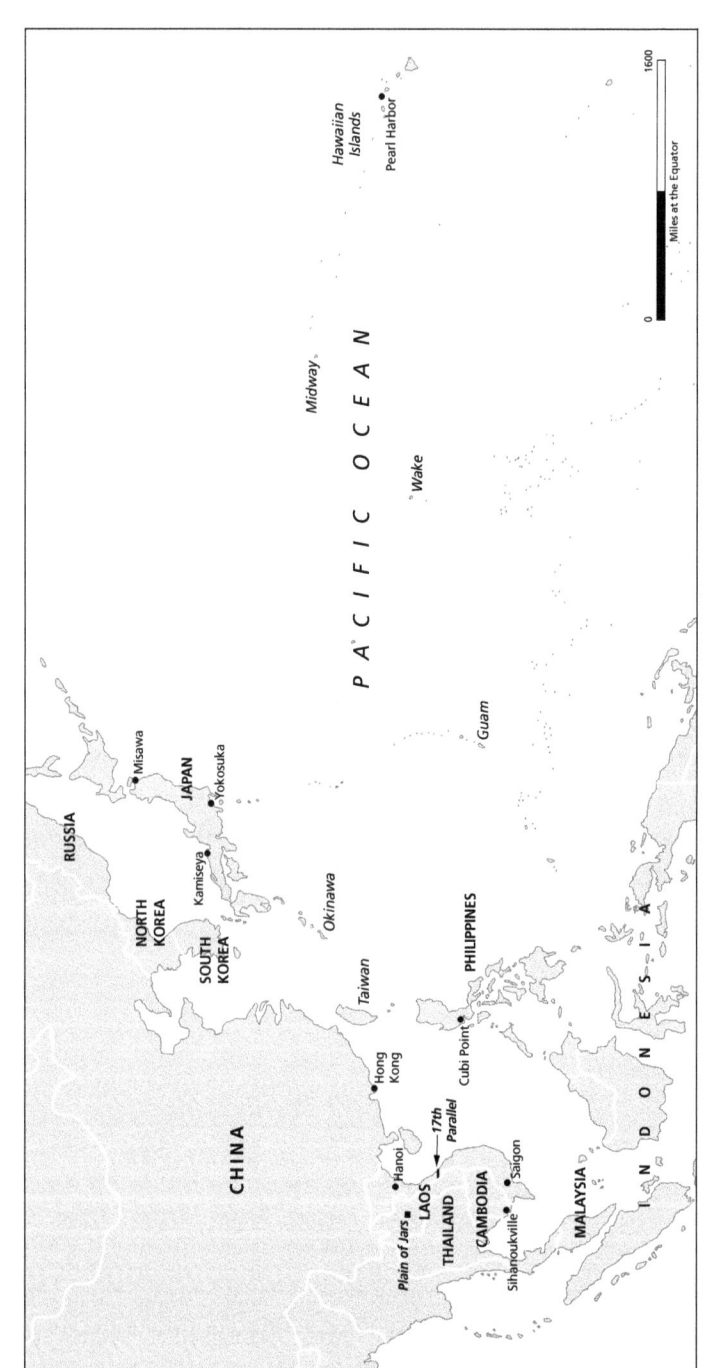

MAP 1
Southeast Asia, theater orientation

quickly changed. The airspace over Southeast Asia went from dangerous to lethal and then deadly in less than a year. All forms of tactical airborne intelligence collection, especially tactical signals, quickly became essential for mission success and aircrew survival. The first air missions into Laos before the United States became deeply involved in Vietnam provided insight into the problems.

Navy Lt. Charles "Chuck" Klusmann of VFP-63 rolled his unarmed RF-8A Crusader photoreconnaissance aircraft level. A pilot in the "Eyes of the Fleet," Light Photographic Squadron VFP-63, Klusmann was making a photographic-reconnaissance pass over the Laotian Xiangkhoang Plateau, called the "Plain of Jars" (Map 1). Thousands of stone jars, possibly ancient burial sites, were scattered across the vast archaeological site. Reports indicated that Communist Pathet Lao forces had placed newly acquired anti-aircraft artillery (AAA) there. Klusmann quickly found the AAA reports accurate. He received a volume of ground fire that damaged his aircraft, forcing him to limp back to his aircraft carrier, USS *Kitty Hawk*.[40]

On June 6, 1964, sixteen days after his first encounter with Communist AAA, Klusmann's luck ran out. Flying a similar mission profile, he ran into a buzz saw of AAA. His aircraft on fire and descending, Klusmann bailed out. He evaded, but the Pathet captured him. It was the first U.S. aircraft lost to the Vietnam conflict but would not be the last. During the failed search-and-rescue effort, the VF-111 Sundowners, also in *Kitty Hawk*, lost another F-8D Crusader to the same AAA.[41]

Three days later, on June 9, a U.S. Air Force F-100 Super Sabre squadron, quickly forward deployed to Da Nang, Vietnam, from the Philippines, attacked the AAA sites on the Plain of Jars. The attack was a disaster. One participant described the clumsy, fumbling assault as an embarrassing "group grope."[42] The two flights of Sabres had logistics, weapons, and targeting problems. The mission resulted in only one flight hitting the right target with little effect. The second flight struck a target twenty-five miles away, ran low on fuel, and diverted to Thailand despite being told not to do so for political reasons. To add insult to injury, upon landing in Thailand one aircraft burst a tire and skidded across the runway. The commanding officer of the Sabre squadron had led the second flight; he was also the pilot of the burst tire aircraft and was relieved of command over the fiasco.

The Sabre flights suffered from a lack of intelligence as well as a lack of tactical combat experience. There were limited detailed maps of Laos, almost no radar coverage, and few navigation aids. And these were just a few of the problems. The Sabres attacked without proper target packages; no photographic target identification existed or any understanding of the operating environment.[43] The Indochina region lacked detailed intelligence analysis of the battle space and the enemy. A better understanding of the air defenses the pilots faced was required if there were to be future missions—and there would be many more missions. Navy air intelligence and the IOIC learned, side by side with the aircrew, how to support a modern hyper-lethal air war.

Even before the disastrous June 1964 *Kitty Hawk* missions the Navy already knew it had a conventional-arms operational problem. Navy ships patrolled the South China Sea throughout the 1950s, observing the ongoing struggle in Indochina. President Eisenhower had ordered a Navy and Marine task force to Southeast Asia in the 1950s to support beleaguered partners of the recently created Southeast Asia Treaty Organization (SEATO). The French then lost Vietnam (Indochina), militarily defeated by the Việt Minh in 1954. By 1956 the French had pulled out, leaving a divided Vietnam and a power vacuum. The Democratic South was fragile and faced a Communist insurgency from the North. In response, the United States increased its Military Assistance Advisory Group (MAAG) efforts to stop the growth of Communist insurgencies in Vietnam and elsewhere in Southeast Asia.[44]

Airborne nuclear-strike missions and limited conventional war were on polar ends of the range of military options, creating tension for the Navy. Its traditional expeditionary conventional-war skill set had atrophied while chasing the strategic atomic weapons mission during the 1950s. Vice Chief of Naval Operations Vice Adm. Claude Ricketts (1961–1964) was new to the VCNO position and quickly recognized the problem. In a handwritten note on a copy of a September 1961 memorandum from Secretary of Defense McNamara, Ricketts wrote that the Department of Defense budget had "vast sums for space and other expensive projects of little military virtue" but little for the execution of a limited war seemingly on the horizon. "If this [budget approach] continued," he lamented, "we'd [Navy] soon be unable to stop a communist infiltration in the jungle of Laos, or prosecute an anti-submarine war, or engage in a limited conflict of any description."[45]

That the crisis in Vietnam seemed inevitable, even though no policymaker wished to engage to prevent it, shows how confused and murky the understanding of Southeast Asia and communist threat were at the time. The same was true of Washington's ad hoc policymaking and U.S. military strategy and planning. As Deputy National Security Advisor Robert Komer warned in a memorandum of October 31, 1961, to his boss George McBundy, no one wanted the United States involved in a war in "another squalid, secondary theater in Asia." But, Komer lamented, "We'll end up doing so sooner or later anyway, because we won't be willing to accept another defeat."[46] Despite a strong pacification effort that included sending additional U.S. troops to MAAG Vietnam throughout 1961 and 1963 as a deterrent, Vietnam slid further toward civil war.

The 1964 shootdown of the two *Kitty Hawk* Crusaders and the bungled Sabre attacks on the Plain of Jars further escalated military intervention. Less than two months after the incidents, on August 2 USS *Maddox* was attacked by North Vietnamese patrol boats.[47] *Maddox* was operating in international waters, conducting much-needed signals intelligence collection, called DESOTO (DeHaven Special Operations off TsingtaO) missions, against the growing North Vietnamese threat. The Navy launched retaliatory strikes, Operation Pierce Arrow, three days later from aircraft carriers *Ticonderoga* and *Constellation*. U.S. air, ground, and naval forces were moved into Southeast Asia to deter North Vietnam. Most of those forces would not leave until the end of U.S. involvement in Vietnam.[48]

On August 7 Congress approved the Southeast Asia Resolution, known as the Gulf of Tonkin Resolution, providing the legal basis for U.S. President Johnson to retaliate and escalate the war in Vietnam, which he believed necessary to maintaining international peace.[49] The die was cast.

Two Air Force B-57 bomber squadrons, part of the force buildup for Pierce Arrow, deployed to the South Vietnamese Biên Hòa Air Base northeast of the capital, Saigon. The bombers increased a substantial U.S. Air Force presence at Udorn Air Base, Thailand. Navy Lieutenant Klusmann, held in captivity for over two months by this point, finally saw his luck turn for the better. Using a driving rainstorm as cover, he managed to escape from his Pathet captors, making his way through the jungle for three days, until he finally stumbled upon Royal Lao forces. He was turned over to the U.S. Air Force at Udorn on September 3, 1964. Klusmann was the first U.S. service member to be captured in the Vietnam conflict and the first U.S. prisoner of war to escape.[50]

The IADS and Rolling Thunder

In March 1965 President Johnson authorized the commencement of the Operation Rolling Thunder bombing campaign. The smoldering war in Vietnam turned hot. By this time the North Vietnamese had improved their air defenses, adding Soviet-supplied radar-guided SAM and Soviet-built Chinese-supplied jet fighters. The complex operating environment forced suppression strikes against air-defense systems, allowing the striking force to reach the primary target. Postmission airborne reconnaissance followed the strike, often conducted by a Vigilante or an RF-8 Crusader. These missions were complex and required detailed preparation. The "accurate and timely" exploitation of imagery and electronic-intelligence data provided by the IOIC improved planning and increased mission success and aircraft survivability.[51]

Between 1965 and 1973 Navy aircraft flew more than 144,556 attack sorties against targets in Vietnam. The "harsh arbitration of combat" demanded an effective Intel Center organization.[52] Each day of flight operations was another "rep," and every deployment another "set," contributing to learning, adaptation, and evolution for the Intel Center. Like a bodybuilder lifting weights to build muscle, the more reps and sets the air wing and aircraft carrier completed, the more effective the organization became. In peacetime, strike mission training allowed for limited reps and sets. Military-organization effectiveness slows to a crawl in peacetime operations.[53] For the new Intel Center, the air war in Vietnam and dealing with the IADS threat became an anvil upon which organizational change was "hammered out." The heavy "change" hammer of the missile age was about to fall on the Intel Center.

A MiG-17 fighter downed the first U.S. strike aircraft during the Thanh Hóa Bridge attack in April 1965.[54] The air-to-air kill was a wake-up call. In that same month U.S. airpower would get a slap to the face. A U-2 Dragon Lady reconnaissance aircraft observed an SA-2 Guideline SAM site under construction near Hanoi. That a Soviet-made advanced SAM site was under construction was somewhat of a shock to the Joint Chiefs of Staff in Washington. They immediately requested permission to strike the construction zone. Concerns over such strikes killing Soviet or Chinese technicians working on site, escalating the conflict, forced Secretary of Defense McNamara to deny the multiple requests. By July at least five SAM sites were within twenty miles of Hanoi.[55]

U.S. Air Force Capt. Richard P. Keirn and his weapons officer, Capt. Roscoe Fobair, flew cover for F-105 Thunderchiefs en route to strike the Lang Tai explosive plant fifteen nautical miles east of Hanoi. Keirn and Fobair's F-4 Phantom was at twenty thousand feet, above most of the AAA weapons' range. A warning call came over the radio: possible SA-2 activity in their area. An Air Force electronic-surveillance aircraft, EB-66 Destroyer, detected a Fan Song radar signal, the tracking and fire-control radar associated with the SA-2. Moments later, two or three Guideline missiles came screaming at the F-4s. The missiles looked like "telephone poles with fins." One hit Keirn and Fobair's Phantom. Another, likely using a proximity fuse, exploded near the group, peppering three Phantoms with shrapnel.[56]

On fire and descending out of control, Keirn ejected from his stricken aircraft. Fobair, possibly killed by the Guideline's impact, remained in the plane as it hit the Vietnamese countryside. On only his fifth mission over Vietnam, Keirn was captured and became a prisoner of war. His life seemed plagued with bouts of bad luck: This was his second time as a POW. In 1944 on his first B-17 mission, he had been shot down over Leipzig, Germany, and held captive for nineteen months. His stay in North Vietnam would be much longer.[57]

PHOTO 1.5
North Vietnamese SAM crew in front of SA-2 launcher, date unknown NATIONAL MUSEUM OF THE U.S. AIR FORCE

The SA-2 was dangerous; its semi-active radar-guided missile garnered significant interest from the airpower communities. However, the limited number of fixed SA-2s caused less loss of U.S. aircraft than the ubiquitous mobile AAA pieces. The North Vietnamese forces, officially Democratic Republic of Vietnam (DRV) forces, launched an estimated 3,500 to 5,000 SA-2 missiles, destroying eighty U.S. aircraft (at a ratio of between forty-four and sixty-three to one).[58] The SA-2 presented a high-altitude threat, forcing striking aircraft into lower altitudes where AAA was deadly. During the three years of the Rolling Thunder bombing campaign, the DRV developed an increasingly sophisticated and deadly integrated air defense system (IADS). An IADS comprises three elements: air surveillance sensors (active and passive), battle-management command and control (C2), and weapons-employment control. Integrating these three elements helps solve the air-defense time-space-force problem by detecting, tracking, engaging, and destroying enemy aircraft at the speed of jet aircraft warfare.[59] Air surveillance provides an early warning (time) and an operational picture (space) needed for C2 to coordinate and synchronize defensive counter–air weapons (force). Creating defensive zones enhances C2 and weapons application by deconflicting intercepting aircraft engagements from missile and AAA engagements. Usually fighter engagements occurred farther away from the protected zones, with AAA used for point defense of infrastructure and protecting long-range SAMs.

The DRV's air-defense headquarters at Hanoi's Bach Mai Airfield contained a control center, a situation center, and air-weapons control staff. The headquarters (HQ) served to centralize battle management, providing a common air-defense picture and performing C2 duties. HQ assigned subordinate air-defense sectors airborne targets via landline telephone and radio communications. Each sector assigned MiG fighters and SAM/AAA batteries across the battlespace to intercept airborne targets. The ground control intercept (GCI) radar stations guided the airborne pilots in "hit-and-run"–style attacks against inbound U.S. aircraft.[60] While active sensors were at the heart of the DRV's IADS, passive sensors, intelligence collection, and visual observers played essential roles. At the beginning of Rolling Thunder an estimated forty visual observation (VISOB) posts were in North Vietnam. The number of posts grew. VISOB posts were a low-technology, resource-intensive approach to early warning. Signals intelligence collection by the DRV intelligence organizations of U.S. communications enhanced DRV's radar and VISOB-fed air-surveillance picture.[61] The DRV's IADS was effective, and while some of the communication and C2 processes were less sophisticated, they were reliable and resilient. The results chewed up offensive airpower, muting the American way of war reliant on lethal strategic bombing.

U.S. Air Force and Navy airpower stumbled into the DRV's IADS through a mix of hubris and poor understanding of the Communist support network in Southeast Asia. A decade earlier, while the National Intelligence Estimate (NIE) of November 1955 predicted that by 1960 the Sino-Soviet bloc would have improved and integrated air-defense systems, the intelligence community (IC) dismissed the idea, saying any improvements would "fall considerably short of providing air defense of the scale and nature required" to defeat Western air capabilities. The IC believed in the late 1950s that the Soviets had provided only a few SA-2s to China and were unlikely to offer sophisticated SAMs to Vietnam.[62]

By July 1961 the IC's tone had changed, in part owing to the shootdown of U.S. Air Force Maj. Francis Gary Powers' U-2 by a Soviet SA-2 Guideline over Sverdlovsk Oblast, southern Russia, on May 1 the year prior. Analysis suggested the Soviets had been putting considerable effort into expanding the deployment of SA-2s, developing new weapons, and creating a more-integrated air-defense system. After the Cubans shot down another U-2 during the October 1962 Cuban Missile Crisis, the NIEs leading up to the 1965 Rolling Thunder air campaign made it clear the IC now understood the level of threat. At the same time, however, the IC still felt Soviet air-defense systems would "still have great difficulty in coping with a large-scale air attack employing . . . sophisticated tactics."[63] In other words, the thinking went, the U.S. airpower approach to strategic bombing used advanced technology and was so sophisticated that it would overwhelm any Soviet IADS. The IC also thought Vietnam would not receive SAMs, and even if they did the IC presumed Soviet bloc satellite states' IADS would be even less effective. Thus, as the decision to employ conventional bombing assets against North Vietnam grew, there seemed little concern about DRV air defense being an issue.

One possible reason for a lack of concern about the IADS stemmed from the IC's misunderstanding of the Sino-Soviet split on the DRV. During the 1950s Chinese communist doctrine diverged from traditional Russian Marxism-Leninism, and the relationship rapidly declined in 1960; the split was formalized in 1962. The IC believed the split had forced the DRV to choose China, its neighbor. In so doing, it was assessed, the DRV would have sacrificed Soviet aid, reducing access to technical weapons.[64] The belief that the DRV had lost access to high-end SAMs underpinned an assessment provided at a conference in June 1964. Secretary McNamara declared that the DRV "lacked surface-to-air missiles and simply did not have the resources to provide air defense for all their key targets."[65] McNamara's belief ignored the reality of competition within the Communist sphere. The competition has been described as the "pedaling" of two different perspectives: anti-capitalism (class warfare) in the case of the Soviets and anti-imperialism (decolonization) for the Chinese. If China supported Communist North Vietnam, the Soviets must also help them or risk losing credibility within the Communist sphere. The escalating levels of support from both sides benefited the DRV.[66] The Soviets provided the high-end technological aid required to fight U.S. airpower that the Chinese could not.

For the IC, Soviet IADS was another of its "estimate" problems. Intelligence and national-strategy literature discuss "bomber" and "missile gap" estimates. As noted by the late historian John Prados, the IC struggled to produce "definitive and unassailable" estimates because "the exercise was inherently one of attempting concrete prediction in the midst of uncertainty."[67] U.S. Intelligence often fails to uncover innovation in weapons and tactics because of a "mix of perceptions" about the character and conduct of future war. Thomas Mahnken writes that a "cognitive anchor" widens the gap between perception and reality, especially during times of peace.[68] For example, in a November 1962 Moscow military parade, the Soviet Troops of National Air Defense (PVO Strany) displayed a high-altitude SAM dubbed the SA-5 Griffon (later the NATO designator for the system changed to Gammon). The Joint Analysis Group (JAG), comprised of analysts from the Defense Intelligence Agency (DIA) and CIA, reported in 1963 that the Griffon was an air and missile defense system. However, in the follow-up 1963 NIE, the CIA downplayed its capabilities, questioning whether the radars observed in the parade were associated with ballistic missile defense (BMD), not general air defense.[69]

Not everyone in the IC agreed with downplaying these capabilities. Under pressure, the U.S. Intelligence Board supplemented the priority national intelligence objectives four times in 1964 to increase the understanding of the Soviet BMD and IADS. The Soviet economy was declining, as was noted in the December 1964 NIE. However, the assessed economic decline conflicted with the observed growth of Soviet BMD and anti-ballistic missile equipment. Finally, Secretary McNamara believed that despite "considerable uncertainty" in intelligence the SA-5

Griffon was an IADS designed to destroy aircraft, not ballistic missiles.[70] For the pilots flying and the air intelligence personnel supporting them in the early stages of the Vietnam War, indecision in Washington created a more dangerous operating environment. At the time of Operation Pierce Arrow in 1964 the DRV's air-defense systems comprised around 1,400 anti-aircraft artillery pieces with four AAA fire-control radars, twenty-two acquisition radars, and no fighter aircraft. By March 1965, when Operation Rolling Thunder began, DRV air-defense capabilities had grown to nine AAA fire-control radars, thirty-one acquisition radars, and thirty Soviet Mikoyan-Gurevich (MiG)-15 Fagot, MiG-17 Fresco, and the MiG-19 Farmer fighters.[71]

In the near term, the U.S. Air Force and Navy developed strike tactics to counter this growing IADS threat. In response the DRV invested in counter-countermeasures. By December 1965 seventy MiG fighters operated from North Vietnam bases. Even more MiGs operated out of southwest China, including the new supersonic MiG-21 Fishbed fighters. The SA-2 Guideline missile system was integrated with over eight thousand AAA pieces (37-mm, 57-mm, and 100-mm weapons). The air-defense capabilities engaged attacking aircraft up to forty thousand feet (twelve km altitude). By the end of Rolling Thunder in 1968 there were more than ten thousand AAA pieces and two hundred SA-2 SAM sites. The airspace over North Vietnam was described as "the greatest concentration of anti-aircraft weapons that has ever been known in the history of defense of any town or any area in the world."[72] U.S. airpower needed to understand the IADS and how it employed the SA-2 to defeat the system. Since the IADS was a science- and technology-centered problem, a technical intelligence (TECINT) planning, collection, exploitation, and all-source-fusion-analysis approach was required. The TECINT challenge was another formative experience for afloat air intelligence and Navy Intelligence organization culture.

CHAPTER 2
Adapting the Intel Center

North Vietnamese intelligence organizations were an important part of its integrated air defense system (IADS). The Việt Minh (later the DRV) relied on a mix of World War II U.S. and British equipment and training when the war with its French colonizers began. The Soviet Union was reluctant to support the revolutionary Việt Minh during the war with the French. China, however, saw the proximity of the Indochina war as a vital interest and so began offering limited military and intelligence assistance in 1950.[1] The Soviets changed their mind by 1958.

From a Soviet-intelligence perspective, providing the DRV with advisers, training, and signals-intelligence-collection equipment provided two benefits: First, it gave them access to the collection of human intelligence by the DRV's two intelligence organs. Second, within its cooperation with the DRV, the Soviet intelligence apparatus could conduct intelligence operations against the United States, South Vietnam, DRV, and China.[2] Gaining access to China through Vietnam was vital for the Soviets, as Nikita Khrushchev had withdrawn thousands of advisers and most KGB agents from China during the Sino-Soviet split, losing an understanding of China's global and regional intent.[3]

The leading Soviet intelligence agency was the Committee for State Security—better known to English speakers as the Komitet gosudarstvennoy bezopasnosti, or KGB. They obliged the DRV's request for a signals intelligence (SIGINT) collection capability, sending a limited supply of electronic equipment, a radio-intercept unit, and a team of advisers to train the DRV's public-security personnel. In 1959 more was requested, and the Soviets again obliged, establishing a SIGINT-focused program named "Vostok"—after the first Soviet spacecraft—which lasted well into the 1970s. The KGB appears to have provided expertise and code-breaking tools to crack French and U.S. encrypted messages.[4]

Unlike the KGB, the Soviet foreign military apparatus, the Main Intelligence Directorate (Glavnoye razvedyvatel'noye upravleniye, or GRU) focused its intelligence support at the operational and tactical levels, supporting electronic intelligence (ELINT) and the interrogation of captured U.S. military personnel. Archival material shows that GRU support included information from Soviet Navy *Vishnya*-class intelligence-collection trawlers (AGIs) deployed in the South China Sea. The *Vishnya* were a constant presence, monitoring U.S. Navy aircraft carriers and reporting launch time and aircraft composition. The GRU support included technical ELINT-collection equipment, training, and advisers,[5] which allowed the DRV to counter suppression-of-enemy-air-defenses (SEAD) operations and disrupt U.S. airborne early warning radar (AEW) operations by the Navy's E-2 Hawkeye and the Air Force's EC-121 Warning Star aircraft.[6]

When GRU advisers left in 1968, the DRV had an entire ELINT-collection battalion focused on "detecting, studying, identifying, and exploiting American electronic jamming signals, especially from B-52 bombers."[7] Technical intelligence (TECINT) assistance from the GRU researched new American hardware. The DRV established a special "Research Committee" that included DRV and Soviet electronic-warfare specialists to study captured American airpower equipment. The research effort reportedly obtained the entire cockpit of a downed U.S. Air Force F-111 Aardvark, one of the Air Force's newest combat aircraft, entering service in March 1968. The GRU also gained access to captured U.S. personnel, likely interrogating them to glean the tactics and techniques used with advanced electronics.[8]

In addition to passive sensors (VISOB) and intelligence collection, the North Vietnamese IADS used overlapping active-sensor (radar) coverage. Early warning (EW) radars could see 215 nautical miles, providing a long-range threat notification. Height finding (HF) radar complemented EW radars, providing altitude discrimination between air contacts and helping assign appropriate weapons (fighters, SAMs, or AAA). Ground control intercept (GCI) radars increased detection and identification capability, which was lacking in the EW radars. Finally, fire-control radar guided the AAA pieces onto inbound targets. The DRV's radar coverage warned the Air Defense Headquarters of U.S. aircraft refueling over Laos and the Gulf of Tonkin before their ingress. The MiGs presented a counterthreat that drove U.S. aircraft down from higher altitudes into the SAM threat. The SAM threat drove them further down into the more deadly AAA threat.[9]

An immediate response to the IADS threat was required; the Rolling Thunder bombing campaign had to continue. Thus, before U.S. intelligence could create a detailed TECINT collection approach suitable to the problem, it had to find an immediate way to suppress those systems. The first SEAD efforts took a brute-force approach, coupling whatever airborne electronic-warfare systems in the theater with bombing missions into a SAM attrition campaign. The first SEAD approach was an avoid-and-fight approach: First, strike missions avoided the SAM threat by flying outside their missiles' range. Of course, the SA-2 was a point-defense system collocated with critical DRV infrastructure—the infrastructure the Rolling Thunder campaign wanted to strike—and flying outside the range was almost impossible. Therefore U.S. airpower had to fight: physically destroy, or "hard kill," the operational SAMs.

Within days of Air Force Captain Keirn's shootdown and capture at the hands of an SA-2, President Johnson authorized an all-out attack on SAMs. The effort failed, costing six of the forty-six F-105s fighter-bombers sent, all downed by AAA. Ironically the SA-2's Fan Song radars meant to be destroyed remained active before, during, and after the attack. SAM sites were quickly added to Rolling Thunder's strategic bombers' target lists, and specific SAM hunter-killer missions, called Iron Hand missions, were initiated. Despite the effort, more and more SAM sites were being identified through photographic and SIGINT reconnaissance.[10]

One of Operation Iron Hand's more successful efforts was the Air Force's Wild Weasel tactic, which they began using in November 1965. It was simple: Fly a pathfinder (bait) aircraft into an SA-2 threat area, and let the SA-2's radars illuminate—and shoot at—the bait aircraft, revealing the SA-2 site's location. Another plane then attacks the SA-2's site with rockets, bombs, and guns. The idea was so insane that when briefed that he would be flying *into* a SAM threat, one F-100 Super Sabre backseat electronics warfare officer (EWO) reportedly cried out, incredulous, "You want me to ride in the back of a two-seat fighter with a teenage killer in the front seat? *You gotta be shitting me!*"[11]

The F-100F carried a radar homing and warning (RHAW) device alerting the aircraft that an SA-2 Fan Song fire-control radar was targeting them, allowing them to take evasive maneuvers to defeat the missile.[12] The trailing F-105 Thunderchief observed the Guideline missile's path and attacked the launch site. After the IADS adapted, and the U.S. developed the AGM-45 Shrike (with range of eight nautical miles) homing anti-radiation missile to destroy (hard kill) SA-2 and AAA radars in a standoff attack. The Shrike was fired inside the SA-2's twenty-one-nautical-mile threat range; it followed the Fan Song's radar frequency back to its source. A "lofting" technique extended the Shrike's range to thirty-five nautical miles, outside the Guideline's threat. In 1966 a new version of Shrike, the AGM-78 Standard ARM, extended the range to forty-eight nautical miles.

A DRV air-defense unit's belief, whether true or not, that a Wild Weasel hunter-killer team was in the vicinity was enough for them to shut down SA-2's radars. Thus the threat of Wild Weasel possibly created more "soft kills" than their Shrike missiles ever created in hard kills.[13]

Iron Hand and Wild Weasel missions helped reduce SAM accuracy but did not stop the DRV from firing missiles in barrage fashion. Avoiding flying telephone poles, even unguided ones, forced U.S. aircraft entering a target area to maneuver, resulting in their descent within the range of the deadly AAA. Part of the solution to lessening barrage SAM firing was eliminating the DRV's inventory of missiles. Network analysis showed that targeting Guideline missile–assembly and –maintenance facilities would result in a reduction. Unfortunately the location of those facilities and the political fallout from possibly killing Soviet or Chinese on-site technicians kept the facilities off the Joint Chiefs of Staff's approved target list.[14]

In the end, direct attrition of SAM missiles and radars had limited effect and cost too many aircraft. A more efficient and sustainable approach to SEAD was required. The U.S. military's intelligence apparatus and the science community became fascinated with the SA-2. Air Force and Navy studies were undertaken, with results issued in October 1965. The studies offered near- and long-term requirements for defeating the SA-2.[15] There was no applicable solution immediately at hand, however, and the Air Force and Navy continued to employ existing systems while experimenting with new tactics recommended by the study. For example, while Iron Hand missions still occurred separately, the study clarified that SEAD and the strike missions must have a supportive relationship: Iron Hand and Wild Weasel missions should proceed inbound strike aircraft, degrading SAM operations. An electronic-warfare aircraft like the EB-66 Destroyer would remain just outside the SAM threat, jamming the single-band guidance radar during the operation. The inbound bombers would then vary their route, making them less predictable, and enter the target area through a blanket of chaff—thin slivers of metal foil that confused the SA-2's tracking radar. These tactics showed some promise, but the DRV was able to adjust, making the situation a never-ending game of countermeasures and counter-countermeasures.[16]

The SEAD-tactics development process was discovery learning, sometimes with deadly consequences, but it did result in some improvements. Long-term recommendations were to improve aircraft survivability by increasing warning and electronic countermeasures for each aircraft. Broadly fielding the radar homing and warning (RHAW) system carried by Wild Weasel and pairing it with a chaff-dispensing system was undertaken. Improving precision day/night navigation for aircraft flying at high speed and low altitude was also recommended.

Intelligence-related requirements topped the list of recommendations. Improved and increased signals, especially electronic intelligence, were a priority. A better understanding of its operation and guidance systems was needed to defeat the missile in flight. More detailed photographic intelligence of the missile sites and improved poststrike photos were required. A complete initial and then continual survey of the SAM sites' locations in connection to the associated transportation networks was needed. Of course the reports also demanded that collection and intelligence reporting be timelier.[17]

Time is always a critical factor, for it is immutable. With improved planning, information automation, and more staffing, more may be done within the time available. For the intelligence professional, anticipating the customer's requirement is a superpower gifted to few. In the case of the DRV SAM problem, it took time to plan a technical intelligence (TECINT) collection approach because, in some cases, the devices needed for the collection had yet to be developed. Once collected and processed, the electronic intelligence exploitation and analysis took longer before revealing relevant assessments.

The TECINT effort explicitly looks to understand the "characteristics, capabilities, and limitations of all foreign military systems, weapons, weapons systems, and materiel."[18] There is little record of Secretary McNamara's thinking about TECINT collection. However, his April 1964 directive tasking the Defense Intelligence Agency with "establishing a single DoD technical intelligence program" was likely an effort to reduce the uncertainty around the Soviet IADS.[19] The Navy led TECINT efforts; the Office of Naval Intelligence had been created in 1882 as "a clearinghouse for technical intelligence" on naval warfare.[20] In October 1944 ONI had established the Technical Intelligence Center (TIC), focused on exploiting captured German and Japanese naval equipment. They worked with the Armed Forces Security Agency (which would become the National Security Agency) to standardize technical-intelligence collection, analysis, and reporting processes. Exploiting Soviet equipment, particularly radars and anti-ship cruise missiles (ASCM), became a priority. In the 1960s the TIC evolved into the Naval Scientific and Technical Intelligence Center (NAVSTIC).[21]

By 1964 space-based collection programs had a growing array of imagery and SIGINT capabilities for broad- and focused-area collection. The director of Defense Research and Engineering (DDR&E) coordinated the development and acquisition of collection systems based on guidance derived from priority national intelligence objectives (PNIOs). TECINT identified intelligence gaps that often drove the PNIOs.[22] The technology-development and -acquisition priorities of the individual services, however, frequently conflicted. The creation of the Joint Reconnaissance Center (JRC) in 1964 synchronized airborne reconnaissance and surveillance in part toward understanding the DRV but more so against Soviet weapons programs globally. There needed to be a single entity providing policy and program guidance for activities in the field and those at science and technology exploitation centers across the Department of Defense. Secretary McNamara directed the Defense Intelligence Agency (DIA) to lead the TECINT effort for the Department of Defense in April 1964.[23]

The DIA recommended TECINT priorities and the realigning of science and technology resources. More important to the Vietnam War effort, the DIA "directly assign[ed] tasks" to analyze and produce exploited scientific- and technical-intelligence collection. The DIA also established uniform "formats and categories" and "standards of dissemination" across the department. However, the Department of Defense was not the only entity within the TECINT community. Though the DIA represented the most prominent TECINT collector in the intelligence community, the military services and the CIA also conducted TECINT. Coordination with the CIA was sometimes challenging and competitive, especially with analytical efforts.[24]

The most important TECINT target, at least at first, was the SA-2 Guideline's semi-active guidance system. In 1965 the U.S. Air Force brought a TECINT-specific collector, the ERB-47H Stratojet, to focus on the Guideline missile. The ERB-47H coordinated with other airborne ELINT collectors to capture several height-finding manual Morse code and voice messages from the SA-2's radar to a filter station. The message from the filter station to the Air Situation Center reported airborne-contact details using a grid system.[25] The intercepted messages were a boon but not fully exploitable as a battlefield advantage at the time.

The Guideline's arming signal was the real TECINT target. There was too much risk to the ERB-47H to fly into North Vietnam to collect the signal. An uncrewed collector was required. Project Long Arm modified a Ryan-built Model 147 "Firebee" high-reconnaissance drone in 1962.

PHOTO 2.1
The U.S. Air Force Ryan AQM-34L Firebee drone "Tom Cat" of the 556th Reconnaissance Squadron flew sixty-eight missions over North Vietnam before being shot down by anti-aircraft fire over Hanoi. NATIONAL MUSEUM OF THE U.S. AIR FORCE

There were two drone variants, one collecting imagery and another using a CIA-provided ELINT collection system. A modified C-130 cargo plane lifted the drone and launched it into North Vietnam. The ERB-47H would act as an airborne controller and receive the drone's collection in flight. The drone would fly into the SA-2's engagement window and, if lucky, would be shot down, hopefully collecting and transmitting the Fan Song's fire-control datalink to the inbound Guideline missile before being hit by the missile.[26]

The first Long Arm drone missions occurred in the summer of 1965. The Ryan drone was to image SA-2 sites and return to a recovery point where the wet film imagery would be removed and developed. Only two drones flew that summer; both had control problems and were lost to ground fire. Later that year the technical ELINT drones flew with better results. In February 1966 a Ryan drone was successful. A Guideline missile destroyed it, and the valuable arming signal was collected and transmitted. With the TECINT collection in hand, scientists adapted self-protection electronic countermeasure pods to disrupt the Guideline's arming signal. More Long Arm flights occurred in late 1966 and throughout 1967; however, many of their successes remain classified.[27]

During this two-year effort to collect on the SA-2's semi-active guidance and missile-arming system, Vigilante and Crusader collection missions filled the gap, allowing the SAM site–attrition effort to continue.

Reps and Sets Hammer Out Afloat Intelligence Organization

There were seemingly endless attack and tactical-reconnaissance sorties. The Intel Center team worked with the pilots to understand the North Vietnamese integrated air defense systems and develop an attack plan that created local air superiority through SEAD. Air superiority was required just long enough for the bombers to get in, bomb the target, and return safely—a difficult task. Mission planning and briefing and the postmission debriefing and analysis were conducted over and over. The endless repetition hammered out a new afloat air-intelligence organizational culture.

The photographer's mate third class (PH3), armpit deep in an aerial film solution tank, would recall operation protocol with bemusement: *When mixing solutions, great care should be taken to keep free of contamination.* This phrase was part of a caution statement in the *Photographer's Mate 3 & 2* rate training manual, the bible for every third- and second-class petty officer PH. The right solution chemistry was essential for processing the RA-5C and RF-8 aerial film. The PH3's arm was anything but clean and free of contamination. However, shipboard experience revealed that the mixing method made no difference: the solutions would still have to be tested and adjusted constantly. Using one's right arm as a stir-stick—a "Sailor modification" to the procedure—made the initial mixing much easier and faster.[28]

The tanks inside the Versamat automated photo-processing unit held the developing and fixing solutions for the automatic film processor located in the Intel Center's photography-development space, or "darkroom." The PH3 could feel the ship maneuvering and gauge ship roll using a jerry-rigged protractor—a piece of string with a nut at its end—hung on an athwartship bulkhead. If the roll was minimal, solution levels in the tanks could be filled to the maximum level, saving work later. In choppy seas with too much heel the chemicals would splash out of the top of the tanks.[29]

PHOTO 2.2
PH3 Robin "Lobster" Hartford prepares to "go dark" and disappear behind the door into the darkrooms. To his right is one of four automatic, self-threading, leaderless roller-transport Kodak Versamat EH-38C processors designed to work rapidly and dry continuous lengths of black-and-white roll films. *SARATOGA* (CV 60), 1975, SELF-PORTRAIT BY R. HARTFORD

The weeks in school only slightly prepared the PH for daily combat operations. In an average thirty-day line period in the Gulf of Tonkin, the PH3 might develop around one hundred thousand linear feet of photography, a far larger amount than the training course had anticipated.[30] Everything the petty officer did now would be based on the doctrine and manuals, but Sailors routinely modified and adapted to simplify the work and easily repeat it to accomplish the mission.

Even six hours before the flight schedule commenced, a ship's Intel Center would be abuzz with activity. Like the PH3, many air intelligence officers and enlisted would already be preparing for the day's strike missions into Vietnam. The Intel Center never slept; the flight schedule stretched from noon until midnight or midnight until noon, depending on how far into the thirty-day line period they were. When the ship was not at flight quarters, it was conducting a replenishment at sea, a four-hour evolution, to top off its jet fuel and bomb stores.³¹ If the Intel Center team was not planning for strike missions, they were preparing to receive the returning aircrews. Debriefing the pilots, processing the collected imagery and signals intelligence, and producing reports from returning missions consumed the rest of their time.

The aircraft carrier conducted "cyclic operations" over twelve-hour periods. The flight deck operated in eight "event" cycles, each spanning an hour and a half. Each event launched and recovered twenty-five to forty aircraft. A *Forrestal* or newer-class aircraft carrier had between eighty and ninety aircraft. A-4 Skyhawks, A-7 Corsairs, and A-6 all-weather Intruder bombers conducted strikes into Vietnam.³² The F-4 Phantom fighters and F-8 Crusaders escorted the bombers and flew combat air patrols (CAPs), defending the aircraft carrier. There were also an E-2 Hawkeye, a turboprop early-warning aircraft, local airborne refueling tankers, helicopters, and logistics aircraft on the flight schedule.

The twenty-five aircraft of the first event launched at noon, and the aircraft of the second event launched at 1330. The first event's aircraft landed immediately after the last aircraft of event two had launched. The returning aircraft were refueled and rearmed, ready to launch again in a later event.³³ Aircraft with longer on-station times, like the E-2 Hawkeye, remained airborne for several cycles, landing two or three events after launch. Long-range strikes used air-to-air refueling and returned several cycles later as well.

An aircraft carrier using cyclic operations consistently puts up one hundred or more sorties daily during a thirty-day line period. Throughout 1965, the first year of the Rolling Thunder bombing campaign, USS *Enterprise*'s cyclic operations produced 211 sorties, 165 listed as attack/strike sorties, almost double normal operations in one twelve-hour flight day. If needed the air wing would conduct an "Alpha Strike," launching all available aircraft—up to ninety, if maintenance allowed—against one target. Alpha Strikes were coordinated with other Navy air wings or the Air Force to penetrate heavy air defenses and create maximum damage to a target complex.³⁴

The morning duties for the PH3 and the rest of the Intel Center would involve making final preparations for the noon launch of event one. The planning for the event would have begun days before. Task Force 77, the three aircraft carriers and supporting surface ships, would have received mission orders from the Air Force's Seventh Air Force (7AF). The rear admiral, in command of Task Force 77, and his staff would have embarked on one of the three aircraft carriers and coordinated air operations with the land-based 7AF.[35] Each Sunday, 7AF released a weekly fragmentary order (FRAGO) providing a flight schedule and the targets for the week (0600 Tuesday through 0600 the following Tuesday). The assigned aircraft carrier's Intel Center and Strike Operations cell would begin the strike mission, reconnaissance planning, and detailed target analysis with the arrival of the weekly FRAGO.[36] A daily FRAGO arrived at 1800 each day, providing updates, changes, and additions to missions previously scheduled in the weekly FRAGO.[37]

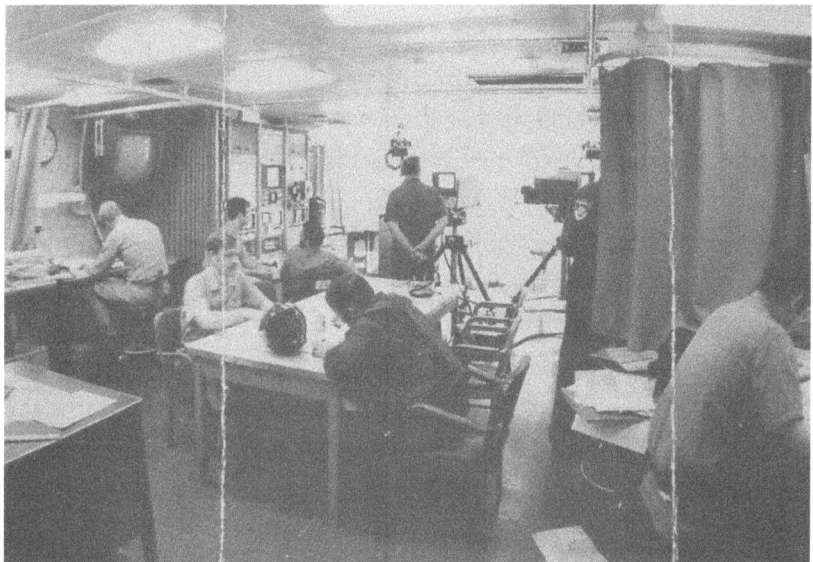

PHOTO 2.3
Mission planning, CVIC, OZ Division, *Saratoga* (CV 60), 1974. Mission planning is where the brief was assembled and broadcast via a closed-circuit television system (9TV) to the ready rooms of the squadrons involved—in color, no less! The table in the center was where mission planning occurred, even while the brief was being delivered. PHOTO BY R. HARTFORD

The Brief

Seven hours before event one launched, the photographic intelligenceman, third class (PT3), would be working with a squadron air intelligence officer to prepare maps for the event's briefing—always held two hours before its launch.[38] The briefing was a fusion of safety-of-flight and air-operations information, such as weather and flight restrictions, with enemy threat and target intelligence, the quintessential fusion of operations and intelligence.[39] The brief was broadcast to the eight squadron ready rooms and air-operations spaces (called outstations) via a closed-circuit television system, 9TV. The briefing charts, mounted to sliding corkboards or placed on easels, were positioned in the back of the Mission Planning work center. Cameras, mounted on rolling tripods and operated by enlisted personnel, broadcast the briefer's presentation to television sets in each outstation. The outstations could ask the briefer questions using a handset attached to the television's channel control panel.[40] The Intel Center's Mission Planning and Brief and Debrief work centers were staffed primarily by squadron AIs and enlisted personnel. The interaction between the pilots and these work centers improved with familiarity; each squadron dealt with squadron intelligence personnel, sometimes their own, led by the carrier air group's senior air intelligence officer (CAGAI).[41]

The aircraft carriers operated from "Yankee Station," an area in the Gulf of Tonkin roughly between the Vietnamese Demilitarized Zone and the Chinese island of Hainan. The PT3 in Mission Planning used Chartpak-brand adhesive graphic tape to mark the route on the briefing chart.[42] Most charts were marked up by hand; others were bespoke maps printed using the IOIC's database and plotter. The Electronic Evaluation (EE) work center printed charts showing the enemy air, SAM, AAA, and radar site locations. These charts, pinned to sliding cork boards, were updated by hand throughout the day; they were ready references during mission planning. The EE work center scrutinized the early morning 7AF's daily intelligence summary (DISUM) message and the individual operational reports (OPREPs) from previous missions (Air Force, Army, Marine, and Navy). EE's personnel fused the reporting and compared it to their current database. Punch cards and machine-readable messages

PHOTO 2.4
A squadron AI delivers the mission event brief. *Saratoga* (CV 60), 1976, Mediterranean deployment. PHOTO BY M. TONKLI

allowed the Q-20 to ingest the updates and corrections into the database. A specific chart "zoomed in" to the target location, providing a detailed look at the current tactical picture. The briefers would then annotate charts in the event briefs with the new intelligence.[43]

The EE work center was not alone in poring over the classified daily DISUMs and OPREPs message traffic. The messages were printed and hung on D-ring clipboards called "read boards"—required reading for most Intel Center personnel. Some messages were specific analysis products or intelligence assessments. Many Navy and non-Navy intelligence producers provided analysis, like the Fleet Intelligence Center Pacific (FICPAC) in Hawaiʻi, the Fleet Intelligence Center Pacific Facility (FICPACFAC) in the Philippines, the ONI, and the DIA.[44]

The PT3 and the AI prepared the base brief for the day's events. Each subsequent briefer would update the brief as the day went on. The other AI on the morning shift would be busy double-checking the accuracy of the Card of the Day, fresh from the ship's printshop. Copies of the card were sent to the squadron ready rooms, one copy for each pilot.[45] The evening briefer would have prepared the Card of the Day the night before. The card contained the check-in frequencies, navigation data, search-and-rescue information for that day's missions, and vital information for aircrew flying into the DRV IADS.[46] Briefed, the aircrew would then gear up and climb to the flight deck and their awaiting aircraft. The Intel Center team would already be preparing the brief for the next event.

The Debrief

The aircraft would slam onto the flight deck with a *ka-chunk!*, simultaneously spooling its engine to full military power. Its tail hook would catch a cross-deck pennant (arresting gear), stopping the aircraft and allowing the pilot to pull back the engine's throttle. In the Intel Center, just below the flight deck, the sound of aircraft recovering was deafening. The returning planes signaled to the personnel in the Debrief work center that they were about to become busy. Pilots went from the aircraft directly to the Intel Center, or their ready room, to debrief their mission.[47]

The Intel Center's coffee urns would hiss, signaling freshly made coffee was ready. The first group of returning pilots would enter the Intel Center. Thirsty and exhausted, still in flight gear, the pilots would quickly drain the urns. Two or more AIs, assisted by enlisted personnel, would be waiting at a table in the Mission Planning spaces to debrief the pilots. A printed form with specific questions guided the debrief. The questions asked about the flight, including fuel consumed, route, and ordinance expenditure, were required by Task Force 77 planners and air wing maintenance. The intelligence, such as SAM and AAA firings (known as SAFIRE), enemy ground movements, and the pilot's observation of their bombing's effect, would be the focus of the debrief. The SAFIRE reports were important and immediately included in the following event brief in progress in the Mission Briefing work center. A yeoman would type up a postevent mission report called an Operational Report-3 (OPREP-3), almost in real time as the debriefs occurred. CAGAI reviewed and then routed the OPREP-3 for comment through the IOIC supervisor and the Task Force 77 staff. The aircraft carrier operations officer released the message using the ship's Communications (radio room) Department.[48] A second message would be sent later, containing the time-consuming processing, exploitation, and analysis of the imagery and SIGINT collection.

The PH3 would wait in the darkroom to receive the film canisters from the PHs assigned to service the aircraft. The film was delivered via a pass-through window into EDP and through another pass-through into the darkroom.[49] The Kodak automatic film processor was a substantial improvement in film development. Some claimed that the processor and stereo comparison viewers (SCVs) allowed photographic prints to be produced and analyzed in less than ten minutes.[50] Even under peacetime operations, the short timeline claim was a stretch. PH3 Robin Hartford in *Saratoga* in 1973 offered that the processor developed about fifteen feet of photography a minute. A short burst by the camera produced 150 feet of exposed film! That length of film took ten minutes to process and an additional ten minutes to create a film positive from the developed negative for the Multi-sensor Interpretation work center's SCV before interpretation could even begin.[51]

Photo interpreters and photographic intelligence (PTs), under the guidance of the IOIC imagery officer in the Multi-sensor Interpretation work center, analyzed the imagery. The photo interpreters quickly scanned the imagery, looking for targets requiring restrike. The Immediate Photo Interpretation Report (IPIR) described the initial analysis. The IPIR message might transmit from the radio room to 7AF as a "flash" (highest priority) message if it recommended a restrike.[52] Immediate strikes on any SAM or AAA site might occur, especially if the photo interpreters found the site on any reconnaissance photography from the mission. Often the pilots and navigators of a Vigilante would review the imagery they collected with the photo interpreters, providing additional details to help with the analysis. In return the Vigilante crews wanted confirmation that they had successfully collected relevant imagery: their reward, the satisfaction of a job well done.[53]

A thorough analysis of the images occurred later comparing against historical images, some only days old, held in the database. If the reconnaissance mission was a poststrike bomb-hit assessment, the analyst would compare its new images to prestrike images.[54] An end-of-day

Supplemental Photo Interpretation Reports (SUPIRs) message would summarize the detailed analysis of all imagery missions. The entire roll of developed film, but most often just the critical prints, would then be sent to 7AF on the first carrier on board (COD), an S-2 Tracker, or the new C-2 Greyhound aircraft heading to shore.[55] That day's process would now be complete, yet preparations for the following day would already be underway; the Intel Center never slept when the aircraft carrier was on the "line" off the coast of Vietnam.

Conclusion

The mission reps and sets shaped the organization and the individuals in the Intel Center. As the officers and enlisted left the operational commands and transferred ashore, they carried the shipboard Opintel perspective. The operators who worked with the Intel Center changed their perspective on the usefulness of shipboard air intelligence. As the Vietnam War continued, the airpower Navy continued to adapt. With the new Intel Center, the Navy's operators began to see opportunities to improve the approach to the targeting methodology supporting the Vietnam bombing campaign. They required the Intel Center's support to develop new thinking about targeting.

Understanding IADS became a cornerstone of afloat Navy Intelligence for the next six decades. Every AI (135x) and then the intelligence officer (163x) brought from the Vietnam air war hard-won lessons concerning the details of an IADS and the strike mission planning that dealt with them. From the start of Operation Rolling Thunder on March 2, 1965, every Intel Center was focused on supporting strike missions through the lens of penetrating the deadly IADS. The constant pressure and close working relationship with the pilots shaped the Intel Center organization by creating a new performance orientation. Sortie after sortie evolved the Intel Center.

TECINT efforts cut across the national intelligence community, and because it is scientific and technology-focused, it consumed many resources. The somewhat-competitive nature of intelligence in general and TECINT in particular does not mean that individual organizations within the U.S. intelligence community do not cooperate and collaborate.

The use of the Ryan drone to collect the Guideline's arming signal shows one successful collaboration. There were many more successes, but most remain hidden in the classified archives. While the SA-2 was an early focus of TECINT efforts, the increasing hazard posed by the DRV's air-to-air fighter capability required attention. Since the SA-2 and the fighters were part of an integrated system, the TECINT effort shifted to understanding the strengths and weaknesses of the IADS's command, control, and communications aspects.

In January 1970 Navy Intelligence's TECINT element, NAVSTIC, moved to Suitland, Maryland, and occupied a floor in the Naval Reconnaissance and Technical Support Center. NRTSC created and maintained the IOIC storage-and-retrieval databases, among a growing number of other technical-intelligence collection methods. As the character of warfare became more electronics-infused, so did the intelligence collection systems. NAVSTIC remained the Navy's science and technology intelligence arm. It conducted TECINT specific to naval warfare and played a critical communication- and information-management role by linking the Air Force and Army Foreign Science and Technology divisions with the Navy and DIA's TECINT efforts. In 1972 NAVSTIC merged with NRTSC, becoming the Naval Intelligence Support Center.[56]

The U.S. bombing campaign in Vietnam between 1965 and 1972 was the nation's most extended in the twentieth century. 1.2 million fixed-wing sorties delivered over eight million tons of ordnance during the Vietnam War, 87 percent more than was dropped on Germany during the massive bombing raids of March 1945.[57] Over 3,500 U.S. aircraft were lost during the course of the Vietnam War, most due to DRV combat actions. The human toll was significant; thousands of airmen were killed and over seven hundred captured; 80 percent of POWs were airmen. In March 1973, 591 POWs returned to American soil during Operation Homecoming. Capt. Richard "Pop" Keirn was one of them. He had been a POW for seven years. Over nine years of Pop's thirty-three in the U.S. military were spent in captivity. He retired from the Air Force as a colonel in 1976 and passed away on May 25, 2000, at the age of seventy-four.[58]

CHAPTER 3

Air Combat and New Thinking about Targeting

The first strike against the Dragon's Jaw bridge in 1965 did minor damage. The 540-foot-long steel bridge spanning across the Ma at Thanh Hóa was anchored on either side by the Mount of Dragon and Jade Mount hills—hence its nickname.[1] Two Navy F-8 Crusaders were caught unaware as a pair of DRV MiGs slashed through their formation, gone before the Navy fighters could respond. In their wake, the MiGs left one Crusader damaged, peppered with 23-mm cannon holes. The Crusader diverted to Da Nang, making a hairy but safe emergency landing. The MiG attack was the first of many to come.[2]

U.S. Air Force leadership seemed unconcerned about the MiG attack on the Navy aircraft. They were, however, upset that the Thanh Hóa Bridge was still standing. If the Navy could not do the job, the Air Force would. They doubled down and ordered a larger strike to knock the Jaw out of the Dragon. To U.S. airpower, the MiG-15s and -17s, while agile, were half the size of and equipped with fewer technical capabilities than the Air Force and Navy's top fighters. And while the DRV's pilots had Soviet and Chinese training, they were certainly not a match for U.S. airmen.

This was all true on paper, but in the air and having the initiative, DRV's MiGs caused problems and were sometimes deadly. Within the IADS the MiGs were the most flexible and versatile part. The MiGs' attacks meant more combat air patrols (CAP) and escort missions had to be flown to cover the vulnerable bombers flying strike missions. Air-to-air combat with the MiGs often forced U.S. aircraft down into the deadly AAA weapons envelopes. Only sixty-seven U.S. aircraft were lost to MiGs but 1,443 to AAA. On the other side, U.S. airmen shot down 196 MiGs during the entirety of the Vietnam conflict.[3]

The second strike on the Thanh Hóa Bridge went ahead. As the Air Force F-105s circled, waiting to make a run on the bridge, this time with heavier bombs, the MiGs slashed in again. Four MiGs, guided by ground control intercept (GCI) radar direction, descended on the loitering Thunderchiefs. Heavily laden, the Thunderchiefs were sitting ducks. The MiGs pummeled two unaware aircraft as they zoomed through the formation; the MiGs were gone before anyone could react. The two Air Force planes spiraled into the ground with their pilots still in the cockpits. They were the first and second losses to MiGs in the war.[4] And the Dragon's Jaw remained. It took over eight hundred sorties against the bridge before it finally fell in 1972.

The focus on suppressing the MiG and SAM threats garners most of the Vietnam War's historical airpower narrative. The two problems were technological issues most familiar to the aviation community. Thus strategic, operational, and tactical intelligence support was required to solve them. MiGs and SAMs revealed a weakness in the efficacy of the nuclear weapons–based deterrence strategy. It highlighted an imbalance in the mix of skills U.S. airpower possessed. Even as Air Force and Navy aviators prepared for conventional war in Vietnam, nuclear strike missions held primacy. In the early 1960s Air Force fighter-bomber units flew "only one [nonnuclear strike training] event per aircrew per year."[5] Nuclear weapons delivery qualifications were required for F-105 pilots, even those en route to combat in Southeast Asia. The pilots lacked close-fight aerial combat skills. They also lacked the air surveillance, battle management, and C2 structures needed to employ their standoff air-to-air weapons. Identifying a friend from a foe beyond the visible range in the air domain was challenging.

Restrictive rules of engagement (ROE) required airmen to visually identify (VPID) the target, bringing them to a merge and within 1.5 to 2.5 nautical miles before firing.[6] The killing range of the AIM-7E Sparrow semi-active air-to-air missile was sixteen nautical miles, beyond-visual-range (BVR) missile. Firing the Sparrow within the 2.5 nautical miles

VPID range limited the weapon's effectiveness. The F-4 Phantom could use its AIM-9 Sidewinder (with a range of nine nautical miles) infrared sensor missile only if it engaged the target at 1 but no more than 2.5 nautical miles away.[7] Owing to these restrictions the effectiveness of U.S. air-to-air missiles was dismal. Between 1965 and 1968 U.S. airpower's success rate was 8.9 percent for the Sparrow and 16 percent for the Sidewinder missiles.[8]

Any aerial combat that close was a quintessential "dogfight" of aviation lore. In the nuclear weapons delivery era, neither the Air Force nor the Navy considered dogfighting a part of modern airpower. The MiGs pilots, however, understood that neutralizing U.S. firepower in the air and on the ground required that they execute a close fight at close range. DRV commanders referred to the tactic as "grabbing them by the belt buckle" fighting. The hit-and-run, ambush-style attacks used by the MiGs allowed them to get in close, where their guns did the most damage and the U.S. fighter's missiles were less effective. In the early days of the Rolling Thunder bombing campaign, the Air Force's F-105 Thunderchief and the Navy's F-8 Crusader were the only fighters with air-to-air guns, each carrying a 20-mm cannon. The Air Force and Navy quickly added 20-mm cannon pods to non-gun-equipped fighters and later integrated the cannons into the fuselage. The Thunderchief and Crusader were eventually upgraded with lead-computing gunsights. Adding a gun was a short-term solution. Giving up on the standoff fight ceded U.S. airpower's technological advantage. Thus solving the BVR problem was the ultimate solution.[9]

In the near term, arming U.S. aircraft with cannons did not improve the air-to-air kill ratio. U.S. airmen had lost the art of conventional dogfighting. In this regard the Navy made more advances than the Air Force. When the Rolling Thunder bombing paused in 1968, the Navy analyzed its aerial combat. The Ault Report recommended 242 improvements to Navy aviation systems and procedures. The recommendations centered on improving training and tactics in using weapons and sensors. In March 1969 the Navy opened a postgraduate course in fighter weapons, tactics, and doctrine at Naval Air Station Miramar, California. Top Gun, as it came to be known colloquially, would eventually improve the Navy's kill ratio from 3.7 to 1 during Rolling Thunder to 13 to 1 during the 1972 Linebacker I and II bombing campaigns.[10]

The VF-121 Peacemakers, a replacement air group squadron (RAG), received the task of creating the new fighter weapons school. The Peacemakers cobbled together a team of nine instructors, four pilots, four radar intercept officers (RIO), and one air intelligence officer. Though the Ault Report did not mention "intelligence" once in its 494 pages, most of the recommended tasks required a foundation provided by strategic intelligence and Opintel.[11] In his memoir Dan Pedersen, first commander of Top Gun, describes establishing the school in under one year. Regarding the importance of his AI, Pedersen wrote that finding "Spook" was essential: "He was a human vacuum cleaner" of information. Without him, "Top Gun would have needed many more years to emerge as a research library for fighter pilots and the center of knowledge that it quickly became."[12]

Naval Air Station (NAS) Miramar, California, had no AI manning for such an advanced school.[13] However, there was no lack of AIs at Miramar. The twenty-one fighter squadrons, five air wings, the RAG, and a photo-reconnaissance squadron (RF-8) on the base each had at least one AI—twenty-eight AIs altogether.[14] The Navy's bureaucratic processes were rigid; it could not quickly create specific billets for Top Gun. In typical adaptation fashion, Pedersen used personal relationships and informal coordination to pluck "Spook" from the available talent pool already on Miramar.

Top Gun, as a center of excellence for the air combat community created a reservoir of expertise. The tactics and techniques taught there soon spread across the fleet. For the AIs, the reciprocating influence of knowledge and organizational culture coming from Top Gun was formative. Every squadron expected its AI to work informally with a Top Gun AI and bring new intelligence back from the weapons school. Every AI in the shipboard IOIC learned from AIs exposed to Top Gun. The only thing holding back the knowledge exchange was the lack of security clearance for the new highly classified intelligence.

Even with better dogfighting training, being "grabbed by the belt" was a stupid way for third-generation multimillion-dollar aircraft and

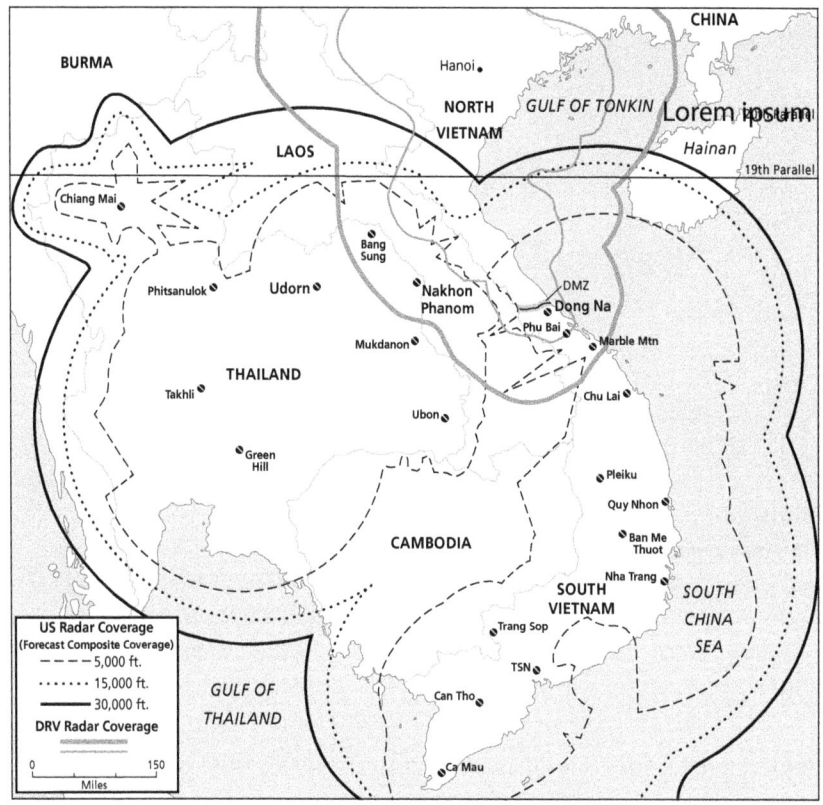

MAP 2
A comparison of U.S. versus DRV radar coverage, 1968. This composite map uses data from Michael Hankins' "Teaball Solution" (2016) and Robert Hanyok's *Spartans in Darkness* (2002).

highly trained airmen to fight. U.S. airpower needed to fire effectively first, which required airspace awareness and the ability to distinguish between friend and foe electronically.

Bolo to Picture Warfare

Finally it was a free-fire zone for the Phantoms! Nine Sparrow missiles slammed into four North Vietnamese MiG-21 Fishbeds. Seven AMI-9 Sidewinders slammed into three more Fishbeds. One-third of the DRV's most advanced fighters were smoking on the ground. A U.S. Air Force RC-130 Silver Dawn communication intelligence collection aircraft reported the

PHOTO 3.1
The Mikoyan-Gurevich MiG-21PF "Fishbed-D," the aircraft pictured, carried air-to-air missiles but no guns. It is painted to represent a plane from North Vietnam's elite 921st Fighter Regiment. Although U.S. forces lost about fifty aircraft to North Vietnamese MiG-21s, Air Force fighters shot down sixty-eight MiG-21s in air combat. PHOTO AND DESCRIPTION FROM THE NATIONAL MUSEUM OF THE U.S. AIR FORCE

MiG-21 pilot's reactions during the engagement. Fishbed pilots exclaimed to their ground controllers, "The sky is full of F-4s" and "Where are the F-105s?? You briefed us to expect F-105s!" GCI governed the MiG pilot's actions so totally that another Fishbed pilot notified his controller, "I'd like to come down now."[15] The Air Force's Operation Bolo was a triumph!

The brainchild of the two-time fighter-ace and charismatic Air Force leader Brig. Gen. Robin Olds, Bolo used deception and airspace management to create identification of MiGs beyond the visual range. "The ruse was simple," Olds wrote of the 1967 operation. Intelligence told them that the DRV listened to their communications and tracked the emissions from the electronic countermeasure (ECM) pods, the QRC-160, carried by the F-105s. Olds' F-4 fighters would mount the QRC-160 pods, pretend to be F-105s, and jump the MiGs. By clearing the airspace of all friendly aircraft, any aircraft detected by the F-4s AN/AWG-10 fire-control radar system was hostile and could be engaged.[16] The operation was successful, but its large SEAD and support packages consumed too many resources.

It was an unsustainable approach. What was needed was a proper electronics-based system to determine "identification—friend or foe."

IFF systems, as they are known, were not new; they had developed during World War II. By the 1960s virtually all aircraft carried an IFF transponder receiving electronic queries and automatically responding with an encoded signal that identified them. Only a positive response from an interrogated IFF transponder provided clarity, assuring it was friendly. No IFF response meant that the "bogey" (unknown) aircraft was *either* a friendly aircraft with a malfunctioning IFF transponder or a "bandit" (enemy).[17]

In 1971 the AN/APX-81 Combat Tree system made BVR shots possible under almost any operational conditions. Combat Tree was a passive and active IFF interrogator. Passively it received and processed IFF replies from a MiG's transponder being queried by its GCI radars. In the passive mode Tree allowed U.S. fighters to identify their quarry without revealing they had done so. In its active mode it allowed the interrogation of aircraft IFF transponders on bogeys flying at high and low altitudes. The improved active interrogation mode defeated the MiG tactic of GCI vectoring around and below U.S. combat air patrols to surprise them from behind.[18]

Operation Bolo's success came from surveillance, reconnaissance, and TECINT analysis efforts identifying weaknesses in the North Vietnamese's IADS command and control communications. Physics and proximity denied the U.S. ground-, sea-, and airborne-based radar systems from seeing deeply into North Vietnam. The lack of radar created the air battlespace awareness deficiency; it left strike missions flying "alone and unafraid" when entering North Vietnamese airspace.[19] The solution to the air picture deficiency lay within the IC's TECINT and SIGINT collection efforts.

The DRV had an excellent radar picture of aircraft operating in their airspace (see map 2). Visual observations and communication intelligence collected on U.S. bases augmented the DRV radar-based air picture. The solution to U.S. airpowers' problem was simple: the intelligence community needed to steal the DRV's air picture. Stealing the picture was complex, and the effort to penetrate, collect, and exploit the North

Vietnamese's electronic environment leveraged a network of ten thousand U.S. and allied cryptologists and intelligence professionals.[20] The counter-SA-2 TECINT and SIGINT effort developed intelligence tradecraft and an organizational culture suited to pulling off an air picture heist.

The U.S. Intelligence Board provided the overall direction of SIGINT collection for the Vietnam War. However, the Air Force's Strategic Air Command (SAC) controlled airborne SIGINT operations, the actual missions, in the Pacific. These operations collected a baseline of Việt Minh and then DRV communication activity to understand the Communist sphere before the war. By the late 1950s the signals collection site at Clark Air Force Base, Philippines, and the Navy's at San Miguel provided only about 450 daily hours of SIGINT intercept coverage on North Vietnamese communications.[21]

In 1961 the U.S. Intelligence Board approved communication-intelligence collection to directly support the South Vietnamese government. The U.S. Army led the mobile ground-based collection effort. Both the Air Force and Navy conducted airborne SIGINT collection against Vietnam. NSA supported the collection by leading much of the analytic effort. In 1964, with growing U.S. military involvement, the Joint Chiefs of Staff created the Joint Reconnaissance Center (JRC) to coordinate all SIGINT and imagery collections.[22]

Collection platforms and capabilities improved continuously, as did their tactics. Several signal-collection platforms were operating against the DRV's IADS. The Navy's VQ-1 squadron flew EC-121 Constellation land-based airborne SIGINT-collection aircraft. Shipboard RA-5C Vigilantes and EA-3B Skywarriors also collected over land in North Vietnam. The Air Force flew EC-121s, RC-135 Stratolifters, RB-66 Destroyers (based on the EA-3), and the high-speed, high-altitude SR-71 Blackbird. The collection was processed, exploited, and analyzed in the theater and provided to those few with clearance for special compartmented information (SCI). Analysts at the NSA (Fort Meade, Maryland), DIA (Arlington, Virginia), and Office of Naval Intelligence (Washington, D.C.) exploited the collection as well.[23]

The constant SIGINT collection and monitoring of the IADS paid off. In early 1965 analysts identified a series of manual Morse code messages in the HF and VHF ranges associated with IADS command and control. The messages reported aircraft held by DRV radar in a single-line "pro forma" message: a series of digits and letters reporting an aircraft's direction, altitude, speed, identity, and type. The DRV's Air Situation Center at Bac Mai Hanoi Airfield broadcasted the messages to the MiG airfields and SAM/AAA sites to share an air-operational picture.[24]

The DRV used weak encryption and plain language to move messages quickly. U.S. cryptologists easily broke the coded messages. The intercepts were operational SIGINT gold, allowing the U.S. military to expand its air-surveillance picture by incorporating the information on intercepted DRV messages. The processing and exploitation of the messages was slow, and the classification of the messages as SCI trapped them behind high-level security's "green door." For a time the advantage of the SIGINT goldmine was limited by an inability to exploit the information promptly.[25]

Automation and information-management tools were needed. NSA established Project Hammock as a dedicated effort to exploit the pro forma message. Under Hammock, Air Force cryptologists at Monkey Mountain, Da Nang, South Vietnam, decrypted the intercepted messages. Then they manually converted the DRV contacts into the U.S. "lateral-tell" track format, allowing the track to be inserted into their air-defense picture. The process created the illusion that the inserted tracks were from U.S. radar, hiding the source of information. The process was still slow. Due to security not every U.S. radar picture received the "special" tracks. The 7AF's Tactical Air Control Center–North Sector (TACC-NS) controlled reporting of the tracks and provided warnings to U.S. aircraft. However, significant security restrictions and poor C2 limited TACC-NS' ability to make the cumbersome system effective.[26]

By December 1966 most restrictions on displaying the "special" tracks had been removed. A centralizing effort brought all airborne reconnaissance and surveillance flights under one controller. Tactical airborne communication intelligence, technical ELINT reporting, and the "special" tracks were now inputs into a more-fused U.S. air defense and warning system. Though the process was slow, the Da Nang TACC-NS battle commander sent MiG and border-crossing warnings directly to airborne controllers or pilots.[27]

U.S. air surveillance and warning improved, but nothing had turned the intelligence into a feed consistently supporting operations. An actual air battle management solution giving an upper hand to U.S. airpower still did not exist. The DRV's centralized GCI doctrine was a labor-intensive but effective air battle management approach. Some in the U.S. airpower community envied the DRV's system. The Air Force suffered from a cultural identity that valued airborne autonomy to create initiative. However, they also needed the warning and, on occasion, the battle direction DRV pilots enjoyed.[28]

Using a form of GCI was not new for the U.S. military, even in the Vietnam theater. The Navy used a semi-automated GCI approach called "Red Crown," which provided limited warning and battle direction to airborne Navy fighters, an advantage the Air Force pilots lacked.[29] The Air Force, however, wanted more than just the voice warning calls of the Red Crown system. They wanted a broadly shared air battlespace picture that fused multisource intelligence into their radar picture in almost real time. Again the Air Force's desire was not new. The Navy had created the Combat Information Center (CIC) concept and the Navy Tactical Data System (NTDS) with the same idea. But in this case the myriad of information-security restrictions limited fusion expertise for NTDS and what the Air Force was attempting. The lack of automated systems and the weaknesses in communication capability restricted the Air Force's efforts.

Advancing Project Hammock became vital. The manual system was limited to ten tracks. The "time from intercept to the consumer was usually 8 to 10 minutes," in which time an aircraft could travel 150 miles.[30] A computer-based information-management system was needed to automate Hammock's manual airspace plot. NSA's research division was given a computer system called IronHorse and directed to create a "visual display of SIGINT derived tracking of aircraft reflecting DRV Air Defense communications." The IronHorse system was revolutionary and ready for use in March 1968, seven months before Rolling Thunder ended, too late to change the bombing campaign's outcome. In April 1969 an explosion at the Marine Corps ammunition dump at Da Nang destroyed the IronHorse complex.[31]

For Navy Intelligence, TECINT efforts exposed them to new areas of technical-collection techniques and new intelligence sources. The field was on the leading edge of what Christopher Ford and David Rosenberg called a "new era of 'INTs.'" A revolution in various intelligence sources, like SIGINT and its subcomponent ELINT, acoustic intelligence (ACINT), and specialized imagery intelligence (IMINT, formerly photo intelligence). The Intel Centers afloat had limited access to many INTs because of security-classification restrictions and physical-space limitations. Those Navy intelligence officers exposed to the new INTs while in shore-based commands returned to sea. Once on the ship they demanded access to new sources and methods. They found informal ways to modify, borrow, and use personal connections to get the intelligence their commanders demanded. The exposure to and increasing access of the highly classified INTs began the transition of the Intel Center capability from bringing in air intelligence only to including Opintel. The Navy and the U.S. military-intelligence community would catch up to the INT revolutions and formalize the new processes. For example, as the Vietnam War continued, the DIA, which controlled the highest security levels for the military, recognized the need for the tactical forces to have more access and began a process to expand that access.

While IronHorse sank into the depths of history, the desire for a shareable common operational picture that drove the effort remained. IronHorse showed a way to expand information fusion to include classified intelligence sources. For the next three decades Navy Intelligence's afloat Opintel teams strived to create an all-source, fused, shareable common intelligence picture that supported a common operational picture.

As for the Thanh Hóa Bridge, the Dragon's Jaw dished out more lessons for Navy aviation and the Intel Center.

Targeting and Intelligence, a Force Multiplier

The Rolling Thunder bombing campaign struggled to achieve cohesion; it sought to serve too many masters. President Johnson wanted punitive damages on North Vietnam, coercing the leadership to stop the Viet Cong insurgency in the South. U.S. ground commander General Westmoreland,

USA, wanted the bombing campaign to interdict supplies from North Vietnam to the Viet Cong. The bombing targets were all part of one political-military system. The combined effect of bombing against the system should have produced the desired coercive effects, but the piecemeal approach ensured failure. "Gradualism" took hold. If some bombing was not working, more might. Bombing increased quantitively but not qualitatively; it never targeted the critical nodes that made a difference.[32]

Theater commanders, the Joint Chiefs of Staff, and senior cabinet members nominated the Rolling Thunder bombing campaign's targets. The president approved the targets vetted through a loathed process. For Task Force 77 from 1965 through early 1966, theater and national-intelligence organizations produced the target list and the accompanying "target folders" and delivered them to the aircraft carriers. The folders contained the details of the target, such as the facility's construction, the desired damage, the type of weapon to be used, and the chosen mean point of impact (DMPI) for the bombs.[33]

Since most of the targets were in the *Basic Encyclopedia of Targets*, some information existed in the Storage and Retrieval system located in the Intel Center. There were five thousand military targets listed in the *Encyclopedia* for Vietnam, and "1,700 of these had been hit," Secretary McNamara noted; as of October 1967, 412 "important fixed targets" remained.[34] Because the enemy continued to adapt and rebuild, there was no way to hit every target. Adding new and updating other targets required the ONI and FICPAC to update the IOIC database regularly. Updates came in hard copy target installation files (TIF), punch cards, machine-readable messages, magnetic tape, and MITRAN cards.[35]

The strike-mission planning team assembled in the aircraft carrier's Intel Center with the target folder. The team included the strike and elements' lead pilots for the mission, the strike operations officer, and the carrier air group staff AI (CAGAI). A Mission Planning work center squadron AI was assigned to each planning team. Gathered around one of the Mission Planning work center tables, with event briefings conducted nearby, the strike lead reviewed the strike-mission order. Someone from the Multi-sensor Interpretation work center might present a target analysis using images of the target. The Mission Planning AI often presented the IADS picture, using the order of battle charts kept up to date in Mission Planning.[36] The strike leads hashed out the route, fuel, weapons, and tactics. The AI presented the expected weather for the mission because it played a significant role in mission success, especially during the typhoon season.[37] The planning was hot and fast, guided by the muscle memory of many previous planning evolutions. Once complete, the strike plan made its way through the chain of command for approval by Task Force 77.[38]

"Operations on Yankee Station were a twenty-four-hour grind," Cdr. Wynn Foster, USN, said of attack squadron VA-163. The air wing conducted "armed reconnaissance" missions for which no specific target had been assigned. Mockingly called "truck hunting," the missions looked for targets of opportunity to strike, often supply trucks. Once Soviet-made SA-2 Guideline missiles became a factor, SAM "hunting" search-and-destroy missions, officially called Iron Hand, were added. The grinding operational tempo, seemingly senseless targeting plan, and complicated rules of engagement (ROE) restrictions worsened the missions. Even Foster's carrier air group (CAG) commander, Capt. James Stockdale, USN, a consummate leader in all conditions, was frustrated with the war. Foster recalled Stockdale muttering to him after a mission-planning briefing, "We fly through flack thick enough to walk on, directly past the world's largest hydroelectric plant, to bomb some blankety-blank JCS-approved outhouse in the middle of a rice paddy."[39]

Rolling Thunder air operations grew eightfold in 1966 but could not achieve the results needed. In early 1966 the DIA wrote that it was hard to "paper over the failures of *Rolling Thunder*."[40]

By August 1966 the new Task Force 77 commander, Rear Adm. David Richardson, USN (1914–2015), was noting that more targets were being assigned, each "less significant, and more thoroughly defended."[41] Secretary McNamara's effectiveness measurement for Rolling Thunder seemed to be sortie production. Richardson saw the flaw in this measurement, recalling that his operations officer, Capt. Robert Hunt, USN, explained the situation best: Improving flight deck operations any further was difficult; it might increase sortie generation by 5 percent. But by choosing targets more wisely, the task force could "multiply," doubling or tripling its bombing effectiveness. It was bombing effectiveness, not sorties, that was the true measure of success.[42]

Choosing better interdiction targets, the only targets Richardson had the latitude to select, required an improved target-planning system. Hunt had one in mind; it married operator and intelligence officers in "communion."[43] Hunt and the Intel Center teams took a "systems of systems" analysis approach that went beyond a single target, looking "rather [at] the relationship of one target to other targets in a grouping."[44] Hunt's approach exploited operational intelligence to its fullest. Richardson and Hunt noted that there was no need to strike "large target complexes because they were large, nor big bridges because they were big."[45] The goal was to stop the enemy's transportation system. In doing so the enemy was forced to ship materiel another way that would be slower and possibly even more vulnerable to the task force's interdiction tactics.

Richardson required all the carriers in the Vietnam operating area to use the new target-analysis model. The Fleet Intelligence Center Pacific Facility (FICPACFAC) in Subic Bay, Philippines, changed its primary mission from imagery distribution to target analysis, assisting the shipboard teams.[46] The targeting model was tested in September 1966 when Task Force 77 attacked the railway line south of the infamous, seemingly indestructible Thanh Hóa Bridge, the "Dragon's Jaw."[47]

The Air Force and the Navy attacked the Thanh Hóa Bridge multiple times. Its destruction illustrates tactical problem-solving using lessons and technology. The Air Force began the airpower learning journey by delivering almost one hundred tons (181.4 metric tons) of high explosives to the bridge with little effect. The bridge was new, sturdily constructed by Chinese engineers in 1964, and heavily defended by air defense systems and fighter jets. The 750-pound (340-kg) M117 general-purpose, unguided bombs and strike-mission tactics were not up to the task.

The bombing problem required precision weapons; "dumb" gravity bombs were insufficient. The Air Force used an older video-guided weapon to solve the precision problem, the AGM-12 Bullpup. The Bullpup improved precision but created limited effects with its 250-pound

PHOTO 3.2
U.S. Navy A-4E Skyhawks from Attack Squadrons VA-163 Saints and VA-164 Ghost Riders, USS *Oriskany* (CVA 34), attacking the Phuong Dinh railroad bypass bridge, ten kilometers north of Thanh Hóa, North Vietnam, on September 10, 1967. Endless bombings with low-yield weapons had produced only limited damage to the well-engineered bridge, even when it looked impressive. PHOTO TAKEN BY LT. CDR. JERRY BREAST VA-163, U.S. NAVY, U.S. NAVY NATIONAL MUSEUM OF NAVAL AVIATION PHOTO NO. 1996.488.031.033

(113-kg) charge. Pilots dropped and guided one weapon at a time, forcing them to violate a golden rule: never make a second pass on a target. The chances of getting shot down increased with each pass, and with such a small warhead it was hardly worth the additional risk.[48]

The Navy took over attempts on Thanh Hóa in December 1965. The effect was the same, and the cost of pilots and planes was high. Despite the losses the Navy dropped another 130 tons of bombs on the bridge in 1966 with little effect. The defiant Dragon's Jaw became legion, a symbol of resilience to the North Vietnamese and a nemesis to U.S. airpower.

The Thanh Hóa Bridge represented several converging tactical problems. First, the military required a precision air-to-ground weapon with enough high explosives to destroy an overly engineered bridge. Second, it required standoff weapons-delivery capability that sidelined the North Vietnamese IADS. Third, disrupting the IADS' air surveillance, targeting systems, and C2 required new attack and electronic-warfare tactics.

But Richardson saw a fourth way: using a network-analysis approach that improved bombing results. In fact Richardson and his team used a network-analysis approach to choose targets that achieved the desired results with the available weapons and tactics—an approach to targeting that should be the standard and applied before effort went into developing new weapons. Richardson's approach was simple: Afloat operational intelligence, supported by FICPACFAC's imagery analysis, analyzed the DRV's transport systems. They found several smaller, less "attractive-looking" bridges within the transport system that, if destroyed, significantly disrupt DRV logistics—the actual objective of the entire effort.[49]

In early September 1966, Task Force 77 destroyed all the temporary bridges south of the Thanh Hóa Bridge, closing the rail line and trapping several trains; the follow-on attacks against the trains destroyed over one hundred railroad cars and rolling stock. The arrival of trucks to offload supplies from the stranded rail cars presented further targets.[50] It was the first real success against the Thanh Hoa area transportation system. Follow-on task force commanders seemed less enthusiastic about Richardson's network-analysis approach, returning to direct strikes on the Dragon's Jaw with newly fielded, longer-range precision weapons.

Conclusion

Sailor modifications were incorporated as the hammer of combat sorties pounded out, with rep after rep, the kinks in the Intel Center's processes and organizational weaknesses on the anvil of the air war. The Navy's afloat intelligence teams passed along the knowledge of its Sailor modification, often informally, to teams preparing to deploy to the waters off Vietnam. More successful modifications and adaptations were written down, and "lessons learned" were shared with the fleet-training organizations for formal incorporation. The Vietnam air war changed the Navy Intelligence and shipboard Intel Center organizations, their culture, and their identity. Those changes are reflected in today's Navy Intelligence.

In June 1967, his tour as Task Force 77 commander completed, Richardson was back in Washington, advocating use of intelligence as a force-multiplier targeting model. The new CNO, Adm. Tom Moorer, USN, tasked Richardson with discerning whether or not the Navy was succeeding in the interdiction war in North Vietnam. Using a multi-source approach heavily reliant on imagery, Richardson's intelligence team showed that "each [primary] target was losing its significance as more and more . . . systems were . . . bypassing damaged areas." Richardson's final analysis was blunt: "We simply were not winning. . . . Our improvements were not keeping up with the rate of improvement that the North Vietnamese were able to achieve."[51]

Neither Richardson's report nor other bombing analyses made any difference; the campaign continued for another year. Rolling Thunder finally came to a close on November 1, 1968. Its legacy is one of great destruction for little gain. For Richardson, his efforts to integrate the power of Opintel, shipboard and shore-based, into afloat operations became part of his raison d'être. Reflecting on being given command of the Navy's Sixth Fleet in 1968, Richardson later said, "I was sent there [to Sixth Fleet] to bring lessons learned in Southeast Asia" to the Mediterranean theater.[52] Richardson's Sixth Fleet efforts were at the van of creating the Ocean Surveillance Information System (OSIS).

As for the Dragon's Jaw . . . on October 6, 1972, Lt. Cdr. Leighton W. "Snuffy" Smith, USN, a future vice admiral, leveled and slowed his A-7 Corsair. He confirmed that his wingman had done the same. "Lock on," Smith instructed his wingman. Both pilots trained their video scopes on the western side of the bridge's center piling, then launched their two thousand–pound (907-kg) AGM-62 Walleye II "Fat Albert" bombs. The two weapons hit almost simultaneously. An RA-5C Vigilante captured a poststrike bomb-hit assessment image confirming the damage. The Thanh Hóa Bridge spanning the Ma River, the bloody Dragon's Jaw was finally down! The victory was short-lived. The Dragon's Jaw reopened less than a year later after the United States had left the war. Much of the DRV's army crossed the bridge in 1975 to conquer Saigon.[53]

CHAPTER 4
Learning and Adapting

For Navy Intelligence's afloat air intelligence, the Vietnam conflict's air war was a "discovery learning" period leading to significant organizational change. Learning occurred at the speed of the conflict as prior knowledge and doctrine were applied uniquely to counter the IADS and support strike execution. The entire endeavor focused on survival and winning. Both required learning more quickly than the enemy.

Trent Hone explains that the U.S. Navy has always been a learning organization. An example of an adaptive and innovative organization whose capacity to learn while engaged in combat operations made it successful against the Imperial Japanese Navy during World War II.[1] Janine Davidson, U.S. deputy assistant secretary of Defense for Plans, writes that military organizational learning occurs in a scan-interpret-act manner. When scanning is experiential, it becomes discovery learning. Davidson points out that even when military organizations have mechanisms to codify discovery-learning observations (lessons learned), they rarely incorporate their interpretations into organizational changes.[2] From a broader perspective, an organization's learning must overcome institutional inertia and military organizational identity that resist change. The Vietnam War is such an example.

Discovery learning in war is most relevant at the tactical level. Combat experience is visceral, and adaptation is immediate for survival. Naval theorist Milan Vego offers that personal combat experience reaffirms old lessons learned but now misapplied. In other cases it reveals deep insights into technological, tactical, operational, and strategic issues. When gathered and appropriately analyzed these lessons are valuable at all levels of war.³ The Intel Center operated at the tactical level. The experiences and learning that occurred happened on personal and subculture levels. As those individuals moved up throughout their Navy careers they imparted those experiences and lessons to others, creating organizational learning that rose from the bottom of the organization to the top. Still, as those individuals leave the Navy and combat experience fades, the skill sets atrophy. Peacetime exercises can never replace the learning occurring in combat.

The factor of time plays a vital role in organizational learning. More time between the experiences allows the lessons to be absorbed and incorporated into doctrine and training—evolution.⁴ However, the Vietnam War experience, especially regarding penetrating the DRV's IADS, reinforces the immediacy of applying combat lessons in achieving operational objectives in a complex and adapting environment. Lessons came hot and fast during the war; changes to organizational structures were made and then made again, with little time to document them. The Vietnam War experience shows that changes may last only one deployment cycle, one year for most U.S. military personnel during the war. The changes, violently relearned when new personnel replace previous ones, often disrupt organizational learning. The loss of the IronHorse is such an example; its development was a hard-sought revolution that solved a significant gap in air-battlespace management. When the system was lost, there was little effort to re-create it. This is not to say that the concept of IronHorse learned at the individual level died; as we will see later, it did not. The Thanh Hóa Bridge and IFF for beyond-visual-range engagement problems illustrate that solutions are developed when enduring organizational and technological lessons are applied over time. The Thanh Hóa Bridge experience, in which the Air Force and Navy continued unsuccessfully using the same tactics while waiting to develop more powerful weapons, reinforces those solutions to military problems. At least for the Navy the solution seems more often to be technologically than organizationally focused.

The Navy's afloat operational-intelligence organization learned, informally adapted, learned more, and adapted again. Shipboard intelligence required space to work on multisource fusion, more people to conduct the fusion, and access to large amounts of data. The IOIC provided all three. However, a caveat regarding data access must be added: As the "INT" revolution gained momentum, access to data required access to the highly classified compartmented data and intelligence. By 1970 access to special compartmented intelligence (SCI) and spaces to handle the material at sea remained limited, but informal and formal efforts were underway to change those conditions.[5]

The IOIC was responsible for a leap forward in information-management technology. More information was available to the shipboard Intel Center team than had ever been before. Though better, the fusion of available material was a multisource, not all-source, approach. Further, operational intelligence lacked the timeliness needed for tactical decision-making. Navy Vice Adm. Lowell "Jake" Jacoby, USN (Ret.), described the capabilities of the Intel Center as limited to air intelligence "threat presentation" and deliberate strike-mission targeting.[6] These air-intelligence capabilities laid a foundation, particularly in shipboard intelligence operations and organization, that remains today.

The Intel Center was simultaneously centralizing and decentralizing. The larger space with advanced information-management tools centralized the air-intelligence professionals. This centralization also created "space" in the form of freedom to innovate. At the same time the increased access to information decentralized the knowledge previously held only at shore-based intelligence commands and provided it to the afloat intelligence professional. Thus the Intel Center had emergent potential, the freedom to self-organize, and evolvability. Aircraft carrier operations during the Vietnam War increased complexity and created enabling constraints guiding organizational change through action and feedback to action. The potential and constraints shepherded the Intel Center's evolution, allowing it to adapt, self-organize, and innovate with a specific purpose, a customer-focused purpose to improve the effectiveness of the strike missions and save pilot lives.[7]

These changes to the afloat organizational culture influenced the entirety of Navy Intelligence. However, the Intel Center's organizational change was different in every ship. Every ship in the fleet was crewed and organized similarly, but how they approached adaptation to new electronic technology varied. Louis A. Zurcher Jr. explains these informal shipboard changes in "The Sailor Aboard Ship." He points out that shipboard organizational change begins as personnel seek effectiveness and efficiency. Informal changes become institutionalized or formalized over time. In the case of navies, technology sometimes arrives on the ship piecemeal. New communication equipment is an example. During a refit period, new communications equipment materializes. If the Communications Division planned and a school was available, a Sailor or two would be sent for training on the new system. The nominally school-trained Sailors would then train the rest of the division. Inevitably "reality shock"—the sudden realization of the disparity between how a job is envisaged and trained for ashore and the actual work shipboard—sets in. The division adapts. An informal organization emerges within the division, seeking the practical, if not pragmatic, effectiveness needed to make the new technology work. The entire division changes in the process.[8]

The informal changes, seen as new cultural norms, are carried back to the "general population" of Navy culture.[9] The U.S. Atlantic and Pacific Fleets have sizable unit level training organizations capturing best practices, refining them, and returning them to the fleet as doctrine. For example, the Training Command, Atlantic Fleet (TraLant), provided unit-level training in ship operations, weapons, and combat operations at training bases along the East Coast of the United States. Most important TraLant's Underway Training Unit conducted at-sea instruction onboard each ship as part of the ship's "workup" before deployment. The training command's instructors had all recently transferred from fleet ships and were "abreast of ever-changing [Navy] world conditions and technology." The instructors understood the informal organizational changes and "sailor modifications" or "workarounds" used to create effectiveness in deployed ships.[10]

The Integrated Operational Intelligence System (IOIS) was a different type of change—not incremental but an entire package, including plane, sensors, processing, exploitation, and analysis center. The Intel Center (IOIC) was designed and built based on the Navy Bureau of Air's (BuAir) required operational-capability specifications and projected operational-environment assessments.[11] The BuAir requirements drove the necessary staffing and training to operate the Intel Center, but each ship decided what "best" looked like. The staffing of the Intel Center is where the most significant organizational changes occurred.

Changes to Shipboard Organization

Forrestal- and *Kitty Hawk*–class aircraft carriers and *Enterprise* IOICs had five to seven junior rank AIs (135x) plus twenty-one enlisted personnel. Each person had a specific duty designed to optimize the IOIC, at least on paper.[12] Once on the ship, however, the additional personnel fell in on the existing Operations Department's OP division organization. Each OP division determined the most effective way to operate the IOIC and conduct its other photographic duties. Air intelligence was not new to OP, but now it dominated its mission.

OP's other tasks were recording flight deck operations, photographing the seemingly ever-present Soviet Navy ships, supporting the ship's public-affairs posture, and producing the ship's cruise book. OP's central photo lab, located below the mess deck, next to the printshop on deck three, was six decks below the Intel Center on the O3 level.[13] The OP division's missions were as far apart as their physical distance on the ship.

Beginning in 1963 the distinctions in the OP's mission began to bifurcate the organization. Cruise books between 1963 and 1965 show two OP organizational identities, the photo lab personnel separate from those in the Intel Center. For example, *Kitty Hawk*'s 1963 cruise book breaks OP into "OP Division—Photography" and "OP Division—Intelligence."[14] *Forrestal* on its 1965–1966 cruise took a similar approach; its cruise book shows OP dedicated to photography and a new "AIO division" focused on air intelligence.[15] The informal changes occurring in *Kitty Hawk* and *Forrestal* preceded but likely anticipated the IOIC installation on each ship. *Saratoga* and *Independence* received their IOIC installations in 1962, the first and second systems installed.[16] OP divisions on subsequent

IOIC ships were likely informally reorganizing based on observed best practices from *Saratoga* and *Independence*, as seen in Rock Ore's audacious request for more space in *Forestall*.

Before the installation of the IOIC, OP consisted of around forty personnel: three to four officers, one to three chief petty officers, and the rest enlisted. After the installation OP crew jumped to around seventy officers and enlisted.[17] When *Forrestal* received her IOIC in 1967, Intel Centers had been operational in combat for over two years. Consolidating best organizational practices and performance orientation resulted in institutionalizing distinct photography and intelligence roles. *Forrestal* created a separate division dedicated to Opintel and operating the IOIC—the OZ division. By 1970 all *Forrestal*- and *Kitty Hawk*–class and *Enterprise* cruise books show an OZ division for the Intel Center and an OP division, usually controlled by the ship's senior intelligence officer (IOIC supervisor), for photo lab, ship's photography, and public-affairs tasks.

The informal learning within the Intel Center occurred as new ways to use and maintain the technology were found. Maintenance of electronic equipment is another type of organizational change. Former *Saratoga* IOIC Supervisor Capt. Jerry Soriano, USN (Ret.), cautioned about the center's computer components. "Lest you conclude all was rosy with the IOIC," Soriano wrote, "the system, as advertised, never really lived up to the promotional hype." The IOIC, he says, had been oversold by NAA.[18]

To keep the systems operational, the Navy had an additional contract with NAA for afloat technical support. Even so, Soriano wrote, success only came from "well-trained dedicated people [enlisted and officers]" who knew the air intelligence business and adapted the IOIC's equipment as needed."[19] Soriano disliked the NAA technical-representative system and refused to take the NAA technical representative on deployment. It was contentious, but Soriano felt his team could handle any technical problems. *Saratoga*'s 1967 Mediterranean Sea deployment, sans technical representative, had no IOIC problems the crew could not handle.[20]

Not every IOIC could keep their systems working, even with informal changes. For example, loading the rolls of film into the SCV was cumbersome. With up to three Vigilante combat missions per day, the PHs and photographic intelligencemen (PT) struggled to keep up. Eventually the imagery volume and time constraints forced drastic informal changes.[21] For example, at the end of *Ranger*'s 1969 deployment to Vietnam the IOIC supervisor deinstalled one of the SCVs because "it did not work at all," writes Capt. Nels Litsinger, USN (Ret.) "The second [SCV] (sometimes 'coaxed' into working) was tossed [overboard into the sea]" during *Ranger*'s first workup period of the 1970 deployment. Smaller, simpler, and easier-to-use motorized light tables replaced the SCVs. Two to three deck-mounted and stabilized single-station light tables fit in the space of one SCV, giving the photography interpreters similar capacity with less trouble.[22]

Staffing Consolidation

In 1964 CNO Adm. David L. McDonald ordered a review of the officer subspecialty and specialty-designation areas. The intelligence designator (163x) was of particular interest. The last such review had been the 1959 Keith Board, which had established a plan to reduce specialty officer areas, filling the requirements instead with regular officers given postgraduate education—more subspecialists. The subspecialty officers did their primary line job and the subspecialty one only when required. Driving the subspecialty approach was the assumption that the average Navy officer's knowledge of emerging technologies would be enough for the modern Navy. It was thought that too much specialization in one technology area diminished flexibility in the officer corps. Specialization was just not efficient in a smaller post–Second World War Navy.[23]

The Keith Board's plan plunged the engineering duty officer (EDO) and intelligence-specialty communities into crisis. They lacked sufficient qualified personnel to fill a growing set of technical requirements. A 1962 review of the problem by a Bureau of Ships study group summed up the situation for EDOs: "The Bureau feels trapped in a vicious cycle spiraling into self-destruction."[24] It was unable to meet expanding technical and managerial requirements. Navy Intelligence was in the same state but with an additional complication: it had three separate intelligence communities—the intelligence officer (163x), the air intelligence officer (135x), and the subspecialty intelligence line officer. The aviation community funded the air intelligence officers and assigned positions in squadrons, aircraft carriers, and air wings. Navy Intelligence funded and detailed the intelligence officers, including some subspecialist line officers.[25] Interestingly the distinction between two of the communities, 135x and 163x, was illustrated in their footwear. Only aviators wore brown shoes with their khaki uniform; all others wore black shoes. The 163xs referred to themselves as "Black Shoes," primarily supporting flag officer's staff and working ashore.[26] Air intelligence officers (AI, 135x) were from the "Brown Shoe" air community, primarily supporting squadrons aboard aircraft carriers.[27]

Both the 135x and 163x communities had a personnel-inventory problem. The creation of the Defense Intelligence Agency (DIA) in 1961, an intelligence centralization effort, had forced ONI to provide approximately 350 officers, enlisted personnel, and civilians to the new organization. The subspecialist intelligence 163x line officers were a low-density, high-demand group, and being forced to fill additional positions was difficult. In 1959, for example, there were 229 intelligence officers (163x) and 501 unrestricted line intelligence subspecialists. Not all subspecialists were available for intelligence duty.[20] The intelligence officers filled an array of intelligence staff, analysis billets, counterintelligence, or investigative positions at District Intelligence Offices and attaché positions.[29] The few direct Opintel positions were at theater command staffs (fourteen positions), fleet staff (seven positions), Fleet Intelligence Centers (seven positions), ONI's CNO intelligence plot (four positions), amphibious task group staff (three positions), and the new Navy Field Operational Intelligence Office (NFOIO) at Fort Meade, Maryland (six positions).[30] Most of the intelligence officers had never before been to sea and were in commander rank and above. On the other hand the AI (135x) personnel number was closer to nine hundred, mainly in the pay grades of lieutenant and below.[31] The IOIC had grown in scope, doubling the staffing demands and stretching thin the 135x inventory.

The study ordered by CNO McDonald in 1964 became known as the Combs Board. The resulting report acknowledged the problems in the intelligence officer (163x) community. Though not considered a specialty designator, the AI (135x) community's problems were also reviewed by the Combs Board. The report noted that the AI's problems were acute. For example, the AIs were fodder for other ground-aviation duties, like legal officer in a squadron or administration officer at an air station when not assigned as an AI in a squadron.[32] This jack-of-all-trades approach to the AI's career path resembled a subspecialty intelligence line officer path. Worse yet AIs were forced to compete against pilots for promotion, resulting in low AI promotion (10 percent) and a dismal retention rate. In contrast an intelligence-officer promotion board comprised one 163x and seven line officers. Thus it was the intelligence officer's customers who selected the promotee. Unlike the AI's dismal promotion rate, the intelligence officers had around a 95 percent promotion rate to lieutenant commander and 75 percent to commander.[33] The intelligence officer only competed in the selection board against the other intelligence officers of the same grade.

The Combs Board recommended increases to the intelligence officer community's numbers and correcting the AI's promotion rate by incorporating the AIs into the intelligence officer community. An added benefit of this intelligence organization centralization would be the improvement of advanced intelligence technical training.[34] In December 1965 the first twenty-five AIs (135x) converted to intelligence officer (163x).[35] AIs would continue to convert over the next five years, lifting the intelligence officer community's numbers from around 200 to 1,100 by 1970.[36] Rock Ore and twenty-four other 135x AIs converted to 163x in 1966, the merger's second tranche of 135x line transfers.

The forced merger of the 135x into the 163x community resulted in an intelligence officer 163x community that was 1,300 strong by 1970. No matter their shoe color, brown or black, they were now all special duty intelligence officers. The swelling of the community had career implications for both the ex-135xs and the traditional 163xs officers. The former 135xs lacked the Opintel experience of traditional 163xs—a career path that provided 163xs with expertise in the character of Opintel focused on tracking Soviet submarines, supporting strategic planning, counterintelligence, regional and technical intelligence, and attaché work.[37] The 163x Opintel experience, on the other hand, lacked the air-intelligence experience. The intelligence officer detailer, now managing the careers of one community, assessed that the ex-135xs were not disadvantaged. "Many 1630 billets old and new require only a good intelligence specialist," the detailer wrote. Thus they were theoretically open to all 1630 officers, ex-135xs included.[38]

The same was not necessarily true for the traditional 163x officer. The 1967 *Intelligence Newsletter* offers that "air intelligence billets of high responsibility [lieutenant commander and above] must be filled by officers with qualifying air intelligence experience. This is a necessity and makes good sense."[39] For traditional 163xs the writing was on the wall. The new performance orientation essential for promotion was shipboard Opintel duty on an aircraft carrier or aircraft carrier division (CARDIV) flag officer's staff. The aviation community, still the resource sponsors for air-intelligence billets, desired only experienced air-intelligence officers (ex-135xs) to fill positions on the aircraft carrier. Serving on a CARDIV staff as the senior intelligence officer (N2), a commander rank, or as an aircraft carrier senior intelligence officer, a lieutenant commander rank, resulted in an officer fitness report signed by a senior aviator, a line officer of admiral or captain rank. Line surface, aviation, and submarine officers composed the selection boards for intelligence officers.[40] Therefore an intelligence officer without a good fitness report from a senior line officer in operational command had difficulty competing for promotion against one who did.

The traditional 163x's lack of air-intelligence experience was a problem almost impossible to overcome, so few tried. According to Rear Adm. Thomas Brooks, USN (Ret.), the first traditional 163x to attempt a CARDIV N2 job was in 1969 by Cdr. Ralph "Norm" Channell, USN (Ret.).[41] The "black shoes [traditional 1630s] shrieked in horror," Brooks noted of Channell's efforts to get to sea duty as a CARDIV N2. "You are truly heroic," Brooks recalls cautioning Channell. "You don't know anything about being an AI [135x]!" Going to a CARDIV staff ill-prepared could destroy a career, and Brooks said many black shoe 163xs thought, "Why would you do that?" To them Channell offered a simple, and insightful answer: "This is the future of our community."[42]

Though the move was risky, Channell saw the opportunity in shipboard Opintel. His successes, first at convincing the aviation-placement officer and CARDIV 3's commander to accept him and then in performing well there, demonstrated the art of the possible for traditional 163xs. Channell's efforts were a watershed moment and solidified for the "new" 163x community that Opintel sea duty was the organization's present and future performance orientation.[43]

The Importance of Integrated Proximity

The Intel Center changed how the customers—the line officer warfighters—interacted with the AIs. "You can't avoid each other; a ship's a small little world," said Vice Adm. Thomas Wilson, USN (Ret.), a former Multi-sensor Interpretation (MSI) officer in *Kitty Hawk* (1975). There was "integrated proximity," as he called it; living and working in close quarters as friends and supporting warfighters created togetherness. The AI must understand the operator's culture and the operator the AI's. It is a situation of almost total cultural immersion.[44] The Intel Center became in many ways the "family room" of the AI and operator relationship. It was where the customer (the warfighter) and the supplier (the Opintel team) transacted the business of understanding the adversary for mission success.

In every relationship there is a power dynamic. Within the Intel Center "the operational mission was our mission," says Nels Litsinger. "We never had a separate 'intelligence mission.'"[45] The Intel Center's effectiveness hinged on organizational power that reduced friction. The performance orientation concentrated on customer satisfaction through innovation and excellence. Using organizational power was not done for personal gain but to accomplish a higher performance orientation. The success of the Intel Center ultimately meant promotion opportunities for all its members.

The pre-IOIC Air Intelligence Office had less shipboard organizational power than the new Intel Center. The IOIC supervisor, as the ship's intel officer (SIO), led two divisions (OP and OZ) with seventy to ninety personnel.[46] When the air wing embarked, all the squadron intelligence personnel were assigned to the Intel Center, adding another twenty officers and enlisted. There could be upward of one hundred personnel working for the IOIC supervisor.[47] OP and OZ made up one of the largest organizations in the Operations Department. Rock Ore notes that on *Forrestal* the Intel Center's size, both in square feet and personnel numbers, and its essential mission "gave the intelligence officer [senior intelligence officer (SIO)] some power" with the ship's leadership.[48]

Ore's "power" relates to the importance of his suborganization within the ship. Power distance, or the comfort with unequal power distribution, describes Ore's observation. Wong and Gerras note that "deference to those higher in rank is often viewed as a prerequisite to a military organization['s]" power distance.[49] The Navy likely has the highest power distance within the U.S. military; it maintains a clear division between officers and enlisted personnel.[50] To many, the closer one worked with the center of power, or near the "flagpole"—referring to the headquarters building—the more power one garnered.[51] The power is part of a "halo effect," wherein the leader's authority casts over those in proximity. However, power is more likely earned and lost in line with performance benefiting the organization than gifted from above.[52]

Ore's point is that the Intel Center gave him access to senior leaders because he had intelligence only they were cleared to see. "You could influence the CO [commanding officer]," Ore said, because you had access to him, and access "helped with any problems [you had]."[53] Being close to the flagpole gave Ore some sway, but the proven performance of the Intel Center earned him power. Ore used his power to increase the size of the Intel Center during its installation. He also used the power to maintain his division's staffing and shield it from administrative distractions.[54] The leadership continued demanding more of the Intel Center as long as it continued to prove useful. Their reward for success reinforced the Intel Center's importance and its part in the organization's culture.

In the Navy, power distance plays a role in the evolution of performance orientation. The Navy's 1971 publication *Personnel Management* summarizes the enlisted and officer personnel administration, its processes, and its procedures. Like any military organization, the Navy is a hierarchy, a series of "pyramids, with many personnel at the base and successively fewer at each higher level." Not all can reach the top. "Personal characteristics and performance" determine whether the individual is selected for promotion or "perhaps considered unfit for retention."[55] The primary tool of the promotion board is the officer's fitness report, written by the commanding officer.[56] The fitness report provides the officer's history, qualifications, and character statement. The report is subjective, the personal views of the commanding officer. But those views are decisive in an officer's career. The fitness report has a duality, both incentivizing and offering recognition in the present, and promising promotion as a future reward.[57] Promotion equates to power, and under this duality today's officer looks to make good use of whatever power is available, hoping to earn more in the future.[58] Thus the fitness report and the promotion process shape the individual's career and, therefore, the organization's performance orientation, present and future. The report is the cornerstone of today's U.S. military's "up or out" system.

Exceptionalism and In-Group Collectivism

The Intel Center was a mystery for most of the crew on the aircraft carrier. It is a place hidden "behind the green door" where "spooks" and "spies" do whatever it is those people do.[59] Those spooks took pride in their exclusive club. What had once been a small, uninteresting-looking Air Intelligence Office in the 1950s was now a sophisticated Intel Center—a hub of activity supporting combat missions. People working inside the Intel Center were set apart from the rest of the ship's crew; they felt exceptional. The multisource analysis and mission planning created interdependence and cohesion among the IOIC work centers, a catalyst for a subgroup identity.[60] The Intel Center took on its own culture, distinguishing itself from the ship and the Navy Intelligence organization.

"I would dare say I felt 'special,'" offered former PH3 Robin Hartford of his work in the Intel Center. "I think the rest of us did too. After all, you had to obtain a security clearance and keep it to stay there."[61] Hartford was right to feel special. Working in the Intel Center also required a Navy rating and enlisted code (NEC), which can be gained only through completing unique, often-challenging schools. To be a PH or PT required that the applicant first show "enough know-how" to learn the many skills and tasks needed for the rating.[62] To determine the nature of each recruit's know-how, the Navy used a basic test battery (BTB), consisting of five tests covering cognitive reasoning, vocabulary, math, mechanical skills, and clerical skills. Analysis of the BTB test showed that a recruit with a score above a certain level was most likely to complete the associated training for the rating. "Such a minimum score for admission to a school" and the rate, noted the Navy's *All Hands Magazine* "is known as the 'Cutting Score.'"[63]

The PH and PT ratings required "substantially above average" scores on verbal and cognitive reasoning testing and on the arithmetic test (ARI) measuring mathematical reasoning. The PH and PT "A-schools," or initial rate-training courses, were in the top twelve for student attrition in a 1972 study by the Naval Personnel and Training Research Laboratory. The PH A-school had 7.4 percent attrition, while the PT A-school had 17.9 percent, the fourth highest attrition of all Navy A-schools.[64] The difficulty in becoming a PH and PT, plus the security-clearance requirement, placed those sailors in the upper echelon of personnel. Those working in the Intel Center were viewed as "prima donnas" by the rest of the crew. The separation and sense of exceptionalism was reinforced through group artifacts—like artwork posted on the center's door or the wearing of specially made patches.

Collectivism extended to divisions within the ship and the ship or squadron itself. The heraldic emblems adorning the interior spaces of the aircraft carrier were so important that the cruise books included them. Most naval warships have a crest and motto representing the "best qualities of the ship, its crew, and its mission." U.S. Navy fighter squadrons are notorious for having the most imaginative, colorful, and racy emblems.[65]

Crews often created new emblems, called "patches," representing participation in a deployment or special mission. These emblems, patches, and mottos are symbols of belonging in organizational culture, reinforcing in-group collectivism and organizational identity. They stabilize organizational changes by expressing pride, paying "homage to their lineage," and extolling the privilege of organizational membership" of the Intel Center.[66]

Saratoga's bright yellow and red crest is adorned with a crown and a trident within a shield. Perched atop the shield, on a black shadow of the aircraft carrier, was a fierce red and black fighting cock, ready to strike.[67] *Saratoga*'s Intel Center took a humorous view of the ship's crest and "unconquered fighting cock" motto; they painted their bulkhead with a giant cartoon of Foghorn Leghorn holding a spyglass, standing next to reels of film, throwing missile-looking darts at a dartboard.[68]

Forrestal, CVA 59, provides another example; its Intel Center produced a symbol based on its leadership. Rock Ore, IOIC supervisor, was short in stature. Lt. Cdr. Ron Tarkowski, USN, assistant IOIC supervisor, was taller. The cartoon shows "Rocky," a squirrel character with the number 59 on his chest, surrounded by punch cards and reels of film. The words "IOIC Forrestal" are below the squirrel.[69] Why a squirrel? Tarkowski was a large man, Rock Ore said, and "the enlisted man that drew that cartoon made me Rocky to Tarkowski's Bullwinkle"—a reference to the squirrel and moose characters from *The Adventures of Rocky and Bullwinkle and Friends* cartoon, which aired on television between 1959 and 1964.[70] Ore said the IOIC team liked the cartoon so much that he agreed to let them put it into the 1967 cruise book.

Opintel members assigned to air squadrons saw themselves first as members of that squadron and second as members of the Intel Center. "My squadron was like family," wrote PT3 Mario Tonkli, USN. "We all took care of each other." His loyalty to the squadron was "100%," and he was proud to announce it. "[I] only got 1 tattoo in my entire life (back when only sailors and bikers got tattoos), and that's of my squadron logo." It seems there is enough pride in the identity of the aircraft carrier's air wing intelligence personnel to go around. "I can proudly claim sailing the *Saratoga*," he added.[71]

AI had levels of loyalty as well. Many began their Navy career in a flight program before ending up in air intelligence. AI ranks were filled with these "fallen angels"—those who washed out of flight training, chose not to fly, or could not fly any longer. "Fresh-caught" ensigns who had gone through Aviation Officer Candidate School (AOCS) directly into the AI training pipeline were few in the 1960s.[72] "Non-flying officers always were somewhat of a second class [citizen] in the ready room," former squadron AI Nels Litsinger wrote.[73] The specific culture of the aviation community—the uniforms, the lingo, the sense of humor—was unique. Pilots were demigods, and the intelligence officer was a lower being. Lt. (jg) Stephen Cox describes the AI's culture shock to the squadron:

> The fleet squadron aviation intelligence officer (AI) is a rare species. Found alone or in pairs, he is often the youngest, most junior member of the wardroom, and as a non-aviator, is also usually the object of a steady stream of ready-room humor. If he is to adapt to "the squadron environment," he must learn a new language, using terms such as "roger" and "check your six," and hand signals such as the two-finger "let us go" wave. The intelligence officer is often camouflaged in a flight jacket (complete with patches), brown shoes, and aviator sunglasses—and can usually travel virtually unnoticed among aviators, thereby easing the transition into squadron life.[74]

The squadron may abuse their AI, but God help anyone else who dared. Once an AI proved competent and was accepted, loyalty to and from the squadron was resolute. "I never had any problem figuring out who I worked for," Litsinger said of squadron versus IOIC loyalty. My "CO [commanding officer of] VF-154 signed my fitness report, and that was where my first loyalty was directed." Litsinger steadfastly reminds us that devotion to the operational mission was ultimately the focus regardless of the intelligence officer's squadron loyalty.[75]

Conclusion

In the post–World War II airpower Navy, every aircraft carrier had a small, dedicated space for air combat–operations intelligence. The intelligence spaces and staffing were inadequate for modern power projection against shore targets. The Vigilante's air-reconnaissance system allowed consolidation and expansion of operational intelligence functions afloat. The expansion and modernization of Navy operational intelligence and collocating it with the operational commander was necessary, as was the merger of the AI (135x) into the intelligence officer (163x) community to centralize Navy Intelligence operations and better support afloat and ashore intelligence requirements.

By 1970 the Intel Center had proven its value. In the debate to modernize the Navy's aircraft carriers, the Intel Center became one of the old aircraft carriers' five specific weight, space, and capability deficiencies. They were arguing for a new, larger aircraft carrier capable of carrying the heavier, larger aircraft (weight and space), and large enough to house new technology equipment and the electricity and air-conditioning for new electronics. "There is no growth potential left" in the *Essex-* and *Midway-*class aircraft carriers, said Rear Adm. James L. Holloway III, USN, in his 1970 congressional testimony. The old carriers were too small to install the IOIC or operate larger advanced aircraft, he said, urging Congress to fund the nuclear-powered *Nimitz-*class to replace the *Essex-* and *Midway-*class carriers and eventually the *Forrestal-*, *Kitty Hawk-*, and *Enterprise-*class super aircraft carriers.[76]

Holloway's statement to Congress clarified that shipboard-automated, multisensor-fusion operational intelligence was required to succeed in modern naval combat. The Intel Center had been tested in the Vietnam War, and the experience was formative to the systems and processes; it shaped Navy Intelligence for half a century. From a carrier-design perspective the IOIC was now an embedded part of Navy airpower, and thus was the Intel Center part of aircraft carrier design. The Intel Center was the shipboard operational-intelligence model, an institutionalized norm within Navy aviation's organizational culture. Today every aircraft carrier, large-deck helicopter/vertical short takeoff and landing (VSTOL) amphibious warship, and command and control ship commissioned in the U.S. Navy has an intelligence center modeled after the IOIC.

The air intelligence officer's (135x) culture, based on a performance orientation supporting aircraft carrier aviation missions, had squadron-like in-group collectivism. When the 135xs combined with the 163xs their aviation-centric culture became dominant. The traditional intelligence officer (163x) career path had changed from shore command to shipboard-centric. Thus junior intelligence officers' performance and learning orientations (135x in one 163x community) also changed. The aviation-squadron culture imprinted itself with its artifacts and antics, becoming one with the air intelligence and Opintel subcultures. In simple terms, combining the 135x AIs into the 163x community and establishing the Intel Center changed the entire organizational culture of Navy Intelligence. Opintel as a process became an amalgamation of the two characters, air intelligence and Opintel, supporting the operational and tactical levels more than ever before—a perspective of Opintel dominated by the aviation community's mission.[77]

The increased access to multisource intelligence brought about by the IOIC's automated storage and retrieval systems allowed shipboard and shore-based Opintel to provide dynamic intelligence support across various operational missions. Rear Adm. David Richardson's quest to seize the dynamic nature of multisource Opintel continued throughout the 1960s. He left the Vietnam War in late 1967 to bring his ideas to the Mediterranean theater as Sixth Fleet commander. He leveraged Opintel to improve mission effectiveness through integration—both in planning and mission execution—of operations and intelligence. Richardson was a driving force in implementing the 1970s Ocean Surveillance Intelligence System (OSIS), an all-source fusion concept.

The creation and fielding of the IOIC was successful because the Navy found an innovative way to deal with President Kennedy's shift away from carrier-based strategic bombing; it was a fortuitous event. The size of *Forrestal*-class aircraft carriers provided the space required for consolidation, not just the addition of more electronics. The dedicated intelligence space, access to significant intelligence reporting, and extra personnel allowed for improved target analysis and mission planning. These would be critical improvements needed for the conflict growing in Southeast Asia.

As for Rock Ore in *Forrestal*, he would never get to test his new, larger Intel Center in combat. *Forrestal* arrived at Yankee Station off North Vietnam on July 14, 1967, and began strike missions a week and a half later on the 25th. A devastating fire broke out on July 29 as she prepared to launch the second strike mission of the day. An unguided five-inch (127-mm) Mk-32 "Zuni" rocket had ignited and launched from an F-4 Phantom, hitting an A-4 Skyhawk waiting behind the portside waist catapults. The rocket did not detonate, instead tearing a hole in the Skyhawk's fuel tank. The resulting fire detonated ordnance, ripping a hole into the armored flight deck and engulfing other aircraft on the flight deck and the hangar bay below. One hundred thirty-four men died, some while sleeping in the aft berthing below the explosion. Twenty-one of the seventy-three aircraft on board were destroyed, and forty more were damaged. It was the most significant loss of life on a U.S. Navy ship since World War II.[78] *Forrestal* limped back to the United States and spent more than a year in the shipyard. Rock Ore transferred from *Forrestal* near the end of its yard period, reporting to NRTSC in 1968.

Forrestal's Vietnam War experience had been cut short, and she would never return to the Pacific theater. But the war's lessons for Navy Intelligence were far from over. While the air war over North Vietnam was still raging, the DRV was supplying insurgent forces, the Viet Cong, operating in the Mekong Delta, south and west of the South Vietnam capital of Saigon. A joint and combined U.S. Navy, U.S. Army, and South Vietnamese navy interdiction effort was required. The "brown water" of the maze-like Mekong Delta was hazardous. The dangers on the ground in the south differed from those in the air over the north. Supporting interdiction operations, a form of close blockade, would require a new all-source fusion Opintel approach.

PART II
The Vietnam War: Adapting to Naval War

It was a certainty that the DRV was using the sea to infiltrate supplies into South Vietnam, a fact not yet supported by data. The North Vietnamese were already supplying the Viet Cong insurgent forces through the overland "Ho Chi Minh Trail." The time-space-force equation showed the certainty that the DRV used the sea to supply the Viet Cong. With over 870 nautical miles of coastline and 3,000 nautical miles of delta waterways, the Viet Cong had ample maritime routes to exploit. Intercepting these supplies and denying them maneuver in the delta and littorals was a crucial Navy mission.

A blockade was necessary, and it had to be a close blockade of the littorals and the inland waterways of the Mekong River Delta. The Navy was ill-prepared for such a task; it lacked the right mix of ships and an intelligence organization to support the effort. The Navy had successfully conducted a distant blockade against Cuba three years earlier, but it was a near-run thing and done over the open ocean. The Navy's decisions to rely on presence and interdiction within the delta and coordinated air and surface patrols in the littorals were bold choices that relied on a yet-untested operational-intelligence organization. The experience of the Navy intelligence officers who supported, from bases floating in the brown waters of the Mekong or at the land-based maritime patrol squadrons, was formative to the individual and the community.

CHAPTER 5

A Close Blockade

The Republic of Vietnam Navy (RVNN, South Vietnam) reported to the U.S. Military Assistance Advisory Group (MAAG) that the Viet Cong were using the delta to infiltrate military supplies. No one listened, determining the VNN reporting to be spurious, despite the DIA's and CIA's separate assessments agreeing that seaborne infiltration was occurring.[1] The Navy attaché in Saigon reported on RVNN's claims, but not all his reports were forwarded. The MAAG delayed any reports criticizing them or the VNN, Capt. Donald "Mac" Showers (1630), USN (1919–2012), PACFLT N2, told DNI Rear Adm. Rufus Taylor, USN, in 1963.[2] By late 1964 the weak RVNN had ceded most of the northern Mekong Delta to the Viet Cong.[3]

The Navy's in-country Vietnam intelligence personnel comprised about five intelligence officers (163x) and two line intelligence subspecialist advisers across the MAAG and RVNN headquarters (HQ).[4] Access to special compartment intelligence (SCI) for the advisers was almost nonexistent. By late 1964 intelligence officer advisers forwarded a recommendation for airborne reconnaissance and surveillance to assist the RVNN in proving that seaborne infiltration was occurring. In 2004 Capt. Ralph "Norm" Channell, USN (Ret.), (the same officer discussed in the previous chapter), adviser to the RVNN, recalled that a few old Navy P-5B Marlin seaplane patrol flights had occurred but not nearly enough.[5]

In February 1965 things changed. A U.S. Army medivac helicopter swung wide, cutting across Vũng Rô Bay en route to the Army's 8th Field Hospital in Nha Trang, fifty nautical miles south. Fishing boats in Vũng Rô Bay were typical, but Army pilot Lt. James S. Bowers, USA, had noticed something odd: a 130-foot steel-hulled trawler. Odder still was that the trawler was painted in camouflage and unloading crates on the beach! He called the sighting in. South Vietnamese A-1H Skyraider attack aircraft arrived on the scene, sinking the trawler and bombing the stacked crates on the beach. RVNN ships arrived a day later, finding over one hundred tons of military supplies, most still intact and stacked on the shoreline.[6]

U.S. Seventh Fleet admitted that the captured trawler was "positive proof that sea infiltration is occurring . . . [and that] at least a portion of the unconfirmed reports of the past were, in fact, true."[7] U.S. Army General Westmoreland, commander, Military Assistance Command Vietnam (MACV, which had replaced the MAAG), requested that the Navy establish a blockade against military supplies and personnel infiltration into South Vietnam. Operation Market Time began on March 24, 1965, interdicting ships transporting supplies in the seas and littorals. Operation Game Warden started in December 1965, conducting presence operations to interdict supplies on the lower Mekong River Delta. Operation Sealords (Southeast Asia Lake, Ocean, River, and Delta Strategy) began after the 1968 Tet Offensive. It focused on offensive operations interdicting supplies in the northern delta rivers along the Cambodian border.

Market Time was primarily a Navy and U.S. Coast Guard effort; Game Warden and Sealords were joint operations between the Navy Riverine forces and the U.S. Army's 9th Infantry Division. In July 1965 commander Patrol Forces Seventh Fleet, now in command of Market Time, complained that a lack of intelligence was hampering operations. Since the beginning of the operation airborne and surface scouting had been ad hoc. The lack of intelligence-collection assets was a problem, but the limited coordination between RVNN surface patrols and the Navy's efforts was the true issue. Fusing airborne and surface reconnaissance and surveillance reporting with SIGINT collection to create an operating picture of Viet Cong and DRV activity was proving inadequate. Maritime airborne surveillance, called the "air barrier," had begun in March 1965, using a few P-2V Neptune land-based maritime patrol and reconnaissance aircraft (MPRA). Norm Channell, fellow intelligence officer (163x) Frank Noll, and a few RVNN officers volunteered to fly on the Neptune

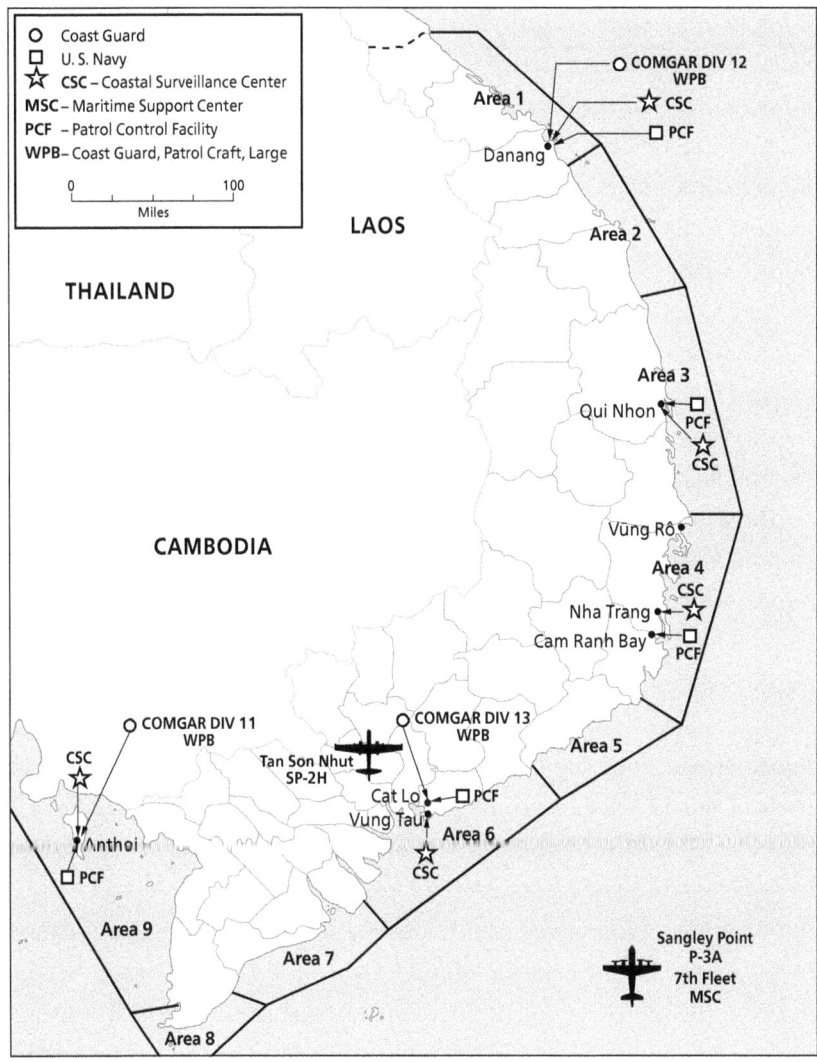

MAP 3

Southeast Asia theater of operations, showing Market Time surface-barrier patrol areas, 1966 DATA FROM A PERIOD MAP FOUND AT THE NAVAL HISTORY AND HERITAGE COMMAND'S HAMPTON ROADS MUSEUM, TITLED "OPERATION MARKET TIME."

missions. Maritime contacts were radioed to RVNN ships, guiding their interdiction efforts. Debriefs from the flights occurred at Naval Advisory HQ and RVNN HQ. The burden of briefing and debriefing the MPRA crews fell to their squadron air intelligence officer (AI, 135x).[8]

By July 1965 more coordinated air and surface search barriers were in place. The coastal water space was divided into patrol areas, and Coastal Surveillance Centers (CSCs) coordinated patrols and conducted some fusion of the reports (see map 3). Navy intelligence officers (163x) coordinated air and surface patrols and maintained a plot of merchant and possible infiltration activity. There were still inadequate identification tools to assist the patrols and limited integration of SIGINT reporting. Not until 1967 did the Naval Reconnaissance Technical Support Center (NRTSC) finally provide photographic-identification booklets to aid air- and surface-barrier operations.[9] The number of MPRA assets applied to the air-barrier mission grew. The new, more capable P-3A Orion took on most of the air-barrier effort.

There weren't enough intelligence professionals and facilities to support Market Time and the soon-to-commence Game Warden operations (December 18, 1965, to March 1973). In April 1965 a Navy All Navy (ALNAV) message went out to the fleet requesting volunteers for Vietnam duty. The 1965 *Intelligence Newsletter* wrote that eleven officers (163x) had already volunteered to join the seven in Vietnam. Demands increased, and the *Newsletter* pointed out that "all of our LTJG, LT and many of our LCDRs and some CDRs will get their chance to serve" in Vietnam. By 1966 thirty-two 163x and line intelligence subspecialist officers were in-country Vietnam.[10]

What Nels Litsinger offered about the needs for shipboard Opintel for all-source fusion held for Market Time and Game Warden fusion analysis. Having more intelligence officers was good, access to special compartmented intelligence (SCI) material was better, and a place where the officer could fuse SCI and create useful assessments was best. Bringing the three elements together in South Vietnam was as challenging as it had been on the aircraft carrier. Navy intelligence officers set about rectifying these deficiencies.

Control of Market Time operations switched in 1965 from the Seventh Fleet to the Naval Advisory Group (NAG) located in Saigon. Construction began of a Navy SCI facility (SCIF) and special-communications facility (SpintCom) for the NAG's intelligence section (N2) situated on the MACV compound. Unfortunately, because they were in a combat area, the two Navy intelligence officers (163x) assigned to oversee the SCIF had been "read out" of the SCI program as a precaution. Lt. Cdr. Don Tuthill, USN, a line intelligence subspecialist, passed through Saigon to meet his ship. Still "read in" to SCI, Tuthill was grabbed by the two NAG intelligence officers and co-opted to smooth out the SCIF construction details.[11] Access to SCI was an afterthought and often an ad hoc affair supporting combat operations.

The DIA established a special security officer (SSO) system in January 1962. It centralized the "responsibility for the operational control, management and supervision for: . . . storing and disseminating Special Intelligence [SCI] and other highly sensitive information" across the Department of Defense. The security-clearance system tied specific personnel billets (positions) to SCI material access, thus limiting the total number of personnel with access. The control of the defense special security communications system (DSSCS), the SpintComs, also fell to the DIA.[12] The SSO and SpintCom systems created structure and improved security. However, linking billets and SCI access limited the flexibility and adaptability needed to sustain combat operations.

Lacking creativity and looking for simple solutions for improving security often resulted in an approach that restricted access to the material. The access problem was not new; it was seen during the World World II and the Korean Wars. Withholding vital, highly classified intelligence from operators and military decision-makers was scornfully called the "green door syndrome." Keeping intelligence behind the "green door" protected vital intelligence sources. However, many pilots and infantry saw it as a practice that resulted in unnecessary casualties.

The intelligence community's fear of losing highly sensitive sources was not unfounded. Too many personnel sharing the intelligence was a risk to national security. Understanding that U.S. military forces' poor operational security in Vietnam was the fundamental security problem would take years and cost lives. On Christmas Day 1969, almost four years after the conflict had begun, a sweep of Bình Dương Province (north of Saigon) uncovered a North Vietnamese COMINT collection site. The captured documents proved what the NSA had assessed: the DRV's most valuable intelligence source was the information it collected from poorly secured U.S. communications.[13] Communication security (COMSEC) had been an afterthought in U.S. military planning. Expediency, hubris, and poor understanding of communication vulnerabilities exposed U.S. military operational details to Soviet- and Chinese-trained North Vietnamese intelligence collection.

The NSA suspected a significant operational-security problem existed and needed someone to prove it. The NSA pressed the JCS to assign Rear Adm. Donald "Mac" Showers (1630), USN, former PACFLT N2, to investigate. The Purple Dragon Study led by Showers created a communication security (COMSEC) and operational security (OPSEC) monitoring program that revealed extensive "leakages" of operational details to the DRV. Despite efforts to create awareness, improve procedures, and increase field cipher technology, COMSEC and OPSEC problems continued throughout the war.[14]

Navy intelligence officers (163x) were familiar with all-source Opintel fusion used to track Soviet submarines. Market Time operations were irregular war, meaning human intelligence was the most important. Overt HUMINT collection was an aspect of Navy intelligence's naval attaché system. However, few 163x had experience in HUMINT operations of any kind or the required analytic tradecraft. Navy intelligence had a small counterintelligence and investigative capability embedded within its district intelligence offices (DIO) but not much else. Navy Intelligence's HUMINT approach was insufficient for Market Time, Game Warden, and later, Sealords counterinfiltration operations. Secretary of the Navy Paul Nitze and DNI Rear Adm. Rufus Taylor, USN, recognized the problem. So too did Norm Channell, advising the RVNN as a liaison officer in 1965.

The RVNN had a network of informants, and Channell's efforts started there. "I suppose [I was] the first 'bag man' from [US] Naval Intelligence in [the] South," Channell wrote. He "delivered the first cash [money] to the Vietnamese Naval Intelligence officers" to help them recruit informants. A U.S. Army HUMINT organization already existed in Vietnam.

Channell thought the Navy should leverage the Army's efforts, not build its own.[15] Whether due to parochialism or organizational realism, in March 1966 the Navy established a HUMINT element, the Naval Field Operations Support Group (NFOSG), or Task Force 157.[16] Most pedestrian investigative and counterintelligence duties remained outside TF 157, which focused on more-covert operations. The DIO structure was insufficient to handle the growing counterintelligence duties, and the over–two hundred personnel in DIOs across the globe were reorganized into the new Naval Investigative Service Offices (NISO) in 1966.[17]

In April 1966 Market Time command shifted from the Naval Advisor Group (NAG) to Naval Forces Vietnam (NAVFORV), a component command under MACV. Operation Game Warden began the following month. NAVFORV had a few enlisted intelligence rates and six 1630s: a captain (N2), a commander (N2A), three lieutenant commanders, and one lieutenant. By 1968 NAVFORV had fifteen 1630s and fifteen enlisted intelligence personnel. The NISOs in Saigon and Da Nang, South Vietnam, each had one 163x lieutenant commander. By 1970 the Vietnam NISOs had grown to five offices supported by twelve enlisted, twenty-one 163x and civilian special agents, and eight Vietnamese employees. The NISOs worked with the Vietnamese national police to stop Viet Cong sapper attacks against U.S. Navy installations.[18]

The Viet Cong had HUMINT sources as well, and NISO counterintelligence efforts attempted but failed to stop their espionage. At the time little was understood about how deeply and broadly the Viet Cong had penetrated South Vietnam's civilian and military organizations. "After the war was over," lamented Vice Adm. Earl "Rex" Rectanus, USN (1926–2010), then a captain and Zumwalt's NAVFORV N2 in Vietnam, "we found even some of the most trusted (South) Vietnamese . . . were deep informants all along."[19]

Operation Game Warden required additional tactical-intelligence support.[20] In 1967 Navy Intelligence added sixteen Naval intelligence liaison officer positions (NILO), describing them as a rewarding and unique experience in the 1968 *Newsletter*. Indeed, lieutenant junior grade and lieutenant 1630s were sent into the province, often alone, to support

PHOTO 5.1
A U.S. Navy river patrol boat (PBR) crew conducting an inspection in one of the rivers of the Mekong Delta. Like their counterparts on Operation Market Time, the PBR Sailors inspected thousands of craft, turning suspects over to South Vietnamese authorities.
COURTESY OF ROBERT E. MOESER, U.S. NAVY HISTORY AND HERITAGE COMMAND

operations and work with their Vietnamese counterparts directly. The duty carried a tremendous amount of responsibility and significant danger.[21] NILOs were a vital addition, one Norm Channell recalls as an alternative for building an in-country Navy HUMINT network. He wrote that he and the other intelligence advisers pitched the NILO idea up the chain of command to Pacific Fleet HQ. Even with the risks the NILO concept provided an opportunity to solve the lack of intelligence-to-operations integration of the maritime interdiction effort.²²

Capt. Earl "Rex" Rectanus' arrival in the spring of 1968 coincided with future CNO Adm. Elmo R. Zumwalt Jr., USN (1920–2000), new commander of NAVFORV, creating Sealords. Rectanus, a CINCPAC intelligence officer before becoming the NAVFORV N2, followed the intelligence effort supporting Market Time. He brought new energy and a different perspective to intelligence support and counterinfiltration operations. Rectanus centralized his intelligence organization.

First, Rectanus moved the NILOs from RVNN HQ's senior U.S. naval adviser's control to his own. By controlling the NILOs, Rectanus aligned their training, collection efforts, and reporting processes. The NILOs collated their data, conducted first-phase analysis, and disseminated reports directly, not through other sections, to NAVFORV's intelligence section. Second, Rectanus brought in more tactical ground and air SIGINT-intercept

PHOTO 5.2
Lieutenant commander "wetting down," Vietnam, November 30, 1968. Vice Admiral Zumwalt (*back row, center*) is shown with members of his NAVFORV staff. Then-captain Rectanus (*front row, center*) is kneeling in front of his boss. PHOTO FROM THE EARL F. "REX" RECTANUS PERSONAL ARCHIVE, COURTESY OF EARL F. RECTANUS JR.

PHOTO 5.3
Captain Rectanus (*front row, far left, kneeling*) and his Da Nang First Coastal Zone Officers, 1968 PHOTO FROM THE EARL F. "REX" RECTANUS PERSONAL ARCHIVE, COURTESY OF EARL F. RECTANUS JR.

capability. Third, he improved the relationship with the RVNN's intelligence section. The RVNN shared information from its informants, and Rectanus in return provided heavily sanitized COMINT reports.[23]

Rectanus' organization now had plenty of information but lacked long-term analytical capacity. As a source HUMINT requires credibility consideration. Fusing HUMINT with other sources required analytic tradecraft expertise Opintel intelligence officers (163x) lacked. Leveraging HUMINT knowledge and training from the Army and the new Navy TF 157 helped. Rectanus' intelligence section was small but provided predictive-analysis capabilities when appropriately organized. Thus he created three divisions, collections, analysis, and current intelligence, to provide a breadth of operational-intelligence support.[24]

The collection division planned traditional operational-level reconnaissance and surveillance source collections like IMINT and SIGINT. It also planned clandestine HUMINT operations. Placing different source and collection methods under one division layered the collection plan, creating improved all-source, not just multisource, analysis opportunities. Under Cdr. Bill Hegeman (1630), USN, the analysis shop handled longer-term analysis, at least relative to the tactical environment. Intelligence support to planning also fell to the analysis division.[25]

During Operation Sealords, the current intelligence division was the "tactical intelligence" work center supporting the fast-paced, evolving tactical situation. It handled reporting significant activities, maintained an intelligence plot, and conducted briefings. Rectanus recalled in a 1982 interview that the current intelligence division "put on dog-and-pony shows [briefs] for anybody and everybody that we could get to listen."[26] The briefs created transparency and credibility, advancing the N2's analytically driven argument that many infiltration operations into Vietnam were originating in Cambodia.

The analysis division fused all-source intelligence, looking for enemy operating patterns. "The enemy has the same problem as any military," Rectanus said of the Viet Cong; "their supply lines were pretty well standard."[27] Once an operating pattern was detected, a collection plan leveraged assets to gather more intelligence and track and target the infiltrators. A significant part of the collection plans consisted of field reconnaissance, surveillance, and raids to capture documents and Viet Cong prisoners for interrogation.

Rectanus used his analysis and current intelligence divisions' efforts to bring the U.S. intelligence community (IC) to a consensus regarding Cambodia's complicity in the seaborne infiltration network. The covert U.S. submarine collection, airborne SIGINT and IMINT, and low-level HUMINT collection focused on Sihanoukville, Cambodia. The collection provided indications of infiltration operations but nothing definitive enough for Washington to accept. In 1969 Rectanus used a clandestine TF 157 HUMINT network called "Sunshine Park" to send collectors into Cambodia. The effort seemed to confirm the offloading and shipping of Chinese weapons to the Viet Cong. Under normal conditions the burden of proof regarding Cambodia's complicity in the infiltration would have been met for the IC. However, the analysts at the CIA and the DIA "couldn't be budged," Rectanus later recalled, because doing so

MAP 4
The Mekong River Delta, area of operations for Operations Game Warden and Sealords
DATA FROM MOBLEY AND MAROLDA'S *KNOWING THE ENEMY* (2015)

had strategic, not just military, implications. "Whether it was the [CIA and DIA] analysts themselves . . . [who] didn't believe our analysis was as good as it was . . . [or] they were told by Washington" not to concur was unclear.[28] In June 1969 a CIA agent delivered a bill of lading proving the Sihanoukville connection. CIA Director Helms said they had "egg on our collective faces" for not having listened to Rectanus' analysis. In March 1970 U.S. and South Vietnamese forces invaded Cambodia, erasing any doubt about that country's complicity.[29]

The NILO Experience

The NILO experience was formative for Navy Intelligence because the intelligence officer's being forward with the operator created a closeness that built credibility. The air war in North Vietnam had a similar effect on air-intelligence credibility building with aircrew. However, the NILOs in the south were, as some there would say at the time, "in the shit" with their customer.

The Vàm Cỏ Đông and Vàm Cỏ Tây rivers flowed from Cambodia into the Mekong Delta (see map 4). Both rivers allowed the Viet Cong to maneuver and access the northern territory outside Saigon. Much of Sealords took place on these two rivers. Sealords pushed floating armored stations called sea floats upriver to create operating bases for the riverine patrol crafts.[30] Life on a sea float was sparse, fast-paced, and dangerous. Up to seven hundred personnel might live on the twelve barges making up the floating city anchored in the middle of the river. The enemy kept constant surveillance and pressure on the floating fortress. At night the enemy upped the terror level by conducting harassing fires.[31]

The forward-floating bases established a bubble of control on the river from which denial operations were conducted. The armed patrols

PHOTO 5.4
Operation Sea Float ammunition pontoons are towed up the Cửa Lớn River to old Năm Căn city. Dated July 1969. NAVAL HISTORY AND HERITAGE COMMAND

launched from the sea floats provided denial effects and "pulsed" the environment to force observable "spikes" in enemy activity. These "operating to know" tactics are effective but dangerous in complex environments.[32] The interaction with the local villagers was almost as crucial as the denial operations, creating the trust and legitimacy needed to gather HUMINT from the cooperating villagers.[33]

Some of the heaviest combat actions for NILOs occurred during Sealords.[34] Capt. John E. Vinson, USN, and Cdr. Peter B. Decker, USN, operated from Vàm Cỏ Đông River locations. Vinson was the NILO at the riverine operations advanced tactical support base (ATSB), a strip of land along the river at Trà Cú. The ATSB was in a remote, marshy trouble spot of enemy activity. Located fifteen miles north, Decker was the NILO at the Navy border-control station collocated with the divisional combat assistance team (D-CAT 99) at Đức Hòa. The runway at Đức Hòa allowed Decker to conduct airborne patrols from a small O-1 Bird Dog (Cessna 160). The Bird Dog was a single-engine, two-seat aircraft made of a tubular metal frame covered in canvas fabric; its service life was usually short. Decker's had a .50-caliber M-60 "Sailor-modified" machine gun suspended out of the passenger door by some parachute cord.[35]

The ATSB at Trà Cú monitored an unattended ground sensors (UGS) line called Duffle Bag. The UGS collected seismic, magnetic, infrared, and acoustic information along assessed Viet Cong infiltration routes. Duffle Bag reports were passed to NAVFORV and used tactically to deploy patrols or engage infiltration forces. In 1969 Decker conducted airborne reconnaissance of an abandoned farm in his Bird Dog. Vinson radioed Decker from Trà Cú that Duffle Bag had detected machine-gun fire bursts from a nearby farm. Decker already knew; he'd been on the receiving end of the fire. While the pilot frantically maneuvered the Bird Dog, Decker returned fire with his Sailor-modified M-60 and called for help over the radio.[36]

Standby air and land forces from Đức Hòa and artillery from a distant U.S. Army battery descended on the farm. "A North Vietnam Infantry Company was literally decimated with the final body count exceeding 300 enemies KIA [killed in action]."[37] Vinson later received the recovered

PHOTO 5.5
Cdr. Jack Graf, USN, holding a variation of the Smith and Wesson S76 submachine gun, stands next to Cessna O-1 Bird Dog liaison and observation aircraft during the Vietnam War. No date. FROM THE VICE ADMIRAL EARL F. (REX) RECTANUS COLLECTION, VIETNAM CENTER AND SAM JOHNSON VIETNAM ARCHIVE, TEXAS TECH UNIVERSITY

documents and an annotated map describing the destroyed infantry company's objective: the destruction of Vinson's ATSB at Trà Cú, the province HQ, and the riverine boat resupply facility eight miles north of Đức Hòa.

Death of a NILO was always a possibility, but the concern that a NILO might become a POW seemed more of an operational concern. With their access to classified material, a captured NILO might be a treasure trove for the DRV and their associated Soviet and Chinese intelligence organizations. Only one NILO fell to such a fate, Lt. Cdr. (1630) Jack Graf, the Fourth Coastal Zone intelligence officer. In 1969, on his second tour of duty, Graf was shot down. His Bird Dog aircraft crashed in the mudflats along the river in Kiến Hòa Province. Graf, who had access to

SCI, and his pilot, Capt. Robert White, USA, evaded but were quickly captured by Viet Cong forces. COMNAVFORV N2, Capt. Robert Pyle, was concerned, and the U.S. Army's Joint Personnel Recovery Center (JPRC) offered him little help; the Kiến Hòa Province was too distant and dangerous to mount an uncoordinated rescue effort without better intelligence, they argued.

Pyle spoke with the commanding officer of the NIS office in Vietnam (NISOV), Lt. Cdr. Thomas Brooks, USN (Ret.) (a future DNI), asking that he leverage their HUMINT connections with the RVNN. The request resulted in an RVNN lieutenant junior grade officer riding his motorcycle through VC-controlled areas to his relatives' farm in Kiến Hòa. His relatives had seen Graf, and the officer made the hazardous journey back to report the sighting. Even with the credible intelligence on Graf's location, the JPRC moved cautiously. Every second wasted took Graf and White farther away with their Viet Cong captors. On his own Brooks cobbled together a rescue force of "Vietnamese irregulars and former VC (known as Kit Carson Scouts)" and helicoptered to Graf's last known location. It was twenty-four hours too late; Graf and White had moved. Another month was spent looking for Graf, but it was in vain.[38]

Graf spent three months in a jungle cage. White, who remained a prisoner and survived the war, later reported that Graf defied the Viet Cong's torture and eventually made an escape attempt. While chased, Graf attempted to swim across a river. He was gunned down and drowned before he could be recaptured.[39]

Summary

The customer, the Navy's warfighters, added the new performance orientation of in-country Vietnam Opintel support. Therefore NISO, NILO, and NAVFORV staff assignments in Vietnam were as crucial as those in the shipboard Intel Center. The intelligence officer (163x) experiences matched the aviation and line intelligence subspecialist officers', the customers who selected them for promotion. The 1970 *Intelligence Newsletter* wrote, "Insofar as possible, qualified officers departing Vietnam are given first consideration for available openings."[40] Preferential treatment in future assignments was another reward for in-country Vietnam tours. A Vietnam veteran might "scoop up" a more prestigious position, further improving chances for promotion.

The 1971 *Newsletter* made the promotion benefits clear. A report reviewing the latest commander-rank promotion board noted that "Washington Duty" and "Joint Duty" were career-enhancing. The duty increased the promotion rate to 86 percent (27 percent for those without the duty) for the former and 79 percent (50 percent without the duty) for the latter. "Viet Nam Duty" and "Naval Investigative Duty" resulted in a higher promotion rate, at 86 percent. Those without "Viet Nam Duty" had only a 63 percent promotion rate. Those with "HUMINT, Attache and CTF-157 Tours" had a 100 percent promotion rate.[41] If the promotion numbers did not make the importance of having Vietnam duty apparent, then upon becoming the DNI in 1971 Rectanus certainly did.

NISO, NILO, and NAVFORV staff duty exposed officers to all-source Opintel fusion analysis, collection planning, HUMINT tradecraft, and counterintelligence operations. The training pipeline for in-country jobs could be up to sixty-four weeks, including collection systems, HUMINT tradecraft, and Vietnamese-language and -culture training.[42] Officers with these skills had a better understanding of expeditionary warfare, which significantly influenced the evolution of the Navy Intelligence organization. The lieutenant and lieutenant junior grade 163xs who served in Vietnam later served at Ocean Surveillance Information System (OSIS) nodes. Their all-source Opintel-fusion tradecraft and collection knowledge shaped the development of those organizations. Those officers also returned to sea in the 1970s as lieutenant commanders holding shipboard Opintel leadership positions, where their influence was tremendous.

MPRF Supporting a Close Blockade

Navy intelligence officers honed their air-combat and strike-support Opintel skills in the North and HUMINT tradecraft supporting counterinfiltration and counterinsurgency operations in the South. The surface Navy and the land-based maritime-patrol community led the South China Sea and littoral sea close-blockade effort. The air intelligence officers (135x, the community merger with the 163x had yet to occur) supporting the maritime-patrol squadrons learned another form that merged air intelligence with Opintel.

The four-week air intelligence officer course (135x) held in 1959 at Fleet Air Intelligence Center Atlantic (FAITCLANT) was attack aviation–focused. Graduates viewed VA (attack) squadron duty as an elite assignment. The top AI graduate of each course earned the first choice from the list of available jobs. Lt. (jg) William Cracknell, top graduate in the 1959 course, picked the Black Falcons of VP-7. His choice upset the Naval Air Forces Atlantic (AIRLANT) N2. "Cracknell, you're attack-trained; you should go to an attack squadron!" Enlisting in the Naval Reserves in 1949, Cracknell had horrible eyesight but an excellent memory; he'd passed the eye exam by reciting the eye-chart lines the candidate ahead of him had shouted out. He'd flown as an enlisted rating in various castoff two-seat attack aircraft operated by the Naval Reserve.[43]

Cracknell responded to the N2's admonition by pointing out that he could not fly in an attack squadron (VA) but could fly as aircrew in a patrol VP (fixed wing patrol) squadron. "Besides," added Cracknell wryly—never one to miss an opportunity to quip—"and I really upset him [N2] with this," he recollected later; "I said, 'I think ASW [anti-submarine warfare] is the future of the Navy.'"[44]

Maritime patrol duty was not "sexy" in aviation community parlance. Patrol aircraft flew long missions at relatively low speeds, often more than eight hours (up to fourteen hours by shutting down and feathering an engine). Many joked that the only essential equipment on the old P-2 Neptune and new P-3 Orion was their large-capacity coffee maker and onboard head (toilet). Cracknell was right, at least from a naval strategy perspective; maritime patrol was critical for nuclear-war deterrence. Maritime patrols were also necessary for the counterinfiltration operations in South Vietnam; they played a crucial operational scouting (find, fix, and track) role.

Cracknell did get to fly, and fly a lot. He qualified as a navigator on one of VP-7's twelve combat aircrews. Until 1963, when the Naval flight officer (NFO) program began, navigators had typically been Naval air observers (NAO) like Cracknell or another pilot.[45] The typical crew of a P-2 in the early 1960s had four or five officers, two to three of them pilots, one navigator, and one tactical coordinator (TACCO). Six or seven enlisted ratings operated sensors and onboard aircraft equipment. A patrol squadron had nine to twelve planes, 250 enlisted, and fifty officers. To operate the more-sophisticated aircraft and fly the complex missions, as those P-3C flew, fifteen additional officers but not more aircraft were added to the squadron.[46]

There were twenty-six active-duty and fifteen reserve patrol squadrons in 1970. Active-duty squadrons were split in half: thirteen in Patrol Wings Pacific, eight at Moffett Field, California, and five at Barber's Point, Hawai'i. Patrol Wings Atlantic had seven squadrons in Brunswick, Maine, and six in Jacksonville, Florida.[47] The squadrons deployed in several manners, sometimes as a whole, to one forward site. The mass deployment did not mean all the aircraft remained at that site. Often the squadron dispatched aircraft to other theater locations. For example, when Cracknell joined VP-7 in Rota, Spain, in November 1959 most of its P-2V aircraft were scattered across the theater, supporting various exercises and patrols.[48]

Supporting Operation Market Time narrowed the locations and rotation windows to squadrons deploying to the western Pacific; it required participation of the entire maritime patrol and reconnaissance fleet at one time or another. Most deployments were to the Philippines—Naval Stations Sangley Point or Cubi Point. Airfields in Japan were also used. Due to the theater's geometry the Philippines and Japan provided access to Market Time and western Pacific patrol areas; after all, Soviet and Chinese naval operations in the Pacific also required watching. Detachments from the Philippines– or Japan-deployed squadrons were sent to South Vietnam airfields near Saigon (Tan Son Nhut Air Base) and Naval Station Cam Rahn Bay. The Royal Thai airbase at U-Tapao, Thailand, was also a detachment site used to patrol the Gulf of Thailand, looking for infiltration from Cambodia. The South Vietnam air bases were austere, with limited P-2 and P-3 maintenance facilities. Additionally the danger of sapper and mortar attacks on the airfields made forward-detachment duty dangerous.

By mid-1967 Market Time's integrated-radar, airborne-reconnaissance, and surface-patrol efforts had cut trawler infiltration by more than half. 1968 saw the Viet Cong–led Tet Offensive (January to October), which meant Market Time patrol forces had their work cut out for them. For example, the "four trawlers incident" of March 1968 began as Market Time interdiction operations had been designed: A P-2 Neptune from the White Lightnings of VP-17's Ton San Knut detachment patrolling east of Da Nang, just above the demilitarized zone (DMZ), detected a steel-hulled trawler making for the coast of Vietnam. They then detected a second trawler. The P-2's plane commander, Lt. Norm Cook, USN, and his aircrew covertly tracked both trawlers as they made the slow transit toward the coast. Cook notified the coastal surveillance center at Da Nang. The interdiction piece of Market Time spun into action.[49]

U.S. Coast Guard Lt. (jg) Gerald A. McGill, in command of the USCG *Point Welcome* (WPB 82329), an eighty-two-foot *Point*-class cutter, had just returned to Da Nang after a patrol. Within thirty minutes, *Point Welcome* was back underway, en route to intercept the trawlers. At 0100 the following day McGill arrived on the scene, one hundred nautical miles south of the DMZ. Four trawlers, not two, were strung out to the northeast, making for the coast. Another USCG cutter and several U.S. Navy *Swift*-class boats joined the *Point Welcome*. The first trawler was only eleven nautical miles from entering the Sông Trà Khúc River. Illumination rounds lit the sky, and the U.S. interdiction forces unleashed .50-caliber machine-gun and mortar fire into the trawlers, sinking two of them. Under *Point Welcome*'s fire, the third trawler detonated a powerful scuttling charge, blasting shrapnel into *Point Welcome* five hundred yards away, blowing out its pilot-house windows and embedding a carbine bayonet into its hull. The fourth trawler turned tail and headed toward Haiphong, North Vietnam. The interception and destruction of four trawlers during the Tet Offensive caused the DRV to stop using steel-hulled trawlers for over a year.[50]

VP-17's Ton San Knut detachment was mortared three days later, damaging one aircraft, which was repaired, but injuring no personnel. The White Lightnings of VP-17 were relieved by the Blue Dragons of

PHOTO 5.6
Coast Guard *Point*-class patrol boats were the workhorses of Market Time patrols. Here USCGC *Point League* stands by after forcing ashore a one hundred–foot North Vietnamese trawler on June 20, 1966. The trawler was found to be carrying an estimated 250 tons of weapons and supplies for the Viet Cong. The trawler is afire, just to the left of *Point League*'s bow. NAVAL HISTORY AND HERITAGE COMMAND

VP-50 at the end of March 1968. VP-50 and VP-17 were decommissioned in 1992 and 1995, respectively. Lieutenant Cook received the Distinguished Flying Cross for his actions. McGill received a Bronze Star for *Point Welcome*'s part in the action, among other interdiction actions. *Point Welcome* never left Vietnam; she was transferred to the Republic of Vietnam Navy as RVNS *Nguyễn Hẩn* (HQ 717) on April 29, 1970. The U.S. Coast Guard played a significant yet unrecognized role in Operation Market Time.[51]

CHAPTER 6

A Distant Blockade, in All but Name

The operational intelligence support to Operation Market Time had similarities to the all-source-fused tracking and plotting (Opintel) of Soviet submarines that the typical intelligence officers (163x) were accustomed to. During the Cold War finding, fixing, and tracking enemy combatants required a combination of terrestrial and space-based collection and surveillance at sea. The oceans are vast and surveillance assets few. Balancing the surveillance time-space-force equation requires airpower and, in growing increments, space-based satellites. The Navy's Maritime Airborne Patrol and Reconnaissance Forces (MPRF) were busy hunting steel-hulled trawlers in the South China Sea. However, the United States still needed them to track Soviet submarines as well.

Submarine-launched, atomic weapons–tipped ballistic missiles were the Soviet's second-strike weapon. Not until the mid-1970s did the Soviet Navy possess a ballistic missile submarine, Project 667B *Delta*-class SSBN, and a long-range missile, the SS-N-18 Stingray SLBM, of which the continental United States was within range from the North Atlantic, Barents Sea, and Arctic Seas operating areas. Before that Soviet SSBNs had to penetrate the Atlantic Ocean via the Greenland-Iceland-United Kingdom (GIUK) gap. The GIUK gap and other choke points were underwater and terrestrial geography channeling surface and subsurface vessels. These areas became the hunting grounds for the Navy's sea-control forces.[1]

The land-based patrol aircraft augmented sea-based scouting efforts. There are two types of MPRF squadrons: The fixed-wing patrol (VP) squadrons hunted submarines and conducted broad ocean-surveillance or maritime patrols (MARPAT). The fixed-wing air-reconnaissance (VQ) squadrons provided airborne SIGINT collection. These large, multi-engine aircraft had the flexibility to adapt to changes in the character of warfare. They also carried various weapons to conduct armed reconnaissance if required, a necessity for sea control-or-denial operations.

For the intelligence officer (135x and, after the merger, 163x) operating as the squadron's air intelligence officer (AI), a tour in VP or VQ exposed them to new types of intelligence operations, both in collection and fusion analysis. The VP and VQ aviation culture differed from the fighter and attack squadrons'. The patrol mission forced AIs to operate simultaneously within the air-intelligence and all-source fusion characteristics of Opintel. Junior intelligence officers left the MPRF world for shipboard and shore-analysis center tours, sharing their insights into collection operations and all-source fusion tradecraft. This reciprocal increased the emergent potential and evolvability of shipboard Opintel and Navy Intelligence.

Scouting (reconnaissance and surveillance) efforts are sometimes just a footnote of naval battles, belying the tremendous effort and the significant impact they have on the outcome. The diminution of scouting is understandable; finding a target is less fascinating (or "sexy," in aviator jargon) than the following killing battle. Scouting is part of operational intelligence and is integrated into the broader fires-centric effort. Scouting's effectiveness comes in degrees. At best, ship-based scouting aircraft provided a measure of control in only a limited "vital" area around the capital ship.[2] Therefore, as the demands for maritime battlespace awareness increased, scouting assets chased technology for increased range, detection capabilities, and payload. Physics, however, dictated that only land-based aircraft could provide tactical long-range-detection and -tracking capabilities.

From a naval-strategy perspective, airborne maritime patrol enhanced sea control-and-denial measures in war while influencing the maritime domain during peace. MPRF operations during Market Time, the close blockade against North Vietnamese infiltration in South Vietnam, demonstrated the P-2V Neptune's and P-3 Orion's importance to sea control-and-denial efforts. What of their usefulness in peacetime? Professor Milan Vego suggests that no sea control exists in peacetime, only sea influence as part of competition and cooperation.[3] Indeed, a fine line exists between control and influence when kinetic weapons are not employed. Wartime sea control considers how much sea must be controlled for how long and by what amount of force. When not in control of a portion of the sea, one can still deny or contest its use by the enemy. In peacetime the sea is, as Alfred Thayer Mahan once described it, a "great global common," free for all to use. If the sea is accessible to all for trade and movement, what does influence mean, and is it different from control?

According to late naval strategist J. C. Wylie, control began with the "complete knowledge" of everything that moves by sea.[4] This domain understanding created peacetime situational awareness, allowing a navy to disperse its fleets to develop regional or global influence. Understanding maritime activity allowed a navy to concentrate its forces operationally in times of tension. The concentration deterred, compelled, or reassured nations into acting in a desired manner, preventing war.[5] From Wylie's perspective, combat potential and omnipresent surveillance defined maritime influence. The mixture of power and understanding regulates a competitor's behavior. However, Wylie says, control is not truly established until the concentration of naval force—or the "man on the scene with a gun"—occurs.[6] Thus influence in the Cold War is illustrated when a Soviet ballistic missile submarine sorties and a U.S. submarine and P-3s track it.

Commander in Chief of the Soviet Navy Admiral Sergey Gorshkov, SN, had grievances. He complained that the United States' form of maritime influence used "harassment tactics." He particularly denounced the "buzzing" of his ships by low-flying naval-patrol aircraft.[7] His complaints rang hollow; the Soviet Navy had the same ideas and used similar tactics. The two navies came into increasing contact with each other. Author David Winkler described the competition for maritime influence as a "growing seriousness of at-sea confrontations with the Soviet combatant vessels." There were also "incidents with merchant ships, fishing trawlers, and AGIs [intelligence collection ships]."[8] Both sides protested the many

PHOTO 6.1
A YP3V-1 Orion buzzes a submarine during anti-submarine warfare testing, 1960.
COURTESY OF L. M. AERO

collisions between the two navies' vessels. On multiple occasions the U.S. Navy invited the Soviet Navy to meet and negotiate an agreement regarding safety at sea. By November 1970 the Soviet Navy agreed that the incidents had been too many and the risk of escalation significant. Two years later, in May 1972, the United States and the Soviet Union signed the Prevention of Incidents on the High Seas and the Air Space Above Them (INCSEA) agreement.[9] The agreement provided rules for the maritime-influence competition.

Rules are, of course, a form of control. INCSEA managed escalation and reduced harassment of operations at sea. For the U.S. Navy INCSEA removed some distractions, allowing it to invigorate its anti-submarine-warfare (ASW) and war-at-sea naval tactics. It grew its surveillance of the Soviet Navy's operations. Strategically, finding, fixing, tracking, and targeting Soviet ballistic missile submarines (SSBN)—and holding them at risk of attack—was an essential deterrence objective.

Navy writings from the early 1970s describe the holding-at-risk operations against Soviet submarines as "sortie controls." However, Professor Geoffrey Till argues that the effort was a "form of distant blockade all but in name."[10] As the Navy had learned during the Cuban Missile Crisis, calling a sea denial operation a "blockade" in peacetime had bellicose undertones. Nonetheless the strategy exploited geography, creating choke-point control, especially in the northern Atlantic. Multiple ASW mechanisms contributed to the blockade. A passive underwater sound surveillance system (SOSUS) detects the submarine (find). The P-3s, using air-dropped sonobuoys, fixed, tracked, and targeted Soviet submarines. By 1973 most of the Navy's ASW aircraft carriers (*Essex*-class) had been decommissioned. Attack aircraft carrier battlegroups with a "mixed wing" of ASW and strike aircraft conducted ASW barrier patrols in coordination with the VP squadrons.[11] The mix of ASW assets, including destroyers and frigates using towed sonar array sensor systems (SURTASS), checked the Soviet Navy attack submarines' anti-carrier operations. The efforts strengthened the distant blockade with a layered ASW defense, increasing maritime influence and sea-control potential.

The most important force multiplier in the distant blockade was intelligence. The combination of space, surface, subsurface (SOSUS and attack submarines), and airborne collection allowed all-source fusion at the new shore-based Ocean Surveillance Information System (OSIS) centers. The analysis translated into effective ASW operation and Navy asset concentration when required. The OSIS system better understood where Soviet nuclear submarines were than did the Soviet Navy. *The Admirals' Advantage* quotes Vice Adm. Thomas Wilson recollecting that the Soviets knew "that we were very good at our OPINTEL mission and therefore good at our operational mission. . . . They realized we were good at finding them, attacking them if necessary."[12]

The Soviet Navy focused on getting through the detection and tracking-focused distant blockade. Because this was ostensibly peacetime, they had access to the oceans. Access, however, was not guaranteed during wartime; thus the Soviet Navy grew its "blue water" capabilities to ensure access beyond the choke points. That blue water force also gave the Soviet

Navy defense-in-depth protection of vital SSBN operating "bastions," located in the Barents Sea and the Sea of Okhotsk, needed to launch second-strike ballistic missiles. Despite the Soviet Navy's growth, the U.S. Navy's operations sent the intended message (whether true or not): *We can destroy your submarines, ships, and aircraft at will.*

P-3s proved a more efficient way to hold submarines at risk. Overtly holding their SSBNs at risk sent a powerful political message to Soviet high command. Times were changing, and the Navy's ASW operations would be airborne, forward, and persistent. "There was a new era beginning," author David Reade wrote of the new P-3 patrol aircraft, and "it belonged to *Orion* 'The Hunter.'"[13]

The Mad Foxes of VP-5's P-3A Orion circled the Soviet Navy ship *Moskva*. Simultaneously a second aircraft took photographs. The Orion conducted a "nine-point rig," taking pictures of the ship's quarters, beams, and nadir in standard MARPAT fashion. The *Moskva* was another highlight for the Mad Foxes in an already-busy four-month 1970 deployment to Naval Air Station, Sigonella, Sicily. VP-5 was typical of MPRF; it had evolved with technological improvements and changes in the character of war while retaining its maritime-patrol roots. The patrol squadrons were the birth of Navy aviation. Though Eugene Ely flew off a Navy ship in November 1910, aircraft carrier aviation did not begin in earnest until 1922. The Navy ordered its first aircraft six months after Ely's flight, in May 1911—a Curtiss A-1 seaplane. Three years later, in 1914, a few Navy seaplanes supported the siege of Veracruz, Mexico. During the First World War, Navy airmen flew a mix of French, Italian, British, and a few American seaplanes against Imperial German Navy submarines and support facilities.[14]

Because patrol and reconnaissance squadrons have legacies back to 1921, historical confusion surrounds them. The Mad Foxes' lineage is typical and described to provide a context of the Navy MPRF evolution. Established in January 1937 in Seattle, Washington, as Patrol Squadron Seventeen-F (VP-17F), the squadron was redesignated three times during World War II—first to VP-17, then VP-42, and then again to Bombing Squadron 135 (VB-135) in 1943. Now called the Mad Foxes, they were redesignated two more times to VPB-135 and then VP-135 in 1946. In 1948, VP-135 was redesignated Medium Patrol Squadron Five (VP-ML-5) and given the specifically designed patrol aircraft P-2V Neptune. It was again redesignated to VP-5 in 1948, becoming the second squadron assigned the VP-5 designation. Today Navy policy prevents the reuse of a squadron designation, and no other squadron will ever be named VP-5. The Mad Foxes were the last squadron to fly the SP-2E and transitioned to the P-3A Orion in July 1966.[15] Like most squadrons, they conducted patrols supporting Market Time off Vietnam.

The P-3A was a significant improvement over the P-2V. Both were anti-submarine warfare aircraft, but by 1959 new sensors and electronic equipment had increased Neptune's gross weight by 40 percent. Lockheed, the maker of the P-2V, modified the design of its commercial L-188 Electra aircraft into the P-3 Orion to meet the Navy's patrol requirements. The most important feature of the new Orion was its capacity for technological improvements and modifications. The first Orion operational flights supported the "quarantine" during the 1962 Cuban Missile Crisis. It remained in Navy service for almost sixty years.[16]

The P-3A's powerful APS-80 radar and improved internal navigation systems, the ASN-42, the Doppler APN-122, and APN-70 LORAN, provided an excellent long-range surface-radar picture. Its maneuverability allowed the P-3 to operate at high and low altitudes, descending as low as 250 feet to photograph surface contacts. With its manual teletype (TT-264/AG TTY) the P-3 relayed maritime contacts directly to Navy surface-patrol craft and the Coastal Surveillance Centers. In 1967 the P-3C's new CP-901 avionics computer was compact and powerful, collating all analog data on the tactical coordinator's (TACCO) scope. The CP-901 let the airborne Naval Tactical Data System (ANTDS) pass APS-80 radar tracks to the shipboard Naval Tactical Data System (NTDS) via Link 11. NTDS used encrypted "pro forma" machine-readable messages between the systems over a duplex datalink (Link 11).[17]

The Orion was a submarine hunter. Because sound propagated easily through the water, the noise from the submarines was used to locate them. The speed at which sound travels in water depends on the sound's intensity and the characteristics of the body of water: depth, salinity, temperature, and solid features influence sound propagation in the ocean. By 1955 the Navy had a passive sound surveillance system (SOSUS)—deployed arrays of hydrophones, recorders, and analysis centers—listening for Soviet submarines in the North Atlantic.[18]

The airborne processor/recorder AQA-1 Jezebel collected sonar signals from passive and active sonobuoys. The air-dropped sonobuoys contained a deployable hydrophone and a transmitter. When the Tactical

PHOTO 6.2
P-3 Orion sensor operators "worth their weight in gold," 1970s NAVAL HISTORY AND HERITAGE COMMAND

Navigation Modification (TACNAVMOD) was fielded in 1975, the Jezebel was on version seven, a much-improved computer processor using a family of advanced sonobuoys. The passive Directional Frequency Analysis and Recording (DIFAR) sonobuoy (SSQ-53) and the active Directional Command Activated Sonobuoy System (DICASS) sonobuoy (SSQ-62) allowed an Orion to localize a submerged contact more quickly with increased accuracy.[19]

The acoustic system and operators were so proficient in the Orion that Capt. Don Miskill, USN (Ret.), a pilot with VP-50 in 1975, recalled that he was getting play-by-play of the submarine's movement. "Hang on, TACCO," Miskill recalled one operator saying of one submarine being tracked; "I think he's gonna make a turn. I think he's making a depth change." There was a constant chatter from the sensor operators over the internal communications system when following a Soviet submarine. The sensor operators were "worth their weight in gold," Miskill reminisced.[20]

Squadrons conducted split deployments; sending aircraft and maintenance detachments to two or more locations was a tactic developed in the 1950s and 1960s. This allowed one squadron to support Market Time and Soviet submarine–tracking operations in the Pacific. Don Miskill participated in a unique form of split deployment. His aircraft left Moffett Field, Alameda, California, patrolling the northern Pacific before landing at Adak, Alaska. He patrolled from Adak, conducting several missions over multiple days before performing a long-range patrol, landing in Guam. The pattern repeated itself: from Guam to Iwakuni, Japan, then Iwakuni back to Adak, then from Adak back to Moffett. The pattern used all the squadron aircraft to create a depth of surveillance and opportunities for logistical support to each deployment site.[21] Unlike a VA or VF squadron deployed to an aircraft carrier, patrol-squadron deployment schemes presented AIs with unique challenges and opportunities.

By 1973 Navy Intelligence had about 5 percent of its commander-and-below billets dedicated to the MPRF effort. More than twenty-four lieutenant junior grades, or almost 14 percent, spent time in the MPRF community.[22] The percentage, in reality, was higher as the theater Fleet Intelligence Centers (FIC) also provided additional intelligence officers for maritime-patrol mission support. The patrol (VP) or reconnaissance (VQ) squadron tours were challenging. Junior AIs faced operational-intelligence support and leadership tests that most fighter and attack AIs did not. A VP or VQ tour was a different type of crucible that blended Opintel's air intelligence and all-source fusion analysis characteristics.

There were obvious challenges. How would an AI in Adak provide threat presentations and the premission brief for several patrols flying from different locations and with various objectives? How would the target analysis be conducted, not for dropping bombs but for collecting imagery, acoustics, and SIGINT? Images and data on the targets, the submarine or surface ship, were necessary to improve intelligence collection. All-source fusion Opintel was vital because it shrank the area of probability (AOP) where the submarine or surface vessel was likely to be found. Fuel and weather were operational concerns AIs had to understand. A small AOP allowed the aircraft to transit at high altitudes, using less fuel, before starting its patrol; the tactic created a longer on-station time over the collection area.

The patrol squadron AIs had help with these challenges. Like the fighter and attack squadron AIs deployed to the aircraft carriers, VP squadrons had centralized-intelligence support, the Tactical Support Center (TSC). Primary P-3 deployment sites had a TSC, but many detachments flew from fields that did not. The centralization of intelligence support and analysis at the TSCs had similarities with the creation of the shipboard IOIC/Intel Center. Like the Intel Center, the TSC had permanently assigned intelligence personnel but relied on personnel from the deployed squadrons to conduct intelligence operations. The TSC, unlike the Intel Center, provided more C2 for the actual flights. Real-time mission planning and air-space control came from the TSC. In-flight support for the eight-hour-plus missions came via a Fleet Broadcast System (FBS) controlled by the TSC. Like the Intel Center, the TSCs evolved.[23] Thus by the 1970s most AIs were inundated with pre- and postmission and in-flight support requirements. Cracknell's description of his time as an AI in VP-7 in the early 1960s was not typical. Most AIs did not fly as much or become part of a flight crew as Cracknell had.

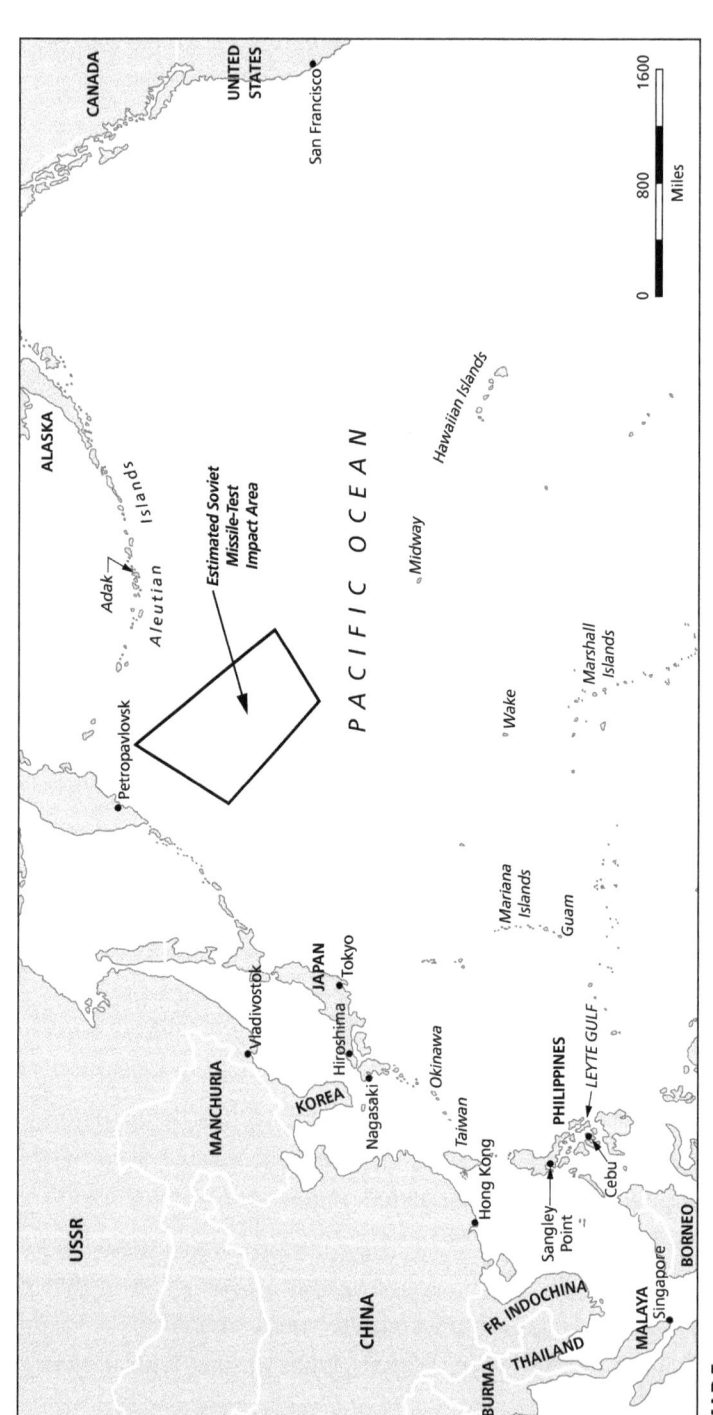

MAP 5

The northern Pacific operating area, 1975

New technology and the growing threat of the Soviet Navy consumed the AI's time, and there was little left for flight-duty tasks. Beyond a few familiarization flights, most AIs were grounded, toiling away in a brick building with few windows near the flight line.

Dale Thompson, AI with the Blue Dragons of VP-50 in 1975, provides insight into a "day in the life" of a typical P-3 squadron AI. When the squadron conducted its 1975 split deployment, Thompson and his intelligence team went to Adak and remained at the TSC. The SOSUS network and patrolling Navy attack submarines produced much information on Soviet naval activities. Reading reports and fusing intelligence was constant and overwhelming for Thompson's small intelligence cell. Blue Dragon flights launching from Guam patrolled over two thousand nautical miles and landed eleven hours later in Adak. The TSC at Guam debriefed and provided premission briefs for Thompson's crews. The premission brief was like the event brief on the aircraft carrier; it included operational data, the safety-of-flight information, and a current intelligence picture. The patrol plane commander (PPC), the TACCO, and the enlisted aviation anti-submarine warfare operators (AW rating) received sanitized intelligence regarding Soviet operations. The AWs operated the P-3's sonar system—the sensor stations (SS) 1 and 2 positions. The mission brief provided the TACCO with the target submarine's operating AOP, created from Opintel analysis, and recommended an initial ASW search pattern. Real-time changes in tasking or intelligence updates arrived to the crew via the encrypted FBS to the aircraft's TT-264 teletype.[24]

The imagery capabilities of the P-3 were essential for MARPATs. It allowed the P-3 to return high-quality images of ships, revealing new operating patterns or technology. Some of the imagery uncovered startling changes to Soviet naval capabilities. A squadron PH assigned to the base's photo lab loaded film into the P-3's two cameras. The cameras were of the same family used in the RA-5C Vigilante. The KA-74 Hycon still-image camera was nose-mounted and repositionable, taking images straight down or from a forward or left-right oblique position. Below the aircraft the belly-mounted panoramic KB-18A had a 180-degree field of view from nose to tail. The crew also took 35-mm handheld images through a fuselage blister window.[25]

When the aircraft landed in Adak, the PHs downloaded the wet film and took it to the base photo lab for development. An hour later the images were exploited on light tables in the squadron's hangar AI spaces. The AWs in sensor station (SS) 1 and 2 took their recordings of the sonobuoy collection, both the sizable magnetic tape reels and the paper printouts (called the "grams"), to the TSC for processing. The postmission report was called a "Purple," and the air-mission tasking order, called the "Green," were Rainform human-machine-readable-formatted messages. The TACCO filled out the operational part of the Purple, fuel use, for example, and the collection data (log of surface and subsurface contacts) before landing. Depending on the mission, the AI debriefed part or all of the crew and then reviewed the imagery and sonar-collection reports. The AI fused the analysis into the report, completing and releasing the Purple long after the crew had left.[26]

The mission debriefs were straightforward affairs for the most part. If a mission had been specifically heady, collecting many contacts, the AI's debrief of the crew became detailed and time-consuming. Such missions occurred during the northern Pacific portion of the Soviet Navy's exercise Okean 75 (1975).[27] The exercise happened off Petropavlovsk, not Vladivostok, Russia, where intelligence assessments had anticipated it would be (see map 5). Thompson, one of two AIs at the TSC in Adak, Alaska, was quickly dropped into a frenzy. Extra P-3s and electronic-collection EP-3s from VQ-1 descended on the airfield. "All hell" broke loose as Thompson tried to cover all the briefing and debriefing for VP flights. As it played out, the Soviet naval exercise displayed anti-submarine warfare and simulated anti-carrier attacks by surface ships. The P-3s were in a fertile hunting ground, and the intelligence community was thirsty for information and photographs of the Soviet Navy and naval air forces' activity.[28]

During this increased mission tempo, one crew imaged a *November*-class nuclear-powered attack submarine (SSN) "sitting on the surface." Thompson released a Rainform initial intelligence report (IIR). The

"November submarine had an unusual attachment to the sail," and the IC became fascinated and demanding. The collection resulted in phone calls from intelligence organizations in Washington, asking, "When will we see these photos?" Thompson responded, "Well, at least a week." The classified images had to be mailed or couriered from Alaska. Many secure phone calls occurred between Thompson and the inquiring intelligence organizations as he detailed the images and answered their questions. The intelligence gain added to Thompson's already-packed schedule.[29]

The IC did not always trust the forward-deployed AI's analysis. The AI who relieved Thompson in 1976, Lt. (jg) Ann Rondeau (intelligence subspecialist and a future vice admiral), had a similar experience while deployed to Misawa, Japan, in 1978. IS1 B. J. Harrison found a Soviet *Delta*-class SSBN while exploiting a postmission photograph; he brought the image to Rondeau, reporting that he had discovered a North Sea Fleet *Delta* missile boat off Kamchatka, Russia, "that shouldn't be here." Harrison convinced Rondeau that the analysis was correct. Before releasing the IIR, Rondeau needed to persuade the squadron commanding officer (CO). The CO was hesitant to trust his IS and junior AI. If she were in the Intel Center on an aircraft carrier, Rondeau would have had at least two senior 1630 intelligence officers to review her analysis. As it was, she was on her own to convince her leadership of the report's value. Rondeau put the situation into context for the CO: *Being wrong is better than being right and not having made the report.* "I would rather be called wrong than negligent," Rondeau later said.[30]

The DIA responded to the IIR within hours. "You could not possibly have seen this," they said of the report; "it's not there." By then the CO and the wing commander had looked at Harrison's analysis and believed him to be correct. Nothing more was heard from the DIA. Sure enough, when the next monthly DIA Intelligence Update came in the classified mail, among the pages was a picture of the *Delta*, without credit to VP-50.[31]

Imagery intelligence was critical, but the acoustic signature of the Soviet submarines was the intelligence prize. The sonobuoy data on the magnetic tapes went to the Sonar Information Center (SIC) inside the TSC. An ACINT field team from the Naval Scientific and Technical

Intelligence Center's (NAVSTIC) Undersea Warfare Intelligence Section, assisted by assigned AWs, staffed the SIC. Using the Acoustic Intelligence Data System (AIDS), the SIC conducted a "preliminary screening" of the data on the tapes. They determined the collection's value and then shipped the tapes for further processing and exploitation to NAVSTIC in Suitland, Maryland. The development of AIDS and the ACINT field teams had resulted from previous processing, exploitation, and analysis failures at ONI.[32]

The Navy invested heavily in SOSUS. However, they failed to invest appropriately in the systems and technicians required to process and exploit the vast amounts of acoustic data. By 1959 ONI was receiving unprocessed recordings at an increased rate, about seven hundred tape reels yearly. ONI was the control point for ACINT, but the Bureau of Ships (BuShips) owned the two small acoustic-processing labs. The labs were a year or more behind in working through received materials. To solve the analysis problem Navy Intelligence took several steps. In 1962 the Acoustic Intelligence Analysis Facility opened at the Naval Observatory, Washington, D.C., shifting tape processing away from BuShips. In 1965 NAVSTIC created the Undersea Warfare Intelligence Section and ACINT field teams. AIDS was fielded in 1972. The field teams were vital because they triaged ACINT collection, sending only significant recordings for analysis. The triage lessened the exploitation burden, allowing time to analyze Soviet and Chinese submarine development trends. The field teams also improved the P-3's ACINT collection capability by providing timely feedback to the collectors, critiques of NAVSTIC analysis, and support to mission planning. ACINT processing was so technical and highly classified that most AIs were too busy to participate in ACINT exploitation.[33]

The lessons regarding the need for better access to highly classified intelligence from the air and anti-infiltration operations in Vietnam did little toward addressing the "green door syndrome" for the VP community. SCI material influenced theater-level collection planning and where and when patrol planes flew their missions. However, it did little to inform the squadron's tactical planning. Even Thompson, the AI, was not read in to SCI during the first half of his tour. In 1976 VP-50's CO, executive officer (XO), operations officer (Ops O), and AI billets were finally coded for SCI clearances. Once the squadron had SCI clearances, access to the material remained limited. SpintCom and SCIFs were located at communications stations or a SIGINT collection facility, not the TSC. Thompson recalled that when in Misawa, Japan, the closest SCIF was three miles away, he used the base's bus to go to the SCIF about once a week.[34]

The tempo of operations limited Thompson's ability to access SCI reports. However, that same tempo also created a balance; it lowered the expectations and thus the demand for SCI material by the few with clearances. Thompson wrote that the aircrews were happy and "never really asked" for SCI intelligence for most missions.[35] He incorporated SCI material where possible, but only if it supported their tactical missions. At the Misawa SIGINT site, when he could catch the bus to get there, Thompson had full access to all their message read-boards. He was not supposed to, but "they left me to fend for myself, so I looked at *all* their message boards. Shame on me," he offered with a chuckle. He pulled the relevant analysis and gave it to his TACCO in private one-on-one meetings after the mission brief. As they say, a good intelligence officer is resourceful and must find ways to get the intelligence that makes their customers successful. Thompson's efforts are another example of the initiative every AI was expected to have. His experience with SCI access was common for AIs across all U.S. naval aviation.[36]

Sometimes SCI material was required for mission success even if the entire crew was not cleared (read-in) to receive it. Thompson recalled that one aircrew flying Pony Express missions attended a briefing held under a tent at Midway Islands. The briefing was at a level well above the crew's clearance. Thompson inquired whether or not he needed to complete an inadvertent-disclosure report. "Forget about it," the Wings Pacific N2 told him. "Sometimes operational contingencies trump the niceties of clearances and access."[37] Pony Express was one of those missions. It was a collection effort against Soviet missile testing. The Soviet submarine-launched ballistic missile, the SS-N-18, was a long-range weapon with multiple independent reentry vehicles (MIRV) and a particular focus of Pony Express missions.[38]

Pony Express was a multisensor technical intelligence (TECINT) effort like the ones executed against the Soviet-built North Vietnamese–operated air-defense systems in the war. The intercontinental ballistic missile (ICBM) development was part of the Strategic Arms Limitation Talks (SALT) meant to control nuclear-weapons escalation. Monitoring each other's ICBM development was essential to complying with SALT. There was constant debate over the encryption of missile telemetry signals as part of SALT. Not until 1979 with SALT II's ban on the deliberate denial of telemetric information was compliance verification somewhat obtainable.[39] Telemetry intelligence (later called foreign instrumentation signals intelligence, FISINT) was a specific form of SIGINT. By 1972 the NSA had created a network that provided indications and warnings of upcoming Soviet launches and a series of stations that collected and processed FISINT.[40]

Soviet ICBM test ranges used impact zones on the Kamchatka Peninsula, Russia, and the sea northwest of Midway Island (see map 5). The Pony Express mission was the U.S. Navy's part of the FISINT collection network. Two purpose-built space vehicle–tracking ships, the USNS *Arnold* and *Hoyt Vandenberg* (operated by Air Force FISINT teams), were dedicated to the mission. Four converted *Claud Jones*–class destroyer escorts (DE) operated by Naval Security Group (NSG) personnel were also committed. VP and VQ assets flew Pony Express missions in support at various times.[41]

The critical and most challenging part of the FISINT operation was placing the collection ships near the missile's impact zone. Maritime law required that the Soviets notify mariners (NOTAM) of an upcoming test-missile impact area. Soviet NOTAMs covered large swaths of ocean and were issued a day or so before the event. The notice was not timely. The NSA and the Navy used intelligence collection to predict impact areas and reposition their collection units. Underway Soviet missile range instrumentation ships (SMRIS) indicated an upcoming missile test. The VP squadron's role was to track and report on the SMRIS and other Soviet combatants patrolling potential impact sites. They also laid sonobuoys to detect the missile's impact into the water.[42]

PHOTO 6.3
The Soviet missile range instrumentation ship (SMRIS) *Marshal Nedelin* at sea in the Pacific Ocean monitoring a long-range ballistic missile test, 1989 NARA

In 1964 the Department of Defense established the Defense Special Missile and Astronautics Center (DEFSMAC). It conducted all-source fusion analysis to advise the decision-makers in developing a Pony Express collection plan. DEFSMAC provided a sanitized warning message that predicted the likely missile launch time to the Navy's surface and airborne collection assets. The surface collection ships left Pearl Harbor while the VP and VQ assets began Pony Express missions from Adak, Alaska, and Misawa, Japan. VP-50's mission in 1975 flew from Adak, sometimes landing at Midway Islands. The facilities at Midway were limited; hence the briefing was held in a tent near the airfield.[43] Once the SMRIS were located, usually by patrol plane, the surface collectors proceeded to the location. *Vandenberg*, *Hoyt*, and the *Claud Jones*–class destroyers stayed within visual sight, less than nineteen nautical miles off the SMRIS vessels, the best position to collect the telemetry downlink from the missile. Once a Soviet test missile hit the water, the on-station P-3 searched for debris, guiding the *Claud Jones*–class DE to the site for recovery. At the same time the Soviet Navy's ships were attempting to collect the debris. The operations created tense moments observed by the

P-3 circling overhead. The collection of COMINT by VQ aircraft during these interactions helped provide a warning when Soviet assets might feel threatened or looked to escalate.[44]

Platform Flexibility and Special Reconnaissance Missions

VP and VQ AIs faced a steep learning curve in electronic warfare and signals collection. Airborne electronic reconnaissance played a significant role in the victory over Japan in World War II. After the war, maritime patrol continued, but electronic-reconnaissance efforts were scaled back. By the late 1940s fear of the Soviet Union invigorated airborne SIGINT reconnaissance. Available platforms, particularly the PB4Y-2 Privateer seaplanes and the new P-2V Neptune, were modified, sometimes in an impromptu "Sailor mod" fashion, for SIGINT collection.

The Navy had sold most of its electronic-reconnaissance equipment as surplus after World War II. Now it needed to purchase some of it back. Don East writes that the Navy sent two electronic technician chief petty officers (ETC) to locate and buy back some of the equipment. Disguised in civilian clothes and paying cash, the two ETCs purchased all the "intercept receivers, direction finders, pulse analyzers," and other electronic reconnaissance equipment they found.[45]

The Navy called its reconstituted reconnaissance SIGINT program the Special Electronic Search Project (SESP). Patrol squadrons took a mission-support approach, providing detachments of a few patrol aircraft with SIGINT-collection equipment installed and operated by squadron personnel. The approach was an informal one, an innovation that filled mission needs. In 1951 the Navy decided to formalize the effort. They removed the SESP detachment from VP-26, establishing them as the Batmen (later renamed the Sandeman) of Fleet Air Reconnaissance Squadron (VQ-2). The Sandeman supported the Sixth Fleet, based out of Port Lyautey, Morocco, and later Rota, Spain.[46]

At the same time, a similar "mission support" approach emerged in the Pacific fleet. Four P4M-1Q Mercators were assigned to the Special Projects Division at Naval Station Sangley Point, Philippines. The Mercators, a significant improvement over the Privateer seaplane, became a detachment within the Typhoon Trackers of VW-1 in 1953 and moved to Guam. Two years later the SIGINT detachment was removed and established as the World Watchers of Fleet Air Reconnaissance Squadron (VQ-1). From 1955 until 1991, VQ-1 and -2 flew a mix of EC-121M Constellation (1954–1974), EA-3A/B Skywarrior (1958–1991), and EP-3 aircraft.[47]

In 1970, VQ-1 tested two modified P-3Bs, redesignated as EP-3B. The EP-3B proved so successful that the Navy gave Lockheed a contract to convert twelve P-3As to EP-3E Aries SIGINT reconnaissance aircraft. The Aries had a modern solid-state signal-intelligence suite dedicated to SIGINT collection in the new sophisticated electronic environment. The Orion series' tail-mounted magnetic-anomaly detector (MAD) "stinger" was removed. Delivery of the EP-3Es began in July 1971. Each squadron received six EP-3Es by the end of 1972.[48]

The VQ squadron's mission was SIGINT reconnaissance, collecting ELINT and COMINT, which differed from VP's maritime-patrol, surveillance, and ACINT mission. The EP-3E Aries carried no weapons. It provided direct SIGINT support to the fleet, providing indications and warning to airborne aircraft and ships at sea. The control of the airborne SIGINT collection mission was contentious.

The NSA centralized SIGINT collection-planning authority under United States Signal Intelligence Directive 1 (USSID 1), controlling SIGINT's overall direction and security strictures. However, USSID 1 allowed for decentralized execution of SIGINT collection.[49] An Aries was a Navy airborne SIGINT asset. Its onboard Navy SIGINT technicians, the cryptologic direct support element (CDSE), fell under a local Naval security group (NSG). The NSG worked directly for the theater's Navy component commander. The NSA provided analytical and technical support and received data and reports from the missions through the NSG.

The relationship between the centralized control of SIGINT authority and decentralized operations benefited both the strategic and operational levels. It diffused the NSA's bureaucratic control over all things SIGINT. Though they tried several times, the NSA could never directly control the CDSEs. Regarding the situation, Robert E. Morrison quotes intelligence officer (163x) Capt. Sidney Wood, USN: "This is what we [VQ-1] were all about—Direct Fleet Support. Real-time tactical fleet combat support." Collecting signals and sending them back to the NSA at Fort Meade for evaluation resulted in little "evaluation" returning to the western Pacific SIGINT collection entities or operational fleet. To Wood, direct fleet support "differentiated [the] VQ/SECGRU team's mission from all other air collectors. The NSA types could never accept that and constantly tried to get us into 'their mode' of national security support."[50] AIs across the fleet, on the aircraft carriers but especially at the VQ squadrons, quickly learned the cryptologic officers' (161x) SIGINT collection-management intricacies, including the delicate command relationships between the NSG and the NSA. AIs witnessed and often participated in more than one "shouting match" with the NSA's representatives "sent to mend our ways," Morrison writes.[51]

The ELINT and COMINT components of the VQ's SIGINT mission exposed AIs to national-level SCI intelligence. The collection systems were highly technical. An Aries mission aircraft had a similar flight crew to a P-3: two to three pilots, a navigator, a TACCO (or sensor coordinator), and several in-flight technicians. A cryptologic team led by an NSG cryptologic officer (161x) consisted of technicians (CT rating) operating the systems and linguists working on COMINT collection. Altogether up to twenty-four personnel might be onboard an Aries mission aircraft. As part of blockade operations, airborne SIGINT provided vital awareness needed to support the theater and afloat commanders' operational decision-making.

The Aries and other reconnaissance and patrol aircraft flew dangerously close to the enemy to support the fleet. The Peacetime Aerial Reconnaissance Program (PARPRO), led by the U.S. Air Force, provided warning support to imagery and SIGINT reconnaissance flights on the periphery of the Soviet Union and other hostile Communist states. The PARPRO system used designated flight paths and radio brevity codewords (condition codes) to provide threat warning and evasion directions for the reconnaissance aircraft. The system had flaws; the shootdown of VQ-1's EC 121 by North Korean forces in 1969 occurred under PARPRO support. At that time the support lacked the direct signals analysis and warning support of the NSA's global SIGINT enterprise.[52]

The loss of the EC-121 forced the NSA to realize that its focus on strategic SIGINT priorities weakened the support provided to the tactical signals collectors. The Vietnam War, the attack of the SIGINT collection vessel USS *Liberty* (AGER-5) during the 1967 Six-Day War in the eastern Mediterranean Sea, and the capture of the *Liberty*'s sister ship USS *Pueblo* (AGER-2) by North Korean forces (1968) pushed a reluctant NSA back into providing tactical-intelligence support to the fielded forces. The NSA became more inclusive with the Navy and its NSG during SIGINT-collection planning and direct-warning support during operations. In July 1972 the long-awaited National SIGINT Operations Center (NSOC) opened, providing global SIGINT support to theater operations. The NSA, however, continued to have a "national-level monopoly" on Soviet C3 (command, control, and communication) exploitation.[53]

Some sources claim that the PARPRO system was replaced in 1965 or 1969. However, interviews with patrol squadron personnel reveal they conducted PARPRO flights well into the late 1980s. On his second deployment with VP-50 in 1976 Dale Thompson was a qualified PARPRO briefing officer. He said that the warning system had five indications and warning "conditions" determined by the PARPRO center, supported by the NSA NSOC, on Yokota Air Base in Japan. A "periphery line" drawn around the Communist country established a warning boundary for U.S. aircraft. The boundary was close enough to allow for collection operations but far enough away for U.S. aircraft to flee before being attacked.[54] COMINT collection supplied the enemy's understanding of the tactical situation and intentions. Intercepted air-defense radar pro forma messages (like those DRV air-defense messages exploited during the Vietnam War) showed the enemy's understanding of the U.S. aircraft's position. Intercepts of the voice communications between the ground control and enemy-interceptor aircraft warned of potential intercepts.

The PARPRO warnings were short and straightforward. In 2021 Thompson described the system used in 1975. The PARPRO center might issue a "condition" setting over the radio. Condition 1 was the lowest, and condition 5 was the highest. For example, condition 4 translated to "The enemy's radar has determined that you have flown into the periphery. . . . Check your navigation and back off [from the periphery line]." Condition 5 was meant, "You are about to be attacked!"[55]

Because the P-3 Orion had almost no electronic countermeasures (ECM), it could not provide self-protection. The standard patrol aircraft's only defense was the PARPRO system and any direct support warning the airborne VQ Aries provided with its onboard COMINT intercepts. "We [VP] were the poor step-children of that whole system," Thompson lamented. "We were totally dependent on and at the mercy of the PARPRO system to keep us safe."[56] Relying on the PARPRO system meant that some aircrew needed to understand the SCI material supporting the warning analysis. VP-50's SCI-cleared leadership attended SCI intelligence briefings at Atsugi, Japan. The briefs gave them insight into PARPRO missions the VQ aircraft were flying.[57]

Whether conducting PARPRO or fleet-support missions, the operational intelligence demands of a VQ squadron were more than one AI could handle. In 1972, VQ-1's intelligence team had seven officers: a commander (N2), three lieutenants (two in the AI role, one Opintel fusion analyst), two lieutenants junior grade (a special security officer and an Opintel fusion analyst), and an intelligence warrant officer. Because VQ-2 had shipboard detachments in the 1970s, their intelligence team was lean, consisting only of a lieutenant commander (N2) and a lieutenant (assistant N2). In addition several enlisted personnel handled intelligence and security duties (four at VQ-2 and likely six to eight at VQ-1). Each squadron had a SpintCom managed by a lieutenant commander.[58]

The intelligence department supported briefing and debriefing aircrew, mission and collection planning, and many security-related issues surrounding SCI access and material storage. The details of the VQ's intelligence collection and analysis remain classified for the most part. What is clear is that it was complex dealing with theater and national intelligence, not to mention the classified security system—a sufficiently dynamic challenge to require the seniority and experience of an intelligence officer in the rank of commander, the same rank as the squadron's commanding officer. Postmission reports carried the SCI classification level and used an SCI Rainform version of the VP Purple report. The onboard cryptologic detachment sent separate reports through the NSG. The N2 was responsible for overseeing the initial analysis, triaging the mission's collection, and sending the most vital intercepts back to the IC for further analysis.

The MPRF community continued to create mission-support packages to regain the acoustic-detection advantage. One example in declassified contract documents is the CNO special project program K-0416, "Bear-Trap." The project rapidly applied new technology, often commercial computers and prototyping, to improve the search, detection, and tracking of Soviet submarines by airborne ASW aircraft.[59] Dale Thompson described the BearTrap effort against Soviet *Yankee*-class SSBNs during his 1975 deployment. The SOSUS system or SCI signals or human intelligence cued a BearTrap mission. Standard P-3s might find and track the Soviet submarine, usually a ballistic missile boat. Then a BearTrap mission aircraft took over, using its specially calibrated sonobuoys to record the submarine's source propagation level (SPL).[60]

Limited declassified government records of BearTrap missions are available. The P-3 History Project records the first P-3 airframe to have a BearTrap modification as Bureau of Aeronautics number (BuNo) 152727, assigned to VP-23 in September 1967. The second, BuNo 157323, was assigned to VP-56 in July 1970. Two P-3 aircraft, BuNo 158574 and BuNo 158913, assigned to VP-47 and VP-16 respectively, were modified in 1973. Other aircraft were modified in 1975, 1982, 1984, 1985, and 1999.[61] Interviews with VP-50 personnel indicate that BearTrap aircraft were "crossdecked" or moved from the returning squadron to a deploying squadron.

A 1982 Department of the Navy justification submission to Congress requested $6.2 million to support the BearTrap program.[62] NAVAIR's Naval Air Systems Command (NAVAIRSYSCOM) oversaw the BearTrap program, and the Naval Air Warfare Center Aircraft Division (NAVAIRWARCENACDIV) laboratory developed the technology. The Fleet Electronic Warfare Support Group (FEWSG) conducted the engineering and installation of the avionics suites in Orion aircraft.

Navy contracts from the 1990s show the new Maritime Patrol and Reconnaissance Aircraft (MPRA) Program (PMA [air] 290) responsible for BearTrap. Sensors for the program were developed by the Naval Signal Processors Program Office (PMS [ship] 428) "to replace the AQA-7(V) signal processing system with a UYS-2A based system" in November 1995.[63] The linkage to the AQA-7(V) may confirm Dale Thompson's recollections about BearTrap and its acoustic experimentation. A 2007 expense-justification exhibit for program K-0416 notes that BearTrap provides "Sound Pressure Level (SPL) quality recordings of targets of interest and . . . the BEARTRAP Environmental data collection program provides passive and active acoustic and non-acoustic data essential for the . . . calibrated(ing) recording systems, advanced detection and tracking systems, special sensors, advanced processing systems and techniques."[64]

Project BearTrap attempts to solve two problems Don Miskill discussed: the quieting of enemy submarines and the need to filter out the ocean's ambient noise. First, making the algorithms that filtered ambient noise required a deep catalog of those noises. Second, an index of enemy submarine signals being sought was needed to gain an advantage by reducing ambient noise, thus increasing submarine detection. Analyzing the enemy submarine signals allowed the assessment of operational patterns and new technologies. The detailed ACINT data collected from airborne sensors was vital to improving the SOSUS network that supported the distant blockade-based deterrence strategy. Intelligence officers exposed to the new technology carried it to their other tours. More importantly those officers witnessed innovation in action. They learned the art of the possible within an organization imbibed with emergent potential and evolvability.

At the Van of Change

An AI tour in a 1970s VP squadron put a junior intelligence officer (now all 163xs) into an operational world in which high-end competition with the Soviet Navy occurred daily. The squadron was where the two characters of air intelligence and Opintel combined. A well-honed squadron with congealed aircrews did magical things in the distant blockade effort.

The "crews determined greatness," offered then–lieutenant junior grade and future vice admiral Ann Rondeau, USN (Ret.). ASW was a complex, multilayered process that began with intelligence providing a starting point. With the help of intelligence, aircrews knew the Soviet submarine and its submariner; they developed a "sixth sense," anticipating the submarine's tactical actions. By doggedly fixing, tracking, and targeting Soviet submarines, the Navy's understanding of the threat and its ability to message deterrence grew.[65]

William Cracknell's quip in 1959 was partially correct; the Navy focused on ASW, yes, but not at the expense of power projection. Though the Navy's submarine community was gaining power, the aircraft carriers and the airpower Navy still controlled most of the Navy's direction. As intelligence officers rotated in and out of these squadrons, they carried a new form of Opintel to their next assignment. Cracknell's time in aviation and as the AI/Navigator in VP-7 prepared him well. He converted with other 135x to the active-duty 1630 designator; in Cracknell's case it was back to 163x in 1967. In 1968 he attended the U.S. Naval War College in Newport, Rhode Island, publishing a paper titled "The Role of the U.S. Navy in Inshore Waters."[66] The paper captured his experience supporting Operations Sealords and Game Warden during a tour in Vietnam. Cracknell became Carrier Division Four's N2 and embarked on USS *John F. Kennedy* (CV 67) in 1972. He remained his own man. The *Kennedy*'s cruise book photograph shows the bearded and bespectacled William Cracknell wearing his beloved leather flight jacket—a maverick within the staff. In 1988 Cracknell retired from the Navy as a captain after having completed a tour as commander, Naval Intelligence Command, Suitland, Maryland.[67] He passed in October 2005.

Like other junior intelligence officers in the VP world, Rondeau and Thompson learned that they were part of a large intelligence apparatus as bureaucratic and parochial as any behemoth organization. When asked if her patrol squadron AI tour made a difference to her career, Rondeau, like other AIs, offered an emphatic "Yes!" She offered that obtaining the rank of vice admiral was due to "my nearly four years at VP-50," a period "defining to me as a naval officer."[68]

An AI tour provided experience about the operational Navy needed to put intelligence into context. Dale Thompson agreed with Rondeau, adding that his VP-50 tour had prepared him for his time at a Fleet Ocean Surveillance Information Facility (FOSIF). Further, Thompson said, unlike AIs on an aircraft carrier, he was not focused "on that AI thing on the [aircraft] carrier; I was focused on the Soviet Navy, [their] overall naval activities." He "just picked up from there" at FOSIF, tracking Soviet submarines and other maritime activities as he had before.[69]

To Rondeau "ASW became a proficiency area for the naval officer who was involved in it" because it was an "integrated, cross-platform skill set." Intelligence collection and analysis were done ashore, at SOSUS and FOSIF, at the TSC, and on the aircraft carrier at sea. Rondeau said there "was a friendly competition in that orbit of anti-submarine warfare" between the shore and operational forces. The ASW find-fix-track competition increased proficiency in the "art of ASW" that brought the rest of the Navy along. It prepared the Navy for the hyperlethal fight at sea.[70]

Thompson and Rondeau each had a deeper understanding of Soviet and Navy platforms' operational capabilities and limitations. The exposure to SCI material was also eye-opening, especially in a VQ squadron. An AI tour in VQ provided unique insight into the command, control, and communication (C3) used by the Soviet Navy. Understanding the cryptology world and the NSG/NSA organizational dynamics were "bonus" lessons from a VQ tour, which later paid significant dividends at Ocean Surveillance Information System (OSIS) nodes and afloat Opintel assignments.

By their nature VQ and VP squadrons operated where the most dangerous threats existed. Aircraft mishaps occurred. Some states reacted aggressively against airborne-collection operations, and the interactions sometimes resulted in losses. The intense operational tempo forced an AI to learn quickly about the enemy, the environment, and themselves. Squadron AI tours in VP and VQ came with dynamic deployments that forced adaptation and creativity. AIs learned about their capabilities and resilience. Most importantly they understood the importance of tapping into the Navy Intelligence's intelligence officer network at the various

TSCs, OSIS nodes, and Fleet staff headquarters and, most importantly, on the aircraft carriers at sea. As the Navy sailed in the mid-1970s toward a go-forward naval strategy against the Soviets, MPRF supported aircraft carrier battlegroups directly or indirectly. Often maritime patrols anchored a battlegroup's surface and subsurface search coordination (SSSC) efforts.

Social Change: Women AIs and MPRF

Rondeau's tour at VP-50 represented the social changes occurring in the Navy and Navy Intelligence, she later said. The post–Vietnam War social contract between the Navy and U.S. youth was on shaky ground. CNO Zumwalt recognized the problems. The inequalities in treatment, based on race and gender, reduced opportunities for Sailors. Worse, the Navy had an organizational culture that encouraged excessive use of alcohol and tobacco and that tolerated discrimination. Retention was low, and desertion and unauthorized absences were high. To knock off these "irritating and unproductive barnacles" of social injustice, Zumwalt conducted studies, gathered data, and released directives called Z-Grams directly to the fleet.[71] After two years of Z-Grams, in August 1972 Zumwalt finally arrived at Z-116, "Equal Rights and Opportunities for Women in the Navy." He wrote that Z 116 "visualized, perhaps wrongly it now appears, the imminent passage of the Equal Rights Amendment."[72] The amendment never passed, though it remains debated in Congress to this day.

Zumwalt could not overturn legislation restricting women from serving in combat aircraft and surface combatants. However, he could initiate "a series of administrative actions that enabled the Navy to make full use of women" when the law changed or the definitions were liberalized.[73] One change affecting Navy Intelligence was Z-116's announcement authorizing "Unrestricted Line Officer women to serve in Restricted Line (RL) billets."[74]

A note from the December 1975 *Intelligence Newsletter* highlights the significance of the 1972 decision. "The number of Women Officers working in our community as subspecialists continues to grow," the *Newsletter* reported. Women with the "necessary intelligence training and experience" may fill all intelligence subspecialist billets "not aboard combatant ships or aircraft." The number of women serving in 163x billets was growing. A WAVE (Women Accepted for Volunteer Emergency Service) captain had been nominated to become the first woman Naval Attaché.[75]

Z-116 resulted in a pilot program for women to serve aboard ships. In November 1972 the USS *Sanctuary* became the first ship with a mixed-gender crew. The Navy, however, may not have been as progressive as it was pragmatic. In the post–Vietnam War era they were having trouble recruiting and retaining enough personnel to crew the fleet. Women provided a personnel resource for noncombat positions that freed the men to go to sea.[76]

In 1974 tugboats and other service vessels became open to women. How "vessels of the Navy" were defined changed the law's restrictions. The Navy considered "vessels" to be those that "go to sea," meaning ships that deploy for extended periods on the high seas. Service craft were not deployed to sea, making them available for women.[77] In June 1975 CNO Holloway took further steps to reduce restrictions, deciding to "permanently open the Restricted line officer community to women" beginning in the spring of 1976.[78] Navy Intelligence allowed women to designate as 163x and "follow normal 163X professional development patterns." Almost all shore-duty billets in Navy Intelligence were open to female officers.[79]

Legislative changes were slower than Navy policy updates. Living and working conditions at the land-based patrol, transport, and helicopter squadrons made integration easier than on the aircraft carrier and surface forces.[80] In 1955 the Navy's first female officer completed a solo flight at Air Basic Training Command. The aviation community seemed more—though only slightly—willing to experiment with including women as genuine line officers.[81] The aviation community allowed some women into flight training in the spring of 1973. Women could still not deploy on aircraft carriers; thus the only assignment equivalent to "sea duty" for women aviators was posting overseas. Seven of the first twelve women to complete flight training in 1973 and 1974 went to transport or research

squadrons flying multiengine, land-based aircraft like the P-3 and C-130. Only two of the seven were assigned to overseas squadrons.[82] In 1979 the Secretary of the Navy rolled out a new policy permitting female pilots flying support aircraft to land on ships (temporary duty only). Women could also be assigned to "shore duty combat aircraft squadrons in billets not requiring women to fly combat missions."[83]

The maritime-patrol community's construct appeared to mitigate some restrictions on women on operational duty. Still, the P-3 was a combat aircraft, and women pilots could not fly P-3s in an active patrol squadron until the law changed. They continued to push the boundaries, and by 1980 a female pilot flew in VQ-2 as a temporary duty assignment for eight months. It was not until the 1990s that MPRF would open to female pilots.[84]

Navy Intelligence was at least two years ahead of Holloway. Upon arriving at VP-50 in 1974 Dale Thompson found that two squadrons already had women intelligence line (nonwarfare-qualified) subspecialist AIs. One of the women, Capt. Gail Harris, USN (Ret.), then a lieutenant-junior grade, was the first African American woman officer to serve in a squadron.[85] The women line subspecialists tested the waters while Navy Intelligence brought onboard 163x women officers. In 1976 three women—two lieutenants and one lieutenant junior grade—laterally transferred from 110x line to the 163x community. All three were assigned to fleet commands (Pacific and Atlantic) and OpNav. Also in 1976 two women "fresh caught" from the civilian sector graduated from Air Officer Candidate School and AFAITC along with their male 163x counterparts. The two ensigns went to PATWING ONE, Kadena, Japan, and VP-1, Barbers Point, Hawaiʻi.[86]

Oddly enough Rondeau, a 110x line (nonwarfare-qualified) officer, applied to transfer to 163x but was denied. Her path to VP-50 in 1976 was through the subspecialty route, but even that path was nontraditional. As an ensign she worked in "cryptology and communications security" on the CINCPACFLT staff. She recalled that she "wanted to do something operational," and her detailer "worked an assignment to VP-50 for me—a BearTrap squadron, by the way."[87]

Rondeau attended the Navy's strike-mission-focused introductory intelligence course at AFAITC in Denver. "It was tough getting training in many ways as a young officer," she recalls. "I found some modest training, but much was 'pickup learning.'" Like many intelligence officers with high achievement motivation (HAM), Rondeau made her own training opportunities. "As I went on, I had some good teachers in the squadron, and I just studied hard," she says. Learning from and leveraging her male counterparts' expertise at the squadrons and TSC on Moffett Airfield helped. "My mind was nearly all Navy. I just worked hard. I was dedicated and effective. I was curious and hungry to learn," she said in a 2022 interview. The efforts made her work trustworthy, and she trusted—essential traits for intelligence officers.[88]

Credibility and competency were important, especially for a woman entering the male-dominated Navy. Hard work positioned Rondeau to seize opportunities within the squadron. In times of crisis, competence trumps social prejudice, especially in the pragmatic aviation community. In the late 1970s pilots left for commercial airlines, creating a shortage. VP-50 filled its vacant pilot department-head positions with competent junior officers. Rondeau had proven herself one of the Blue Dragons' most competent officers. She was asked to write the daily flight schedules, usually a job done by a junior pilot. The pilot shortage and operation tempo of the squadron simultaneously grew. Rondeau went from writing schedules to being the Blue Dragons' operations officer (Ops O).[89]

Being the Ops O is a big deal; being a nonpilot woman Ops O in 1979 is extraordinary. Here again Rondeau's competency as an AI made the position possible. The squadron required the wing commander's approval to make the change. The wing commander readily acquiesced. He "knew me as my time as an AIO," Rondeau said, "because I had filled in for the Wing's missing AI," often providing intelligence briefings to the commander. As the Ops O, Rondeau understood that she needed to balance the organizational culture with the dynamics of her role. She needed to be part of the group to be effective. Her established AI-to-customer relationship helped in her Ops O role. She reached out to the pilots and maintenance crews, incorporating their operational expertise and opinions, creating inclusion and lessening friction. Being both the AI and Ops O meant Rondeau was "really busy," but "I worked hard" to meet the demands of the squadron. After returning from deployment Rondeau retained the Ops O position, leaving in 1980 for graduate school at Georgetown University.[90]

The Navy worked through the integration of women; by 1980 almost 15 percent of VP-50 were women. Still, Rondeau remained the only female Blue Dragons officer. VP along with a few other non-CV/CVN aviation squadrons were on the pioneering edge of the integration of women. As such, the structures and culture to support leaders in the newly diverse environment were nearly nonexistent. The wardrooms and chief petty officers' messes were only as productive and healthy in organizational change as their leaders, who struggled to find suitable approaches to the gender-integration challenges. The command master chief, who was "flummoxed" by the challenges, asked Rondeau if she would serve in the antiquated role of the "women's division officer." Rondeau went to the executive officer to talk about the character of leadership. Following the Navy's *Standard Organization and Regulation Manual* (SORM) was "considerably better than leading by gender," Rondeau offered. The XO immediately agreed, and she became a division officer like any other Navy junior officer.[91]

The path ahead of them remained long, but by 1980 women were well on their way to serving as full members of the Navy. Sadly it would not be until the 1990s that women intelligence personnel could serve in shipboard Opintel roles. Gender diversity improved the Opintel fusion analysis by providing new perspectives. The reciprocating influence of shore-based all-source centers on shipboard Opintel benefited. For shipboard Opintel, diversity would bring creative problem-solving and unique, informal adaptation to post–Cold War revolutions in military affairs.

Conclusion

Close-blockade operations during the Vietnam War and the distant blockade of Soviet submarines afterward shaped Navy Intelligence, reinforcing the need for ocean surveillance. Navy Intelligence's discovery-learning into human intelligence (HUMINT) sources and fusion analysis increased maritime domain awareness against Viet Cong infiltration networks. The effort reduced Viet Cong supplies delivered via maritime modes and influenced Opintel's performance orientation and collectivism.[92] Despite considerable efforts, however, the outcome of the war did not change.

The Navy realized that sea control, denial, and interdiction operations in the southern Vietnam theater required understanding enemy and friendly activity within the maritime domain. Intelligence regarding the enemy's size, location, and intent at sea, elements of the traditional 163x character of Opintel, were essential to position interdiction forces. Distinguishing an enemy transport vessel from similar friendly craft was vital to targeting and interdiction operations. At least in concept some similarities existed between tracking resupply vessels and Soviet submarines. Both problems are force-space focused; there are too few forces to surveil too much space. The function of intelligence is a critical balancing mechanism.

In tracking Soviet submarines, effective surveillance focused on their bases and the choke points through which they passed. A similar surveillance approach used in Operations Market Time, Game Warden, and Sealords had varying levels of success.[93] The HUMINT collection brought fusion analysis closer to all-source intelligence operations. Adding highly classified SIGINT and ACINT intelligence from the maritime patrol and reconnaissance forces moved Opintel toward truly all-source fusion. Thus the reciprocating influences between the various characters of airpower at sea on the aircraft carrier and ashore at the VP and VQ squadrons shaped Opintel as a process and an organizational culture. The creation of the Ocean Surveillance Information System (OSIS) became a melting pot of Opintel's character and a crucible for intelligence officers, shaping an Opintel identity across Navy Intelligence.

PART III
Decentralizing

The boatswain's pipe twilled over the 1 MC, quickly followed by the blaring drone: "Attention, all hands. This is the captain speaking." *Liberty* had been attacked, the captain said, and the "Mighty Massey" had been directed to proceed south at flank speed to render aid. The engines of the *Allen M. Sumner*–class destroyer USS *Massey* (DD 778) spooled up, the screws bit deep into the sea, and the destroyer squatted as she leaped forward at twenty-five knots. Traveling south, away from the *America* (CV 66) and Task Group 60.1, the *Massey* increased speed to twenty-seven knots. USS *Davis* (DD 937), a *Forrest Sherman*–class destroyer, fell in with *Massey*, and both accelerated to thirty-one knots, the max speed of the *Davis*.[1]

Massey and *Davis* steamed at flank speed for thirteen hours, arriving at *Liberty*'s location as the sun rose on Friday, June 9, 1967. The *Liberty* was hard to make out, obscured by a dense fog. The two destroyers went "all stop" on their engines and drifted. It was quiet. Lookouts on *Massey* reported hearing the "eerie sound of waves splashing" on the side of the yet-invisible ship. *Liberty* came into view; she was listing badly, a thirty-nine-foot hole torn into her hull. A lookout reported seeing what appeared to be bodies floating in water. Another lookout reported two Soviet warships shadowing *Massey* and *Davis*.[2]

Israeli fighters had strafed *Liberty*, killing eight crewmen. Thirty minutes later *Liberty* was torpedoed by Israeli Navy attack boats, killing twenty-five crewmen in the cargo hold converted into research spaces. In the final count *Liberty* had thirty-four Sailors dead and another 171 wounded.[3] The Department of Defense downplayed *Liberty*'s mission and the horrific attack. The media correctly speculated, however, filling in the details missing from the censored inquiry report released in late

June 1967. The papers, as did the Pentagon, focused on communication failures as the cause of the incident: the delay in delivering radioed orders directing *Liberty* to pull back from the coast was at root of the horrific incident.[4]

To newly promoted Vice Adm. David C. Richardson, USN, fresh from Vietnam duty and preparing for his new assignment as commander of the Sixth Fleet, the *Liberty* incident foreshadowed a change in the operational environment within the Atlantic Ocean and Mediterranean Sea. The problems he saw were not just communication-related but also concerned intelligence support to operations.[5]

MAP 6
The Mediterranean theater, 1968

CHAPTER 7
To Not Be Surprised

In the aftermath of the 1967 Arab-Israeli War the Soviet Navy doubled its number in the Mediterranean Sea to twenty-four combatants and auxiliaries.¹ The sea was congested, and interactions were complex. The Israeli attack on the *Liberty*, a signals-collection ship, was a cautionary tale for Vice Admiral Richardson. He felt the attack highlighted operations-intelligence integration failure as much as it did a communication and command one. The *Liberty* attack followed by the capture of her sister ship, USS *Pueblo* (AGTR-2), by the North Koreans in January 1968 reinforced the need for ocean surveillance, improved situational awareness, and better warning. Concerned about being surprised, Richardson found that "there was no available intelligence [about the Soviet operations] worthy of the name" when he arrived to take command of the Sixth Fleet.² He needed warning intelligence and better operation-intelligence integration to command a fleet in this contested environment.

The idea of "warning" regarding enemy military action or one state's move against another has always existed. The World Wars framed warning, or lack of it, as an intelligence function. The World War II battle at Midway Islands illustrated operational-warning success—a lesson the Navy held dear. In the Cold War, budgetary issues and processes forced the intelligence community (IC) to define "warning intelligence" so that they could fund it. What *is* warning intelligence? It meant different things to different decision-makers, depending on what level of national security from which they viewed it. In her influential work *Anticipating Surprise* Cynthia M. Grabo wrote that providing "warning could be said to be an almost unlimited responsibility of the intelligence system" and one that potentially covers any development anywhere in the world.³

Strategic warning is the most discussed form of warning intelligence. At the strategic level of war warning is somewhat ambiguous, especially regarding the timing of future action. Strategic warning, viewed as a long-term analysis effort, provides the "earliest possible warning . . . the warning system is supposed to provide." The problem with warning is that it is a "judgment about the probability of military action in the future," Grabo points out, that may be "unrelated to the imminence of [its] action."[4] Details within the warning can be accurate, but if the assessed timing of the attack is wrong, it is still considered a failure. In their recent book *Warning Intelligence* John A. Gentry and Joseph S. Gordon use the 2001 attack on the World Trade Center as an example. A strategic warning had been given—that a terrorist attack on a major city was probable, and the 1993 bombing of the World Trade Center made New York City a likely candidate—but a tactical warning failed to provide the target and attack timing, meaning only so much preparation could be made and resources directed in advance to respond to a grave yet vague caution.[5]

Tactical warning tends to be a concern of commanders in the field. They use local sensors to detect tactical enemy-force movements. The problem is that modern war has no distinct line between strategic and tactical warnings. An attack on a Navy aircraft carrier, a strategic asset, may result in the same strategic response as an attack on American soil.[6] Additionally, most threats to deployed U.S. forces come from beyond the range of their tactical-warning sensors. Therefore national-intelligence collection sensors serve operational-intelligence needs by bridging strategic and tactical warning.[7]

More complex is warning-intelligence analysis itself. Michael S. Goodman considers the myriad ways the puzzle pieces of individual data may be overlooked or pieced together wrongly, in the end creating a distorted picture that obfuscates rather than informs. "Mirror imaging"— or viewing an adversary's actions through one's own lens—is a common and often dangerous bias compounded by confirmation bias. Analysts may cherry-pick information, only regarding the data in support of their original assessment, which may or may not be flawed, or in support of their preferred point of view, which may or may not reflect reality. The result is a perseverance to adhere to a line of thought despite lack of evidence or even when presented with evidence to the contrary. Teasing apart enemy intent and capability is a critical challenge; just because a state *can* launch an attack does not mean it will. Neither does the will to attack without the ability to succeed mean they will not attack. "There is a relationship between capabilities and intent, but it is not a linear or simple one," Goodman writes; "the two are usually only joined when considering 'threat,' not the intent."[8] All strategic or tactical warnings in the Cold War required consideration of political and military developments together. Therefore interpreting tactical-warning intelligence requires help from strategic-warning intelligence in the political context. Without the context the aggressive competition witnessed between the U.S. and Soviet Navies, for example, might lead to an escalation spiral where one was not warranted.[9]

Warning intelligence itself uses a depth of knowledge gained through long-term analysis. Foundational intelligence, part of long-term analysis, provides a comprehensive understanding of the adversary's capabilities and history. Current intelligence offers details concerning what the adversary is doing now. Relying only on current intelligence to formulate a warning clouds judgment and leads to alarmism or, worse, failure to see past recent reports and regard the bigger picture. Supporting a dedicated warning-intelligence organization is preferable to relying on long-term and current intelligence organizations alone.[10] Assembling, funding, and supporting a specific body that produces warning intelligence is a typical approach—like Britain's Joint Intelligence Committee, about which Goodwin writes. Ensuring the body is large enough to handle the vast amounts of long-term and current intelligence and provide the judgment needed for warning intelligence is a challenge.[11] Gentry and Gordon have considered the U.S. intelligence community as a whole and recommend a hybrid warning-organization model. They conclude that warning intelligence is best conducted under a moderated version of the model currently used in the United States and Britain in which EAAWA, or "Every Analyst is A Warning Analyst." EAAWA uses a small, specialized warning office led by a senior warning analyst with units producing strategic warning intelligence.[12]

No matter the warning intelligence organization, Grabo offers, in the end creating warning is problematic because it "is an intangible, an abstraction, a theory, a deduction, a perception, a belief." Such a hypothetical "can be neither confirmed nor refuted until it is too late" and an attack has occurred.[13] Sir David Omand says that to be useful a warning must provide decision-makers with four critical elements: situational awareness, an explanation regarding the observed situation, an estimation of the possible outcomes, and notification. What makes the "intangible" warning credible, Omand says, is a "strong knowledge claim" by the subject-matter expert providing the warning. What makes the warning useful, he says, is placing it into context and providing the "so what?"—or why the warning matters and why the current policy or military posture is inadequate or critical.[14]

Omand's wisdom is relevant to understanding the U.S. Navy's position on warning intelligence. Harsh conditions and dynamic combat at sea that necessitate rapid on-the-ground analysis and response have created a tradition of independence in operations.[15] The complexities of the sea multiply those of combat; the commander must use guidance, experience, and tactics creatively. There is little time to reach back to shore for information. Therefore the relationship between the commander and the intelligence officer is essential. A vital warning with less certainty is better received from an intelligence officer the commander "owns" and trusts than from an anonymous intelligence center ashore. After all, the decision-maker must be able to listen to a warning for the warning to be helpful, and proximity and hard-won trust make that more likely. The shipboard intelligence officer regularly provides the situation, explanation, and estimation in context to the commander's current operations, and the commander provides the so-what.

Independence at sea is valuable for command but not for warning-intelligence production. The U.S. Navy's shipboard Opintel team required assistance with long-term analysis from shore organizations as the need for more specific operational warnings about Soviet Navy intent grew in the 1970s. Richardson cared little for the theory and challenges of warning intelligence. His desire was simple: to not be surprised by Soviet or Arab action in the Mediterranean Sea.

Richardson, Sixth Fleet, and Ocean Surveillance

The respected Wayne Hughes has noted that winners in war-at-sea "have outscouted the enemy."[16] For some time the Navy desired an ocean surveillance system that provided global scouting, gave strategic warnings, monitored adversaries' navies, and supported tactical force allocation.[17] The origin of the modern ocean-surveillance project started with a 1964 study by the Director of Naval Intelligence. In *Network-centric Warfare* Norman Friedman traces the general and specific operating-requirement memorandums issued between 1966 and 1971 by the Radar, Electronic Warfare, Sonar (REWSON) Project at the Naval Electronics Systems Command. The requirements documents capture the operating forces' demands for the inclusion of funding for ocean surveillance within the Navy and Department of Defense planning and budgeting process.[18] The reality, however, was that the Ocean Surveillance Information System (OSIS), as it would come to be called, was "a concept arrived at by many ... through a convergent evolution driven by fleet operators' urgent need for such a capability."[19] The operator who likely made the most significant contribution to the concept and structure of OSIS was Admiral Richardson. His less-formal and iterative efforts at Sixth Fleet anticipated rather than coincided with the technical systems envisioned.

It was not that the Mediterranean theater lacked adequate surveillance; a NATO radar system was established in Greece and Turkey, and U.S. airborne- and surface-patrol assets were active.[20] However, most surveillance activities were not centralized, and the reporting was not fused and assessed. Richardson and all the fleet commanders wanted "warning," not just surveillance. In an interview shortly before his death, Capt. Robert Tolle, USN (163x), Richardson's assistant intelligence officer, recalled that Richardson referred to his personal copy of the *Liberty* incident report when discussing the need for better operations-intelligence integration, warning intelligence, and C2.[21] Richardson was uninterested in the Navy bureaucratic problems that prevented operational intelligence improvements in warning intelligence; he demanded better, not perfect, tangible, not theoretical, operational intelligence that provided warning, and he wanted it *now!* Richardson used his rank and position to make people listen, Tolle offered. "He never gave up; he fought for whatever he wanted."[22]

Richardson understood the theory of all-source fused intelligence from his time as commander of TF-77 in the Gulf of Tonkin off Vietnam. He believed that by driving the Sixth Fleet's operational intelligence toward all-source fusion he would avoid being surprised by the Soviets. "I was sent there to bring lessons learned in Southeast Asia," Richardson said of his time with the Sixth Fleet, especially to introduce the use of "special intelligence" materials.[23]

When in August 1968 he walked aboard the Sixth Fleet flagship, the cruiser USS *Little Rock*, Richardson found a small and like-minded Opintel team. The signals-intelligence section operated from a newly installed special intelligence communications (SpintCom) space.[24] The ocean-surveillance concept was simple: "systematic observation of the sea" using all-source information to discern operational patterns of the adversary. The challenge was creating a place with analysts who could fuse the information. New space-based reconnaissance systems produced lots of data, adding to the existing surveillance networks.[25] Additionally, persistent surveillance by terrestrial systems produced a flood of information, more than his small team in the cramped spaces of *Little Rock* could analyze and fuse.[26]

The technical collection's success required maintaining the information sources' security. Thus the intelligence community tightly controlled and centralized the material through information-security caveats. Space-based systems collected "national" intelligence and produced analysis at a strategic level that supported strategic military decisions. That same intelligence also provided indications and warning indispensable to military operations.[27] The lessons from the Vietnam War reinforced the need for more access to the highly classified special compartmented information. However, getting the IC to decentralize that SCI material was the problem. The Special Security Office (SSO) at the DIA and within the Navy slowly coded more billets for SCI access, but more decentralization was still required.

Richardson envisioned having an ocean-surveillance cell like the one he'd seen at the Navy's Field Operational Intelligence Office (NFOIO) in Fort Meade, Maryland. He set about leveraging his position to create access to the material and assemble the needed expertise.[28] His first effort was to gain access to more national-intelligence products.

Access to national intelligence was problematic; the classification and caveats created a have versus have-not situation at Sixth Fleet. By law, operational commands were not authorized access to national-intelligence imagery and SIGINT products for tactical exploitation.[29] Only a few people on Richardson's staff were cleared to receive the SIGINT intelligence briefed by detachment cryptologists at the Naval Security Group (NSG). Richardson had Commander E. R. Sourbeer, USN (1630), his N2, fuse signals intelligence with other intelligence sources to force all-source integration and fused intelligence for the staff. The sanitized brief provided context, allowing the operators, pilots, and surface line officers to understand the situation.[30]

In a 2019 interview Capt. Louis Giacchino, USN (1610) (Ret.), then a lieutenant commander and the staff cryptologist, spoke about signals intelligence integration during his time at Sixth Fleet. The staff intelligence officer N2 (1630) "was and should be the focal point of intel to the flag [Richardson]," he said. "I had access to the flag, but there should be great rapport [between] the top intel guy and the flag," he added.[31] Signal intelligence is, after all, only one source of information. Combining two forms of signals intelligence—for example, communication and electronic intelligence—is a multi-intelligence but not all-source approach. While seductive, multi-intelligence combinations often lack analytic depth.[32] The NSG detachment, Opintel team, and Richardson understood the need for broad intelligence collection-and-analysis synergy that would provide a deeper understanding of the enemy's activity.

Even with the addition of raw COMINT intercepts and other compartmented information, the analysis at Sixth Fleet was only "nearly all-source."

Richardson's Opintel team still lacked access to satellite-collected Talent Keyhole (TK) imagery. Before September 1970 TK material was reserved for strategic forces and not authorized for use by tactical units. Richardson put in a request to the Chief of Naval Operations for TK material. The request garnered interest from other theater commanders who wanted access, forcing the CNO to lobby for the limited release of certain TK materials to Sixth Fleet. Though his Opintel team now had access to more SCI material, Richardson still lacked space and personnel to conduct fusion analysis; he needed a shore-based Intel Center.[33]

A Sixth Fleet Analysis Center

In the spring of 1969, Chief of Naval Operations Admiral Moorer, USN, arrived to review Richardson's Sixth Fleet—especially his intelligence efforts. Moorer's visit was the culmination of meetings with Richardson the previous summer,[34] and in the interim Richardson had been relentless. His fledgling Opintel team had shown results, and his "strong voice and experience" legitimized their efforts.[35] Now the CNO and DNI were in Italy with a proposal.

DNI Rear Adm. Fredrick "Fritz" Harlfinger, Richardson recalled, observed that the Navy was "struggling for

PHOTO 7.1
Vice Admiral Richardson (*right*) shakes hands with CNO Adm. Thomas Moorer on the Sixth Fleet flagship USS *Little Rock*, spring 1969. PHOTO COURTESY OF THE BUFFALO AND ERIE COUNTY NAVAL AND MILITARY PARK

some time with the creation of an Ocean Surveillance Information System." Harlfinger noted that what Richardson's Opintel team was doing on the *Little Rock* "might be the answer." Harlfinger then offered to establish an Opintel fusion center at the naval base in Rota, Spain, dedicated to supporting the Sixth Fleet.[36]

If Richardson were to maintain the tasking authority of the ocean surveillance and analysis cell in Rota, there would be several advantages to Harlfinger's proposal. First, more space and a dedicated workforce could conduct all-source fusion Opintel twenty-four hours a day.[37] Second, Rota was home to essential surveillance and analysis assets like the Naval Security Group (NSG), the Fleet Air Reconnaissance Squadron Two (VQ-2), Maritime Patrol Squadrons (VP), and the Navy's only European Fleet Weather Center (FWC), allowing for increased integration.[38] Most importantly a shore facility in Rota would allow assured communications because of the large modern station there.[39] Richardson agreed to the arrangement. Cdr. George Pressly, USN (1630), and several "brand-new intelligence officers (1630)" arrived later in the summer of 1969 and set up a Fleet Ocean Surveillance Information Facility (FOSIF) inside the Fleet Weather Center's building.[40]

In addition to Harlfinger, Moorer brought along three CIA representatives to the *Little Rock* meeting. Richardson's new FOSIF required HUMINT collection to fuse with the SIGINT and IMINT to make it all-source Opintel. Richardson recalled that the CIA representatives offered a clandestine boat to collect against Soviet ships operating in the Mediterranean Sea. Several months after the meeting with the CIA representatives, Richardson received a small yacht he nicknamed "Attsa My Boat"—in homage to its provenance. The boat had been "leased from Italians, manned by Italians," and "had special collection equipment" onboard.[41] The boat was likely operated not by the CIA but by Navy Intelligence's Task Force 157. Quite probably Attsa My Boat was TF 157's yacht, *Big Smoke*, itself probably named after Thomas Duval, one of the founders of Navy HUMINT and nicknamed "Big Smoke" for the large cigars he enjoyed.[42] In 1963 Duval had established HUMINT operations in Guantánamo, Cuba, for the Office of Naval Intelligence.[43]

Since its creation in 1966, Task Force 157 had been conducting clandestine collection operations in several critical European ports, maritime choke points in the Mediterranean Sea, and in Vietnam. In Bremerhaven and Frankfurt, Germany, clandestine operations provided information on Soviet bloc merchant ships. Operations in Istanbul, Turkey, provided information regarding Soviet Black Sea Fleet operations and merchant activity. Another office established in Naples supported Sixth Fleet. Jeffrey T. Richelson once wrote that TF 157 used boats and yachts to get within fifty feet of Soviet combatants entering the harbor or operating near the coast. The yachts, sometimes equipped with "special nuclear intelligence sensors," would then be used to collect signals intelligence.[44]

The Fleet Ocean Surveillance Facility in Rota, Spain, was the first node in the Ocean Surveillance Information System (OSIS). FOSIF began simply by using "brute force" analysis; it had limited automation but good communications. The NSG's SpintCom and SI communication system allowed FOSIF to coordinate analyst to analyst, though time-delayed, with intelligence organizations in Europe and Washington, D.C. Access to the tactical reporting networks of the Anti-submarine Warfare Forces, Sixth Fleet, the underway aircraft carriers, and the airborne patrol and reconnaissance squadrons decreased tactical reporting times.[45] The tactical networks also allowed FOSIF Rota to relay "tippers"—or tip-offs, indications about Soviet activity—which they would share back and forth via the high-frequency direction finding (HFDF) radar networks and other collectors within the Mediterranean theater.[46]

After only four months of operation, FOSIF Rota had proven its worth, even if it had yet to be officially commissioned. The 18,500-ton Soviet Navy ship *Moskva*, the largest in the Soviet Navy, was underway in the Black Sea. The *Moskva*, listed as an aircraft-carrying cruiser by the Soviet Navy, was configured as a helicopter carrier and was the Soviets' premier anti-submarine warfare platform.[47] The NSG's signals-intercept station picked up messages with the *Moskva*'s call sign. The intercepts were not unusual, especially considering the Soviet Navy was coming off its New Year's stand-down period and returning to its standard training cycle. When *Moskva* changed her radio call sign, analysts at NSG and FOSIF

Rota grew suspicious.[48] The sweeping gaze of ocean surveillance allowed FOSIF Rota to observe Soviet Navy operational patterns and understand its command, control, and communications (C3). FOSIF's all-source and longer-term analysis provided a warning to the Sixth Fleet. Richardson and Navy Intelligence had essentially created a version of the every-analyst-is-a-warning-analyst model to prevent operational surprise.

Most Navy line officers lacked the security clearance to view SCI material. Thus discussing the details of the *Moskva*'s movement with Sixth Fleet units was difficult. Essential details of the intelligence were "laundered" to hide the source of information but allow the distribution of operationally crucial elements.[49] FOSIF Rota, with access to the NSG, sanitized some but not all compartmented material by fusing it with other collections. What intelligence FOSIF analysts could not sanitize was used to cue terrestrial-collection assets, like a maritime patrol aircraft, to gather similar information at lower classification levels.

FOSIF, in constant contact with Sixth Fleet staff on the *Little Rock* (Gaeta, Italy), made them aware that the *Moskva* might leave the Black Sea. FOSIF then tipped the surveillance networks in the eastern Mediterranean to look for the *Moskva*. Richardson demanded that his staff be responsive to warning intelligence, a lesson he'd taken away from the 1967 *Liberty* incident. One of the most proactive members of his staff was Cdr. James Aloysius "Ace" Lyons Jr., USN, the anti-submarine staff officer.[50]

Lyons received the report of *Moskva*'s movement and FOSIF's request to divert an airborne VQ-2 electronic surveillance EA-3B to the northern Aegean to look for her. The EA-3B subsequently picked up electronic emissions from the *Moskva*'s long-range air search Topsail radar.[51] FOSIF was now tracking and reporting the *Moskva*'s plodding movement toward the Dardanelles. There was no surprise when the *Moskva* made her Montreux declaration a day later. By then Lyons had a fleet photography team flying from Naples, Italy, to Athens, Greece. The photography team boarded USS *Warrington* (DD 843) and steamed to the North Aegean, meeting the *Moskva* thirty nautical miles south of the Strait of the Dardanelles.[52] "That had to tell them something," Richardson wryly surmised of Soviet reaction to *Moskva*'s intercept. "Making intelligence interactive with operations in real time" was finally closing the gap between the two, giving Navy commanders an operational advantage in the Mediterranean theater.[53]

FOSIF Rota was fully operational and commissioned in April 1970, just as the Soviet Navy's Okean 70 global naval exercise commenced.[54] "The realm of Ocean Surveillance," announced a 1970 issue of the *Intelligence Newsletter*, "has come into its own this year." Navy Intelligence had added new billets at the Navy Ocean Surveillance Information Center (NOSIC) in Suitland, Maryland, and at FOSIF Rota and Fleet Ocean Surveillance Information Center (FOSIC) Europe (London).[55] By 1972 the Naval Field Operational Intelligence Office (NFOIO) was supporting a decentralized OSIS. Every major theater of operations had an OSIS node dedicated to its fleet. Besides FOSIC London, there were facilities or centers in Kamiseya, Japan (Western Pacific Fleet), Pearl Harbor, Hawai'i (Pacific Fleet), and Norfolk, Virginia (Atlantic Fleet). NOSIC, installed in 1971, had coordination responsibilities for the centers and the facility at Rota. However, Rear Admiral Brooks later noted that "coordination" somewhat overstated NOSIC's role; it was more of a "central repository of expertise."[56] New datalinks and dedicated communication circuits kept all the OSIS nodes connected. The entire OSIS system envisioned in 1964 was finally alive and growing. However, not everyone was happy about Navy decentralization of national intelligence.[57]

Developing a penetrating understanding of the adversary is part of "long-term" analysis, customarily conducted by support agencies like the NSA or the DIA. To Washington, operational intelligence conducted in theater provided regionally focused current intelligence. Only the IC in Washington provided the heavy lifting for long-term analysis.[58] However, Sixth Fleet's Opintel team in Rota, like the NAVFORV team under Rex Rectanus in Vietnam, was unwilling to cede to Washington the role of subject-matter expertise on threats Sixth Fleet was facing. Rota blurred the traditional organizational lines of intelligence analysis to provide context, the so-what specific to its afloat units under Sixth Fleet.[59]

The breadth of current intelligence and the depth of long-term intelligence defined normal Soviet naval operations in the Mediterranean. "Normal" was buried within the patterns observed in Soviet C3 procedures over time. From its understanding of the normal, Rota created indicators that predicted Soviet operations. More importantly those indicators could identify, as early as possible, when Soviet activity was not as expected and was possibly aggressive.[60] Analysis of Soviet C3, FOSIF Rota proved, must be timely, fleet-focused, and done in-theater.

Warning intelligence, like all intelligence, is a team sport, and Rota needed help from the Navy's cryptologic community. The Navy Field Operational Intelligence Office (NFOIO), located with the NSA at Fort Meade, Maryland, and the NSG in Rota gave Navy Intelligence access to raw SIGINT. However, that access was tightly tied to strategic-level decision-making. The Vietnam War had pushed a reluctant NSA back into providing tactical-intelligence support to fielded forces. In July 1972 the long-awaited National SIGINT Operations Center (NSOC) opened, providing global SIGINT support to theater operations. The NSA, however, continued to have a "national-level monopoly on [Soviet] C3 exploitation."[61]

FOSIF Rota had a good relationship with the Naval Security Group and in 1972 moved into the NSG's building. When NSOC opened its doors FOSIF bombarded it with Mediterranean-related SIGINT requests. The NSA quickly grew annoyed. The NSG created an embedded Cryptologic Support Group (CSG) at FOSIF to sweeten the soured relationship with the NSA. The CSG provided the specific SIGINT analysis FOSIF was asking of the NSOC. It also broke down a historical divide between intelligence and cryptologic roles that impeded timely all-source fusion.[62] Rota's cryptologic security group had about twenty personnel, led by a Navy cryptology officer (1610). The CSG occupied the same spaces as FOSIF, providing direct support to them while working administratively for the NSG.[63]

The CSG personnel supported the four-section FOSIF watch and the "day shops"—or long-term-analysis work centers. A FOSIF watch team had three members: a watch officer (an intelligence officer, 163x or line subspecialist), a SIGINT analyst (an enlisted CSG cryptologic technician

[CT], usually a petty officer first or second class), and a plotter analyst (an enlisted yeoman [YN], photographic intelligenceman [PT], or intelligence specialists [IS], petty officer first or second class). Located in the center of the FOSIF spaces, the watch had access to the day shops and to the NSG's communication center (SpintCom, reporting designator USN-24) and production and reporting center. On the wall opposite the watch officer's desk was affixed a large chart of the Mediterranean theater. The plotter analyst marked all units' positions both on the wall map and on a backup copy kept at the workstation. The plot and the daily intelligence report production were done by hand, using little automation. "When I got there," Capt. Nels Litsinger, USN (Ret.), recalls of his 1977 arrival at FOSIF, "we were still manually plotting positions on an overlay of a map of the Mediterranean. I mean, the plotter analyst literally plotted things in different colors on the sheet!"[64]

The SIGINT analyst, as a CSG member, had direct access to the NSG and exploited raw communication intercepts. "We had a very, very close relationship with them [CSG]," Litsinger later recalled, noting, however, that only the CSG members had access to the signals "intercept side" of the NSG. The "crypies [cryptologists] didn't discuss it [intercepts], period. . . . If we had a question for a collector," Litsinger said of the NSG reports, the CSG member of the watch team would get the answer.[65] The NSG also gave FOSIF access to the highly classified electronic intelligence (ELINT) collection. Classic Bullseye, the NSG's twenty-one worldwide high-frequency direction finding (HFDF) stations, and the National Reconnaissance Office's space-based Poppy ELINT collection constellation helped correlate emitters with specific Soviet hulls.[66] HULTEC, or hull-to-emitter correlation, created an electronic, communications, and acoustics "fingerprint" of each Soviet unit used to track them.[67] Computer-based information management like the Naval Intelligence Processing System (NIPS) allowed analysts to lift the "fingerprints" from collected signals data.

After two years of operations FOSIF Rota had settled on several standard daily products (record messages) disseminated to the Sixth Fleet's ships, Flag Officer staff, and the intelligence community. Updated or amplified messages, called "spot reports," were released as necessary to warn of changes to Soviet unit activity. "The most important message we sent was the 0100 submarine report," Litsinger recalled. The Mediterranean Submarine Summary, referred to by Rota watch teams as the "0100," was a highly classified Soviet submarine activity summary. The 0100 had "every [classified information] compartment we had access to," Litsinger recalled. Rota's reporting was current intelligence, but its focus on understanding Soviet C3 within the theater had long-term analysis roots. The 0100, produced at night, had several versions, each with a different classification, released throughout the early morning hours. The message release times supported the various Sixth Fleet staff battle rhythms, particularly the preparation of the morning commanders' update brief.[68]

The watch officer used a Wang Laboratories word processor connected to the Digital Equipment Corporation PDP 11/45 computer to write the messages, print a hard copy, and create a punched-paper tape for message transmission. The system, Litsinger lamented, while an improvement

PHOTO 7.2
FOSIF Rota's watch floor, 1970s. Keeping a twenty-four-hour watch was critical to current and long-term analysis and providing indication and warning to the fleet. U.S. NAVY PHOTO REPRODUCED IN FORD AND ROSENBERG'S *ADMIRALS' ADVANTAGE* (2005)

over the cumbersome stand-alone HP word processor, was challenging to use.[69] "You were constantly walking over to the manual plot [at the plotter analyst's station] . . . then walking back to write your product," Litsinger recalls. You used "whatever SI [special intelligence] products that came in to . . . give you the background to do your analysis." The final product, a human-machine-readable record message called a "Rainform" format, was punched out on paper tape and given to the Naval Security Group's communication center for release.[70]

The 0100 was a huge message, around twenty-five pages, and included the analysis of any signal intercept potentially originating from a Soviet unit. The multisection message took an hour or more to transmit at seventy-five baud, one hundred words per minute. "The operators kind of trusted our analysis," Litsinger says, but not always the other intelligence officers. The shipboard Opintel teams and Sixth Fleet task force's staff needed all the data for each contact to analyze and answer their operator's questions. With the 0100 completed for the day, a sanitized general-service secret version would be prepared for transmission at 0200.[71] Removing the technical-source information and reducing the contact's location to an innocuous geographic point "in the vicinity of" the actual origin sanitized the highly classified report. A "latest and greatest" update of the 0100 summarizing any changes went out at 0500, before the 0600 Sixth Fleet staff briefing.[72]

By the time the Arab-Israeli War broke out in October 1973, FOSIF Rota was consistently producing quality Opintel and operational-warning products. They were almost too good for the NSA's liking; Rota dominated the reporting on Soviet activity in the Mediterranean theater, sparking a "cryptologic world 'turf' battle," recalled Rear Adm. Jim McFarland, USN, the first CSG officer in charge at FOSIF Rota.[73] The NSA thought Rota was intruding on NSA bureaucratic dominance and was concerned about sanitization issues. In 2016 McFarland quoted from one report written by a flustered senior civilian at the NSA:

> There is no distinction between the FOSIF and the CSG [personnel]. . . . They all share the same space! Worse yet, the CSG . . . has

access to RAW SIGINT. . . . It is reporting first on many Med-related events. . . . The CSG Officer in Charge knows the [NSA] system and is only concerned with supporting the fleet in whatever manner he can with or without a proper charter. We have created an unchecked monster in Rota.[74]

Sixth Fleet and the Navy were pleased with the Opintel support produced by FOSIF Rota, which was able to quickly respond to unfolding events in the Middle East. They "worked miracles" to supply relevant operational and warning intelligence to Sixth Fleet units "eyeball to eyeball" with the Soviet Navy as the Arab-Israeli War raged and tensions rose. Vice Adm. Daniel Murphy, USN, then Sixth Fleet commander, praised FOSIF Rota publicly, calling the Soviet C3 report—likely the 0100 message—"the most important single intelligence report he received during the war."[75]

CHAPTER 8

OSIS Revolution to Opintel Evolution

Iron sharpeneth iron; so a man sharpeneth the countenance of his friend.

—PROVERBS 27:17 (*KJV*)

FOSIF Rota's operations officer (Ops O), a lieutenant commander (163x), pulled into the parking lot at 0500. He rubbed the sleep from his eyes as he walked into the building. It was hours yet from sunrise, but it did not matter; the building had no windows to the outside anyway. He needed to read the boards before his day began at 0600. The metal trifold binders filled with administrative, intelligence assessments, and tasking record messages—the "read-boards"—were in high demand. These boards were required to be read by all personnel, and reading the boards first gave an individual a head start over their peers on any task or critical warning intelligence. Not reading the boards assured that he'd miss something essential and—to use a bullfighting analogy—he'd be "gored" in the FOSIF Rota competition arena.

The assistant officer in charge (AOIC) of FOSIF, also a lieutenant commander (163x), arrived a little later, finding the Ops O with the boards in one hand and a cup of coffee in the other. Determined to get the boards first, the AOIC arrived at 0430 the next day. When the Ops O arrived at 0500, the AOIC smiled and looked up from his reading. The two FOSIF high achievers—as high achievers do—created a competition over the read-boards. The Ops O began arriving at 0415. The AOIC at 0400 the next day. The silent battle, much to the watch teams' amusement, escalated until both men arrived at 0330 one morning. Eventually the two reached a truce. They had to; they were in a "self-goring" spiral, victims of FOSIF's "competition and rivalry."[1]

Organizations use internal competition to shape their members into the desired archetype. Writing about the American corporate environment in the 1950s, organizational analyst William Whyte noted that modern corporations emphasize work and management through competition and cooperation.[2] The intelligence officer's Cold War training and career pipeline mirrored Whyte's observations in many ways. Because Opintel had changed swiftly, Navy Intelligence used the competition to develop leaders who adapted more quickly than the environment changed.

In a 1975 issue of the *Intelligence Newsletter* Rear Adm. Bobby Ray Inman, USN, described the reinforcing mechanism of competition for the Opintel performance orientation; it was "not only promotion opportunity" that was being decided but also access to the "most demanding and rewarding assignments."[3] The competition and cooperation between Opintel leaders, analysts, and watch teams was the "steel that sharpened steel" as the Navy had never before seen. Opintel was "primus inter pares—a 'fast track' career" in which "the best officers . . . [were] normally assigned to these [OSIS] facilities."[4] Navy Intelligence leveraged the up-or-out military promotion system to develop the "combat scholars" it wanted.[5] The promotion system supported competition by favoring individuals with problem-solving skills who were intrinsically driven by high-achievement motivation (HAM) and reacted positively to criticism.

In their article "Winning Isn't Everything," social psychologists John M. Tauer and Judith M. Harackiewicz look at intrinsic motivation in a competitive context. Individuals high in achievement motivation, the HAMs, enjoy their work, especially when they perceive themselves to be winning (succeeding). Those low in achievement motivation, the LAMs, dislike being evaluated and avoided achievement situations. For HAMs, winning is a drug. Positive and negative feedback encourage them to continue competing. Thus HAMs have high intrinsic or internal motivation and seek competence value from external feedback. Positive feedback is beneficial, but Tauer and Harackiewicz find that most HAMs both enjoy the competition and work harder when given negative feedback. The competition does not end for the HAMs; in most cases, they continue to work on tasks during their free time.[6] The competition raises competence valuation for all participants, HAMs and LAMs alike. FOSIF Rota was a HAM's heaven and a LAM's hell.

Vic Socotra, the pen name of a former FOSIF Rota watch officer from the 1980s, describes FOSIF as a "bullring"—appropriate for its location in southern Spain. Seeing himself as the matador and his watch team as the cuadrilla, Socotra casts the customers and other watch officers as the bulls. He saw the twelve-hour coffee-, nicotine-, and adrenaline-fueled watch as a professional life-or-death event. On the watch floor "you could get gored professionally in all sorts of different ways for the smallest misstep." Getting past being a "novillo" and becoming a real Opintel matador meant the difference between "retiring [from the Navy] as a Captain vs. Commander," Socotra writes.[7]

Socotra's perception emphasizes a survival-of-the-fittest concept William Whyte observed during his studies. The duality Whyte noted in the internal, competitive culture of corporate America could easily be applied to the Navy. "To get ahead, of course, one must compete— but not too much, and certainly not too obviously," Whyte wrote of personal ambition. The HAMs' drive to get ahead fueled the steel-sharpening-steel aspect within the Navy's organizational culture. Blind personal ambition, however, would destroy the organizational culture. Finding the internal competition sweet spot was the task of the organization's leadership. The balance between ambition and cooperation was often itself a competition. "To get ahead, he must co-operate with the others—but co-operate better than they do," Whyte wrote. Any "eager beaver" unable to work with others was "exposed and brought to heel" by evaluation and management practices.[8]

The Navy's command structure and evaluation process effectively managed ambition and cooperation but only when leadership wielded those tools wisely. Nels Litsinger, a watch officer at FOSIF Rota from 1977 to 1979, agrees with Socotra. There was much competition and pressure on the watch officers to "write better products and make better assessments." To put Socotra's observation about FOSIF into context, Litsinger acknowledged the competition but said, "Any attempt to undermine or sabotage another watch team or watch officer would have been seen as an attempt to make the command look bad." There was enough oversight and criticism of the FOSIF products from external sources, and no one wanted internal criticism piled on top. "Dissension within [FOSIF] would be intolerable," and those offenders were quickly brought to heel.[9] Socotra's and Litsinger's observations underscore the ebb and flow of internal competition and the leader's challenge to balance ambition with cooperation.

In some cases knowledge became a weapon. The HAMs sought out the information needed for any competitive advantage. For example, working with the analysis "day shops," even if that meant staying after their watch, increased understanding of the adversary's C3, the available intelligence source material, and an understanding of the SCI communication circuits' complexities. Armed with this knowledge, a HAM had a competitive advantage. Many HAMs looked to maintain such advantages, unwilling to share knowledge with other watch officers. Some HAMs recognized the problems caused by knowledge disparity among watch personnel. "Reasonable people," Socotra wrote, "would have tried to help you [whether HAM or LAM] to ensure mission success [and] not seek any personal gain at your expense."[10] Litsinger echoes Socotra. "I did feel that a lot of common knowledge, useful terminology, and background data had not been efficiently shared." In the spirit of cooperation, Litsinger created and shared helpful information in what he called the "SWO [Senior Watch Officer] Gouge" book. The document ensured everyone had "access to a body of common knowledge."[11]

Even LAMs put in additional time to increase their knowledge; to let a knowledge gap grow would invite unwanted negative attention—an even deeper circle of hell for a LAM. William Whyte observed that in the corporate culture no one could risk assuming that everyone would survive within the promotion-of-the-fittest system. On some level everyone recognized that sliding behind the pack or standing still was as bad as an outright failure. Even if they wished to do "okay" and stay as a due course officer, LAMs needed to work extra hours like those who sought promotion.¹² This way everyone benefited from the competitive environment, especially the Navy. Anyone wishing to remain in the shrinking intelligence officer (163x) community, even if only to retire at a lower rank, had to compete or be culled.

Further competition came from the analysts in FOSIF Rota's day shops. "The product's [read-]board was the venue for peer review," Litsinger said. The "day ladies," the derisive term the watch teams used for those working day-shift hours in the analysis shops, "would just slice you apart . . . on the products," Litsinger lamented.¹³ Creating the highly classified 0100 submarine summary message was the main event, the "Corrida Goyesca de Ronda," Socotra writes.¹⁴ The 0100 was the watch officer's message, and "you were judged upon it. . . . It was a rite of passage and really made the difference between being a good FWO [FOSIC Watch Officer] and a great one."¹⁵ The day ladies were mainly men: Navy senior enlisted cryptologists, intelligence officers who had moved from the watch, and civilians from the Naval Security Group (NSG). They conducted long-term analysis during the day shift.¹⁶ Interaction with the analysis process, the constant feedback—often negative—and collaboration with subject-matter experts were new for the junior intelligence officers. It was a formative environment. Everyone—the day ladies and the command leadership of FOSIF and NSG alike—commented through the read-boards on every product that went out. "So—man—sometimes you'd come back in, and your message had red [ink] writing all over it! I mean, it was just brutal! But you got better, and you didn't make mistakes, or you had consequences," Litsinger recollected.¹⁷

It was sink or swim for FOSIF Rota personnel. Criticism was not anonymous, and "unfair criticism was subject to rebuttal and anything deemed personal or detrimental to good taste might garner a take-aside [of the offender] by the FOSIF or CSG [Cryptologic Security Group] OIC [Officer in Charge]" for counseling.¹⁸

The competition results were displayed in the officer-fitness report, the decisive document to an officer's promotion hopes. The Navy evaluation system forces reporting senior officers to rank their personnel periodically. For example, all lieutenants are evaluated simultaneously on the last day of June. The periodic fitness reports were a one-to-*n* personnel ranking—the best at the top and the worst at the bottom. Intelligence officers were ranked against others of the same grade; the performance rank generally corresponded to performance-trait scores on the fitness report. Sailors coveted receiving a mark indicating they were "one of the top few" or receiving an "early promote" recommendation, indicating they were the number-one-ranked officer in grade. A lower stratification within the cohort was a "due course" officer grouping, designating "an excellent officer of value to the service," "a fine and effective officer," and "entirely satisfactory in present grade."[19] Most officers were due course; they hoped to improve or have "one of the top few" officers transfer from the command, allowing them to move up in the ranking. Only an officer who presented grievous character flaws received the lowest "unsatisfactory" rank on a fitness report.

Some officers sank. Litsinger recalled that a few 163x and line intelligence subspecialists struggled in the FOSIF crucible. A few watch officers "used to go out and cry in the parking lot" after an especially trying watch. One naval aviator, an EA-3 sensor officer (a line subspecialist), was so fed up with the challenges of the watch that he asked for reassignment. Officers who could not cope, consistently made mistakes, or did the minimum were replaced or moved aside.[20] A watch officer showing disciplined initiative, taking calculated risks in their predictive assessments, and aggressively communicating with the afloat units could make some mistakes but recover and improve.[21] Officers who were not the fittest might survive FOSIF but do little more in the Navy Intelligence community. The steel would strike and either be honed against steel to make better intelligence officers or plunge deep into the heart, ending careers.

Aviation Community Collectivism at Rota

More intelligence officers flourished at FOSIF Rota than foundered. Litsinger noted that all the officers during his time were promoted to at least captain, one even making vice admiral.[22] Most officers sent to FOSIF in the 1970s had a common background: shipboard Opintel duty in aviation squadrons. Ready-room hijinks among Navy pilots were legion, and their loyalty to the squadron and fellow aviators was a thing of lore. Gallows humor, also a norm for Navy pilots in high-stress environments, fit nicely within FOSIF Rota's "bullring" environment.[23] Thus OSIS node organizations adopted aspects of aviation culture.

As much because reading them was required as because of the credibility they conferred to any information printed on them, the read-boards became a vehicle for intra-unit hijinks. Much read-board mischief focused upon administrative issues, ensuring the joke did not negatively impact the mission. Vic Socotra describes how it was managed:

> Us wags would find the real stupid shit upper-level policy-related messages and post them along with a blank sheet for "comments"—something I learned early on when I was back in the [aviation] squadron. I carried on that tradition there [FOSIF] since you could do it anonymously. Anyone could slip something onto the [admin] read-board without anyone knowing who did it.... Anything on the read-board then was taken as gospel. Caveat emptor.[24]

Fake messages preyed on the "gullibility of read-board junkies." An excellent fake message "looked and smelled real" and played on the often-absurd Navy bureaucracy. Socotra and the less gullible would see "how deep we could sink the rusty fishhook into the mouths of the unprepossessing" and let the joke play out for days before revealing the farce. As Socotra wrote regarding the hijinks, "[an old] Naval Aviation adage says, 'If you're not having fun, then you aren't doing it right.'"[25]

Aviation culture sometimes takes "fun" to new levels. The motto *Work hard, play hard* is breathlessly chanted. There is no off switch for competition, even during playtime. For example, zapping—or placing an adhesive sticker of the squadron's crest, a zap, in unique places—rose to an art form that took the competition in new directions.[26] Specific mottos or humorous sayings, usually from a typical Navy bureaucratic farce that had played out, were translated into cartoon characters for a patch a Sailor could wear on a flight jacket or a zap. Most patches were offensive and irreverent, sometimes even lewd.

The FOSIF patch was rimmed in bright red, featuring the head of an unattractive, bright green frog with the words "FOSIF ROTA" in red letters on its chest. A bright red banner around the frog contained the black-typed motto, *Today the Pond, Tomorrow the World*, reinforcing the Opintel team's identity of exceptionalism as they toiled in the Mediterranean "pond," achieving an omnipotence that would eventually leak out into the rest of the world's oceans.[27]

The unattractive frog was a callback to an actual ceramic frog that had been placed in the building, Litsinger recalls. The frog became a sort of "capture the flag" totem, periodically disappearing, stolen by another organization and ransomed. Like in the squadrons, zapping played a role at FOSIF and the ship's CVIC. The more "obnoxious the placement," the better the zap. The best zaps were "all over officer's clubs, women's restrooms, and under/inside the desks of admirals," Litsinger recalls. The zaps eventually made their way into most command centers and watch floors in Europe, Washington, D.C., and Norfolk, Virginia. "Every bar in the gut of Naples, Rota, and pubs in London had at least one," he said. And for good measure those zaps "were not all that easy to remove."[28]

Those at FOSIF Rota worked hard and played hard in true aviation fashion. They wanted everyone to know who FOSIF was and that they were great at what they did. The bullring competition and sink-or-swim pressure were grueling; those who excelled "fast-tracked" their careers. All that left Rota carried a new performance orientation and organizational culture shaped by technical and all-source warning intelligence tradecraft. When those FOSIF/FOSIC graduates returned to the fleet, they exposed the tradecraft to the afloat Opintel organization. Vic Socotra wrote that while in USS *Midway* and then in *Independence* he applied the analytical ideas he learned at FOSIF Rota, instilling the analytical tradecraft and ideas into those junior intelligence officers he led. "I instructed our Strike Cell [targeting cell within CVIC] to create a cliché a day," Socotra wrote; the effort made the intelligence officers genuine Opintel analysts who wrote using "critical analysis" just like those at the OSIS nodes. The products conveyed to the consumers the so-what ensuring they would be informed and "even be entertained." These were not the typical "cut-and-paste rip-offs ... spewing rambling diatribes with no contextual value" often seen by less-informed aircraft carrier intelligence centers (CVIC) Opintel teams.[29]

The FOSIFs and FOSICs were an Opintel melting pot and an intelligence officer crucible, impacting not only Navy Intelligence but the fleet as a whole. Improved intelligence operations increased battlespace awareness and offered more timely warnings. The fleet would leverage these improvements to evolve as well. OSIS became an immensely influential reciprocating influence on afloat Opintel, a continual driving force in its evolution.

Resulting Shipboard Command and Control Changes

The OSIS nodes decentralized national intelligence ashore to better support the fleet at sea. At the same time, significant organizational changes occurred to the fleet. CNO Zumwalt shifted the attack aircraft carriers from power projection into a multimission role. He mixed strike and anti-submarine warfare (ASW) aircraft within the same air wing. The "mixed wing" plan ran the risk of preventing the aircraft carriers from performing either mission well; it was a risk Zumwalt needed to take. Decommissioning the antiquated ASW carriers freed the budget to modernize the fleet. Covering the vital sea-lanes would be difficult with only the twelve aircraft carriers left after the decommissioning. The S-3 Viking anti-submarine aircraft and the Light Airborne Multi-purpose System (LAMPS) equipped SH-3 Sea King helicopter were exceptional new scouting and sea-control assets that mitigated some risks.[30] The developing F-14 Tomcat interceptor was expensive but necessary to handling Soviet long-range aviation threats. Getting new platforms and systems out to the fleet took time; integrating them and creating new warfighting doctrine was challenging.

Back in 1959 William Cracknell had predicted that "ASW was where the Navy was going." By 1975 the trajectory was undeniable. Yet many senior officers on the aircraft carrier still focused on land-attack competencies.[31] Even with installation of the new ASW equipment and the "mixed wing," aircraft carrier officers were slow to accept the ASW and sea-control roles. Their reluctance was likely due to a lack of knowledge about conducting those missions.

The Anti-submarine Classification and Analysis Center (ASCAC), a formal systems package, was installed in *Saratoga* in 1971.[32] The Navy also installed electronic warfare (EW) systems to manipulate electromagnetic signals within the electromagnetic spectrum, complicating Soviet attempts to track and target the aircraft carriers.[33] A new anti-submarine warfare division, OX, was added to the Operations Department of *Saratoga* to run the ASCAC. The OX division was staffed by four Navy aviation officers and a mix of ten enlisted aviation warfare systems operators or aviation anti-submarine warfare technicians.[34] The ASCAC focused on understanding the undersea warfare environment and directing the escorting ships to protect the aircraft carrier from enemy submarine attacks. Near-real-time analysis of acoustic signals from sonobuoys deployed by the S-2 Tracker (and later the S-3 Viking) occurred within the ASCAC. The acoustic information helped detect and classify the submarine type and coordinate an attack against the submarine.[35]

The disparity between the envisaged and the actual ASCAC and EW systems work situations forced each aircraft carrier to adapt their organization differently.[36] In 1973 *Kitty Hawk* became the first West Coast aircraft carrier to receive the ASCAC. Unlike *Saratoga*, she used OW as the ASCAC division designator, while OX was designated the Electronic Warfare Division. Other aircraft carriers—USS *Constellation*, *America*, and *Ranger*—used OX to designate the Operations Department Administration section, not the Electronic Warfare Division or ASCAC division. *Kitty Hawk*'s and *Independence*'s uses of OW for their electronic warfare division was further confusing.[37] The shipboard organizational variation associated with unique differences in the Atlantic and Pacific fleets was amplified by a lack of clear Navy doctrine and operating procedures.

The new ASW and EW warfare missions required different types of information and intelligence, particularly regarding the locations and activities of Soviet naval units. However, physics limited the shipboard radars' detection ranges, and many of the Soviet threats had weapons that launched well outside the Navy's shipboard-sensor horizons. Spreading picket ships away from the aircraft carrier increased detection ranges but lost the defensive benefits of massing the ships for anti-air warfare.[38] The scouting and protection tactics used in the aircraft carrier battlegroup of the early 1970s were essentially the same as those that had been used during World War II. The approach was to circle the wagons around the carrier, so to speak. The escorting ships were placed around the aircraft carrier at different ranges, providing a layered detection and defense structure. The Intel Center—now renamed the Aircraft Carrier (CV) Intelligence Center (CVIC)—would supply a threat presentation to the aircraft carrier's operations officer, who then worked with the air wing and flag staff to design the best surface- and aircraft-scouting and protection plan in defense of the carrier.[39] This World War II–style scouting approach required many aircraft to cover a vast surveillance area. The mixed-wing concept limited aircraft and made relying solely on airborne surveillance a losing proposition.

A new approach, surface-subsurface surveillance coordination (SSSC), was developed as a sustainable integrated scouting and counterforce plan that took advantage of new technology. SSSC integrated and leveraged land-based maritime-patrol aircraft sweeping the choke points and known enemy-operating areas with the aircraft carrier battle group's organic defenses. The E-2 Hawkeye was an essential "quarterback'" directing airborne SSSC platforms.

In 1965 the Airborne Tactical Data System (ATDS) was installed in the Hawkeye and deployed to the Vietnam War. The Hawkeye's twenty-four-foot saucer-shaped radome housed a long-range surface- and air-search radar. The Link 11 tactical datalink enabled the ATDS to transmit its radar picture via encrypted pro forma messages to the shipboard NTDS, extending the battle group's surveillance ranges by several hundred miles.[40] The Hawkeye executed command-and-control functions for airborne SSSC and anti-air warfare using an aircraft-to-aircraft datalink (Link 4). "When ATDS worked, it worked well and was highly appreciated," David Boslaugh wrote.[41] During operations in the Gulf of Tonkin it became standard operating procedure to always have at least one Hawkeye airborne. Unfortunately there were never enough Hawkeyes to keep one constantly airborne.

Even when Hawkeyes *were* available to provide constant surveillance, the additional radar inputs provided taxed NTDS's decade-old design. The system often bogged down, the screens flickering or freezing as the computer processor data locked. Not all contacts detected by the radar became tracks within NTDS when overloaded. A complete replacement of NTDS was required, but the cost was prohibitive. Instead "NTDS was developed to death," squeezing every bit of capability out of the antiquated hardware and software.[42]

For the aircraft carrier battlegroup, NTDS's limited battlespace field of regard, 512 nautical miles by 512 nautical miles, seemed inadequate for the high-speed and long-range threats of the modern jet age.[43] Another problem was correlating all the tracks surveillance generated. In such a vast space it was impossible to achieve 100 percent correlation of radar contacts to an actual platform (that is, determining whether the signal had originated from a merchant, combatant, friend, or foe). With little chance for a new NTDS, the aircraft carriers looked inward for solutions.

At its core the problem was a time-space-force one. The ship looked for ship and shore Opintel to help purchase time to balance the space-force equation; the increase in time improved the survivability of the aircraft carrier.[44] The Combat Information Center (CIC) needed time to deal with an overloaded system, the air wing needed more aircraft maintenance and pilot rest time, and the flight deck needed time for aircraft launch and recovery. Eking out those extra precious hours and minutes required better information, intelligence, and warning, allowing commanders to anticipate future operational needs. Intelligence had to provide better situational awareness of operating conditions beyond the radar horizon, allowing faster decision-making.

Long-Range Aviation Problem

Dealing with the long-range Soviet aviation (LRA) problem became an enabling constraint driving organizational evolution. The air wing's battle against LRA bombers flying simulated strike missions on the aircraft carrier was called the "outer air battle" because it was meant to be fought well beyond the horizon, 150 to 250 nautical miles from the aircraft carrier.[45] On Sunday, November 22, 1971, a *New York Times* headline said that the Navy and Soviet LRA were playing "chicken of the sea" with these close-quarter aircraft interactions in the Mediterranean Sea. Growing concern over Soviet LRA anti-aircraft carrier tactics swept through the Navy. Sixth Fleet, for example, had the shortest tactical warning time of a possible airborne attack against an aircraft carrier, measured in minutes, not hours.[46] Guidance from CNO Admiral Moorer to all aircraft carriers and battlegroup commanders in 1969 was simple: *Do not be overflown by an unescorted Soviet aircraft!* The directive would remain in place for the rest of the Cold War.

A cartoon in *Ranger*'s 1976 western Pacific deployment cruise book depicts the Soviet bomber–overflight problem. The cartoon shows the ship's commanding and flag officers calling the operation's divisions, asking, "Will a Bear [TU-95 bomber] overflight occur?" "No," all the divisions respond. In the next panel a Bear bomber overflies the *Ranger*.[47] The cartoon takes up an entire page of the cruise book; too much space is dedicated for the joke to not be rooted in an uncomfortable truth: a Bear overflight might cost an aircraft carrier commanding officer's job and career. The Soviet LRA overflight problem was about tactics and time; there is no sea control without air control in the modern age. The overflights were also about the changing peacetime Navy. Anti-submarine warfare (ASW) was as big and probably more complex than the LRA problem. However, only aviators commanded aircraft carriers, and successfully commanding one was the only way to be promoted to admiral rank. Not every officer could reach the top in the up-or-out career model. A 20 percent reduction in the officer corps came from the decrease in the number of aircraft carriers.[48] Promotions were now riding not on a battle lost but a chance overflight by a Soviet aircraft.[49] Therefore the LRA problem was interesting to the airpower–airpower-centric Navy. An old adage guided shipboard Opintel's priorities: *What my boss finds interesting I find fascinating!*

Initially the shipboard Opintel team had little to offer in tactical-warning support. The demands on Opintel were for timelier, more-tactical intelligence that could create a comparative advantage in war at sea, a type of combat not seen since the ending of World War II. The CNO's directives were all well and good in theory, but executing them with the resources on hand was another story. Bruce Powers, an analyst assigned to Sixth Fleet from 1968 to 1970, later reflected on the implausibility of a particular 1969 instruction concerning TU-16 bombers. "The Moorer stricture that Badgers [TU-16 bombers] should be escorted within 100 [nautical miles] of a carrier was met only to the degree that the average intercept distance was 50 [nautical miles]," he recalled. In the Mediterranean an early warning was critical to interception success, yet warning was either nonexistent or limited to announcing the takeoff of the Badgers, which was too late to make a difference. "The incidents [of warning] were highly variable," wrote Powers, who worked for the Center for Naval Analyses. "More often than not, interceptors were launched later than they should be."[50]

The Navy Intelligence's OSIS nodes successfully used all-source fusion to track Soviet warships and submarines. FOSIF Rota's Soviet

PHOTO 8.1
A Soviet Tupolev TU-95 "Bear" Reconnaissance Plane is escorted by a VF-74 F-4J "Phantom" fighter as it flies past USS *Nimitz* (CVN 68), July 15, 1976. NAVAL HISTORY AND HERITAGE COMMAND

submarine and surface-intelligence summaries provided increased battlespace awareness.[51] Lessons from World War II pointed to a solution to the LRA warning problem: access to national SIGINT. Few on the aircraft carrier understood the highly classified signals intelligence. In some cases SCI materials were familiar to Opintel practitioners only as rumors. Necessity drew all-source-seeking Opintel practitioners toward a closer relationship with the OS Division, where the special-intelligence material was received.

Most of the SCI messages came from the intelligence community or OSIS node products. Opintel practitioners, seeking access to the analysts producing the reports, embarked on a crash course in OSIS. Comprehending the detailed analysis found in the OSIS products took a lot of work for most shipboard Opintel practitioners. Nels Litsinger found that a lack of a deep understanding of the subject, the Soviet Navy, or the technical collection used were the main barriers, yet many intelligence officers needed to understand the classified OSIS node products. "I read the words," Litsinger said, "but [had] absolutely no idea what they meant. . . . We never saw that stuff [SCI reports on the Soviets] before."[52]

Shipboard Opintel strengthened its relationship with OSIS through the OSIS nodes. They used back-channel message traffic over dedicated communication circuits (OpsComm) to engage in a question-and-answer learning method. The OpsComm circuit was simplex, meaning the ships could not send and receive simultaneously. Back-channel message exchanges were slow, and so was the learning. The relationship between the OSIS nodes and the shipboard Opintel team was leveraged to try and "make the outer air battle as 'outer' as we could," said Vice Adm. Lowell Jacoby, USN, of the Opintel teams' attempts to find, fix, track, and warn of Soviet activity as far away from the carrier as possible.[53] The extreme ranges added a "complexity and time-sensitive nature" to tactical decision-making.[54] Providing warning intelligence regarding the Soviet LRA threat to the aircraft carriers became part of a beyond-the-horizon fight the Navy was wrestling with. The entire effort was a formative experience, shaping shipboard Opintel's performance orientation and organization.

CHAPTER 9
OSIS and Ship Opintel Evolve

The organizational change that made fighting a beyond-the-horizon battle at sea possible began in 1969. "The Commanding Officer who tries to run a 'one man' show will lose his ship," one Navy report advised.[1] This piece of wisdom was never more applicable than during the tactical complexity of the battle for the first salvo, of which the LRA problem was a quintessential example. The multithreat tactical battle demanded distributed command and control (C2). The commanding officer needed someone specially trained to merge digital systems with tactical naval warfare: a tactical action officer (TAO). The TAO exploited the battlespace-awareness information pouring into the Combat Information Center (CIC) to "fight the ship."[2] The idea of the TAO was helpful, especially on board the destroyers. Unfortunately the size of and increased complexity of the aircraft carriers slowed adoption of the concept almost to a halt.

The Opintel team was feeling its way inside the new information demands. The CVIC, assisted by the shore-based FOSIF/C, determined through long-term analysis the likely types of Soviet bombers and their ingress routes to the aircraft carrier. It allowed the commander to preposition ships, spot alert aircraft, decide what weapons to use, and coordinate air-to-air refueling assets.[3] Understanding Navy capabilities, naval tactics, and the commander's decision cycle was challenging but critical to Opintel's success. An issue of the 1974 *Intelligence Newsletter* wrote, "An Intelligence Officer should feel as much at home in the CIC as he does in the IC [Intelligence Center] or his own squadron's ready room."[4] Indeed, it was a poignant comment, but feeling at home in the surface-warfare environment of the CIC was awkward for an aviation culture–indoctrinated intelligence officer.

The information flow from the Intel Center had other hindrances more significant than CIC shyness. Even with distributed C2 and the interactive information and decision exchange of NTDS, the individual warfare modules found themselves in an information stovepipe. Their systems were delivering so much tactical data that they could not accept information from CVIC. The situation was described in a 2020 interview by Commander Donald Durr, USN, intelligence officer on *Kitty Hawk* from 1974–1976. "There was no formal process for the Intel Center [CVIC], ASCAC, EW folks, CIC to work together," he said. "It's terrible to say . . . we worked together when we could, but it just didn't [always] seem necessary or helpful."[5]

Another challenge was fielding intelligence officers (1630) with experience supporting the new S-3 aircraft and the ASW mission. Gaining experience meant intelligence officers required more time at sea. A 1974 issue of the *Intelligence Newsletter* advised that Navy Intelligence would fill specific shipboard billets with more senior intelligence officers, creating second and third ship tour officers.[6]

The presentation of the air threat was familiar to CVIC. However, less of its effort focused on the threats to aircraft en route to land targets and more on those threats to the aircraft carrier itself. The ship's Operations Department suborganizations were changing, shifting their performance orientation to meet the war-at-sea threats. The CVIC had changed little from the Integrated Operational Intelligence Center (IOIC) layout of the early 1960s. Nor had the OZ Division, staffing CVIC, and the OP Division, providing photographic support, changed since the mid-1960s. The battle-tested methods of cyclic air-wing operations still controlled the battle rhythm, but the mission had changed from strikes to SSSC. The location and activity of Soviet subsurface, surface, and long-range aviation comprised a primary portion of the premission event brief.

In the mid-1970s, when aircraft carrier battlegroups conducted local operations in the western Pacific, the air wing focused on air-to-air combat and some ASW training. A few RA-5C Vigilantes conducted overwater collection missions, though the aircraft was leaving service.[7] Aircrew debriefs now focused on Maritime Force Reports (MAREPS), often called "locators," reporting vital subsurface, surface, and surveillance coordination (SSSC) information. Locators were passed to the CIC and sent off the ship to the shore operation and intelligence centers. Along with the E-2 Hawkeye's inflight radar reporting, locators helped validate tracks held in NTDS, essential for sea-control operations and possible war-at-sea scenarios.[8]

The Atlantic and Mediterranean theaters were more active than the Pacific in the mid-1970s. First, the Mediterranean theater was congested on the sea and in the air. The Soviets used a variable-presence model to manage crises in the Mediterranean while reducing maintenance issues. They increased their average number of ships and maintained air assets throughout the decade.[9] Second, the Atlantic contained two critical northern maritime choke points: the GIUK gap (the Soviet's entrance into the Atlantic basin from the Norwegian Sea), and the Strait of Gibraltar (the entrance to the Mediterranean Sea).

The CVIC Mission Planning and Brief and Debrief work centers in aircraft carriers operating for Sixth Fleet in the Mediterranean had their hands full. The Mediterranean contained Soviet and Arab units as well as NATO forces. Keeping pilots abreast of political sensitivities and safety-of-flight issues, like no-fly areas, was consuming. "The idea of creating and maintaining a real-time [intelligence] plot [in CVIC] was just beginning to take hold," Litsinger wrote of his time in *Saratoga* the late '70s.[10] Maintaining and briefing an extended surface plot for SSSC awareness required an all-source fusion approach using OSIS node and "locator" reporting. Updates to the intelligence plot were often briefed hourly over the "9-TV" closed-circuit television systems (CCTV), adding complexity to CVIC's operational tempo.[11]

The shipboard SupRad/SpintCom, now called the Ship's Signals Exploitation Space (SSES), grew as the special-intelligence reporting increased. In 1970 the NSG detachments became a permanent part of the ship's OS Division on the aircraft carrier. By 1973 every aircraft carrier had an OS Division operated by a cryptologic officer (161x) and six enlisted cryptologic technicians (CT). OS Division's original purpose was to provide "round-the-clock special communications support and timely tactical information to the embarked commander."¹² The OSIS node all-source analysis and the CSG relationship were so successful ashore that a similarly close relationship resulted on the ship. The importance of shipboard tactical signals-intelligence collection grew. So important was the OS Division to all-source Opintel that the OS Division officer worked directly for the ship's intelligence officer (163x), who drafted the OS Division officer's fitness report.¹³

Meanwhile the PH3 in the CVIC darkroom had less Vigilante strip film to develop. The late-1970s fielding of the Tactical Air Reconnaissance Pod System (TARPS) would return the CVIC darkroom to a high level of strip-film processing. But in the meantime the demand to develop 35-mm handheld camera film was the priority. Handheld photography of the Soviet combatants and intelligence collection (AGI) vessels and high-interest merchants were obligatory. The aircraft carrier's surveillance team, the SNOOPIE team (Ship's Nautical Or Otherwise Photographic Intelligence Exploitation), took handheld photographs of the ever-present Soviet "tattletales" from the ship's observation decks.¹⁴ The CVIC darkroom processed SNOOPIE team photographs from all battlegroup ships. SSSC aircraft flew with handheld cameras and took many pictures. Of course any intercept of Soviet long-range aviation (LRA) required handheld imagery of the intercepted aircraft. Thus the darkroom in CVIC was awash with 35-mm film to process and print.¹⁵

Handheld photography of Soviet ships was valuable, providing imagery for analyzing new Soviet electronic-warfare capabilities and weapon systems. The intelligence specialists (IS) analyzed the 35-mm photographs in the Multi-sensor Imagery work center, identifying and assessing any changes. The analysis and the images were assembled in an initial information report (IIR). The report was sent as a Rainform message. Prints of the photographs were flown off the aircraft carrier to the in-theater Fleet Intelligence Center and then on to the Office of Naval Intelligence for further analysis. Identification keys from handheld photographs, for example, helped operators, SNOOPIE teams, and imagery analysts identify Soviet units.¹⁶

Interactions with Soviet LRA were increasing. The reps and sets of Vietnam power-projection missions had hammered out the IOIC's identity. Now the CVIC of the 1970s was repping and setting its way through the outer air battle toward a tactical decision-making support identity. The Soviet TU-95 Bear bomber and its maritime patrol variant, the TU-142 Bear-F, was a paw that continually reached out from the Soviet shore to the Navy's aircraft carriers.

New Reps and Sets of Evolution

Saratoga swung gently, placing the aircraft carrier's bow into the wind. The starboard Catapult One thumped. Seconds later Cat Two on the port side did the same. The two Alert Five F-4 Phantoms were off the deck screaming upward in afterburner. The E-2 Hawkeye, waiting behind Cat Two, moved up, hooked up, and was launched to follow the Phantoms. The E-2's long-range radar guided the Phantoms hurtling toward an inbound Soviet TU-95 Bear bomber. As the Navy F-4 Phantom closed on the Soviet Bear, the pilot keyed the mic and radioed the side number of the Bear aircraft and its course, speed, and altitude. Intercepting Soviet aircraft was almost a daily occurrence for Navy aircraft carriers operating in the Mediterranean Sea in the 1970s. One of the Bear's leather-helmeted aircrew waved at the Phantom as the large bomber descended. The Phantom matched the maneuver. At three hundred feet above the water the Bear and Phantom made a close pass of *Saratoga*.[17] The Phantom pilot ensured his aircraft was between the Bear and *Saratoga*. The Navy required the second Phantom to photograph the Bear, Phantom, and *Saratoga* alignment to reduce the Soviet propaganda value of the flyby.[18]

The ship's operations officer (Ops O) swung by CVIC to see the ship's intelligence officer (SIO). The Ops O said the Bear intercept had occurred at one hundred nautical miles; the skipper was pleased with the Opintel team's early warning. A chain of indications and tactical warning from FOSIF Rota fused with other reporting by the CVIC Opintel team had been critical to the intercept. The day before the intercept the Opintel team had briefed of indications that a Soviet

LRA flight might occur the next day; the Ops O and air-wing commander had heeded the warning. Understanding the operating pattern of Soviet LRA provided by CVIC had ensured that two fighters and an E-2 were on alert for an early-morning launch. An indication that a Bear likely launched from its base earlier than previously assessed came via a special-intelligence message early the following day. The air operations officer increased the alert posture of the two F-4 Phantoms, launching them early. The chain of events was an example of intelligence and operator integration.

The LRA and outer air-battle problems illustrate the reciprocal influence between OSIS nodes and shipboard Opintel teams. The teams were now part of the tactical sea-control decision-making process, not just overland strike-mission support. Tactical-warning intelligence was a growing performance orientation, and a supporting relationship between OSIS nodes ashore and shipboard Opintel developed. Thus the OSIS node–to–shipboard Opintel relationship changed most of Navy Intelligence's performance and learning orientation.

Shipboard and FOSIF Rota experiences provide examples of competition reinforcing and embedding the new all-source, fusion-driven warning-intelligence culture. From shipboard Opintel teams to OSIS nodes and back, officer and enlisted rotation cycles further reinforced the performance orientation through reciprocation. The close relationship between the FOSIF/C and their Navy Cryptologic Support Group (CSG) resulted in a similarly close relationship between CVIC and the aircraft carrier's Ships Signals Exploitation Space (SSES) staffed by Naval Security Group (NSG) personnel.

As the ship's intelligence officer (SIO) walked forward on the 03 level, the ship's pitching became more pronounced. He steeled himself to enter *Kitty Hawk*'s SSES. Its location, twenty feet from the bow and directly under the trough holding Cat One's steam-driven running gear, made it the "worst space" on the ship for any work center. "Every launch you had the aircraft right over your head in afterburner," recalled Cdr. Don Durr, USN (Ret.). The noise was tremendous and punctuated by the shuttle slamming into a "water break" at the end of its run. The noise and vibration just added to the unpleasantness of working in a compartment that moved twenty to thirty feet vertically up and down as the ship's bow plowed through the high seas. Despite an inhospitable SSES, the cryptologists "were a tremendous asset," Durr said firmly.[19]

During World War II and in Korea the NSG had performed exceptionally well, providing communications intelligence directly to the fleet.[20] A review of *Forrestal-*, *Kitty Hawk-*, and *Enterprise-*class cruise books for 1972 and 1973 shows that all had a dedicated cryptology section, OS Division. The division had one cryptology officer (161x designator), one cryptologic technician (CT) chief petty officer, and around four enlisted CTs. Theater fleet NSG elements augmented OS Division. The augmentees were language interpreters, collectors, and equipment technicians with subject-matter expertise both on the targets and the collection equipment; they were brought aboard for deployment periods. Together the OS Division and augmentees made a powerful SIGINT team.[21]

Kitty Hawk's SSES quickly found ways to provide signals intelligence against the Soviet LRA overflight warning problem. Some message traffic "tippers" or warnings of LRA activity came into SSES from national sources. The tippers, however, were not timely enough for immediate warning but did provide indications of future activity. The U.S. SIGINT enterprise became expert at collecting low-level communications (COMINT) and conducting traffic analysis on the external parts of the intercepts. Layered with electronic intelligence (ELINT) collection on Soviet radars, the low-level COMINT indicated individual Soviet unit activity.[22] Durr recalls that the OS Division officer's initiative on *Kitty Hawk* teased out relevant SIGINT details that made tactical warning of inbound LRA successful.[23]

Having a deep understanding of Soviet airfield operations, for instance, provided valuable indicators. Routine aircraft-maintenance messages were often not encrypted but yielded useful information. For example, intercepting an unencrypted radio-call request for fuel could indicate an LRA flight for the next day. Before takeoff LRA aircraft checked their radar and communication systems, providing collectible

ELINT indicating imminent flight operations. Once in the air, GCI provided navigation to the bomber, and HF signals were quickly collected, indicating the bomber's flight path.[24]

The ability to collect and receive SIGINT reporting through the SSES did not always equate to a deeper understanding of the operating environment. The shipboard Opintel teams needed more education and training to support the new tactical-decision-support-type of Opintel. A 1973 conference on intelligence officers (163x) and enlisted Opintel rates (YN and PT) identified the lack of understanding of OSIS across the Navy as an issue.[25] New Navy intelligence officers attended a twenty-week accession-intelligence training course at the Air Force's Technical Training Center (AFAITC). The course, the conference report noted, was inadequate because it was Air Force–centric and had "minimal commonality" with naval warfare.[26]

The Navy's new intelligence officers entered an environment wherein vast quantities of technical signals, imagery, and acoustic "INTs" from various highly classified space- and terrestrial-based collection systems were available.[27] Understanding the technical details of the collection was one aspect; managing the information collected was another. Intelligence officers and enlisted personnel required training in information-management systems like the Naval Intelligence Processing System (NIPS). Most important the intelligence officers were required to comprehend the new naval-warfare concepts. Operators, on the other hand, needed to learn about new intelligence capabilities.[28]

Exposing Navy Opintel practitioners to "INTs" required access to SCI material, something AFAITC lacked until 1973.[29] By 1975 most personnel working in CVIC required a top-secret clearance with eligibility to access SCI.[30] Even having access to some SCI could not prepare officers and enlisted Opintel personnel for a close relationship with cryptologists, access to raw SIGINT, and interactions with senior analysts.

Enlisted Opintel professionals had the same SCI limitations as the intelligence officers. A 1973 professional workshop, separate from the training conference, identified the need for a specific enlisted intelligence rate.[31] In 1975 the photographic intelligenceman (PT) and yeoman

(YN-2505) combined into a new intelligence specialist (IS) rate.[32] Mario Tonkli, serving in *Saratoga* at this time, saw his rate change from PT3 to IS3, but nothing about his job responsibilities altered.[33] It took time to create new schools, like a specific intelligence specialist (IS) A-school, and improve the Naval Intelligence Processing System (NIPS) schools. Later, enlisted NSG cryptologic technicians (CT) were added as instructors to incorporate SIGINT collection and reporting methods early in the IS rate training.

By 1977 AFAITC's training had improved, but the 1973 assessment of its inadequacy for the Navy still rang true. "The geo-location on an Air Force base [in Colorado] made no naval sense," said Capt. Richard Noble, USN (Ret.), former Navy AFAITC commanding officer. "The Air Force had no interest in submarine warfare or the surface navy. They evinced no interest in naval air."[34] AFAITC was unsuitable and had never really been for the new character of shipboard Opintel. The shipboard junior officers and enlisted personnel of the mid-1970s evolved Opintel the old-fashioned Navy way through discovery learning, collaboration across the waterfront, and on-the-job training provided by the few OSIS node graduates who had returned to the fleet. It would not be until the 1980s that Navy Intelligence would create an appropriate accession-level intelligence-training facility, at Dam Neck, Virginia.

Competition, Friendly Rivalries

The desire was always to have ocean-surveillance information processed aboard the aircraft carriers and command ships. Communications technology was the limiting factor. In a 2019 interview Vice Adm. Jake Jacoby, USN (Ret.), described the 1970s OSIS situation as driven by communications- and information-management technology limitations. Therefore many intelligence officers assert that "real" Opintel was only conducted at the all-source accessible shore-based OSIS nodes, not in the CVICs at sea. "The concept [of Opintel] really was that particularly [to] the FOS-IFs," Jacoby said. "Reading, plotting, digesting" reports from the FOSIF allowed shipboard intelligence to conduct "threat presentation and targeting" for the commander but not much else.[35] The relationship between

OSIS nodes and shipboard Opintel teams was increasingly divided by their perspectives on the character of Opintel. Thus a big brother/little brother division emerged.

In any family the little brother inevitably feels he must prove to his big brother that he is an equal family member.[36] The competitive Little Brother Syndrome began to emerge slowly within the Navy Intelligence's Opintel family. In the early 1970s shipboard Opintel teams lacking unfettered access to compartmented SIGINT material took an OSIS node's assessments at face value. They had to; there was nothing else. As long as the OSIS nodes operated as designed, with the afloat commander as their primary customer, the afloat Opintel teams were fully supported and content. However, OSIS node support was so valuable that many fleet commanders used it as their direct intelligence support. The "FOSIC in Pearl," recalled Commander Durr, gave "a tremendous amount of support to the CINCPAC fleet commander and his staff. They were almost his N2."[37] Thus a combination of professional curiosity and variable support from overtaxed OSIS nodes drove shipboard Opintel teams to learn OSIS. As the afloat Opintel teams gained more access to SCI material, they started, as HAMs do, to question OSIS node assessments. The afloat little brother HAMs were competing with the OSIS big brother HAMs.

The 1977 Soviet TU-95 Bear overflight of *Saratoga* off South Carolina exemplifies the family competition. Nels Litsinger recalled that Bears were flying out of a base in Cuba. "Myself and the ship's intelligence officer went down to SSES," Litsinger recounted. "We had an inkling that perhaps they [Bears] were doing something unusual." The FOSIC in Norfolk, Virginia, disagreed; they assessed that the Bears currently airborne over the Atlantic were returning to Cuba and would not overfly *Saratoga* on the return. Litsinger insisted that the indicators pointed otherwise. The FOSIC watch officer insisted the Bears were "no problem—they're going back to Cuba!" Litsinger and SIO told everyone who would listen that the Bears *would* fly on *Saratoga*. The embarked flag officer, a rear admiral, unwilling to change the ASW exercise schedule over an ambiguous warning that went against the theater FOSIC's assessment, disregarded the recommendations that he put two fighters on Alert-5 for an intercept of the Bears. A short time later, as the first orange light of dawn broke over the Charleston Operations Area, a single Bear overflew *Saratoga*.[38]

Once it was reported, *Saratoga*'s commanding officer was "called to Norfolk immediately." The commander in chief Atlantic "was absolutely torqued" about an unescorted Bear overflight. Litsinger and the ship's assistant intelligence officer questioned the OSIS node in Norfolk over their Bear assessment using the teletype OpsComm circuit. The FOSIC watch did not respond. The problem with many of the OSIS nodes Litsinger offered was a lessening amount of close coordination between them and the afloat customer. When there was communication, the OSIS nodes framed it as "We know the problem; you guys afloat don't." There was little exchange of views and discussion about the assessment; big brother gave it, and little brother had to accept it. "It was kind of a mess," Litsinger said.[39]

At the time a question arose: *Is the OSIS node an extension of shipboard Opintel, or is shipboard Opintel an extension of the OSIS node?* Where you sit is where you stand on the question. Most ships' commanding officers and battlegroup admirals cared little either way: They neither understood Opintel's organization nor cared to; they just wanted a timely warning.

Afloat commanders prefer "choke-con," or the ability to figuratively "choke" a subordinate to get what they wanted from them, Opintel included.[40] "If they [commanders] were dissatisfied [in their Opintel support], it was usually with the part [of the Opintel team] not on the ship," Jacoby observed. "Commanders wanted the shore to be supportive . . . [and] would get their intel guys to get on the teletype [OpsCom] and ask more questions."[41] The shipboard leaders could not "choke" the shore intelligence command, but they could pressure their Opintel team to squeeze FOSIF for everything available. The fact that shipboard leaders (that is, CO, squadron CO, and flag officers) wrote the intelligence officers' fitness reports reinforced the performance orientation. If an intelligence officer did well, meaning there were no surprises for the boss, the reward was a positive fitness report and a better chance for promotion. If the little brother shipboard Opintel team could "scoop" big brother OSIS node on a warning call along the way, all the better.

Conclusion

Richardson was relieved by Vice Adm. Isaac C. "Ike" Kidd Jr., USN, as the Sixth Fleet commander in August 1970. Kidd and Richardson were like-minded on intelligence and operations integration, and FOSIF Rota flourished. With his large family in tow, Richardson flew directly to Hawai'i, taking over the role of deputy commander in chief, U.S. Pacific Fleet (CINCPACFLT). Under CINCPAC commander Admiral Clarey, Richardson was again heavily involved in Navy planning for Vietnam War operations. A shifting geopolitical landscape and a change in the Navy under new CNO Zumwalt's efforts added complications to the effort.

The United States was looking for an exit strategy from the Vietnam War. In March 1972, to force the North Vietnamese back to the negotiation table, President Nixon authorized Operations Linebacker I and II. Planning the bombing campaign fell to Richardson. He assembled a team from the 7th Air Force, Strategic Air Command, and Navy planners.[42] Operation Linebacker succeeded: airpower was once again in good favor. Richardson retired from the Navy on July 1, 1972.

Richardson pursued two primary efforts in his retirement: getting SCI directly to the afloat commander and nurturing a desire for intelligence among senior Navy leaders. His work as a contractor meant he could grow his understanding of intelligence-operations linkages as the challenges of the 1970s unfolded.[43] For example, he served on a panel examining the U.S. IC's seeming inability to predict the 1973 Arab-Israeli War. He learned that intelligence had been received in advance of the Egyptian attack and a warning had been issued, yet the decision-makers had failed to listen. "Nobody should expect intelligence officers to be mind readers. That is not their business," Richardson said of the ignored intelligence warning. Intelligence can tell you what is happening and provide an assessment, but the "significance of that information is an operational responsibility. . . . Don't expect the intelligence people to make operational decisions."[44]

For Richardson, the intelligence-operations integration only grew through improved C3 procedures, requiring a better application of "computer-aided information management." Getting sensitive information from the national-intelligence systems to the operator had been the aim behind opening FOSIF Rota. Now his efforts were coming full circle. Starting in 1975 he was associated with and influenced the direction of a new tactical command center effort. The concept of the tactical exploitation of national capabilities (TENCAP) was explored through the "Outlaw" series of experiments. The effort demonstrated how over-the-horizon targeting was possible during a war-at-sea missile fight.[45] Richardson's support to Navy Intelligence and his efforts to improve the intelligence-operations linkages made him a perfect keynote speaker for the 1998 Opintel Lessons Learned Conference at the Navy and Marine Corps Intelligence Training Center in Dam Neck, Virginia.[46] Richardson passed away at the age of 101 in June 2015.

What made Richardson's effort more important was a shift within the Navy to a go-forward view of its strategy. James "Ace" Lyons had been Richardson's forward-looking intelligence-operations-focused ASW watch officer in 1970. Soon after he embarked on a study of strategy at the National War College and the Naval War College. Throughout the '70s Lyons went on to hold strategy positions in the Pentagon as an action officer in OP-60 and planner in OP-60, a junior flag officer in OP-60, and a flag aide in OPNAV. By the time he made captain, he was groomed and ready to be a Navy planner and eventually served as an admiral. Retired Capt. Peter Swartz, USN, said, "No Navy captains today have that kind of background in N3/N5."[47]

Lyons believed that his strategy and planning efforts should focus on deterring the Soviet bloc and disabusing Washington of the notion that should war break out, the Navy would only "haul stuff across the Atlantic," leaving the Army to do the real fighting in the Fulda Gap. Lyons saw deterrence through power, said Swartz. He "wanted to scare the crap out of the Soviets and make sure they knew that if they came outside [the Barents Sea or northern Pacific] they'd die." Lyons' attitude and strategy acumen shaped the perspectives of Navy planners throughout the late-1970s and John Lehman, future Secretary of the Navy under President Reagan. "Lyons taught Lehman and made Lehman, Lehman," Swartz said in a 2019 interview.[48] The growth in C2 capabilities that allowed improved operational and tactical decision-making underpinned Lyons' view of an aggressive strategy. He and Lehman would display the Navy's new lethality and go-forward approach in the early 1980s.

PART IV
Formalizing

"The alarmed Soviet command mobilized all available ships and aircraft to find the carrier strike groups," former secretary of the Navy John Lehman writes in *Oceans Ventured*. The 1981 Exercise Northern Wedding, part of an extensive series of exercises called Ocean Venture, was led by the aggressive and unorthodox Rear Adm. James "Ace" Lyons. As commander of the Second Fleet and NATO's Striking Fleet, Lyons put eighty-three NATO ships into the North Atlantic virtually undetected by the Soviet Navy. A flight of fighters, launched from the aircraft carriers, flew over a thousand miles, surprising several Soviet Tu-95 Bear bombers off Murmansk, Russia. The 540-knot F-14 Tomcat flyby of the Tu-95 Bears was Lyons' way of letting them know that the U.S. Navy had a new strategy.[1]

The Ocean Venture exercises displayed the aggressive "go forward" strategy that had developed over the past five years. The strategy harnessed new computers and weapons to older aircraft carriers and surface combatant technologies to fight a war America, especially the U.S. Navy, liked—mass attrition using conventional precision, hyperlethal weapons. Operating in the far northern waters of the Pacific and Atlantic basins, the areas traditionally reserved for the Soviets, required aggressive naval strategists like Adm. Isaac C. Kidd Jr., USN, commander in chief of the Atlantic (CINCLANT), Adm. Thomas Hayward, USN, commander of the Pacific-based Seventh Fleet (and future CNO), and Lyons. To make the strategy viable, the Navy required a beyond-the-horizon operating picture and targeting capabilities—all things supported by intelligence. Computers powered the concepts, creating a coordinated cognitive-to-action warfighting paradigm that operated forward at a tempo the Soviets could not match.

CHAPTER 10
Shipboard Tactical-Decision Support

The U.S. struggle in Vietnam became death throes that ended with the SS *Mayaguez* incident. The U.S.-flagged *Mayaguez*, transiting seventy nautical miles southwest of Sihanoukville, Cambodia, was boarded by the Khmer Rouge on May 12, 1975, and her crew taken hostage. The United States launched a large military rescue mission that included assault forces and the bombing of Cambodian airfields. The strong tones of reprisal were unmistakable; one postmission report noted, "The performance of the U.S. forces was inspiring." That being said, the operation played out with anything but military efficiency. Forty-one U.S. servicemen were killed, twenty-three in a nonbattle accident. Over one hundred Cambodians were killed. The *Mayaguez*, released by Cambodia just before the assault, was safe but at staggering cost.[1]

At the time, the *Mayaguez* incident seemed like a footnote, a little realpolitik drama. But it proved a "harbinger of things to come."[2] First, the disproportional use of force was, as national security author Christopher Lamb described, decision-making "using force as an 'emotional catharsis'" for the failures of Vietnam.[3] Saigon's chaotic, almost-farcical shambles of an evacuation had been mere weeks before the *Mayaguez* incident. Vice President Nelson Rockefeller displayed the emotionality that shaped U.S. reaction to the capture of the *Mayaguez*: "If we do not respond violently," he said, "we will get nibbled to death." He then argued for what Lamb calls "unrestrained action," saying, "if the communists do not think that you will react strong and fast, they will keep on doing this."[4]

The outsized military response sent a message: The United States' prestige mattered, it would not "tolerate provocation by small powers," and China and Russia had better take responsibility for their client states.

Chinese Foreign Minister Qiao Guanhua chided the United States: "You are too emotional in your actions," he said, calling the *Mayaguez* "totally unnecessary." China was more vocal than their Communist ally, suggesting a "conscious policy decision" by the Soviets "to avoid using the issue as a platform to criticize the United States in the aftermath of the fall of Indochina."[5] The military action was a return to expeditionary crisis-escalation management, thus resting primarily on the Navy's shoulders. The "excessive" force reassured Asian and European partners, particularly South Korea. It may have been outright deterrence, forcing China and the Soviets to reconsider the U.S. approach to achieving strategic objectives. The excessive use of force would become a foundational aspect of future U.S. military responses.

The Vietnam War "shattered the U.S. Army, and to a lesser extent the other services," wrote Norman Friedman. Modernization focused on implementing the lessons learned, driven by a "never again" mantra.[6] The Arab-Israeli War reinforced the need for a new doctrine that exploited hyperlethal air-war capabilities, enhancing land-power warfighting. The never-again mantra forced an increase in the number of SCI security clearances granted to military intelligence officers, enlisted, and operators. The IC changed too. The tight controls on national intelligence, particularly SIGINT and IMINT, were slowly loosened. New information-management and communication technology improved all-source Opintel fusion and dissemination processes. Finally, the SCI material created opportunities for intelligence officers to work elbow to elbow with operators, developing strategies, doctrine, and new tactics. The desire to have OSIS afloat drove Navy Intelligence's thinking, and revolutions in shipboard computerization seemed to show great promise in realizing the dream. It would be decades before technology could allow a true OSIS-like plot for a shipboard environment.

The Soviet Threat, Computers, and Money

By the 1976 U.S. presidential election, there were real concerns over Soviet intentions and the West's diplomatic approach. The Soviet ability to mobilize a proxy, Cuba, and support operations at great distances offered further dangers. Ronald Reagan, running on a hardline platform against Soviet aggression, had failed to gain the 1976 Republican Party's nomination—though he would go on to win the 1980 election. Shortly after Democrat Jimmy Carter's presidential inauguration the following January, Reagan said he had a simple answer to the Soviet problem: We win, and they lose.[7] Future British prime minister Margaret Thatcher denounced Soviet conduct as well: "We must remember that there are no Queensbury rules in the contest that is now going on," she said in a January 1976 speech, referencing the rules governing boxing that mandated the use of gloves; "And the Russians are playing to win."[8] The strategic tensions, especially the importance of rebuilding NATO, provide context for developing over-the-horizon (OTH) weapons and improved C2. More special compartmented information facilities (SCIF) were needed on the aircraft carrier to allow Opintel practitioners space to analyze SCI material and provide assessments at sea, supporting the commander's tactical decision-making.

The disadvantageous global-security environment brought about new political realities. The West's strategic concerns, fostered by heightened Soviet military adventurism, created a conventional arms race. This revolution in military affairs leveraged computers and microelectronics to develop conventional "smart weapons." These weapons created hyperlethal attrition by shooting farther and faster; they accelerated the track, target, and engage decision cycle. Some believed that in the new military environment, conventional force created an opportunity to achieve strategic outcomes before atomic weapons could be employed.

The Soviets aggressively used their military to influence the world order and spread Communism. Their military supported an evolving conventional war–based strategy. Led by the rising General Nikolai V. Ogarkov, in 1971 the Soviet military explored a way to exploit advanced conventional weapons in keeping with their "deep battle" doctrine. Their Theater Strategic Operations (TSO) military strategy was to act across multiple fronts and use maneuver tactics to attack quickly, penetrate deeply into Europe, and occupy vital European areas and capitals.[9] Building an enormous force and exercising battlefield tactics revealed the

Soviet strategy to NATO observers.[10] Restoring NATO force capabilities, especially the United States', was a counterforce deterrence strategy.

President Jimmy Carter was more dove than a hawk. However, even he became convinced of the need to reinforce NATO, increasing defense spending by around $8 billion. It was the most significant peacetime increase in U.S. defense spending to that point in U.S. history. Most importantly, Carter focused money on research and development and increasing military readiness.[11]

The Soviets did not expect NATO growth or the resulting strategic unity.[12] What took the Soviets even more by surprise was NATO's technological advancements. The United States' hyperlethal offset strategy was coming up to speed. The result was asymmetry, complicating Soviet defense calculus and creating more strategic options for the United States.[13] The "smart weapons" were lifted and improved from the Vietnam and Middle East battlefields.

When the U.S. military rolled out Project Assault Breaker in 1978, Ogarkov and the Soviets realized how devastating computerization would be. Assault Breaker integrated several technologies, including lasers, electro-optical sensors, microelectronics, data processors, and radars. Its surveillance and targeting system supported surface- and air-launched long-range weapons. The weapons delivered a mass of "smart" submunition (bomblets), destroying tanks and armored vehicles within a wide area, breaking any TSO maneuver assault. Ogarkov's plan hinged upon computerization too, but there was little industry capacity for mass computer production in the Soviet system. Social and Soviet ideological issues created continuous resistance against computers and restricted the industry.[14]

Fear of the Communist threat and memories of Japan's exploitation of U.S. open-trade policy before World War II resulted in an embargo against the Soviet bloc. Exports of military-related machinery, tools, electronics, and technology were restricted. The United States leveraged its Marshall Plan aid to compel European nations to comply with export restrictions. The embargo became another tool to contain Communism.[15]

There were over five hundred items embargoed from the Soviet bloc and China. Embargoes are double-edged weapons, impeding the West's economic expansion. Historian Frank Cain offers that the embargo policy created a growing divide "between the UK and USA concerning whether trade should prevail over ideology." The United States continued to expand the number of export controls while Britain and many U.S. corporations wanted reductions. Thus keeping the allies and industry on-side regarding the embargo on computer technology was challenging. Britain disagreed with many export strictures and used "exception provisions" to justify the sale of computers as part of the advancement of science. Further, the Soviet bloc's "general progress toward self-sufficiency" made some export controls obsolete. The U.S. intelligence community assessed the West as "at least four years" ahead of the Soviets in computer technology. The sale of the slower and lower memory–capable machines seemed harmless to national security.[16]

In 1950 Soviet journalists savaged the new American computer technology glorified in the *Time* magazine article "Can Man Build a Superman?" Soviet social and ideological issues created continuous resistance to computers and restricted Russia's industry. Authoritarian control maintained the Soviet state by limiting access to information, especially about cybernetics. The Soviet military, however, recognized the need for computers and microelectronics. Of the Soviet computer industry's dilemma, history of mathematics professor Slava Gerovitch writes that in "a classic example of 'doublespeak,' the Soviet Union began secretly pursuing military computing while condemning the West for doing the same."[17]

By the 1960s the Soviets planned to create a "unified system" linking their enterprises into one computer network to optimize their economy. Most of the hardware and software had been purchased or stolen from the West. The United States was concerned. Economics was one issue, but the same computer technology had reached the Soviet military. In 1969 equipment was embargoed that manufactured printed circuits, transistors, memory disks, and drums.[18] Apprehension about computer-technology transfer to the Soviet bloc dominated the hearings associated with the Trade Reform Act of 1973. Georgia representative Bob B. Blackburn summarized the concerns: Computers purchased to assist crop planning also computed trajectories for intercontinental ballistic missiles.[19]

The technology situation became worse for the Soviets in the 1970s and '80s. The fateful decision, or maybe the addiction to the West's better computer technology, forced the Soviets to reverse-engineer and steal (take) instead of developing (make) computer technology themselves. The make-or-take decision of the 1960s haunted the Soviet computer industry for four decades.[20] The net result was a lack of computers for advanced communication tools required for their reconnaissance-strike and -fires complex.[21] In contrast, the United States produced more powerful, compact, reliable computers and at lower cost. Microcomputers allowed tactical users to assimilate and share vast amounts of information. Most revolutionary was the application of microcomputers to create a shared operational "picture." The shared picture synchronized U.S. and NATO military activity across theaters and the globe. The new form of picture-based command and control increased the tempo of the U.S. operations and its allies'. The Soviets, lacking computers, could not compete.[22]

A New Way of War

The hyperlethal air combat of Vietnam and the Arab-Israeli Wars reinforced the idea that more effective command and control (C2) led to victory. Warfighting heuristics said faster and more accurate coordinated fires carried battles at sea.[23] Increasing the tempo of war through maneuver and computer-assisted decision-making gave the enemy no time to cope with rapidly unfolding circumstances. Such a tempo induced a type of mental paralysis in the enemy, U.S. Air Force Col. John Boyd opined. New computers processed the flood of data from netted sensors. They shared the information machine to machine across a digital network, allowing U.S. commanders to quickly make better decisions than their adversaries could.[24]

The Navy surface platform's sensor-to-shooter kill chain was created through its Naval Tactical Data System (NTDS). The aircraft carrier air wing, and then ASCMs, provided the airborne part of the kill chain. By the late 1970s the cost of making weapons go faster and farther was not as useful as making them more accurate. A shift to a "military sensor and communication revolution" began.[25]

NTDS required new computer hardware. In 1977 the Navy began replacing all NTDS hardware and looking for a new system. The AEGIS integrated a phased-array radar and advanced missile and digital C2 systems. It incorporated NTDS's C2 functions into a new, longer-range Battle Group Antiair Warfare Coordination (BGAAWC) program. AEGIS revolutionized distributed lethality and war at sea.[26] The results were beyond anything the Soviet reconnaissance-strike complex could match. The problem with AEGIS and the upgrades to NTDS was their fielding. AEGIS would not be available until the new USS *Ticonderoga*-class cruiser was launched in 1983; that same year the new Tomahawk long-range subsonic cruise missile and the new NTDS were scheduled to enter the fleet.

The Navy's operators could see the future of the over-the-horizon (OTH) battles. They immediately began developing informal and formal tactics, techniques, and procedures for such a future. In the mid-1970s the Navy was still digesting the missile-warfare lessons of the 1973 Arab-Israeli War. The Israeli Navy had won two missile battles at sea using salvo warfare that took advantage of detection, deception, and timing. Most importantly the Israelis coordinated their forces, allowing their distributed lethality to concentrate against the opposing units. The U.S. Navy of the 1980s would need to fight similarly, leveraging the aircraft carrier battlegroup's broad and flexible warfighting capabilities.[27] Such a force needed individual units to share an understanding of the strategic situation that was combined into a single visualization of the tactical and operational environment.

The complexity of the battlegroup required a tremendous amount of coordination to be effective. Distributed air and surface lethality created overlapping weapons zones. Without proper real-time coordination, multiple systems could engage the same target. Worse, confusion could slow reaction time, resulting in no engagement at all.[28] The C2 for this type of warfare required a "command by negation" structure, a modern U.S. Navy version of the German's nineteenth-century *Auftragstaktik* concept. Using "mission tactics," as it translates, the commander sets clear objectives and provides resources that subordinates then have the latitude to use as they deem most appropriate to realizing the objective.[29] The composite warfare commander (CWC) concept embarked on the primacy of the *Auftragstaktik* commander's intent. Developed at the Tactical Training Group Pacific (TACTRAGRUPAC) in the 1970s, CWC became the Navy's new battlegroup C2 construct. Under CWC individual warfare commanders, Air and Missile Defense Warfare, Strike Warfare, and Anti-submarine Warfare were empowered by the officer in Tactical Command (OTC), the battle group commander. These individual warfare commanders were guided by the OTC's intent to execute missions independently within their warfare area until told to "stop"—the negation of command. CWC supported offensive multidomain war-at-sea requirements while allowing simultaneous control of defensive counterforce operations.[30]

Applying the CWC warfighting concept required better intelligence. At the time, better intelligence often equated to more information. Multiple redundant tactical data streams were flowing from shore to the battlegroups. The archaic record message format created a capacity shortage and overloaded the commander with data, not intelligence. A better way to present more intelligence in a form easily consumed by the battlegroup commander was needed.[31] In a 2019 interview Rear Adm. Thomas Brooks, USN (Ret.), senior intelligence officer (N2) for the Second Fleet commander in 1976, described early-1970s Navy Intelligence's thinking about the C2 principles. Brooks believed in a "two squares of linoleum" approach to supporting the commander: "My advertised purpose," Brooks said of the Opintel section he led on the Second Fleet flagship USS *Mount Whitney*, was that "the admiral should be able to plant his feet on two squares of linoleum and without moving see the 'red' picture [enemy], the 'blue' picture [his forces], and be able to communicate direction to his units."[32]

Brooks and his shipboard Opintel team owned the "red" picture. The Opintel team kept a manual plot on a chart to display it. The plot was difficult to share across the battlegroup, and creating a record of individual red-unit movement over time for pattern analysis was almost impossible.[33] A digital plotting and sharing system was needed.

Embracing the Two Squares of Linoleum

Shipboard decision support and warning-intelligence demands only grew. The new CWC concept required a dedicated fused "picture." The Opintel team provided the long-range common intelligence plot (CIP) to contextualize battlegroup operations with the enemy's actions. The battlegroup commander, the OTC, would fight the battlegroup from those two squares of linoleum. However, where those squares would be and how the commander received a fused intelligence and operational plot were in development.

Naval warfare improvements in the offing left the current fleet grasping at anything providing a comparative advantage. Therefore the fleet innovated faster than the Navy's bureaucracy. Thus informal efforts to

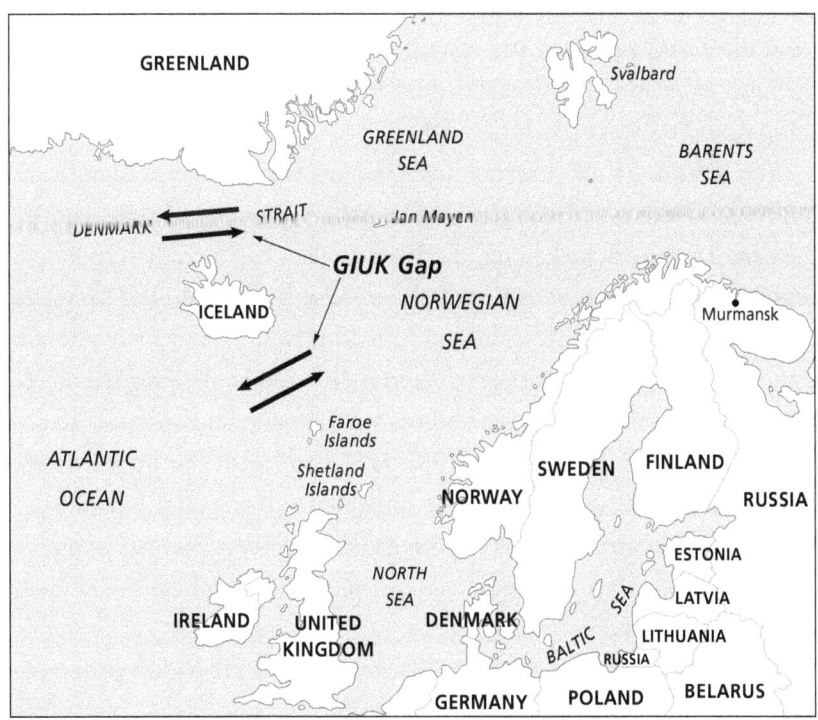

MAP 7
The North Atlantic and Norwegian Sea area of operations

improve beyond-the-horizon naval-battle decision-making came in two forms: improved information management and creating a physical and digital space for tactical-decision support. The Enhanced Calculator Link Processing Systems (ECLIPS) was an informal, bootstrap approach to creating a digitized intelligence plot.

The ECLIPS computer crashed again; it had happened several nights in a row. The technicians scrambled to get the system online again. Then-commander Thomas Brooks, Second Fleet N2, onboard the flagship *Mount Whitney* in the North Atlantic, wondered what the hell was going on. The picture had been fine when he'd gone to bed. On one cathode-ray tube display on the flag bridge the ECLIPS displayed Link 14 data—"blue" (or friendly) ship positions, "red" (or adversary) ship positions, and "white" (or merchant) ship positions. Having the three sets of "tracks" automated and displayed on one screen was progressive. Second Fleet commander Vice Adm. John "Black Jack" Shanahan liked ECLIPS's plot because it aided tactical decision-making. The Opintel team liked and yet hated the system too. Now, in the middle of one of the most extensive NATO exercises of 1976, if not the decade, the damn thing would only work half of the time![34]

The Teamwork '76 exercise followed on the heels of a significant NATO land exercise, Reforger, held in early September of that year. By the time Teamwork kicked off, the Warsaw Pact had already responded, beginning an extensive land and air exercise in Poland. The exercises were massive, with eighty thousand troops and ten nations in Teamwork alone. At stake was the efficacy of deterrence based on denying the objective. Brooks needed to provide his boss with situational awareness across the entire theater. He knew that ECLIPS, also called the Link System, would help Shanahan's staff better understand the spatial relationship between the hundreds of NATO, Soviet, and Warsaw Pact navy ships.[35] The intelligence picture it showed was imperfect, but it helped—at least, when it worked at all.

It took time to bring the 1971 Hewlett Packard HP 9830A programmable calculator, the heart of the Link System, back online. A small magnetic tape cassette held the computer program language operating the system. There was no longer a need to ingest the operating system using cumbersome punch cards. However, reading, installing, and running the program from the cassette still took precious time. Once the program was running, the OSIS message feeds containing red and white tracks and the Link 14 feed containing blue tracks from NTDS were connected, and the data was ingested. Once in the system, the track's data must be scrubbed and verified and duplicate or ambiguous tracks corrected or deleted. The direct feed of the messages into the calculator versus the cumbersome paper-tape method made displaying the tracks faster and updatable. Even when ECLIPS worked properly, the digital plot of the Norwegian Sea was already lagging. The OSIS nodes in London and Rota sent most intelligence-summary messages on a schedule, not in real time. The system's crash delayed the plot further still.[36]

Trying to solve the mystery of nightly Link System crashes, Brooks arrived on the flag bridge of *Mount Whitney* early in the midwatch. The Link System was working; maybe the problem had been solved, maybe not. Brooks waited. A young Sailor arrived with a floor buffer; the flag bridge's blue square linoleum tiles identified the space as "Flag Country," dedicated to senior staff officers, and his to buff every night. While Brooks observed, the Sailor dutifully plugged the buffer into a bulkhead outlet and switched it on. *Pop!* Instantly the Link System machine shut off. The electrical circuit could not handle the load. "We solved the problem," Brooks later recalled, by telling the Sailor to "plug your damn buffer in over there!" pointing to another bulkhead power outlet. "That's how crude the system was in those days," he later reflected. The Link System "was quite sophisticated," he emphasized, but "not by today's standards."[37]

Brooks used a system not designed for Opintel but for non-NTDS-equipped combatants. The Link System processed a Link 14 message; a person could read the messages only if they understood the format and what each line's header meant.[38] Personnel on non-NTDS ships manually plotted the tracks from the message onto a map.[39] Surface line officer Cdr. Clifford Willoz, USN (Ret.), served in one of the U.S. destroyers lacking NTDS. To Willoz, plotting Link 14 tracks by hand was criminal. Non-NTDS-capable combatants did not stand a chance in combat. They would be overwhelmed and paralyzed by the flow of information in a mass Soviet air attack.[40] In 1968 Willoz ran a section within OpNav OP92U/ Naval Intelligence Command, Applications Department (NIC-AD). His team provided daily intelligence briefs regarding Soviet undersea activity. Willoz was "appalled by the lack of any automated/technical tools to assist in the briefings" at NIC-AD. He looked around for a solution and "discovered the magical world of HP calculators." Willoz acquired funding to purchase a Hewlett Packard (HP) programmable calculator, X/Y pen-plotter, and punch-card reader, creating the Calculator Link Processing System (CLIPS). The system automatically produced a paper plot from Link 14 machine-readable messages.[41]

In August 1971 Rear Adm. Emmet Tidd, USN, former chief of staff to CNO Admiral Zumwalt for Operations and Decision Coordination during Project Sixty, took command of Cruiser Destroyer Flotilla Six.[42] Tidd took notice of Willoz's efforts with CLIPS and assigned him to his staff. With money from the Secretary of the Navy's Independent Study Program, Willoz solved the manual-plotting problem for Tidd's non-NTDS destroyers; he found a way to feed the digital teletype stream directly into the HP calculator, eliminating running paper-tape messages through a reader. Later he added a cathode-ray tube (CRT) display, replacing the pen-plotting system, and renamed it the "Enhanced" CLIPS—or ECLIPS. Willoz programmed ECLIPS to accept the Rainform Red–formatted classified messages containing the OSIS node intelligence reports.[43] He was not alone in his desire for automation; the Royal Canadian Navy had begun running the Automatic Data Link Plotting System (ADLIPS) in 1973. It is unclear whether ECLIPS influenced ADLIPS, though the timing indicates it may have.[44]

In 1972 Naval Surface Forces Atlantic (SURFLANT) funded about fifteen systems, seeing ECLIPS as a low-cost tactical-decision aid. SURFLANT offered the Link Systems to deploying aircraft carriers. By 1976 SURFLANT supplied Link Systems to the Atlantic Ocean– and Mediterranean Sea–deploying flagships like *Mount Whitney*, aircraft carriers, and some large-deck amphibious ships.[45] A few ships in the Pacific Fleet were deployed with ECLIPS. With only a limited number of systems,

SURFLANT rotated, or cross-decked, them from returning to deploying ships.[46] ECLIPS was never an official program of record, and limited documentation about the system exists. Before 1979 little or no Link System training was provided to the deploying unit.[47] The system's success was hit or miss based on the ship's Intelligence and Automated Data Processing (ADP) officers' initiative.

Possibly as early as 1974 the Link System deployed with Opintel teams. It was usually placed in CVIC or on the flag bridge. These were secret-level information compartments, and the Link System only displayed sanitized secret OSIS and Link 14 reports. Later, placing ECLIPS into SCI-cleared spaces provided the Opintel team with a more-detailed SCI-level automated intelligence plot. Command ships, aircraft carriers, and large-deck amphibious ship Opintel teams were, to a degree not previously seen, able to offer battlespace awareness to the afloat commander only provided at the OSIS nodes ashore.[48]

CHAPTER 11
Formal "Two Squares" Effort

When Admiral Zumwalt was elevated to CNO on April 14, 1970, he was given the remit to modernize the Navy. It was no small task. To respond to the Soviet threat Zumwalt had to do no less than improve active and passive electronic warfare, command-control-communications (C3), and weapons and sensors.[1] The idea was to use technology to create an asymmetry, countering the growing quantitative advantage of the Soviet Navy with the qualitative one. Zumwalt decided that the best way to make these needed technology changes was to centralize policymaking under one organization. He modified his OpNav staff to create an office with the authority and remit to centralize the direction of the development and fielding of new technologies. Command Support Systems (OP-094) would be led by then-DNI Rear Admiral Fredrick "Fritz" Harlfinger, USN (later vice admiral) and work to centralize the policy and programming associated with the growing technology and concepts of C3. It was the Navy's first attempt at institutionalizing information warfare. OP-094 brought under one aegis the functions of intelligence, communications, meteorology, cryptology, space systems, and the Navy's portion of the Worldwide Military Command and Control System (WWMCCS, pronounced Wimex).[2]

In unpublished interviews with U.S. Naval Institute Press historian John T. Mason, Harlfinger describes when his vision of OSIS support to the commander at sea faced organizational challenges. During several briefings held in the early days of Zumwalt's tenure as CNO, Harlfinger had been explaining how the space-based and terrestrial-signals intelligence-collection missions operated. The details of missions, the importance of oceanographers, the need for exploitation, and analysis centers

PHOTO 11.1
Naval Intelligence Command Change of Command, Leutze Park, Washington Navy Yard, Washington, D.C., July 22, 1971. *Left to right:* Vice Admiral Harlfinger, Rear Admiral Rectanus, possibly VCNO Admiral Ralph W. Cousins, and CNO Admiral Zumwalt.
OFFICIAL NAVY PHOTO, VICE ADMIRAL EARL "REX" RECTANUS PERSONAL ARCHIVE, COURTESY OF EARL RECTANUS JR.

to coordinate—the list of interconnected elements grew. Finally Zumwalt broke in. "Well, why don't you just take charge of all of it?" Halfinger recalls him saying.[3] That would not be possible, Harlfinger pointed out, because he was the Director of Naval Intelligence. Harlfinger stood up OP-094 on March 15, 1971, and then turned the Naval Intelligence directorship to Rear Adm. Rex Rectanus in July of that year.

As a former submarine skipper and one of the directors of Program C in the highly classified National Reconnaissance Office (NRO), Harlfinger was well-placed to understand the growing complexities of space-based satellite reconnaissance, C2, C2 warfare (C2W), and their value to the afloat commander. He led the Navy's satellite-reconnaissance program consisting of representatives from the Naval Research Laboratory, PME-106, SPAWAR, the U.S. Navy Electronics Command, and the Naval Security Group—all located in Washington, D.C., and nearby Maryland.[4]

Building a robust and adaptable communication system was a primary objective for Harlfinger's OP-094. In the past communications had singularly focused on transmitting voice. Now passing data in a duplex or multiplex manner was more important. The data exchange allowed for the creation of a shared near-real-time picture. Author Norman Friedman calls this type of warfare "picture-centric warfare." It was the heart of OSIS and eventually Wimex.[5] Picture warfare was embodied in the Naval Tactical Data System (NTDS), but that system had limited capabilities. Harlfinger was trying to perfect the OSIS system, now two years old, by designing a communication relay that connected the geographic commander in chief (CINC) theater commands to Wimex and the national command center and connected the CINCs to their subordinate task forces. That OSIS picture provided a common intelligence picture that, if integrated with the NTDS common operating picture, could make a powerful battlespace and integrated-targeting tool. That was all well and good, but only for the strategic level of war. Afloat commanders were faced with fast-traveling weapons fired from well beyond the current shipboard sensor horizon. To have a comparative advantage the Navy had to master the over-the-horizon targeting (OTH-T) process.[6]

In 1972 the Reconnaissance, Electronic Warfare, Special Operations, and Naval Intelligence systems (REWSON) office, under OP-094, would begin fusing multisource information—primarily space-based national-satellite intelligence, OSIS-fused intelligence, and tactical surveillance—in a shipboard environment. The information-management goals set in 1972 were expanded as the Navy realized gathering and correlating multisource information was only part of the task. The fleet and task force commanders must be able to share threat information. They must also be able to "display and assess that information, and to communicate reliably, quickly and securely with higher authority and dispersed units."[7] Satellite-based high-speed datalinks require computer systems to manage, automatically correlate, and exchange vast amounts of data in real time.

By 1975 REWSON had made progress and was ready to demonstrate to the entire fleet the fruits of four years of research and development.

The demonstration was called "Outlaw"—the code word for tactical use of satellite-collected data able to be forwarded from OSIS nodes for tactical use at sea. Outlaw Hawk, the first of two demonstrations in the mid-1970s, created a crude battlespace "picture" for the afloat commander.[8] It showed that an OSIS-produced common intelligence picture (CIP) could support Navy C2 systems at sea. Those systems were developed as part of the Tactical Flag Command Center (TFCC) project and were presented in the second Outlaw demonstration in 1976, "Outlaw Shark."[9]

Creating one common operating picture (COP) that would be shared globally throughout U.S. Navy installations was a daunting task—not least because none of the systems yet connected. Running earlier and somewhat parallel to Outlaw Hawk was a brute-force-analysis approach. Beginning in 1971, OP-094 sponsored several experiments and demonstrations under a Fleet Flagship System program. The program continued work on an afloat C3 system—called an Extended Surface Plot (ESP)—that would fuse nationally collected signals intelligence.[10] From the start the experimental development was robust. Simultaneously testing began in Sunnyvale, California, on a Multi-source Correlation Facility. The MSCF created a common intelligence picture (CIP)—a similar effort to that underway in the OSIS nodes—but with attempts to further automate processes. The next goal was to fuse the MSCF concept with a shareable COP that could simultaneously display enemy and friendly units.[11]

In late 1975 the Navy converted the Fleet Command Support Centers (FCSCs) to Flag Command Centers. The FCC manually correlated the OSIS, ASW command-control-communications system (ASW CCCS), and Wimex. The resulting picture showed the unit's name, location, and assessed activity. It was translated into a human/machine-readable Link 14 or Rainform Red message and sent to a new Tactical Flag Command Center (TFCC) onboard flagships. The message's information was manually plotted on a chart in the TFCC.[12]

Tests on the Pacific-based *Kitty Hawk* in 1975 showed that the FCC-TFCC process had already improved the commander's situational awareness to 650 nautical miles, much farther than what NTDS provided. The concept was good, but without computer automation the process was untenable. The computers placed in the first interim-TFCC (ITFCC) configuration installed in *John F. Kennedy* in 1976 were developed from *Kitty Hawk*'s Outlaw Hawk demonstration. The Navy began reconfiguring some aircraft carriers with interim-TFCCs and a dedicated SCI material Opintel fusion space called the Supplemental Intelligence Plot (SupPlot).[13]

Outlaw Hawk and the interim-TFCC focused on support to decision-making at sea. Outlaw Shark, the second demonstration, focused on OTH-T for developing a new tactical long-range Tomahawk anti-ship cruise missile (TASCM). Unlike Outlaw Hawk, which looked at information-fusion processes, Shark developed an afloat computer system incorporating automated multisource correlation and fire control. The new software displayed a fused plot of information from multiple sources (e.g., radar, visual, sonar, HFDF, satellite-derived, and OSIS) for multiple contacts. The contacts—called "tracks"—were displayed on a digital plot.[14]

IronHorse Rides Again?

Outlaw Shark's approach to picture warfare was similar to the U.S. Air Force's IronHorse system, destroyed in Da Nang in April 1969. IronHorse had two AN/GYK-9 computers (CP-818) designed explicitly for the NSA. The GYK-9's Univac design was compatible with the Navy's AN/UYK-1/7 and the USQ-20 systems used in the IOIC and NTDS. Input into the GYK-9 came from twenty-two AN/GGC-15 manual Morse code collection stations. Cryptologists processed the "pro forma" message intercepts, sending them to the first GYK-9. Voice COMINT intercepts were input using MOD-35 teletype keyboards (non–Morse code voice intercept).[15] The process was labor intensive, requiring over fifty personnel to operate and probably triple that to maintain continuously.

The two GYK-9 computers took in the vast intercept data and created a bearing and range report. They then rationalized the data, decrypting and editing it into U.S. radar–compatible tracks. The tracks were digitally plotted onto a crude map of the battlespace and displayed on a cathode-ray tube (CRT). New tracks on display appeared as a "blinking trace," or track, for a CRT analyst to manually review. The GYK-9 used algorithms to "detect and reject irrelevant chatter," or duplicate tracks, assisting in the analyst's review of the tracks. Any "unrecognizable format" track data was displayed on an "edit console" for the analyst to correct and reenter the track.[16]

The Tactical Air Control Center's (TACC) Backup Interceptor Control System (BUIC) electronically distributed tracks to the Air Force's tactical air-control system (Combat Lightning). Sanitized tracks (with classified track data removed) went to the Navy's TF 77 NTDS at sea and the Marine Corps Tactical Data System (MTDS) in Da Nang. IronHorse handled 120 tracks—twelve times the capacity of the Hammock system—and "reduce[d] the intercept-to-consumer time from 10 minutes to a matter of seconds."[17]

Outlaw Shark had autocorrelation capabilities and depicted what IronHorse called "irrelevant chatter" as "ambiguous tracks." Unlike IronHorse, Shark retained historical data on each track and displayed previous positions and movements as a line of the plot's contact tracks. Shark also allowed an analyst to examine, to a limited degree, the data used to derive a track's position. A track in Shark was derived using multiple fixes, like HFDF or spaced-based systems. Shark displayed major and minor ellipses of the fixes. Though limited, the ellipses combined to show the uncertainty regarding the unit's position represented by the track.[18] The ellipses created an area of uncertainty (AOU) surrounding the track and the vessel it represented. Tightening the AOU by gaining more fixes shrank the ellipses; thus a small AOU was essential to the OTH-T process. The confluence of ethical issues associated with firing long-range weapons at moving targets not visually identified was at the heart of OTH-T efforts. Smaller AOUs meant increased certainty, but the effort took more time. A TASM could take thirty to sixty minutes to reach a moving target; when it arrived near the target, even more uncertainty might exist. The situation was a classic time-space-force conundrum that only all-source intelligence improved.[19]

Though only nine Outlaw Shark systems were produced, the concepts and software significantly influenced OTH fire control and Opintel for generations. The capabilities embedded in its software were incorporated into the Shore Targeting Terminal (STT), the MK-117 digital fire-control system, and the Tomahawk Common Weapons Control System. The Shark's computers were developmental, supporting the creation of the AN/USQ-81 (V) computers that supported the TFCC. The OSIS system benefited from new datalinks and correlation capabilities developed by the Outlaw demonstrations. Most of those capabilities were incorporated into the OSIS Baseline upgrade and a 1980s Prototype OSIS Terminal (POST) installed in SupPlots. Thus Outlaw Hawk led to the TFCC, and Outlaw Shark influenced TFCC operations, SupPlot, and long-range fire-control processes. Shipboard Opintel now focused on tactical-decision support through the CIP-to-COP relationship embodied in SupPlot and the TFFC supporting the afloat commander.[20]

Regarding IronHorse, after the April 1969 explosion destroyed the complex at the Marine Corps ammunition dump in Da Nang, the system had been rebuilt in July 1969. The explosion had convinced the Air Force to make the system more mobile, and so they placed the intercept positions in cramped vans. Communication and software problems degraded the system, and in April 1971 an upgraded IronHorse II was operating at Ramasun Air Force Base, Thailand. But the air war in Vietnam was winding down, and IronHorse II still had software problems. So the equipment was disassembled and shipped to the NSA at Fort Meade, Maryland, and with that IronHorse became lost to history.[21] Nothing indicates that IronHorse influenced Outlaw Shark, but the concepts have eerie similarities.

SupPlot, Formalizing Shipboard Tactical-Decision Support

The AN/UGC 25 Model 28 compact receive-only teleprinter tapped away at sixty-five words per minute.[22] It was printing the top-secret special-intelligence summary from the FOSIC detachment at CINCLANT in Norfolk, Virginia. *America*'s Signal Exploitation Spaces (SSES), located all the way forward on the 03 level, received the message and redirected it to SupPlot's printer. Located amidship on the 03 level, SupPlot was close to the CIC and next door to the TFCC. In addition to the teleprinter, SupPlot contained an OpsComm teletype circuit connected to FOSIC

Norfolk. Across from the teletype in the small compartment were an NTDS terminal, an ECLIPS, and the Outlaw Shark system.

The red light on the OpsComm teletype circuit switched on, indicating an incoming message. The teletype, louder and faster than the teleprinter, banged out "cip," shorthand for "come in, please." The watch at FOSIC Norfolk wanted to pass information to *America*'s SupPlot watch officer. *America* was in the Atlantic, just east of Bermuda, and en route to the Mediterranean Sea for her 1979 deployment. The SupPlot watch officer, an intelligence officer (1630) in the rank of ensign, responded with "ga," shorthand for "go ahead." The OpsComm circuit light switched red. The teletype quickly banged out the message: INDICATIONS: TWO SOVIET TU-142/95 BEAR-F HEADING *AMERICA*'S WAY. The ensign took two strides across the fifteen-by-ten-foot SupPlot to the map board mounted on the bulkhead. Curling two fingers and his thumb, he extended his pinky and forefinger, making a simple divider to measure distance on the map. Walking his fleshy divider from the Kola Peninsula to *America*'s position showed that the Bear-F could be overhead *America* around 0900 that morning. The ensign typed a few questions about the source of the indications on the OpsComm teletype. He received the shorthand response "w81," or "wait one," as the distant end gathered information. "GROUND CONTROL INTERCEPT (GCI) COMMUNICATION AND ELECTRONIC EMISSIONS FROM THE ONBOARD RPB-3 TUCHA WEATHER RADAR" banged in response. The ensign signed off and moved to ECLIPS.[23]

ECLIPS lacked any correlation tools; it displayed a classified-secret common-intelligence picture (CIP) derived from the LINK 14, Rainform Red messages, and manual track inputs from the watch officer. Unlike the NTDS, which displayed contacts in relative terms from a designated link reference point (DLRP), both ECLIPS and Outlaw Shark displayed track positions in latitude and longitude. A 9TV camera mounted to the overhead broadcasted ECLIPS's cathode-ray tube screen, showing the plot to twenty-five outstations throughout *America*. To help NTDS operators determine relative bearing and range, the CIP placed *America* in the center of the display, with range rings out every one hundred nautical miles. The primary intelligence plot was still maintained on charts mounted on large sliding metal boards affixed to the bulkhead; no one trusted that the ECLIPS computer would not crash.[24] With ECLIPS updated, the ensign reached for the secure internal-communication circuit, the 12MC's black handset mounted on the bulkhead nearby. He sanitized the warning intelligence, removing any indications of the source. Pressing the 12MC's chrome button labeled "CIC," he put the handset to his ear and mouth, depressing the handset's push-to-talk button as he spoke: "CIC, SupPlot. Indications of probable Soviet Bear overflight at approximately 0900, over." The sharp response: "SupPlot, CIC, roger, we see your plot update on 9TV, out." Following a notification list taped to his desk, the ensign passed the Bear warning intelligence to other parts of the battlegroup's command-and-control structure. F-14 Tomcat and E-2 Hawkeye alert postures increased. The intercept of the Bears occurred flawlessly later that morning.[25]

SupPlot's primary role was supporting the admiral's watch, located next door. The ensign sometimes passed warning intelligence in person to the admiral's watch officer in the TFCC. Since the ensign maintained the CIP supporting the TFCC, the personal interaction built rapport. The ensign stepped past the other SupPlot watch stander, an intelligence specialist (IS) still waiting for the teleprinter to tap out the twenty-five-plus-page intelligence summary. Passing through a thick black security curtain, the ensign opened SupPlot's door and stepped over the lifted threshold into the small passageway. As the SupPlot door began to close, he opened the door to the TFCC, directly across from SupPlot, and stepped inside the compartment.[26]

America's TFCC was more than twice the size of its SupPlot, about thirty-by-twenty feet. The TFCC was not cleared for SCI material, but some watch standers were. SCI intelligence was passed verbally to cleared personnel. The ensign knelt and whispered the report to the TFCC's battle watch officer.[27] *America* was the third *Forrestal*-class aircraft carrier reconfigured in 1978 with a version of the TFCC and its supporting SupPlot. *Kitty Hawk* and *Kennedy* were the first ships in the Outlaw Hawk demonstrations, which spanned from 1975 to 1977. *America*'s TFCC had critical communication improvements to its HF, UHF, and VHF secure voice and data systems. The NTDS in the CIC and TFCC were upgraded, solving lost-data problems and improving their digital displays.[28] A secure radio terminal was connected to the fleet satellite-communication system (FLTSATCOM), assuring data and voice services across the distributed battlegroup.[29] Unfortunately the large-screen display and networked command-center equipment were still developing. Even incomplete the installation of the TFCC and SupPlot legitimized the CWC concept. In the TFCC the admiral had a tactical picture (NTDS), a theater CIP broadcast over the secure closed-circuit television system (9TV), and secure communications with his warfare commanders—the realization of the "two-squares of linoleum" C2 concept.

Shark, Aircraft Carriers, and New Correlation Tools

America's Outlaw Shark terminal was developmental. Congress demanded that the Navy present a feasible plan to solve the over-the-horizon targeting problem or lose its TASM funding. The Shark demonstrations accelerated and expanded as a result. *America*'s Shark terminal was a holdover system from "CNO Project 310–1, Over-the-Horizon Targeting Concept Demonstrations" conducted in 1977 and 1978.[30] Capt. Lynn Wessman, USN (Ret.), Outlaw Shark project lead (1977–1979) for commander, Submarine Group Eight (COMSUBGRU 8), wrote that using *America* was an obvious continuation of the demonstration. Integrating new Shark technology beyond the submarine community into the TFCC and CWC was an outgrowth of Project 310–1.[31]

Wessman noted that Shark's computers automated the manual plot using processes demonstrated by the Outlaw Hawk project. Outlaw Hawk sparked the Naval Command and Control System (NCCS) creation effort, and Shark added to it. The NCCS drove the attempt to baseline OSIS computer and communications systems with standard equipment. Technology improved so quickly that baseline installations were immediately obsolete. Nothing was a baseline because it constantly evolved. It was not until 1977 that there was enough stability that a semblance of a baseline existed. The baseline was at least enough to embark on the first in a series of codified OSIS-node system upgrades.[32] However incomplete, the upgrades helped with the flood of information from new space-based systems. FOSIF Rota, for example, received electronic intelligence (ELINT) collection from the latest "Classic Wizard" satellite system and other global terrestrial collection systems. Wizard was reportedly "capable of detecting signals from a ship's radar up to 2,000 miles (3,200 kilometers) away," allowing radar-system classification.[33] Thousands of satellite collection "hits" were processed and correlated daily to make Wizard useful.

NCCS improvements and the Shark demonstrations occurred in parallel, each developing new technological applications that improved the other. Electronic and computer improvements came "hot and fresh" from informal and formal efforts. The Outlaw Shark demonstrations used four nodes: a shore-based node located at COMSUBGRU-8 headquarters in Naples, Italy, a submarine node (an available submarine), a surface node (the cruiser USS *Josephus Daniels*) equipped with a "Classic Outboard" ELINT collection suite, and an air node (EP-3E aircraft, callsign *Ranger 25*). Airborne and surface collection by *Ranger 25* and the high-frequency direction finding (HFDF) Classic Outboard system on the cruiser, respectively, transmitted their collection over an HF link or UHF satellite communication (Gapfiller) simplex datalink to Naples. The duplex datalink between Rota and Naples, a landline connection, allowed Rota's intelligence data to pass to Outlaw Shark's plot-fusion center in Naples.[34]

Rainform pro forma human/machine-readable messages transmitted the track data for the system. Wessman recalls that Shark's data fields were more numerous than the human/machine-readable Rainform Red message. The Shark program's modification to Rainform Red became the foundation for the OTH-T Gold Rainform message format instituted in 1979.[35] ECLIPS could only digest track data in Link 14 and the standard Rainform Red message formats. To allow ECLIPS to read the new version of Red and then the Gold messages, the Shark's engineers helped rewrite its software.[36]

There is little unclassified archival information to describe the Rota-to-Naples datalink or its interaction with the Shark program. Wessman recalled that the landline datalink from FOSIF Rota to the Shark system in Naples was "a full 75 baud teletype data link . . . [that] operated 24/7 even during non—[Outlaw Shark] test periods." The feed from FOSIF provided a "current 'Red Force' data picture in the COMSUBGRU-8 OPCON [operation control room]" driving the Shark's plot.[37] Not all FOSIF personnel knew they were supporting the Shark test. Nels Litsinger at FOSIF Rota recalled that support for Shark was not "transparent to the watch at FOSIF." There was no capability to "query" or "pull" data from Rota; all unit "locational data was kept in OSIS Baseline, and the watch could answer specific queries," but the plot itself was kept manually on a large map on the watch floor. Thus to Litsinger the intelligence summary messages were the only dissemination of unit data FOSIF released.[38]

The reality was that the Shark program was testing a bidirectional system where new OSIS baseline upgrades and OTH-T Gold message format would allow Rota to automatically push out timely "event-by-event" digital reporting to Naples. The link to Shark in Naples was full-duplex reporting. Thus Rota also received "event-by-event" reporting from the Shark system during the test periods, allowing them to update their manual plot.[39] The near-real-time aspect of the duplex information exchange between Rota and the Shark cell in Naples was significant.

In the spring of 1979 the Shark project further tested the datalink's capability. They deployed the Shark-equipped *Ranger 25* to observe a real-world Warsaw Pact naval exercise near the GIUK gap. While airborne, *Ranger 25* detected Warsaw Pact naval units (red), created unit tracks in Shark, and pushed those tracks via a SATCOM datalink to COMSUBGRU-8 in Naples. The tracks went to Rota via the duplex landline datalink and then from Rota to FOSIC Norfolk via another satellite-communications OSIS datalink. Within minutes of the unit's detection Navy leadership in Norfolk saw tracks of those detected units almost in real time.[40]

Through versions of OP-094 in the 1980s, the Navy continued to evolve its command-support duplex-data networks and improve the FLTSATCOM. It created duplex data and voice links, called the Officer in Tactical Command Information Exchange System (OTCIXS), and its surveillance- and targeting-information subsystem, the Tactical

Data Exchange System (TADIX), between shore command centers and shipboard TFCC/SupPlot. A tactical-intelligence datalink, TACINTEL, allowed SCI data exchanges between OSIS nodes and shipboard SupPlots in the 1980s.[41]

The similarities in concept between Outlaw Shark and the Air Force's Vietnam War IronHorse air-battle management system are inescapable. Both sought to fuse all- or multisource intelligence into a common, shareable picture. Shark used all-source system information, including space-based, while IronHorse was more multisource SIGINT from airborne collection systems. By 1977 computer technology had advanced, making the version of the CP-818 used in IronHorse obsolete. Shark used smaller, commercial-off-the-shelf (COTS) computers for development and testing. The software was eventually integrated into the ruggedized mini-computer ROLM-1602, designated AN/UYK-19(V), and integrated into the AN/USQ-81(V), the designator given to the production version of the Shark computer system.[42]

Correlation Tools

A poster of a large, ominous, teeth-baring great white shark was taped to the Shark Fusion Room's door. The hull number of the current Outlaw Shark–equipped submarine was written on its dorsal fin. The words "OUTLAW SHARK . . . is a mean mutha!" were printed in bold black letters around the shark's outline. Inside the fusion room an operator sat at a Shark terminal. The terminal was commercial hardware—two "Tektronix CRT displays with a dark-green background . . . the landmass and contacts drawn . . . in a lighter green color," Wessman wrote.[43] The operator used a joystick to position the cursor over the track representing the vessel or aircraft. She clicked a button to select or "hook" the track. The hooked track's information was displayed in four orange-colored alpha-numeric lines, giving its position and description. The data was in two categories: location and classification. The location data was shown in "data fields," or categories, and included the unit's name, its hull number, its platform type (air, surface, subsurface), its position (in latitude and longitude), the time of the position, the unit's course, and its speed.[44]

The tracks were oriented on the screen to give the operator a spatial understanding of the physical operating environment. The track's classification came from the collection source: visual, radar, sonar, shore-based HFDF (Classic Bullseye), ship-based HFDF (Classic Outboard), or Classic Wizard. Each source provided further details. For example, visually identified units reported through a locator message included a description of the vessel or its activity in the four-line "free text" field. Radar-identified units might include the NTDS track number or the platform that held radar contact on the unit. HFDF and Wizard provided electromagnetic spectrum data like the frequency, PRF (pulse repetition frequency), and PRI (pulse repetition interval) of the signal collected. HFDF and Wizard reports provided the area of uncertainty (AOU) for the detected unit's location.[45]

The operator sitting at the Shark's analysis terminal looked at the screen. Of the fifteen tracks displayed, five were ambiguities. When new track data arrived, the system used an algorithm to correlate it against current tracks. The automated correlation was better than IronHorse's, which had sought only to reject "clutter" and identify incomplete tracks for review. The Shark algorithm weighted the data fields; the platform's name and hull number carried a heavier algorithmic weight. It correlated and automatically merged new data into an existing track. For example, if the update provided new location coordinates, the track moved to its new location. The system automatically created a new platform or ambiguity track if the data could not be correlated. The operator intervened, applying analysis to reconcile the plot's tracks, but the automation made the process much quicker.[46]

The datalink from FOSIF Rota was at the SCI classification level. Only the Shark Fusion Room received the SCI data. Though the Shark in *America* was in the SCI-cleared SupPlot, it and the other deployed systems received a classified-secret Shark feed. To release track updates at the secret level, the operator manually reviewed each track's data and sanitized anything classified above secret using the "sanitizer" computer console. Once reviewed and cleared, the track update entered a transmit queue.[47]

The operator took a last look at the Shark's plot and then the transmit queue. Twelve tracks were ready for release to the other Shark systems, ten previous tracks with three new correlations, and two new tracks. She created a new platform track, labeling it "MSG 21." Shark was a data-only system; there were no voice circuits. The operators used the four free-text lines in a "dummy track"—in this case MSG 21—to pass "shorthand" notes developed from OpsComm circuit communication. She typed, "Shipshark, Oldshark, and Airshark, 21st update time 0430Z. Have a gr8 Navy day. SheShark out." SheShark, the operator, was a female lieutenant (1100 designator, nonwarfare-qualified line officer) on loan from Naples' Telecommunications Station. She addressed the Sharks on the cruiser (ShipShark), submarine (OldShark), and *Ranger 25* (AirShark). SheShark sanitized the MSG 21 dummy track and added it to the transmit queue. She chuckled; whenever a Shark-equipped platform arrived in Naples, someone would come to COMSUBGRU-8's headquarters trying to meet SheShark.[48]

PHOTO 11.2

"SheShark," Cdr. Laurel Hargan-Wessman, USN (Ret.), then a lieutenant, sits at an Outlaw Shark computer terminal. Another Outlaw Shark analyst is working at another terminal to her left. Naples, Italy, 1978. COURTESY OF LYNN WESSMAN

Outlaw Shark had weapons-targeting and -tracking correlation algorithms. It could generate a "predicted area of uncertainty" for target and nontarget tracks. A separate system, the TASM route-planning program, helped the fire-control operator select waypoints for the missile's flight path that would avoid nontargets (e.g., "white" merchant shipping) identified by the Shark system. The TASM route brought the weapon to a place where it could guide onto the target.[49] A missile time-on-target was sent to the designated firing platforms synchronizing the attack. Using Shark information to help develop the TASM's flight path from each firing platform, positioned at different ranges and bearings, helped to deliver their weapons onto the target simultaneously.[50] No missile launch occurred during the demonstrations in 1977 and 1978, but Shark performed well in attack simulations. The commander, Naval Forces Europe, saw Shark as "the best effort to date to provide the capability to transmit, correlate, and evaluate sensor data quickly enough to provide the complete surface picture" required for over-the-horizon targeting (OTH-T) decisions.[51]

A "best effort" was not good enough. Exercises in the 1980s using the AN/USQ-81(V) and MK-117 fire-control system developed by Shark showed only a 12 percent TASM accuracy. Out of all simulated firings, 38 percent hit other enemy ships; 6 percent hit white shipping; the rest, 54 percent, missed their assigned targets altogether. There was a lack of confidence in the system. Data lag, up to sixty minutes, was a problem. Commanders questioned the accuracy of the combined intelligence and operations picture and what exactly they were shooting at.[52] More development went into the USQ-81(V), incorporating it into a Common Weapons Control System (CWCS). The Tactical Data Information Exchange System-Broadcast (TADIXS-B) was also developed. In the late 1980s and 1990s, TADIXS was replaced with Tactical Receive Equipment (TRE) and related Applications (TRAP) broadcasts. No TASMs were ever fired in combat, and after the Soviet Union collapsed they were pulled from the inventory.[53]

Outlaw Shark's fusion and track-management processes became a standard approach to creating and maintaining a CIP for the Opintel community. The Outlaw demonstrations reinforced the benefit of timely all-source fusion collocated with the commander at sea. The operator's belief that targeting-quality data could be sent directly from the "sensor to shooter" without fusion analysis was questioned. Consequently SupPlot solidified the importance of Opintel's tactical-decision support and warning role. Over the next few years, technological improvement and Vice Adm. Jerry O. Tuttle's initiative made the Outlaw Shark–type operational picture a reality throughout the fleet.

As a captain, Vice Admiral Tuttle was the aircraft carrier *John F. Kennedy*'s commanding officer from 1977 to 1978. In 1979 Tuttle, now assistant director, Plans and Policies, DIA, returned to *Kennedy* to observe operations.[54] *Kennedy* had been equipped with the second TFCC and SupPlot installation and had conducted the Outlaw Hawk TFCC demonstrations in 1976.[55] Tuttle likely deployed with ECLIPS as *Kennedy*'s commanding officer. He had a vision of a shared COP that incorporated the best technologies he'd encountered during his time in *Kennedy* and at the DIA. In 1981 Tuttle, now a rear admiral in command of Carrier Group Eight (COMCARGRU EIGHT), was on the ECLIPS-equipped USS *Eisenhower*—"Ike"—during the Ocean Venture '81 exercises. He saw the art of the possible and put his energy into making an integrated shared operational picture a reality. Tuttle used AIRLANT funds to purchase HP commercial computers, creating the Joint Operations Tactical System (JOTS).[56]

Tested during wargames at the Naval War College in 1982, JOTS combined tactical-decision aids and tactical-search and -surveillance displays. AIRLANT made JOTS a program of record in 1982. The distribution of stand-alone systems to every aircraft carrier battlegroup began in 1983. The officer in Tactical Command Information Exchange System (OTCIXS) and the Tactical Data Information Exchange Subsystem (TADIXS) datalinks improved the JOTS-supported COP and the CWC concept. Shipboard Opintel continued to improve its fusion analysis, broadening the CIP-to-COP linkage into a theater-wide visualization displayed using JOTS.[57] A commander never needed to leave those "two squares of linoleum" to activate the force.

CHAPTER 12
A Period of Evolution

When asked how vital SupPlot was to Opintel, former DNI Vice Adm. Lowell "Jake" Jacoby wrote, "The power of the direct feeds and visualization capabilities provided by the automated displays were clear. They enhanced [the] flow of information . . . to the BG [battlegroup] command and control space."[1] Because SupPlot was a SCIF, it had special intelligence data feeds and all-source fusion. Access to the highly classified intelligence in the compartment next door allowed real-time integration into the battlegroup C2. SupPlot, Jacoby wrote, "was where I went for information, and it was basically my 'battle station.'" SupPlot's engagement with the admiral in the TFCC became routine, he noted. The "near real-time injection of intelligence under the supervision of the N-2 made intel much more relevant and integral to BG [battlegroup] operations and decision making."[2] OSIS had decentralized national intelligence, bringing it to the Navy's operational fleets. SupPlot decentralized OSIS and brought it to the battlegroup's flagship, the aircraft carrier.

ECLIPS and Outlaw Shark were revolutionary sparks that drew the shore-based OSIS nodes closer to shipboard Opintel. The vision of shipboard OSIS had always been clear. The evolutionary path to formalized shipboard OSIS-like tactical-decision support was a matter of technology and time. The two characteristics of Opintel, the air intelligence mission and the tracking of enemy units, merged into tactical-decision support—Opintel at sea. However, the Navy's speed of evolutionary change, how it crewed, trained, and equipped for new performance orientations, was always plodding. The increased speed of computer-driven military affairs made the Navy's formal adaptation processes seem almost glacial. Formal changes would have to catch up later. SupPlot created shipboard Opintel as we know it today, and it embedded and reinforced an Opintel identity for the Navy Intelligence organization. As with most revelational technological applications in ships, the following evolution is never straightforward. SupPlot was an enabling constraint for the organization, but all the Navy's aircraft carriers and command ships required alterations. There was neither "white space" in the fleet's deployment schedule nor in the shipyard's capacity to alter the entire fleet simultaneously. Each ship had to wait for alteration, but that did not mean the afloat commanders would. The Opintel professionals would find a way to meet their commander's intelligence demands.

Leveraging Evolvability, Provisional Measures

In 1981, when Rear Adm. Jerry Tuttle launched the "Ike" battlegroup's part of the Ocean Venture exercise, he was in Ike's combat information center (CIC), not a TFCC.[3] Ike, recalled Capt. Nels Litsinger, USN (Ret.), did not yet have the formal TFCC or the SupPlot ship alteration. Instead Ike had created informal versions of the TFCC and SupPlot.[4] The USS *Nimitz*, like Ike, also lacked the TFCC alteration. "Flag Plot," a small conference room outside the CIC, was a provisional TFCC for both ships. Inside the CIC a high-backed bridge chair was placed on a slightly raised platform and an NTDS consul embodied the admiral's C2 over the battlegroup, his "two squares of linoleum." Capt. Paul Lasko, USN (Ret.), the N2 and Flag's watch officer in *Nimitz*'s 1979 deployment, recalled in 2020 that while on watch he sat in the admiral's chair or at the NTDS terminal monitoring battlegroup operations. When the admiral entered the CIC, the Flag's watch officer quickly exited the admiral's chair! The Flag watch's role was to ensure the battlegroup followed the day's plan. Permission from the officer in tactical command (OTC), the Flag, to execute battlegroup events, such as flight operations, was requested and approved by the Flag through the watch officer.[5] However, without the dedicated TFCC, the Flag's watch officer did not really "fight the battlegroup" as the tactical action officer (TAO) did for the ship.

Aircraft carriers lacking the SupPlot/TFCC ship alteration (ShipAlt) created informal versions of SupPlot. The *Nimitz*-class were more fortunate than the *Forrestal*-class aircraft carriers. The *Nimitz*-class SSES was moved aft from the bow to amidship, closer to the CIC. On Ike, Litsinger recalled that his predecessor had carved out a SupPlot-like compartment around 1979 or early 1980. The compartment, called a tactical analysis plot (TAP) by Ike, was inside the Multi-sensor Interpretation (MSI) work center within CVIC. Though small the TAP had the same capability and layout as the ShipAlt-installed SupPlot on *America*. The TAP's ECLIPS, however, lacked a direct communications circuit. Ike's communications officer strictly interpreted the strictures against connecting commercial computers, which ECLIPS technically was, to classified circuits. Without ECLIPS's automatic updates, manual plotting using magnetic pucks placed on bulkhead-mounted charts was faster. The TAP's watch team resembled a smaller version of an OSIS node's team because Litsinger had been a FOSIF Rota watch officer before arriving in Ike.[6]

The "Indy," USS *Independence* (*Forrestal* class), provides another example of an informal SupPlot. Cdr. Tom Terlizzi, USN (Ret.), a SupPlot watch officer in 1979, noted that Indy had yet to receive the TFCC ShipAlt. So the ship's workforce converted a small ten-by-twelve-foot storeroom next to Flag Plot into an ad hoc SupPlot. Indy's SupPlot had an ECLIPS with a printer and an NTDS terminal. The manual-intelligence plot was on the bulkhead with its charts and magnetic pucks. ECLIPS, Terlizzi recalled, sounded with a *ding*, alerting the watch when a message containing a report of a Soviet Navy combatant arrived. He could open a nonwatertight door (NWTD) between the SupPlot and Flag Plot and pass the Flag's watch information on any critical contact, just like *America*'s SupPlot discussed earlier.[7]

Terlizzi wrote that Indy's SupPlot was a "baby step" and did not have the full capability of the ShipAlt versions. It was "a simple SI-level [SCI] plot." Less fusion analysis occurred because SupPlot lacked a circuit to receive reports or an OpsComm teletype to communicate with OSIS node analysts. It was probably for the best that Indy had a limited SupPlot, Terlizzi offered; its watchstanders lacked the experience to interpret the SCI intelligence materials. "We were a relatively junior, eager group," he wrote; "there was a clear lack of leadership to develop our understanding of how we [SupPlot] fit into the whole [battlegroup operations] picture."[8]

Across the fleet, aircraft carriers implemented Opintel for tactical-decision support informally and in the best way possible. Aircraft carrier intelligence staffing was not changing as quickly as the performance orientation. Formal and informal SupPlots were crewed "out of hide" from the existing billet structure.[9] For example, Rear Adm. Tony Cothron, USN (Ret.), then an ensign standing the nightshift SupPlot watch in *America*, was billeted to the aircraft carrier as the subsystem photographic interpretation (PI) officer.[10] There were no shipboard billets for SupPlot watches.

Aircraft carriers' OZ Divisions still used the Integrated Operational Intelligence Center (IOIC) workforce structure to crew CVIC. The 1979 *Intelligence Newsletter* shows *Forrestal-* and *Kitty Hawk*–class ships and the *Enterprise* had six intelligence officers (163x) holding the billets of intelligence officer, assistant intelligence officer, storage and retrieval officer, subsystem PI, subsystem electronic evaluator (EE), and electronic warfare officer. The new *Nimitz*-class had four 163x officers in the billets: an intelligence officer, a storage and retrieval officer, a photographic intelligence officer, and an electronic warfare officer.[11] Aircraft carrier cruise books from 1978 through 1980 show that each carrier, despite class, had between twenty and twenty-five enlisted. Most OZ Division enlisted personnel were intelligence specialists (IS). Two or three data processingmen (DP), one or two draftsmen (DM), and a yeoman (YN) were also assigned.

The extra personnel assigned during the Vietnam War were gone. Cruise books of the time give the impression that the formal OZ Division staffing had changed little in size since the early 1960s. However, the reality was that the aircraft carriers never had a full personnel complement in the 1970s. CVICs were chronically understaffed across the fleet. Litsinger recalled that while Ike's staffing document called for twenty-nine ISes, he never had more than nineteen onboard. Despite the staff shortage, "standing TAP watch eventually became a perk for the IS," he noted. For the officers, on the other hand, "TAP became double duty . . . [and] a burden on them."[12] Whether seen as a perk or burden, standing SupPlot watch was "personally enriching" and enhanced the officer and enlisted members' promotion chances.

The junior officers and enlisted watch personnel had little to no experience in that character of Opintel work. Navy Intelligence, working toward but still unable to find a suitable replacement, continued accession-level training at the Air Force's Air Intelligence Training Center (AFAITC) in Colorado. AFAITC's training had improved, but the 1973 assessment of its inadequacy for the Navy still rang true in 1979. "The geo-location on an Air Force base [in Colorado] made no naval sense," note Capt. Richard Noble, USN (Ret.), a former Navy AFAITC commanding officer. "The Air Force had no interest in submarine warfare or the surface navy. They evinced no interest in naval air," he wrote in 2020.[13] Opintel's focus on supporting CWC tactical decisions was not part of the AFAITC curriculum.

Informal training took place on the ships to fill the tactical-decision support and warning-intelligence tradecraft deficiencies. OSIS node veterans provided reciprocating influence, teaching new SupPlot watch officers and enlisted watchstanders OSIS tradecraft. "There was no 'textbook,'" Litsinger wrote. He used his experience at FOSIF Rota to teach TAP watchstanders the basics: plotting, scanning message traffic, compiling items of interest, and writing intelligence summaries. The human-machine-formatted intelligence messages were complex. The ship's cryptologist, the OS division officer, provided necessary signals intelligence (SIGINT) training to help TAP watchstanders understand the messages because they needed to "understand the [SIGINT] data and where it came from." ECLIPS provided some data-management functions. It stored, recalled, and displayed a unit's track history, crudely mimicking the track-management functions seen in Outlaw Shark.[14]

For tactical-decision support Opintel needed to be relevant to the commander and timely. "We used General Quarters drills as training sessions," Litsinger wrote. During the ship's combat-training exercises they found opportunities to practice tactical-decision support. As much as the TAP needed training, so did its customers. Litsinger noted that he held training sessions with the ship's TAOs because "we wanted them to understand what [intelligence] was being passed over the 12MC and to have trust in the data." Litsinger had success with his broad approach to training Opintel and its customers. "It got to the point," he wrote, "where the TAOs were stopping by TAP for an update prior to going on watch in CIC."[15]

Like at FOSIF Rota, all cleared shipboard Opintel personnel read the message boards and the Read Book and reviewed the CIP's status. Both in knowledge and Opintel proficiency the competition seen at OSIS nodes emerged on the ship. "Steel sharpened steel" for shipboard Opintel as well.

The on-the-job (OJT) approach to training SupPlot watchstanders was hit or miss. On Indy in 1979 Terlizzi lacked a ship's intelligence officer (SIO) with Litsinger's OSIS background. "The JO's [junior officers] recognized we had two in a row weak [S]IO's—nice guys, but [they] never really 'taught' us anything," Terlizzi lamented. He did attend a weeklong ECLIPS class before his deployment; however, the course never discussed Opintel fusion analysis, instead focusing on maintaining the system. Once underway a technician came aboard to groom the system, making it operational. The formal training was "pretty weak stuff," Terlizzi wrote. Only when the Flag N2, Capt. Paul Lasko, embarked did Terlizzi receive any contextual Opintel-analysis training. Lasko "showed us how ECLIPS could be a good tool for getting a heads up on Bears [TU-95/142], etc.," Terlizzi wrote.[16] SupPlot training eventually became formalized through schoolhouse-provided Opintel fusion-analysis tradecraft training.

In June 1981 Navy Intelligence created a formal two-phase, four-week OSIS/SupPlot training pipeline. The enlisted intelligence specialist (IS) rate reinforced the OSIS/Opintel analysis-fusion specialty by assigning Naval enlisted codes (NEC) that classified training. ISes heading for shore-based OSIS nodes received the 3903 NEC after training. Some 3903s went to aircraft carrier SupPlots. The other character of Opintel, carrier-based strike warfare, also required further specialization. Thus the "carrier-based strike warfare Opintel analyst" 3902 NEC was a separate code with additional strike-mission-planning training. Those heading to Fleet command and control ships (LCC) or multipurpose amphibious landing ships (LHA) received the 3904 NEC and specialized training. An

OSIS baseline system installed at the Fleet Intelligence Training Center Atlantic (FITCLANT) in Norfolk, Virginia, was used for training. For ISes going to the aircraft carriers as strike-warfare analysts (3902 NEC), secure closed-circuit television (SCCTV, 9TV) and the new mission-briefing systems (MBS) operator's course completed their pipeline training. All ISes received Naval Intelligence Processing System (NIPS) operator training as part of the intelligence specialists' (IS) primary A-schooling.[17]

Intelligence officer training included limited OSIS fusion-analysis elements at AFAITC in 1981. In general, however, little formal all-source fusion-analysis training was available to them. Depending upon the shipboard billet assigned after AFAITC, specialized training occurred en route to their follow-on command. No specialized training in fusion analysis existed since no designated SupPlot billets existed. Officers learned any tactical-decision support Opintel OJT from those senior officers with experience.

Midgrade intelligence officers with academic qualifications and better-than-average performance records might be screened for postgraduate education. The education slots were few—a total of twenty-two in 1979. In Washington, D.C., the Defense Intelligence School provided the most opportunity, offering five degrees, two of which focused on intelligence-analysis tradecraft. The Naval Postgraduate School in Monterey, California, provided degrees in Naval intelligence programs, computer systems management, and international relations. The Naval War College and National War College provided opportunities for senior intelligence officers to pursue professional military education with their line counterparts. By 1980 a midcareer Naval intelligence training program (MNITP) was added to help midgrade officers, senior enlisted, and civilians gain critical insight into operational intelligence's changing landscape.[18]

Automating Strike-Mission Planning

Strike-mission planning had not changed much since the Vietnam War. It was time-consuming and cumbersome; it lacked the tactical agility that quick-response strikes required. Operational factors of time, timing, space, and workforce constrained and restrained strike-mission planning.

Fuel was always a primary planning concern. Incomplete target analysis occurred in CVIC, and targets not contained in the *Basic Encyclopedia* or NIPS were described vaguely. Air-defense systems protecting targets are depicted more in possibilities than probabilities. Ingress and egress route planning was often heuristic, and comparing alternate routes and strike-force composition options was difficult. Therefore the limited planning time resulted in settling on a strategy that was unlikely to yield the best outcomes.[19]

The air wing planned strike missions using paper charts. The pilots flew with strips of paper charts, showing the ingress and egress route waypoints fastened to a small board, a "kneeboard," strapped to their thigh. The Mission Planning work center in CVIC maintained thousands of paper charts. After all, an aircraft carrier could deploy anywhere with little notice. CVIC's chart vaults were unventilated storerooms outside CVIC in the 02- or 03-level outboard areas. In Indy the chart vault was under the portside waist catapults. The ISes kept the charts updated, hand-marking any changes or additions. Maintaining the charts was a heavy burden made more difficult by the "off-gassing [of] very toxic, eye-burning fumes" from the decomposing charts into the unventilated storerooms.[20]

Air wing–strike planning was ripe for computerization. In 1974 development began on computer-based decision and strike-planning aids. One of the first decision aids, the Air Strike Timing Decision Aid (ASTDA), used Monte Carlo simulation models to identify uncertainties for air-to-air, air-to-ground, and ground-to-air engagements. ASTDA helped planners decide on mission-aircraft composition.[21] Another aid, the Air Strike Outcome Calculator (ASOC), helped planners consider strike-package and weapons-composition options to meet the desired mission outcome. A route-planning tool, the Route Planning Aid, compared possible ingress and egress routes, aiding in choosing the most effective and least risky route.[22] All the decision aids required input from CVIC's Opintel team regarding the adversary and the targets.

The computer power of NIPS ran some air wing mission–planning aids. In 1976 *Kennedy*'s CVIC received the Compartmented Mode Processing System (CMPS). It modified NIPS's Storage and Retrieval subsystem, providing a shared computer system for target intelligence, mission planning, electronic evaluation, and SSES functions. The CMPS also integrated the EA-6B Prowler's Aircraft Electronic Intelligence Mission Data Processing Subsystem.[23] The Harpoon and Tomahawk missiles' automated air mission–planning tools were developed in parallel to air wing decision-aid development. The Theater Mission Planning System (TMPS) was shore-based and created Tomahawk attack-route packages for the missile's onboard computer-navigation system. These packages included route details like speed changes, turns, climbs and dives, and navigational waypoints to the target.[24] The utility of the TMPS for aircraft carrier strike planning was evident. By the mid-1980s CVICs had the Tactical Automated Mission Planning System (TAMPS), significantly improving time-sensitive strike-planning capability.[25] TAMPS also printed out mission-specific maps and kneeboard cards. The ISes still had to maintain charts, but the digital maps in TAMPS helped reduce the number of paper charts required.

Access to national imagery, particularly space-based collection, was missing from shipboard Opintel fusion analysis. Time-sensitive strike-mission planning against ad hoc targets was especially disadvantaged. During the Vietnam War, Navy Fleet Intelligence Centers (FICs) had used national and tactical imagery to build strike-target folders. The folders were then flown out to the aircraft carriers in the Gulf of Tonkin. The process was slow. Restrikes on targets used poststrike, bomb-hit, and damage imagery from air wing–reconnaissance assets.[26] North American Rockwell tested an imagery-transmission system between the Integrated Operational Intelligence Centers (IOIC) and the FIC in Pearl Harbor, Hawai'i. Rockwell IOIC contract manager Nolan Leatherman said the image-transmission capability was "the next step" in strike mission–planning support. "We had only one system at Pearl," he recalled; "there was talk of putting one in Italy or somewhere in the Mediterranean," but the contract never supported the expansion.[27]

The Fleet Intelligence Center Europe-Atlantic (FICEURLANT) was one of five theater sites receiving national imagery. FIC's imagery teams were part of a federated process and "read out" or analyzed the imagery pertinent to their theater of operations. An initial photographic interpretation report (IPIR) focusing on air and naval order-of-battle details was sent to the fleet within two hours of the image download.[28] The IPIR was important, but strike-mission planning and target analysis required the actual image to determine the type of ordinance and the desired mean point of impact (DMPI) to achieve the specific damage. Building on earlier work, CVICs began receiving Fleet Imagery Support Terminals (FIST) in 1979. FIST allowed FICs to "fax an image (slow line scan) of a target photo to afloat units," recalled Terlizzi. "Very crude, but [it] improved timeliness."[29]

In 2017 Vic Socotra wrote that *Midway* had NIPS and FIST in 1979.[30] He lamented that neither had worked very well. FIST only worked "on the Admiral's privacy circuit, and if he wasn't using it at night, it may have been possible to get an image or two."[31] FIST helped; the system went through several upgrades during the 1980s. The problem with FIST had to do more with its reproduction capabilities; there was a significant loss of detail. According to a 1984 CIA review, the hard-copy printout of the image was poor.[32] Like the IOIC's stereo comparison viewers (SCVs), FIST's limitations created acrimony. "When I got to USS *Coronado* (AGF-11), they still had a FIST (Fleet Imagery Support terminal) onboard. I told them to throw it over the side," Socotra wrote.[33] However, not everyone felt the same way. "I do not share JR's [Vic Socotra] low opinion of FIST," wrote Litsinger; the FIST in Ike in 1981 had allowed him to meet Rear Admiral Tuttle's tremendous appetite for all relevant national imagery. "It took an average of 9 minutes to send or receive an image," Litsinger later recalled, good enough to keep Tuttle satisfied.[34]

Flag Staff's Intelligence Demands Grow

Capt. Paul Lasko, recalling the importance of SupPlot to the admiral and his staff, offered that CVIC is where he as N2 went for "archival information, historical information, or stuff like that—pictures of stuff." If he needed to know where the Soviets were and what they were doing, "we'd go to SupPlot, or we'd go to SSES."[35] SupPlot's location next to the TFCC reinforced its importance to the senior decision-maker. Even so SupPlot was "owned and operated" by the ship's Opintel organization, not the Flag officer's. The demand signal of the aircraft carrier's commanding officer had primacy. The Flag officer and staff generally used the output from CVIC as it was. The N2 had some communication access, through SSES, to shore-based SCI analysis, as did SIO. Now, however, the N2 spent more time in SupPlot than had ever been necessary in CVIC. As the Flag's demands on SupPlot grew, so did the friction. The N2 presented demand signals but provided no staffing support. The afloat Opintel organizational culture, now in its second decade, bristled at what they saw as stakeholder interference in the long-standing ways. Inevitably the question arose, *Who does SupPlot work for?*

SupPlot's dilemma is common in changing organizations. Seth Rosenbloom and Michelle J. Markus offered three mechanisms at work-during-change events: force coercion, rational persuasion, and shared power. Forced coercion is most common in the military. The N2, close to the senior leader, uses power distance to influence and, if needed, threats to coerce SIO. In the rational-persuasion approach the N2 might wield expertise or experience as a form of persuasion. Rosenbloom and Markus offer that the shared-power approach is the least-successful tool in the hierarchical military because it involves the stakeholders in planning and implementing change. For Navy intelligence officers the standard career path and small organizational size make the shared-power mechanism effective.[36]

"Ownership" of SupPlot is complicated, and in the struggle to tailor SupPlot's mission all three change mechanisms occurred. Because of each aircraft carrier and battlegroup staff's individuality, SupPlot's ownership was litigated repeatedly at the start of each battlegroup training cycle. The organizational structure was shaped through trial and error during exercises and operations until it matched the battlegroup's organizational character.

By 1979 two aircraft carrier battlegroup staffs had emerged: the carrier group (CARGRU) and the cruiser-destroyer group (CRUDESGRU). A naval aviator and a surface warfare officer (SWO) led the carrier group and the cruiser-destroyer group. The cruiser-destroyer group was an offshoot of the new SWO designation. The criticality of distributed lethality in defense of the battlegroup increased awareness of the importance of surface combatants. CNO Admiral Zumwalt, a surface line officer, institutionalized the surface line's place in the Navy by creating a distinct community. As was common in the aviation and submarine communities, Zumwalt used a warfare pin as an artifact of the SWO's identity. To increase the new community's influence, it needed command of the Navy's primary power projection and sea-control force, the aircraft carrier battlegroup. Zumwalt succeeded in placing the SWO-led cruiser-destroyer groups in command of aviation platforms. Aviators, however, still commanded the aircraft carriers themselves.[37]

CARGRU had additional intelligence staffing resources, which CRUDESGRU lacked. The CARGRU N2, a commander in rank, was given an assistant N2, a lieutenant commander, and one or two ISes. CRUDESGRU had an N2 and one or two ISes. The N2s tailored Opintel products, using analysis available in message traffic or SupPlot, to meet the Flag's staff needs. "You had to travel from Minsk to Pinsk," described Paul Lasko, N2 on the *Nimitz*, in seeking out the analysis for the Flag's staff. "I had a good relationship with the SIO," Lasko recalled; "he knew what his job was, and I knew what mine was." The two intelligence officers collaborated and cooperated to ensure each had success.[38]

Litsinger, SIO in Ike, took a more proactive approach. The TAP produced a daily "Read Book" that included tailored intelligence summaries and SCI intelligence messages of interest. The book was hand-carried by the TAP's enlisted watch personnel to the aircraft carrier commanding officer and the ship's operations officer. The Read Book pushed intelligence out to the decision-makers. The courier helped answer any questions or provide background on a report. Litsinger offered that carrying the Read Book was an opportunity for the IS to get face time with leadership, improving their chances for promotion.[39] The N2 took the TAP's Read Book to the cleared Flag's staff members and the admiral. The Read Book provided the N2 with a format and opportunity to pass along even more tailored analysis.

The late 1970s and 1980s saw more senior leaders gaining access to highly classified compartmented intelligence. The Navy's new Maritime

Strategy, founded on intelligence, made the importance of Opintel more apparent to those at sea; however, more access created more demands on SupPlot. The operators cared little about who controlled SupPlot if they received the intelligence they needed. The operator could always "choke" personalized intelligence out of intelligence officer. However, every Opintel practitioner had an opinion regarding who should control the flow of intelligence from SupPlot and SSES. Personalities and perspectives regarding execution of the CWC concept shaped the organizational environment. Each Flag had a different perspective. For example, "CARGRU EIGHT and CRUDESGRU TWO pretty much let the ship provide the [intelligence] support," Litsinger wrote of Opintel operations on Ike from 1981 to 1983. CARGRU SIX, however, "wanted to play a larger role in controlling the flow [of intelligence]."[40]

When a battlegroup entered the Mediterranean Sea, part of the Sixth Fleet staff became Combined Task Force 60 (CTF 60, also designated as CARGRU 6) and embarked on the aircraft carrier. CTF 60, Sixth Fleet's Battle Force, often displaced the original battlegroup staff, assuming all duties as the officer in tactical command (OTC).[41] CTF 60's position on shipboard Opintel operations revealed the differing views between the intelligence officers (163x) and cryptologic officers (161x).

A CTF 60 cryptologist (161x) proposed a "signals warfare coordinator" (SIWAC) concept in 1979. The SIWAC would control and coordinate all cryptologic support. The intelligence officers (163x) were concerned that such a position might "result in a bifurcated intelligence support stream and potentially confusing intelligence data," Litsinger recalls. CTF 60 believed otherwise and by 1982 had attempted to use force-coercion to implement control over all shipboard Opintel in Ike. Using a "Flagship Instruction," CTF 60's N2 attempted to wrest control of Opintel operations from Ike's SIO. "When CTF 60 came aboard . . . the [CTF 60] N2 insisted that CVIC [including the TAP] worked for him," Litsinger later recalled. The cryptologist (1610) attempted to "take control of SSES," even restricting the ship's company OS Division personnel's access to their work center, SSES.[42]

At Litsinger's behest Ike's commanding officer used a rational-persuasion argument with CTF 60's admiral to counter the forced coercion:

after an entire workup cycle and part of an Atlantic deployment, Ike had a smoothly working Opintel process, the commanding officer argued; attempting to segregate essential Opintel functions, including TAP and SSES, compromised the integrity of the tactical-decision support and warning intelligence needed to fight the ship and battlegroup. Ike's commanding officer won the argument, though the Flag's cryptologist insisted that when he was in the CIC "all SSES support go through him to the TAO." Litsinger wrote that since the TAP's reporting "still went to the TAO via 12MC" the compromise meant little change to Opintel's actual processes, "so we lived with it!"[43]

New technology, like the Prototype OSIS Terminal (POST) and Vice Admiral Tuttle's JOTS, emerged in the 1980s. The friction arose over who controlled the source feed through the tactical intelligence broadcast (TACINTEL) and where the CIP and COP were maintained.[44] In some cases N2s and SIOs used shared-power and rational-persuasion approaches. They collaborated to refine processes and products to create "one size" that suited most customers. The approach worked since the N2 and SIO were of the same rank and generally of the same experience. Still, some SIOs and N2s fought, often making the deployments painful for all Opintel team members. Those instances of deep friction seem to have been rare; cooperation, not competition, assured the most operational and professional success. As an N2 in the late 1980s, Vice Adm. Lowell Jacoby, like many N2s, chose to reduce tensions by only involving himself in Opintel lines of operations the Flag required, mainly SupPlot. The shared-power approach worked. "I spent little time in CVIC and did that consciously," Jacoby wrote. He "made sure that it was clear to all that the Ship's Intel Officer ran that [CVIC] operation in coordination and collaboration with the Air Wing AI [CAGAI]." Jacoby did not ignore the SIO and CAGAI but "drew on them for information about ship and air wing operations and planning, but it was purposefully infrequent and as required." His visits to CVIC were often "more social and to show that I still had interest [in CVIC operations]."[45]

The creation of SupPlot formalized shipboard Opintel's role of providing warning and decision support to the battlegroup. SupPlot was a revolutionary milestone brought about through the advancement of technology that increasingly improved the ability to access and fuse all-source intelligence into an intelligence picture. ECLIPS and Outlaw Shark, though not a realization of OSIS afloat, demonstrated that the vision of a shareable and continuously updated picture was possible. SupPlot and the TFCC concepts were proven so successful that all aircraft carriers would receive one. Starting with USS *Carl Vinson* in 1980, the *Nimitz*-class aircraft carriers modified their architecture to include a full SupPlot and TFCC. To this day all Navy large-deck amphibious ships and aircraft carriers have an expeditionary plot—ExPlot in the case of the former or a SupPlot in the latter—supporting a TFCC.

Organizationally, in the mid- to late 1970s, SupPlot added to shipboard Opintel's performance orientation, modifying the evolutionary path. At its core the changes to Opintel were about preparing for the possibility of supporting commanders in a war at sea with the Warsaw Pact navies; providing tactical-decision support, preventing surprise, and helping with OTH targeting required better education and training for the intelligence professionals afloat. Navy Intelligence began to improve in these areas, but the demands of SupPlot moved more quickly than the Navy's ponderous staffing, training, and equipping process. Shipboard changes occurred, and the existing billet structure was informally modified to crew the new performance orientation. Personnel were trained informally on the job by OSIS node veterans. The discovery learning used to meet the commander's Opintel demands was challenging, but the organization rose to it. In doing so shipboard Opintel infused Navy Intelligence with an Opintel organizational identity.

If Navy Intelligence was going to make a difference, it needed the operators to better understand the function of Opintel and those professionals conducting intelligence operations. As U.S. naval strategy took on a more aggressive hue, intelligence and shipboard Opintel took more prominent roles. The United States and NATO alliance navies hoped to apply pressure on the Warsaw Pact navies that increased deterrence and compliance mechanisms' effectiveness. The pressure came from operating "forward" into historically Soviet naval operating areas in the

Norwegian Sea and northern Pacific. But such operations risked creating an escalation spiral. Therefore strategic and operational levels of war intelligence had to help policymakers and afloat commanders better understand how the Soviets might act and had to warn them to anticipate reactions.[46] In the late 1970s a new understanding of the Soviet Navy's strategy emerged from a decade of technical-intelligence collection. It challenged assumptions used to design the Navy during the previous three decades. Navy Intelligence had to convince the operators of the validity of the latest assessments.

CHAPTER 13
"Selling" Opintel
Reinforcing and Embedding Mechanisms

Rear Adm. Bobby Ray Inman, USN (Ret.), recognized that OSIS's success and the evolution of shipboard Opintel created strategic, operational, and tactical opportunities. The opportunities reinforced the role of operational intelligence. There were more problems than opportunities when Inman took over as the DNI in 1974. He wrote a letter to the intelligence officer (163x) community soon after his promotion:

> We are rapidly approaching an extraordinarily difficult time ... when expected resources will be far short of clearly delineated requirements. We must and we will question every function now being performed, to ask "Why are we doing this?", and "What does it really support?" The finest effort by all of you will be essential to ensure that the resulting smalling intelligence effort will be the best possible, fully dedicated to and supporting of the operating forces.[1]

Navy Intelligence needed to remain relevant if it was to survive. The distrust descending upon the intelligence community (IC) worsened the situation. The Schlesinger Report, a series of *New York Times* articles, and the congressional-driven shakeup of the CIA had been damaging.[2]

Inman understood the inner workings of OpNav. He had been the first restricted line officer to be an executive assistant for the vice chief of Naval Operations, Adm. Maurice Weisner, in 1972.[3] The early 1970s were a reduced-resources environment, a "smalling" of the Navy. Inman's experience told him the "budgetary knives" would first cut things that did not sail or shoot. Navy Intelligence might be left with less funding when new operational concepts demanded more, not less, operational intelligence. He needed to "sell" the importance of Opintel to its Navy customer, the operators. He first embedded and reinforced the Opintel organizational identity using a talent-management approach. Then he showed the Navy's operators the necessity of Opintel to succeed in war at sea and at power projection in the competition against the Soviet Navy.

The talent-management tool that Inman planned to use leveraged the Navy organization's culture of competition that was decades old. The highest-performing intelligence officers represented the Opintel corporate brand. Inman paired the best with up-and-coming line flag officers. The approach "sold" the Opintel brand one flag officer at a time to the Navy. Inman controlled his talent-management and corporate-branding approach for eight years and continued to influence the approach for almost another decade. Inman built what *The Admirals' Advantage* describes as a "reservoir of operator trust and credibility" gained through Opintel professionals working "side by side" with operators.[4] Inman's approach paid off when it mattered most: convincing the U.S. Navy that the Soviet Navy was a defensive force. The change in the Soviet Navy's mission assessment was a seminal event and led to an effective "go forward" naval strategy that helped bring the Cold War to an end.

Creating Opintel Talent Management

In June 1974 Adm. James Holloway became Chief of Naval Operations. Three months later he selected Rear Admiral Inman as the forty-ninth DNI. Inman quickly focused on managing active-duty and reserve intelligence officers (1630 and 1635). In a 2020 interview Inman described his intelligence-officer management intent: put the best performers in front of the flag officers on their way up to dramatically increase the appreciation of the 1630 field.[5]

Inman understood that delivering intelligence to a commander is personal. The Opintel professional must interact directly with the customer. High-confidence-tailored Opintel builds legitimacy and trust. Being sophisticated with intelligence tradecraft and technical systems is essential. Understanding the tactics, techniques, and procedures the commander uses and being able to talk "red," the adversary, in context to "blue's" mission is vital. These qualities give the intelligence officer access to the commander's inner circle. That access and a close relationship with the commander is critical in the art of Opintel; it gives the gift of anticipation that separates the Opintel professional from other staff members. Inman needed to manage the talent of the Navy Intelligence and position officers to access the commander's inner circle.

To achieve his talent-management goal, Inman needed two things: First was the authorization to personally detail intelligence officers. As DNI he influenced intelligence-officer detailing and placement. However, the tangled administration of the Bureau of Naval Personnel (BuPers) often muted his influence. Second, he needed a process that analyzed the Navy's competitive personnel-performance process to identify intelligence and line officers' top performers. Third, he needed a method to match intelligence-officer HAMs—individuals high in achievement motivation—to the line communities' HAMs.

CNO Holloway understood Inman's plan and saw the talent-management ideas in action as his N2 at 7th Fleet. Holloway personally called the chief of BuPers, instructing him to give Inman detailing authority for all active-duty intelligence officers (1630) and line intelligence-subspecialty officers. To detail reserve intelligence officers (1635), Inman benefited from access to a consolidated reserve structure that had been created earlier by Admiral Weisner.[6]

With detailing authority secured, Inman set about identifying top performers. Here he benefited again from Weisner. As Weisner's executive assistant Inman had taken notes (in the role of recorder) during several line officer slating committees. The slating committee comprised the CNO, VCNO, and chief of BuPers. They decided on placement and future billet assignments for the rear admirals (lower and upper half). As the meeting's recorder, Inman recalled, he was exposed to the process and "who were the up-and-comers, particularly of the new flag selectees." He also saw which flag officers were moving to command afloat and up to the numbered fleets.[7]

Rank mattered, and Inman needed to put the proper grade of intelligence officer in the critical billets. The 1975 *Intelligence Newsletter* announced that "upgrad[ing] the rank of the officers sent to the most demanding LCDR and LT billets at sea" would occur in the billet slatings for fiscal years 1976 and 1977.[8] Placing a lieutenant commander in some shipboard lieutenant billets began in 1974.[9] The aircraft carrier SIO and the flag's staff N2 became commander-grade positions. The upgrading of the SIO and N2 billets had two positive effects: First, it allowed intelligence officers to get another operational sea tour, honing their shipboard Opintel tradecraft, before becoming N2s or SIOs. Second, it created more parity with the other battlegroup staff officers. A commander's rank carried additional credibility when advising the battlegroup commander or the aircraft carrier commanding officer.

Weisner also provided Inman guidance and insight into the general talent-management philosophy of the slating process. Inman used that experience and the slating-committee process as a framework. He gathered four Navy Intelligence chief warrant officers to review the records of the intelligence officers and line intelligence-subspecialty officers.[10] The warrant officers created a one-to-n list of the top officers. The list was helpful information, but it probably told Inman what he already knew. "Bobby Inman," wrote fifty-fourth DNI, Rear Adm. Thomas Brooks, "kept card files and records on other members of the (then very small) 1630 community." Inman knew who was good and who was not. He knew the intelligence officer community better than anyone else; after all, he'd been following the careers of his peers and juniors for years. With a clear understanding of who the intelligence officer HAMs were, Inman "pushed them ahead." Brooks described the process as "mentoring"; today it is considered talent management. Inman, Brooks offered, "ensured that senior Flag Officers who were obviously destined for higher command were served by only the top 1630s. . . . Thus, he enhanced the community's prestige in the eyes of senior URLs [line officers]."[11]

Inman personally detailed the officers in the top half of the list, and the officer detailer assigned the others. "The very best I had [in the grade of captain] went to those number fleets where the flag was selected to four stars," Inman said. The group below was sent to the staffs of the Atlantic and Pacific Fleet commanders in chief. He sent the top commanders to the CARGRU and CRUDESGRU afloat commands.[12]

Building a Corporate Brand

Today Inman's approach is called corporate branding through talent management practices. His total effort to "sell" Opintel's legitimacy, credibility, and indispensability to the Navy was primarily public relations. Managing information from the organization to the consumer to improve its perception is the essence of public relations. It is a broad field as old as civilization.[13] One of the best-known public-relations experts or "press agents" is American Edward Louis Bernays (1891–1995). Bernays' understanding of human nature and the psyche allowed him to craft advertising campaigns that sold everything from cigarettes and bacon to opinions and ideologies. One of his critical understandings was, "If you can influence the leaders, either with or without their conscious cooperation, you automatically influence the group they sway."[14]

Discussing "selling" or public relations associated with intelligence is dangerous to some. It smacks of the politicization of intelligence or the use of intelligence to advance personal or policy agendas. The definition of politicized intelligence, however, is not so simple. There are many forms—manipulation of analysis, bias and embedded assumptions, and parochialism being the most common. Mark Lowenthal, noted author on intelligence issues, offers that policymakers may ask for the opinion of their intelligence officers and may even reject the analysis and opinions, but policymakers cannot present *their* alternative views as intelligence analysis. "There are no hard-and-fast rules here," Lowenthal says of the intelligence-policy interaction, "but there is an unwritten rule."[15] World War II- and Cold War–era CIA director Sherman Kent tried to define the rule; having more information and academic objectivity maintained the divide, he said, reducing corruption between intelligence and policy.

Kent's contemporary, Willmore Kendall, disagreed with Kent's Ivy League elitism and analytic methods. Conducting analysis far away from the customer and focusing only on predictions, not understanding, was less useful to the decision-makers, he felt. President Nixon also disagreed with Kent and made some reforms in 1971.[16] Fifty years later CIA Director Robert Gates would argue along Kendell and Nixon's lines: Intelligence is only helpful if produced near the policymaker and focused on their decisions. The "objective" versus "actionable" debate—or the Kentian versus Kendall/Gatesian schools of debate—exposed the role of proximity as necessary to intelligence support and a possible vector of politicization.[17] Operational intelligence must retain the Kentian objectivity yet with Gatesian proximity, Navy Intelligence came to recognize. Thus Opintel straddles the divide, its practitioners caught in a virtuous cycle: The Opintel practitioner relies on credibility and objectivity to gain proximity. They need proximity to understand the commander's requirements to tailor the intelligence. Thus by being within the inner circle they risk losing objectivity and their credibility in the process.

Inman's public-relations approach remained at the operational level of war, somewhat avoiding the policy entanglements of strategic intelligence. He focused on quality support to the customer, not the politicization of intelligence that resulted in a loss of credibility. Every intelligence officer needed to represent the corporate brand of Navy Intelligence to influence the Navy's leaders. That brand was the Opintel enterprise of OSIS-based tactical-decision support and its strike-mission support-at-sea character. The brand was also its people: Smart officers who understood Opintel, the enemy, and the commander's mission. Servants who took the initiative, often working tirelessly beyond their remit, to support operations. Inman knew the last fifteen years of sea, shore, back-to-sea rotations, and internal competition had honed the Opintel identity. The Opintel organizational identity was the brand, and the brand was its identity.[18]

A corporate brand is a complex mix of organizational identity and product offering. The brand is the customer's perception of the organization, while the identity is the employees' perception. The two perspectives are linked and represent a total value proposition to customers and employees.[19] Credibility is critical to the intelligence field's corporate brand and organizational identity.

"A credible source is a believable source," wrote Andrea Baertl Helguero, an On Think Tanks research officer.[20] Credibility has two components: expertise and trustworthiness. For a Navy intelligence officer, service experience represents expertise and competency. In a hierarchical Navy a person's rank embodies their experience level. For example, an officer of an ensign rank usually has been in the Navy for only two years and has less specialty experience than does an officer in the rank of a commander with at least fifteen years of experience.

Competency is relative to experience and thus linked to the individual's rank. An ensign's competency level can be high but only for tasks and analysis expected of an ensign. Though it could be that the ensign's competency would not be expected to be the same for tasks at a commander's level. The ribbons (awards) pinned to the uniform give insight into the individual's performance level, representing competency and experience. However, the belief that rank equates to experience and competency only works if one believes the Navy's promotion system never makes mistakes, only ever promoting those who are competent and experienced.

The intelligence officer career path is, among other things, a talent-development process. It ensures that the officer gains knowledge through training and postgraduate education. The career path makes the rank of the officer commensurate with experience and thus knowledge. The entire intelligence-officer career path and detailing process allows a flag officer to assume that the intelligence officer carries specific expertise upon meeting.

Like credibility, trustworthiness has many components. Trustworthiness is honesty, forthrightness, and a willingness not to deceive. To the customer, intelligence, trustworthiness, and credibility combine when considering the product. Is the assessment credible? Is the source reliable? The commander "must have confidence," writes Capt. Frank P. Notz, USN, "that you [his intelligence officer] are loyal to him and 100% reliable."[21] In the aggregate the intelligence officer's credibility is a judgment by the customer regarding the trustworthiness, experience, and competency of the intelligence and the intelligence officer.

Of course, "credibility is judged subjectively by individuals," writes Helguero; judgments are based on "previous experience . . . hearsay, on reputation, on official or professional credentials." Here Helguero points out that heuristics matter: people use "rules of thumb" and their personal experiences to make decisions about credibility.[22] Since operational commanders rarely have the motivation or time to conduct an in-depth evaluation of the intelligence or the intelligence officer, heuristics become the primary source of judgment. The lens of personal experience is substantial; it makes military leaders prefer familiar things.

This familiarity principle, or "mere effect," relies on similarity. Believing there is a similarity with someone is often grounded in the past. People look for similarity through comparable "backgrounds" in social culture and experiences.[23] Through Opintel at sea the intelligence officer's (163x) career path creates a common operational background with future commanders. Inman's perception allowed him to match intelligence officer HAMs with similarities to line flag officer HAMs to create perceived if not actual familiarity.

Similarity, however, goes beyond background, and so does compatibility. Each commander has a leadership style and view of the intelligence function. The intelligence officer needed credibility, but being the most credible might not make them the proper intelligence officer for a particular commander. The "Inman touch," part press agent and part social scientist, made the difference, bringing credibility and compatibility together. "The bottom line," Inman said, "is that it took focus[ing] on performance record, aptitude, intellect, and who they would be working for" to create success for Navy Intelligence and the intelligence officer.[24] Inman leveraged talent management to create a brand. He then sold the Opintel brand to the Navy by selling it first to its up-and-coming flag officers.

Success Follows Success

Inman's approach paid off. In his first efforts Inman "sent four very capable lieutenant commanders" to Naval Forces Europe (NAVEUR). When the commander-grade selection list came out, four of the six NAVEUR personnel selected for promotion were intelligence officers—the four Inman had directly detailed there. The NAVEUR commander telephoned

Inman, "thanking me for sending topflight talent." In another effort Inman chose captain-grade officers with Defense Intelligence School (DIS) degrees. After assessing their records he detailed the best officers to "key jobs where they could be observed" by senior up-and-coming flag officers. Five of the group made flag rank, an astounding number.[25]

The process "worked across the board," Inman said. The success was apparent not only in the performance reports but also in the selection-board results. Detailing for the Sixth Fleet commander and future CNO Adm. James Watkins offers another example Inman recalled,

> [Vice Adm.] Jim Watkins was skeptical when I told him I was sending [Captain] Bill Studeman out to be his EA [executive assistant]. . . . [Later, Watkins], on his way to being CINCPACFLT, he had the courtesy to tell me that if he had to leave the staff and go with only one officer he would have taken Studeman to be that person.[26]

The process worked to "sell the brand," Inman said. However, it only worked through personal effort, with Inman's unique touch. Consistency in the human product requires maintaining the talent-management process to preserve the brand. It was an effort that required Inman's constant oversight.[27]

In 1976 Inman was promoted and moved to the Defense Intelligence Agency. No longer DNI, Inman was still the senior intelligence officer. "The senior Flag in the community is designated as the Code Sponsor," Rear Adm. Thomas Brooks wrote. "By tradition, the Code Sponsor is consulted on all community matters, including senior detailing."[28] CNO Holloway, recognizing the success of Inman's efforts, decided to continue allowing him to personally detail intelligence officers. He "told the chief of Personnel [BuPers] that I would continue to oversee this process as long as I was on active duty."[29] When Inman became deputy director of the Central Intelligence Agency in 1981, the law prevented him from remaining the code sponsor.

Nonetheless Inman continued to dialogue with the DNIs for several more years. "Candidly, I continued," he said, "even after my retirement."[30]

It did not hurt Inman's talent-management efforts that he was the first intelligence officer to become a four-star admiral. Brooks clarified the significance of Inman's long-term influence:

> Often, the DNI is not the senior Flag and not the Code Sponsor. But Inman was both while DNI (3 years) and remained Code Sponsor while DIRNSA [Director of the National Security Agency] (3 more years) and then while Deputy DCI (2 more years). He was very active in the detailing process for more than 8 years—enough time to influence the structure of the community for a decade to come. No one else ever was Code Sponsor that long.[31]

Nothing lasts forever, and Inman's influence began to wane in the late 1980s. DNIs who had benefited from the "Inman touch," like Rear Adm. William Studeman (fifty-third DNI) and Brooks (fifty-fourth DNI) continued to seek his talent-management advice. By the term of the fifty-sixth DNI, Rear Adm. Michael Cramer, USN, Inman's influence and the talent-management process had "slipped." In 1994 Rear Admiral Cramer "abandoned the whole process. . . . He stopped managing career development from his level," Inman said.[32] That does not mean that others did not try to use elements of Inman's talent-management approach. Vice Adm. Lowell "Jake" Jacoby (fifty-eighth DNI, 1997–1999), a former junior and senior intelligence officer detailer, tried modernizing the talent-management approach. Jacoby was a "vocal proponent of implementing the sea duty screening process" that would "institutionalize ADM Inman's emphasis on sending the best talent to sea."[33]

The efforts to formalize and institutionalize talent management through administrative selection boards reinforced and further embedded Opintel's tactical-decision support and warning-intelligence performance orientation. One could argue that the tactical decision–support orientation became most significant because it represented OSIS's transition from shore to sea. Jacoby wrote that in either strike-mission planning or tactical-decision support the emphasis on "the importance of excellence in sea duty performance" throughout a career reinforced Opintel's brand.[34] It made sea-duty jobs highly desirable and critical to promotion opportunities. Shipboard Opintel was and remains Navy Intelligence's brand.

Why Inman's Efforts Made a Difference

Since the post–World War II era and the start of the Cold War, the Soviet's grand strategy, particularly the naval component of their military strategy, had been much debated. By design the independent intelligence organizations within the U.S. intelligence community did not always agree on intelligence assessments.[35] By the late 1970s, based on a vast amount of signal and human intelligence, Navy Intelligence concluded that the Soviet Navy's strategy was most likely defensive, ballistic missile submarine (SSBN) protection–focused. The strategy created deterrence because it defended "bastions," allowing Soviet Navy SSBNs to operate undetected within them, poised to deliver a nuclear-weapon second strike. Not everyone in the Navy agreed. The competing assessments on the Soviet naval strategy between ONI and CIA became heated. The former believed the Soviet's naval strategy was offensive, while the latter thought it defensive. The Center for Naval Analyses (CNA), contracted by the Navy, agreed with the CIA.[36] Neither the CIA's nor the CNA's analysis supported the early-1970s narrative regarding how the U.S. Navy was modernizing. Defense analyst Peter Swartz observed that the assessment of a defensive Soviet naval strategy would be proven correct. However, the "authors [CIA, CNA, and those in Navy Intelligence] were for some time prophets without honor in their own country."[37]

A defensive Soviet naval strategy was, for many, impossible to accept. Not only did the assessment reverse what the IC had been saying for over a decade, but skeptics also pointed to the aggressive Soviet shipbuilding program as an incongruency. Therefore Navy line officers who had spent a career preparing for a third Battle of the Atlantic required convincing. Even the Navy's submarine community who better understood the "nuclear correlation of forces" was reluctant to accept the new assessment.[38] Fundamentally, a defensive Soviet naval strategy, it was thought, reduced the amount of threat that a resurging U.S. Navy was designing its new modern fleet to defeat.

Throughout the late 1970s Navy Intelligence had been doing yeoman's work to communicate highly classified intelligence to the fleet. The credibility of the assessment hinged upon the relationship currency between intelligence officers and the Navy's senior line flag officers—a currency that Inman's talent-management efforts had banked. *The Admirals' Advantage* likens convincing the fleet to accept the new intelligence assessments to Protestant Christian revivalism. The "evangelical" movement leveraged the operator-intelligence officer trust built by the two groups working cheek by jowl at sea. The preaching circuit of classified briefings was constant.[39]

CNO Thomas Hayward (1924–2022) believed in an aggressive go-forward operational approach to dealing with the Soviet Navy. The idea of a defensive Soviet naval strategy gave him an opportunity, but only if he could draw the budget and warfighting concepts together. As Tom Hone writes in *Power and Change*, Hayward recognized what his predecessor Zumwalt had: the Navy needed a unifying concept around which to plan and program.[40] Hayward needed a maritime strategy to align planning, programming, and budgeting with warfighting. Navy Intelligence showed Hayward, through the new assessment, a Soviet navy vulnerability that his go-forward approach could exploit.

In 1980 Inman was in his second year as director of the NSA and still influencing Navy Intelligence. That year Director of Naval Intelligence (DNI) Rear Adm. Sumner "Shap" Shapiro, USN (1926–2006), created OP-009J at the Office of Naval Intelligence (ONI). Shapiro brought Rich Haver, senior civilian analyst and technical director, over to the Pentagon from the Navy Field Operational Intelligence Office (NFOIO) at Fort Meade, Maryland, to set up 009J, an analysis section focused on the new intelligence. Haver had been working with the highly classified intelligence on the Soviet Navy for some time. Shapiro received direct reports from 009J, and their analysis helped inform CNO Hayward's decision-making.[41] With the analysis, Hayward laid the groundwork for restructuring his staff (OpNav) to further exploit the intelligence's insights.

As Americans prepared to go to the polls and elect the new president in November 1980, Ronald Reagan, courting the hawks, began arguing that the Soviets were using détente to gain an advantage under President Jimmy Carter's watch. The argument took, and Reagan won in a landslide. He argued that the West needed to change its goal of not losing the Cold War: it was time the West played to win.[42] The sea became a gameboard, and the U.S. and Soviet navies were "eyeball-to-eyeball," playing a dangerous, high-stakes game. Policy, strategies, and intelligence were converging.

It was in 1981 that the Navy and the IC fully agreed with the new assessment of a defensive Soviet naval strategy. The U.S. Navy, with an Ace Lyons F-14 Tomcat flyby off Murmansk, Russia, had already begun its application of a new go-forward strategy. In April 1981 CNO Hayward asked the Naval War College to create the Center for Naval Warfare Studies to support a new Strategic Studies Group (SSG).[43] In 1982 he moved OP-095, director of Antisubmarine Warfare Programs, to director of Naval Warfare. A new "net assessment" office (OP-96N) under Navy intelligence officer Capt. William H. J. Manthorpe was also created. OP-095 created "Team Charlie," a group of mostly Navy line officers tasked with assessing the analysis provided by Haver's 009J.[44] To translate Team Charlie and SSG efforts into a political and budgetary context Hayward created the Strategic Concepts Branch (OP-603) in 1982. To guide the entire process and evaluate its efforts Hayward restructured the Advanced Technology Panel (ATP), which had been created in 1975. He loaded the panel with senior officers who could make actionable recommendations. Together these new organizations took on a wholesale revision of Navy doctrine.[45] Guided by credible and trustworthy intelligence presented by intelligence officers, the decision-makers knew and trusted that policy and naval strategy had begun to align.[46]

As Hayward's tenure ended he finally had what he desired: "Cells of bright officers" to develop a unifying maritime strategy and "communicate it throughout OpNav." His successor, Adm. James D. Watkins, USN (1927–2021), built upon Hayward's foundation. Watkins had a better relationship with Secretary of the Navy John Lehman than Hayward had. The relationship helped refine the new Maritime Strategy, which became the central argument for creating a larger Navy. Lehman made the Navy Secretariate, not OpNav, the focal point for Navy policy supporting the new strategy, not just the center of Navy budget programming. He argued in Congress and with the secretary of Defense that the Navy and its new strategy was the most effective use of resources for a wide range of conflicts.[47]

CHAPTER 14
Observations

> *What gift do you think a good servant has that separates them from the others? It's the gift of anticipation. And I'm a good servant. I'm better than good; I'm the best; I'm the perfect servant. I know when they'll be hungry, and the food is ready. I know when they'll be tired, and the bed is turned down. I know it before they know it themselves. I'm the perfect servant; I have no life.*
>
> —MRS. WILSON, *Gosford Park*[1]

Lest you imagine, Rear Adm. Tom Brooks offered, "that there was some master plan for Opintel, there was no such thing."[2] If there was not a master plan, then what drove the shipboard Opintel evolution? Undoubtedly the Navy's hierarchical organization was an influence. Intelligence has always responded to the demand signals from the organization's leadership. However, as Brooks notes, the Navy organization could not, beyond the simple aspiration for better operational intelligence, dictate a five-, ten-, or twenty-year master plan for Opintel. The world and the Navy were too complex and ever-changing for such a thing. The shipboard organization's "evolvability," or willingness to adapt by modifying their behavior, provided the only chance for effectiveness within the complexity.[3]

Organizations tend to develop around a central task or a demand that creates a guiding constraint. If the constraint is driven from above, a top-down constraint, mechanisms, structures, and behaviors are created to accomplish the task. However, once competent in the task, organizations can become trapped and unwilling to adapt beyond those things that perform the task. On the other hand, learning organizations look beyond the top-down constraint to the intended better future it is meant to create. These organizations avoid the competency trap, because the constraint becomes an enabling one that produces innovation. From a learning perspective, innovation driven by these enabling constraints matters more, for example, than the technology that may have created the constraint itself because it fosters evolvability—the ability of an organization to adapt and self-organize to new complex constraints informally.[4]

We have seen three crucial elements of the Opintel organization's evolvability. First, the shared sense of purpose was critical. Shipboard Opintel served the operators. No matter how the shipboard organization changed, its guiding principle was to provide the commander with relevant and timely operational intelligence. The second is the idea of coordination without hierarchy, or decentralization, and informal organizational compensation that leads to innovation and adaptation. The third is the influence of the favorable qualities of Navy organizational culture, most notably the aviation community's habitual desire to innovate.

A Servant Ethos

Those interviewed for this study, when describing their role as intelligence officers, almost invariably used terms like "supported," "worked for," "loyal to," and "served." The choice of words is not surprising. An intelligence professional serves the mission, and the commander embodies the mission. The commander's staff, the operations, intelligence, logistics, and communications officers, serve as a type of privy council. The devotion and trust of these privy council servants to the commander, and the commander to them, is fundamental to mission success.

Doctrinally the commander is the master of the intelligence cycle, whose requirements drive the intelligence officer's efforts. Many authors of military-intelligence books reinforce the servant relationship of intelligence to the commander. For example, Donald McLachlan writes that "intelligence is the servant and not the master."[5] Most Navy intelligence officers agree and approach the customers' needs as a devoted civil servant approaches a minister, governor, or sovereign.[6] The intelligence officer's perspective of the relationship with the commander as servant-master is a critical enabling constraint on Opintel's evolvability.

The central task of supporting the master requires that the servant be competent in their field and devoted to the master's efforts. Writing on the servant ethos in military intelligence, the late professor of Naval strategy at the U.S. Naval War College Michael Handel shared a quotation from an intelligence officer serving Field Marshal Sir Bernard Montgomery:

> It was my task, as I saw it, to know my Chief, to know how his mind worked so well that I could happily deputize for him in his absence, either in the field or at the conferences he so hated to attend; to know him so well that I might sense when to put forward a suggestion and when to bide my time; when to wake him or let him sleep.[7]

The servant ethos in the shipboard Opintel organization provided a navigational North Star for change. Adaptation and innovation, the foundations of organizational learning, served only as solutions the Opintel organization used to solve challenges in the operating environment and the mission of their master.

Shipboard Opintel personnel became comfortable with complexity, uncertainty, and change; it became part of their Opintel identity. The servant ethos also made them comfortable managing the delicate chemistry with the commander. A good intelligence officer-to-commander relationship allows a direct exchange of new intelligence that reveals dangers threatening an operational plan. A great rapport also creates the ability to anticipate the commander's needs. The intelligence officer can anticipate a report's impact—the "so what"—and present new challenges and opportunities resulting from the change in the operating environment offered to the commander through a discussion.[8]

The intelligence officer's role is relegated to the background. Many Opintel professionals bristle at this. They should not. As Handel notes, intelligence, "like logistics, should always play a supportive role; yet the word supportive as used here is *not* synonymous with secondary or unimportant."[9] Quite the opposite: Opintel is vital, providing the commander with a force multiplier, often a key to success. It is a fact that any servant's critical role is frequently thankless. There are few cases in which intelligence success receives contemporary praise. Even military history tends to focus more on intelligence failures than successes. Handel illustrates the necessity that the intelligence officer accept the servant position with another quotation from Sir Bernard Montgomery's intelligence officer:

> At the height of the Battle of Alamein, I spoke privately to Montgomery about new intelligence from our "Y" services that indicated a change in enemy dispositions. . . . He not only altered the plan as commander; it became, in his own mind, his own decision, his own proposal, and was referred to as such in his diaries. . . . I did not feel any disappointment at this subsequent failure to give credit. . . . Such appropriation of ideas and designs is the very basis of command.[10]

Thus nothing evolved in the shipboard Opintel organization that did not serve the commander. Any organizational innovation that is not effective is modified or abandoned, any effective but inefficient process improved, often through informal arrangements within the ship or Navy Intelligence organization. Formal structures imposed by the hierarchical organization that did not improve Opintel's effectiveness were quietly ignored or informally worked around.

Why Informal Changes Made the Difference

The "miracle of the OSIS system" and all Opintel "was how totally decentralized it was," Rear Admiral Brooks wrote. "There was no single entity in charge from an operational perspective . . . and it flourished because of that!"[11] Brooks' statement seemed the antithesis of what one expects in a hierarchical military structure. Interviewees continually used words like "informal," "decentralized," "learning," "innovative," and "adapted" to describe shipboard Opintel changes. These terms point toward multiple evolvability mechanisms at play. If no master plan and decentralization was limiting the formal organizational structures, why was shipboard Opintel's evolution successful? The answers may lie in the power of informal, decentralized, and interdependent multiorganizational structures.

Professor Donald Chisholm, U.S. Naval War College, explored informal coordination mechanisms in his 1989 book *Coordination without Hierarchy*. He saw the informal processes as critical to making interdependent organizations perform more effectively than some hierarchical ones. I argue that Chisholm's analysis explains much of the evolution of the Navy's Opintel organization. Informal changes and relationships were powerful instruments in the evolution of shipboard Opintel. For example, OSIS and SupPlot were born from innovations that had begun with informal coordination processes. Even the IOIC, developed ashore and installed on the aircraft carrier as a complete package, evolved through informal shipboard organizational changes. Personal relationships and communication with other IOIC supervisors created informal feedback loops that significantly enhanced organizational learning.

Informal approaches to problem-solving are not new to the Navy. In his book *Learning War* Trent Hone examines the Navy's interwar and World War II problem-solving and learning processes. Hone's discussion of the Navy's gunnery and Combat Information Center (CIC) development shows that each ship individually experimented with solutions to war-at-sea problems. His description of a fragmented-experiment approach to problem-solving, or what I am calling "Sailor modifications," represents informal innovation. The Sailor's innovations and adaptation represented learning, an essential element of organizational evolution. In sharing what the crews learned with other ships, the Navy learned. The sharing of knowledge through feedback loops from one officer to another throughout the Navy has been a consistent fixture of the service since the creation of the Naval War College in the late nineteenth century. Knowledge sharing was no different during the evolution of shipboard Opintel.[12]

What made these informal systems possible is the complex, adaptive Navy system.[13] As discussed previously, Hone frames the evolving interdependent relationships' fundamental governing aspects as "constraints." In modern U.S. military terms, constraints are activities one *must do*, and restraints are those one *cannot do*.[14] These are both internal and external control mechanisms. Physics, for example, and tradition place constraints and restraints on capabilities and organizations. As a sizable historical organization, the Navy has learned and adapted to constraints and restraints over centuries. When enough constraints are applied, the organization reaches a new level of specialization, creating what Hone calls a "symmetry break"; with this, a new self-organization emerges. Adaptation and innovation within constraints are often small, iterative, evolutionary, and informal. Innovation becomes more revolutionary when restraints are removed, such as by developing computers and microelectronics to overcome operational obstacles.[15] These revolutionary innovations, followed by evolutionary adaptations, are the foundation of this book's methodology.

Hone points out that when internally placed restraints ("can't do") become too many, the organization becomes centralized, reducing its evolvability.[16] The Navy is a hierarchical military organization, and by design; it desires centralization where constraints and restraints are balanced and controlled. Within the Opintel evolution, the importance of decentralization and informal organizational changes exposes an incongruency. Donald Chisholm's work helps explain the disconnect and why informal structures within multiorganizational systems are essential to adaptability. In some regards, his work helps us understand the mechanisms in Hone's description of evolvability in a complex adaptive system.

Hierarchic organizations, Chisholm says, use centralization to correct perceived ineffectiveness or inefficiency. Centralization is seen as a corrective panacea for organizational problems. Decentralization is not usually an organization's first choice in corrective measures. However, war often creates a necessity for decentralization or fragmentation. Chisholm notes that decentralization may be a pragmatic solution that increases the "speed of operations" and "expands the activities of the war effort." However, the nature of organizations is always to stop fragmentation and return to centralization. Where a multiorganizational system exists, the hierarchy desires consolidation.[17]

Too much control or overcentralization may create rigidity. Chisholm uses the rigid research and development effort of the post–World War II military as an example. Military research's centralization limited adaptive responses to the rapidly changing Cold War operational environment.[18] OSIS provides another example of the success of decentralization. Supporting the increased speed of decision-making required more access to national intelligence; the OSIS nodes decentralized national intelligence, placing it in the hands of the fleet's frontline decision-makers. As communications improved, a second decentralization occurred, pushing OSIS intelligence through SupPlot, to the ship and battlegroup decision-makers at sea.

Navy Intelligence created what Chisholm describes as "informal organizations and loosely coupled systems" when it decentralized national intelligence. The OSIS nodes also exemplify the self-organization accompanying a symmetry break and the resulting decentralization. Self-organization manifesting as order, driven by a shared understanding of the mission and a servant ethos, is created from the new informal organization. Thus decentralization is not without some intracentralization.[19] Contrary to the belief that informal and loosely coupled suborganizations are anathema to effectiveness, Chisholm's work shows that such conditions establish effective coordination. This coordination using "informal channels, behavioral norms, and agreements" grounded through personal relationships and shared goals proved highly effective in the Opintel evolution.[20]

In current U.S. military doctrine, "command is central to all military action, and unity of command is central to unity of effort."[21] This hierarchical organizational thought does not always hold. For example, coalitions represent complex adaptive systems that function better not as hierarchical but as loosely coupled systems. The critical component of coalition operations, just as it is for decentralized intelligence or the shipboard multiorganization system, is the unity of effort that drives unified action. The servant ethos of shipboard Opintel represents unifying effort, synchronization, and cooperation that leads to coordination. If needed, coordination integrates functions and aligns suborganizations to achieve unity of action during a designated period.[22] Chisholm notes that the informal organization's role, both intra- and interorganizational, is continuously redefined based on "experience, and specific tasks are determined by negotiation. The parties to the bargain are determined not by an organizational chart but by the character of the issue at hand."[23]

The shipboard Opintel team is an example of an informal organization and a loosely coupled system improving evolvability. As discussed, formal suborganizations controlled certain areas of operational intelligence within the Navy. The aviation community, for example, recognized early in its evolution the need for air combat–specific operational intelligence, paying for air-intelligence billets within each squadron, the air wing, and the aircraft carrier. After the air intelligence (135x) and intelligence officer (163x) merger, Navy Intelligence provided minimally aviation-trained original intelligence officers (163x) to serve in those aviation-owned air-intelligence billets. It also provided intelligence officers to Flag staffs and the national intelligence community. The formal design of Opintel support did not extend much beyond the intelligence officer billet structure and accession training; informal organizational mechanisms took over within the Intel Center or at the Flag staff to meet the specific requirements.

Neither the battlegroup staff N2, nor the ship's senior intelligence officer (SIO), nor the carrier air wing's air intelligence officer (CAGAI) had the command authority or resources to execute shipboard Opintel alone. The N2 had little to no personnel to contribute to Opintel operations. However, the N2's power distance and direct interaction with the battlegroup commander contributed direction and guidance—an intelligence demand signal. The SIO contributed the bulk of the personnel, equipment, and systems. The other ship's departments provided communications, systems support, and hotel services (messing, berthing, laundry, etc.). The SIO met the aircraft carrier commanding officer's tactical intelligence demands and coordinated with the N2 to meet the Flag's demands. The CAGAI, while owning no personnel, managed to provide the air group commander's tactical air-intelligence demands. When embarked, the CAGAI temporarily managed the individual squadrons'

Opintel personnel. The squadron AIs and intelligence specialists were detailed as additional duty (ADDU) to the aircraft carrier's intelligence center (CVIC) to work under CAGAI.

We have explored the growing Opintel demands of the battlegroup commander in the late 1970s. The demands were beyond the capabilities of the formal organization as it was. Even with the formalizing of cryptologic support from the ship's signal exploitation space (SSES), neither the SIO, nor CAGAI, nor the N2 could answer the demands alone. The growing tension between increasing tactical-decision support demands emerged, in many ways, as a struggle over the control of SupPlot. Attempts to use a centralizing organizational mechanism, force-coercion, to align SupPlot created limited centralization and almost no organizational sustainability. Interdependency between SSES, SupPlot, the SIO, CAGAI, and the N2 created informal compensation for the formal organizational limitations. The informal mechanisms worked because Navy Intelligence was a small community wherein informal communication channels flourished. Even with a promotion system driven by competition, as we saw at FOSIS Rota, informal cooperation and coordination solved most Opintel organizational problems.[24]

At sea the N2, SIO, and CAGAI relied on personal relationships to find the openness necessary to discuss solutions rationally. As Chisholm discusses in his work, this informal interaction was spontaneous informal multiorganizational problem-solving.[25] Considering that informal shared power is the least successful tool in a hierarchical military, we have to ask, why did it work for shipboard Opintel? Navy and the aviation community's culture, the intelligence officer's career path, and the small organizational size of Navy Intelligence provide part of the answer. Self-regulating the personalities and egos of the high-achieving (HAM) intelligence officers is another part. The three HAMs, N2, SIO, and CAGAI, created a delicate, informal cooperation balance. Cooperation benefited all, but it could be undone if the individuals reverted to the formal structure's parochialism of Opintel resource "ownership." Significant emotional and interpersonal communication resources were constantly applied to manage the informal multiorganizational structure.

Formal organizations conceived of in theory and committed to paper often in practice failed to understand the current and future shipboard realities. Chisholm calls the planned-versus-reality delta a formal organizational structure failure. The IOIC's original structure is an example of formal organizational failure compensated through informal mechanisms. Innovation and adaptation through informal compensation mechanisms emerged inside the ship's IOIC and Operations Department. The IOIC adaptation during the Vietnam War illustrates these mechanisms. To adapt to the high volume of combat missions, the personnel in the IOIC self-organized into sustainable groups able to conduct repeatable processes for an extended time. Eventually the environment changes, relieving the need for informal compensation, or the formal organization adopts the informal practices—or what we've been calling "catching up"—centralizing the informal compensation practices.[26]

Catching up is complicated for the Navy because of the tension between the extreme sense of urgency and the budgetary cost of making changes. Formalizing organizational change should be considered only if supported by sufficient empirical evidence—though there is often little time to gather such evidence. Tactical and operational doctrine provides a place to articulate the common understanding of the problem and how formalization might improve military action. Military doctrine, Milan Vego writes, expresses the "will and philosophy of an organization and specifies premises and actions to sustain its effort."[27] Sound doctrine links theory with practice; it includes considerations of service culture and technology, both now and in the future. Current operating concepts result in tactical and operational doctrine derived from the warfighters' recent experiences and their informal solutions during combat. Conversely, future operating concepts are still under development but usually, not always, describing a vision based on lessons learned from studying war, for the future application of technology.[28]

For Navy Intelligence, catching up occurred through changes to the intelligence officer and enlisted billet structure. Codifying informal change by realigning billets was a decision within the "lifelines" or scope of Navy Intelligence's decisional power; it was a change made easily and, most importantly, quickly. However, formalizing in this manner robs the organization of open debate that creates a shared understanding of the problem, solutions, and future operating concepts.

Some tactical-level doctrines, usually ship or air wing operating procedures, capture current practices without considering theory and operating concepts. When asked in 2019 about Navy operational intelligence doctrine in the 1960s and 1970s, Rear Admiral Brooks wrote, "To my knowledge . . . the first Intelligence related NWP [Naval Warfare Publication] was not published until the 1980s." He said, "There were numerous *ONI Review* articles and other semi-official references to OPINTEL, but I know of no official OPNAV INSTR [instruction] or similar document directing or defining it."[29]

When formalizing change, choosing speed over a measured-analysis approach carries risk. The risk comes in scale. After the tactical defeats at Guadalcanal in 1942, the quick changes in radar and the Combat Information Center (CIC) created operational victories. In the case of the early days of U.S. airpower in Vietnam, Washington's choice to quickly formalize an Operation Rolling Thunder bombing-target selection process meant the risks to both the military mission and the airmen flying the missions were little understood. Rear Admiral Richardson's study of the Rolling Thunder failures led him to create an informal network assessment–based targeting process that proved to be better. Unfortunately Richardson was unable to formalize his process.

However, in peacetime there is no accurate test. Thus concepts should be "subjected to rigorous testing, experimentation, and frank debate" before resulting in doctrinal changes.[30] Again, there must be time and a desire to conduct such testing and debate. One could argue that the technological revolutions and resulting evolutions happened so quickly in the 1970s that there was little time to consider them. Additionally, since Navy Intelligence lacked doctrine in the first place, there was no doctrine to change, further dampening the desire to create any from whole cloth.

The lack of formal doctrine did not derail Opintel's evolutionary efforts from 1960 to 1980. Most of the informal and formal decisions were sound. Having a singular enemy, the Soviet Navy, was an enabling constraint and helped channel change and decisions toward appropriately solving specific tactical and operational problems. To say that a formal centralized organization failed to meet the intelligence demand inaccurately describes the organizational structure. Navy Intelligence did not design an informal shipboard organizational system. Nor did they knowingly create a flawed, formal, centralized one.

The fact is that all formal organization structures are susceptible to failures, especially inside the dynamic naval and shipboard environment. Informal organization compensation emerges from an endosymbiosis relationship, an informal organization existing inside the formal one. Commanders who hold too tightly to the formal centralized organization structures in the face of changing environments often undo informal compensation. They break the endosymbiosis relationships and their ship's internal cohesion.

Centralization and formalization are not the antitheses of innovation and adaptation; they are instead foundational and essential mechanisms. Chisholm notes that informal elements left unchecked can weaken an organization. Formal organizational mechanisms must periodically consolidate or realign informal organizational elements to correct any weaknesses.[31] For example, maintaining a Navy requires vast sums of money. Informal organization structures create military force design and management issues. Without centralization and formal organizational structure, planning, program, and budgeting of monies to build and run a naval force or the Opintel process that serves it is impossible.

There is also an inherent cohesion within formal organizations that resists entropy. Cohesion is essential; while too much cohesion may make an organization brittle, too little can disrupt unity. Formal organizations are challenging to break into a loose organizational system by design. The stability of centralization and formal mechanisms are keystones within the larger organizational structure. Chisholm notes that maintaining from the beginning a loosely coupled organization system, especially if the stakeholders feel it works well, is easier than trying to create one later. Indeed, no military organization, even one that espouses a desire to "flatten" its structure, sets out to design a loosely coupled organization.

OSIS is a perfect example. The OSIS nodes were never intentionally designed as a loosely coupled multiorganizational system, but that is what occurred. New high-speed datalinks and reciprocal influences allowed informal coordination among OSIS nodes and other intelligence organizations to drive adaptation and innovation. Crew resource planning, dedicating trained personnel to the nodes, and computer baselining were formal "catch-up" actions. Trying to centralize OSIS more than it was would have undone a successful structure.

As difficult as it is to forcibly decentralize an existing formal organization, bringing one back together is equally challenging.[32] The Sixth Fleet CTF 60 staff's effort to control *Eisenhower*'s Opintel organization in the early 1980s presents an example. Another example is the NSA's attempt to tame the "unchecked monster" of the Cryptologic Support Groups (CSGs) at FOSIF Rota or the fleet support–centric airborne cryptologic direct support elements (CDSE) flying in VQ aircraft in the Pacific. The critical component often missing in recentralization and formalization efforts is trust in the leader: if the organization's members recognize competency, credibility, and authority legitimization in the leader, they are better prepared to push past long-received practices that required using only the minimum necessary constraints and restraints. Sixth Fleet CTF 60's attempt to centralize created too many new constraints (must-do) and restraints (cannot-do) on an already-successful interdependent multiorganizational system. Thus the centralization attempt was abhorrent from an Opintel-culture perspective. From the perspective of Ike's Opintel organizational structure, CTF 60's attempt would only result in degrading the organization by destabilizing and weakening it.

The CTF 60 shipboard and OSIS node examples also reinforce the critical role of leadership within organizations. Allowing a loosely controlled, interdependent multiorganizational structure to exist requires a courageous leader. History abounds with examples in which a leader's proclivity to centralize organization created fatal rigidity. Naval hierarchical C2 certainly desires centralization. Nevertheless, shipboard Opintel had three decentralized Opintel power poles—the N2, SIO, and CAGAI. The inception of the three poles likely began not by design but through a struggle over operational-intelligence equities and scarce resources. The informal evolution processes took care of the rest. The multiorganization structure prevented rigidity, even if not by design. Fortunately Navy Intelligence and the broader Navy understood, or were forced to understand, by rapidly changing conditions that aggressive centralization efforts of the Opintel organization were unwise. One reason may have been a "do-not-fix-something-that-works-fine" mentality. Another may be the Navy and aviation community's underlying organizational culture that saw value in some decentralization to adapt to the new speed of modern war.

Whatever the reason, allowing informal mechanisms to continue was essential to the evolution of shipboard Opintel. Still, the tension of formal centralization of Opintel resources always lurked in the background. The tension was mostly good, creating a sinusoidal wave of decentralization (informal) and recentralization (formal) efforts. Shipboard Opintel's evolvability benefited from the process.

The Outlaw experiments are an example of the benefits. The afloat commanders were exposed to the tactical-warning intelligence OSIS provided and wanted more. Informal compensations had reached their limits, and more access to OSIS all-source information required money. The Navy caught up to the demand and funded formal innovation in the Outlaw experiments. Tactical Flag Command Centers (TFCCs) and SupPlot were a formalizing outgrowth of the innovation. From creating the IOIC to SupPlot, the sinusoidal wave from formal to decentralization and back to recentralization proved effective in creating a learning organization during the Cold War. It continues to this day.

Why Aviation Culture Was Important

Before aviation, Navy culture was dominated by the surface line community, the "battleship Navy." By 1900 progressivism had made surface line officers into "warrior engineers" with naval warfare and industrial technology expertise.[33] The aviation community's lineage, culture, and identity are born from the surface line community. Aviation's role envisioned through the lens of the larger Navy was supporting battleships.

The aviators, however, saw themselves through a different lens, allowing them to develop a specific naval-aviation identity.

The aviation community's influence on Opintel comes first from the inextricable linkage between airpower and intelligence. In "10 Propositions Regarding Air Power" author Phillip Meilinger writes, "Technology and air power are integrally and synergistically related." Because aviation is more technologically focused, Meilinger argues, its "unique characteristics necessitate that airmen centrally control it."[34] Thus airmen believe only other airmen could provide the required air intelligence. This line of thinking was not unique; the surface line community believed similarly about who delivered their operational intelligence.

Second, Meilinger writes, "Air Power is targeting, targeting is intelligence, and intelligence is analyzing the effects of air operations." Indeed, "a skeptic could argue that a history of air strategy is the history of the search for the single, perfect target."[35] The strategic and tactical bombing of World War II supports Meilinger's assertions regarding the importance of intelligence. Brian Vlaun adds to Meilinger's thoughts, writing, "The growth of airpower cannot be thoroughly comprehended without an understanding of the maturation of its air-intelligence component."[36]

After World War II, the Navy eliminated or outsourced much of its air intelligence. The failures during the Korean War reinforced the aviation community's requirement for assured access to air intelligence. The need was so crucial to the aviation community that they were willing to pay for upward of nine hundred air intelligence officer (135x) billets. The investment made aviation the largest customer of Navy Intelligence then and now.

In the Cold War Navy, the aviation community became dominant. Since only aviators could command aircraft carriers, more made Flag officer rank. Consequently their influence was considerable both in performance orientation and organizational culture. It was not just the growing power of the aviation community that mattered. Their culture had an identity that focused on trust in technology. The trust in technology and the possibility of its failure created a cultural identity that is comfortable with complexity and risk, managed through interdependence. Aviation culture embraces, some more so than others, supporting and supported interdependent organizational relationships.[37] Because of its organizational perspectives, the aviation community left air intelligence somewhat to its own devices. If the aviator had quality targeting and detailed threat presentations, they were happy to allow a decentralized intelligence structure to operate. However, not every airpower organization saw its operational intelligence in the same way. Here the U.S. Air Force provides a contrast.

Newly separated from the U.S. Army in 1947, the Air Force was, like the Navy—myopically focused on new technology. The Air Force represented airpower as a strategic asset. Its World War II missions of air defense, strategic bombing, air-naval cooperation, and air support to ground troops had been equal in idea but not equally resourced.[38] The Air Force focused on strategic bombing, especially atomic weapons delivery, partly out of self-interest. Bombing with atomic weapons required a different approach to targeting. Air Force intelligence used increasingly technical collection and analysis methods to produce targets and bombing routes. The approach required the centralization and specialization of its intelligence analysts.[39]

The Air Force consolidated its intelligence officers (Air Force designator 14Nx) and specialized them into six fields: human (HUMINT), signals (SIGINT), imagery (IMINT), geodesy applications, targeting, and staff and command. The result was "intelligence officers [that] had a high degree of technical expertise (depth) but little understanding of the big picture (breadth)."[40] Despite a similar squadron and aviation culture, the Navy's centralized approach to operational intelligence differed significantly from the Air Force's. One reason for the difference is Navy aviation's expeditionary, or tactical- and operational-focused, mission.

By 1970 Navy Intelligence was specialized but only insomuch as it was special duty, separate from line officer duties. Intelligence officers (163x) always conducted operational intelligence, no matter their assigned platform. Unlike the Air Force, the Navy chose to keep its intelligence officers as operational-intelligence generalists. The generalist's career path exposed them to IMINT, SIGINT, HUMINT, and other forms of intelligence gathering, but only from the perspective of providing support to the operationally deployed forces. There was little space on the aircraft carrier to conduct specialized technical analysis. Rear Adm. John Marocchi, USN (1630), summarized the Navy's position: "There will not be room at the top for one who is a specialist in a particular facet of intelligence," he wrote in 1974. "Too much specialization within a specialty," Marocchi wrote, or too much depth and not enough breadth is a bad thing. At sea, redundancy and breadth ensure survivability. For Navy intelligence officers, breadth and some depth allowed the officer to adapt to the battlegroup's evolving operational environment and multi-mission role.[41]

In 1953, after the Korean War, the Air Force, owing to its specialization, became the executive agency for the Department of Defense's Air Target Materials Program (ATMP). The DIA, desiring efficiency, centralized the ATMP. An almost-singular focus on atomic weapons and strategic bombing resulted in the DIA and the Air Force both mainly ignoring conventional-targeting tasks. The Vietnam War showed that targeting for conventional operations was still necessary. For the Air Force the war reinforced that operational intelligence and their intelligence officers (14Nx) needed to directly support the squadron and wing commanders in their forward operating locations. By 1975 the record of poor Air Force intelligence support to the tactical bombing force was common knowledge. The Air Force reconsidered its focus on intelligence depth without breadth as it constructed its future intelligence officer corps. They created the Armed Forces Target Intelligence Training Course to improve tactical targeting.[42] To ensure breadth at the operational- and tactical-intelligence support levels, the Air Force returned intelligence officers to the wings and squadrons, noting that "having the intelligence officer physically in the squadron aids the development of rapport—in fact, it is essential. . . . When the crews know their intel officer, and when he is frequently in the squadron, they are much more likely to take intel questions directly to him, and have them answered in a timely manner."[43] The Air Force came to understand what naval aviation already had: delivering operational intelligence is a personal, if not an intimate, exchange between the customer and intelligence officer.

President Kennedy's elevation of the Navy's Polaris submarine-launched ballistic missile as a strategic asset over its A-5 bomber was a seminal event. Though naval aviation continued to practice Strategic Integrated Operations Plan (SIOP) bombing, it was freed from the shackles of the strategic-bombing role. Focusing on tactical conventional-strike missions improved the Navy's expeditionary capabilities. The conversion of the A-5 to RA-5C and the creation of the IOIC institutionalized shipboard Opintel. The focus on sea control as a critical requirement supporting expeditionary strike, forward presence, and power projection shaped Opintel by blending its two characters, air intelligence and tracking enemy units, into a single integrated support character for the multimission role. The intelligence officer (163x) needed to be a generalist, a jack-of-all-trades to support the breadth of missions. In many ways Kennedy's Polaris decision and the Navy's reaction to it saved Navy Intelligence from an organizational misalignment like the U.S. Air Force's.

Innovation

The aviation community's comfort with innovation points to another essential reason its culture was influential. In *New Ways of War: Understanding Military Innovation*, author Stephen Rosen notes that in both war and peace, in victory and defeat, naval aviation has continuously innovated. Military innovation has two components: organizational and intellectual. Navy aviation combined new thinking (intellectual) on how to win wars with organizational structures that exploited the thinking. Innovation requires the protection of the people who offer the ideas—something only those senior leaders who believe in the ideas can provide. Sustaining innovation required organizational structures that protected innovators who had strayed from the traditional career path from being "shunted aside into a dead-end specialty that does not qualify him for flag rank."[44]

In the 1920s Admirals William Sims, USN (1858–1936, president of the Naval War College), and Joseph M. Reeves, USN (1872–1948, commodore of fleet aviation squadrons), along with Rear Admiral William A. Moffett, USN (1869–1933, chief of the Bureau of Aeronautics), interacted professionally to exchange ideas, support wargaming, and advance the concept of the aircraft carrier. Thereby the three created the opportunity for a new aviation culture to develop. These were influential officers with long careers who were receptive to innovation. Together they successfully gained control over their community and created the conditions for innovation.[45]

In Navy Intelligence, U.S. Navy officers like Vice Adm. Frederick "Fritz" Harlfinger II, Vice Adm. Earl "Rex" Rectanus, Rear Adm. Sumner "Shap" Shapiro, Rear Adm. Thomas Brooks, and many others played significant roles in developing modern shipboard Opintel. They helped innovate Opintel both in technology and organizational design. Adm. Bobby Ray Inman's longevity and influence over intelligence officer talent management played a significant innovative role. His influence resembles Rear Adm. William Moffett's. Known as the "architect of Navy aviation," Moffett was chief of Aeronautics for twelve years—an influential period, four years longer than Inman's over Navy Intelligence. Inman, like Moffet, had vision, longevity, and respect within the Navy, allowing him to protect junior innovators and create viable career paths for them.[46]

Not all Opintel innovations came from intelligence officers. Vice Adm. David Richardson, an aviator and Opintel customer, had significant influence. He advocated for better Opintel and operators to improve their understanding of its use in decision-making. Richardson advocated for Opintel throughout the Navy staff (OpNav) and protected the careers of innovators. Inman's effort to "sell Opintel" created more similar-minded advocates like Richardson: the more advocates, the more protection for Opintel innovators. The result was significant improvements in Opintel learning and adaptation throughout the Navy.

EPILOGUE
Afloat, at Last

NATO's Teamwork '88 exercise, the largest multinational naval exercise of the decade, was in full swing.[1] Capt. Jake Jacoby, USN, Second Fleet N2, stood in SupPlot, looking at the digital-intelligence plot displayed on the experimental Advanced Tracking Prototype (ATP) system. An improved version of the Prototype Ocean Surveillance Terminal (POST) fielded in the early 1980s, the ATP incorporated Outlaw Shark and ECLIPS-like elements. Jacoby's system was a technological bridge to an advanced correlation system (ACS) in development.[2]

The most important feature of the ATP was its direct downlink from the Classic Wizard satellite ELINT collection system. The ATP's correlation capability was its second-best feature. With the ATP, shipboard Opintel teams had similar access and capabilities as those at the OSIS nodes. The ATP also had dissemination tools. It sanitized and down-transferred tracks to the Joint Operations Tactical System (JOTS), displaying the common operating picture (COP). JOTS fed the Combat Information Center (CIC) and the Tactical Flag Command Center (TFCC) displays. Together the intelligence plot and COP enhanced tactical decision-making.[3]

Eleven years earlier, then-commander Tom Brooks, the Second Fleet's N2, stood on the same ship in the same ocean conducting Teamwork '77. At the time, it was the largest NATO naval exercise of the 1970s. Brooks' new technology, crude compared to Jacoby's ATP, improved the intelligence plot's display. In just a decade, shipboard Opintel had made significant technological and organizational advancements. The fragile ECLIPS, stymied by a floor buffer–caused power problem in 1976, had led to OSIS-like capabilities being afloat. A decade earlier, the analysis and dissemination only done by a sizable Opintel team at a shore-based

OSIS node could now be done at sea next door to the afloat operational commander.

Jacoby believed he provided more timely warning intelligence with the ATP than the OSIS nodes. He needed data to prove his assertion, and the Soviet Navy provided it. "The Soviets came at us [with] a lot with Backfire [TU-122], Bears [Tu-95], and Badgers [TU-16]," Jacoby recalled in a 2019 interview. Purposefully, Jacoby's team isolated the FOSIC reports from their own. Comparing the "time difference of arrival [information from the satellite to system]" between the reports, "our finding was that the SIGINT system [through the OSIS node] could not deliver on the [warning] requirement" needed to execute the new Maritime Strategy."[4]

"Unintentionally, what I was saying was that with these capabilities [ATP], we don't need the shore OSIS, the FOSICs, and the FOSIFs [for event-by-event reporting]," said Jacoby. "You have some sense of how popular that was," referring to his assessment and report. The little brother was in some regards now equal to big brother. Jacoby never proclaimed that OSIS was entirely afloat, only that it was moving further toward that goal. The truth is the symbiotic (supported to supporting) relationship between shipboard and shore Opintel, between operational and strategic warning intelligence, was almost unbreakable. The term "OSIS afloat," Jacoby noted, "was coined later. It became a useful moniker for seeking money for the afloat capabilities . . . [like] increased bandwidth to deliver capabilities to carriers and big decks . . . [capabilities like] imagery afloat which became of increased importance in terms of timeliness as precision strike capabilities increased."[5]

The OSIS nodes had not failed Jacoby in 1988; their warning intelligence suffered from scale and scope issues. Jacoby's warning problem on *Mount Whitney* was scaled to only the specific operations area. Warning intelligence from the OSIS nodes in Norfolk, London, and Rota was on a multitheater scale, covering the North Atlantic Ocean and the Baltic, Mediterranean, Norwegian, and Black Seas. It was also decidedly more concerned with Soviet SSBNs than surface navy activity. Jacoby's scope was limited; he only supported the afloat commander and staff. The OSIS nodes supported the entire theater-level command and all the underway units. The OSIS nodes' larger theater scale and scope enabled the shipboard Opintel teams' more detailed focus. Even more important was the continuity the OSIS nodes offered. Battlegroups came and went, creating gaps in coverage and knowledge the OSIS nodes had to cover. The little brother afloat in SupPlot lacked the capacity for theater-wide, beyond-the-horizon warfare without its larger sibling. Conversely, the OSIS nodes big brother needed the tactical details only little brother, at sea, eyeball-to-eyeball with the Soviet Navy, provided. Though competitive in many ways, the relationship was always one of alternating supported and supporting efforts.

There was another problem at the OSIS nodes; they had become victims of their success. Their all-source fusion model successfully pushed the operational intelligence that theater commanders desired. The Navy's "watch standing" approach to operational intelligence allowed it to "push" information to its customers. The U.S. Army and U.S. Air Force took a requirements-based or "pull" approach, mainly producing only intelligence products their customers requested. Those products were scheduled and not necessarily on-demand.[6] Customers, especially at the theater commander level, liked having "pushed" and "pulled" intelligence. Thus the OSIS nodes became essential to the theater commander's intelligence staff. Some within Navy Intelligence argued that the new demands distracted the OSIS nodes from their traditional fleet focus. Others saw the demands as admiration that assured funding for Navy Intelligence in the austere fiscal environment.

Defense Reform, Centralization

Previous defense reform efforts focused on the "tides" of reform: scientific management consolidation, antiwaste efforts, increased "openness" and transparency, and increased management effectiveness. By the mid-1980s pressure had mounted. The "tides" had converged into a wave of demand for a more comprehensive reform bill. The Goldwater-Nichols National Defense Reform Act was passed in September 1986.[7] The Navy was a particular focus for reform. The act attempted, yet again, "to rescind the Navy's historically independent operating role."[8] The bill had broad expectations.

It looked to correct decades of civilian discontent in operational and acquisition capabilities and wasteful spending by all the military services.[9] In particular the idea of "jointness," or a more integrated decision-making and operations execution across the services, was a desire. Like reform bills in the past, the Goldwater-Nichols Act took significant time to implement. The military services often delay implementing elements of reform they dislike. This reform effort would be different because the world was rapidly changing; the Soviet Union was crumbling.

In a 1990 visit to the aircraft carrier *Theodore Roosevelt* the future chief of the Soviet Navy Staff, Rear Admiral Gromov, summed up the U.S. military's dilemma: "We are going to do the worst thing to you: we are going to take away your threat."[10] By 1988 the poorly performing Soviet economy had collapsed and the state-party apparatus torn itself apart.[11] General Secretary Mikhail Sergeyevich Gorbachev's perestroika and glasnost policies had provided too much freedom, undermining Communist Party control. In November 1989 the East Germans, fiscally on the verge of bankruptcy, lost control and opened their border to West Germany. The Berlin Wall fell, Germany unified, and the Warsaw Pact collapsed. It was the beginning of the end of the Cold War.

In April 1990 Jacoby arrived as the new N2 for commander in chief, U.S. Pacific Fleet (CINCPACFLT). Calls to slash defense funding, the "peace dividend," were loud, and the Department of Defense was looking to get ahead of any significant budget cuts.[12] Jacoby knew he needed to use centralization to meet the 33 percent budget cut "or forfeit [the] decisions to 'bean-counters' in Washington." His plan was simple: Combine the three existing intelligence centers in Oʻahu, Hawaiʻi, into a joint center subordinated to USCINCPAC.[13] It was a bold proposal. To many in Navy Intelligence, Jacoby was "selling the farm" by sacrificing the fleet-focused OSIS node in Hawaiʻi. Those more pragmatic, like Rear Adm. Tom Brooks, DNI since July 1988, knew what Jacoby knew: the Soviet Navy's reduced activity meant centralization and "jointness" were the only way to save *any* fleet OSIS support.[14]

The U.S. military's overwhelming dominance against Iraq during the Gulf War (Operation Desert Shield/Desert Storm, 1990–1991) rang the final bell: the Cold War was over.[15] While a victory, the Gulf War performance had failed to meet civilian leadership's "jointness" expectations. The reform efforts accelerated across the Department of Defense. Jacoby's centralizing approach provided a road map for the other theaters.[16]

The Joint Intelligence Center Pacific officially stood up on July 3, 1991. In some regards only the "bean counters" were happy with JICPAC. Many of Pacific command's service components complained. Some components increased their intelligence-production demands to protect their equities. The Navy, mainly intelligence officers (163x) and senior line officers, chose to grumble vehemently.[17] The complaints pointed out that JICPAC's support was much less than that the FOSIC and Fleet Intelligence Center (FIC) had provided to the fleet. JICPAC, as operational intelligence in every theater, had a classic conundrum: customers could have timely, high-quality, or cheap operational intelligence but not all three simultaneously.

JICPAC was overcommitted; it had too many production demands. Jacoby, now JICPAC commander, centralized further to mitigate the challenges. JICPAC instituted a requirement-based system with more "pull" than "push" in supplying operational intelligence. Jacoby aligned personnel with analysis and production efforts by producing products on requirements approved and prioritized by the USCINCPAC J2. New information-management and -dissemination technologies helped the effort, and the requirements-based approach worked. By 1993 JICPAC was fully operational and the model for all other theater intelligence centers.[18]

The last OSIS node officially closed at midnight on July 1, 1996, when FOSIF Rota passed the watch to the Joint Analysis Center (JAC) at Royal Air Force Base Molesworth in the United Kingdom. FOSIF Rota was the alpha and omega of the OSIS system; it is fitting that such a successful operational-intelligence approach ended where it had begun.

Navy Opintel practitioners filled the new Joint Intelligence and Analysis Centers with their Opintel culture. The other services had nothing resembling the Navy's all-source-fusion Opintel process. Ford and Rosenberg write in *The Admirals' Advantage* that "it fell to veterans of the OSIS system to help build the mechanisms for all-source intelligence fusion on the new 'purple' [joint] watchfloors."[19] To some Navy intelligence officers (163x), raising joint operational intelligence "up" meant "shortchanging" the fleet. "It did not seem the Navy was bringing the other Services up," wrote Capt. James "J. R." Reddig, USN (Ret.) (aka Vic Socotra) in 1998, but, "rather, . . . the [Joint] system was dragging OPINTEL support down." Joint operational intelligence had changed Navy Intelligence through the same reciprocating influences seen between OSIS and SupPlot. No matter what Navy intelligence officers felt about joint duty, it had become a critical part of their career path. DNI Rear Adm. Mike Cramer, USN, declared in 1996 that "the Naval Intelligence Community had only three types of assignments: The Fleet, Joint, or preparation to go to one or the other."[20]

More Centralization

The electromagnetic spectrum is essential in modern naval warfare. The Yom Kippur War's naval battles off Latakia, Syria, and Baltim, Egypt, emphasized the point. The Israeli Navy had used electronic warfare tactics to employ the short-range Gabriel anti-ship missile with deadly effect, defeating the Syrian and Egyptian missile boats.[21] The sea control and denial battles during the 1982 Falklands War again underscored electronic warfare's importance.[22] What made command and control warfare (C2W) in the latter part of the Cold War revolutionary was an information environment built by high-speed computing and networked communications.[23] Fundamentally C2W was about using information to make better decisions faster than the enemy, while at the same time using deception and denial to disrupt their decision process. U.S. Air Force Col. John Boyd's observe-orient-decide-act (OODA) model and its idea of creating strategic paralysis in an adversary underpinned C2W.[24]

In January 1995 the secretary of Defense formed an executive board to investigate the idea of information warfare (IW). There was confusion surrounding what "information warfare" is. In 1996 the U.S. Army developed the first comprehensive IW doctrine, Field Manual 100-6, "Information Operations."[25] The Army articulated the concept of "information dominance," or a "degree of information superiority that allows . . . [one] to achieve an operational advantage in a conflict."[26]

The RAND Corporation produced several studies on IW: *Strategic Information Warfare: A New Face of War* (1996) and *Strategic Appraisal: The Changing Role of Information in Warfare* (1999) helped refine the role of information warfare.[27] The Navy struggled with evolving IW concepts. Their professional magazine, the U.S. Naval Institute's *Proceedings*, was full of articles arguing varying points regarding IW's definition and application for naval warfare. In January 1998 Vice Adm. Arthur K. Cebrowski, USN (1942–2005), noted that warfare had shifted from "platform-centric" to "network-centric."[28]

Cebrowski's *Proceedings* article created a seismic shift in how the Navy saw future warfare. The economy, new computing, and computer networking, especially the Internet, Cebrowski argued, created an adaptable information environment. The information environment created new areas for competition. With the right approach, one competitor could create information superiority over others. "Network-centric warfare," Cebrowski wrote, "enables a shift from attrition-style warfare to a much faster and more effective warfighting style characterized by the new concepts of speed of command and self-synchronization." He advocated obtaining "information superiority" by exploiting networked information systems to create information dominance over an adversary, as the Army described in its doctrine.[29] The Navy fell in love with network-centric warfare. The concept fit into Cold War OpNav thinking that treated technology as a replacement for strategy. Indeed, no one would argue against a new warfighting concept that promised to gain the information high ground, disrupt an opponent's decision cycle, and win conflicts quickly.

The attacks of September 11, 2001, on the World Trade Center and the Pentagon and the following conflicts in Afghanistan and Iraq reinforced the importance of IW. More importantly the fight against violent extremist groups, not state actors, highlighted that network-centric warfare, as envisioned by Cebrowski, was open to everyone. The Navy doubled down on network-centric approaches, looking to Navy Intelligence to create information superiority. However, the basic structure of the battlegroup's Opintel organization had not ostensibly changed since the late 1970s. In a 2003 *Proceedings* article Capt. Eileen F. MacKrell, USN (Ret.), described a way to operationalize network-centric warfare inside the shipboard Opintel organizational structure. MacKrell leveraged SupPlot and new network accesses to pull and push information and intelligence to and from shore-based long-term national and theater intelligence-analysis centers. High-speed communications allowed her team to create a maritime domain awareness-centric form of information superiority for the commander and the ships within the battlegroup (now called a carrier strike group).[30]

The Navy needed to centralize its information and intelligence capabilities to gain information dominance. In 2009 it created the Information Dominance Corps (IDC), the most significant change to Navy Intelligence since the 1968 merger of the air intelligence officers (135x) into the intelligence officer (163x) community. The IDC centralized four officer communities and associated enlisted ratings under the deputy chief of Naval Operations for Information Dominance/Director of Naval Intelligence. The Navy combined two OpNav functions: intelligence (N2) and communications (N6).[31] The 16xx officer designator was changed to an 18xx designator for the new corps, combining oceanography specialists (180x) and cryptologic warfare specialists (181x), and later creating cyber warfare engineers (184x), information professionals (182x), and intelligence officers (183x). In 2010 the Navy authorized an information dominance warfare officer (IDWO) warfare insignia (an artifact), like those in the aviation, seemingly legitimizing the new community.[32]

Part of the reorganization came from the ideas of information dominance. Most reasons, however, were based on the realities of an ongoing land-centric asymmetrical conflict with nonstate violent extremists. Left without a significant role in the conflict, the Navy augmented Army and Marine Corps units operating in Afghanistan and Iraq. Navy Intelligence augmentees were in high demand but were insufficient in number. An internal augmentation structure, oddly enough, provided personnel to meet the external augmentation demand. Implemented in April 2009,

OpNav N2/N6 removed about two-thirds of the aircraft carrier's OZ Division crew requirement. The two intelligence officers (163x) assigned to the air wing intelligence officer (CAGAI) as the targeteer and imagery officer in the early 1990s were also removed. Most of the removed personnel filled billets at intelligence centers of excellence at the Office of Naval Intelligence (ONI) and the Naval Air and Strike Warfare Center (NASWC) at Fallon, Nevada. Others went to the Navy's numbered fleets at the theater combatant commands. The numbered fleets used the additional crew resources to create fleet intelligence adaptive force (FIAF) detachments augmenting Afghanistan and Iraq units. ONI and NASWC created fleet intelligence detachments (FID) that returned to the carrier strike groups as augmentees assigned to the staff's intelligence officer (N2).[33]

The shipboard Opintel teams decried the FID model primarily because it had changed the nearly four-decades-old crew resource structure. However, the FID concept improved Opintel, targeting, and all-source analysis tradecraft. With the FID, the N2 now provided more than one-half of the SupPlot and imagery-analysis personnel to the shipboard Opintel team. The N2 also owned the targeting portion of the FID, but the CAGAI managed those personnel in practice. The crew-resource restructuring did not ostensibly change the decentralized shipboard Opintel organization, just the resource balance between the N2, SIO, and CAGAI. Servant ethos and coordination without hierarchy retained primacy despite the N2 and the ship's intelligence officer (SIO) reaching resource parity.

The 2010 "U.S. Navy's Vision for Information Dominance" emphasized that "information in warfare and information as warfare" was no longer a supporting activity. It described IW as a "main battery of 21st century American seapower" and that it "will be treated as a weapon."[34] These words echoed Cebrowski's writings from the late 1990s. Cebrowski had said that making information dominance a reality required specialization through investment in intellectual capital. The argument was that if information was a warfare domain, those working there deserved "warfighter status."[35] The IDC's 2011 "Navy Strategy for Achieving Information Dominance" caused alarm, especially among the intelligence officer (183x) community. In a 2014 article Capt. Henry Stephenson, USN (1830) (Ret.), argued that information was an enabler, not a warfare area equivalent to surface, air, subsurface, and land. "Information dominance as a naval warfare pillar itself—is not a fact," Stephenson wrote. He also criticized the IDC's new cross-detailing approach, wherein IDC officers served in leadership roles outside their specialty.[36]

To Stephenson an even worse trend had emerged: the IDC was trying to restructure itself to mirror the line communities. The restructuring was part of a disturbing centralization proposing to "incorporate most—perhaps all—IDC elements on afloat staff under a single IDC senior officer."[37] Like Stephenson, Capt. William R. Bray, USN (1830) (Ret.), argued in 2016 that intelligence is not information warfare and cannot stand equivalent to the Navy's authentic warfare communities. Bray's article came on the heels of the Navy's renaming of the IDC to the Information Warfare Community (IWC).[38] Many intelligence officers (183x) saw a disturbing trend: the IWC believe it was no longer an enabler or servant but a warfighter intended to command forces at sea and carry a line officer designation. Not all IWC officers saw information warfare as some of the intelligence officers; some believed what was espoused by then-DCNO of N2/N6 Vice Adm. Ted Branch, USN (Ret.), a pilot. The Navy was "stress[ing] the importance of Information Warfare and . . 'double dog doubling down' on Information Warfare."[39] To many doubling down was a good thing.

The IWC was also doubling down on organization centralization. The composite warfare commander (CWC) concept recognized the importance of information in warfare at sea. The information operations warfare commander (listed as IWC in doctrine but referred to as IWCmdr in this book) was a designated warfare commander within the CWC construct. The designation as a warfare commander, not a functional commander, made the IWCmdr equal to the air and missile defense (usually a surface warfare officer), antisubmarine warfare (usually a surface warfare officer), strike warfare (usually the carrier air group commander), and the surface warfare (usually a surface warfare officer) commanders.[40] The new IWC believed they should fill the IWCmdr role. In a 2015 experiment a senior IWC officer became the IWCmdr on a carrier strike group staff. By the end of 2016 the plan to fill all IWCmdr billets with senior IWC leaders was approved, and an administrative IWCmdr selection board was also held.[41] In 2017 two information warfare officers (1810), formerly called cryptologic warfare specialist officers, deployed as the IWCmdr for two carrier strike groups.[42]

Thus, the logic goes, if the IWCmdr was a legitimate warfare commander and the IWC filled that position, then the IWC is a legitimate line warfare area. Further, all the other warfare commanders are from line communities; the IWC should be a line officer, not a restricted line officer community. Some within the Navy, especially intelligence officers (183x), voiced concern over the equation of IWC education, training, and experience with that of line officers who have commanded forces afloat.[43]

One of the most significant organizational changes was the centralization of all afloat IWC functions under the IWCmdr. This centralization was of significant concern for the intelligence officer (183x). In their minds the commander-rank career-milestone positions, strike group intelligence officer (N2) and the aircraft carrier senior intelligence officer (SIO), were no longer senior positions. Being subordinated to an IWC captain in the position of the IWCmdr, the argument went, devalued those roles. The argument went further: If the IWC was now the operator/warfighter and not the servant, would it undermine the intelligence officer's raison d'être? Will the effort to create tactical command credibility distract from the IWC's focus on the "informational side of the warfighting decision loop?"[44]

Others disagree, seeing the IWCmdr as a logical next step. One needs to remain competitive in the future cyber- and artificial-intelligence-dominated global battlespace. They argue that consolidating information-related capabilities and individual IWC functions is necessary to win the next war. Many believe centralizing those functions under the IWCmdr and creating a formal hierarchy is the only secure organizational method for success.[45]

The National Defense Authorization Act, signed January 5, 2021, struck section 8137 from Title 10 of the U.S. Code—"Regular Navy: officers designated for engineering duty, aeronautical engineering duty, and special duty." In law, any restriction to command at sea for the restricted line communities disappeared. Essentially it took the "R" out of "RL," so to speak.[46] The IWC could now have command at sea. The change in law was a milestone, as had been the inclusion of engineering duty officers under the Naval Reform Act of 1899. The march toward taking the "R" out of the "RL" had begun in 2015 with CNO Adm. Jonathan Greenert, a submarine officer. Efforts continued under the leadership of CNO Adm. John M. Richardson, also a submarine officer, and finally succeeded under the current CNO, Adm. Michael M. Gilday, a surface warfare officer.

The repeal happened; few IWC officers were aware. Those who took notice waited for IWC leadership to explain what it meant. On November 16, 2021, in a meeting with IWC members at the U.S. Naval War College, Vice Adm. Kelly Aeschbach, USN (Ret.), commander Naval Information Forces (NAVIFOR), provided a succinct description: the removal of the "R" provided flexibility for a future, ill-defined character of war dominated by actions in the information environment. Information operations, electromagnetic maneuvers, and cyber actions would significantly influence any war's outcome. Aeschbach quickly addressed the concern over promotion opportunities. Unlike the past 135xs, who had competed and lost out to pilots, IWC officers would compete inside an information warfare (IW) line category, not against the traditional line categories (air, surface, submarine, SEAL, and EOD). Most of the audience did not understand the nuanced and challenging aspects of creating a new competitive officer-categories section for IW.

The line competitive categories are a narrow, platform-centric interpretation of Title 10 law. The Secretary of the Navy's policy maintained a balance between the three primary warfighting "unions," as Admiral Zumwalt had called them in the 1970s. Repealing part of Title 10 opened the way to changing Navy policy. "To change a Navy policy simply requires the Navy to issue a new one, which could happen quickly," a 2005 RAND study offered on the process.[47] Indeed, simple administrative policies are easily changed. However, the officer communities hold power within the Navy's organization. Each community's authorized billets are part of a zero-sum equation; adding to one must take from another. Changes to the "Officer Competitive Categories for the Active Duty List" (SecNavInst 1400.1C) provoke parochial battles: if the IWC can have command at sea, someone from the "unions" might not. The IWC had climbed up the U.S. Title 10 legal mountain, one step at a time, only to find another much larger Navy "administrative" mountain.

The SecNavInst 1400.1C is typically reviewed and updated every three years. Creating new IW line competitive categories requires "complete justification" and an evaluation of "advantages and disadvantages" for the proposed category. The change also must support the Navy's total warfighting capability and officer corps.[48] Thus the advantages of warfighting capability that the IWC argues it brings must outweigh the disadvantages of accession, retention, and promotion for the entire officer corps. Further, if the IWC is essential, it could grow, removing flag officer billets from a "union"! Climbing the policy mountain comes with parochial "fistfights" with every step.

Fear, it seems, plays a significant role in the angst associated with the IWCmdr and the removal of the restriction for command at sea. With an uphill Navy policy battle ahead, the IWC leadership feared having an internal battle simultaneously. On the one hand, they feared a buildup of resistance "antibodies" inside the IWC to the changes. The cited articles in this chapter show that the leadership's fear of resistance was not unfounded. The IWC leadership tended to keep their analysis and planning close to their vest. They did so hoping to reduce friction and create space to develop a fully formed plan quickly.

On the other hand IWC members below the senior-leadership level feared the move weakened the tradecraft of their specialty and jeopardized their careers. Not privy to the thinking, the members filled in the knowledge gaps for themselves. In both cases fear stems from what business theorist Chris Argyris calls "defensive reasoning" brought about by asymmetrical knowledge and a reluctance to expose reasoning to criticism.[49]

As we have seen in our exploration, Navy Intelligence tends to formalize through administrative tools (billet restructuring) within its decision "lifelines." Such formalization robs the organization's members of their agency in the learning process. The creation of the IWCmdr and the move toward the "IW line" are further examples. The IWCmdr concept was piloted and formalized in less than two years. According to OpNav N2N6, no whitepapers or results of the experiment were written. Instead several PowerPoint presentations and postdeployment reports captured the observations and opinions of strike group commanders. From those briefings the resource sponsor approved the recommended changes in the billet structure for IWCmdr to any IWC captain (1850 designator). Leadership wanted to "move faster," and the decisions for billet structure were within their "decision space."[50]

The change was undoubtedly "unorthodox" and fast but supposedly "well-informed," at least at the senior-leadership level. The IWCmdr was not a new role. Navy Warfare Publication 3–56, "Composite Warfare: Maritime Operations at the Tactical Level of War," already defined it but not necessarily the same way the IWC was. There was still confusion. The IWC's vision of the IWCmdr and its importance in career progression were ill-defined. The only understanding of the IWCmdr was from a negative vision, not informed by any concepts or theory, only peacetime experience. Milan Vego offers that intellectual change must occur before doctrinal change, and doctrinal change before force-structure changes. Thus the IWCmdr formalization should have been preceded by a document articulating the new operating concept and some draft doctrinal changes that allowed for "frank intellectual debate."[51] If such documents existed, they were not provided to the lower leadership, nor was "frank debate" encouraged.

"Without an open debate," Vego writes, "good ideas would have a hard time becoming accepted." He uses network-centric warfare as an example. Proponents were "unwilling to get involved in, or . . . openly hostile to, any serious discussion of not only the advantages (there are many) but also some serious vulnerabilities (there are quite a few) of the entire concept."[52]

Vego offers that the lack of open debate creates "major problems with the entire concept of information warfare."[53] Here information security is offered as a reason. Indeed, security classification is a consistent problem but only if one confines the discussion to the tactical level. Doctrine comes from the interpretation of the theory and experience. Information warfare's role in force/counterforce theory is ill-defined. What theory exists is mostly unclassified. The discussion should start with those theories, but it has not.

Asking *What do we want?* is not the same as asking *What do we want to avoid?* says American systems scientist Peter M. Senge. The IWC leadership has a positive vision, he says, while many in the lower part of the organization have a negative one. Everyone needs to have the same understanding of the positive vision because negative ones are limiting. Bringing the two visions together often occurs when the organization's survival is threatened. Without a credible catalyst, either vision will not be accepted on its intrinsic merit.[54] Understanding what the IWC is and what the IWCmdr does must be articulated in operating concepts and draft doctrine to share the vision, conduct debate, and accept the concept.

Of course the vision problem is also a generational one. Soon those who were 163x and remember the old system will be gone. The new generation of IWC officers only knows of the current formalized system. As we've seen, informal change led to the evolution of the Navy's afloat Opintel, and informal changes only occur from a centralized, formalized system that retains emergent potential and evolvability. Thus any weakness in the new organization will result in informal compensation, adaptation, and innovation—a perpetual cycle.

In an All Navy Message, Secretary of the Navy Carlos Del Toro reclassified IWC officers from restricted to "line officers performing information warfare duties."[55] The newly established information warfare (IW) line will be more fully defined by SECNAVINST 1400.1D, which establishes officer competitive-promotion categories across the force. Vice Adm. Michael Vernazza, commander, Naval Information Forces (NAVIFOR), clarified that "this now opens the door for command at sea for Information Warfare officers, but that those officers will not be competing with URL officers."[56] The IWC climbed the policy mountain and triumphed in the parochial "fistfight."

Conclusion

Royal Navy Commodore Betton's question *Why this way?* exposed that modern-day Navy intelligence practitioners have a shallow understanding of shipboard Opintel. This subsequent exploration has reinforced several evolutionary themes considered in previous Navy operational intelligence–related works but through the lens of analyzing the importance and interrelationality of technology, all-source fusion, support to the commander, and the importance of personnel. What we have found is a story of informal and formal reciprocal influence between shipboard and shore-based Opintel organizations looking to solve operational problems.

Military organizational evolution especially but all organizations generally are problem-solving-focused. However, deciding *what* problems must be solved is not straightforward. During the Cold War, when a single existential threat was the enabling constraint, organizational change seemed easier. There is no master plan for an organization's evolution, even when an explicit enabling constraint exists in the form of an enemy. The complex adaptive systems at play prevent precise predictions regarding the outcomes of relationships and interactions. What is clear from our study is that the application of new technological advances often drives change within navy organizations.

Three operational intelligence–related naval systems—the Integrated Operational Intelligence Center (IOIC), the Ocean Surveillance Information System (OSIS), and Outlaw Shark-SupPlot—provided scaffolding on which the examination of technology and the evolution of organizations that wielded it sat in balance. We have analyzed the revolutionary "sparks" from those technological systems and the evolutionary organizational innovations that have followed. This methodological approach provided us a chronology that cohered the historical narrative: It is not the technology alone that explains why shipboard Opintel has developed the way it has, but rather, it is how the organization has adapted to the new technology that has proven more interesting and informative. We have seen that informal adaptation by the people using the systems is as important as the systems themselves in their evolution.

The importance of decentralization emerges when we consider the evolution of Opintel. Decentralizing national intelligence to the OSIS nodes, for example, proved critical; however, further decentralization of shipboard Opintel suborganizations, not just national intelligence, was essential in creating evolvability. Decentralization, we've seen, created an interdependent multiorganizational environment. This environment fostered informal communication and coordination, leading to innovation and adaptation essential to evolution. Often decentralization occurs informally, and organizations usually react by reestablishing formal centralization. The decisions made by Navy Intelligence leaders and their line community customers about informal decentralization are important.

Navy Intelligence allowed the multiorganizations to coordinate without hierarchy—or at least didn't impede it—which in the afloat and shore-based OSIS nodes was probably the most advantageous but hardest "nondecision" made for the evolution of shipboard Opintel. What resulted was a safe environment wherein experimentation and adaptation flourished, and those "Sailor-mods" described in this book flourished. Within that environment resided the evolvability Trent Hone describes. The personal decisions by those afloat Opintel professionals to leverage their peers for support and to cooperate by sharing their successful and failed experimentations and adaptations were probably the bravest decisions in the context of organizational evolution, especially considering the Navy's personnel-competition framework. However, if asked those same professionals would not call it bravery but operational necessities. Why? Because within the afloat and OSIS Opintel world the servant ethos was the driving enabling constraint: serving their commander had primacy.

The servant ethos does not only guide the Opintel professional; it is fundamental at all levels of successful organizations. The Opintel organizational culture was born in a Navy schema shaped by the traditional missions of naval diplomacy and war. The three primary line communities—aviation, submarine, and surface—all have individual suborganizational characters. As customers of Opintel, each line community, through its demands for intelligence, influenced the performance orientation and identity of Navy Intelligence. The aviation community provided the most significant organizational cultural influence on the Opintel organization: merging a much larger air intelligence officer (135x) community into the intelligence officer (163x) community resulted in an aviation-dominated organizational culture. Indeed we have seen the influence of the "squadron culture" on competition, coordination, and esprit de corps in both shipboard and shore Opintel organizations.

Another critical aspect of aviation's cultural influence comes from the nature of airpower itself. Airpower is targeting, and targeting is intelligence. Put differently, power projection from the sea is targeting, and targeting is intelligence. World War II showed that surface vessel naval gunfire support, like aircraft bombing, required good targets to achieve desired effects. In the Cold War, fighting beyond the horizon was required, and Opintel became even more vital for its warning intelligence and power protection targeting. This is not to say that other line communities did not have some influence; rather, that influence was limited to those associated with a customer's demand signal for intelligence. For example, the surface line community was limited by shipboard space and a Navy battlegroup construct in which surface ships defended aircraft carriers; this meant that Opintel was provided to surface ships, not produced on them. Thus the surface line relied more on its short-range onboard sensors and operational intelligence produced through a process they had little association with. That lack of association with Opintel at sea limited the surface line community's influence on the Opintel organization's identity.

Most important to the evolution of the Opintel organization is the Navy aviation culture's level of comfort in using informal compensation to adapt formal organizational structures that are too rigid for the changing environment. Inside aviation culture, decentralization, informal coordination, and interdependence were acceptable if not encouraged features. These cultural characteristics worked because intra- and inter-squadron-supported and -supporting roles were common in aviation. The servant ethos of Opintel was embedded and reinforced by aviation culture and became a unifying mechanism in the multiorganizational environment in which informal coordination flourished.

The aviation community also offered a different perspective on constraints (must do) and restraints (cannot do) as subjective, a gray area open to interpretation and subject to pragmatic solutions required to achieve a mission. Because of this perspective the threshold for symmetry break was lower and informal organizational change more common. Constant innovation, creative thinking, and adapting for efficiency occur—a form of endless "tinkering" on the organizational structure. This tinkering, almost to a detriment, abounds in "squadron culture" because the organizational environment creates a safe "space to fail that encourages it."[1] Any good idea was valid, and the best ideas gained traction within the squadron or air wing. Therefore a propensity to lean toward decentralization and informal processes became practice in shipboard Opintel culture. The reciprocal influence between shipboard Opintel and OSIS organizations transferred, embedded, and reinforced a decentralized view of organizational elements throughout Navy Intelligence.

The aviation community imparted a final element to Navy Intelligence: talent management. To embrace innovation meant protecting innovators. The formal Navy career path and promotion structure loathe deviation. Most effective innovators work outside the standard career path, facing career ruination. The aviation community found ways to protect and promote innovators for the organization's good, primarily by having senior officers champion junior innovators. The longevity of the senior officer made the protection of innovators effective. When it mattered most to Navy Intelligence, Admiral Bobby Inman protected innovators; he matched high-performing intelligence officers (163x) with like-minded up-and-coming senior line flag officers. As a resource sponsor Inman's willingness to wield his power beyond his time as director of Naval Intelligence had a long-lasting positive influence; it created a new, enduring culture. His collaboration with his successors—Rear Admirals Sumner "Shap" Shapiro (DNI 1978–1982), John L. Butts (DNI 1982–1985), and William O. Studeman (DNI 1985–1988)—produced similar results to the aviation community's collaboration between Rear Admiral Moffett and Vice Admiral Reeves.

What we have found in our study is that centralization and formal organization, far from being deficient or obsolete, are critical to decentralization and informal adaptation. It is the creative tension over centralism that enhances organizational evolvability. Centralized and strong formal organizational structures created too much rigidity for the shipboard Opintel process in the 1960s and '70s. In the face of the formal organization's weakness, the OZ Division (CVIC and SupPlot), OS Division (cryptologists), and shore-based OSIS nodes informally coordinated to create solutions. Later the formal organization adopted and consolidated some of the informal solutions; in other words, it caught up. Consolidation, usually through organizational billet restructuring within Navy Intelligence, is its primary aspect of evolution. However, overreliance on codifying change through resources (billet restructuring) robbed the organization of needed debate regarding theory, concepts, and shared understanding, leading to greater organizational learning.

The influence of the aviation community, we have seen, has been significant, but the importance of the Vietnam War NISO and NILO experience was as well. The "in-country" experience in collecting and using human intelligence was formative. The visceral experiences of those Naval Intelligence liaison officers operating in the northern part of the Mekong River Delta—under fire, elbow to elbow with the operator—carried significant influence. The intelligence officers (163x) returned from Vietnam with new performance orientations and tradecraft. Their promotion opportunities increased comparatively. Similarly the importance of the VP squadron experience is also limited. Both nonshipboard experiences reciprocally carried new perspectives to OSIS nodes and shipboard Opintel.

Finally, understanding that centralization at the tactical level is not necessarily beneficial does not mean it is not beneficial at higher levels of command. Intelligence's role during and after the Vietnam War provides insight into higher organizational-level centralization. Vice Admiral Rectanus' intelligence operations at NAVFORV show the benefit of centralization at the operational level. The implied efficiencies created by centralization are believed to make intelligence more effective. The example of the intelligence community's reform in the 1970s reinforces the belief. The 1971 Schlesinger Report, for example, was one of many such reform attempts. Usually reform focused on applying "management" to the IC to achieve better results for policymakers. President Nixon's desire in 1971 to increase knowledge provided at a lower cost sometimes clashed with IC desire for complete objectivity.

However, perfect intelligence is impossible, and the decision-makers' desire to reduce risk through information superiority always exists. The result is that decision-makers are increasingly seeking reassurance from intelligence organizations.[2] Intelligence, however, is never perfect, and risk aversion leads to possible decision-making paralysis. The Opintel professional at sea must always balance the tension inherent in the opposing constraints of obtaining accurate intelligence, delivered quickly, with limited resources.

So What?

Navy Intelligence's future success centers on learning from Opintel's Cold War–era organizational evolution. Leadership is an essential component to successful change, and today's leaders must find the courage to nurture the servant ethos as a critical part of organizational evolvability—no easy ask when much of the organization sees itself as a warrior. Leaders must also create an environment in which it is safe to fail and that encourages critical and creative thinking, innovation, and informal adaptation.

Making a "nondecision" at the right time is more challenging but vitally important for today's leaders: choose to *not* step in with more top-down guidance and instead let an organization wrestle with and informally adapt to the new technology or operational problem at the lowest level. Allow informal decentralization; recognizing a revolutionary spark or symmetry break and letting it play out is critical to military organizational evolution. Become comfortable with accepting uncertainty surrounding low-level organization evolution; this is associated with a loss of centralization and low-level intra- and interorganizational coordination without hierarchy. The informal adaptation may not take, but it probably won't be a complete failure either; the organization will tinker and adapt again, building on the goods and correcting the rest.

Before deciding to "catch up" and centralize, consider the lessons learned during the evolution and examine the tinkering to see where new concepts emerge. Publish those concept papers and openly debate them. Listen to the debate. Decide, and then publish the decision, even if the conclusion is yet more billet restructuring. Then aggressively implement centralization: control the narrative through transparency of the positive view of the change vision. Now let the cycle repeat itself.

During the Cold War Navy Opintel evolved successfully amid competition. This history can guide the Navy as it navigates the new era of great power competition now upon us.

NOTES

Preface

1. For a snapshot of the early days of U.S. Naval intelligence in the modern era, see the "Intelligence Assignment and Placement" section of the 1972 issue of the Bureau of Naval Personnel's *Naval Intelligence Newsletter.*

    Throughout this work, I will be pointing the reader to the "Intelligence Assignment and Placement" section of back issues spanning 1960 through 1980, all of which are held among the personal papers of Rear Admiral Thomas A. Brooks Archive, personal papers, Arlington, VA.

2. Wyman H. Packard, *A Century of U.S. Naval Intelligence* (Washington, DC: Office of Naval Intelligence, Naval Historical Center, 1996), archived online at https://archive.org/details/centuryofusnaval00wash. Background on Packard's effort to write the book can be found in Bryan Leese, "NHHC Archive Research Strategy Meeting with Curtis Utz," meeting notes, Naval History and Heritage Command, Washington, DC, April 20, 2018, author's personal papers.

3. Christopher A. Ford and David A. Rosenberg, *The Admirals' Advantage: U.S. Navy Operational Intelligence in World War II and the Cold War*, with Randy Carol Balano (Annapolis, MD: Naval Institute Press, 2005), particularly xii–xiv.

4. I was given access to the ONI archive and transcribed over ten of the eleven VHS tape recordings of the conference. While they informed my research and led me to interview people who had participated in the conference, the transcripts have never been declassified by the Office of Naval Intelligence.

    One unclassified memorandum describes to prospective attendees the history of the Lessons Learned project and offers details of the September 1998 symposium; it is the only symposium-related document released by ONI from the archive. See David A. Rosenberg, "Memorandum for OPINTEL Lessons Learned Symposium Panelists and Commentators; With History of Modern OPINTEL Chronology Enclosure," OPINTEL Lessons Learned Symposium, box 1 of 2, Office of Naval Intelligence Archives, Suitland, Maryland, June 8, 1998.

5. Norman Friedman, *Network-centric Warfare: How Navies Learned to Fight Smarter through Three World Wars* (Annapolis, MD: Naval Institute Press, 2009); Trent Hone, *Learning War: The Evolution of Fighting Doctrine in the U.S. Navy, 1898–1945*, Studies in Naval History and Sea Power (Annapolis, MD: Naval Institute Press, 2018); Thomas Hone and Curtis A. Utz, *History of*

the *Office of the Chief of Naval Operations, 1915–2015* (Washington, DC: Naval History and Heritage Command, Department of the Navy, 2020), 2023 ed. available for download at https://www.history.navy.mil/research/publications/publications-by-subject/opnav-100.html; Thomas Hone, *Power and Change: The Administrative History of the Office of the Chief of Naval Operations, 1946–1986*, Contributions to Naval History no. 2 (Washington, DC: Naval Historical Center, Department of the Navy, 1989), archived online at https://archive.org/details/powerchangethead00wash/mode/2up.
6. For more on SIGINT, see Martin E. Dempsey, "Joint Intelligence," Joint Publication (JP) 2-0, doctrine for the Armed Forces of the United States, chairman, Joint Chiefs of Staff, Washington, DC, October 22, 2013, s.v. "SIGINT," p. B-5, archived online at https://irp.fas.org/doddir/dod/jp2_0.pdf.
7. Bryan H. Leese, "The Evolution of U.S. Navy Operational Intelligence in the Cold War," PhD diss., King's College London, 2023.

Prologue

1. Central Intelligence Agency, "Consequences of U.S. Troop Withdrawal from Korea in Spring, 1949," ORE 3-49, February 28, 1949, https://www.cia.gov/readingroom/docs/DOC_0000258388.pdf; and Central Intelligence Agency, "Current Capabilities of the Northern Korea Regime," ORE 18-50, June 19, 1950, https://www.cia.gov/readingroom/docs/DOC_0000258828.pdf. And see Packard, *Naval Intelligence*, 29, https://archive.org/details/centuryofusnaval00wash/page/28/mode/2up.
2. Norman Friedman, *The Fifty-Year War: Conflict and Strategy in the Cold War* (Annapolis, MD: Naval Institute Press, 2000), 155–57.
3. James A. Field Jr., *History of United States Naval Operations: Korea*, fore. Ernest McNeill Eller, Online ed. (San Francisco: University Press of the Pacific, 2001), chap. 3, part 1, https://www.history.navy.mil/content/history/nhhc/research/library/online-reading-room/title-list-alphabetically/h/history-us-naval-operations-korea/chapter3-war-begins.html.
4. Field, chap. 3, parts 1–2, https://www.history.navy.mil/content/history/nhhc/research/library/online-reading-room/title-list-alphabetically/h/history-us-naval-operations-korea/chapter3-war-begins.html.
5. The x in 135x and 163x represents a placeholder for either active-duty designator 0 or reservist 5. The 163x designator was made law through the Officer Procurement Act of 1947. The first 163xs were selected in 1948. Packard, *Naval Intelligence*, 27, https://archive.org/details/centuryofusnaval00wash/page/26/mode/2up.
6. Packard, 28, https://archive.org/details/centuryofusnaval00wash/page/28/mode/2up.

7. There is a lack of literature and other source materials on the development of enlisted personnel for Navy intelligence. More research and interviews are required to increase this area of the historiography.
8. Packard, 31–33, https://archive.org/details/centuryofusnaval00wash/page/30/mode/2up. And see Michael Stead, "Origins and Early Development of the Naval Intelligence Officer (1630) Designator," *Naval Intelligence Professionals Quarterly*, December 2004.
9. Scott Mobley, *Progressives in Navy Blue: Maritime Strategy, American Empire, and the Transformation of U.S. Naval Identity, 1873–1898*, Studies in Naval History and Sea Power (Annapolis, MD: Naval Institute Press, 2018). Also see Packard, *Naval Intelligence*. For a discussion on intelligence's role in strategy formulation, see "Intelligence as a Tool of Strategy," in *U.S. Army War College Guide to National Security Issues*, ed. J. Boone Bartholomees Jr., 5th ed, (Carlisle, PA: Strategic Studies Institute, U.S. Army War College, 2012), 263–77.
10. Packard, *Naval Intelligence*, 321, https://archive.org/details/centuryofusnaval00wash/page/320/mode/2up.

    Also see Dudley Wright Knox and David Kohnen, *21st Century Knox: Influence, Sea Power, and History for the Modern Era*, 21st Century Foundations (Annapolis, MD: Naval Institute Press, 2016), 9–13. For more on the First World War Navy and U.S. Naval War College, see William Sowden Sims and Benjamin Armstrong, *21st Century Sims: Innovation, Education, and Leadership for the Modern Era* (Annapolis, MD: Naval Institute Press, 2015), 8. And John B. Hattendorf, B. Mitchell Simpson III, and John R. Wadleigh, *Sailors and Scholars: The Centennial History of the United States Naval War College* (Newport, RI: Naval War College Press, 1984), archived online at https://archive.org/details/sailorsscholarsc00hatt/mode/2up.
11. Stead, "Origins of 1630 Designator," 33. And see Louis E. Denfeld, "Naval Intelligence Manual (1949)," ONI 19B, Director of Naval Intelligence, Office of the Chief of Naval Operations, U.S. Department of the Navy, May 1949 (updated 1952), p. 47, archived online at https://ncisahistory.org/wp-content/uploads/2017/06/ONI-19B-Naval-Intelligence-Manual-June-1949.pdf.
12. The U.S. Naval School (Naval Intelligence), or Naval Intelligence School, was a subordinate activity of the Naval Postgraduate School. *Curricula: Intelligence and Language* (U.S. Naval Receiving Station, Washington, DC: U.S. Naval School (Naval Intelligence), 1949), 1–1a, https://ncisahistory.org/wp-content/uploads/2019/10/US-NAVAL-INTELLIGENCE-SCHOOL-CURRICULA-1949.pdf.
13. Stead, "Origins of 1630 Designator," 20. For details on ONI's school, see Packard, *Naval Intelligence*, chap. 30, "Officer Training in Naval Intelligence," https://archive.org/details/centuryofusnaval00wash/page/364/mode/2up.
14. Denfeld, "Naval Intelligence Manual," ONI 19B.

15. Lowell E. Jacoby, "Operational Intelligence: Lessons from the Cold War," *Proceedings*, U.S. Naval Institute, 125, no. 9, 1,151 (September 1999): 1.
16. Jacoby, 1. At the 1998 OPINTEL Symposium, Vice Adm. David Richardson referred to the intelligence officer's relationship to the operational commander as one of "cheek by jowl."
17. Michael M. McCrea, Karen N. Domabyl, and Alexander F. Parker, "The Offensive Navy since World War II: How Big and Why; A Brief Summary," research memorandum, Center for Naval Analyses, Alexandria, VA, July 1989, p. 2, archived online at https://www.history.navy.mil/research/library/online-reading-room/title-list-alphabetically/o/the-offensive-navy-since-world-war-ii-how-big-and-why-a-brief-summary.html.
18. Jaques Elliott, *The Changing Culture of a Factory* (London: Tavistock Publications, 1951); William J. E. Crissy, Review of *The Changing Culture of a Factory*, by Elliott Jaques, *Psychological Bulletin* 50, no. 1 (January 1953): 66–67, https://doi.org/10.1037/h0051516.
19. S. Rebecca Zimmerman et al., "Movement and Maneuver: Culture and the Competition for Influence Among the U.S. Military Services" (RAND Corporation, Santa Monica, CA, 2019), 5.
20. Peter R. Mansoor and Williamson Murray, eds., *The Culture of Military Organizations* (New York: Cambridge University Press, 2019), 5, https://www.cambridge.org/core/books/culture-of-military-organizations/67053E4FCE8B18077EFF8076D49992D6 (paywall).
21. J. C. Wylie, "Why a Sailor Thinks like a Sailor," *Proceedings*, U.S. Naval Institute, 83, no. 8 (August 1957): 811–14, https://www.usni.org/magazines/proceedings/1957/august/why-sailor-thinks-sailor.
22. Geertz's work described in Zimmerman et al., "Movement and Maneuver," 4. And see Clifford Geertz, *The Interpretation of Cultures: Selected Essays* (New York: Basic Books, 1973).

    Mansoor and Murray (*Culture of Military Organizations*, 1) describe culture similarly but cite the military organization culture–focused work of Jeffrey W. Legro, *Cooperation Under Fire: Anglo-German Restraint During World War II* (Ithaca, NY: Cornell University Press, 1995), 19–25. Also see Mats Alvesson, *Understanding Organizational Culture* (London: SAGE, 2002), 3–4, https://epdf.pub/understanding-organizational-culture.html.
23. Leonard Wong and Stephen J. Gerras discussed in Mansoor and Murray, *Culture of Military Organizations*, 19–25. Edgar Schein proposed his organization-analysis framework in 1980; see Edgar H. Schein, *Organizational Culture and Leadership* (Hoboken, NJ: Wiley, 2010).
24. Wong and Gerras discussed in Mansoor and Murray, *Culture of Military Organizations*, 19.

25. Geert Hofstede proposed his model in the late 1970s and published his findings in 1980; see Geert H. Hofstede, *Culture's Consequences: International Differences in Work-Related Values*, abridged ed., Cross-Cultural Research and Methodology Series (Beverly Hills: Sage Publications, 1984). The late Robert J. House founded the GLOBE project in 1993, and the project's work continues today; for more information, visit the project's website at http://www.globeproject.com. Also see Robert J. House, *Strategic Leadership Across Cultures: The GLOBE Study of CEO Leadership Behavior and Effectiveness in 24 Countries* (Thousand Oaks, CA: SAGE Publications, 2014).
26. Wong and Gerras discussed in Mansoor and Murray, *Culture of Military Organizations*, 20–21.
27. Dictionary.com, s.v. "evolution," https://www.dictionary.com/browse/Evolution.
28. Larry E. Greiner, "Evolution and Revolution as Organizations Grow," *Harvard Business Review* 76, no. 3 (May–June 1998): 55–60, 62–66, 68, https://hbr.org/1998/05/evolution-and-revolution-as-organizations-grow.
29. Burke, memo dated October 16, 1949, "Trends in Unification," A1/EM-3, OP-23, p. 1, as quoted in Hone, *Power and Change*, 25n34. And regarding Burke's support for Eisenhower's New Look program, see *Power and Change*, 35.
30. Roger W. Barnett, *Navy Strategic Culture: Why the Navy Thinks Differently* (Annapolis, MD: Naval Institute Press, 2009), 74.
31. Hone, *Learning War*, 16. And Mobley takes a close look at the Navy's late-1800s modernization, using the term "insurgents" to describe change agents, in *Progressives in Navy Blue*
32. The Naval Reform Act of 1899 and the Navy's reintroduction of special duty engineering officers in the restricted line after World War II are addressed in Zach Kopin, "Convergent Corps: Line Officers, Staff Officers and the Modernization of the U.S. Navy," Naval Historical Foundation, NavyHistory.org, April 30, 2013, https://navyhistory.org/2013/04/convergent-corps-line-officers-staff-officers-modernization-us-navy/; and in Justin L. C. Eldridge, Ryan Peeks, and Greg Bereiter, "Navy and Defense Reform: A Short History and Reference Chronology," Navy History and Heritage Command (website), December 22, 2016, p. 28, https://www.history.navy.mil/research/library/online-reading-room/title-list-alphabetically/n/navy-defense-reform.html.
33. John T. Kuehn in Mansoor and Murray, *Culture of Military Organizations*, 356.
34. For more on the Line Personnel Act of 1916, see Hone, *Learning War*, 42–48.
35. Engine-technology developments focused on using high-octane fuel. Britain led the way, with their engines running on 100-octane, while the Germans' ran on 84- and 87-octane fuel. Engines running 100-octane, like the famed

Merlin engines in the Spitfire, produced upward of 1,600 horsepower. During the Battle of Britain, Reich Marshal Hermann Göring asked his airmen what they needed to win the air battle: "More powerful 605 engines with 100-octane," one officer said. Another responded wryly, "Equip my wing with Spitfires." As told in Robert Goralski and Russell W. Freeburg, *Oil and War: How the Deadly Struggle for Fuel in World War II Meant Victory or Defeat* (Quantico, VA: Marine Corps University Press, 2021), chap. 3, "Octane and the Battle of Britain."

36. Roger Thompson, "Brown Shoes, Black Shoes, and Felt Slippers: Parochialism and the Evolution of the Post-war U.S. Navy," research paper no. 5.95, Center for Naval Warfare Studies, Strategic Research Department, U.S. Naval War College, Newport, RI, September 11, 1995, archived online at https://apps.dtic.mil/sti/pdfs/ADA299970.pdf.

37. Thompson, "Brown Shoes," 15.

38. John Lewis Gaddis, *Strategies of Containment: A Critical Appraisal of American National Security Policy During the Cold War*, rev. and exp. (New York: Oxford University Press, 2005), 136.

39. Robert Martinage, "Toward a New Offset Strategy: Exploiting U.S. Long-Term Advantages to Restore U.S. Global Power Projection Capability," Center for Strategic and Budgetary Assessments, CBSAonline.org, 2014, p. 9, https://csbaonline.org/uploads/documents/Offset-Strategy-Web.pdf. And see Robert Tomes, "The Cold War Offset Strategy: Origins and Relevance," *War on the Rocks*, November 6, 2014, https://warontherocks.com/2014/11/the-cold-war-offset-strategy-origins-and-relevance/.

40. Peter D. Haynes, "American Naval Thinking in the Post–Cold War Era: The U.S. Navy and the Emergence of a Maritime Strategy, 1989–2007," PhD diss., Naval Postgraduate School, June 2013, p. 28, archived online at https://calhoun.nps.edu/server/api/core/bitstreams/116e3ac4-7a28-4997-ae6c-36dc9aa8e12e/content. Also see David Alan Rosenberg, "The Origins of Overkill: Nuclear Weapons and American Strategy, 1945–1960," *International Security* 7, no. 4 (Spring 1983): 3–71, https://doi.org/10.2307/2626731, archived online at https://ia600704.us.archive.org/view_archive.php?archive=/24/items/wikipedia-scholarly-sources-corpus/10.2307%252F2589218.zip&file=10.2307%252F2626731.pdf.

41. Adm. Elmo R. Zumwalt Jr., a surface line officer, was CNO from 1970 to 1974; "Chief of Naval Operations," Naval Historical Center, June 28, 2006, archived link https://web.archive.org/web/20071218005946/http://www.history.navy.mil/faqs/faq35-1.htm.

42. Describing Rickover in Thompson, "Brown Shoes," 19; John T. Kuehn's chapter in Mansoor and Murray, *Culture of Military Organizations*, 360; Zumwalt's assessment of the difficulties in dealing with Rickover in Elmo R.

Zumwalt Jr., *On Watch: A Memoir* (New York: Quadrangle/New York Times Book Co., 1976), 85–122.
43. Thompson, "Brown Shoes," 20 and 43. Regarding the nuclear-deterrence triad, see Haynes, "American Naval Thinking," 32. On submarines and the Rickover influence, see John T. Kuehn in Mansoor and Murray, *Culture of Military Organizations*, 362.
44. Hone, *Learning War*, 4–9.
45. Norman Friedman, *Network-centric Warfare*, 206–10.

Part I. Institutionalizing Shipboard Operational Intelligence

1. Rosenberg, "Origins of Overkill," 52.
2. "Text of President Kennedy's Special Message to Congress on Defense Spending; Cutback in Bases Requested by President," *New York Times*, March 29, 1961, p. 16, https://www.nytimes.com/1961/03/29/archives/text-of-president-kennedys-special-message-to-congress-on-defense.html.
3. Vice Chief of Naval Operations, Office of the Chief of Naval Operations, U.S. Department of the Navy, "Debrief of SECDEF Meeting on Program Package #6, Saturday 9 September 1961," (OP-09), p. 2, box 19 (Memoranda for the Record of 1961), OP-09 (Vice Chief of Naval Operations), Organizational Records: The Office of the Chief of Naval Operations 1946–2000, Archives Branch, Naval History and Heritage Command, Washington, DC. On McNamara's plan for survivable weapons, see Friedman, *Fifty-Year War*, 290–91.

   There is an important evolutionary footnote to the development of U.S. Navy cruise and ballistic missiles. The Loon missile program began during World War II, building off of German "buzz bomb" and V2 rocket technology. At the close of the war the program was canceled. But by then a thousand missiles had been built. Those leftover Loons were used to experiment and prototype, resulting in a series of submarine- and surfaced-launched missiles and eventually the Polaris. Robert Farley, "Loon: America's Forgotten World War II Cruise Missile," *The National Interest* (website), Center for the National Interest, February 23, 2021), https://nationalinterest.org/blog/reboot/loon-americas-forgotten-world-war-ii-cruise-missile-178680.
4. Robert R. "Boom" Powell, *RA-5C Vigilante Units in Combat*, Osprey Combat Aircraft no. 51 (Oxford: Osprey Publishing, 2004), 10. Also see Norman Polmar and Minoru Genda, *Aircraft Carriers: A History of Carrier Aviation and Its Influence on World Events*, 1st ed (Washington, DC: Potomac Books, 2006), 204. And "Vigilante Planes Ordered by Navy; $150-Million Will Be Spent for Electronic Aircraft," *New York Times*, April 5, 1967, p. 26, https://www.nytimes.com/1967/04/05/archives/vigilante-planes-ordered-by-nayy-150million-will-be-spent-for.html.

Chapter 1. The Integrated Operational Intelligence Center

1. Actor Albert Finney playing Uncle Henry in Ridley Scott, dir., *A Good Year* (Los Angeles: 20th Century Fox, 2006), 118 min.
2. Capt. William "Rock" Ore, USN (Ret.), in discussion with the author, October 14, 2019. These measurements are based on a scale drawing found in O. R. Osburn, "CVA Integrated Operational Intelligence System," *NAESU Digest*, May 1969, Nolan Leatherman Papers. I compared this with the USS *Saratoga* 03 level A schematic, provided to me by Robin Hartford, PH3, USN, via email, on November 5, 2019.
3. Captain Ore first spoke with me about the IOIC installation on March 7, 2019, with follow-up discussion on October 14. The four-month IOIC supervisors course was held at Naval Air Station Sanford, FL.
4. Packard, *Century of U.S. Naval Intelligence*, 173; Friedman, *Network-centric Warfare*, 181–82.
5. Friedman, *Network-centric Warfare*, 181–83.
6. For a broad discussion on the late-1950s debate about the U.S. Navy position on the Polaris missile system as a minimum or "finite" deterrent concept, see William Burr, ed., "'How Much Is Enough?': The U.S. Navy and 'Finite Deterrence'; A Moment in Cold War History When the Fundamentals of the U.S. Nuclear Posture Were at Stake," *The Nuclear Vault*, National Security Archive Electronic Briefing Book no. 275, May 1, 2009, https://nsarchive2.gwu.edu/nukevault/ebb275/index.htm. Also see Arleigh Burke, "Views on Adequacy of U.S. Deterrent/Retaliatory Forces as Related to General and Limited War Capabilities," memorandum, March 4, 1959, Department of the Navy, Office of the Chief of Naval Operations. Navy Archives, Flag Officers "Dope," CNO Personal Newsletter and Memorandum #44-49 May–June 1959, National Security Archives, https://nsarchive2.gwu.edu/nukevault/ebb275/07.pdf.
7. Nolan Leatherman, lead contract supervisor for North American Aviation (NAA), in telephone discussion with the author regarding IOIC, 2017 and 2018. ONI was directed to support the IOIS with an associated database, per a letter (no. 005187P92) dated June 6, 1962, from Vernon L. Lowrance, director of Naval Intelligence; cited in Packard, *Naval Intelligence*, 178. For A-5 fleet entry, see Powell, *Vigilante in Combat*, 9, 204. Also see "Altitude Record Is Set by New Jet, Navy Says," *New York Times*, December 16, 1960, https://timesmachine.nytimes.com/timesmachine/1960/12/16/99979553.html.
8. Quotation from Friedman, *Network-centric Warfare*, 330n1. And see Powell, *Vigilante in Combat*, 8–11.
9. The ventral "canoe's" name came from its resemblance to a Native American bark canoe strapped to the bottom of the aircraft.

10. Camera designations: KA-51A; KA-53A; and KA-50A, 62A/B, 53A. The KA-series cameras were manufactured by Chicago Aerial Industries and were proven technology, flying successful missions in the F8U-1P/RF-8A Crusaders during the Cuban Missile Crisis. Michael Grove and Jay Miller, *North American Rockwell A3J/A-5 Vigilante*, Aerofax minigraph 9 (Arlington, TX: Aerofax, 1989, dist. Osceola, WI: Motorbooks International, 1989), 31–33. See also "MCARA Aircraft F8U-1P/RF-8A Crusader," *MCARA: Marine Corps Aviation Reconnaissance Association*, 2010, https://www.mcara.us/F8U-1P_RF-8A.html. Regarding the loading of the camera package, see Douglas E. Campbell, *Flight, Camera, Action! The History of U.S. Naval Aviation Photography and Photo-Reconnaissance* (Washington, DC: Syneca Research Group, 2014).

11. Cue to 09:15 in U.S. Department of the Navy, *The Integrated Operational Intelligence System: Electronic Intelligence Station*, U.S. Navy Training Film no. MN-100005f, 27:36, Audio Productions, 1967, National Archives identifier 330-dvic-920, archival resource key ark:/13960/t7jr0gd3w, archived online at https://archive.org/details/330-dvic-920. The PECM system was designated AN/ALQ-161.

12. The SA-2's target acquisition radar, the Fan Song, operates within the G-Band (4–6 GHz) and the SA-3's Low Blow radar within the D/I Bands (1–2 GHz and 9–10 GHz). See Central Intelligence Agency, "Soviet Capabilities in Guided Missiles and Space Vehicles," National Intelligence Estimate NIE 11-5-59, November 3, 1959, CIA FOIA Electronic Reading Room, https://www.cia.gov/readingroom/docs/DOC_0000267656.pdf, p. 8; and see U.S. Department of the Navy, *IOIS: Electronic Intelligence Station*, 09.15 mins. The PECM system was designated AN/ALQ-161.

13. Rod Anderson, "IOIC-IOIS—The Logbook," accessed April 15, 2019, https://sites.google.com/site/50yearsagointheflightlog/main-1/flying-the-ra-5c/ioic-iois. For a detailed explanation of the code-matrix block and the stereo comparison viewer (SVC), cue to 03:58 minutes in *The Integrated Operational Intelligence System: Photo Interpretation Station*, U.S. Navy Training Film no. MN-100005e, 24:36, Audio Productions, 1967, National Archives identifiers 330-dvic-914, archival resource key ark:/13960/t3vv14x9g. Archived online at https://archive.org/details/330-dvic-914.

14. Capt. Wayne Perras, USN (Ret.), interview with the author about operating the PECM system, February 13, 2019. Regarding the PECM's recording system, see U.S. Department of the Navy, *IOIS: Electronic Intelligence Station*.

15. The size of the space was estimated based on the three bays of the IOIC. Ore, interview with the author, October 14, 2019.

16. Everything unclassified and not being used for planning was stored in voids, small compartments not suitable for office, living, or electronics

equipment. "Boys Town" is a joking reference to the 1938 film of the same name about an orphanage, starring Spencer Tracy and Mickey Rooney. Ore, interview with the author, October 14, 2019.

17. The gallery deck is the first half deck or partial deck below the flight deck. See Bureau of Naval Personnel, U.S. Department of the Navy, *Basic Military Requirements*, Navy Training Courses, NAVPERS 10054 (Washington, DC: U.S. Government Printing Office, 1957), 323, archived online at http://hdl.handle.net/2027/uiug.30112098015719. An example of the equipment for installation for both ShipAlts is found in "IOIC Installation, Constellation," enclosure (3), page 1, and enclosure (4), for ShipAlt CVA 2620 and CVA 2285, found in Bureau of Ships, U.S. Navy, "USS *Constellation* (CVA-64); 120 Day Letter for Authorized Alterations," work order, January 4, 1965, archived in record group RG-19, box 113, entry P40, National Archives at College Park. Information on the ASSC is found in Campbell, *Flight, Camera, Action!*, 448–450.

18. Ore, interview with the author, October 14, 2019. Space size based on scale drawing in Osburn, "CVA Integrated Operational Intelligence System," and compared with USS *Saratoga* 03 level schematic provided by Hartford in emails to the author, 2019.

19. Description of work centers found in Osburn, "CVA Integrated Operational Intelligence System," 8. For a good description of the IOIC work centers, see H. G. Karsten, ed., *USS Enterprise (CVAN 65) WestPac Cruise Book, 1965–66* (Westbury, NY: Hallmark Graphics, n.d.), p. 249, archived online at https://www.navysite.de/cruisebooks/cvn65-65/219.htm.

20. Ore, interview with the author, October 14, 2019.

21. Using the inflation rate, $1 in 1967 equals $7.81 in 2020. Approximately 430.04 million BP. See https://www.dollartimes.com/inflation/inflation.php?amount=1&year=1967.

22. Individual contract awards to NAA/R for IOIC in February 1966 and September 1968 under contract N00019–68-C-0552. RA-5C contract N00019–68-C-0190 and RA-5C repair parts contract N00383–69-A-005–0033.

See "Defense Procurement: Air Force" in each of the following issues of the U.S. Department of Defense's *Defense Industry Bulletin*:

Vol. 2 (1966), archived online at https://babel.hathitrust.org/cgi/pt?id=uc1.c2790783&view=1up&seq=1: no. 1 (January): 59; no. 2 (February): 44; no. 7 (July): 27; no. 8 (August): 27; no. 10 (October): 43.

Vol. 3 (1967), archived online at https://babel.hathitrust.org/cgi/pt?id=uc1.c2790784&view=1up&seq=1: no. 8 (August): 35; no. 11 (November): 36; and no. 12 (December): 36.

Vol. 4, no. 9 (September 1968): 35, archived online at https://archive.org/details/defenseindustryb4119wash.

Vol. 5 (1969), archived online at https://babel.hathitrust.org/cgi/pt?id=uc1.c2790786&view=1up&seq=1: no. 2 (February): 36; and no. 8 (August): 35–36. Vol. 6, no. 8 (August 1970): 39, archived online at https://babel.hathitrust.org/cgi/pt?id=uc1.c2790787&view=1up&seq=1.

And see "Vigilante Contract Is Let," *New York Times*, August 18, 1960, https://www.nytimes.com/1960/08/18/archives/vigilante-contract-is-let.html (paywall); and Clare M. Reckert, "Major Companies Plan Big Mergers; North American Aviation in Consolidation Talks with Rockwell-Standard Corp.," *New York Times*, March 22, 1967, https://www.nytimes.com/1967/03/22/archives/major-companies-plan-big-mergers-north-american-aviation-in.html.

23. Ore, interview with the author, March 7, 2019. And see Powell, *Vigilante in Combat*, 16.

24. Information regarding the SCV installation is courtesy of Ore, interview with the author, March 7, 2019; and Capt. Nelson Litsinger, USN (Ret.), emails with the author, 2017 and 2021. On the development of computers for the NTDS program, including the UYK and ECMU, see David L. Boslaugh, *First-Hand: No Damned Computer Is Going to Tell Me What to Do; The Story of the Naval Tactical Data System, NTDS*, ebook (n.p.: n.p., revised April 12, 2017), https://ethw.org/w/index.php?title=First-Hand:No_Damned_Computer_is_Going_to_Tell_Me_What_to_DO_-_The_Story_of_the_Naval_Tactical_Data_System,_NTDS&oldid=154739.

For more on processors, see "The US Navy Launches NAVSAT, the First Operational Satellite Navigation System: 10/4/1957 to 1960," *History of Information*, accessed November 9, 2019, http://www.historyofinformation.com/detail.php?id=83. Cue to 01:48 of this training film to see how the UYK-1 is the processor for the SCV; in U.S. Department of the Navy, *The Integrated Operational Intelligence System: Photo Interpretation Station*.

25. U.S. Department of the Navy, *IOIS: Photo Interpretation Station*, 02:03–03:49 mins.

26. Boslaugh, *First-Hand*, chap. 5, "Testing the Naval Tactical Data System," sec. "Getting Ready for Service Test."

27. U.S. Department of the Navy, *IOIS: Electronic Intelligence System*, 03:51–04:22.

28. Packard, *Naval Intelligence*, 243. Data management has been and will be a problem for the Navy; for a modern discussion of the same issue facing the Navy in the late 1950s, see Isaac R. Porche III et al., "Data Flood: Helping the Navy Address the Rising Tide of Sensor Information," product page, RAND, Santa Monica, CA, May 1, 2014, available for download from https://www.rand.org/pubs/research_reports/RR315.html.

29. Packard, *Naval Intelligence*, 186.

30. Previously called the Naval Photographic Interpretation Center (NPIC). It took two years for NRTSC to assume full control of all IOIC-related efforts. NRTSC also provided intelligence support to targeting, including the Single Integrated Operational Plan (SIOP). Packard, 186 and 243.
31. Packard, 243. For images of the electronic cabinets view minutes 04:23–05:19 in U.S. Department of the Navy, *The Integrated Operational Intelligence System: Reconnaissance Mission Planning and Intelligence Data Flow*, U.S. Navy Training Film no. MN-100005c, 19:18, Audio Productions, 1967, National Archives identifier 330-dvic-915, archival resource key ark:/13960/t3sv73510, archived online at https://archive.org/details/330-dvic-915. Storage and Retrieval space size estimated from scale drawing in Osburn, "CVA Integrated Operational Intelligence System," 8.
32. Packard, *Naval Intelligence*, 243, 245.
33. Ore, interview with the author, March 7, 2019.
34. On ONI's connection to the IOIS/IOIC and the creation and maintenance of the databases, see Friedman, *Network-centric Warfare*, 167. On the development of IOIC databases, see Ford and Rosenberg, *Admirals' Advantage*. Also see Packard, *Naval Intelligence*, 244. NAR may have been working on NIPS-associated storage and display equipment for some time; see "NIPS Video Integration," North American Rockwell contract-proposal brochure, c. 1968, Nolan Leatherman Papers.
35. Packard, *Naval Intelligence*, 245–46.
36. Ford and Rosenberg, *Admirals' Advantage*, 33.
37. Perras, emails with the author, November 12, 2019. See the first seventeen minutes of the Navy training video for a description of the airborne ELINT collection system in U.S. Department of the Navy, *IOIS: Electronic Intelligence System*.
38. Perras, emails with the author, November 12, 2019. See also U.S. Department of the Navy, *IOIS: Electronic Intelligence System*, 24 min. mark.
39. Actor Jim Grimshaw as Maj. Gen. Kinnard in discussion with an unnamed general, in Randall Wallace, dir., *We Were Soldiers*, film (Los Angeles: Paramount Pictures, 2002), 138 mins.
40. The support to Laos was part of the Southeast Asia Treaty Organization (SEATO) effort to counter growing Communist threats. Royal Laos forces had a number of setbacks in their fight, and U.S. military assistance through the Military Assistance Advisory Group (MAAG Laos) would help forestall the toppling of the government for the next decade. Jack Schulimson, *The Joint Chiefs of Staff and the War in Vietnam, 1960–1968, Part 1*, History of the Joint Chiefs of Staff (Washington, DC: Office of Joint History, Office of the Chairman of the Joint Chiefs of Staff, 2011), 38–40, https://www.jcs.mil/Portals/36/Documents/History/Vietnam/Vietnam_1960-1968_P001.pdf.

The Pathet Lao were closely aligned with the North Vietnam Communist Việt Minh. The Pathet conquered Loas in 1975, after the Laotian Civil War. For a detailed discussion on the relationship with Vietnam, see Paul Fritz Langer and Joseph Jeremiah Zasloff, "Revolution in Laos: The North Vietnamese and the Pathet Lao," memorandum RM-5935-ARPA, RAND Corporation, September 1969, https://www.rand.org/content/dam/rand/pubs/research_memoranda/2008/RM5935.pdf.

41. J. L. Butts, USS *Kitty Hawk* (CVA 63), Aviation Historical Summary, March 31–September 30, 1964, p. 3, https://www.history.navy.mil/content/dam/nhhc/research/archives/command-operation-reports/ship-command-operation-reports/k/kitty-hawk-cv-63-ii/m64-s64.pdf. For more on the Navy carrier aircraft during the Vietnam conflict, see Norman Polmar and Edward J. Marolda, *Naval Air War: The Rolling Thunder Campaign*, The U.S. Navy and the Vietnam War (Washington, DC: Naval History and Heritage Command, 2015). See also Norman Polmar and Minoru Genda, *Aircraft Carriers: A History of Carrier Aviation and Its Influence on World Events*, 1st ed (Washington, D.C: Potomac Books, 2006), 230–32.

42. Dario Leone, "The Story of the First, Ill Fated F-100 Super Sabre Combat Mission of the Vietnam War," *Aviation Geek Club* (blog), January 20, 2020, https://theaviationgeekclub.com/the-story-of-the-first-ill-fated-f-100-super-sabre-combat-mission-of-the-vietnam-war/.

43. Leone.

44. For a detailed history of the policies leading toward increased MAAG support, see Schulimson, *Joint Chiefs of Staff*, 1.8ff, "Vietnam Policy in the Eisenhower Administration."

45. Vice Chief of Naval Operations, Office of the Chief of Naval Operations, U.S. Department of the Navy, "Debrief of SECDEF Meeting."

46. Gaddis, *Strategies of Containment*, 244–45. And Komer memorandum from Frank L. Jones, *Blowtorch: Robert Komer, Vietnam, and American Cold War Strategy* (Annapolis, MD: Naval Institute Press, 2013), chap. 5, "Pacification Czar."

47. The August 2 attack on the *Maddox* did occur, but notifications of August 4 night attacks on the *Maddox* and *Turner Joy* have since been determined to have been false radar contacts. Even so, the faulty reports proved to be pivotal in the decision regarding the scale of the U.S. retaliation, not whether or not a retaliation would occur. Schulimson, *Joint Chiefs of Staff*, 1:106.

48. Graham A. Cosmas, *The Joint Chiefs of Staff and the War in Vietnam, 1960–1968, Part 2*, vol. 2 of 3, History of the Joint Chiefs of Staff (Washington, DC: Office of Joint History, Office of the Chairman of the Joint Chiefs of Staff, 2012), 104–8, https://www.jcs.mil/Portals/36/Documents/History/Vietnam/Vietnam_1960-1968_P002.pdf.

49. Cosmas, 2:108–10.
50. Ruddy Cano, "How Naval Aviator Charles Klusmann Escaped a Vicious POW Camp," *We Are the Mighty* (website), last updated September 22, 2022, https://www.wearethemighty.com/mighty-history/how-naval-aviator-charles-klusmann-escaped-a-vicious-pow-camp/.
51. In 1965 the Soviets signed an economic and military support agreement with North Vietnam. China provided MiG-15 and -17 fighters. See Richard A. Mobley and Edward J. Marolda, *Knowing the Enemy: Naval Intelligence in Southeast Asia*, U.S. government official ed., U.S. Navy and the Vietnam War (Washington, DC: Department of the Navy, 2015), 41–43. On North Vietnamese air defense buildup, see Robert F. Dunn, "Navy Air Strike North Vietnam," *Naval History*, U.S. Naval Institute, 141/112/1.354, 29, no. 6 (December 2015), https://www.usni.org/magazines/naval-history-magazine/2015/december/navy-air-strike-north-vietnam (paywall). On the rivalry between the Soviet and Chinese leading to Soviet support to North Vietnam, see Friedman, *Fifty-Year War*, 314.
52. Wayne Thompson, *To Hanoi and Back: The United States Air Force and North Vietnam, 1964–1973* (Washington, DC: Air Force History Office, 2000), 303, https://web.archive.org/web/20151017014122/http://www.dtic.mil/dtic/tr/fulltext/u2/a439924.pdf. See also Mansoor and Murray, *Culture of Military Organizations*, 455.
53. In bodybuilding, repetition (reps) of movement with weight over a number of sets builds strength and mass. Discussing training in terms of reps and sets is common in the post–Cold War Navy. See Dmitry Filipoff, "How the Fleet Forgot to Fight, Pt. 1: Combat Training," CIMSEC.org, Center for International Maritime Security, September 17, 2018, https://cimsec.org/how-the-fleet-forgot-to-fight-pt-1-combat-training/. Regarding peacetime organization change, see Mansoor and Murray, *Culture of Military Organizations*, 455.
54. Benjamin S. Lambeth, *The Transformation of American Air Power*, Cornell Studies in Security Affairs (Ithaca, NY: Cornell University Press, 2000), 41.
55. Jacob Van Staaveren, *Gradual Failure: The Air War over North Vietnam, 1965–1966* (Washington, DC: Air Force History and Museums Program, United States Air Force, 2002), 163, https://media.defense.gov/2010/May/26/2001330292/-1/-1/0/GradualFailure.pdf.
56. Van Staaveren, 163.
57. "Keirn, Richard Paul," Bios, *P.O.W. Network*, accessed September 5, 2023, https://www.pownetwork.org/bios/k/k046.htm.
58. Lambeth, *American Air Power*, 17. See also Michael C. Press, "Tactical Integrated Air Defense System," master's thesis, U.S. Army Command and General Staff College, 1978, p. 10, available for download from https://www.hsdl.org/c/view?docid=722828.

59. Press, "Tactical IADS," 10–13; John J. Deeney IV, "Finding, Fixing, and Finishing the Guideline: The Development of the United States Air Force Surface-to-Air Missile Suppression Force During Operation Rolling Thunder," master's thesis, U.S. Army Command and General Staff College, 2010, chap. 2, "North Vietnam's Integrated Air Defense System," archived online at https://apps.dtic.mil/sti/pdfs/ADA524369.pdf.
60. Deeney, "Finishing the Guideline," chap. 2. See also Carl O. Schuster, "The Rise of North Vietnam's Air Defenses," HistoryNet, July 27, 2016, https://www.historynet.com/13703647.htm. And Lambeth, *American Air Power*, 34–36.
61. Deeney, "Finishing the Guideline," chap. 2, sec. "Sensors and the Air Surveillance Function." Regarding DRV collection of COMINT, see Sharon A. Maneki, "Remembering the Lessons of the Vietnam War," *Cryptologic Quarterly* 23, nos. 1–2 (Spring/Summer 2004): 1–3, NSA Archive, https://www.nsa.gov/portals/75/documents/news-features/declassified-documents/cryptologic-quarterly/remembering_the_lessons.pdf.
62. Allen Dulles, "Air Defense of the Sino-Soviet Bloc, 1955–1960," National Intelligence Estimate NIE 11-5-55, from the director of Central Intelligence, CIA, July 12, 1955, p. 3-4, CIA FOIA Electronic Reading Room, https://www.cia.gov/readingroom/docs/DOC_0000269426.pdf. The NIE mentions AAA weapons are being provided to North Vietnam. Regarding the SA-2, the CIA noted that they "have no reliable evidence indicating the deployment of surface-to-air missiles [by the Soviets] in China, although some deployment [SAM batteries] may have taken place or be planned for the future." However, no assessment is provided on the likelihood of providing the SAMs to North Vietnam. Allen Dulles, "Sino-Soviet Air Defense Capabilities through Mid-1965," National Intelligence Estimate NIE 11-3-61, from the director of Central Intelligence, CIA, July 11, 1961, p. 2, CIA FOIA Electronic Reading Room, https://www.cia.gov/readingroom/docs/DOC_0000267736.pdf.
63. Dulles, "NIE 11-3-61," 6.
64. John McCone, "The Outlook for North Vietnam," Special National Intelligence Estimate SNIE 14-3-64, from the director of Central Intelligence, CIA, March 4, 1966, pp. 2 and 13, CIA FOIA Electronic Reading Room, https://www.cia.gov/readingroom/docs/CIA-RDP80R01720R000200010006-9.pdf.
65. Cosmas, *Joint Chiefs of Staff*, 2:76.
66. See mins. 15:00–17:00 of Sally Paine, "Who Lost the Vietnam War?" lecture and discussion, NWC INS Lecture Series, Newport, RI, October 15, 2021, 58:00 mins., https://www.youtube.com/watch?v=tjXlvIBQmU0.
67. John Prados, "Certainties, Doubts, and Imponderables: Levels of Analysis in the Military Balance," in Herman and Hughes, *Intelligence in the Cold War*, 35.

68. Thomas G. Mahnken, *Uncovering Ways of War: U.S. Intelligence and Foreign Military Innovation, 1918–1941* (Ithaca, NY: Cornell University Press, 2009), 2.
69. The SA-5 based IADS was called the "Tallinn System," but the NATO designation later changed to Gammon. John Prados, *The Soviet Estimate: U.S. Intelligence Analysis and Russian Military Strength* (New York: Dial Press, 1982), 151–57.
70. Prados, 158.
71. Lambeth, *American Air Power*, 15–17.
72. Schuster, "Rise of North Vietnam's Air Defenses"; quoting Gen. John P. McConnell, Air Force Chief of Staff (1965–1969). Also see Lambeth, *American Air Power*, 15–17.

Chapter 2. Adapting the Intel Center

1. Merle L. Pribbenow II, *The Soviet-Vietnamese Intelligence Relationship During the Vietnam War: Cooperation and Conflict*, Cold War International History Project, working paper no. 73 (Washington, DC: Cold War International History Project of the Woodrow Wilson International Center for Scholars, 2014), 2, https://tinyurl.com/ah3mtnbh.
2. Pribbenow, 13–16.
3. Christopher M. Andrew and Oleg Gordievsky, *KGB: The Inside Story of Its Foreign Operations from Lenin to Gorbachev*, 1st ed. (New York: HarperCollins, 1990), 491–94.
4. Pribbenow, *Soviet-Vietnamese Intelligence Relationship*, 5–8. U.S. Navy Chief Warrant Officer John Walker provide cryptographic keys to the Soviets, helping them decipher U.S. messages as early as 1968; Andrew and Gordievsky, *KGB*, 525–31.
5. Pribbenow, *Soviet-Vietnamese Intelligence Relationship*, 10–11.
6. Michael Hankins, "The Teaball Solution: The Evolution of Air Combat Technology in Vietnam, 1968–1972," *Air Power History* 63, no. 3 (Fall 2016): 13–16, https://www.afhistory.org/airpowerhistory/Air_Power_History_2016_fall.pdf.
7. Pribbenow, *Soviet-Vietnamese Intelligence Relationship*, 10–12.
8. Pribbenow, 10–12.
9. Deeney, "Finishing the Guideline," sec. "Sensors and the Air Surveillance Function: Regarding the Fielding of Air Defense Equipment in the Late 1950s." And see Dulles, "Sino-Soviet Air Defense." For a discussion of the understanding of Soviet radars in the 1960s, see Central Intelligence Agency, Office of Research and Reports, "Annex 8 of Soviet Bloc Land Radar Equipment in Cuba as of October 1960: Electronics Facilities in Cuba," CIA/RR EP 60-73-S8, November 1960, CIA FOIA Electronic Reading Room, https://www.cia.gov/readingroom/docs/DOC_0000493869.pdf.

10. Van Staaveren, *Gradual Failure*, 164–65.
11. And with that apocryphal exclamation, the YGBSM initialism was proudly adopted by Wild Weasel squadrons and was stitched into patches of that time. Quoting from Ted Spitzmiller, *Century Series: The USAF Quest for Air Supremacy, 1950–1960; An Illustrated History*, Schiffer Military History (Atglen, PA: Schiffer Publishing), https://archive.org/details/centuryseriesusa0000spit/mode/2up; and see Dario Leone, "You Gotta Be Shitting Me! The Story of the First U.S. SAM-Hunters in Vietnam," *The Aviationist* (blog), March 13, 2014, https://theaviationist.com/2014/03/13/wild-weasel-f-100/.
12. Radar warning receivers (RWR) and chaff were available for most Air Force bombers by 1957. Bernard C. Nalty, "The Air Force in Southeast Asia: Tactics and Techniques of Electronic Warfare; Electronic Countermeasures in the Air War Against North Vietnam, 1965–1973," monograph (Office of Air Force History, Washington, DC, August 16, 1977), 16–17, https://media.defense.gov/2011/Mar/23/2001330092/-1/-1/0/AFD-110323-034.pdf.
13. Deeney, "Finishing the Guideline," chap. 3, "Find, Fix, Finish." For details on the Wild Weasel's tactics, see Nalty, "Air Force in Southeast Asia," 31–52.
14. On November 27, 1965, the USAF did strike a suspected SAM assembly and maintenance complex at Dong Em, twenty-two miles from Hanoi; such targets were generally restricted by the Joint Chiefs until the 1972 Linebacker I and II campaigns. See Stanley J. Dougherty, "Defense Suppression: Building Some Operational Concepts," master's thesis, Air University, 1992, p. 13, https://media.defense.gov/2017/Dec/28/2001861734/-1/-1/0/T_DOUGHERTY_DEFENSE_SUPPRESSION.PDF.
15. Van Staaveren, *Gradual Failure*, 195–96.
16. Van Staaveren, 196; Dougherty, "Defense Suppression," 12. The British developed chaff (called Window), radio jamming (Cigar), and radar jamming (Mandrel); see Nalty, "Air Force in Southeast Asia," 13–16.
17. Van Staaveren, *Gradual Failure*, 195–96.
18. This is from p. 2 of the Vance memorandum, "Establishment of the Defense Special Security Communications System," dated November 4, 1964, as reproduced in Deane J. Allen and Brian G. Shellum, eds., *Defense Intelligence Agency: At the Creation, 1961–1965* (Washington, DC: DIA History Office, 2002), 344–52, https://archive.org/details/DTIC_ADA578664/page/344/mode/2up.
19. Vance memorandum, pp. 374–78, in Allen and Shellum.
20. Mobley, *Progressives in Navy Blue*, 116.
21. Packard, *Naval Intelligence*, chap. 11, "Technical Intelligence."
22. Prados, *Soviet Estimate*, 172–74. For more on the DDR&E and acquisition, see William D. O'Neil and Gene H. Porter, "What to Buy? The Role of Director of Defense Research and Engineering (DDR&E): Lessons from the 1970s," IDA

paper P-4675, Institute for Defense Analysis, Alexandria, VA, January 2011, https://apps.dtic.mil/sti/pdfs/ADA549549.pdf.
23. See pp. 2–4 of DoD Directive 5105.28, "Defense Intelligence Agency (Technical Intelligence)," dated April 27, 1964, as reproduced in Allen and Shellum, *Defense Intelligence Agency*, 379–85.
24. DoD Directive 5105.28, p. 5, in Allen and Shellum.
25. Robert J. Hanyok, *Spartans in Darkness: American SIGINT and the Indochina War, 1945–1975*, United States Cryptologic History 6, vol. 7, *The NSA Period: 1952–Present* (Fort Meade, MD: Center for Cryptologic History, National Security Agency, 1998), 238, https://www.nsa.gov/portals/75/documents/news-features/declassified-documents/cryptologic-histories/spartans_in_darkness.pdf.
26. William Cahill, "Strategic Air Command SIGINT Support to the Vietnam War," *Air Power History* 66, no. 4 (Winter 2019): 32–33, https://www.jstor.org/stable/26872699 (paywall).
27. Cahill, 32–33. Over five hundred variants of uncrewed vehicles (intelligence collection and artillery spotting) were shot down during the war.
28. Bureau of Naval Personnel, U.S. Department of the Navy, *Photographer's Mate 3 & 2*, Rate Training Manual, NAVPERS 10355-A (Washington, DC: Bureau of Naval Personnel, 1972), 631, https://books.google.com/books?id=3-sRsGu4-NwC&pg=PA560&lpg=PA560&dq=Kodak+Color+Aerial+Film+Processor,+EH73&source=bl&ots=y36L1GhIIm&sig=ACfU3U2jemupwhGRw2zsFPpu7iOUPfxQeA&hl=en&sa=X&ved=2ahUKEwimh96ttrXnAhUblXIEHRoaCKUQ6AEwAHoECAgQAQ#v=onepage&q&f=false; Hartford, email exchange with the author, March 29, 2019.
29. Hartford, email to the author, March 29, 2019, which included a photograph of the "heel protractor."
30. In a fifty-four-day line period in 1965, USS *Ranger*'s Vigilantes flew forty-two missions, resulting in 174,355 linear feet of photography. Mobley and Marolda, *Knowing the Enemy*, 33. For PH history and training, see the 1975 *Naval Aviation News* article reprinted in Campbell, *Flight, Camera, Action!* 472–75.
31. For a description of the daily replenishment-at-sea operations, see James L. Holloway III's presentation "Tactical Command and Control of Carrier Operations," part of "Command and Control of Air Operations in the Vietnam War," seminar 4 of the Naval History and Heritage Command's conference proceedings of the Colloquium on Contemporary History, Navy Yard, Washington, DC, January 23, 1991, https://www.history.navy.mil/content/history/nhhc/research/library/online-reading-room/title-list-alphabetically/c/command-control-air-operations.html. See also James L. Holloway, *Aircraft

Carriers at War: A Personal Retrospective of Korea, Vietnam, and the Soviet Confrontation (Annapolis, MD: Naval Institute Press, 2007), 195–201.
32. For a comparison of the nominal air wings by class of aircraft carrier, see Polmar and Genda, *Aircraft Carriers*, 240–41.
33. Holloway, "Tactical Command and Control of Carrier Operations."
34. Holloway, *Aircraft Carriers at War*, 194. Also see James L. Holloway, command history 1965 of USS *Enterprise* (CVA (N)-65), from the commanding officer to the Chief of Naval Operations, doc. ref. OPNAVINST 5750.7, February 2, 1967, p. 7, Naval History and Heritage Command, https://www.history.navy.mil/content/dam/nhhc/research/archives/command-operation-reports/ship-command-operation-reports/e/enterprise-cvn-65-viii/pdf/1965.pdf.
35. Holloway, "Tactical Command and Control of Carrier Operations."
36. There is no consistency with use of the Strike Operations cell. The *Enterprise* specifically identifies the cell in its cruise book. Other carriers do not, instead only noting the traditional Air Operations (OC Division) or Carrier Control Area (CCA) work center as responsible for coordinating the carrier-specific flight schedule. See H. G. Karsten, ed., *USS Enterprise (CVAN 65) WestPac Cruise Book 1965–66* (Westbury, NY: Hallmark Graphics, n.d.), 262, archived online at https://www.navysite.de/cruisebooks/cvn65-65/232.htm.
37. Directorate, Tactical Evaluation (Contemporary Historical Evaluation of Combat Operations), "Project CHECO: Southeast Asia Report," Seventh Air Force Tactical Air Control Center, Operations, HQ PACAF, October 15, 1968, p. 49, https://archive.org/details/DTIC_ADA485188/mode/2up. And much of the information pertaining to the IOIC's daily schedule comes from the author's email exchanges with Capt. Nelson H. "Nels" Litsinger, USN (Ret.), November 11, 2019.
38. The PT rating was established in 1958 by converting some yeomen (YNs) with intelligence specialties and photographer's mates (PHs). Campbell, *Flight, Camera, Action!* 410.
39. Basic description of the premission brief provided by Litsinger in email to author, November 11, 2019. Description of premission brief provided by Mario Tonkli, PT/IS, USN, in email to author, April 20, 2019. Also see Campbell, *Flight, Camera, Action!*
40. By 1966 a variety of closed-circuit television systems (CCTV) were employed on the aircraft carrier as well as surface combatants. See U.S. Bureau of Naval Personnel, U.S. Department of the Navy, *Shipboard Electrical Systems*, major revision, NAVPERS 10864-B (Washington, DC: Bureau of Naval Personnel, 1966), 394–96.
41. Litsinger, email to author, November 11, 2019. On the importance of shipboard integration of intelligence with operators, see Ford and Rosenberg, *Admirals' Advantage*, 50–51.

42. "Chartpak" is a name-brand graphic design product still used today. Dymo Industries' handheld embossing label maker was also used to mark locations on the charts. Tonkli, emails to author, 2019. For a description of Yankee Station and the five route packages, see Polmar and Marolda, *Naval Air War*, 6–7. U.S. Navy strike missions were primarily flying Route Pack I missions in 1967–1968. See Directorate, Tactical Evaluation (Contemporary Historical Evaluation of Combat Operations), "Project CHECO," 26.
43. Litsinger, email to author, November 11, 2019; Tonkli, email to author, April 20, 2019; and Perras, email to author, November 12, 2019.
44. For a discussion on FICPAC and FICPACFAC production, see Packard, *Naval Intelligence*, 447–54.
45. The Card of the Day was a controlled item, every card accounted for at the end of each day. Litsinger, email to author, May 4, 2020.
46. Frequencies came from the 7AF, the aircraft carrier's Carrier Air Operation's Strike Operations Cell. Litsinger, email to author, February 7, 2020. The Navy handled all over-water pilot recovery. For more detail on 7AF and the Joint Search and Rescue Center (JSARC), see Seventh Air Force, U.S. Air Force, "Seventh Air Force In Country Tactical Air Operations Handbook (7AFP 55-1)," Headquarters Seventh Air Force, San Francisco, March 20, 1968, 111–17, archived online by the C7A Caribou Association, http://www.c-7acaribou.com/history/7AF/7AFP_55-1.pdf. For details on the JSARC operations center, see Directorate, Tactical Evaluation (Contemporary Historical Evaluation of Combat Operations), "Project CHECO," 37, 42–44.
47. There was limited standardization of the debrief process, some aircraft carriers preferring to conduct them in IOIC, others in the squadron ready rooms. Campbell, *Flight, Camera, Action!* 433.
48. Litsinger, emails to author, November 11, 2019, and February 7, 2020.
49. Hartford, emails about darkroom operations with author, November 5 and 9, 2019. For a description of PHs working pre- and postmission flight deck duties, see Campbell, *Flight, Camera, Action!* 448–49.
50. Mobley and Marolda, *Knowing the Enemy*, 34.
51. Hartford, email to author, February 14, 2020. "Quick look" analysis of the negative image could be done, but the SCVs used positive images only; Litsinger, interview with author, March 8, 2018.
52. Packard, *Naval Intelligence*, 98; "Seventh Air Force In Country Tactical Air Operations Handbook (7AFP 55-1)," 85.

    Regarding Immediate Air Requests, see Directorate, Tactical Evaluation (Contemporary Historical Evaluation of Combat Operations), "Project CHECO," 21.
53. For a discussion on the SAM and AAA threat and counters to the threat, see Polmar and Marolda, *Naval Air War*, 29–33. Also see Mobley and Marolda,

Knowing the Enemy, 45. Regarding aircrew assisting with imagery interpretation, see Campbell, *Flight, Camera, Action!*
54. Shipboard imagery analysis is considered phase 1 analysis; it determines whether or not a bomb hit the target, not the amount of damage caused. Bomb damage assessments were conducted at intelligence centers ashore, such as the Fleet Intelligence Center, Pacific, located in the Philippines, or at 7AF's headquarters. Packard, *Naval Intelligence*, 448.
55. "Tactical Air Ops Handbook," 86. For more on the C-1 and C-2 COD aircraft, see Sean Sims, "History of the Carrier Onboard Delivery (COD)," *The Hangardeck*, January 7, 2020, http://www.thehangardeck.com/news/2019/1/7/history-of-the-carrier-onboard-delivery-cod. On Navy shore photo interpretation, see Packard, *Naval Intelligence*, 98.
56. Packard, *Naval Intelligence*, 188.
57. Lambeth, *American Air Power*, 13.
58. American Forces Press Service, "Operation Homecoming for Vietnam POWs Marks 40 Years," U.S. Air Force, AF.mil, February 12, 2013, https://www.af.mil/News/Article-Display/Article/109716/operation-homecoming-for-vietnam-pows-marks-40-years/https%3A%2F%2Fwww.af.mil%2FNews%2FArticle-Display%2FArticle%2F109716%2Foperation-homecoming-for-vietnam-pows-marks-40-years%2F.

Chapter 3. Air Combat and New Thinking about Targeting

1. For a detailed discussion of the campaign against the Dragon's Jaw, see A. J. C. Lavalle, ed., *The Tale of Two Bridges and The Battle for the Skies over North Vietnam*, USAF Southeast Asia Monograph Series, vol. 1, monographs 1 and 2 (Washington, DC: Office of Air Force History, 1985).
2. Van Staaveren, *Gradual Failure*, 106. See also John T. Correll, "Against the MiGs in Vietnam," *Air and Space Forces Magazine*, October 1, 2019, https://www.airandspaceforces.com/article/against-the-migs-in-vietnam/.
3. Correll, "Against the MiGs in Vietnam."
4. Van Staaveren, *Gradual Failure*, 106–8. See also Correll, "Against the MiGs in Vietnam." And see Lavalle, *Tale of Two Bridges*, 38–39.
5. Lambeth, *American Air Power*, 36.
6. John Stillion, "Trends in Air-to-Air Combat: Implications for Future Air Superiority," Center for Strategic and Budgetary Assessments, Washington, DC, 2015, p. 10, https://csbaonline.org/uploads/documents/Air-to-Air-Report-.pdf.
7. Semi-active guidance says that the firing aircraft's radar illuminates the target, and the Sparrow follows the reflected energy until it strikes it; Stillion, 12–13.
8. Lambeth, *American Air Power*, 43.
9. Lambeth, 41–43.

10. Lambeth, 47–48. The U.S. Navy officially stylizes it "TOPGUN." The program is officially called Fighter Weapons School, however. The Ault Report echoed the December 1966 conclusions from the Air Force's Project Red Baron analysis.
11. Read the full report at Frank Ault, "Report of the Air-to-Air Missile System Capability Review, July–November 1968 (The Ault Report)," Naval Air Systems Command, Washington, DC, January 1969, Naval History and Heritage Command, https://www.history.navy.mil/content/history/nhhc/research/histories/naval-aviation-history/ault-report.html.
12. Dan Pedersen, *Topgun: An American Story*, 1st ed. (New York: Hachette Books, 2019), 114.
13. Two billets for commander, Fleet Air (COMFAIR) Miramar (one lieutenant commander and one lieutenant), first appeared in 1969 but not assigned to Top Gun. See p. 37 of the "Intelligence Assignment and Placement" section of the November 6, 1969, issue of *Naval Intelligence Newsletter*. For all such similar references to issues of the newsletter hereafter, the reader should note that this is a publication of the U.S. Department of the Navy's Bureau of Naval Personnel, copies of which are found in the personal papers of Rear Admiral Thomas A. Brooks Archive.
14. U.S. Department of the Navy, Office of the Chief of Naval Operations, "Naval Aeronautical Organization for Fiscal Year 1970; Promulgation Of," OPNAV notice 05400, Washington, DC, July 1969, Naval History and Heritage Command, https://www.history.navy.mil/content/dam/nhhc/research/histories/naval-aviation/Naval%20Aeronautical%20Organization/1968-1977/jul1969.pdf.
15. Joseph Trevithick, "Spies Helped the USAF Shoot Down a Third of North Vietnam's MiG-21s," *War Is Boring* (blog), December 30, 2014, https://medium.com/war-is-boring/spies-helped-the-usaf-shoot-down-a-third-of-north-vietnams-migs-ae81e42e50e7; Hanyok, *Spartans in Darkness*, 7:254.
16. Robin Olds, *Fighter Pilot: The Memoirs of Legendary Ace Robin Olds*, with Christina Olds and Ed Rasimus, 1st ed (New York: St. Martin's Press, 2010), 272. See also Walter J. Boyne, "MiG Sweep," *Air Force Magazine*, November 1, 1998, p. 49, https://www.airandspaceforces.com/article/1198sweep/.
17. Stillion, "Air-to-Air Combat," 17–18.
18. Stillion, 17–18. See also Hankins, "Teaball Solution," 10.
19. Hankins, "Teaball Solution," 12.
20. This declassified analysis was completed during the Vietnam War and is a good companion to Hanyok's declassified work. William D. Gerhard, "Southeast Asia, SIGINT Applications in U.S. Air Operations; Part One: Collecting the Enemy's Signals, February 1972," NSA Cryptologic History Series,

February 1972, Governmentattic.org, https://www.governmentattic.org/5docs/NSA-SAIUSAO_1972.pdf.
21. Hanyok, *Spartans in Darkness*, 7:73.
22. Hanyok, 7:123. Covert collections were controlled by multiple entities: the President's Foreign Intelligence Board (PFIB), the National Security Council, and the "Special Security Group." For more on covert actions, see John Prados, *Safe for Democracy: The Secret Wars of the CIA* (Chicago: Ivan R. Dee, 2006), 377–79.
23. Cahill, "SIGINT in Vietnam." See also Deeney, "Finishing the Guideline," sec. "Signals Intelligence."
24. Hanyok, *Spartans in Darkness*, 7:235–37.
25. Hanyok, 7:235–37.
26. Hanyok, 7:248–50.
27. Hanyok, 7:250–51.
28. Teaball was an early attempt at creating a weapons control center providing intelligence inputs and a friendly radar air picture, giving commanders and controllers an improved view of North Vietnamese airspace. Hankins, "Teaball Solution," 12. For more on North Vietnamese GCI operations, see Hanyok, *Spartans in Darkness*, 7:238–39.
29. Operation of Red Crown in Boslaugh, *First-Hand*, chap. 7, "The Naval Tactical Data System in Combat," https://ethw.org/First-Hand:The_Naval_Tactical_Data_System_in_Combat_-_Chapter_7_of_the_Story_of_the_Naval_Tactical_Data_System. Discussion of Red Crown advantage is found in Hankins, "Teaball Solution," 12–13.
30. "IronHorse: A Tactical SIGINT System," *Cryptolog* 2, no. 10 (October 1975): 24, https://www.nsa.gov/portals/75/documents/news-features/declassified-documents/cryptologs/cryptolog_13.pdf. The system has variously been styled "IronHorse" and "Iron Horse"; I chose the former to reflect the usage found in this 1975 article.
31. Hanyok, *Spartans in Darkness*, 7:258. See also "IronHorse," *Cryptolog*, 25.
32. Mark Jacobsen, "Washington's Management of the Rolling Thunder Campaign," in Naval History and Heritage Command, "Command and Control of Air Operations in the Vietnam War." On "gradualism," see W. Hays Parks, "Rolling Thunder and the Law of War," *Air University Review* 33, no. 2 (January–February 1982): 2–23, https://www.airuniversity.af.edu/Portals/10/ASPJ/journals/1982_Vol33_No1-6/1982_Vol33_No2.pdf. For the history of the Rolling Thunder campaign decision-making, see Cosmas, *War in Vietnam*. For a detailed discussion on targeting and bombing during the war, see BDM Corporation, *A Study of Strategic Lessons Learned in Vietnam*, vol. 6, *Conduct of the War*, book 1, *Operational Analyses*, and book 2, *Functional Analyses*

(McLean, VA: The BDM Corporation, 1980), archived online at https://archive.org/details/DTIC_ADA096429 and https://documents.theblackvault.com/documents/vietnam/ADA096430.pdf, respectively.

33. On CINCPAC's operational plan and target folders, see Cosmas, *War in Vietnam*. Regarding the DIA's role in developing target lists, see Michael B. Petersen, "The Vietnam Cauldron: Defense Intelligence in the War for Southeast Asia," Defense Intelligence Historical Perspectives no. 2, Defense Intelligence Agency, Historical Research Division, Washington, DC, 2012, pp. 11–13, https://nsarchive2.gwu.edu/NSAEBB/NSAEBB534-DIA-Declassified-Sourcebook/documents/DIA-46.pdf. On FICPAC's target folders, see Packard, *Naval Intelligence*, 447. For perspective on the JCS targeting adjudication and orders, see Charles M. Simpson, transcript of oral history of Charles M. Simpson, with comments by John McCarthy, interview 1, conducted by Ted Gittinger, May 5, 1984, pp. 3–13, LBJ Library Oral Histories, Lyndon Baines Johnson Library and Museum, Austin, TX, https://www.discoverlbj.org/item/oh-simpsonc-19840502-1-84-79. Shipboard strike-planning processes were discussed in Litsinger, email to the author, February 17, 2020.

34. On the development of the basic encyclopedia numbers (BEN), see Stephen J. Collier and Andrew Lakoff, "The Bombing Encyclopedia of the World," in "The Total Archive," ed. Boris Jardine and Christopher M. Kelty, *Limn*, no. 6 (March 2016), https://doi.org/10.70312/LIMN. And see Lyndon B. Johnson, "October 4, 1967—7:02 p.m. McNamara, Rusk, Rostow" folder, p. 6, Cabinet Room meeting notes on bombing campaign and progress of war, Papers of Tom Johnson, box 1, LBJ Presidential Library, https://www.discoverlbj.org/item/pp-johnsontom-mtgnotes-b01-f45.

35. NRTSC became responsible for the IOIC in February 1964 and fell under ONI's control in August 1965. The creation of TIFs and the use of the AUTODIN communications network allowed some machine-readable message updates, but most updates to the onboard database used punch card and magnetic tape flown out to the aircraft carriers. Packard, *Naval Intelligence*, 186, 452, 449.

36. There were scheduled planning events, but during the constant strain of Rolling Thunder cyclic operations the planning could be ad hoc. The flight leads and at least one Mission Planning AI were planning-team constants. Litsinger, emails with the author, February 2 and 17, 2020.

37. Discussion of the impact of weather on the bombing campaign found in David C. Richardson, *The Reminiscences of Vice Admiral David C. Richardson, U.S. Navy (Retired)*, interview conducted by Paul Stillwell, 1992 (Annapolis, MD: U.S. Naval Institute, 1998), 193–94.

38. On strike mission tasking and planning approval, see James L. Holloway, "Tactical Command and Control of Carrier Operations," in Naval History and

Heritage Command, "Command and Control of Air Operations in the Vietnam War." Air wing strike mission planning in Litsinger email to the author, February 17, 2020.

39. Foster discusses the struggles with restrictive ROE, armed reconnaissance, and Iron Hand missions. James Bond Stockdale would be shot down during the USS *Oriskany* (CV 34) 1965 deployment and held captive in Hanoi. Stockdale would receive the Medal of Honor and rise to vice admiral. Wynn F. Foster, *Captain Hook: A Pilot's Tragedy and Triumph in the Vietnam War* (Annapolis, MD: Naval Institute Press, 1992), 54, 60, 82–83, and 98–99. On the disheartening rule of engagement imposed by Secretary of Defense McNamara, see Malcolm W. Cagle, "Task Force 77 in Action Off Vietnam," *Proceedings*, U.S. Naval Institute, 98, no. 5, 831 (May 1972): 66f, https://www.usni.org/magazines/proceedings/1972/may/task-force-77-action-vietnam. For more on targeting and ROE problems, see Cosmas, *War in Vietnam*.

40. For analysis of the Rolling Thunder campaign, see Cagle, "Task Force 77." There were differing assessments on the bombing campaign within the intelligence community; only the State Department/INR dissented, saying Hanoi would increase attacks, not suspend them. INR was correct. Petersen, "Vietnam Cauldron," 13. See also Bruce Palmer Jr., "US Intelligence and Vietnam," *Studies in Intelligence*, Central Intelligence Agency (December 1984), https://documents.theblackvault.com/documents/vietnam/usvietnamintel.pdf. See also "Vietnam Bombing Evaluation by Institute for Defense Analyses," *New York Times*, July 2, 1971, p. 10, https://www.nytimes.com/1971/07/02/archives/vietnam-bombing-evaluation-by-institute-for-defense-analyses.html.

41. Richardson, *Reminiscences*, 207.
42. Richardson, 195.
43. Richardson, 191.
44. Cagle, "Task Force 77."
45. Richardson, *Reminiscences*, 192–93.
46. Commander Seventh Fleet approved Richardson's operator/intelligence officer model. The commander in chief of Pacific Fleet approved the mission modification of FICPACFAC; Richardson, 195. Regarding FICPACFAC helping to disseminate target installation file (TIF) to the IOIC-equipped aircraft carriers, see Packard, *Naval Intelligence*, 449.
47. Regarding the bridge at Thanh Hóa, see Cosmas, *War in Vietnam*, 2:234–35. For a discussion on the September 9, 1966, attack on the bridge and the shootdown of CAG-16 commanding officer James Stockdale, see Foster, *Captain Hook*, 103–8.
48. Don Hollway, "Slaying the Dragon," *Vietnam Magazine*, October 2015, http://donhollway.com/thanh_hoa/. See also John Darrell Sherwood, "From

Thanh Hoa to Sarajevo: The Odyssey of Admiral Leighton W. Smith," in *Nixon's Trident: Naval Power in Southeast Asia, 1968–1972*, U.S. Navy and the Vietnam War (Washington, DC: Naval Historical Center, U.S. Department of the Navy, 2009), 62–63, archived online at https://archive.org/details/NixonsTrident/page/n67/mode/2up.

49. Richardson, *Reminiscences*, 192–93.
50. Cagle, "Task Force 77." Rear Admiral Richardson provided a briefing to the Naval War College on his interdiction-targeting process; it used the September 1966 attack on the temporary bridges south of Thanh Hóa as an example. The transcript of the brief is missing, but Richardson's slides showing the pre- and poststrike imagery remain in the archive. See David C. Richardson, "Slides from Presentation on Attack Carrier Striking Forces, 1968, May 2," record group RG-15 (Guest Lectures, Transcripts), box 39, folder 24 (Mixed Materials), U.S. Naval War College Archives, Newport, RI, https://usnwcarchives.org/repositories/2/archival_objects/24824.
51. Richardson, *Reminiscences*, 207. Postwar analysis thirteen years later would come to a similar conclusion; see BDM Corporation, *Study*, vol. 6, *Conduct of the War*, book 1, *Operational Analyses*, 7–44.
52. Richardson, *Reminiscences*, 225.
53. Hollway, "Slaying the Dragon."

Chapter 4. Learning and Adapting

1. Trent Hone, *Learning War*.
2. Janine Davidson, *Lifting the Fog of Peace: How Americans Learned to Fight Modern War* (Ann Arbor: University of Michigan Press, 2011), 16–19. See also Peter M. Senge, *The Fifth Discipline: The Art and Practice of the Learning Organization*, rev. and updated (New York: Crown Business, 2006), 219.
3. Milan N. Vego, *Joint Operational Warfare: Theory and Practice* (Newport, RI: U.S. Naval War College, 2009), XI.44–49.
4. Vego, XI.44–49.
5. Litsinger, in interview with the author, March 8, 2018.
6. Interview with Vice Adm. Lowell E. "Jake" Jacoby, USN (Ret.), interview with the author, May 9, 2019.
7. Regarding evolvability, see Hone, *Learning War*, 2–6.
8. Louis A. Zurcher Jr., "The Sailor Aboard Ship: A Study of Role Behavior in a Total Institution," *Social Forces* 43, no. 3 (March 1965): 393–400, https://doi.org/10.2307/2574769 (paywall).
9. Mansoor and Murray, *Culture of Military Organizations*, 353. See also Zurcher, "Sailor Aboard Ship," 393–94.

10. Bureau of Naval Personnel, U.S. Department of the Navy, "TraLant: Atlantic Fleet University," *All Hands*, no. 626 (March 1969): 25–35, https://media.defense.gov/2019/Jul/25/2002162322/-1/-1/1/AH196903.PDF.
11. ONI helped with the design of the database for the system. Packard, *Naval Intelligence*, 178; BuAir would become incorporated into the Bureau of Weapons in 1966. See Hone, *Power and Change*, 65–68.
12. Packard, *Naval Intelligence*, 243.
13. Hartford, in email to the author, March 7, 2020. Photo Lab compartment is located 3-97-01-Q. See plate 13, "Third Deck," in M. Rosenblatt and Son, "USS *Saratoga*, Aircraft Carrier CV-60: Redacted Booklet of General Plans," prepared for New York Naval Shipyard, Brooklyn, NY, June 24, 1957, archived online at https://www.navsource.org/archives//02/0260bj.pdf.
14. Raymond R. Preddy et al., *USS Kitty Hawk (CVA 63) WestPac Cruise Book 1962–63* (n.d.), 130–31, archived online at https://www.navysite.de/cruisebooks/cv63-63/index.html.
15. C. G. Gardner et al., *USS Forrestal (CVA 59) Mediterranean Cruise Book 1965–66*, (Cambridge, MD: William W. McAllister, [1966]), 219–20, 224, archived online at https://www.navysite.de/cruisebooks/cv59-66/index.html.
16. The *Saratoga* was the test ship for the IOIC and had the first installation in late 1962. The RA-5C did not become operational in the fleet until 1963. The *Independence* received the second IOIC installation in 1962 as well. See Packard, *Naval Intelligence*, 243; and see O. R. Osburn, "CVA Integrated Operational Intelligence System," *NAESU Digest* (May 1969): 9, Nolan Leatherman Papers.
17. These numbers have been determined by examining ship cruise books. OP division crewing is difficult to determine as Navy Manning Plans do not always have a 100 percent fill rate for all billets. During the Vietnam War most IOICs were overstaffed to handle the demands of constant combat operations.
18. Capt. Joseph "Jerry" R. Soriano, USN (Ret.), in email exchanges with the author, March 15 and 19, 2019.
19. Soriano, email exchange with the author, March 15, 2019.
20. Soriano, email exchange with the author, March 15, 2019.
21. Litsinger, email exchange with the author, November 1, 2019. For the assessment on the IOIC's shortcomings, see also J. S. Earman, "The Navy's Integrated Operational Intelligence Center," memorandum to the Director of Central Intelligence, May 14, 1965, CIA-RDP80B01676R000300050004-2, p. 2, CIA FOIA Electronic Reading Room, https://www.cia.gov/readingroom/docs/CIA-RDP80B01676R000300050004-2.pdf.
22. Litsinger, email with the author, November 1, 2019. For an example of a motorized light table, see "Cutler-Hammer AIL 1540 Light Table," National Air and Space Museum, Smithsonian, accessed March 15, 2020, https://

airandspace.si.edu/collection-objects/cutler-hammer-ail-1540-light-table/nasm_A20050091000.
23. Charles R. Peck, "Engineering Duty Officers: The Dwindling Muster," *Proceedings*, U.S. Naval Institute, 91, no. 12, 754 (December 1965), https://www.usni.org/magazines/proceedings/1965/december/engineering-duty-officers-dwindling-muster.
24. Quoting from the "Bureau of Ships Study Group for Management Review of the Department of the Navy, September 1962," in Peck, "Engineering Duty Officers."
25. Thomas A. Brooks, "History of the Air Intelligence Community," *Naval Intelligence Professionals Quarterly* (October 2002). Fleet Adm. Ernest J. King, commander in chief, U.S. Fleet, directed a continuation of special-intelligence training in a memo dated October 9, 1945; see Packard, *Naval Intelligence*, 374–76. Also see Stead, "Origins of 1630 Designator," 52.
26. Director of Naval Intelligence Rear Adm. Rufus Taylor reportedly declared, "We don't send junior 1630s to sea"; in Ford and Rosenberg, *Admirals' Advantage*, 38–39.
27. "Intelligence Assignment and Placement," *Naval Intelligence Newsletter* (September 1, 1965). See also Packard, *Naval Intelligence*, 34. And see Stead, "Origins of 1630 Designator," 51–53. For a discussion of warfare-community parochialism, see Thompson, "Brown Shoes, Black Shoes."
28. Packard, *Naval Intelligence*, 32.
29. For more on District Intelligence Offices, see Sherman, "Naval Intelligence Manual (1949)," 13. For attaché and District Intelligence collection on merchant shipping, see Packard, *Naval Intelligence*, 49–50, 84–86, 132–33, and 248–49.
30. "Intelligence Assignment and Placement," *Naval Intelligence Newsletter* (January 15, 1963): 11–15.
31. Packard, *Naval Intelligence*, 32 and 34.
32. "Intelligence Assignment and Placement," *Naval Intelligence Newsletter* (September 1965): 4–5; Brooks, interview with the author, October 31, 2019.
33. James R. Thomson, "Navy-Style Officer Selection Boards Practice Ideal Management System," *Navy Management Review* 11, nos. 10–11 (November 1964): 15; "Intelligence Assignment and Placement," *Naval Intelligence Newsletter* (May 11, 1966): 2.
34. Packard, *Naval Intelligence*, 34; Stead, "Origins of 1630 Designator," 51–53.
35. "Intelligence Assignment and Placement," *Naval Intelligence Newsletter* (May 11, 1966): 9.
36. Stead, "Origins of 1630 Designator," 53. The passing of HR 13050 in 1968 allowed the remaining 135x officers into the 163x community. It would take three to five more years to complete the transition; see "Intelligence Assignment

and Placement," *Naval Intelligence Newsletter* (July 1, 1968): 2. Some senior 1350s refused to convert to 1630. The 1630 detailer would continue to detail them to intelligence billets until they left the service. Brooks, interview with the author, October 31, 2019.

37. See Office of Naval Intelligence, "Typical Career Assignment Pattern for Code 163X Officers," *Intelligence Officer (163X) Newsletter*, November 1957, personal papers of Rear Adm. Thomas A. Brooks. Regarding career progression, see "Intelligence Assignment and Placement," *Naval Intelligence Newsletter* (January 15, 1963): 5–6.

38. "Intelligence Assignment and Placement," *Naval Intelligence Newsletter* (July 1, 1967): 12. Similar language is found on p. 2 of the newsletter's May 11, 1966, issue.

39. "Intelligence Assignment and Placement," *Naval Intelligence Newsletter* (July 1, 1967): 12. Similar language is found on p. 9 of the same issue of the newsletter.

40. Information regarding the board member structure and the importance of fitness reports signed by a line admiral from Brooks, interview with the author, October 31, 2019. Today restricted line promotion boards are made up of two restricted line officers and five line officers; "Active Duty Officer Promotions," slide 9, accessed January 12, 2025, https://www.mynavyhr.navy.mil/Portals/55/Boards/Active%20Duty%20Officer/documents/Active%20Promotion%20Brief.pdf#:~:text=Performed%20twice%20per%20year%2C%20AFQOL%20%231%20in%20May,following%20the%20anniversary%20of%2024%20months%20in%20grade.

41. Brooks, interview with the author, October 31, 2019. Channell's assignment can be found in "Intelligence Assignment and Placement," *Naval Intelligence Newsletter* (June 1969): 28.

42. As recounted by Brooks, in an interview with the author, October 31, 2019.

43. Channell was promoted to captain in 1976; see "Intelligence Assignment and Placement," *Naval Intelligence Newsletter* (March 1977): 18.

44. Wilson quoted in Ford and Rosenberg, *Admirals' Advantage*, 51.

45. Litsinger, email with the author, March 5, 2020.

46. The OP and OZ Divisions on the *Forrestal*, for example, had a total of ninety-four ship's company personnel. "Dog" Davison, ed., *USS Forrestal (CVA 59) Vietnam Cruise Book 1967* (Marceline, MO: Walsworth, n.d.), 233–34 and 242–45, archived online at https://www.navysite.de/cruisebooks/cv59-67/index.html.

47. Staffing for squadron, air wing, IOIC, and flag varied; see "Intelligence Assignment and Placement," *Naval Intelligence Newsletter* (November 1969): 37–38, 43–44. There were between five and seven officers for the IOIC, but the

total staffing fluctuated based on personnel turnover and mission, especially during the Vietnam War "plus up," notes in Packard, *Naval Intelligence*, 243.
48. Ore, interview with the author, March 7, 2019.
49. Wong and Gerras in Mansoor and Murray, *Culture of Military Organizations*, 24.
50. For a discussion on the officer and enlisted divide, see Donald W. Chisholm, "Naval Personnel since 1945: Areas for Historical Research," February 12, 2018, chap. 15, "The Great Divide," archived at the Navy Department Library, Naval History and Heritage Command, https://www.history.navy.mil/research/library/online-reading-room/title-list-alphabetically/n/needs-opportunities-modern-history-us-navy/naval-personnel-since-1945-areas-for-historical-research-1.html.
51. The "flagpole" is a term used to represent the headquarters or where the most senior leaders are located.
52. Jin Li et al., "Power Dynamics in Organizations," CSIO working paper no. 0139, Center for the Study of Industrial Organization, Kellogg School of Management, Northwestern University, Evanston, IL, December 2015, p. 2, http://www.jin-li.org/uploads/1/1/4/5/114595093/7_li_power_dynamics_in_organizations_2015.pdf.
53. Ore, interview with the author, March 7, 2019.
54. Ore, interview with the author, March 7, 2019.
55. Bureau of Naval Personnel, U.S. Department of the Navy, *Personnel Management*, NAVPERS 10848-E, rev. ed. (Washington, DC: U.S. Government Printing Office, 1971), 274, archived online at http://hdl.handle.net/2027/uc1.d0002280634.
56. There are several types of fitness reports (FitRep): regular, submitted annually for all officers of the same grade; concurrent, submitted when an officer has been assigned temporarily to another reporting senior; and special, covering positive and negative distinguishing performance. Bureau of Naval Personnel, U.S. Department of the Navy, *Personnel Management*, 276–77.
57. Bureau of Naval Personnel, U.S. Department of the Navy, *Personnel Management*, 275.
58. Current and future agency costs of power are discussed in Li et al., "Power Dynamics in Organizations," 2.
59. The "green door" is a reference from a song alluding to the happy crowd of a mysterious club located behind a green door. Jim Lowe, *The Green Door*, with the High Fives, phonograph recording (Hollywood, CA: Trinity Music, BMI, 1956), 2:11, video archived online at https://www.youtube.com/watch?v=vle44kNHxDg.

60. Leonard Wong and Stephen J. Gerras in Mansoor and Murray, *Culture of Military Organizations*, 18–19.
61. Hartford, in email with the author, March 5, 2020.
62. Bureau of Naval Personnel, U.S. Department of the Navy, "Basic Test Battery Helps Determine Navyman's Future," *All Hands*, no. 431 (January 1953): 48, https://media.defense.gov/2019/Apr/27/2002122133/-1/-1/1/ah195301.pdf. For more detail on the assessment process, see Bureau of Naval Personnel, U.S. Department of the Navy, *Personnel Management*, 74–75.
63. Bureau of Naval Personnel, U.S. Department of the Navy, "Basic Test Battery," 48–50. On the use of cutting scores, see Bureau of Naval Personnel, U.S. Department of the Navy, *Personnel Management*, 78–79.
64. Cutting score for PH and PT was 105 to 109, the cumulative GCT and ARI scores; it was one of the highest cutting scores, the attrition of Polaris missile electronics technicians (48.7 percent), electronic technician (22.5 percent), and radarman (20.4 percent) being higher. Patricia J. Thomas, "The Relationship Between Navy Classification Test Scores and Final School Grades in 98 Class 'A' Schools," research report SRR 72-22 (Naval Personnel and Training Research Laboratory, San Diego, CA, April 1972), 8, 47, and 50, https://apps.dtic.mil/sti/tr/pdf/AD0741688.pdf. "Substantially above average" equated to a score in the top 24 percent of all enlisted taking the tests; see Bureau of Naval Personnel, U.S. Department of the Navy, *Personnel Management*, 77.
65. Michael Ravnitzky, "Consequential Words: Ship Mottos," *Proceedings*, U.S. Naval Institute, 146, no. 2, 1404 (February 2020): 48, https://www.usni.org/magazines/proceedings/2020/february/consequential-words-ship-mottos; Joy Bright Hancock, "Naval Aviation Insignia," *Proceedings*, U.S. Naval Institute, 59, no. 6, 364 (June 1933), https://www.usni.org/magazines/proceedings/1933/june/naval-aviation-insignia.
66. Wong and Gerras in Mansoor and Murray, *Culture of Military Organizations*, 23.
67. The 1958 insignia of the U.S. Navy Aircraft Carrier USS *Saratoga* (CVA 60) can be seen online at the Naval History and Heritage Command's website, at https://www.history.navy.mil/our-collections/photography/numerical-list-of-images/nhhc-series/nh-series/NH-64000/NH-64888-KN.html.
68. Leghorn is a cartoon rooster (white body, bright red head and plume) with human characteristics who speaks as a hard-of-hearing, blustery Southern politician with a penchant for using catchphrases. See Keith Scott, "The Foghorn Leghorn Story," *Cartoon Research*, 2008, https://cartoonresearch.com/index.php/the-origin-of-foghorn-leghorn/; J. C. Gartland, ed., *USS Saratoga (CVA 60) Mediterranean Cruise Book 1964–65* (Marceline, MO:

Walsworth Publishing, n.d.), "Operations Department, " p. 100, archived online at https://www.navysite.de/cruisebooks/cv60-65/index.html.

69. In 1969 Tarkowski would be the IOIC supervisor of the USS *Kennedy*. Davison, *USS Forrestal (CVA 59) Vietnam Cruise Book 1967*, 254; and see "Intelligence Assignment and Placement," *Naval Intelligence Newsletter* (November 1969): 33. Durr served as the air wing intelligence officer (CAGAI) during the deployment; Capt. Donald G. Durr, USN (Ret.), interview with the author, May 28, 2020.

70. The serialized adventures of a quick-witted flying squirrel (Rocky) and a dim-witted moose (Bullwinkle). Lawrence Christon, "Tales of Jay Ward and the Bullwinkle Gang: How the Subversive Silliness of Rocky and Bullwinkle Sprang into Our Living Rooms," *Los Angeles Times*, November 13, 1988, https://www.latimes.com/archives/la-xpm-1988-11-13-ca-447-story.html; Ore, interview with the author, December 19, 2019.

71. Tonkli converted to the intelligence specialist rating and was promoted to IS2 before leaving the Navy. Tonkli, email with author, March 7, 2020.

72. On officer accessions and Aviation Officer Candidate School, see Bureau of Naval Personnel, U.S. Department of the Navy, *Personnel Management*, 208–11.

73. Litsinger, email with the author, March 5, 2020.

74. Quoting from Cox's 1992 *Proceedings* article "Alone and Unafraid with the Brown Shoe," found in Thompson, "Brown Shoes, Black Shoes," 30–31.

75. Litsinger, email with the author, March 5, 2020.

76. U.S. Congress, Joint Senate–House Armed Services Subcommittee on CVAN-70 Aircraft Carrier, *CVAN-70 Aircraft Carrier: Joint Hearings, Ninety-First Congress, Second Session . . .* (Washington, DC: U.S. Government Printing Office, 1970), 297.

77. Rear Adm. Thomas A. Brooks, USN (Ret.), in discussion with the author at the Naval Intelligence Professionals Annual Meeting, October 11, 2019.

78. Hank Stewart, "How the 1967 Fire on USS Forrestal Improved Future U.S. Navy Damage Control Readiness," *The Sextant* (blog), July 28, 2017, https://usnhistory.navylive.dodlive.mil/Recent/Article-View/Article/2686245/how-the-1967-fire-on-uss-forrestal-improved-future-us-navy-damage-control-readi/.

Chapter 5. A Close Blockade

1. Judith C. Erdheim, "Market Time (U)," report, CRC280, Center for Naval Analyses, Operation Evaluation Group, Arlington, VA, September 1975, pp. 5–6. Naval History and Heritage Command, https://www.history.navy.mil/research/library/online-reading-room/title-list-alphabetically/m/market-time-u-crc280.html.

2. Packard cites a personal message from Capt. Donald M. Showers to Director of Naval Intelligence Rear Adm. Rufus L. Taylor, OP-922, held in H4 files, OA, at the Naval History and Heritage Center, Naval Yard. See Packard, *Naval Intelligence*, 89.
3. On the Viet Cong controlling river in early 1960s, see Earl F. "Rex" Rectanus, unpublished transcript of interview, conducted by Paul Stillwell, parts 1 and 2, November 19, 1982, p. 12, box 01, folder 11, Admiral Elmo R. Zumwalt Jr. Collection, Oral History Interviews, Vietnam Center and Sam Johnson Vietnam Archive, Texas Tech University, Lubbock, TX, available for download from https://www.vietnam.ttu.edu/virtualarchive/items.php?item=6260111001.
4. The merger of the air intelligence 135x community into the intelligence officer 163x community had yet to occur.
5. Norm Channell, "Naval Intelligence in South Viet Nam," *Naval Intelligence Professionals Quarterly* (June 2004): 11, NIP Quarterly Archive.
6. Edward J. Marolda, *The Approaching Storm: Conflict in Asia, 1945–1965*, The U.S. Navy and the Vietnam War (Washington, DC: Naval History and Heritage Command, Department of the Navy, 2009), 75–77; on the Vũng Rô Bay Incident, see "Week of February 19, 2023: Week of February 19–February 25, 2023; American Special Forces Adviser Killed During Rescue, February 19, 1965," *Vietnam War Commemoration*, VietnamWar50th.com, accessed October 28, 2023, https://www.vietnamwar50th.com/education/week_of_february_19_2023/. For more on the U.S. Army's medical system in Vietnam, see Spurgeon Neel, *Medical Support, 1965–1970*, Vietnam Studies (Washington, DC: Department of the Army, 1973), 1991 reissue archived online at https://www.history.army.mil/html/books/090/90-16/index.html.
7. Mobley and Marolda, *Knowing the Enemy*, 58.
8. Channell, "Naval Intelligence l South Viet Nam."
9. NRTSC produced three identification guidebooks to support interdiction operations: *Friendly Small Boats in Vietnam*, *Waterborne Logistic Craft in North Vietnam*, and a bilingual *Vietnam Infiltration Trawler Identification Guide* (INTRIGUE). Packard, *Naval Intelligence*, 187. For the best breakdown of the surveillance and interdiction plan throughout the operations, see Erdheim, "Market Time."
10. "Intelligence Assignment and Placement Section," *Naval Intelligence Newsletter* (September 1965): 7. And see Erdheim, "Market Time," 17.
11. Don Tuthill, "The Early Days of Naval Intelligence in Viet Nam," *Naval Intelligence Professionals Quarterly* (December 2003): 42.
12. "Establishment of the Defense Special Security Communications System," memo, November 4, 1964, and "The Security, Use and Dissemination of

Communications Intelligence (COMINT)," January 26, 1965, both found in Allen and Shellum, *Defense Intelligence Agency*, 333–52.
13. Maneki, "Lessons of Vietnam," 19
14. For an extensive review of the COMSEC and OPSEC problems and Purple Dragon monitoring, see Maneki, "Lessons of Vietnam."
15. Channell, "Naval Intelligence in South Viet Nam," 12.
16. Paul H. Nitze, "Instructions for the Coordination and Control of Navy's Clandestine Intelligence Collection Program," memorandum from the Secretary of the Navy, December 7, 1965, archived online at https://nsarchive2.gwu.edu/NSAEBB/NSAEBB46/document1.pdf. For a detailed discussion of Task Force 157's creation, operations, and demise, see Jeffrey T. Richelson, "Task Force 157: The US Navy's Secret Intelligence Service, 1966–77," *Intelligence and National Security* 11, no. 1 (January 1996): 106–45, https://doi.org/10.1080/02684529608432346 (paywall).
17. Packard, *Naval Intelligence*, 279.
18. Packard, 264–67.
19. Mobley and Marolda, *Knowing the Enemy*, 80–81.
20. On Game Warden and Mobile Riverine Forces (MRFs), see William C. McQuilkin, "Operation Sealords: A Front in a Frontless War; An Analysis of the Brown-Water Navy in Vietnam," master's thesis, US Army Command and General Staff College, 1996, pp. 9–14, https://apps.dtic.mil/sti/pdfs/ADA331787.pdf.
21. "Intelligence Assignment and Placement Section," *Naval Intelligence Newsletter* (July 1968): 11.
22. Channell, "Naval Intelligence in South Viet Nam," 12.
23. Rectanus interview, 18–30, 34.
24. Rectanus interview, 31.
25. Rectanus interview, 31.
26. Rectanus interview, 31.
27. For example, operations by the Navy's Sea, Air, and Land (SEAL) teams. Rectanus interview, 30–31. For SEAL activity, see also Mobley and Marolda, *Knowing the Enemy*, 77–80.
28. Rectanus interview, 44–45. See also Rectanus' comments refuting Helms' claim that Sunshine Park was a CIA operation, in Donald M. Showers, "Commentary: VADM Rectanus on Former CIA Director Richard Helms's Book *A Look over My Shoulder* (Random House 2003)," *Naval Intelligence Professionals Quarterly* 19, no. 4 (December 2003).
29. On Sunshine Park and CIA's admission, see Mobley and Marolda, *Knowing the Enemy*, 66–67.
30. Zumwalt, *On Watch*, 39–40. For a detailed examination of the operation, see McQuilkin, "Operation Sealords," chaps. 2, 3, and 4.

31. "Sea Float: Ca Mau Peninsula, Cua Lon and Bo De Rivers," PCF45.com, accessed October 29, 2023, http://pcf45.com/sealords/seafloat/seafloat.html.
32. Drew Cukor, "Operate to Know: An Operations and Intelligence Design for the Operational Level of War," master's thesis, U.S. Joint Command and Staff College, 2014, p. 58, https://apps.dtic.mil/sti/pdfs/ADA600189.pdf.
33. As an example of building goodwill, see Erdheim, "Market Time," sec. "Psychological Operations." See also McQuilkin, "Operation Sealords," 68–70.
34. Mobley and Marolda, *Knowing the Enemy*, 75.
35. John E. Vinson and Peter B. Decker, "Bad Things Happen When You Take a War Littorally (A Tale of Two NILOs)," *Naval Intelligence Professionals Quarterly* (January 2007): 34–35. See also Mobley and Marolda, *Knowing the Enemy*, 88–89.
36. Vinson and Decker, "A Tale of Two NILOs," 34–35. See also Mobley and Marolda, *Knowing the Enemy*, 88–89.
37. Vinson and Decker, "A Tale of Two NILOs," 35.
38. Thomas A. Brooks and William Manthorpe, "NIS in Vietnam," *Naval Intelligence Professionals Quarterly* (January 1992): 3–4, archived online at https://ncisahistory.org/wp-content/uploads/2021/09/NIS-in-Vietnam.pdf; Mobley and Marolda, *Knowing the Enemy*, 87–88.
39. Many NILOs were wounded. Only two NILOs died; in addition to Graf, Al Hollowell died in an O-1 Bird Dog crash. Mobley and Marolda, *Knowing the Enemy*, 86–88.
40. "Intelligence Assignment and Placement Section," *Naval Intelligence Newsletter* (June 1965): 16.
41. "Intelligence Assignment and Placement Section," *Naval Intelligence Newsletter* (September 1971): 6.
42. Some billets had only three-weeks of Vietnam orientation, others thirteen to sixty-four. "Intelligence Assignment and Placement Section," *Naval Intelligence Newsletter* (September 1971): 19–20.
43. Cracknell commissioned an ensign in the Reserves as a 1635 intelligence officer in 1957. He converted to 1355 in 1958 and back to 1630 in 1969. He retired as a captain following command of the Naval Intelligence Command, Suitland, Maryland, in 1988, and passed away in 2005. William H. Cracknell, transcript of unpublished interview, conducted by A. D. Baker, circa 2000, tape 1, pp. 3–7, Manthorpe Collection, Office of Naval Intelligence, National Intelligence Maritime Center, Suitland, MD.
44. Cracknell, interview, 27–29.
45. On NAO warfare designator, see Edward M. Brittingham, *Sub Chaser: The Story of a Navy VP NFO; A Chronicle of the Development of Anti-submarine Techniques by U.S. Naval Aviation Patrol Planes in the Atlantic Ocean and*

Mediterranean Sea During the Cold War Era, 1962–1985 (Richmond, VA: ASW Press, 2004), 11–13.

46. Cracknell, interview, 33–34. For an example of P-3C squadron composition, see Russell K. Schulz, command history report (OPNAV Report 5750-1) for 1975 of Patrol Squadron Seventeen (VP 17), 50:VLK:wg, 5750, Ser C3 27, February 27, 1976, pp. 22–25, Naval History and Heritage Command.
47. Tom Spink, ed., *Pacific Patrol: A History of Patrol Aviation During the Cold War in the Pacific; A Collaboration* ([Seattle]: Kindle Publishing, 2020), 44–46.
48. Cracknell, interview, 30–31.
49. "Operation Market Time History," VP/VPB Summary Page, *U.S. Navy Patrol Squadrons* (website), VPNavy.org, accessed November 5, 2023, https://www.vpnavy.org/vp_operation_market_time.html.
50. Gerald A. McGill, "The Trawler Incident (1 March 1968)," *Operation Market Time* (blog), April 5, 2020, https://operationmarkettime.com/2020/04/05/the-trawler-incident-1-march-1968/. For a detailed description of a 1967 interdiction of a trawler, read Charles R. Stephan, "Trawler!" *Proceedings*, U.S. Naval Institute, 94, n. 9, 787 (September 1968), https://www.usni.org/magazines/proceedings/1968/september/trawler. For analysis on the result of the four trawler sinking, see Erdheim, "Market Time," 33.
51. Michael D. Roberts, *The History of VP, VPB, VP(HL) and VP(AM) Squadrons*, vol. 2 of *Dictionary of American Naval Aviation Squadron* (Washington, DC: Naval Historical Center, Department of the Navy, 2000), 97–99 and 299, https://www.history.navy.mil/content/dam/nhhc/research/histories/naval-aviation/dictionary-of-american-naval-aviation-squadrons-volume-2/pdfs/Prelim.pdf; McGill, "The Trawler Incident (1 March 1968)."

Chapter 6. A Distant Blockade, in All but Name

1. Andrew Metrick, "(Un)mind the Gap," *Proceedings*, U.S. Naval Institute, 145, no. 10, 1,400 (October 2019), https://www.usni.org/magazines/proceedings/2019/october/unmind-gap.
2. Wayne P. Hughes and Robert Girrier, *Fleet Tactics and Naval Operations*, 3rd ed., fore. John Richardson (Annapolis, MD: Naval Institute Press, 2018), 185–87. See also John F. Keane and C. Alan Easterling, "Maritime Patrol Aviation: 90 Years of Continuing Innovation," *Johns Hopkins APL Technical Digest* 24, no. 3 (2003): 242–44, https://secwww.jhuapl.edu/techdigest/Content/techdigest/pdf/V24-N03/24-03-Keane.pdf.
3. Milan N. Vego, interview with the author, June 28, 2019.
4. J. C. Wylie, *Military Strategy: A General Theory of Power Control* (Annapolis, MD: Naval Institute Press, 2014), 34.

5. On concentration versus dispersal of naval forces, see Milan N. Vego, *Operational Warfare at Sea: Theory and Practice*, 2nd ed., CASS Naval Policy and History Series (London: Routledge, Taylor and Francis Group, 2017), 58–61.
6. Wylie, *Military Strategy*, 72. For an examination in the use of Navy assets to influence and de-escalate crises, see Joseph F. Bouchard, *Command in Crisis: Four Case Studies* (New York: Columbia University Press, 1991).
7. Edward J. Marolda et al., "Conflict and Cooperation: The U.S. and Soviet Navies in the Cold War," presentation at the Colloquium on Contemporary History 1989–1998, seminar 10, Naval Historical Center, Washington, DC, June 12, 1996, https://www.history.navy.mil/research/library/online-reading-room/title-list-alphabetically/c/conflict-coop-us-soviet-navies-cold-war.html.
8. David F. Winkler, *Cold War at Sea: High-Seas Confrontation Between the United States and the Soviet Union* (Annapolis, MD: Naval Institute Press, 2000), 57.
9. See David F. Winkler's presentation, "The 1970 Soviet Decision to Negotiate an Incidents at Sea Agreement," as part of Marolda et al., "Conflict and Cooperation."
10. Geoffrey Till, *Seapower: A Guide for the Twenty-First Century*, 3rd ed. (New York: Routledge, 2013), 182.
11. On the mixed-wing concept, see Elmer B. Staats, "The Navy's Multimission Carrier Airwing: Can the Mission Be Accomplished with Fewer Resources?" Government Accountability Office Secret Report LCD-77-409, Comptroller General's Report to Congress, September 12, 1977, unclassified version doc. LDC-77-451, published November 16, 1977, archived online at https://www.gao.gov/assets/103996.pdf.
12. Ford and Rosenberg, *Admirals' Advantage*, 107.
13. David Reade, *The Age of Orion: Lockheed P-3, an Illustrated History*, Schiffer Military/Aviation History (Atglen, PA: Schiffer, 1998), 15.
14. On the development of Navy aviation, see Roberts, *History of VP Squadrons*, 2:1–14.
15. Roberts, 2:42–51.
16. Reade, *Age of Orion*, 8–15.
17. Reade, 14–22. On the development of ATDS, see Boslaugh, *First-Hand*, chap. 8, "The Marine Tactical Data System and the Airborne Tactical Data System," sec. "The P-3 Orion Land Based Maritime Patrol Craft," https://ethw.org/First-Hand:The_Marine_Tactical_Data_System_and_the_Airborne_Tactical_Data_System_-_Chapter_8_of_the_Story_of_the_Naval_Tactical_Data_System#The_P-3_Orion_Land_Based_Maritime_Patrol_Craft. Also see "VP-5's Threefold Mission in Vietnam," *Naval Aviation News* (March 1968): 29, https://www.history.navy.mil/content/dam/nhhc/research/histories/naval-aviation/Naval%20Aviation%20News/1960/pdf/mar68.pdf.

18. See Gary E. Weir's "SOUS, the Navy, and Bell Labs," pp. 47–60, in Shannon A. Brown, ed., "Providing the Means of War: Perspectives on Defense Acquisition, 1945–2000" (U.S. Army Center of Military History and Industrial College of the Armed Forces, Washington, DC, 2005), https://www.history.army.mil/html/books/070/70-87-1/CMH_Pub_70-87-1.pdf.
19. Project Jezebel was part of the original Bell Lab contract. Brown, 55–56; Reade, *Age of Orion*, 21–27.
20. Capt. Donald Miskill, USN (Ret.), interview with the author, October 8, 2021.
21. Miskill, interview with the author, October 8, 2021. For a full listing of deployments and deployment sites, see Roberts, *History of VP Squadrons*.
22. Total commander-and-below billets, 910. Lieutenant billets, 277; lieutenant junior grade billets, 177. Billets dedicated to MPRF at squadron, wing, and theater level, 49. "Intelligence Assignment and Placement," *Naval Intelligence Newsletter* (1972): II.1–19.
23. TSCs were renamed Anti-submarine Warfare Operations Centers in 1972 but reverted to TSC by 1980. H. Halpin and H. Wilson, "TSC: The Missing Link," *Naval Aviation News* (August 1970): 25, https://www.history.navy.mil/content/dam/nhhc/research/histories/naval-aviation/Naval%20Aviation%20News/1970/pdf/aug70.pdf.
24. Information courtesy of Cdr. Dale P. Thompson, USNR (Ret.), interview with the author, October 19, 2021; Miskill, interview with the author, October 8, 2021; and Vice Adm. Ann E. Rondeau, USN (Ret.), interview with the author, December 3, 2021.
25. Bureau of Naval Personnel, U.S. Department of the Navy, *Photographer's Mate 3 & 2*, 565–70.
26. Regarding Rainform Green and Purple, see Spink, *Pacific Patrol*, 91.
27. On Okean 75, see James F. Clarity, "Soviet Exercises Seek to Prove Navy's Readiness," *New York Times*, April 15, 1970, https://www.nytimes.com/1970/04/15/archives/soviet-exercises-seek-to-prove-navys-readiness.html. On Okean 70, see Norman Polmar, "Norman's Corner: Analyzing Exercise Okean," Naval Historical Foundation, February 20, 2013, https://navyhistory.org/2013/02/normans-corner-analyzing-exercise-okean/.
28. Thompson, interview with the author, October 19, 2021. About the exercise, see "Vast Soviet Naval Exercise Raises Urgent Questions for West," *New York Times*, April 28, 1975, https://www.nytimes.com/1975/04/28/archives/vast-soviet-naval-exercise-raises-urgent-questions-for-west.html.
29. Thompson, interview with the author, October 19, 2021.
30. Rondeau, interview with the author, December 3, 2021.
31. Rondeau, email exchange with the author, January 23, 2022, and interview with the author, December 3, 2021.

32. Packard, *Naval Intelligence*, 192.
33. Packard, 190–92; Thompson, interview with the author, October 19, 2021.
34. Thompson, email exchange with the author, January 6, 2022.
35. Thompson, email exchange with the author, January 6, 2022.
36. Thompson, interview with the author, October 19, 2021.
37. Thompson, email exchange with the author, January 6, 2022.
38. Mark Borgerson, *The SECGRU Years: Five Years in the Naval Security Group* (USA: privately published, 2019), 110.
39. Regarding verification, see Prados, *Soviet Estimate*, 273.
40. Richard L. Bernard, "Telemetry Intelligence (TELINT) During the Cold War" (National Security Agency Center for Cryptologic History, Fort Meade, MD, 2016), 1–14, https://www.nsa.gov/portals/75/documents/about/cryptologic-heritage/historical-figures-publications/publications/misc/telint-9-19-2016.pdf.
41. Borgerson, *Five Years in SECGRU*, 110–12.
42. MPRF imagery and tracking of SMRIS in the 1960s. Packard, *Naval Intelligence*, 405, 448. Regarding Pony Express operations, Thompson, interview with the author, October 19, 2021.
43. On Pony Express missions from Midway Islands, see Spink, *Pacific Patrol*, 99–100, 152, and 285.
44. Borgerson, *Five Years in SECGRU*, 118–27.
45. See the subsection titled "The New Threat Arises" in Don C. East, *A History of U.S. Navy Fleet Air Reconnaissance, Part 1, The Pacific and VQ-1*, and *Part 2, The European Theater and VQ-2*, Web, VPNavy.org, sec. "The New Threat Arises," accessed October 2, 2021, http://www.vpnavy.com/vq1_1950.html.
46. Odd-numbered squadrons were Pacific Ocean–based, even-numbered ones Atlantic-based. John R. Schindler, *A Dangerous Business: The U.S. Navy and National Reconnaissance During the Cold War* (Fort Meade, MD: Center for Cryptologic History, 2001), 4–5. On "mission support" versus dedicated squadron approach, see East, "History of U.S. Navy Fleet Air Reconnaissance," sec. "The New Threat Arises."
47. East, "History of U.S. Navy Fleet Air Reconnaissance," sec. "The Development of a Dedicated Pacific Unit"; Packard, *Naval Intelligence*, 107–8. For a complete accounting of all VQ-1 and 2 aircraft, see Rich Haver, "Electronic Counter Measures Aircraft Life Histories (VQ-1 and VQ-2), 1949–," Aircraft history charts, 1949–1991, *VQ Association* (website), accessed April 20, 2020, http://vqassociation.org/wp-content/uploads/2019/06/062-VQ-Aircraft-History-Charts-HQ.pdf.
48. "New Orion Scheduled (EP-3E)," *Naval Aviation News* (July 1971), 4–5, https://www.history.navy.mil/content/dam/nhhc/research/histories/naval-aviation/Naval%20Aviation%20News/1970/pdf/jul71.pdf.

49. Original SIGINT authority came from the September 1958 National Security Council intelligence directive (NSCID) no. 6; see Noel Gayler, "United States Signal Intelligence Directive (USSID 1)," National Security Agency, September 29, 1971, NSA Archive, https://www.nsa.gov/portals/75/documents/news-features/declassified-documents/nsa-60th-timeline/1970s/19710921_1970_Doc_3987512_USSID1.pdf.
50. Robert E. Morrison, "Fleet Support Detachment, Da Nang, Republic of Vietnam (Det Bravo): Command History" (Virginia Beach: privately published, 2017), 6n9, https://www.navycthistory.com/pdf/HistoryofDetBravoDaNang.pdf.
51. Morrison, 6n9.
52. Keane and Easterling, "Maritime Patrol Aviation," 250.
53. Ford and Rosenberg, *Admirals' Advantage*, 57–58. For more on the shootdown, see National Security Agency, "The National Security Agency and the EC-121 Shootdown," United States Cryptologic History, Special Series Crisis Collection vol. 3 ([Fort Meade, MD]: Office of Archives and History, National Security Agency, 1989), 47, https://media.defense.gov/2021/Jun/29/2002751426/-1/-1/0/THE%20NATIONAL%20SECURITY%20AGENCY%20AND%20THE%20EC-121%20SHOOTDOWN.PDF.
54. Thompson, interview with the author, October 19, 2021.
55. Thompson, interview with the author, October 19, 2021.
56. Thompson, interview with the author, October 19, 2021.
57. Thompson, email exchange with the author, January 6, 2022.
58. "Intelligence Assignment and Placement," *Naval Intelligence Newsletter* (1972): sec. II, "Billets"; and see Crew of Fleet Air Reconnaissance Two (VQ-2), *VQ-2 Rota Spain Cruise Book, 1973–1974* (Marceline, MO: Walsworth Publishing Company, 1974), 52, https://vqassociation.org/history-docs/00eee%20Rota%20Spain%20VQ-2%20Book.pdf.
59. Another example is the highly modified aircraft of special patrol squadrons, discussed in David A. Fulghum, "Navy Spying Masked by Patrol Aircraft," *Aviation Week and Space Technology*, March 8, 1999, https://archive.aviationweek.com/issue/19990308 (paywall).
60. Thompson, interview with the author, October 19, 2021.
61. The report uses information provided by Lockheed Martin, official Lockheed and USN records, and a series of "plane spotters." Because they are difficult to verify, no plane spotter dates regarding location of aircraft are used in this book. Jaap Dubbeldam and Marco P. J. Borst, "P-3 Aircraft Location History Report," *P-3 Orion Research Group–The Netherlands* (website), October 2021, pp. 33, 36–37, 49, 52, and 54, https://www.p3orion.nl/sneaky.html.
62. U.S. Department of the Navy, "Department of the Navy Justification of Estimates for Fiscal Year 1983: Submitted to Congress February 1982; Procurement

Book 1 of 2, Aircraft Procurement," budget report, govt. accession no. AD A114941, Navy Aircraft Procurement and Weapons Procurement (Department of the Navy, February 1982), 1.55, https://apps.dtic.mil/sti/pdfs/ADA114941.pdf.
63. John Pike, "CNO Project BEARTRAP," Intelligence Resource Program (website), Federation of American Scientists, last updated November 25, 1998, https://irp.fas.org/program/collect/beartrap.htm.
64. U.S. Navy Research Development Test and Evaluation, "Exhibit R-2, RDT&E Budget Item Justification," appropriation/budget activity report, February 2007, p. 1, archived online at https://www.dacis.com/budget/budget_pdf/FY08/RDTE/N/0603254N.pdf.
65. Rondeau, interview with the author, December 3, 2021.
66. William H. Cracknell, "The Role of the U.S. Navy in Inshore Waters," student paper, Naval War College, 1968, record group RG-13, file N420.F82 1968 no. 94, box 280, folder 7, Naval War College Archives Repository, https://usnwcarchives.org/repositories/2/archival_objects/206111.
67. "Intelligence Assignment and Placement," *Naval Intelligence Newsletter* (1972); William H. Cracknell Jr., "William Cracknell Obituary," Legacy.com, accessed January, 14 2025, https://www.legacy.com/us/obituaries/name/william-cracknell-obituary?pid=178641324.
68. Rondeau, interview with the author, December 3, 2021.
69. Thompson, interview with the author, October 19, 2021.
70. Rondeau, interview with the author, December 3, 2021.
71. Zumwalt, *On Watch*, 172–81.
72. Zumwalt, 263.
73. Zumwalt, 261–64.
74. On Z-116's impact in the Navy, see James L. Leuci, "Navy Women in Ships: A Deployment to Equality, 1942–1982" (U.S. Navy, Chief of Navy Reserve, Hampton Roads Naval Museum, Norfolk, VA, 2016), 16–20, https://www.history.navy.mil/content/dam/museums/hrnm/Education/Women%20in%20Ships%201978%2020160207.pdf.
75. "Intelligence Assignment and Placement," *Naval Intelligence Newsletter* (1972): 14.
76. Darlene M. Iskra, "Attitudes Toward Expanding Roles for Navy Women at Sea: Results of a Content Analysis," *Armed Forces and Society* 33, no. 2 (January 2007): 208, https://doi.org/10.1177/0095327X06287883. See also Leuci, "Deployment to Equality."
77. Leuci, "Deployment to Equality," 30.
78. Leuci, 35.
79. "Intelligence Assignment and Placement," *Naval Intelligence Newsletter* (1975): 15.

80. The integration of women in the 1970s discussed with Rondeau, interview with the author, December 3, 2021. For example, on administrative duties, see the photograph captioned "It's a Man's World?" in "On Patrol with the Fleet Air Wings," *Naval Aviation News* (April 1970): 24, https://www.history.navy.mil/content/dam/nhhc/research/histories/naval-aviation/Naval%20Aviation%20News/1970/pdf/apr70.pdf. See also "Editor's Corner: WAVE Maintenance Officers," *Naval Aviation News* (May 1970): 24, https://www.history.navy.mil/content/dam/nhhc/research/histories/naval-aviation/Naval%20Aviation%20News/1970/pdf/may70.pdf.
81. Helen F. Collins, "Women in Naval Aviation: From Plane Captains to Pilot," *Naval Aviation News* (July 1977): 9, https://www.history.navy.mil/content/dam/nhhc/research/histories/naval-aviation/Naval%20Aviation%20News/1970/pdf/jul77.pdf. For a discussion on the restrictions of women officers, see Beth F. Coye, "The Restricted Unrestricted Line Officer: The Status of the Navy's Woman Line Officer," *Naval War College Review* 24, no. 7 (March 1972): 53–64. https://www.jstor.org/stable/44641297.
82. Collins, "Captains to Pilot," 15–16.
83. Regarding SECNAVINST 1300.12, see Leuci, "Deployment to Equality," 55.
84. Leuci, 66–76.
85. Thompson, email exchange with the author, January 18, 2022. Gail Harris laterally transferred to 163x sometime in 1977 or 1978. Her billet in 1979 was at FOSIC WestPac. She retired as a captain in 2001. "Intelligence Assignment and Placement," *Naval Intelligence Newsletter* (1979): 12. See also Gail Harris, "Gail Harris: Professional Biography," *Gail Harris: Captain of Persistence* (website), accessed January 18, 2022, https://gailharrisspeaker.com/gail_bio.html.
86. "Intelligence Assignment and Placement," *Naval Intelligence Newsletter* (1976): 14. New 163x ensigns first to attend AOCS discussed in Collins, "Captains to Pilot," 15. On new women 163x ensign assignments, see "Intelligence Assignment and Placement," *Naval Intelligence Newsletter* (1979): 16–17.
87. Rondeau, email exchange with the author, January 23, 2022, and interview with the author, December 3, 2021.
88. Rondeau, email exchange with the author, January 23, 2022, and interview with the author, December 3, 2021.
89. Rondeau interview with the author, December 3, 2021. For more on the military's pilot-retention issues during the 1970s and 1980s, see Marvin M. Smith, "Pilot Retention in the Military: An Analysis of Alternative Bonus Plans," staff working paper (Congressional Budget Office, U.S. Congress, [Washington, DC], June 1988), https://www.cbo.gov/sites/default/files/100th-congress-1987-1988/reports/doc09_1.pdf.
90. Rondeau, interview with the author, December 3, 2021.

91. Rondeau, interview with the author, December 3, 2021. Regarding the effort to enforce Navy SORM and bridge the gender-leadership divide, see Leuci, "Deployment to Equality," 18.
92. As assessment from a BDM report; see Thomas J. Cutler, *Brown Water, Black Berets: Coastal and Riverine Warfare in Vietnam* (Annapolis, MD: Naval Institute Press, 2012), 134, archived online at https://www.google.com/books/edition/Brown_Water_Black_Berets/mlQJrG0EASAC?hl=en&gbpv=1&dq=study+by+the+BDM+Corporation+Market+Time+vietnam&pg=PA383&printsec=frontcover.
93. On space versus force consideration, see Vego, *Joint Operational Warfare*, III-9 and -10. Corbett suggested focusing on terminal areas to improve maritime trade destruction applies here; he said, "Where the carcase is, there will the eagles be gathered together!" As quoted in Till, *Seapower*, 216–17. For more on the Mekong Delta, see U.S. Department of the Navy, Naval Historical Center, "Riverine Warfare: The US Navy's Operations on Inland Waters" (Government Printing Office, Washington, DC, [1969] 2006), chap. 3, sec. "An Imposing Riverine Environment," https://www.history.navy.mil/research/library/online-reading-room/title-list-alphabetically/r/riverine-warfare-us-navys-operations-inland-waters.html.

Part III. Decentralizing

1. USS *Massey*, "Deck Log Book of the USS *Massey*," (DD 778), June 8, 1967, record group RG-24 (Records of the Bureau of Naval Personnel, 1798–2007), National Archives II, College Park, MD, and archived online at http://www.thelibertyincident.com/docs/Logs25-52.pdf.
2. Charles Cooke, BM2, USN, email exchange with the author regarding USS *Massey* and the USS *Liberty* incident, January 29, 2019.
3. Charles Cooke was a BM2 on *Massey* during the ship's run to render aid to the *Liberty*. Cooke, interview with the author, January 29, 2019. And for more on the *Liberty* incident, see Joint Chiefs of Staff, U.S. Department of Defense, "Report of the JCS Fact Finding Team: USS *Liberty* Incident, 8 June 1967," Washington, DC, archived online at http://www.thelibertyincident.com/docs/JCSreport.pdf.
4. Neil Sheehan, "Order Didn't Get to USS Liberty; Pentagon Reports Message Directing Ship off Sinai to Move Arrived Late Ship 15.5 Miles Offshore," *New York Times*, June 29, 1967, p. 1, https://www.nytimes.com/1967/06/29/archives/order-didnt-get-to-uss-liberty-pentagon-reports-message-directing.html.
5. Richardson took command of Sixth Fleet on August 14, 1968; see Richardson, *Reminiscences*, 226.

Chapter 7. To Not Be Surprised

1. Gordon H. McCormick, *The Soviet Presence in the Mediterranean* (Santa Monica, CA: RAND Corp., 1987), 9–10, available for download from https://www.rand.org/pubs/papers/P7388.html.
2. Richardson refers to his personal copy of the *Liberty* incident report in *Reminiscences*, 237–38; see p. 227 for his own assessment of the available intelligence. For more on the attack on *Pueblo*, see Jack Cheevers, *Act of War: Lyndon Johnson, North Korea, and the Capture of the Spy Ship Pueblo* (New York: NAL Caliber, 2013).
3. Cynthia M. Grabo served as senior researcher and writer for the U.S. Watch Committee throughout its existence (1950–1975) and for its successor organization, the Strategic Warning Staff. She published a compilation of three of her previously classified works from 1972 and 1974 as *Anticipating Surprise: Analysis for Strategic Warning*, ed. Jan Goldman, fore. James A. Williams (Washington, DC: Joint Military Intelligence College, 2002), https://ia600501.us.archive.org/33/items/Anticipating-Surprise-Analysis-for-Strategic-Warning-2002/Anticipating%20Surprise%20-%20Analysis%20for%20Strategic%20Warning%20%282002%29.pdf. The quotation is from p. 2.
4. Grabo, *Anticipating Surprise*, 3–4.
5. John A. Gentry and Joseph S. Gordon, *Strategic Warning Intelligence: History, Challenges, and Prospects* (Washington, DC: Georgetown University Press, 2019).
6. Strategic, operational, and tactical warnings can be influenced by the adversary's target, especially when considering at what level of the U.S. government the response decision is made. Sundri K. Khalsa, email exchange with the author, July 1, 2020; and see Khalsa's report "Terrorism Forecasting: A Web-Based Methodology," occasional paper no. 11 (Center for Strategic Intelligence Research, Joint Military Intelligence College, Washington, DC, November 2004), https://books.google.com/books?hl=en&lr=&id=q43aAAAAMAAJ&oi=fnd&pg=PP5&dq=Terrorism+Forecasting:+A+Web-Based+Methodology+Intelligence+College&ots=bkuRnJhOYn&sig=cVB3vgyQEoX5pXsqK6_w8ax2A3Y#v=onepage&q=Terrorism%20Forecasting%3A%20A%20Web-Based%20Methodology%20Intelligence%20College&f=false.
7. Grabo, *Anticipating Surprise*, 4.
8. Michael S. Goodman, "The Dog that Didn't Bark: The Joint Intelligence Committee and Warning of Aggression," *Cold War History* 7, no. 4 (November 2007): 531–32, https://doi.org/10.1080/14682740701621739 (paywall). For example of mirror imaging and confirmation bias in the U.S. intelligence community, see Mahnken, *Uncovering Ways of War*.
9. Regarding naval interactions and control of the escalation spiral, see Bouchard, *Command in Crisis*.

10. For a detailed discussion, see Grabo, *Anticipating Surprise*, chap. 9, "Improving Warning Assessments: Some Conclusions."
11. Goodman discusses analysis from the British intelligence community, recommending that the Joint Intelligence Community increase warning-intelligence staff, in "The Dog that Didn't Bark," 532–33. And the SIGINT collaboration between Britain's Government Communications Headquarters intelligence body and the United States' NSA to better formulate warnings and understand adversary intent is discussed in John Ferris, *Behind the Enigma: The Authorised History of GCHQ, Britain's Secret Cyber-intelligence Agency* (London: Bloomsbury Publishing, 2020).
12. Gentry and Gordon, *Strategic Warning Intelligence*.
13. Grabo, *Anticipating Surprise*, 4.
14. David Omand, "Learning to Be Less Surprised by Surprise," webinar presented at the Warning, Risk, and Resilience Lecture, King's College London, June 3, 2020.
15. Centuries of naval history provide myriad examples of independent command at sea, the best of which is probably the Royal Navy's Admiral Lord Nelson, discussed in Graham Scarbro, "'Go Straight at 'Em!' Training and Operating with Mission Command," *Proceedings*, U.S. Naval Institute, 145, no. 5, 1,395 (May 2019), https://www.usni.org/magazines/proceedings/2019/may/go-straight-em-training-and-operating-mission-command. Also see Barnett, *Navy Strategic Culture*, chap. 2, "Strategic Culture."
16. Hughes and Girrier, *Fleet Tactics*, 200.
17. Christopher W. Maillefert, "Command and Control: A Contemporary Perspective," Advanced Research Project no. 062, Naval War College, Newport, RI, 1974, p. 50, http://archive.org/details/DTIC_ADB001632.
18. Friedman, *Network-centric Warfare*, 171–76.
19. Ford and Rosenberg, *Admirals' Advantage*, 56.
20. Richardson describes elements of the surveillance in *Reminiscences*, 227, 232–33. Friedman describes the HF/DF, radar, terrestrial, and space-based systems in *Network-centric Warfare*, 177–79.
21. An example is found in Richardson, *Reminiscences*, 237–38.
22. Capt. Robert J. Tolle, USN, interview with the author, February 11, 2019.
23. Richardson, *Reminiscences*, 225.
24. Capt. Louis F. Giacchino (1610), USN (Ret.), served at NSG Rota and VQ-2 before becoming the Sixth Fleet cryptologist and sat in interview with the author, February 16, 2019. And Tolle, interview with the author, February 11, 2019. Regarding new SpintCom, see Richardson, *Reminiscences*, 227.
25. Ford and Rosenberg, *Admirals' Advantage*, 44–45.
26. Richardson, *Reminiscences*, 227. For information on the stations on Cyprus, see Giorgos Georgiou, "British Bases in Cyprus and Signals Intelligence,"

Études helléniques / Hellenic Studies, The Republic of Cyprus: 50 Years After / La République de Chypre: 50 ans après, 19, no. 2 (2011): 8, archived online at https://wikispooks.com/w/images/a/a7/British_Bases_in_Cyprus_and_Signals_Intelligence.pdf. For a review of the Navy and Department of Defense satellite-reconnaissance programs, see Pennsylvania State University Advanced Research Lab, ed., "From the Sea to the Stars: A Chronicle of the U.S. Navy's Space and Space-Related Activities, 1944-2009," rev. ed., spons. Gary A. Federici (Naval History and Heritage Command, [Washington, DC], 2010), 54, archived online at https://www.history.navy.mil/research/library/online-reading-room/title-list-alphabetically/f/from-sea-stars.html.

27. Michael Herman points out that high-level government involvement in intelligence collection began at the diplomacy level long before electronic technology, in *Intelligence Power in Peace and War* (Cambridge: Royal Institute of International Affairs, Cambridge University Press, 1996), 21–28, and the discussion encompassing chap. 3, "Resources, Stages and Subjects," archived online at https://archive.org/details/intelligencepowe0000herm/mode/2up. Also see Mark M. Lowenthal, *Intelligence: From Secrets to Policy*, 6th ed. (Los Angeles: CQ Press, 2015), chap. 5, "Collection and the Collection Disciplines."

28. Richardson had a day-long meeting with the Navy Security Group before departing for Sixth Fleet; Richardson, *Reminiscences*, 226. On the NFOIO ocean-surveillance branch, see Packard, *Naval Intelligence*, 223. Also see Ford and Rosenberg, *Admirals' Advantage*, 33.

29. The restrictions would lessen in 1973 under the Tactical Exploitation of National Capabilities (TENCAP) program, and by 1977 law would require that all satellite-collected intelligence be exploited tactically. See Richardson, *Reminiscences*, 231; and see Dwayne A. Day, "From the Sky to the Mud: TENCAP and Adapting National Reconnaissance Systems to Tactical Operations," *The Space Review*, June 19, 2023, https://www.thespacereview.com/article/4606/1.

30. Tolle, interview with the author, February 6, 2019. Also in Richardson, *Reminiscences*, 230.

31. Giacchino, interview with the author, February 16, 2019.

32. Lowenthal, *Secrets and Policy*, 189.

33. Pennsylvania State University Advanced Research Lab, "Sea to Stars," 73; Richardson, *Reminiscences*, 231–32. For more on the strictures against using national-technical intelligence, see Joshua Boehm, "A History of the United States National Security Space Management and Organization," with Craig Baker, Stanley Chan, and Mel Sakazaki (Commission to Assess United States National Security Space Management and Organization, January 11, 2001), III.B.2, "Evolution of the Navy's Space Objectives, 1970–Present," https://spp.fas.org/eprint/article03.html#23.

34. On meeting with Vice Admiral Schoech and CNO Moorer to apply pressure for ocean surveillance, see Richardson, *Reminiscences*, 226. Also see Vic Socotra, "Operational Intelligence and the Creation of OSIS: VADM David C. Richardson and the Operator's Perspective on the Creation of the Ocean Surveillance Information System," *DailySocotra* (blog), June 14, 2008, https://www.vicsocotra.com/wordpress/operational-intelligence-and-the-creation-of-osis/.
35. Tolle, interview with the author, February 11, 2019.
36. Richardson, *Reminiscences*, 235–36. Rota is strategically located in the province of Cádiz, Andalusia, on the Atlantic Ocean side of the Strait of Gibraltar.
37. Letter from Richardson to Vic Socotra in *DailySocotra* (blog), "Creation of OSIS," https://www.vicsocotra.com/wordpress/operational-intelligence-and-the-creation-of-osis/.
38. Once established, FOSIF Rota had no shortage of work; for one description of its activities, see Drew Middleton, "Role of U.S. Navy Base in Spain Expands as Soviet Fleet Grows," *New York Times*, May 14, 1972, p. 2, https://www.nytimes.com/1972/05/14/archives/role-of-us-navy-base-in-spain-expands-as-soviet-fleet-grows.html.
39. Port Lyautey, Morocco, became a communication station supporting the nearby signals-intercept station in Sidi Yahya, Morocco. The base officially closed in 1976. See John W. Finney, "Senate Unit Finds U.S. Has Secret Base in Morocco for Navy Communications," *New York Times*, July 28, 1970, p. 4, https://www.nytimes.com/1970/07/28/archives/senate-unit-finds-us-has-secret-base-in-morocco-for-navy.html. For more on the signal-intercept station, see Borgerson, *SECGRU Years*, chap. 6, "Sidi Yahia Morocco."
40. Richardson, *Reminiscences*, 236. FOSIF Rota was placed inside the small Special Security Office (SSO) vault. George B. Pressly, "Creating FOSIF Rota," presentation, Operational Intelligence Lessons Symposium, Spring Red Tie Luncheon, Naval Intelligence Professionals, Arlington, VA, April 29, 2016, slide 8, https://navintpro.org/news/2016/05/15/red-tie-summary/.
41. Richardson, *Reminiscences*, 235. The yacht may have been a 1968 Chris-Craft Commander 60.
42. Vic Socotra, "Big Smoke," *DailySocotra* (blog), February 4, 2013, https://www.vicsocotra.com/wordpress/big-smoke/.
43. Attsa My Boat/*Big Smoke* is also theorized to have been a 1965 Christ Craft Constellation 57. Richelson, "Task Force 157," 107.
44. Richelson, "Task Force 157," 115–16.
45. Pressly, "FOSIF Rota," slide 9.
46. Litsinger, email exchange with author, April 20, 2020.
47. The *Moskva* was listed as a cruiser to get around the 1936 Montreux Convention. For reportage on the Regime of the Straits' restrictions on aircraft

carriers, see "Big Soviet Cruiser Sails into Atlantic," *New York Times*, January 20, 1970, p. 8, https://www.nytimes.com/1970/01/20/archives/big-soviet-cruiser-sails-into-atlantic.html.

48. The *Moskva* had made a Montreux Convention declaration seventy-two hours before her southbound transit, insufficient warning for Sixth Fleet to sortie a ship to intercept her without the warning intelligence. *DailySocotra* (blog), "Creation of OSIS."
49. Ford and Rosenberg, *Admirals' Advantage*, 59 and 65.
50. James Lyons eventually rose to vice admiral and played a significant role in the Navy's 1980s-era Maritime Strategy. This via Tolle, interview with the author, February 6, 2019. See also *DailySocotra* (blog), "Creation of OSIS."
51. It was the MR-600 Voskhod "Topsail" 3D air search radar. Richardson, *Reminiscences*, 248.
52. Tolle, interview with the author, February 6, 2019. See also Richardson, *Reminiscences*, 248. *Moskva* exited the Mediterranean around January 16, 1970; see "Big Soviet Cruiser," *New York Times*.
53. Richardson, *Reminiscences*, 249–54.
54. Pressly, "FOSIF Rota"; Richardson, *Reminiscences*, 236.
55. "Intelligence Assignment and Placement Section," *Naval Intelligence Newsletter* (1970): 3–4.
56. Brooks, email exchange with the author, November 18, 2020.
57. Packard, *Naval Intelligence*, 343; Ford and Rosenberg, *Admirals' Advantage*, 60–61.
58. For a discussion of current versus long-term analysis, see Lowenthal, *Secrets and Policy*, 153.
59. Ford and Rosenberg, *Admirals' Advantage*, 56–59.
60. Warning analysis comes from deep understanding of the adversary. See discussion in Grabo, *Anticipating Surprise*, chap. 1, "The Role of Warning Intelligence."
61. Ford and Rosenberg, *Admirals' Advantage*, 57–58. The April 15, 1969, shootdown of a Navy EC-121 was the final straw and forced the NSA to create the support center, which would not open for another eighteen months. For more on the precipitating event, see National Security Agency, "EC-121 Shootdown," 47.
62. Ford and Rosenberg, *Admirals' Advantage*, 57–58. FOSIF moved into the NSG Rota building; see Pressly, "FOSIF Rota," slide 26.
63. Litsinger, interview with author, June 27, 2019. Information regarding the FOSIF, CSG, and NSG relationship from Litsinger, email exchange with author, November 18, 2020.
64. Regarding twenty-four-hour FOSIF operations, see Pressly, "FOSIF Rota," slide 16. Watch officers (163x and URL subspecialty intelligence officers)

discussed in Litsinger, email exchange with the author, November 18, 2020. Also, information regarding the plotter analysts from Litsinger, email exchange with author, December 20, 2020, and interview with the author, June 27, 2019. Regarding conversion of yeoman (2505 NEC) and photographic intelligencemen into the intelligence specialists (IS) rate, see J. H. Bartholomew, "Review of Occupational Standards for the Intelligence Specialist Rating; Request For," Naval Intelligence Command, October 26, 1977, record group RG 24 (Records of the Bureau of Naval Personnel), NAID 6287268, HMS Record Entry ID 156557, HMS/MLR Entry Number A1 1022, case files relating to Navy ratings 1945–1978, box 26 (IC–IS), National Archives II, College Park, MD. RA II.
65. Litsinger, interview with the author, June 27, 2019.
66. On Classic Bullseye, see Matthew M. Aid, *The Secret Sentry: The Untold History of the National Security Agency* (New York: Bloomsbury Publishing, 2009), 108. On the Poppy satellite system, see Dwayne A. Day, "Above the Clouds: The White Cloud Ocean Surveillance Satellites," *The Space Review*, April 13, 2009, https://www.thespacereview.com/article/1351/1. See also Pennsylvania State University Advanced Research Lab, "Sea to Stars," 54–55. A list of collection production is found in Pressly, "FOSIF Rota," 13.
67. Ford and Rosenberg, *Admirals' Advantage*, 62.
68. Litsinger, interview with the author, June 27, 2019.
69. Before the Wang word processor a standalone Hewlett Packard processor was used. The Wang and the PDP 11/45 were part of the OSIS Baseline upgrades made in 1977. Friedman describes Naval Electronics Systems Command's (NAVELEX) struggles with upgrading FOSIF/C systems and high-speed datalinks; the OSIS Baseline Update (OBU) would finally occur in 1982; see Friedman, *Network-centric Warfare*, 174–75, 177. Litsinger described the production process and systems to the author in an interview of June 27, 2019. By "processor" was likely referring to the HP 2100A, introduced commercially in 1971; for more on the HP 2100A word processor, visit the HP Computer Museum online at http://hpmuseum.net/display_item.php?hw=98. And PDP 11/45 specifics are found in "Digital Equipment Corporation: 1957 to the Present" (Digital Equipment Corporation, Maynard, MA, 1978), 22, https://gordonbell.azurewebsites.net/digital/dec%201957%20to%20present%201978.pdf.
70. Litsinger, interview with the author, June 27, 2019. The 0100 message was not all Rainform format; it contained significant "free text" narratives; Litsinger, email exchange with the author, November 18, 2020.
71. Litsinger, interview with the author, June 27, 2019. For more on the CSG being "sanitized freely," see Jim McFarland, "Cryptologic Support Group (CSG) Rota USN-726," presentation, Operational Intelligence Learned Symposium, Spring Red Tie Luncheon, Naval Intelligence Professionals, Arlington, VA, slide

17, archived online at https://slideplayer.com/slide/10445420/. Regarding the "authorization to sanitize SI," see Pressly, "FOSIF Rota," slide 6.

72. Information regarding the sanitization of the space-based electronic-intelligence-collection Ships Emitter Location Report (SELOR) from Litsinger, interview with the author, June 27, 2019; and see Pressly, "FOSIF Rota," slide 20. Litsinger says the secret classified 0500 message was really the "hallmark" product for the operators; email exchange with the author, November 18, 2020. Also see Ford and Rosenberg, *Admirals' Advantage*, 64–65.

73. McFarland, "CSG Rota USN-726," slide 13.

74. McFarland, slide 14. Pressly notes that two senior NSA officials—Richard "Dick" Lord and Milt Zaslow—visited FOSIF to discuss "Tech [SIGINT] Issues" and that NFOIO in Washington had to "oil the waters with NSA"; Pressly, "FOSIF Rota," slide 22.

75. McFarland, "CSG Rota USN-726," slide 22.

Chapter 8. OSIS Revolution to Opintel Evolution

1. Litsinger, interview with the author, June 27, 2019. For recollections of the read-boards, see Vic Socotra, "Point Loma: The Bull Ring," *DailySocotra* (blog), September 30, 2019, https://www.vicsocotra.com/wordpress/point-loma-the-bull-ring/.

2. William H. Whyte, *The Organization Man*, fore. Joseph Nocera (Philadelphia: University of Pennsylvania Press, 2002 [orig. pub. Simon and Schuster, 1956]), 112.

3. Inman would become the first four-star 1630 admiral; see "Intelligence Assignment and Placement Section," *Naval Intelligence Newsletter* (1975): vi.

4. Ford and Rosenberg, *Admirals' Advantage*, 72.

5. This from a 1975 Navy intelligence officer recruiting film, *Combat Scholar*, U.S. Navy Recruiting Command (n.p.: John J. Hennessy Motion Pictures), run time 11:43 mins.

6. John M. Tauer and Judith M. Harackiewicz, "Winning Isn't Everything: Competition, Achievement Orientation, and Intrinsic Motivation," *Journal of Experimental Social Psychology* 35, no. 3 (May 1999): 210–13, 227, https://doi.org/10.1006/jesp.1999.1383 (paywall).

7. Socotra, "Point Loma," sec. "Andalucia—Need I Say More?"

8. Whyte, *Organization Man*, 123–24.

9. Litsinger, email exchange with the author, June 23, 2020.

10. Socotra, "Point Loma," sec. "Andalucia—Need I Say More?"

11. Litsinger, email exchange with the author, June 23, 2020. Creation of a watch officer's gouge book discussed in Litsinger's interview with the author, June 27, 2019.

12. Whyte, *Organization Man*, 160.
13. Litsinger, interview with the author, June 27, 2019.
14. Corrida goyesca de Ronda is a grand bullfight celebrating Francisco de Goya's works.
15. Socotra, "Point Loma," sec. "Juan Antonio Ruiz Román—Espartaco."
16. Litsinger, interview with the author, June 27, 2019. See also Pressly, "Creating FOSIF Rota," slide 22; and McFarland, "CSG Rota USN-726," slides 9, 10, and 21.
17. Litsinger, interview with the author, June 27, 2019.
18. Litsinger, email exchange with the author, June 23, 2020.
19. Bureau of Naval Personnel, U.S. Department of the Navy, *Personnel Management*, 278, 284. The fitness report has changed over time, but the stratification and promotion recommendations remain.
20. Litsinger, interview with the author, June 27, 2019.
21. Socotra, "Point Loma."
22. Litsinger, interview with the author, June 27, 2019.
23. John F. Lehman, "Is Naval Aviation Culture Dead?" *Proceedings*, U.S. Naval Institute, 137, no. 9, 1.303 (September 2011), https://www.usni.org/magazines/proceedings/2011/september/naval-aviation-culture-dead.
24. Socotra, "Point Loma," sec. "Juan Antonio Ruiz Román—Espartaco."
25. Socotra, sec. "Juan Antonio Ruiz Román—Espartaco."
26. Dave O'Malley, "The Zap Heard Round the World," *Vintage Wings of Canada/Les Ailes d'époque du Canada* (website), accessed June 27, 2020, https://www.vintagewings.ca/stories/the-zap-heard-round-the-world. See also Hancock, "Naval Aviation Insignia."
27. For an image of the FOSIF Rota frog patch, see Vic Socotra, "Illegal Alien," *DailySocotra* (blog), March 8, 2016, https://www.vicsocotra.com/wordpress/illegal-alien/.
28. Litsinger, email exchange with the author, May 18, 2020.
29. Socotra, "Point Loma," sec. "Juan Antonio Ruiz Román—Espartaco."
30. Zumwalt, *On Watch*, 77–78.
31. Durr, interview with the author, May 20, 2020.
32. Installation of ASCAC occurred from December 1970 through March 1971; see Commander Carrier Division 6, "CV Evaluation Final Report," November 23, 1971, p. 2, archived in record group RG-18, box 19, folder 2, "Management, 1972–1973," Naval War College Archives, U.S. Naval War College, Newport, RI, https://www.usnwcarchives.org/repositories/2/archival_objects/49268; and see I. J. Rimson, W. E. Stahnke, and M. R. Demarest, eds., *USS Saratoga (CVA 60) Mediterranean Cruise Book 1971* (Norfolk, VA; San Diego, CA: Tiffany Publishing Company, n.d.), 89, Operations Department, archived online at https://www.navysite.de/cruisebooks/cv60-71/082.htm.

33. Hughes' concept of countermeasures can extend to physical and electromagnetic space; see Hughes, *Fleet Tactics*, 199–200. Lessons learned from the naval battles of the 1971 Indo-Pakistani War allowed Israeli missile boats to use electronic countermeasures to defeat Styx ASCM fired from Syrian and Egyptian missile boats. Christian H. Heller, "The Impact of Insignificance: Naval Developments from the Yom Kippur War," Center for International Maritime Security, February 19, 2019, https://cimsec.org/the-impact-of-insignificance-naval-developments-from-the-yom-kippur-war/.
34. Rimson et al., *Saratoga Mediterranean Cruise Book 1971*, 89, Operations Department.
35. Description of ASCAC on p. 31 of M. Bixler, ed., *USS Kitty Hawk (CVA 63) WestPac Cruise Book 1973–74* (n.p.: Pischel Yearbooks, n.d.), found at https://www.navysite.de/cruisebooks/cv63-73/029.htm.
36. On the concept of organizations adapting to new technology, see Zurcher, "Aboard Ship," 393.
37. ASCAC (OW div) had four officers and thirteen enlisted. The ocean systems technician (OT) rate was created in 1969. OX was assigned to electronic warfare and operated by the electronic warfare technician (EW) and cryptologic technicians-maintenance (CTM) ratings. See Bixler, *Kitty Hawk WestPac Cruise Book 1973–74*, 29, Operations Department, https://www.navysite.de/cruisebooks/cv63-73/027.htm. Other examples are found in S. Hoder, ed., *USS Constellation (CV 64) WestPac Cruise Book 1978–79* (n.p.: Josten's/American Yearbook Company, n.d.), 252, Operations Department, found at https://www.navysite.de/cruisebooks/cv64-78/250.htm; and in Thomas F. Jakubiak, ed., *USS Ranger (CV 61) WestPac Cruise Book 1979* (n.p.: American Yearbook Company, n.d.), 122, Operations Department, found at https://www.navysite.de/cruisebooks/cv61-79/118.htm; and in Frederic E. Steiner and Thomas L. Schlosser, eds., *USS Constellation (CV 64) WestPac Cruise Book 1971–72 and Cruise Bravo Cruise Book* (n.p.: Pischel Yearbooks, n.d.), 112–13, Operations Department, found at https://www.navysite.de/cruisebooks/cv64-71/201.htm.
38. Hughes, *Fleet Tactics*, 191.
39. Durr, interview with the author, May 20, 2020.
40. On capabilities, operations, and procurement of the E-2C, see U.S. Senate, Committee on Armed Services, *Hearings Before the Committee on Armed Services, United States Senate, Ninety-Fourth Congress, First Session, on S. 920: Fiscal Year 1976 and July–September 1976 Transition Period Authorization for Military Procurement, Research and Development, and Active Duty, Selected Reserve, and Civilian Personnel Strengths* (Washington, DC: U.S. Government Printing Office, February 1975), 4867–77, archived online at https://babel.hathitrust.org/cgi/pt?id=mdp.39015076083842&seq=1.

41. Boslaugh, *First-Hand*, chap. 8, "The Marine Tactical Data System and the Airborne Tactical Data System," sec. "The E-2B Hawkeye," https://ethw.org/First-Hand:The_Marine_Tactical_Data_System_and_the_Airborne_Tactical_Data_System_-_Chapter_8_of_the_Story_of_the_Naval_Tactical_Data_System#The_E_2B_Hawkeye. On E-2C operations, see U.S. Senate, Committee on Armed Services. *Hearings, FY 1976*, 4876.
42. Friedman, *Network-centric Warfare*, 130–35.
43. Friedman, 134.
44. Information as a factor of time discussed in Vego, *Joint Operational Warfare*, 51–52. Also see Hughes, *Fleet Tactics*, 192.
45. For Opintel's role in this fighting tactic, see Richard L. Wyatt, "Supporting the Naval Outer Air Battle," in DiGirolamo, *Naval Command and Control*, 96–105, originally published under the same title in *Signal* 41, no. 1 (September 1986): 19–28, and archived online at https://books.google.com/books?id=3hgLeKnH5ooC&pg=PA19#v=onepage&q&f=false.
46. William H. Honan, "Russian and American Pilots Play 'Chicken,'" *New York Times*, November 22, 1970, https://www.nytimes.com/1970/11/22/archives/article-34-no-title-one-game-rule-not-to-be-broken-dont-lose-your.html; and see Honan, "The World," *New York Times*, October 10, 1971, https://www.nytimes.com/1971/10/10/archives/us-and-russia-now-hear-this-rules-for-chickenofthesea.html. Also see Winkler, *Cold War at Sea*, 7.
47. The TU-95s are depicted as cartoon animal bears with a propeller belted to their backs. See Jim Smallwood, ed., *USS Ranger (CV 61) WestPac Cruise Book 1976* (n.p.: Josten's American Yearbooks, n.d.), 176, Operations Department, found at https://www.navysite.de/cruisebooks/cv61-76/174.htm.
48. Officer strength dropped from 82,565 officers in 1970 to 66,036 in 1975. "US Navy Personnel Strength, 1775 to Present," Naval History and Heritage Command, History.Navy.mil, last updated July 27, 2020, https://www.history.navy.mil/research/library/online-reading-room/title-list-alphabetically/u/usn-personnel-strength.html.
49. Durr, interview with the author, May 20, 2020. And Litsinger, email exchange with the author, May 3 and 4, 2020.
50. See p. 113 of the transcript of the Bruce F. Powers interview, conducted by Bob Sheldon and Mike Garrambone, Lake Barcroft, VA, May 13, 2015, and published by Military Operations Research Society, Calhoun: Naval Postgraduate School Institutional Archive, Monterey, CA, February 21, 2016, https://calhoun.nps.edu/entities/publication/c1f9552d-6a3a-4d6a-a8c7-9c05cf490282. And Bruce F. Powers, email exchange with the author, March 14, 2019.
51. Durr, interview with the author, May 20, 2020.
52. Litsinger, interview with the author, June 27, 2019.

53. Jacoby, interview with the author, May 9, 2019.
54. Wyatt, "Naval Outer Air Battle," 96.

Chapter 9. OSIS and Ship Opintel Evolve

1. Quoting a report issued from the USS *Sterett* (DLG- 31) in Robert B. Pettitt, "TAOs: To Fight the Ship," *Proceedings*, U.S. Naval Institute, 100, no. 2, 852 (February 1974), https://www.usni.org/magazines/proceedings/1974/february/taos-fight-ship.
2. Quoting a report issued by the USS *Sterett* (DLG-31) in Pettitt.
3. Wyatt, "Naval Outer Air Battle," 101.
4. "Intelligence Assignment and Placement Section," *Naval Intelligence Newsletter* (1974): 9.
5. Durr, interview with the author, May 20, 2020.
6. "Intelligence Assignment and Placement Section," *Naval Intelligence Newsletter* (1974): 6.
7. All photographic squadrons would be decommissioned by 1982, replaced by Tactical Air Reconnaissance Pod System (TARPS), which could be carried by F-4 and F-14 aircraft. Nineteen years of RA-5C service came to an end when RVAH-6 was decommissioned September 28, 1979. Campbell, *Flight, Camera, Action!* 489–95.
8. Durr, interview with the author, May 20, 2020.
9. The Soviets had approximately 150 fighters based in Egypt in 1972, though the number would significantly decrease later. McCormick, *Soviet Presence in the Mediterranean*, 8, 11.
10. Litsinger, email exchange with the author, May 4, 2020; he served in *Saratoga* between 1975 and 1977.
11. The need for a real-time plot in CVIC discussed in Litsinger, email exchange with the author, May 4, 2020. Briefing the surface plot discussed in Tonkli, email exchange with the author, April 20, 2019.
12. Bixler, *USS Kitty Hawk WestPac Cruise Book 1973–74*, 31, Operations Department, https://www.navysite.de/cruisebooks/cv63-73/029.htm.
13. Durr, email exchange with the author, May 25, 2020.
14. Ship surveillance team and SNOOPIE example in U.S. National Archives, "The Adventures of CORTDIV 11," *The NDC Blog*, June 18, 2019, https://declassification.blogs.archives.gov/2019/06/18/the-adventures-of-cortdiv-11/.
15. Discussion regarding the development of Beseler Topcon 35-mm handheld camera film from Hartford, email exchanges with the author, March 5 and 7, 2019. Ship's surveillance team (SNOOPIE) activity discussed in Tonkli, email exchange with the author, April 20, 2019.
16. The importance of the "Foxtrot PI Keys" noted in Pressly, "Creating FOSIF Rota," slide 23. And see Winkler, *Cold War at Sea*, 1.

41. Boslaugh, *First-Hand*, chap. 8, "The Marine Tactical Data System and the Airborne Tactical Data System," sec. "The E-2B Hawkeye," https://ethw.org/First-Hand:The_Marine_Tactical_Data_System_and_the_Airborne_Tactical_Data_System_-_Chapter_8_of_the_Story_of_the_Naval_Tactical_Data_System#The_E-2B_Hawkeye. On E-2C operations, see U.S. Senate, Committee on Armed Services. *Hearings, FY 1976*, 4876.
42. Friedman, *Network-centric Warfare*, 130–35.
43. Friedman, 134.
44. Information as a factor of time discussed in Vego, *Joint Operational Warfare*, 51–52. Also see Hughes, *Fleet Tactics*, 192.
45. For Opintel's role in this fighting tactic, see Richard L. Wyatt, "Supporting the Naval Outer Air Battle," in DiGirolamo, *Naval Command and Control*, 96–105, originally published under the same title in *Signal* 41, no. 1 (September 1986): 19–28, and archived online at https://books.google.com/books?id=3hgLeKnH5ooC&pg=PA19#v=onepage&q&f=false.
46. William H. Honan, "Russian and American Pilots Play 'Chicken,'" *New York Times*, November 22, 1970, https://www.nytimes.com/1970/11/22/archives/article-34-no-title-one-game-rule-not-to-be-broken-dont-lose-your.html; and see Honan, "The World," *New York Times*, October 10, 1971, https://www.nytimes.com/1971/10/10/archives/us-and-russia-now-hear-this-rules-for-chickenofthesea.html. Also see Winkler, *Cold War at Sea*, 7.
47. The TU-95s are depicted as cartoon animal bears with a propeller belted to their backs. See Jim Smallwood, ed., *USS Ranger (CV 61) WestPac Cruise Book 1976* (n.p.: Josten's American Yearbooks, n.d.), 176, Operations Department, found at https://www.navysite.de/cruisebooks/cv61-76/174.htm
48. Officer strength dropped from 82,565 officers in 1970 to 66,036 in 1975. "US Navy Personnel Strength, 1775 to Present," Naval History and Heritage Command, History.Navy.mil, last updated July 27, 2020, https://www.history.navy.mil/research/library/online-reading-room/title-list-alphabetically/u/usn-personnel-strength.html.
49. Durr, interview with the author, May 20, 2020. And Litsinger, email exchange with the author, May 3 and 4, 2020.
50. See p. 113 of the transcript of the Bruce F. Powers interview, conducted by Bob Sheldon and Mike Garrambone, Lake Barcroft, VA, May 13, 2015, and published by Military Operations Research Society, Calhoun: Naval Postgraduate School Institutional Archive, Monterey, CA, February 21, 2016, https://calhoun.nps.edu/entities/publication/c1f9552d-6a3a-4d6a-a8c7-9c05cf490282. And Bruce F. Powers, email exchange with the author, March 14, 2019.
51. Durr, interview with the author, May 20, 2020.
52. Litsinger, interview with the author, June 27, 2019.

53. Jacoby, interview with the author, May 9, 2019.
54. Wyatt, "Naval Outer Air Battle," 96.

Chapter 9. OSIS and Ship Opintel Evolve

1. Quoting a report issued from the USS *Sterett* (DLG- 31) in Robert B. Pettitt, "TAOs: To Fight the Ship," *Proceedings*, U.S. Naval Institute, 100, no. 2, 852 (February 1974), https://www.usni.org/magazines/proceedings/1974/february/taos-fight-ship.
2. Quoting a report issued by the USS *Sterett* (DLG-31) in Pettitt.
3. Wyatt, "Naval Outer Air Battle," 101.
4. "Intelligence Assignment and Placement Section," *Naval Intelligence Newsletter* (1974): 9.
5. Durr, interview with the author, May 20, 2020.
6. "Intelligence Assignment and Placement Section," *Naval Intelligence Newsletter* (1974): 6.
7. All photographic squadrons would be decommissioned by 1982, replaced by Tactical Air Reconnaissance Pod System (TARPS), which could be carried by F-4 and F-14 aircraft. Nineteen years of RA-5C service came to an end when RVAH-6 was decommissioned September 28, 1979. Campbell, *Flight, Camera, Action!* 489–95.
8. Durr, interview with the author, May 20, 2020.
9. The Soviets had approximately 150 fighters based in Egypt in 1972, though the number would significantly decrease later. McCormick, *Soviet Presence in the Mediterranean*, 8, 11.
10. Litsinger, email exchange with the author, May 4, 2020; he served in *Saratoga* between 1975 and 1977.
11. The need for a real-time plot in CVIC discussed in Litsinger, email exchange with the author, May 4, 2020. Briefing the surface plot discussed in Tonkli, email exchange with the author, April 20, 2019.
12. Bixler, *USS Kitty Hawk WestPac Cruise Book 1973–74*, 31, Operations Department, https://www.navysite.de/cruisebooks/cv63-73/029.htm.
13. Durr, email exchange with the author, May 25, 2020.
14. Ship surveillance team and SNOOPIE example in U.S. National Archives, "The Adventures of CORTDIV 11," *The NDC Blog*, June 18, 2019, https://declassification.blogs.archives.gov/2019/06/18/the-adventures-of-cortdiv-11/.
15. Discussion regarding the development of Beseler Topcon 35-mm handheld camera film from Hartford, email exchanges with the author, March 5 and 7, 2019. Ship's surveillance team (SNOOPIE) activity discussed in Tonkli, email exchange with the author, April 20, 2019.
16. The importance of the "Foxtrot PI Keys" noted in Pressly, "Creating FOSIF Rota," slide 23. And see Winkler, *Cold War at Sea*, 1.

17. As reported in Honan, "Russian and American Pilots Play 'Chicken.'"
18. The required airborne photograph alignment for escorting a Soviet aircraft discussed in Litsinger, email exchange with the author, May 3, 2020.
19. Durr, interview with the author, May 20, 2020.
20. Several books describe using COMINT to advantage in major operations during World War II. Milan N. Vego provides an excellent example in *Major Fleet-versus-Fleet Operations in the Pacific War, 1941–1945*, 2nd ed., Naval War College Historical Monograph Series no. 22 (Newport, RI: Naval War College Press, 2016), 35–44. And see Edwin T. Layton, *"And I Was There": Breaking the Secrets; Pearl Harbor and Midway*, with Roger Pineau and John Costello (Saybrook, CT: Konecky and Konecky, 2001); W. J. Holmes, *Double-Edged Secrets: U.S. Naval Intelligence Operations in the Pacific During World War II* (Annapolis, MD: Naval Institute Press, 1979); and, most recently, Elliot Carlson, *Joe Rochefort's War: The Odyssey of the Codebreaker Who Outwitted Yamamoto at Midway* (Annapolis, MD: Naval Institute Press, 2011).
21. Durr, interview with the author, May 20, 2020. Cryptologic detachments in Mediterranean discussed in Giacchino, interview with the author, February 16, 2019.
22. On low-level intercepts of "plaintext" messages and the use of message "externals," see Aid, *Secret Sentry*, 22 and 129. Space-based and airborne direction finding of Soviet units is discussed in Ford and Rosenberg, *Admirals' Advantage*, 62.
23. Durr, interview with the author, May 20, 2020.
24. The use of airfield- and CGI-signal intercepts during the Vietnam War is discussed in Gerhard, "Collecting the Enemy's Signals," 32–34, 50.
25. J. A. Maxwell, "1973 Naval Intelligence Training Conference," report, NAVINTCOM, Suitland, MD (Naval Intelligence Command, September 11, 1973), 11, record group RG 24, A1 1022, box 26, National Archives and Records Administration II, College Park, MD.
26. Maxwell addresses the recommendation to limit AFAITC student numbers and increase Fleet Intelligence Training Center (FITC) Norfolk, VA, students in "1973 Conference," i. For the training pipeline, see Naval Intelligence Command, "Career Planning Information Guide for Intelligence Specialists Officers" (Bureau of Naval Personnel, 1972), fig. 2, personal papers of Rear Admiral Thomas A. Brooks.
27. "INT" was shorthand for the type of intelligence source. Ford and Rosenberg, *Admirals' Advantage*, 61.
28. Maxwell, "1973 Conference," ii, iii, and iv.
29. Maxwell, 5.

30. Hartford discussed the process of obtaining SCI access in an email exchange with the author, March 4, 2019. And Litsinger discussed special-intelligence access in an email exchange with the author, March 7, 2019.
31. Director of Occupational Standards, U.S. Department of the Navy, "Workshop Draft of Occupational Standards: Intelligence Rating," NPPSA-100, June 1973, record group RG 24, A1 1022, box 26, National Archives II, College Park, MD. See also Ford and Rosenberg, *Admirals' Advantage*, 72.
32. M. D. Cullison, "Occupational Analysis of Photographic Intelligenceman (PT) and Related NECs," special report, Naval Personnel Research and Development Laboratory, Bureau of Naval Personnel, Washington, DC, June 1973, archived online at https://apps.dtic.mil/sti/tr/pdf/ADA014488.pdf; Ford and Rosenberg, *Admirals' Advantage*, 72.
33. Tonkli, email exchange with the author, April 22, 2019.
34. Capt. Richard A. Noble, email exchange with the author, October 13, 2020. The Navy and Marine Corps Intelligence Training Center (NMITC) opened at Dam Neck, Virginia, in October 1986, replacing AFAITC. It combined four separate Navy intelligence facilities located in Colorado, Florida, and Virginia. See "NMITC Dedication," *Naval Intelligence Professionals Quarterly* (September 1986): 2.
35. Jacoby, interview with the author, May 9, 2019.
36. Sibling-rivalry behavior—or "little brother syndrome"—to explain organizational or neighboring-state rivalry is discussed in Richard Ellis Hebblethwaite, "The Little Brother Syndrome and Nuclear Proliferation: An Exploratory Analysis of Pakistan and North Korea's Risk Prone Policies," master's thesis, Wright State University, 2013, p. 11, archived online at https://docslib.org/doc/10323760/the-little-brother-syndrome-and-nuclear-proliferation-an-exploratory-analysis-of-pakistan-and-north-koreas-risk-prone-policies.
37. Durr, interview with the author, May 20, 2020.
38. Litsinger, interview with the author, January 29, 2019. The "Alert 5" intercept posture requires the aircraft to launch within five minutes of notification. Thus the crewed aircraft is spotted on the catapult with its the engines running.
39. Litsinger discussed the interaction with FOSIC detachment CINCLANTFLT in Norfolk, Virginia, in interview with the author on May 8, 2019.
40. Describing "choke-con," Ben FitzGerald and Parker Wright, "Digital Theaters: Decentralizing Cyber Command and Control," Disruptive Defense Papers (Center for a New American Security, Washington, DC, April 2014), p. 15, https://www.jstor.org/stable/resrep06146.
41. Jacoby, interview with the author, May 9, 2019.
42. Richardson, *Reminiscences*, 275–77.

43. Richardson served as a contractor with Sanders Associates (1973–1986) and Lockheed Missiles and Space Corp. (1975–1985). Richardson, *Reminiscences*.
44. Richardson, 286–87.
45. Richardson, 287–89.
46. Rosenberg, "Memorandum for OPINTEL."
47. Discussed in Peter M. Swartz, "Oral History of Captain Peter M. Swartz, USN (Ret.)," conducted by Ryan Peeks and Justin Blanton, July 24, 2019, transcr. and ed. Naval History and Heritage Command, U.S. Department of the Navy, 2020, p. 13, https://www.history.navy.mil/content/dam/nhhc/research/publications/publication-508-pdf/Swartz_Oral_History-508.pdf; and discussed in the author's interview with Captain Swartz, USN (Ret.), December 14, 2017.
48. Swartz, "Oral History," 15, 21, 31.

Part IV. Formalizing

1. Ocean Venture '81 is the name given to a series of interrelated naval exercises that included Northern Wedding '81. Technically Ocean Venture was only one phase of the collective exercises. See John F. Lehman, *Oceans Ventured: Winning the Cold War at Sea*, 1st ed. (New York: W. W. Norton, 2018), xvi–xviii and chap. 2, "Ocean Venture '81."

Chapter 10. Shipboard Tactical-Decision Support

1. Daniel P. Bolger dedicates a full chapter to the *Mayaguez* incident and tactical military action in *Americans at War, 1975–1986: An Era of Violent Peace* (Novato, CA: Presidio, 1988), chap. 1, "Marines over the Side."
2. Bolger, 94.
3. Christopher J. Lamb, "The *Mayaguez* Crisis, Mission Command, and Civil-Military Relations," 1st ed. (Join History Office, Office of the Chairman of the Joint Chiefs of Staff, Washington, DC, 2018), 114, https://www.jcs.mil/Portals/36/Documents/History/28270_MayaguezCrisis_web%20corrected.pdf?ver=2019-08-16-124241-780&timestamp=1565973771822.
4. As recounted by Lamb, 115.
5. As recounted in Lamb, 175–76.
6. Andrew J. Bacevich discusses the lessons from Vietnam, including reconsidering post-9/11 neoconservatism and militarism through a never-again lens, in *The New American Militarism: How Americans Are Seduced by War* (New York: Oxford University Press, 2005), 39–75.
7. Reagan's continued campaign against President Carter's foreign policies is a significant part of what won him the 1980 election. Richard V. Allen in the foreword to Sergei Kostin and Eric Raynaud, *Farewell: The Greatest Spy Story of the Twentieth Century*, trans. Catherine Cauvin-Higgins (Las Vegas: AmazonCrossing, 2011), i–iii.

8. Margaret Thatcher, "Speech at Kensington Town Hall ('Britain Awake')) (The Iron Lady)," Chelsea, London, January 19, 1976, Margaret Thatcher Foundation, Speeches etc., https://www.margaretthatcher.org/document/102939.
9. Theater Strategic Operations (*teatral'naya strategicheskaya operatsiya*, or TSO) used maneuver tactics but is not considered blitzkrieg because it acts across multiple fronts, not just one. Mary C. FitzGerald, "Marshal Ogarkov on Modern War: 1977–1985" (Defense Technical Information Center, Fort Belvoir, VA, rev. November 1986), 36, https://apps.dtic.mil/sti/tr/pdf/ADA176138.pdf. Regarding Soviet long-range strikes, see Milan N. Vego, "RECCE-Strike Complexes in Soviet Theory and Practice" (Soviet Army Studies Office, U.S. Combined Arms Center, Fort Leavenworth, KS, June 1990), 1–6, https://apps.dtic.mil/sti/tr/pdf/ADA231900.pdf. And see László Valki, ed., *Changing Threat Perceptions and Military Doctrines* (New York: St. Martin's Press, 1992), 29.
10. For more on the Soviet Theater Strategic Operations concepts see Diego A. Ruiz Palmer, "A Strategic Odyssey: Constancy of Purpose and Strategy-Making in NATO, 1949–2019," Strategy Series research paper no. 3 (Research Division, NATO Defense College, Rome, Italy, June 2019), available for download at http://www.ndc.nato.int/download/downloads.php?icode=598. And see Phillip A. Petersen, "Perceptions in the Cold War Theater Competition—The Soviet Northwestern TVD" (The Potomac Foundation, Vienna, VA, November 18, 2014), https://www.esd.whs.mil/Portals/54/Documents/FOID/Reading%20Room/Litigation_Release/Litigation%20Release%20-%20The%20Northwestern%20TVD%20in%20Soviet%20Operational%20Strategic%20Planning%20%202014.pdf. For a discussion of Warsaw Pact exercise and the Soviet strategy, see Diego A. Ruiz Palmer, "Theatre Operations, High Commands and Large-Scale Exercises in Soviet and Russian Military Practice: Insights and Implications," Fellowship Monograph 12 (Research Division, NATO Defense College, Rome, Italy, May 2018), https://www.ndc.nato.int/news/news.php?icode=1172.
11. On U.S. efforts to strengthen conventional deterrence, see Jeremy Kuzmarov, "The Improbable Militarist: Jimmy Carter, the Revolution in Military Affairs and Limits of the American Two-Party System," *Class, Race and Corporate Power* 6, no. 2 (November 10, 2018), https://doi.org/10.25148/CRCP.6.2.008311. For a detailed discussion of Carter spending, see also Frank L. Jones, "A 'Hollow Army' Reappraised: President Carter, Defense Budgets, and the Politics of Military Readiness," the Letort Papers (Strategic Studies Institute, U.S. Army War College, Carlisle, PA, October 2012), 17–19, https://www.jstor.org/stable/resrep11172.
12. William J. Casey, "Soviet Goals and Expectations in the Global Power Arena," National Intelligence Estimate NIE 11-4-78, director of the Central Intelligence Agency, July 7, 1981, p. 78, CIA Historical Review Program, https://www.cia.gov/readingroom/docs/DOC_0000268220.pdf. And see Colin S. Gray,

Strategy for Chaos: Revolutions in Military Affairs and the Evidence of History, Cass Series, Strategy and History 2 (London: Frank Cass, 2002), 245–50.
13. See Robert Tomes, "The Cold War Offset Strategy: Origins and Relevance," Beyond Offset Special Series, *War on the Rocks*, November 6, 2014, https://warontherocks.com/2014/11/the-cold-war-offset-strategy-origins-and-relevance/. See also Martinage, "Toward a New Offset Strategy."
14. Friedman, *Fifty-Year War*, 448–50. Regarding U.S. computer air-battle-management systems, particularly the systems' success in the 1982 Israeli air victory over Syria in the Beqaa Valley, see Tomes, "Cold War Offset Strategy." Also see Defense Advanced Research Projects Agency (DARPA), "Innovation Timeline," sec. "Assault Breaker," DARPA.mil, accessed August 25, 2020, https://www.darpa.mil/about/innovation-timeline.
15. Congress had codified the restrictions in the "Battle Act" or Mutual Defense Assurance Control Act (MDAC). Frank Cain, "Computers and the Cold War: United States Restrictions on the Export of Computers to the Soviet Union and Communist China," *Journal of Contemporary History* 40, no. 1 (2005): 131–35, http://www.jstor.org/stable/30036313.
16. Cain, 138, 133–37.
17. Slava Gerovitch, "How the Computer Got Its Revenge on the Soviet Union," *Nautilus*, April 2, 2015, https://nautil.us/how-the-computer-got-its-revenge-on-the-soviet-union-235368/.
18. Gerovitch. And on the embargo, see Cain, "Computers and the Cold War," 43–44.
19. Blackburn at p. 1488 in U.S. Senate, Committee on Finance, *The Trade Reform Act of 1973: Hearings; Ninety-Third Congress, Second Session, on H.R. 10710*, 6 vols. (Washington, DC: U.S. Government Printing Office, 1974), https://www.congress.gov/bill/93rd-congress/house-bill/10710#:~:text=10710%20%2D%20An%20Act%20to%20promote,93rd%20Congress%20(1973%2D1974)].
20. David A. Wellman, *A Chip in the Curtain: Computer Technology in the Soviet Union* (Washington, DC: National Defense University Press, 1989), 96, https://apps.dtic.mil/sti/tr/pdf/ADA259360.pdf. Regarding the IBM thesis, see Simon Donig, "Appropriating American Technology in the 1960s: Cold War Politics and the GDR Computer Industry," *IEEE Annals of the History of Computing* 32, no. 3 (April–June 2010): 13–14, doi:10.1109/MAHC.2010.6.
21. For more on the complex, see Vego, "RECCE-Strike Complexes."
22. For a detailed look at the issues surrounding the "computer arms race" and the U.S. military's computerized weapons–lethality role in the strategic competition, see Bryan H. Leese, "The Cold War Computer Arms Race," *Journal of Advanced Military Studies* 14, no. 2 (Fall 2023): 102–20, https://doi.org/10.21140/mcuj.20231402006.

23. Hughes and Girrier, *Fleet Tactics*, 218.
24. Regarding decision-making, operational tempo, and resulting paralysis, see David S. Fadok, "John Boyd and John Warden: Air Power's Quest for Strategic Paralysis," master's thesis, Air University, 1995, archived online at https://archive.org/details/DTIC_ADA291621. Using information networks to improve decision-making is discussed in Friedman, *Network-centric Warfare*; and also see Friedman, *Fifty-Year War*, 445–49.
25. John W. Bodnar, "The Military Technical Revolution: From Hardware to Information," *Naval War College Review* 46, no. 3 (1993): 7.
26. Aegis, the shield of the Greek god Zeus, was referred to as the "shield of the fleet." AEGIS also stands for "advanced electronic-guided interceptor system." James D. Flanagan and George W. Luke, "AEGIS: Newest Line of Navy Defense," *Johns Hopkins APL Technical Digest* 2, no. 4 (December 1981): 237–42, https://secwww.jhuapl.edu/techdigest/Content/techdigest/pdf/V02-N04/02-04-Flanagan_Navy.pdf. And see Edward P. Lee et al., "History of BGAAWC/FACT: Knitting the Battle Force for Air Defense," *Johns Hopkins APL Technical Digest* 23, nos. 2–3 (September 2002): 117–37, https://secwww.jhuapl.edu/techdigest/Content/techdigest/pdf/V23-N2-3/23-02-Lee.pdf. And Boslaugh, *First-Hand*, chap. 9, "Legacy of NTDS," sec. "Building AEGIS," https://ethw.org/First-Hand:Legacy_of_NTDS_-_Chapter_9_of_the_Story_of_the_Naval_Tactical_Data_System#Building_Aegis.
27. "From 'Futuristic Whimsy' to Naval Reality" is Abraham Rabinovich's exploration of the Israeli Navy's development of missile boats, found in *Naval History*, U.S. Naval Institute, 28, no. 3 (June 2014), https://www.usni.org/magazines/naval-history-magazine/2014/june/futuristic-whimsy-naval-reality. And see Wayne P. Hughes, ed., *The U.S. Naval Institute on Naval Tactics*, U.S. Naval Institute Wheel Books (Annapolis, MD: Naval Institute Press, 2015), 62–89. On the use of the aircraft carrier, see Haynes, "American Naval Thinking," 39–40.
28. Chester C. Phillips, "Battle Group Operations: War at Sea," *Johns Hopkins APL Technical Digest* 2, no. 4 (December 1981): 299–300, https://secwww.jhuapl.edu/techdigest/Content/techdigest/pdf/V02-N04/02-04-Phillips_Sea.pdf.
29. *Auftragstaktik* emphasizes commander's intent. In the U.S. Navy the concept is related to command by negation. Donald E. Vandergriff, "How the Germans Defined Auftragstaktik: What Mission Command *Is—and—Is Not*," *Small Wars Journal*, June 21, 2018, https://archive.smallwarsjournal.com/jrnl/art/how-germans-defined-auftragstaktik-what-mission-command-and-not.
30. P. J. Doerr, "CWC Revisited," *Proceedings*, U.S. Naval Institute, 112, no. 4, 998 (April 1986), https://www.usni.org/magazines/proceedings/1986/april/cwc-revisited (paywall).

31. Michael S. Loescher, "Origins of Modern Naval Command and Control," in DiGirolamo, *Naval Command and Control*, 6.
32. Brooks, interview with the author, May 16, 2019.
33. Brooks had photographs taken of the plot; others plotted on tracing paper overlays to keep and share a historical copy; interview with the author, May 16, 2019.
34. Story as relayed during Brooks' interview with the author, May 16, 2019. On Shanahan, see Franklin C. "Chuck" Spinney, "A Personal Remembrance: Black Jack Shanahan, VADM (USN Ret.)," POGO: Project On Government Oversight (website), October 30, 2013, https://www.pogo.org/analysis/personal-remembrance-black-jack-shanahan-vadm-usn-ret.
35. "NATO Wargames," *AP Television*, television broadcast, aired in West Germany, Poland, the North Atlantic, and Norway, 9:00 p.m., September 30, 1976, 12:35, RR7639B, https://newsroom.ap.org/editorial-photos-videos/detail?itemid=0c416b97a0bad6b717b2c2e2b4231769&mediatype=video&source=youtube. On deterrence theory, see John J. Mearsheimer, *Conventional Deterrence*, Cornell Studies in Security Affairs (Ithaca, NY: Cornell University Press, 1983), 165.
36. Cdr. Clifford P. Willoz, USN (Ret.), email exchange with author, May 19–23, 2019. And see "HP 9830A," The Museum of HP Calculators (website), accessed May 23, 2019, https://www.hpmuseum.org/hp9830.htm.
37. Brooks, interview with the author, May 16, 2019; Brooks, email exchange with the author, May 22, 2019.
38. Link-14 messages used NATO Message Text Formatting System (FORMETS). ADatP-3 (Allied Data Publication) describes FORMETS as "providing the rules, procedures and vocabulary to be used in the construction of character-oriented [machine readable] message text formats." Ir. W. A. Levenbach, "Message Handling in a Military Environment," TNO report no. FEL-89-B260, TNO Physics and Electronics Laboratory, Netherlands Organization for Applied Science and Research, The Hague, September 18, 1989, 30–31, https://apps.dtic.mil/sti/pdfs/ADA217929.pdf.
39. This is a greatly oversimplified description. For details on message formats and processing, see Northrop Grumman, "Understanding Voice Data Link Networking," NorthropGrumman.com, December 2014, pp. 1–3, https://dl.icdst.org/pdfs/files/e90d37a9b93e2e607206320ea07d7ad2.pdf. And see Boslaugh, *First-Hand*, chap. 9, "Legacy of NTDS," sec. "Digital Revolution in the Fleet: Spread of NTDS in the Fleet," para. 2, https://ethw.org/First-Hand:Legacy_of_NTDS_-_Chapter_9_of_the_Story_of_the_Naval_Tactical_Data_System#Digital_Revolution_in_the_Fleet. For examples of TTY equipment and message processing, see Nick England, "US Navy Teletype Equipment—1950's & 1960's," *US Navy Radio Communications—1950's & 1960's*, Navy-Radio.com, last updated November 3, 2024, http://www.navy-radio.com/tty.htm.

40. Boslaugh, *First-Hand*, chap. 7, "The Story of the Naval Tactical Data System," sec. "Vietnam, the Real Service Test," para. 5, https://ethw.org/First-Hand:The_Naval_Tactical_Data_System_in_Combat_-_Chapter_7_of_the_Story_of_the_Naval_Tactical_Data_System#Vietnam,_the_Real_Service_Test.

41. Willoz, email exchange with the author, May 28, 2019; Clifford Willoz, email exchange with the author, May 29, 2019.

42. Project Sixty was Zumwalt's plan to modernize the equipment and culture of the Navy. He released the plan after his first sixty days as CNO; hence its name. Berman describes Tidd as a type of overseer of Project Sixty staff work; Larry Berman, *Zumwalt: The Life and Times of Admiral Elmo Russell "Bud" Zumwalt, Jr.*, 1st ed (New York: Harper, 2012), 233.

43. Willoz, email exchange with the author, May 29, 2019.

44. Jerry Proc, "ADLIPS, LINK 11/14, CCS-280, CANEWS, CANEWS 2 and Other Systems," *Radio Communications and Signals Intelligence in the Royal Canadian Navy* (website), last updated September 19, 2024, http://jproc.ca/rrp/rrp2/1980s_adlips_link.html.

45. Naval Air Forces Atlantic (NAVAIRLANT) oversees the Atlantic-based aircraft carriers, not SURFLANT. It is unclear whether or not SUFLANT gave ECLIPS units to NAVAIRLANT or provided them directly; it was most likely the latter. By this time Willoz was no longer involved in the project. He was surprised to hear that the project had not ended when he'd left. Willoz, email exchange with the author, May 20, 2019.

46. Document contained in email from Willoz to the author, May 29, 2019.

47. Cdr. Thomas P. Terlizzi, USN (Ret.), described a week-long ECLIPS course he attended in 1979 on Naval Training Station Dam Neck, Virginia. The course was maintenance and repair, not operator-focused. Email exchange with the author, November 5, 2020.

48. ECLIPS connectivity on USS *Eisenhower* and discussion of USS *Nassau*'s (LHA-4) functional connectivity to the teletype feeds from Litsinger, email exchanges with the author, October 29, 2020, and from Willoz, email exchange with the author, May 23, 2019.

Chapter 11. Formal "Two Squares" Effort

1. Elmo R. Zumwalt Jr., "Project Sixty: Memorandum for All Flag Officers (and Marine General Officers)," OP-00 (CNO), September 16, 1970, Office of the Chief of Naval Operations, U.S. Department of the Navy, Washington, DC, document p. 19, item no. 6230911006, box 09, folder 11, Admiral Elmo R. Zumwalt Jr. Collection: General Subject Files, Vietnam Center and Sam Johnson Vietnam Archive, Texas Tech University, Lubbock, TX, available for download from https://vva.vietnam.ttu.edu/repositories/2/digital_objects/404169.

2. Much of the information on OP-094 was compiled for a manuscript sponsored by the Naval Intelligence Professionals organization. Bryan H. Leese, "C2W and Technology: The Story of OP-094 and the Navy's Attempt to Centralize Systems for Better Decision Making" (unpublished manuscript, last modified October 2024). Regarding the creation of OP-094, see Chief of Naval Operations, U.S. Department of the Navy, "Memo for VCNO, Establishment of the Office of Command Support Programs, OP-094," organizational review, OP-09B, February 26, 1971, Immediate Files of the Chief of Naval Operations, 1971, box 4, series vii (OP-9B, Director of Naval Administration, 1968–1993), Archives Branch, Naval History and Heritage Command, Washington, DC. Admiral Zumwalt's change of command remarks, in "NAVINTCOM Fleet Intelligence Newsletter (FIN)—Change of Command," Commander Naval Intelligence Command, July 1971, Vice Admiral Earl "Rex" Rectanus Personal Archive, courtesy of Dr. Earl Rectanus Jr.
3. Frederick J. Harlfinger II, unpublished transcript of interviews, conducted by John T. Mason. March 11, 1977, interview 9 of 9, p. 477, Archives, U.S. Naval Institute, Annapolis, MD.
4. Clayton D. Laurie and Michael J. Suk, *Leaders of the National Reconnaissance Office: Volume 1, 1962–1992; Directors, Deputy Directors, Staff Directors, Program Directors, Chiefs of Staff, Directorate and Office Managers*, 2nd rev. ed. (Chantilly, VA: National Reconnaissance Office, Center for the Study of National Reconnaissance, 2019), xiv, 51–52, https://www.nro.gov/Portals/65/documents/history/csnr/leaders/Leaders_of_NRO_Vol_I_July_2019_web.pdf?ver=2019-09-18-094920-410&timestamp=1568815046728.
5. Friedman, *Network-centric Warfare*, ix–xi.
6. Leese, "C2W and Technology."
7. U.S. Congress, House of Representatives, Committee on Armed Services, Subcommittee on Research and Development, "House Hearings on Military Posture and H.R. 11500 (H.R. 12438), Department of Defense Authorization for Appropriations for Fiscal Year 1977, House Committee on Armed Services, Subcommittee on Research and Development," Washington, DC, 94th Congress (House), February 25, 1976, p. 515.
8. Friedman, *Network-centric Warfare*, 207. For more on the demonstrations, see Pennsylvania State University Advanced Research Lab, ed, "From the Sea to the Stars," 92–93.
9. The intent to connect the CIP to NTDS went even further. REWSON wished to link all C2 systems—including the Anti-submarine Warfare Centers Command Control System (ASW CCCS) and the Fleet Command Support Centers (FCSC)—in one global COP. The Navy's common picture would then be connected to the strategic Worldwide Military Command and Control System

(WWMCCS). Friedman, *Network-centric Warfare*, 191–95. See also Ford and Rosenberg, *Admirals' Advantage*, 69–71.

10. The effort started with Multilayer Plotting (MLP) and advanced to the ESP in January 1971. Friedman, *Network-centric Warfare*, 190. The MLP and ESP effort is discussed in Harlfinger, interview, 492.

11. Friedman, *Network-centric Warfare*, 191. The Navy's Operational Test and Evaluation Force (COMOPTEVFOR) at Sunnyvale began Fleet Objective-265, a demonstration program to evaluate the feasibility of delivering intelligence from national systems to operators; Pennsylvania State University Advanced Research Lab, ed., "From the Sea to the Stars," 75–76. Also in Leese, "C2W and Technology."

12. Regarding the intent to connect all C2 systems, see Friedman, *Network-centric Warfare*, 191–95.

13. The *Kennedy* was the first to receive an ITFCC. John R. C. Mitchell, command history 1976 of USS *Kennedy* (CV 67), from the commanding officer to the Chief of Naval Operations, doc. ref. OPNAVINST 5750.12B, April 7, 1977, p. 2, Naval History and Heritage Command.

    Friedman notes that the *Kennedy*'s IFTCC was phase 2 of the FCC-TFCC test; *Network-centric Warfare*, 195, 332n6. See also Subcommittee on Research and Development, "Hearings on Military Posture and H.R. 11500 (H.R. 12438)," 515–17.

14. Lynn G. Wessman, USN (Ret.), email exchange with the author, March 3, 2021.

15. Hanyok, *Spartans in Darkness*, 7:258. See also "IronHorse," *Cryptolog*, p. 25. The AN/GYK-9 was a Univac CP-818, 24-bit processor. For remembrances of former technicians who worked with the CP-818 FLEXCOP IronHorse system at the National Cryptologic School in Maryland, see sec. 3.7, "CP-818 (1224)," in "24-Bit Computers, Chapter 51" VIP Club, VIPClubMN.org, last updated August 25, 2024, shttps://vipclubmn.org/CP24bit.html.

16. "IronHorse," *Cryptolog*, 25–26. See also Hanyok, *Spartans in Darkness*, 7:259.

17. Regarding BUIC, see Hanyok, *Spartans in Darkness*, 7:259. Regarding sanitization of tracks to NTDS and MTDS, see "IronHorse," *Cryptolog*, 26.

18. Wessman, email exchange with the author, March 3, 2021.

19. An example of the OTH-T ethical problem is the 1988 sinking of a merchant ship. A harpoon fired from a Navy F/A-18 Hornet aircraft confused the target hulk with the merchant ship within the exercise area. William M. Arkin and Joshua Handler, "Naval Accidents, 1945–1988," Neptune Paper no. 3 (Greenpeace/Institute for Policy Studies, Washington, DC, June 1989), 72, archived online at https://web.archive.org/web/20230308153409/https://uploads.fas.org/2014/05/NavalAccidents1945-1988.pdf.

20. Wessman, email exchange with the author, March 3, 2021. See also testimony by Vice Adm. David F. Emerson, director of Navy Research, Development, Test and Evaluation, in U.S. Congress, House Committee on Appropriations, Subcommittee of the Department of Defense, *Department of Defense Appropriations for 1979: Hearings Before a Subcommittee of the Committee on Appropriations, House of Representatives, Ninety-Fifth Congress, Second Session* (Washington, DC: U.S. Government Printing Office, 1978), 398–99. See more testimony by Vice Admiral Emerson in his capacity as director of Navy RDT&E in U.S. Congress, Senate, Committee on Appropriations, Subcommittee on Department of Defense, *Department of Defense Appropriations for Fiscal Year 1981: Hearings Before a Subcommittee on Appropriations, United States Senate, Ninety-Sixth Congress, Second Session*, part iv, *Procurement/R. D. T. & E. (Pages 1–948), Department of Defense, Department of the Navy* (Washington, DC: U.S. Government Printing Office, 1980), March 27, 1980, pp. 127–28, https://www.google.com/books/edition/Department_of_Defense_Appropriations_for/4hje_az-aJMC?q=Congressional+testimony+AN/USQ-81(V)&gbpv=1#f=false.
21. Hanyok, *Spartans in Darkness*, 7:260.
22. The AN/UGC 25 Model 28 Receive-Only compact printer was the most installed model. England, "US Navy Teletype Equipment."
23. This story provided by Rear Adm. Tony L. Cothron, USN (Ret.), a SupPlot watch officer in *America*'s SupPlot during the 1979 deployment. Email exchange with the author, September 17, 19, and 22, 2020. *America* received its SupPlot and an I-TFCC during a four-month shipyard availability in September 1978; see Thomas R. Sherman, ed., *USS America (CV 66) Mediterranean Cruise Book 1979* (no publication information available), 19, https://www.navysite.de/cruisebooks/cv66-79/016.htm. *America* received its full TFCC with new systems in January 1981; Friedman, *Network-centric Warfare*, 196.
24. Cothron, email exchanges with the author, September 16, 17, 18, 19, and 22, 2020.
25. Sherman, *USS America Mediterranean Cruise Book 1979*, 21.
26. Cothron, email exchanges with the author, September 2020.
27. SCI information was passed to cleared watch standers via headsets connected to the 12MC. Cothron, email exchanges with the author, September 2020. See also Friedman, *Network-centric Warfare*, 196.
28. *America*'s command histories have not been declassified. However, the ship alterations (ShipAlts) were somewhat standard across the class of ship. *America* would have had similar ShipAlts as *Kitty Hawk*'s HF/UHF/VHF upgrades, ShipAlts 4355, 4357, and 4363, respectively. See Edward J. Hogan, command history 1976 of USS *Kitty Hawk* (CV 63), from the commanding officer to the Chief of Naval Operations, OPNAVINST 5750.12 series, April 30,

1977, pp. 23–24, Naval History and Heritage Command, https://www.history.navy.mil/content/dam/nhhc/research/archives/command-operation-reports/ship-command-operation-reports/k/kitty-hawk-cv-63-ii/1976.pdf. The NTDS upgrades (ShipAlt 4644) attempted to meet the new triservices tactical air-control system/tactical air-defense system display standards created for warfighting interoperability across services. See Sammuel W. Hubbard, command history 1975 of USS *Kitty Hawk* (CV 63), from the commanding officer to the chief of Naval Operations, OPNAVINST 5750.12, May 1976, Naval History and Heritage Command, https://www.history.navy.mil/content/dam/nhhc/research/archives/command-operation-reports/ship-command-operation-reports/k/kitty-hawk-cv-63-ii/1975.pdf.

29. For the FLTSATCOM installation (ShipAlt 5056), see Walter Lewis Chatham, command history 1978 of USS *Kitty Hawk* (C V-63), from the commanding officer to the Chief of Naval Operations, OPNAVINST 5850.12, February 17, 1979, p. 49, Naval History and Heritage Command, https://www.history.navy.mil/content/dam/nhhc/research/archives/command-operation-reports/ship-command-operation-reports/k/kitty-hawk-cv-63-ii/1978.pdf. For more on the FLTSATCOM program (begun in 1972 but delayed until 1978) and the Navy's use of commercial "Gapfiller" satellites, see Pennsylvania State University Advanced Research Lab, ed., "From the Sea to the Stars," 78–82, 116–17.

30. CNO Project 310-1 testing was done in three periods—one in the fall of 1977 and two in 1978. Wessman, email exchange with the author, April 29, 2020, and March 2, 2021. On OTH-T, see Pennsylvania State University Advanced Research Lab, ed., "From the Sea to the Stars," 96.

31. Wessman, email exchange with the author, March 3, 2021.

32. FOSIC Norfolk was baselined in late 1977. Upgrades were constant as new computers and electronics were developed. Brooks, email exchange with the author, October 7, 2020. Discussion about upgrades at FOSIF Rota from Litsinger, email exchange with the author, October 2020. With completion of the OSIS Baseline Upgrade (OBU) 1983, fuller integration with other intelligence databases increased. Ford and Rosenberg, *Admirals' Advantage*, 102–3.

33. The satellites were called PARCAE but had an unclassified cover designation of White Cloud, as part of the Naval Ocean Surveillance System (or NOSS). "Classic Wizard" referred to the receiving and processing systems. The collection system consisted of a three-satellite grouping in a larger constellation. There were possibly six satellites, in groups of three, operational within the constellation by July 1978. See Day, "Above the Clouds." The active surveillance counterpart to Classic Wizard was to be Clipper Bow, but the system was never funded. For more on OTH-T satellite systems, see Friedman, *Network-centric Warfare*, 179, 208.

34. The description of system and satellite communications is from Wessman, email exchanges with the author, January 1, 2019; the landline connection to Naples was discussed via email on February 1, 2021.
35. Wessman, email exchanges with author, July 2, 2020, and March 2, 2021, concerning Wessman's belief that the OTH-T Gold message format came out between 1979 and 1982, supporting the new OTCIXS and TADIXS datalink systems. Nels Litsinger notes FOSIF Rota was using OTH-T Gold in 1979 (explained by Wessman in email of February 1, 2021).
36. Wessman, email exchange with the author, July 2, 2020.
37. Wessman, email exchange with the author, March 2, 2021.
38. Litsinger, email exchange with the author, October 6, 2020.
39. It was the description of "event-by-event reporting" in separate correspondence from Wessman (email, March 2, 2021) and Litsinger (email, February 1, 2021) that revealed the true nature of the data exchange.
40. Test and demonstration described by Wessman in email exchange with the author, March 2, 2021.
41. Friedman, *Network-centric Warfare*, 195. For a detailed look at the Navy's data and voice-exchanges systems, see Richard Banks Landolt, "The Officer in Tactical Command and Tactical Data Information Exchange Systems (OTCIXS/TADIXS) and the Transition to the Military Strategic and Tactical Relay System (MILSTAR)," master's thesis, Naval Postgraduate School, 1987, p. 21, https://apps.dtic.mil/sti/tr/pdf/ADA181664.pdf.
42. Ruggednova was the brand of ROLM Mil-Spec computers. Alex Bochanneck, "If It Moves, It Should Be Ruggednova," *CHM Blog*, Computer History Museum, December 4, 2012, https://computerhistory.org/blog/if-it-moves-it-should-be-ruggednova/. See also Pennsylvania State University Advanced Research Lab, ed., "From the Sea to the Stars," 97.
43. Wessman, email exchange with the author, September 17, 2020.
44. Wessman, email exchange with the author, September 17, 2020.
45. The system displayed major and minor ellipses of the fixes. The ellipses combined to show the amount of uncertainty regarding the unit's position represented by the track, the AOU. Tightening the AOU came from more fixes that shrank the ellipses and thus the AOU. Description of the fusion room operations from Wessman, email exchanges with the author, June 30, 2020, and March 3, 2021.
46. Description of the automated data-correlation process from Wessman, email exchange with the author, June 30, 2020.
47. Description of the sanitization from Wessman, email exchange with the author, January 1, 2019.
48. SheShark is Cdr. Laurel Hargan Wessman (Ret.), USN. The use of dummy tracks as an early form of SMS text messaging discussed in author's

email exchange with Lynn G. Wessman, husband of Laurel, September 19, 2020.
49. Wessman, email exchange with the author, September 19, 2020.
50. Wessman described the adoption of Harpoon "Ambush" doctrine for TASM time-on-target simultaneity effort for TASM in an email exchange with the author, March 2, 2021.
51. Friedman, *Network-centric Warfare*, 209.
52. Friedman, 210.
53. Pennsylvania State University Advanced Research Lab, ed., "From the Sea to the Stars," 120, 126–29.
54. Jerry O. Tuttle, command history 1977 of USS *Kennedy* (CV 67), from the commanding officer to the Chief of Naval Operations, March 22, 1978, p. 2, Naval History and Heritage Command; and Lowell R. Myers, command history 1979 of USS *Kennedy* (CV 67), from the commanding officer to the Chief of Naval Operations, OPNAVINST, May 20, 1980, p. 11, Naval History and Heritage Command.
55. Regarding the installation of the Interim Tactical Flag Command Center (ITFCC), see Mitchell, command history 1976 of USS *Kennedy* (CV 67), 14.
56. Jerry O. Tuttle, "A Brief History of JOTS," in DiGirolamo, *Naval Command and Control*, 119. Litsinger notes that Tuttle was very interested in ECLIPS during the Mediterranean Sea portion of the deployment; Litsinger, interview with the author, June 27, 2019.
57. Friedman, *Network-centric Warfare*, 198–200. For Tuttle's personal description of the creation of JOTS, see Tuttle, "Brief History," 119–22.

Chapter 12. A Period of Evolution

1. Jacoby, email exchange with the author, October 14, 2020.
2. Jacoby, email exchange with the author, October 14, 2020.
3. Regarding *Ike*'s participation in Ocean Venture '81, see Lehman, *Oceans Ventured*, xvii, 74–75.
4. Litsinger, interview with the author, May 29, 2019.
5. Litsinger writes that there was a "first iteration" of the TFCC, the Flag Plot; email exchange with the author, May 21, 2020. Lasko was the N2 for Eight (COMCARGRU 8), embarked in *Nimitz* in 1979. Capt. Paul G. Lasko, USN (Ret.), interview with the author, October 17, 2020.
6. Litsinger, email exchanges with the author, September 14 and October 30, 2020, and interview with the author, May 29, 2019.
7. The ding sounded if a line in the message matched a list of Soviet equipment held in the systems memory. For example, if a "Front Door"—the radar associated with the *Juliet*-class SSGN's SS-N-3 Shaddock ASCM—was in a

message, a ding sounded. Terlizzi, email exchange with the author, November 5, 2020.
8. The OpsComm teletype was still located in SSES compartment forward above the bow on the 03 level. Terlizzi, email exchange with the author, November 5, 2020.
9. Litsinger, email exchange with the author, September 14, 2020. "Out of hide" is U.S. militaryspeak for the sourcing of crew from existing military positions.
10. Cothron, email exchange with the author, September 17, 2020.
11. "Intelligence Assignment and Placement," *Naval Intelligence Newsletter* (1979).
12. The Navy provides a basic allowance (BA) of personnel for each ship. It usually only crews to 95 percent (the fill) and then with a goal of 90 percent fit (meaning the right officer designator and enlisted rates) of the BA number for operational commands. Shore commands are often crewed at 80 percent of BA. Litsinger's fill rate was only 65 percent for his 1981 deployment. Litsinger, email exchange with the author, September 14, 2020.
13. The Navy and Marine Corps Intelligence Training Center (NMITC) opened at Dam Neck, Virginia, in October 1986, replacing AFAITC. It combined four separate Navy intelligence facilities located in Colorado, Florida, and Virginia. "NMITC Dedication," *Naval Intelligence Professionals Quarterly*: 2; Noble, email exchange with the author, October 13, 2020.
14. Description of TAP watch personnel training from Litsinger, email exchange with the author, October 29, 2020.
15. Litsinger, email exchange with the author, October 29, 2020.
16. Capt. Paul Lasko, USN (Ret.), was also the N2 on the USS *Nimitz*. Terlizzi, email exchange with the author, November 5, 2020.
17. "Intelligence Assignment and Placement Section," *Naval Intelligence Newsletter* (1979): 28–29.
18. Postgraduate quotas remained around twenty-two during the 1970s and 1980s. See the "Intelligence Assignment and Placement" sections of the *Naval Intelligence Newsletter* issues from (1976): 7–8; (1979): 19–21; and (1980): 28.
19. Description of air wing–strike planning in Friedman, *Network-centric Warfare*, 154–55.
20. Description of the chart vault and CVIC operations from Terlizzi, email exchange with the author, November 5, 2020.
21. This Navy ASW strike-aid study compared fifteen mission-planning aids. Wayne W. Zachary, "Decision Aids for Naval Air ASW," technical report 1366-A (Analytics, Willow Grove, PA, March 15, 1980), 3–3, https://apps.dtic.mil/sti/tr/pdf/ADA085134.pdf.

22. Friedman, *Network-centric Warfare*, 155.
23. Dougherty, command history 1976 USS *Kennedy*, p. 2.
24. Ross R. Hatch et al., "Fifty Years of Strike Warfare Research at the Applied Physics Laboratory," *Johns Hopkins APL Technical Digest* 13, no. 1 (January–March 1992): 119, ttps://secwww.jhuapl.edu/techdigest/Content/techdigest/pdf/V13-N01/13-01-Hatch.pdf. See also Friedman's discussion in *Network-centric Warfare*, 155–56.
25. On the genesis of TAMPS, see "Tactical Aircraft Mission Planning System: Windows on the Future," *Naval Aviation News* (June 1995): 27–28, https://books.google.com/books?id=deiWwyjpQiQC&q=TAMPS#v=onepage&q=TAMPS&f=false; Friedman, *Network-centric Warfare*, 155–56. Both sources offer that the failed attack of December 4, 1983, by Navy aircraft carrier A-6 and A-7 against Syrian targets accelerated the development of TAMPS and a specialized strike-warfare "Top Gun" course in Fallon, Nevada.
26. See the description of Vietnam-era strike-mission planning in chapter 2.
27. The image-transmission system was based on an image-scanner and -transmission system called TINTS (Tactical Intelligence Transfer System), developed as part of the IOIC contract in 1968, discussed with Leatherman in interview with the author, February 5, 2018.
28. FIC Europe (FICEUR) and FIC Atlantic (FICLANT) combined into FICEURLANT in 1968. FICEURLANT was located in Norfolk, Virginia. The last two merged in 1974 to form FIC Europe-Atlantic (FICEURLANT). Terlizzi, email exchange with the author, November 5, 2020.
29. Terlizzi, email exchange with the author, November 5, 2020.
30. *Midway* is the longest-serving aircraft carrier of the twentieth century. She was extensively modernized in the 1970s, adding many of the *Forrestal*-class features and capabilities. *Dictionary of American Naval Fighting Ships*, s.v. "Midway III (CVB 41)," Naval History and Heritage Command, May 30, 2019, https://www.history.navy.mil/content/history/nhhc/research/histories/ship-histories/danfs/m/midway-iii.html.
31. Vic Socotra is the pen name of Capt. James "J. R." Reddig, USN (Ret.); see "Air Intelligence," *DailySocotra* (blog), July 3, 2017, https://www.vicsocotra.com/wordpress/air-intelligence/.
32. Christopher B. Hearn, "Report on the Fleet Imagery Support Terminal (FIST) System," memo from the cochair of the WAIT evolution team to the Washington Area Imaging Transition group, Central Intelligence Agency, August 2, 1984, CIA FOIA Electronic Reading Room, https://www.cia.gov/readingroom/document/cia-rdp91b00776r000100100059-6.
33. Socotra [Reddig], "Air Intelligence."
34. Litsinger, email exchange with the author, February 1, 2021.

35. Lasko, interview with the author, October 17, 2020.
36. Seth Rosenbloom and Michelle J. Markus, "When the Project and the Organizational Culture Clash," paper presented at PMI Global Congress 2010, Project Management Institute, Washington, DC, 2010, https://www.pmi.org/learning/library/project-organizational-culture-conflicts-resolve-6585.
37. Malcolm Muir, *Black Shoes and Blue Water: Surface Warfare in the United States Navy, 1945–1975* (repr. Honolulu: University Press of the Pacific, [1996] 2005), 225–29.
38. Lasko tells an old Jewish tale of a journey from Minsk to Pinsk, illustrating the difficulties found in performing a seemingly simple task. A version of the story is found in Nathan Ausubel, ed., *A Treasury of Jewish Folklore*, abridged ed. (New York: Bantam, 1980), 169. Lasko, interview with the author, October 31, 2020.
39. Litsinger, email with the author, October 30, 2020.
40. Litsinger, email with the author, September 14, 2020.
41. Today the operational Carrier Strike Group in the Mediterranean theater is designated CTF 60. A separate Sixth Fleet staff no longer embarks.
42. Litsinger, email with the author, September 14, 2020.
43. Litsinger, email with the author, September 14, 2020.
44. Litsinger's discussion of his time as the Sixth Fleet N2 in late 1980s from email exchange with the author, September 14, 2020.
45. Jacoby, email exchange with the author, October 14, 2020.
46. Ford and Rosenberg, *Admirals' Advantage*, 77–79.

Chapter 13. "Selling" Opintel

1. Inman in "Intelligence Assignment and Placement," *Naval Intelligence Newsletter* (1974): 5.
2. On CIA misdeeds, the *New York Times* articles, and the Church Committee, see Stansfield Turner, *Secrecy and Democracy: The CIA in Transition* (Boston: Houghton Mifflin, 1985), chap. 4, "The Haunting Past." The Schlesinger Report (officially "A Review of the Intelligence Community") was authorized by President Richard Nixon in 1970 to identify and alleviate factors of ineffectiveness within the IC's organizations. See Michael Warner, "Reading the Riot Act: The Schlesinger Report, 1971," *Intelligence and National Security* 24, no. 3 (June 2009): 387–417, https://doi.org/10.1080/02684520903036974 (paywall). Also see Prados, *Safe for Democracy*, chap. 18, "From 'Rogue Elephant' to Resurrection."
3. Adm. Bobby Ray Inman, USN (Ret.), interview with the author, November 16, 2020. Weisner was VCNO for four months. He was replaced by Admiral Holloway. Inman had previously worked for Weisner at 7th Fleet. See "Naval Operations Vice Chief Is Shifted After 4 Months," *New York Times*, January

3, 1973, https://www.nytimes.com/1973/01/03/archives/naval-operations-vice-chief-is-shifted-after-4-months.html.
4. Christopher A. Ford and David A. Rosenberg, "The Naval Intelligence Underpinnings of Reagan's Maritime Strategy," *Journal of Strategic Studies* 28, no. 2 (2005): 391, https://doi.org/10.1080/01402390500088627 (paywall).
5. Inman, interview with the author, November 16, 2020.
6. Inman, interview with the author, November 16, 2020. The chief of BuPers was Vice Adm. David H. Bagley (February 1972–April 1975), followed by future chief of Naval Operations Adm. James Watkins (April 1975–July 1978).
7. Inman, interview with the author, November 16, 2020.
8. "Intelligence Assignment and Placement," Naval Intelligence Newsletter (1975): 3.
9. The filling of junior officer ranks by more senior officers is discussed in "Intelligence Assignment and Placement," *Naval Intelligence Newsletter* (1974): 6.
10. Inman discussed creation of the board to review records in an interview with the author, November 16, 2020.
11. Brooks, email exchange with the author, October 16, 2020.
12. Inman, interview with the author, November 16, 2020. Vice Admiral Jacoby, the detailer in 1980, discussed Inman's detail plan in an email exchange with the author, October 16, 2020.
13. Barry Alan Marks, "The Idea of Propaganda in America," PhD diss., University of Minnesota, 1957, p. v, archived online at https://www.proquest.com/docview/301928906/citation/E0310AB7450444B0PQ/1.
14. Quoted from Edward L. Bernays, "Edward L. Bernays Beech Nut Packing Co," interview, conducted at Bernays' home in Cambridge, Massachusetts, interviewer and date unknown, posted to YouTube by the Museum of Public Relations, June 13, 2016, 2:44, https://www.youtube.com/watch?v=OI-pO-o-yqI.
15. Lowenthal, *Intelligence*, 5.
16. Probably the most famous case of the politicalization of intelligence is the Vietnam War's "body count and crossover point" measure of performance. The assessed North Vietnamese order of battle numbers that the calculation was based on were hotly debated and rife with bias, embedded assumptions, and parochialism. Warner, "Reading the Riot Act."
17. H. Bradford Westerfield, "Inside Ivory Bunkers: CIA Analysts Resist Managers' 'Pandering'; Part II," *International Journal of Intelligence and CounterIntelligence* 10, no. 1 (March 1997): 19–54, https://doi.org/10.1080/08850609708435332 (paywall).
18. Capt. Frank P. Notz, USN (Ret.), provided a thorough discussion of the intelligence officer's attributes and identity in *Some Thoughts for Naval Intelligence Officers* (Suitland, MD: Office of Naval Intelligence, 1988).

19. For a deeper discussion of corporate branding, see Avinandan Mukherjee and Hongwei He, "Company Identity and Marketing: An Integrative Framework," *Journal of Marketing Theory and Practice* 16, no. 2 (Spring 2008): 111–25, https://www.jstor.org/stable/40470344 (paywall).
20. Andrea Baertl Helguero, "De-constructing Credibility: Factors that Affect a Think Tank's Credibility," Working Paper no. 4, On Think Tanks (website), March 2018, p. 8, https://onthinktanks.org/wp-content/uploads/2018/04/ABaertlHelguero_WP4.pdf.
21. Notz, *Intelligence Officers*, 24. Notz provides advice for and describes the attributes of effective intelligence officers.
22. Helguero, "De-constructing Credibility," 9.
23. For more on the mere effect (familiarity principle), see the original essay by Robert B. Zajonc, "Attitudinal Effects of Mere Exposure," *Journal of Personality and Social Psychology* 9, no. 2 (part 2) (June 1968): 1–27, https://psycnet.apa.org/doiLanding?doi=10.1037%2Fh0025848. For more on "background similarity in hiring, see Yong-Min Kim, "Career Advancement in Managerial Hierarchies in the United States Firms: A Multi-theoretic Model and Empirical Tests of the Determinants of Managerial Promotion," PhD diss., University of Southern California, 1995, archived online at https://www.proquest.com/docview/304220709/?pq-origsite=primo.
24. Inman, interview with the author, November 16, 2020.
25. Inman, interview with the author, November 16, 2020. The commander in chief at CINCUSNAVEUR was Vice Adm. Joseph P. Moorer (1977–1980).
26. Inman, interview with the author, November 16, 2020. Admiral Watkins was commander, Sixth Fleet, from 1978 to 1979 and CNO from 1982 to 1986. Adm. William Studeman became the second 1630 to make four-star rank, Inman having been the first.
27. Inman, interview with the author, November 16, 2020. Jacoby was a detailer during the 1980s and describes the success of Inman's approach in an email exchange with the author, October 16, 2020. Inman's process worked so well that he employed it at the National Security Agency with great success. For more on Inman's talent management and mentoring, including his "30 Rules for Intelligence Officers," see Bryan H. Leese, "Naval Intelligence Professionals: Admiral Bobby R. Inman, 'Great Captain,'" Professional Articles, *Naval Intelligence Professionals Quarterly* (June 15, 2016), https://www.navintpro.org/professional-articles/2016/06/15/admiral-bobby-r.-inman,-great-captain/ (paywall).
28. Brooks, email exchange with the author, October 17, 2020.
29. Inman, interview with the author, November 16, 2020.
30. Inman, interview with the author, November 16, 2020.

31. Brooks, email exchange with the author, October 17, 2020.
32. Inman, interview with the author, November 16, 2020.
33. Jacoby, email exchange with the author, October 16, 2020.
34. Jacoby, email exchange with the author, October 16, 2020.
35. Competitive analysis is a concept based on a belief that analysts looking at the same problems can counter parochial agency views found in assessments. Lowenthal, *Intelligence*, 17–18.
36. Jacob W. Kipp, review of *Soviet Naval Doctrine and Policy, 1956–1986*, by Robert Waring Herrick, Speaking of Books, *Journal of the Historical Society* 3, nos. 3–4 (June 2003): 431–34, https://onlinelibrary.wiley.com/doi/10.1111/j.1529-921X.2003.00071.x. Brad Dismukes and Peter M. Swartz discussed the Center for Naval Analyses' role in the strategy-analysis debate at "Soviet Strategy and Open Source Analysis," lecture and discussion, Arlington, VA, November 7, 2017. CNA was contracted by OpNav to support CNO Zumwalt's Project Sixty planning. Don Boroughs, *The Story of CNA: Civilian Scientists in War and Peace* (Arlington, VA: Center for Naval Analyses, 2017), 35–47.
37. For Swartz's quotation, see Boroughs, *Story of CNA*, 38.
38. Ford and Rosenberg, *Admirals' Advantage*, 88.
39. Ford and Rosenberg, 89. Discussion of wargaming at the Naval War College in Lehman, *Oceans Ventured*, 52–56. Adm. William Small led the ATP; see William N. Small, transcript of oral history of Admiral William N. Small, USN (Ret.), conducted by David F. Winkler, August 1997, Naval Historical Foundation, Washington, DC.
40. Hone, *Power and Change*, 106.
41. Ford and Rosenberg, "Reagan's Maritime Strategy," 387; Thomas A. Brooks and William Manthorpe, "Setting the Record Straight: A Critical Review of *Fall from Glory* by Gregory I. Vistica," *Naval Intelligence Professionals Quarterly* (April 1996), repr. *The Submarine Review*, Naval Submarine League, (April July 1996): 61, archived online at https://s36124.pcdn.co/wp-content/uploads/2021/09/1996-July-OCRw.pdf.
42. Friedman, *Fifty-Year War*, 452.
43. Hone, *Power and Change*, 107–8; Hattendorf et al., *Sailors and Scholars*, 312–13.
44. Dr. Alf Andreassen, chief civilian scientist, led the team. Ford and Rosenberg, "Reagan's Maritime Strategy."
45. The ATP was led by vice CNO Vice Adm. William Small. Ford and Rosenberg, 387, 388–89; Hone, *Power and Change*, 107–8. Also see John B. Hattendorf's discussion in "The Evolution of the U.S. Navy's Maritime Strategy, 1977–1986," Newport Papers 19 (Center for Naval Warfare Studies, Naval War College, Newport, RI, 2003), chap. 2, "Thinking about the Soviet Navy, 1967–1981," https://doi.org/10.21236/ADA422147.

46. Bryan H. Leese, "A Cold War–Education Approach for Today's Military (unpublished manuscript, last modified December 2024).
47. Secretary Lehman's assertiveness, Hone and Utz offer, and his expansive view of his authority led to a clash with CNO Hayward, resulting in their not speaking for most of 1981. The "standoff" was not good for either of them, and so they gradually discovered that they could cooperate when they dealt with the Navy's program because they saw "eye-to-eye generally on programmatic issues" and likely the Maritime Strategy. Thomas C. Hone and Curtis A. Utz, *History of the Office of the Chief of Naval Operations, 1915–2015* (Washington, DC: Naval History and Heritage Command, U.S. Department of the Navy, 2020), 334–35, https://www.history.navy.mil/content/dam/nhhc/research/publications/publication-508-pdf/OPNAV%20100%20508.pdf. Also see Leese, "Cold War Education."

Chapter 14. Observations

1. Helen Mirren as Mrs. Wilson in *Gosford Park*, dir. Robert Altman, writ. Julian Fellowes (UK, USA, IT: USA Films, Capitol Films, The Film Council, Sandcastle 5 Productions, Chicagofilms, Medusa Film, 2001), 137 min.
2. Brooks, interview with the author, May 9, 2019.
3. Trent Hone uses the Bénard cell to describe "emergent potential" and "evolvability" in *Learning War*, 8. For more on organizational evolvability and memory versus learning, see Amit Jain and Bruce Kogut, "Memory and Organizational Evolvability in a Neutral Landscape," *Organization Science* 25, no. 2 (March–April 2014): 479–93, https://doi.org/10.1287/orsc.2013.0841.
4. Hone, *Learning War*, 4–5.
5. Donald McLachlan, *Room 39: A Study in Naval Intelligence* (New York: Atheneum, 1968), 353, http://archive.org/details/room39studyinnav00mcla; Michael I. Handel, *Intelligence and Military Operations* (London: Frank Cass, 1990), 72–73. For another discussion on the commander's role in the intelligence cycle, see Brian J. Tyler's master's thesis from Air War College, 2011, republished as "Intelligence and Design: Thinking About Operational Art," Drew Paper 14 (Air University, Air Force Research Institute, Maxwell Air Force Base, AL, July 2014), chap. 3, "The Practice of Operational Intelligence," https://media.defense.gov/2017/Nov/21/2001847430/-1/-1/0/DP_0014_TYLER_INTELLIGENCE_DESIGN.PDF.
6. Machiavelli provided a pragmatic and considered discussion on the role of civil servants. See Miles J. Unger, *Machiavelli: A Biography* (New York: Simon and Schuster, 2011), https://archive.org/details/machiavellibiogr0000unge/mode/2up.
7. The intelligence officer as quoted in Handel, *Intelligence and Military Operations*, 68.

8. Handel, 67. The importance of personalities in the intelligence officer and commander is discussed in Tyler, "Intelligence and Design," chap. 4, "Operational Intelligence and the Commander."
9. Handel, *Intelligence and Military Operations*, 21, emphasis original.
10. Handel, 68.
11. Brooks, email exchange with the author, November 18, 2020.
12. Hone uses the surface line community to illustrate Navy learning and evolvability, particularly gunnery fire control and the creation of the CIC concept, in *Learning War*, 59–64. For a discussion of informal processes, see Zurcher, "Sailor Aboard Ship."
13. This is called an "open" system; see Simon Reay Atkinson and James Moffat, *The Agile Organisation: From Informal Networks to Complex Effects and Agility*, Information Age Transformation Series (Washington, DC: CCRP Publications, 2005), sec. "Open Systems."
14. On constraints/must-do, restraints/cannot-do, and other physical or authority limitations, see Martin Dempsey, "Joint Planning," Joint Publication (JP) 5-0, chairman, Joint Chiefs of Staff, June 16, 2017, p. III-42, archived online at https://www.airforcespecialtactics.af.mil/Portals/80/Joint%20Pub%20JPUB%205-0%20Joint%20Planning.pdf.
15. Hone uses French biologist François Jacob's work to discuss complex adaptive systems in *Learning War*, 3–4.
16. Hone, 8.
17. Donald W. Chisholm, *Coordination Without Hierarchy: Informal Structures in Multiorganizational Systems* (Berkeley: University of California Press, 1989), 7–9.
18. Quoting from Burton Klein's 1958 *Fortune* article, "A Radical Proposal for R and D," in Chisholm, 9–11. President Eisenhower's New Look program was a response to the need for research and development adaptation; see Richard M. Leighton, *Strategy, Money, and the New Look, 1953–1956*, History of the Office of the Secretary of Defense vol. 3 (Washington, DC: Historical Office, Office of the Secretary of Defense, 2001).
19. Atkinson and Moffat, *Agile Organisation*, secs. 27–41.
20. Chisholm, *Coordination Without Hierarchy*, 11.
21. Martin E. Dempsey, "Doctrine for the Armed Forces of the United States," Joint Publication (JP) 1, chairman, Joint Chiefs of Staff, July 12, 2017, p. xx, https://irp.fas.org/doddir/dod/jp1.pdf. JP-1 explains why unity of command within coalition operations is difficult.
22. Dempsey, "Doctrine," (JP-1), xiii.
23. Chisholm, *Coordination Without Hierarchy*, 12.
24. Another example: during World War II, fire-control officers independently developing CICs created informal knowledge sharing. Hone, *Learning War*, 187, 206, and 248.

25. Chisholm, *Coordination Without Hierarchy*, 22.
26. Chisholm, 20.
27. Vego, *Joint Operational Warfare*, XII-3.
28. Vego, chap. "On Doctrine."
29. Brooks, email exchange with the author, December 4, 2019.
30. Vego, *Joint Operational Warfare*, XII-14. On wartime tactical doctrinal changes, see Hone, *Learning War*, 118–21, 210–49.
31. Chisholm, *Coordination Without Hierarchy*, chap. 7, "Informal Weakness and Formal Compensations."
32. Chisholm, 189.
33. Mobley, *Progressives in Navy Blue*, 2–4.
34. Phillip S. Meilinger, "10 Propositions Regarding Air Power," Air Force Histories and Museum Program (School of Advanced Airpower Studies, Maxwell Air Force Base, AL, 1995), 56, and 49, https://media.defense.gov/2010/May/25/2001330281/-1/-1/0/AFD-100525-026.pdf.
35. Meilinger, 20, 22.
36. Brian Vlaun, "Selling Schweinfurt: Targeting, Assessment, and Marketing in the Air Campaign Against Germany," PhD diss., Air University, 2017, p. 485, https://apps.dtic.mil/sti/pdfs/AD1042098.pdf.
37. For a description of an aircraft carrier's flight-operations organization that illustrates the point, see Gene I. Rochlin et al., "The Self-Designing High-Reliability Organization: Aircraft Carrier Flight Operations at Sea," *Naval War College Review* 40, no. 4 (Autumn 1987): 76–92, https://www.jstor.org/stable/44637690.
38. William J. Fry, "Thickening the Fog: The Truncation of Air Intelligence Since World War II," master's thesis, Air University, June 2010, p. 3, https://apps.dtic.mil/sti/citations/AD1019234. See also Michael Warner, "The Collapse of Intelligence Support for Air Power, 1944–52: Two Steps Backward," *Studies in Intelligence* 49, no. 3 (2005), https://www.cia.gov/resources/csi/static/collapse-intel-support-air-power.pdf.
39. For a discussion of the Air Force's development of intelligence, surveillance, and reconnaissance (ISR) capabilities, see Tyler Morton, "From Kites Through Cold War: The Evolution of United States Air Force Manned Airborne ISR," PhD diss., Air University, 2016, https://apps.dtic.mil/sti/pdfs/AD1030466.pdf. And see John R. Glock, "The Evolution of Air Force Targeting," *Airpower Journal* 8, no. 3 (Fall 1994); repr. pub. and archived online at https://apps.dtic.mil/sti/pdfs/ADA567476.pdf, p. 29.
40. U.S. Department of the Air Force, "AFSC 14NX Intelligence Officer: Career Field Education and Training Plan," CFETP 14NX, in 2 parts, February 13, 2013, p. 31.

41. At the time Marocchi, a 1630, was deputy chief, Central Security Service. See "Intelligence Assignment and Placement," *Naval Intelligence Newsletter* (1974): sec. "Remarks from Rear-Admiral Marocchi (November 4, 1974)," p. 2.
42. Glock, "Evolution of Air Force Targeting," 158–63.
43. The 14Ns would go to the Wing and then be detailed to the squadrons. Reina Pennington, "Behind the Green Door: Is There Intelligence in Fighters," *USAF Fighter Weapons Review* (Summer/Fall 1983); repr. *USAF Fighter Weapons Review*, "USAF Weapons School 50th Anniversary Issue" (Spring/Summer 1999).
44. Stephen Peter Rosen, "New Ways of War: Understanding Military Innovation," *International Security* 13, no. 1 (Summer 1988): 142, https://doi.org/10.2307/2538898 (paywall).
45. Jan M. Van Tol, "Military Innovation and Carrier Aviation—an Analysis," *Joint Force Quarterly* (Autumn/Winter 1997–1998): 103, https://ndupress.ndu.edu/portals/68/Documents/jfq/jfq-17.pdf.
46. Van Tol, 102–3.

Epilogue

The epigraph takes its title from *Mount Whitney*, Second Fleet Flagship, Norwegian Sea, August 1988.

1. U.S. Navy, "Command History, Naval Air Forces Atlantic," Commander, Naval Air Force Atlantic (AIRLANT) (website), sec. "1980s," accessed March 13, 2021, https://www.airlant.usff.navy.mil/Organization/Carrier-Air-Wings/Carrier-Air-Wing-CVW-8/Command-History/.
2. Jacoby, email exchange with the author, February 26, 2021. The Advanced Tracking Prototype (ATP) was an experimental version of the ACS, an Afloat Correlation System (ACS). Using non-ACS-related funds, the Navy upgraded POST. Lynn Wright, Deputy Director of Naval Intelligence (Ret.), remembers Booze Allen contractors working on the ATP in the late 1980s. Regarding correlating capacity, see U.S. General Accounting Office, "Navy Command and Control: Data Fusion Needs and Capabilities for Battle Group Commanders," briefing report to the chairman of the Legislation and National Security Subcommittee, Committee on Government Operations, House of Representatives, GAO/NSIAD-90-69BR, March 1990, pp. 5–7, https://www.gao.gov/pdf/product/77739.
3. Lowell E. Jacoby, "Joint Intelligence Center, Pacific (JICPAC)—Thinking Back 30 Years," Naval Intelligence Professionals, NavIntPro.org, April 21, 2021, pp. 2–3, https://www.navintpro.org/professional-articles/2021/04/21/joint-intelligence-center,-pacific-(jicpac)---thinking-back-30-years/.
4. Jacoby, interview with the author, May 9, 2019.

5. Jacoby, email exchange with the author, March 14 and April 20, 2021.
6. J. R. Reddig describes the different services' approaches to operational intelligence in "The OSIS Culture: Intelligence Support to Naval Operations in the Cold War," course paper, National War College, Washington, DC, February 2, 1998, p. 15, personal papers of J. R. Reddig.
7. Eldridge et al., "Navy and Defense Reform," 2.
8. John H. Cushman Jr., "Congress Endorses Military Overhaul," *New York Times*, September 18, 1986, sec. A, p. 23, https://www.nytimes.com/1986/09/18/us/congress-endorses-military-overhaul.html.
9. Regarding the failures, see Charles Nemfakos et al., "The Perfect Storm: The Goldwater-Nichols Act and Its Effect on Navy Acquisition," occasional paper (RAND Corporation, Santa Monica, CA, 2010), https://www.rand.org/content/dam/rand/pubs/occasional_papers/2010/RAND_OP308.pdf.
10. Said to Mr. Richard Haver, Navy Intelligence civilian analyst and director, during the visit of a high-ranking soviet military delegation to the *Roosevelt* in 1990. Quoted in Reddig, "OSIS Culture," 14. Charles S. Abbot records the visit that included Representatives Les Aspin, Jim McCrery, and Owen Pickett along with other Navy senior leaders in the 1990 command history of USS *Theodore Roosevelt* (CVN-71), from the commanding officer to the Director of Naval History, OPNAV 5750/1, February 27, 1991, pp. 2–3, Naval History and Heritage Command, https://www.history.navy.mil/content/dam/nhhc/research/archives/command-operation-reports/ship-command-operation-reports/t/theodore-roosevelt-cvn-71-i/1990.pdf.
11. Regarding the downturn of the Soviet economy, see Friedman, *Fifty-Year War*, "Part Six: Counterattack and Victory."
12. President George H. W. Bush's 1990–1994 funding for the Future Years Defense Program (FYDP) was reduced by $167 billion. For more on the complicated Defense budget cuts, see U.S. General Accounting Office, "DOD's Budget Status: Fiscal Years 1990–94 Budget Reduction Decisions Still Pending," NSIAD-90-125BR, February 22, 1990, p. 2, https://www.gao.gov/products/nsiad-90-125br.
13. Jacoby, "JICPAC—Thinking Back," 2–3. For more on the closing of all Fleet Intelligence Centers (FIC) in 1991, see A. D. Baker, "Farewell to the FICs," *Naval Intelligence Professionals Quarterly* (January 1992).
14. Regarding the Joint Intelligence Center planning effort, see Jacoby, "JICPAC—Thinking Back," 4. Jacoby discussed being blamed for losing OSIS in an email exchange with the author, December 20, 2020. Brooks discussed the loss of the Soviet Navy threat and its impact on the OSIS system in an email exchange with the author, March 14, 2021.
15. Friedman, *Fifty-Year War*, chap. "Unexpected Victory."

16. There had also been a separate study performed by the General Defense Intelligence Program (GDIP) office; see J. R. Reddig, "The Creation of JIC-JAC," *Naval Intelligence Professionals Quarterly* (October 2001).
17. Litsinger was the PACFLT N2 from 1992 to 1995. Information Navy line communities' complaining about the quality of intelligence support from the Joint system and on FOSIF West Pacific (Kamiseya, Japan) becoming a detachment under JICPAC, preserving some OSIS capability, from Litsinger, email exchange with the author, April 15, 2021.
18. Jacoby, "JICPAC—Thinking Back," 8–12. On the requirements-based system's impact to fleet customers, see Reddig, "OSIS Culture," 16.
19. Ford and Rosenberg, *Admirals' Advantage*, 115.
20. Reddig quotes DNI Cramer on the lack of fleet support in "OSIS Culture," 15–16.
21. Regarding insights into the Israeli thinking on using electronic warfare at sea, see Abraham Rabinovich, "The Little-Known US-Soviet Confrontation During Yom Kippur War," The World from PRX, July 31, 2016, https://theworld.org/stories/2016/07/31/little-known-us-soviet-confrontation-during-yom-kippur-war.
22. Important for this study is the example of the sinking of the *Atlantic Conveyor* during the Falklands War. On May 25, 1982, Exocet anti-ship cruise missiles fired by Argentine Air Force Super Étendards were seduced by chaff dispensed by HMS *Ambuscade*. The missiles missed the *Ambuscade*, instead striking the unarmed *Conveyor*, which *Ambuscade* had been meant to protect. Douglas N. Hime, "The 1982 Falklands-Malvinas Case Study," NWC 1036, Joint Military Operations Department, Naval War College, Newport, RI, June 4, 2010, pp. 34–36.
23. For a deeper discussion on C2W, see Dan Struble, "What Is Command and Control Warfare?" *Naval War College Review* 48, no. 3 (Summer 1995): 89–98, https://www.jstor.org/stable/44642810.
24. For more on Boyd's concepts, see Fadok, "Quest for Strategic Paralysis." For Hughes' discussion of information warfare in naval warfare, see Hughes and Girrier, *Fleet Tactics*, chaps. 12 and 13.
25. Conrad Crane, "The United States Needs an Information Warfare Command: A Historical Examination," *War on the Rocks*, June 14, 2019, https://warontherocks.com/2019/06/the-united-states-needs-an-information-warfare-command-a-historical-examination/.
26. U.S. Department of the Army, "Information Operations," Field Manual no. (FM) 100-6, Headquarters, Washington, DC, August 27, 1996, pp. 1–9, archived online at https://archive.org/details/fm-100-6-information-operations-1996/mode/2up.

27. Roger C. Molander, Andrew Riddile, and Peter A. Wilson, "Strategic Information Warfare: A New Face of War" (RAND Corp., Santa Monica, CA, 1996), https://www.rand.org/pubs/monograph_reports/MR661.html; and see Zalmay M. Khalilzad and John Patrick White, eds., *Strategic Appraisal: The Changing Role of Information in Warfare*, fore. Andrew W. Marshall (Project Air Force, RAND Corp., Santa Monica, CA, 1999), available for download from https://www.rand.org/pubs/monograph_reports/MR1016.html.
28. Arthur K. Cebrowski and John H. Garstka, "Network-centric Warfare—Its Origin and Future," *Proceedings*, U.S. Naval Institute, 124, no. 1, 1,139 (January 1998), https://www.usni.org/magazines/proceedings/1998/january/network-centric-warfare-its-origin-and-future.
29. Cebrowski and Garstka.
30. Eileen F. MacKrell, "Network-centric Intelligence Works," *Proceedings*, U.S. Naval Institute, 129, no. 7, 1,205 (July 2003), https://www.usni.org/magazines/proceedings/2003/july/network-centric-intelligence-works.
31. The OpNav N2/N6 is the resource sponsor for 18xx designators.
32. David J. Dorsett, "The U.S. Navy's Vision for Information Dominance" (Department of the Navy, Chief of Naval Operations for Information Dominance, May 2010), https://apps.dtic.mil/sti/pdfs/ADA522185.pdf; Gary Roughead, "NAVADMIN 058/10 Information Dominance Corps Warfare Insignia," from Chief of Naval Operations to NAVADMIN, U.S. Navy NAVADMIN Library, February 10, 2010, https://navynavadmin.wordpress.com/2010/02/19/information-dominance-corps-warfare-insignia/.
33. Regarding the FID and FIAF process, see Bryan H. Leese, "Nobody Wants a Pacer! Reframe and Reassess the Fleet Intelligence Detachment Program Model," Naval Intelligence Professionals (website), April 19, 2016.
34. Dorsett, "U.S. Navy's Vision," 6, 3.
35. Cebrowski and Garstka, "Network-centric Warfare."
36. U.S. Navy, "Navy Strategy for Achieving Information Dominance 2013–2017: Optimizing Navy's Primacy in the Maritime and Information Domains," Office of the Deputy Chief of Naval Operations for Information Dominance, Washington, DC, 2011, archived online at https://archive.org/details/DTIC_ADA571217/. Regarding cross-detailing, for example, an intelligence officer (183x) might serve as the executive officer of a communication station. And see Henry Stephenson, "Masters or Jacks?" *Proceedings*, U.S. Naval Institute, 140, no. 10, 1,340 (October 2014), https://www.usni.org/magazines/proceedings/2014/october/masters-or-jacks.
37. Stephenson, "Masters or Jacks?"
38. William R. Bray, "Intelligence Is Not Warfare!" *Proceedings*, U.S. Naval Institute, 142, no. 12, 1,366 (December 2016), https://www.usni.org/magazines

/proceedings/2016/december/intelligence-not-warfare. Ted N. Branch, "The 'Information Dominance Corps' Is Now the 'Information Warfare Community,'" *CHIPS, the Department of the Navy's Information Technology Magazine* (January–March 2016), https://www.doncio.navy.mil/chips/ArticleDetails.aspx?ID=7307.

39. Branch, "Information Dominance Corps." For more on the functions of the new IWC, see Richard Mosier, "Navy Information Warfare—What Is It?" *Center for International Maritime Security* (blog), September 13, 2016, https://cimsec.org/navy-information-warfare/.

40. Mark Milley, "Joint Maritime Operations," Joint Publication (JP) 3-32, Change 1, chairman, Joint Chiefs of Staff, December 16, 2020, U.S. Space force and U.S. Department of the Air Force, p. xii, https://irp.fas.org/doddir/dod/jp3_32.pdf.

41. Jacky Fisher, "IW Has a Seat at the Table: Information Warfare Commanders Harness IW Disciplines," Naval Information Forces (NAVIFOR), October 20, 2020, https://www.doncio.navy.mil/CHIPS/ArticleDetails.aspx?ID=14000.

42. Bryan Braswell, "Evolving the Information Warfare Commander," *CHIPS, the Department of the Navy's Information Technology Magazine* (July–September 2017), https://www.doncio.navy.mil/chips/ArticleDetails.aspx?ID=9422.

43. One of the best examples of the debate is Henry Stephenson, "Navy Information Warfare: A Decade of Indulging a False Analogy," *Proceedings*, U.S. Naval Institute, 145, no. 1, 1,391 (January 2019), https://www.usni.org/magazines/proceedings/2019/january/navy-information-warfare-decade-indulging-false-analogy. Another example is William R. Bray, "Information Warfare Should Embrace Dissent," *Proceedings*, U.S. Naval Institute, 143, no. 11, 1,377 (November 2017), https://www.usni.org/magazines/proceedings/2017/november/information-warfare-should-embrace-dissent.

44. Stephenson, "Navy Information Warfare."

45. For a discussion of the functions, tasks, and purpose supporting the new IWCmdr's role of head of the afloat IW organization, see Mosier, "Navy Information Warfare."

46. See U.S. Congress, 10 U.S.C. (Armed Forces), Subtitle C (Navy and Marine Corps), Part II (Personnel), Ch. 815 (Original Appointments), §8137 (Regular Navy), enacted by act of Congress August 10, 1956, section repealed January 1, 2021, https://uscode.house.gov/view.xhtml?path=/prelim@title10/subtitleC&edition=prelim.

47. Roland J. Yardley et al., "OPNAV N14 Quick Reference: Officer Manpower and Personnel Governance in the U.S. Navy; Law, Policy, and Practice, Technical Report," primer, with Samantha J. Merck (National Defense Research

Institute, RAND Corporation, Santa Monica, CA, 2005), vii, https://www.rand.org/content/dam/rand/pubs/technical_reports/2005/RAND_TR264.pdf.

48. Richard V. Spencer, "Officer Competitive Categories for the Active Duty List of the Navy and Marine Corps," SecNav Instruction (SECNAVINST) 1400.1C, secretary of the Navy, U.S. Department of the Navy, April 5, 2019, pp. 2–3, https://www.secnav.navy.mil/doni/Directives/01000%20Military%20Personnel%20Support/01-400%20Promotion%20and%20Advancement%20Programs/1400.1C.pdf.
49. Chris Argyris' work as discussed in Senge, *Fifth Discipline*, 232–40.
50. OpNav staff members in conversation with the author, January 26, 2022.
51. Vego, *Joint Operational Warfare*, XII-14 and -15.
52. Vego, XII-13.
53. Vego, XII-13.
54. Senge, *Fifth Discipline*, 209–15.
55. Carlos Del Toro, "U.S. Navy Regulations, 1990 Interim Change (Corrected Copy)," ALNAV 094/24, Secretary of the Navy, December 18, 2024. https://www.mynavyhr.navy.mil/Portals/55/Messages/ALNAV/ALN2024/ALN24094.txt?ver=FRs4Dgr--DHkM35IF_daUw%3d%3d.
56. Vernazza as quoted in "Information Warfare Community Changes Status: No Longer Restricted Line," News, Naval Intelligence Professionals, NavIntPro.org, December 20, 2024, https://www.navintpro.org/news/2024/12/20/Change-in-Status-for-Information-Warfare-Community/.

Conclusion

1. Hone, *Learning War*, 6–9.
2. Rufus Taylor, forty-third director of Naval Intelligence, shares the story of a run-in with Secretary of the Navy Paul Nitze in 1967. Nitze wanted more intelligence on a subject, but there was no more to give. Taylor then told the angry Nitze, "You'll just have to make the decision on your own, because that's the last step in the intel process. You hear what the intel people have to say, and then you decide what it all means. Now, you are exercising the final command function in intelligence." Rufus Taylor, "The Security of Intelligence—an Oral History," transcript of oral history of Vice Admiral Rufus L. Taylor, USN, circa 1985, pp. 17–18, box 1 of 2, Manthorpe Archive, Office of Naval Intelligence National Intelligence Maritime Center, Suitland, MD.

SELECTED BIBLIOGRAPHY

Selected Interviews

Brooks, Thomas A., Rear Admiral, USN (Ret.), b. *1937*, Intelligence Officer (1630), served 1958–1991. Interviews and email correspondence. Navy tours included: DNI 1988–1991; Amphibious Group 3; NISO Vietnam; N2, COMSECONDFLT; Assistant Naval Attaché, Turkey; FOSIC CINCLANTFLT; NFOIO; J-2, CINCLANT; and J-2, Joint Chiefs of Staff.

Cothron, Tony L., Rear Admiral, USN (Ret.), b. *1955*, Intelligence Officer (1630), served 1978–2008. Interview and correspondence. Navy tours included: DNI 2006–2008; USS *America*; FOSIC Det, Atlantic Fleet; Fleet Intelligence Training Center Atlantic; Navy Opintel Center (NAVOPINTCEN), Director, Fleet Intelligence, Fleet Forces Command.

Donald, Miskill, Captain, USN (Ret.), b. *1948*, Pilot (1310), served 1970–1995. Interviews and correspondence. Navy tours included: VP-50; V-2 Division, USS *America* (CV 66); Commanding Officer, VP-11.

Durr, Donald G., Captain, USN (Ret.), b. *1942*, Ground Officer, Intelligence (1350), converted to Intelligence Officer (1630), served 1964–1987. Interviews and correspondence. Navy tours included: Seven aircraft carrier deployments, including USS *Kitty Hawk*.

Giacchino, Louis F., Captain, USN (Ret.), b. *1934*, Cryptology Officer (1610), served 1956–1986. Interview and mail correspondence. Navy tours included: Sixth Fleet, 1967–1969; VQ-2, Rota, Spain; U.S. Naval Communications Facility Nicosia, Cyprus; and Naval Security Group, Puerto Rico.

Hartford, Robin W., PH3, USN, *1953–2021*, Photographers Mate, Third Class Petty Officer (PH3), USN, served 1972–1976. Interviews and correspondence. Navy tour in USS *Saratoga*.

Inman, Bobby R., Admiral, USN (Ret.), b. *1931*, Surface Line Officer (1110), converted to Intelligence Officer (1630), served 1950–1982. Interviews and correspondence. Navy tours included: DNI, 1974–July 1976; Vice Director, DIA; Director, NSA; and Deputy Director, CIA.

Jacoby, Lowell E. "Jake," Vice Admiral, USN (Ret.), b. *1945*, Intelligence Officer (1630), served 1969–2006. Interviews and correspondence. Navy tours included: DNI, 1997–1999; Director, DIA; VF-24; Seventh Fleet Detachment Charlie, Saigon, Vietnam; CNO Intelligence Plot, Washington, DC; N2 Second Fleet; NFOIO; N2, Carrier Group Eight; and JIC Pacific, Hawaiʻi.

Lasko, Paul G., Captain, USN (Ret.), *b. 1936*, Ground Officer, Intelligence (1350), converted to Intelligence Officer (1630), served 1960–1985. Interviews and correspondence. Navy tours included: N2, Carrier Group Eight; Assistant Attaché, USSR; N2, Atlantic Fleet Tactical Training Group N2; and CO of the Naval and Marine Corps Intelligence Training Center.

Leatherman, Nolan H., *b. 1936*, contracting officer for North American Aviation (NAA), 1960s–1980s. Interviews and correspondence.

Litsinger, Nelson H. "Nels," Captain, USN (Ret.), *b. 1947*, Intelligence Officer (1630), served 1968–1998. Interviews and correspondence. Navy tours included: VF-154; FOSIF Rota, Spain; CAGAI, Carrier Air Wing Three; SIO, USS *Dwight D. Eisenhower*; and DIA.

Noble, Richard A., Captain, USN (Ret.), *b. 1938*, Surface Line Officer (1110), converted to Intelligence Officer (1630), served 1961–1992. Correspondence. Navy tours included: USS *Sterett* (DLG-31); Assistant Naval Attaché, Pakistan; FOSIC Pacific, Hawai'i; PACFLT; CINCPAC; N2, Cruiser Destroyer Group Twelve; and Commanding Officer, Navy AFAITC, Denver, Colorado.

Ore, William E. "Rock," Captain, USN (Ret.), *b. 1933*, Ground Officer, Intelligence (1350), converted to Intelligence Officer (1630), served 1957–1987. Interviews. Navy tours included: VA-113, USS *Forrestal*, DIA, and others.

Perras, Wayne, Captain, USN (Ret.), *b. 1938*, Intelligence Officer (1630), served 1968–1998. Interview and correspondence. Navy tours included: RVAH-6; instructor at AFAITC, Denver, Colorado; FOSIC Pacific, Hawai'i; N2, Carrier Group One; Naval Forces Central Command (TF-157).

Powers, Bruce F., *b. 1939*. Interview and correspondence. Analyst and Department Director, Center for Naval Analyses, 1961–1978; various Defense and Military Operations Research analyst and adjunct professor, 1979–present.

Reddig, James "J. R.," Captain, USN (Ret.) (aka Vic Socotra), *b. 1951*. Intelligence Officer (1630), served 1977–2003. Correspondence. Navy tours included: Squadron, Air Wing, and as a numbered Fleet Intelligence Officer; FOSIF Rota, Spain; FOSIC Pacific, Hawai'i; Intelligence Officer Junior Officer Detailer; and Joint Chief of Staff, J2.

Rondeau, Ann E., Vice Admiral, USN (Ret.), *b. 1951*, Surface Line Officer (1110), served 1974–2012. Interview and correspondence. Navy tours included: PACFLT staff; AI, VP-50, CO, Naval Support Activity, La Maddalena, Italy, and at Naval Support Activity Mid-South in Millington, Tennessee; Commander of Naval Training Center Great Lakes, Illinois; Commander of Naval Service Training Command; and President, Naval Postgraduate School.

Soriano, Joseph R., Captain, USN (Ret.), *b. 1932*, Ground Officer, Intelligence (1350), converted to Intelligence Officer (1630), served 1955–1982. Interview and correspondence. Navy tours included: SIO, USS *Saratoga*; CINC Pacific Fleet staff; and Officer in Charge, FICPACFAC, Republic of the Philippines.

Swartz, Peter M., Captain, USN (Ret.), *b. 1942*, Surface Line Officer (1120), served 1965–1992. Interviews and correspondence. Navy tours included: NILO, An Thớ'i, Vietnam; instructor, Naval Amphibious School; BuPers Human Resources; Strategy, Plans, and Policy for CNOs Zumwalt, Holloway, and Heyward and for SecNav John Lehman.

Terlizzi, Thomas P., Commander, USN (Ret.), *b. 1948*, Enlisted Quartermaster Petty Officer Second Class (QM2(SS)), commissioned as Intelligence Officer (1630) in 1970, served 1965–1993. Correspondence. Navy tours included: USS *Independence*; Fleet Intelligence Center Europe/Atlantic, Norfolk, Virginia; CNO Intelligence Plot, Washington, DC; and SIO, USS *America*.

Thompson, Dale P., Commander, USNR (Ret.), *b. 1948*, Intelligence Officer (1635), served 1973–1995. Interview and correspondence. Navy tours included: AI, VP-50; Watch Officer, FOSIC PAC; Watch Officer, CNO-IP; and Watch Officer, Naval Ocean Surveillance Information Center (NOSIC), Suitland, MD.

Tolle, Robert J., Captain, USN (Ret.), *1936–2019*, Ground Officer, Intelligence (1350), converted to Intelligence Officer (1630), served 1960–1987. Interview and correspondence. Navy tours included: RVAH-NINE; Sixth Fleet staff; NOSIC, Suitland, Maryland; FICPAC, Hawai'i; and Executive Assistant to the DNI.

Tonkli, Mario, IS2, USN, *b. 1953*, Photographic Intelligenceman (PT), converted to Intelligence Specialist Second Class Petty Officer (IS2), USN, 1972–1978. Email correspondence. Navy tour with VA-75.

Vego, Milan N., *b. circa 1940*, served in the Yugoslav Navy (1961–1973) and Third and Second Mate (Deck) in West German commercial ships (1973–1976). Interview and email correspondence. Professor, U.S. Naval War College. Dr. Vego is an expert on operational art, maritime operations, and naval warfare.

Wessman, Lynn G., Captain, USN (Ret.), *b. 1950*, Submarine Officer (1130), served 1971–2001. Correspondence. Navy tours included: SUBGRU 8, Naples, Italy; multiple tours on submarines, including command; and Deputy Commander of Submarine Squadron 8, Norfolk, Virginia.

Willoz, Clifford P., Commander, USN (Ret.), *b. 1940*, Surface Line Officer (1110), served 1962–1982. Email correspondence. Navy tours included: OpNav OP92U, Naval Intelligence Command–Applications Department (NIC-AD); CINCLANT Fleet staff; Cruiser Destroyer Flotilla 6 staff; tours in several combatants, including command of USS *Coontz* (DDG-40).

Books, Articles, and Transcripts

Abbot, Charles S. Command history 1990 of USS *Theodore Roosevelt* (CVN 71). From the Commanding Officer to the Director of Naval History, OPNAV 5750/1,

February 27, 1991. Navy History and Heritage Command, https://www.history.navy.mil/content/dam/nhhc/research/archives/command-operation-reports/ship-command-operation-reports/t/theodore-roosevelt-cvn-71-i/1990.pdf.

Adams, Jefferson. *Strategic Intelligence in the Cold War and Beyond.* The Making of the Contemporary World. New York: Routledge, 2015.

Aid, Matthew M. *The Secret Sentry: The Untold History of the National Security Agency.* New York: Bloomsbury Publishing, 2009.

Allen, Deane J., and Brian G. Shellum, eds. *Defense Intelligence Agency: At the Creation, 1961–1965.* Washington, DC: DIA History Office, 2002. https://archive.org/details/DTIC_ADA578664.

Altman, Robert, dir. *Gosford Park.* Written by Julian Fellowes. UK, USA, IT: USA Films, Capitol Films, The Film Council, Sandcastle 5 Productions, Chicagofilms, Medusa Film, 2001. 137 min.

American Forces Press Service. "Operation Homecoming for Vietnam POWs Marks 40 Years." U.S. Air Force, AF.mil, February 12, 2013. https://www.af.mil/News/Article-Display/Article/109716/operation-homecoming-for-vietnam-pows-marks-40-years/https%3A%2F%2Fwww.af.mil%2FNews%2FArticle-Display%2FArticle%2F109716%2Foperation-homecoming-for-vietnam-pows-marks-40-years%2F.

Anderson, Rod. "IOIC-IOIS—The Logbook." Accessed April 15, 2019. https://sites.google.com/site/50yearsagointheflightlog/main-1/flying-the-ra-5c/ioic-iois.

Andrew, Christopher M., and Oleg Gordievsky. *KGB: The Inside Story of Its Foreign Operations from Lenin to Gorbachev.* 1st ed. New York: Harper Collins, 1990.

AP Television. "NATO Wargames." Television broadcast, aired in West Germany, Poland, the North Atlantic, and Norway, 9:00 p.m., September 30, 1976, 12:35. RR7639B, https://newsroom.ap.org/editorial-photos-videos/detail?itemid=0c416b97a0bad6b717b2c2e2b4231769&mediatype=video&source=youtube.

Arkin, William M., and Joshua Handler. "Naval Accidents, 1945–1988." Neptune Paper no. 3. Greenpeace/Institute for Policy Studies, Washington, DC, June 1989. Archived online at https://web.archive.org/web/20230308153409/https://uploads.fas.org/2014/05/NavalAccidents1945-1988.pdf.

Atkinson, Simon Reay, and James Moffat. *The Agile Organisation: From Informal Networks to Complex Effects and Agility.* Information Age Transformation Series. Washington, DC: CCRP Publications, 2005.

Ault, Frank. "Report of the Air-to-Air Missile System Capability Review, July–November 1968 (The Ault Report)." Naval Air Systems Command, U.S. Navy, Washington, DC, January 1, 1969. Archived online by the Naval History and Heritage Command at https://www.history.navy.mil/content/history/nhhc/research/histories/naval-aviation-history/ault-report.html.

Ausubel, Nathan, ed. *A Treasury of Jewish Folklore.* Abridged ed. New York: Bantam, 1980.

Bacevich, Andrew J. *The New American Militarism: How Americans Are Seduced by War*. New York: Oxford University Press, 2005.

Baker, A. D. "Farewell to the FICs." *Naval Intelligence Professionals Quarterly* (January 1992).

Barnett, Roger W. *Navy Strategic Culture: Why the Navy Thinks Differently*. Annapolis, MD: Naval Institute Press, 2009.

Bartholomees, J. Boone, Jr. "Intelligence as a Tool of Strategy." In *U.S. Army War College Guide to National Security Issues*, 5th ed., 253–77. Carlisle, PA: Strategic Studies Institute, U.S. Army War College, 2012.

Bartholomew, J. H. "Review of Occupational Standards for the Intelligence Specialist Rating; Request For." Naval Intelligence Command, October 26, 1977. Record group RG 24 (Records of the Bureau of Naval Personnel), NAID 6282768, HMS Record Entry ID 156557, HMS/MLR Entry Number A1 1022, case files relating to Navy ratings 1945–1978, box 26 (IC–IS), National Archives II, College Park, MD.

Bernard, Richard L. "Telemetry Intelligence (TELINT) During the Cold War." National Security Agency Center for Cryptologic History, Fort Meade, MD, 2016. https://www.nsa.gov/portals/75/documents/about/cryptologic-heritage/historical-figures-publications/publications/misc/telint-9-19-2016.pdf.

Bernays, Edward L. "Edward L. Bernays Beech Nut Packing Co." Interview, interviewer unknown, Cambridge, MA, date of interview unknown. Posted June 13, 2016, by the Museum of Public Relations, YouTube video, 2:44, https://www.youtube.com/watch?v=OI-pO-o-yqI.

BDM Corporation. *A Study of Strategic Lessons Learned in Vietnam*, vol. 6, *Conduct of the War*, book 1, *Operational Analyses*, and book 2, *Functional Analyses*. McLean, VA: BDM Corporation, 1980. Archived online at https://archive.org/details/DTIC_ADA096429 and https://documents.theblackvault.com/documents/vietnam/ADA096430.pdf.

Berman, Larry. *Zumwalt: The Life and Times of Admiral Elmo Russell "Bud" Zumwalt, Jr.* 1st ed. New York: Harper, 2012.

Bixler, M., ed. *USS Kitty Hawk (CVA 63) WestPac Cruise Book 1973–74*. N.p.: Pischel Yearbooks, n.d. Archived online at https://www.navysite.de/cruisebooks/cv63-73/index.html.

Bochanneck, Alex. "If It Moves, It Should Be Ruggednova." *CHM Blog*, Computer History Museum, December 4, 2012. https://computerhistory.org/blog/if-it-moves-it-should-be-ruggednova/.

Bodnar, John W. "The Military Technical Revolution: From Hardware to Information." *Naval War College Review* 46, no. 3 (1993): 7–21.

Boehm, Joshua. "A History of the United States National Security Space Management and Organization." With Craig Baker, Stanley Chan, and Mel Sakazaki.

Commission to Assess United States National Security Space Management and Organization, January 11, 2001. https://spp.fas.org/eprint/article03.html.

Bolger, Daniel P. *Americans at War, 1975–1986: An Era of Violent Peace*. Novato, CA: Presidio, 1988.

Borgerson, Mark. *The SECGRU Years: Five Years in the Naval Security Group*. USA: privately published, 2019.

Boroughs, Don. *The Story of CNA: Civilian Scientists in War and Peace*. Arlington, VA: Center for Naval Analyses, 2017.

Boslaugh, David L. *First-Hand: No Damned Computer Is Going to Tell Me What to Do; The Story of the Naval Tactical Data System, NTDS*. eBook. N.p.: n.p., revised April 12, 2017. https://ethw.org/w/index.php?title=First-Hand:No_Damned_Computer_is_Going_to_Tell_Me_What_to_DO_-_The_Story_of_the_Naval_Tactical_Data_System,_NTDS&oldid=154739.

Bouchard, Joseph F. *Command in Crisis: Four Case Studies*. New York: Columbia University Press, 1991.

Boyne, Walter J. "MiG Sweep." *Air Force Magazine*, November 1, 1998, https://www.airandspaceforces.com/article/1198sweep/.

Branch, Ted N. "The 'Information Dominance Corps' Is Now the 'Information Warfare Community.'" *CHIPS, The Department of the Navy's Information Technology Magazine* (January–March 2016). https://www.doncio.navy.mil/chips/ArticleDetails.aspx?ID=7307.

Braswell, Bryan. "Evolving the Information Warfare Commander." *CHIPS, The Department of the Navy's Information Technology Magazine* (July–September 2017). https://www.doncio.navy.mil/chips/ArticleDetails.aspx?ID=9422.

Bray, [William R.] "Information Warfare Should Embrace Dissent." *Proceedings*, U.S. Naval Institute, 143, no. 11, 1,377 (November 2017). https://www.usni.org/magazines/proceedings/2017/november/information-warfare-should-embrace-dissent.

———. "Intelligence Is Not Warfare!" *Proceedings*, U.S. Naval Institute, 142, no. 12, 1,366 (December 2016). https://www.usni.org/magazines/proceedings/2016/december/intelligence-not-warfare.

Brittingham, Edward M. *Sub Chaser: The Story of a Navy VP NFO; A Chronicle of the Development of Anti-submarine Techniques by U.S. Naval Aviation Patrol Planes in the Atlantic Ocean and Mediterranean Sea During the Cold War Era, 1962–1985*. Richmond, VA: ASW Press, 2004.

Brooks, Thomas A., and William Manthorpe. "History of the Air Intelligence Community." *Naval Intelligence Professionals Quarterly* (October 2002).

———. "NIS in Vietnam." *Naval Intelligence Professionals Quarterly* (January 1992): 3–6. Archived online at https://ncisahistory.org/wp-content/uploads/2021/09/NIS-in-Vietnam.pdf.

———. "Setting the Record Straight: A Critical Review of *Fall from Glory* by Gregory I. Vistica." *Naval Intelligence Professionals Quarterly* (April 1996). Repr. *The Submarine Review*, Naval Submarine League (July 1996): 60–65. Archived online at https://s36124.pcdn.co/wp-content/uploads/2021/09/1996-July-OCRw.pdf.

Brown, Shannon A., ed. "Providing the Means of War." U.S. Army Center of Military History and Industrial College of the Armed Forces, Washington, DC, 2005. https://www.history.army.mil/html/books/070/70-87-1/CMH_Pub_70-87-1.pdf.

Bureau of Naval Personnel, U.S. Department of the Navy. *Basic Military Requirements*. Navy Training Courses, NAVPERS 10054. Washington, DC: U.S. Government Printing Office, 1957. Archived online at http://hdl.handle.net/2027/uiug.30112098015719.

———. "Basic Test Battery Helps Determine Navyman's Future." *All Hands*, no. 431 (January 1953): 48–54. https://media.defense.gov/2019/Apr/27/2002122133/-1/-1/1/ah195301.pdf.

———. "Intelligence Assignment and Placement." *Naval Intelligence Newsletter*, various issues, 1960–1980. Personal papers of Rear Admiral Thomas A. Brooks, Arlington, VA.

———. *Personnel Management*. NAVPERS 10848-E. Rev. ed. Washington, DC: U.S. Government Printing Office, 1971. Archived online at http://hdl.handle.net/2027/uc1.d0002280634.

———. *Photographer's Mate 3 & 2*. Rate Training Manual, NAVPERS 10355-A. Washington, DC: Bureau of Naval Personnel, 1972. https://books.google.com/books?id=3-sRsGu4-NwC&pg=PA1&dq=Kodak+Color+Aerial+Film+Processor+EH73&source=gbs_toc_r&cad=2#v=onepage&q&f=false.

———. *Shipboard Electrical Systems*. Major revision, NAVPERS 10864-B. Washington, DC: Bureau of Naval Personnel, 1966.

———. "TraLant: Atlantic Fleet University." *All Hands*, no. 626 (March 1969): 25–35. https://media.defense.gov/2019/Jul/25/2002162322/-1/-1/1/AH196903.PDF.

Bureau of Ships, U.S. Navy. "USS *Constellation* (CVA-64); 120 Day Letter for Authorized Alterations." Work order, letter, January 4, 1965. Archived in record group RG-19, box 113, entry P40, National Archives II, College Park, MD.

Burke, Arleigh. "Views on Adequacy of U.S. Deterrent/Retaliatory Forces as Related to General and Limited War Capabilities." Memorandum. March 4, 1959. Department of the Navy, Office of the Chief of Naval Operations. Navy Archives, Flag Officers "Dope," CNO Personal Newsletter and Memorandum #44-49 May–June 1959. National Security Archives. https://nsarchive2.gwu.edu/nukevault/ebb275/07.pdf.

Burr, William, ed. "'How Much Is Enough?': The U.S. Navy and 'Finite Deterrence'; A Moment in Cold War History When the Fundamentals of the U.S. Nuclear

Posture Were at Stake." *The Nuclear Vault*, National Security Archive Electronic Briefing Book no. 275, May 1, 2009. https://nsarchive2.gwu.edu/nukevault/ebb275/index.htm.

Butts, J. L. USS *Kitty Hawk* (CVA-63), Aviation Historical Summary, March 31–September 30, 1964. https://www.history.navy.mil/content/dam/nhhc/research/archives/command-operation-reports/ship-command-operation-reports/k/kitty-hawk-cv-63-ii/m64-s64.pdf.

Cagle, Malcolm W. "Task Force 77 in Action Off Vietnam." *Proceedings*, U.S. Naval Institute, 98, no. 5, 831 (May 1972): 66ff. https://www.usni.org/magazines/proceedings/1972/may/task-force-77-action-vietnam.

Cahill, William. "Strategic Air Command SIGINT Support to the Vietnam War." *Air Power History* 66, no. 4 (Winter 2019): 29–42. https://www.jstor.org/stable/26837699 (paywall).

Cain, Frank. "Computers and the Cold War: United States Restrictions on the Export of Computers to the Soviet Union and Communist China." *Journal of Contemporary History* 40, no. 1 (2005): 131–47. http://www.jstor.org/stable/30036313.

Campbell, Douglas E. *Flight, Camera, Action! The History of U.S. Naval Aviation Photography and Photo-Reconnaissance.* [Washington, DC]: Syneca Research Group, 2014.

Cano, Ruddy. "How Naval Aviator Charles Klusmann Escaped a Vicious POW Camp." *We Are the Mighty* (website), last updated September 22, 2022. https://www.wearethemighty.com/mighty-history/how-naval-aviator-charles-klusmann-escaped-a-vicious-pow-camp/.

Carlson, Elliot. *Joe Rochefort's War: The Odyssey of the Codebreaker Who Outwitted Yamamoto at Midway.* Annapolis, MD: Naval Institute Press, 2011.

Casey, William J. "Soviet Goals and Expectations in the Global Power Arena." National Intelligence Estimate NIE 11-4-78, director of the Central Intelligence Agency, July 7, 1981. CIA Historical Review Program, https://www.cia.gov/readingroom/docs/DOC_0000268220.pdf.

Cebrowski, Arthur K., and John H. Garstka. "Network-centric Warfare—Its Origin and Future." *Proceedings*, U.S. Naval Institute, 124, no. 1, 1,139 (January 1998). https://www.usni.org/magazines/proceedings/1998/january/network-centric-warfare-its-origin-and-future.

Central Intelligence Agency. "Consequences of U.S. Troop Withdrawal from Korea in Spring, 1949." ORE 3-49, February 28, 1949. https://www.cia.gov/readingroom/docs/DOC_0000258388.pdf.

———. "Current Capabilities of the Northern Korea Regime." ORE 18-50, June 19, 1950. https://www.cia.gov/readingroom/docs/DOC_0000258828.pdf.

Central Intelligence Agency, Office of Research and Reports. "Annex 8 of Soviet Bloc Land Radar Equipment in Cuba as of October 1960: Electronics Facilities in Cuba." CIA/RR EP 60-73-S8, November 1960. CIA FOIA Electronic Reading Room, https://www.cia.gov/readingroom/docs/DOC_0000493869.pdf.

Channell, Norm. "Naval Intelligence in South Viet Nam." *Naval Intelligence Professionals Quarterly* (June 2004).

Chatham, Walter Lewis. Command History 1978 of USS *Kitty Hawk* (C V-63). From the Commanding Officer to the Chief of Naval Operations, OPNAVINST 5850.12, February 17, 1979. Naval History and Heritage Command. https://www.history.navy.mil/content/dam/nhhc/research/archives/command-operation-reports/ship-command-operation-reports/k/kitty-hawk-cv-63-ii/1978.pdf.

Cheevers, Jack. *Act of War: Lyndon Johnson, North Korea, and the Capture of the Spy Ship Pueblo*. New York: NAL Caliber, 2013.

Chief of Naval Operations, U.S. Department of the Navy. "Memo for VCNO, Establishment of the Office of Command Support Programs, OP-094." Organizational review, OP-09B, February 26, 1971. Immediate Office Files of the Chief of Naval Operations, 1971, box 4, series vii (OP-9B, Director of Naval Administration, 1968–1993), Archives Branch, Naval History and Heritage Command, Washington, DC.

Chisholm, Donald W. *Coordination Without Hierarchy: Informal Structures in Multiorganizational Systems*. Berkeley: University of California Press, 1989.

———. "Naval Personnel Since 1945: Areas for Historical Research." February 12, 2018. Archived at the Navy Department Library, Naval History and Heritage Command. https://www.history.navy.mil/research/library/online-reading-room/title-list-alphabetically/n/needs-opportunities-modern-history-us-navy/naval-personnel-since-1945-areas-for-historical-research-1.html.

Christon, Lawrence. "Tales of Jay Ward and the Bullwinkle Gang: How the Subversive Silliness of Rocky and Bullwinkle Sprang into Our Living Rooms." *Los Angeles Times*, November 13, 1988. https://www.latimes.com/archives/la-xpm-1988-11-13-ca-447-story.html.

Clarity, James F. "Soviet Exercises Seek to Prove Navy's Readiness." *New York Times*, April 15, 1970. https://www.nytimes.com/1970/04/15/archives/soviet-exercises-seek-to-prove-navys-readiness.html.

Collier, Stephen J., and Andrew Lakoff. "The Bombing Encyclopedia of the World." In "The Total Archive," ed. Boris Jardine and Christopher M. Kelty, *Limn*, no. 6 (March 2016). https://doi.org/10.70312/LIMN.

Collins, Helen F. "Women in Naval Aviation: From Plane Captains to Pilot." *Naval Aviation News* (July 1977): 8–18. https://www.history.navy.mil/content/dam/nhhc/research/histories/naval-aviation/Naval%20Aviation%20News/1970/pdf/jul77.pdf.

Commander Carrier Division 6. "CV Evaluation Final Report." November 23, 1971. Archived in record group RG-18, box 19, folder 2, "Management, 1972–1973."

Naval War College Archives, U.S. Naval War College, Newport, RI. https://www.usnwcarchives.org/repositories/2/archival_objects/49268.

Correll, John T. "Against the MiGs in Vietnam." *Air and Space Forces Magazine*, October 1, 2019. https://www.airandspaceforces.com/article/against-the-migs-in-vietnam/.

Cosmas, Graham A. *The Joint Chiefs of Staff and the War in Vietnam, 1960–1968, Part 2*. Vol. 2 of 3. History of the Joint Chiefs of Staff. Washington, DC: Office of Joint History, Office of the Chairman of the Joint Chiefs of Staff, 2012. https://www.jcs.mil/Portals/36/Documents/History/Vietnam/Vietnam_1960-1968_P002.pdf.

Coye, Beth F. "The Restricted Unrestricted Line Officer: The Status of the Navy's Woman Line Officer." *Naval War College Review* 24, no. 7 (March 1972): 53–64. https://www.jstor.org/stable/44641297.

Cracknell, William H. "The Role of the U.S. Navy in Inshore Waters." Student paper, Naval War College, 1968. Record group RG-13, file N420.F82 1968 no. 94, box 280, folder 7, Naval War College Archives Repository. https://usnwcarchives.org/repositories/2/archival_objects/206111.

———. Unpublished transcript of interview of William H. Cracknell, conducted by A. D. Baker, circa 2000. Tape 1, Manthorpe Collection, Office of Naval Intelligence, National Intelligence Maritime Center, Suitland, MD.

Crane, Conrad. "The United States Needs an Information Warfare Command: A Historical Examination." *War on the Rocks*, June 14, 2019. https://warontherocks.com/2019/06/the-united-states-needs-an-information-warfare-command-a-historical-examination/.

Crew of Fleet Air Reconnaissance Two (VQ-2). *VQ-2 Rota Spain Cruise Book, 1973–1974*. Marceline, MO: Walsworth Publishing, 1974. https://vqassociation.org/history-docs/00eee%20Rota%20Spain%20VQ-2%20Book.pdf.

Crissy, William J. E. Review of *The Changing Culture of a Factory*, by Elliott Jaques. *Psychological Bulletin* 50, no. 1 (January 1953): 66–67. https://doi.org/10.1037/h0051516.

Cryptolog. "IronHorse: A Tactical SIGINT System." Vol. 2, no. 10 (October 1975): 24–26. Archived online at the National Security Archive. https://www.nsa.gov/portals/75/documents/news-features/declassified-documents/cryptologs/cryptolog_13.pdf.

Cukor, Drew. "Operate to Know: An Operations and Intelligence Design for the Operational Level of War." Master's thesis, U.S. Joint Command and Staff College, 2014. https://apps.dtic.mil/sti/pdfs/ADA600189.pdf.

Cullison, M. D. "Occupational Analysis of Photographic Intelligenceman (PT) and Related NECs." Special Report. Naval Personnel Research and Development Laboratory, Bureau of Naval Personnel, Washington, DC, June 1973. https://apps.dtic.mil/sti/tr/pdf/ADA014488.pdf.

Cushman, John H., Jr. "Congress Endorses Military Overhaul." *New York Times*, September 18, 1986, sec. A. https://www.nytimes.com/1986/09/18/us/congress-endorses-military-overhaul.html.

Cutler, Thomas J. *Brown Water, Black Berets: Coastal and Riverine Warfare in Vietnam*. Annapolis, MD: Naval Institute Press, 2012. Archived online at https://www.google.com/books/edition/Brown_Water_Black_Berets/mlQJrG0EASAC?hl=en&gbpv=1&dq=study+by+the+BDM+Corporation+Market+Time+vietnam&pg=PA383&printsec=frontcover.

Davidson, Janine. *Lifting the Fog of Peace: How Americans Learned to Fight Modern War*. Ann Arbor: University of Michigan Press, 2011.

Davison, "Dog," ed. *USS Forrestal (CVA 59) Vietnam Cruise Book 1967*. Marceline, MO: Walsworth, n.d. Archived online at https://www.navysite.de/cruisebooks/cv59-67/index.html.

Day, Dwayne A. "Above the Clouds: The White Cloud Ocean Surveillance Satellites." *The Space Review*, April 13, 2009. https://www.thespacereview.com/article/1351/1.

———. "From the Sky to the Mud: TENCAP and Adapting National Reconnaissance Systems to Tactical Operations." *The Space Review*, June 19, 2023. https://www.thespacereview.com/article/4606/1.

Deeney, John J., IV. "Finding, Fixing, and Finishing the Guideline: The Development of the United States Air Force Surface-to-Air Missile Suppression Force During Operation Rolling Thunder." Master's thesis, US Army Command and General Staff College, 2010. https://apps.dtic.mil/sti/pdfs/ADA524369.pdf.

Defense Advanced Research Projects Agency (DARPA). "Innovation Timeline." DARPA.mil, accessed August 25, 2020, https://www.darpa.mil/about/innovation-timeline.

Del Toro, Carlos. "U.S. Navy Regulations, 1990 Interim Change (Corrected Copy)." ALNAV 094/24, Secretary of the Navy, December 18, 2024. https://www.mynavyhr.navy.mil/Portals/55/Messages/ALNAV/ALN2024/ALN24094.txt?ver=FRs4Dgr--DHkM35IF_daUw%3d%3d.

Dempsey, Martin E. "Doctrine for the Armed Forces of the United States." Joint Publication (JP) 1, chairman, Joint Chiefs of Staff, July 12, 2017. https://irp.fas.org/doddir/dod/jp1.pdf.

———. "Joint Intelligence." Joint Publication (JP) 2-0, doctrine for the Armed Forces of the United States, chairman, Joint Chiefs of Staff, Washington, DC, October 22, 2013. Archived online at https://irp.fas.org/doddir/dod/jp2_0.pdf.

———. "Joint Planning." Joint Publication (JP) 5-0, chairman, Joint Chiefs of Staff, June 16, 2017. Archived online at https://www.airforcespecialtactics.af.mil/Portals/80/Joint%20Pub%20JPUB%205-0%20Joint%20Planning.pdf.

Denfeld, Louis E. "Naval Intelligence Manual (1949)." ONI 19B, Director of Naval Intelligence, Office of the Chief of Naval Operations, U.S. Department of the Navy,

May 1949 (updated 1952). Archived online at https://ncisahistory.org/wp-content/uploads/2017/06/ONI-19B-Naval-Intelligence-Manual-June-1949.pdf.

DiGirolamo, Vinny, ed. and comp. *Naval Command and Control: Policy, Programs, People and Issues.* Foreword by Jerry O. Tuttle. Fairfax, VA: AFCEA International Press, 1991. Archived online at https://archive.org/details/isbn_091615923/.

Digital Equipment Corporation. "Digital Equipment Corporation: 1957 to the Present." Maynard, MA, 1978. https://gordonbell.azurewebsites.net/digital/dec%201957%20to%20present%201978.pdf.

Directorate, Tactical Evaluation (Contemporary Historical Evaluation of Combat Operations). "Project CHECO: Southeast Asia Report." Seventh Air Force Tactical Air Control Center, Operations, HQ PACAF, October 15, 1968. https://archive.org/details/DTIC_ADA485188/mode/2up.

Director of Occupational Standards, U.S. Department of the Navy. "Workshop Draft of Occupational Standards: Intelligence Rating." NPPSA-100, June 1973. Record group RG 24, A1 1022, box 26, National Archives II, College Park, MD.

Dismukes, Brad, and Peter M. Swartz. "Soviet Strategy and Open Source Analysis." Lecture and discussion, Center for Naval Analyses, Arlington, VA, November 7, 2017.

Doerr, P. J. "CWC Revisited." *Proceedings*, U.S. Naval Institute, 112, no. 4, 998 (April 1986). https://www.usni.org/magazines/proceedings/1986/april/cwc-revisited (paywall).

Donig, Simon. "Appropriating American Technology in the 1960s: Cold War Politics and the GDR Computer Industry." *IEEE Annals of the History of Computing* 32, no. 3 (April–June 2010): 32–45. doi: 10.1109/MAHC.2010.6.

Dorsett, David J. "The U.S. Navy's Vision for Information Dominance." Chief of Naval Operations for Information Dominance, U.S. Department of the Navy, May 2010. https://apps.dtic.mil/sti/pdfs/ADA522185.pdf.

Dougherty, Stanley J. "Defense Suppression: Building Some Operational Concepts." Master's thesis, Air University, 1992. https://media.defense.gov/2017/Dec/28/2001861734/-1/-1/0/T_DOUGHERTY_DEFENSE_SUPPRESSION.PDF.

Dubbeldam, Jaap, and Marco P. J. Borst. "P-3 Aircraft Location History Report." P-3 Orion Research Group–The Netherlands (website), October 2021. https://www.p3orion.nl/sneaky.html.

Dulles, Allen. "Air Defense of the Sino-Soviet Bloc, 1955–1960." National Intelligence Estimate NIE 11-5-55, from the Director of Central Intelligence, CIA, July 12, 1955. CIA FOIA Electronic Reading Room, https://www.cia.gov/readingroom/docs/DOC_0000269426.pdf.

———. "Sino-Soviet Air Defense Capabilities Through Mid-1965." National Intelligence Estimate NIE 11-3-61, from the director of Central Intelligence,

CIA, July 11, 1961. CIA FOIA Electronic Reading Room, https://www.cia.gov/readingroom/docs/DOC_0000267736.pdf.

———. "Soviet Capabilities in Guided Missiles and Space Vehicles." National Intelligence Estimate NIE 11-5-59, from the director of Central Intelligence, CIA, November 3, 1959. CIA FOIA Electronic Reading Room, https://www.cia.gov/readingroom/docs/DOC_0000267656.pdf.

Dunn, Robert F. "Navy Air Strike North Vietnam." *Naval History*, U.S. Naval Institute, 141/12/1,354, 29, no. 6 (December 2015). https://www.usni.org/magazines/naval-history-magazine/2015/december/navy-air-strike-north-vietnam (paywall).

Earman, J. S. "The Navy's Integrated Operational Intelligence Center." Memorandum to the Director of Central Intelligence, May 14, 1965. CIA-RDP80B01676R000300050004-2. Archived online at https://www.cia.gov/readingroom/docs/CIA-RDP80B01676R000300050004-2.pdf.

East, Don C. *A History of U.S. Navy Fleet Air Reconnaissance, Part 1, The Pacific and VQ-1* and *Part 2, The European Theater and VQ-2*. Web, VPNavy.org. Accessed October 2, 2021. http://www.vpnavy.com/vq1_1950.html.

Eldridge, Justin L. C., Ryan Peeks, and Greg Bereiter. "Navy and Defense Reform: A Short History and Reference Chronology." Naval History and Heritage Command (website), December 22, 2016. https://www.history.navy.mil/research/library/online-reading-room/title-list-alphabetically/n/navy-defense-reform.html.

Elliott, Jaques. *The Changing Culture of a Factory*. London: Tavistock Publications, 1951.

England, Nick. "US Navy Teletype Equipment—1950's & 1960's." *US Navy Radio Communications—1950's & 1960's*, Navy-Radio.com, last updated November 3, 2024. http://www.navy-radio.com/tty.htm.

Erdheim, Judith C. "Market Time (U)." Report, CRC280. Center for Naval Analyses, Operation Evaluation Group, Arlington, VA, September 1975. Naval History and Heritage Command. https://www.history.navy.mil/research/library/online-reading-room/title-list-alphabetically/m/market-time-u-crc280.html.

Fadok, David S. "John Boyd and John Warden: Air Power's Quest for Strategic Paralysis." Master's thesis, Air University, 1995. https://archive.org/details/DTIC_ADA291621.

Farley, Robert. "Loon: America's Forgotten World War II Cruise Missile." *The National Interest* (website), Center for the National Interest, February 23, 2021. https://nationalinterest.org/blog/reboot/loon-americas-forgotten-world-war-ii-cruise-missile-178680.

Ferris, John. *Behind the Enigma: The Authorised History of GCHQ, Britain's Secret Cyber-Intelligence Agency*. London: Bloomsbury Publishing, 2020.

Field, James A., Jr. *History of United States Naval Operations: Korea.* Foreword by Ernest McNeill Eller. Online ed. San Francisco: University Press of the Pacific, 2001. https://www.history.navy.mil/content/history/nhhc/research/library/online-reading-room/title-list-alphabetically/h/history-us-naval-operations-korea.html.

Filipoff, Dmitry. "How the Fleet Forgot to Fight, Pt. 1: Combat Training." CIMSEC.org, Center for International Maritime Security, September 17, 2018. https://cimsec.org/how-the-fleet-forgot-to-fight-pt-1-combat-training/.

Finney, John W. "Senate Unit Finds U.S. Has Secret Base in Morocco for Navy Communications." *New York Times*, July 28, 1970, p. 4. https://www.nytimes.com/1970/07/28/archives/senate-unit-finds-us-has-secret-base-in-morocco-for-navy.html.

Fisher, Jacky. "IW Has a Seat at the Table: Information Warfare Commanders Harness IW Disciplines." Naval Information Forces (NAVIFOR), October 20, 2020. https://www.doncio.navy.mil/CHIPS/ArticleDetails.aspx?ID=14000.

FitzGerald, Ben, and Parker Wright. "Digital Theaters: Decentralizing Cyber Command and Control." Disruptive Defense Papers. Center for a New American Security, Washington, DC, April 2014. https://www.jstor.org/stable/resrep06146.

FitzGerald, Mary C. "Marshal Ogarkov on Modern War: 1977–1985." Defense Technical Information Center, Fort Belvoir, VA, rev. November 1986. https://apps.dtic.mil/sti/tr/pdf/ADA176138.pdf.

Flanagan, James D., and George W. Luke. "AEGIS: Newest Line of Navy Defense." *Johns Hopkins APL Technical Digest* 2, no. 4 (December 1981): 237–42. https://secwww.jhuapl.edu/techdigest/Content/techdigest/pdf/V02-N04/02-04-Flanagan_Navy.pdf.

Ford, Christopher A., and David A. Rosenberg. *The Admirals' Advantage: U.S. Navy Operational Intelligence in World War II and the Cold War.* With Randy Carol Balano. Annapolis, MD: Naval Institute Press, 2005.

———. "The Naval Intelligence Underpinnings of Reagan's Maritime Strategy." *Journal of Strategic Studies* 28, no. 2 (2005): 379–409. https://doi.org/10.1080/01402390500088627 (paywall).

Foster, Wynn F. *Captain Hook: A Pilot's Tragedy and Triumph in the Vietnam War.* Annapolis, MD: Naval Institute Press, 1992.

Friedman, Norman. *The Fifty-Year War: Conflict and Strategy in the Cold War.* Annapolis, MD: Naval Institute Press, 2000.

———. *Network-centric Warfare: How Navies Learned to Fight Smarter Through Three World Wars.* Annapolis, MD: Naval Institute Press, 2009.

Fry, William J. "Thickening the Fog: The Truncation of Air Intelligence Since World War II." Master's thesis, Air University, June 2010. https://apps.dtic.mil/sti/tr/pdf/AD1019234.pdf.

Fulghum, David A. "Navy Spying Masked by Patrol Aircraft." *Aviation Week and Space Technology*, March 8, 1999. https://archive.aviationweek.com/issue/19990308 (paywall).

Gaddis, John Lewis. *Strategies of Containment: A Critical Appraisal of American National Security Policy During the Cold War*. Revised and expanded. New York: Oxford University Press, 2005.

Gardner, C. G., A. S. Davis, C. W. Clark, R. W. Holdsworth, and B. B. McSorley. *USS Forrestal (CVA 59) Mediterranean Cruise Book 1965–66*. Cambridge, MD: William W. McAllister, [1966]. Archived online at https://www.navysite.de/cruisebooks/cv59-66/index.html.

Gartland, J. C., ed. *USS Saratoga (CVA 60) Mediterranean Cruise Book 1964–65*. Marceline, MO: Walsworth Publishing, n.d. Archived online at https://www.navysite.de/cruisebooks/cv60-65/index.html.

Gayler, Noel. "United States Signal Intelligence Directive (USSID 1)." National Security Agency, September 29, 1971. NSA Archive, https://www.nsa.gov/portals/75/documents/news-features/declassified-documents/nsa-60th-timeline/1970s/19710921_1970_Doc_3987512_USSID1.pdf.

Geertz, Clifford. *The Interpretation of Cultures: Selected Essays*. New York: Basic Books, 1973.

Gentry, John A., and Joseph S. Gordon. *Strategic Warning Intelligence: History, Challenges, and Prospects*. Washington, DC: Georgetown University Press, 2019.

Georgiou, Giorgos. "British Bases in Cyprus and Signals Intelligence." *Études helléniques / Hellenic Studies*, The Republic of Cyprus: 50 Years After / La République de Chypre: 50 ans après, 19, no. 2 (2011). Archived online at https://wikispooks.com/w/images/a/a7/British_Bases_in_Cyprus_and_Signals_Intelligence.pdf.

Gerhard, William D. "Southeast Asia, SIGINT Applications in U.S. Air Operations; Part One: Collecting the Enemy's Signals, February 1972." NSA Cryptologic History Series, February 1972. Archived online at https://www.governmentattic.org/5docs/NSA-SAIUSAO_1972.pdf.

Gerovitch, Slava. "How the Computer Got Its Revenge on the Soviet Union." Technology. *Nautilus*, April 2, 2015. https://nautil.us/how-the-computer-got-its-revenge-on-the-soviet-union-235368/.

Glock, John R. "The Evolution of Air Force Targeting." *Airpower Journal* 8, no. 3 (Fall 1994): 14–28. Reprint published and archived online at https://apps.dtic.mil/sti/pdfs/ADA567476.pdf.

Goodman, Michael S. "The Dog that Didn't Bark: The Joint Intelligence Committee and Warning of Aggression." *Cold War History* 7, no. 4 (November 2007): 529–51. https://doi.org/10.1080/14682740701621739 (paywall).

Goralski, Robert, and Russell W. Freeburg. *Oil and War: How the Deadly Struggle for Fuel in World War II Meant Victory or Defeat.* Quantico, VA: Marine Corps University Press, 2021.

Grabo, Cynthia M. *Anticipating Surprise: Analysis for Strategic Warning.* Edited by Jan Goldman, foreword by James A. Williams. Washington, DC: Joint Military Intelligence College, 2002. https://ia600501.us.archive.org/33/items/Anticipating-Surprise-Analysis-for-Strategic-Warning-2002/Anticipating%20Surprise%20-%20Analysis%20for%20Strategic%20Warning%20%282002%29.pdf.

Gray, Colin S. *Strategy for Chaos: Revolutions in Military Affairs and the Evidence of History.* Cass Series, Strategy and History 2. London: Frank Cass, 2002.

Greiner, Larry E. "Evolution and Revolution as Organizations Grow." *Harvard Business Review* 76, no. 3 (May–June 1998): 55–60, 62–66, 68.

Grove, Michael, and Jay Miller. *North American Rockwell A3J/A-5 Vigilante.* Aerofax minigraph 9. Arlington, TX: Aerofax, 1989. Distributed by Osceola, WI: Motorbooks International, 1989.

Halpin, H., and H. Wilson. "TSC: The Missing Link." *Naval Aviation News* (August 1970): 25. https://www.history.navy.mil/content/dam/nhhc/research/histories/naval-aviation/Naval%20Aviation%20News/1970/pdf/aug70.pdf.

Hancock, Joy Bright. "Naval Aviation Insignia." *Proceedings*, U.S. Naval Institute, 59, no. 6, 364 (June 1933). https://www.usni.org/magazines/proceedings/1933june/naval-aviation-insignia.

Handel, Michael I. *Intelligence and Military Operations.* London: Frank Cass, 1990.

Hankins, Michael. "The Teaball Solution: The Evolution of Air Combat Technology in Vietnam, 1968–1972." *Air Power History* 63, no. 3 (Fall 2016): 7–24. https://www.afhistory.org/airpowerhistory/Air_Power_History_2016_fall.pdf.

Hanyok, Robert J. *Spartans in Darkness: American SIGINT and the Indochina War, 1945–1975.* United States Cryptologic History 6, vol. 7, *The NSA Period: 1952–Present.* Fort Meade, MD: Center for Cryptologic History, National Security Agency, 2002. https://www.nsa.gov/portals/75/documents/news-features/declassified-documents/cryptologic-histories/spartans_in_darkness.pdf.

Harlfinger, Fredrick J., II. Unpublished transcript of interviews, conducted by John T. Mason, 1976–1977. Archives, U.S. Naval Institute, Annapolis, MD.

Harris, Gail. "Gail Harris: Professional Biography." *Gail Harris: Captain of Persistence* (website), accessed January 18, 2022. https://gailharrisspeaker.com/gail_bio.html.

Hatch, Ross R., Joseph L. Luber, and James H. Walker. "Fifty Years of Strike Warfare Research at the Applied Physics Laboratory." *Johns Hopkins APL Technical Digest* 13, no. 1 (January–March 1992): 113–24. https://secwww.jhuapl.edu/techdigest/Content/techdigest/pdf/V13-N01/13-01-Hatch.pdf.

Hattendorf, John B. "The Evolution of the U.S. Navy's Maritime Strategy, 1977–1986." Newport Papers 19. Center for Naval Warfare Studies, Naval War College, Newport, RI, 2003. https://doi.org/10.21236/ADA422147.

Hattendorf, John B., B. Mitchell Simpson III, and John R. Wadleigh. *Sailors and Scholars: The Centennial History of the United States Naval War College.* Newport, RI: Naval War College Press, 1984. Archived online at https://archive.org/details/sailorsscholarsc00hatt/mode/2up.

Haver, Rich. "Electronic Counter Measure Aircraft Life Histories (VQ-1 and VQ-2), 1949–." Aircraft history charts, 1949–1991, *VQ Association* (website), accessed April 20, 2020. http://vqassociation.org/wp-content/uploads/2019/06/062-VQ-Aircraft-History-Charts-HQ.pdf.

Haynes, Peter D. "American Naval Thinking in the Post–Cold War Era: The U.S. Navy and the Emergence of a Maritime Strategy, 1989–2007." PhD diss., Naval Postgraduate School, June 2013. Archived online at https://calhoun.nps.edu/server/api/core/bitstreams/116e3ac4-7a28-4997-ae6c-36dc9aa8e12e/content.

Hearn, Christopher B. "Report on the Fleet Imagery Support Terminal (FIST) System." Memo from the cochair of the WAIT evolution team to the Washington Area Imaging Transition group, Central Intelligence Agency, August 2, 1984. CIA FOIA Electronic Reading Room, https://www.cia.gov/readingroom/document/cia-rdp91b00776r000100100059-6.

Hebblethwaite, Richard Ellis. "The Little Brother Syndrome and Nuclear Proliferation: An Exploratory Analysis of Pakistan and North Korea's Risk Prone Policies." Master's thesis, Wright State University, 2013. Archived online at https://docslib.org/doc/10323760/the-little-brother-syndrome-and-nuclear-proliferation-an-exploratory-analysis-of-pakistan-and-north-koreas-risk-prone-policies.

Helguero, Andrea Baertl. "De-constructing Credibility: Factors that Affect a Think Tank's Credibility." Working Paper no. 4, On Think Tanks (website), March 2018. https://onthinktanks.org/wp-content/uploads/2018/04/ABaertlHelguero_WP4.pdf.

Heller, Christian H. "The Impact of Insignificance: Naval Developments from the Yom Kippur War." Center for International Maritime Security, CIMSEC.org, February 19, 2019. https://cimsec.org/the-impact-of-insignificance-naval-developments-from-the-yom-kippur-war/.

Herman, Michael. *Intelligence Power in Peace and War.* Cambridge: Royal Institute of International Affairs, Cambridge University Press, 1996. Archived online at https://archive.org/details/intelligencepowe0000herm/mode/2up.

Herman, Michael, and Gwilym Hughes, eds. *Intelligence in the Cold War: What Difference Did It Make?* London: Routledge, 2014.

Hime, Douglas N. "The 1982 Falklands-Malvinas Case Study." NWC 1036, Joint Military Operations Department, Naval War College, Newport, RI, June 4, 2010.

History of Information. "The US Navy Launches NAVSAT, the First Operational Satellite Navigation System: 10/4/1957 to 1960." Accessed November 9, 2019. http://www.historyofinformation.com/detail.php?id=83.

Hoder, S., ed. *USS Constellation (CV 64) WestPac Cruise Book 1978–79*. N.p.: Josten's/American Yearbook Company, n.d. Archived online at https://www.navysite.de/cruisebooks/cv64-78/index.html.

Hofstede, Geert H. *Culture's Consequences: International Differences in Work-Related Values*. Abridged ed. Cross-cultural Research and Methodology Series. Beverly Hills: Sage Publications, 1984.

Hogan, Edward J. Command history 1976 of USS *Kitty Hawk* (C V-63). From the Commanding Officer to the Chief of Naval Operations, OPNAVINST 5750.12 series, April 30, 1977. Naval History and Heritage Command, https://www.history.navy.mil/content/dam/nhhc/research/archives/command-operation-reports/ship-command-operation-reports/k/kitty-hawk-cv-63-ii/1976.pdf.

Holloway, Don. "Slaying the Dragon." *Vietnam Magazine*, October 2015. http://donhollway.com/thanh_hoa/.

Holloway, James L. *Aircraft Carriers at War: A Personal Retrospective of Korea, Vietnam, and the Soviet Confrontation*. Annapolis, MD: Naval Institute Press, 2007.

———. Command history 1965 of USS *Enterprise* (CVA (N)-65). From the commanding officer to the Chief of Naval Operations, OPNAVINST 5750.7, February 2, 1967. Naval History and Heritage Command, https://www.history.navy.mil/content/dam/nhhc/research/archives/command-operation-reports/ship-command-operation-reports/e/enterprise-cvn-65-viii/pdf/1965.pdf.

———. "Tactical Command and Control of Carrier Operations." Part of "Command and Control of Air Operations in the Vietnam War," seminar 4, the Colloquium on Contemporary History conference proceedings, Naval History and Heritage Command, Navy Yard, Washington, DC, January 23, 1991, seminar 4. Archived at the Navy Department Library, Naval History and Heritage Command. https://www.history.navy.mil/content/history/nhhc/research/library/online-reading-room/title-list-alphabetically/c/command-control-air-operations.html.

Holmes, W. J. *Double-Edged Secrets: U.S. Naval Intelligence Operations in the Pacific During World War II*. Annapolis, MD: Naval Institute Press, 1979.

Honan, William H. "Russian and American Pilots Play 'Chicken.'" *New York Times*, November 22, 1970, p. 221. https://www.nytimes.com/1970/11/22/archives/article-34-no-title-one-game-rule-not-to-be-broken-dont-lose-your.html.

———. "The World." *New York Times*, October 10, 1971. https://www.nytimes.com/1971/10/10/archives/us-and-russia-now-hear-this-rules-for-chickenofthesea.html.

Hone, Thomas C. *Power and Change: The Administrative History of the Office of the Chief of Naval Operations, 1946–1986*. Contributions to Naval History no. 2.

Washington, DC: Naval Historical Center, Department of the Navy, 1989. Archived online at https://archive.org/details/powerchangethead00wash/mode/2up.

Hone, Thomas C., and Curtis A. Utz. *History of the Office of the Chief of Naval Operations, 1915–2015*. Washington, DC: Naval History and Heritage Command, U.S. Department of the Navy, 2020. https://www.history.navy.mil/content/dam/nhhc/research/publications/publication-508-pdf/OPNAV%20100%20508.pdf.

Hone, Trent. *Learning War: The Evolution of Fighting Doctrine in the U.S. Navy, 1898–1945*. Studies in Naval History and Sea Power. Annapolis, MD: Naval Institute Press, 2018.

House, Robert J. *Strategic Leadership Across Cultures: The GLOBE Study of CEO Leadership Behavior and Effectiveness in 24 Countries*. Thousand Oaks, CA: SAGE Publications, 2014.

HP Computer Museum. "Computer Systems: Early 200s Selection; 2100A." HPMuseum.net. https://hpmuseum.net/display_item.php?hw=98.

Hubbard, Sammuel W. Command history 1975 of USS *Kitty Hawk* (C V-63). From the Commanding Officer to the Chief of Naval Operations, OPNAVINST 5750.12, May 1976. Naval History and Heritage Command, https://www.history.navy.mil/content/dam/nhhc/research/archives/command-operation-reports/ship-command-operation-reports/k/kitty-hawk-cv-63-ii/1975.pdf.

Hughes, Wayne P., ed. *The U.S. Naval Institute on Naval Tactics*. U.S. Naval Institute Wheel Books. Annapolis, MD: Naval Institute Press, 2015.

Hughes, Wayne P., and Robert Girrier. *Fleet Tactics and Naval Operations*, 3rd ed. Foreword by John Richardson. Annapolis, MD: Naval Institute Press, 2018.

Iskra, Darlene M. "Attitudes Toward Expanding Roles for Navy Women at Sea: Results of a Content Analysis." *Armed Forces and Society* 33, no. 2 (January 2007): 203–23. https://doi.org/10.1177/0095327X06287883.

Jacoby, Lowell E. "Joint Intelligence Center, Pacific (JICPAC)—Thinking Back 30 Years." Naval Intelligence Professionals, NavIntPro.org, April 21, 2021. https://www.navintpro.org/professional-articles/2021/04/21/joint-intelligence-center,-pacific-(jicpac)---thinking-back-30-years/.

———. "Operational Intelligence: Lessons from the Cold War." *Proceedings*, U.S. Naval Institute, 125, no. 1, 1,151 (January 1999). https://www.usni.org/magazines/proceedings/1999/january.

Jain, Amit, and Bruce Kogut. "Memory and Organizational Evolvability in a Neutral Landscape." *Organization Science* 25, no. 2 (March–April 2014): 479–93. https://doi.org/10.1287/orsc.2013.0841.

Jakubiak, Thomas F., ed. *USS Ranger (CV 61) WestPac Cruise Book 1979*. N.p.: American Yearbook Company, n.d. Archived online at https://www.navysite.de/cruisebooks/cv61-79/index.html.

Johnson, Lyndon B. "October 4, 1967—7:02 p.m. McNamara, Rusk, Rostow" folder. Cabinet room meeting notes on bombing campaign and progress of war. Papers of Tom Johnson, Box 1. LBJ Presidential Library. https://www.discoverlbj.org/item/pp-johnsontom-mtgnotes-b01-f45.

Joint Chiefs of Staff, U.S. Department of Defense. "Report of the JCS Fact Finding Team: USS *Liberty* Incident, 8 June 1967." Washington, DC. Archived online at http://www.thelibertyincident.com/docs/JCSreport.pdf.

Jones, Frank L. "A 'Hollow Army' Reappraised: President Carter, Defense Budgets, and the Politics of Military Readiness." The Letort Papers. Strategic Studies Institute, U.S. Army War College, Carlisle, PA, October 2012. https://www.jstor.org/stable/resrep11172.

———. *Blowtorch: Robert Komer, Vietnam, and American Cold War Strategy.* Annapolis, MD: Naval Institute Press, 2013.

Karsten, H. G., ed. *USS Enterprise (CVAN 65) WestPac Cruise Book 1965–66.* Westbury, NY: Hallmark Graphics, n.d. Archived online at https://www.navysite.de/cruisebooks/cvn65-65/index.html.

Keane, John F., and C. Alan Easterling. "Maritime Patrol Aviation: 90 Years of Continuing Innovation." *Johns Hopkins APL Technical Digest* 24, no. 3 (2003): 242–56. https://secwww.jhuapl.edu/techdigest/Content/techdigest/pdf/V24-N03/24-03-Keane.pdf.

Khalilzad, Zalmay M., and John Patrick White, eds. *Strategic Appraisal: The Changing Role of Information in Warfare.* Foreword by Andrew W. Marshall. Project Air Force, RAND Corp., Santa Monica, CA, 1999. Available for download from https://www.rand.org/pubs/monograph_reports/MR1016.html.

Khalsa, Sundri K. "Terrorism Forecasting: A Web-Based Methodology." Occasional paper no. 11. Center for Strategic Intelligence Research, Joint Military Intelligence College, Washington, DC, November 2004. https://books.google.com/books?hl=en&lr=&id=q43aAAAAMAAJ&oi=fnd&pg=PP5&dq=Terrorism+Forecasting:+A+Web-Based+Methodology+Intelligence+College&ots=bkuRnJhOYn&sig=cVB3vgyQEoX5pXsqK6_w8ax2A3Y#v=onepage&q=Terrorism%20Forecasting%3A%20A%20Web-Based%20Methodology%20Intelligence%20College&f=false.

Kim, Yong-Min. "Career Advancement in Managerial Hierarchies in the United States Firms: A Multi-theoretic Model and Empirical Tests of the Determinants of Managerial Promotion." PhD diss., University of Southern California, 1995. Archived online at https://www.proquest.com/docview/304220709/?pq-origsite=primo.

Kipp, Jacob W. Review of *Soviet Naval Doctrine and Policy, 1956–1986*, by Robert Waring Herrick. Speaking of Books, *Journal of the Historical Society* 3, nos. 3–4 (June 2003): 431–34. https://onlinelibrary.wiley.com/doi/10.1111/j.1529-921X.2003.00071.x.

Knox, Dudley Wright, and David Kohnen. *21st Century Knox: Influence, Sea Power, and History for the Modern Era*. 21st Century Foundations. Annapolis, MD: Naval Institute Press, 2016.

Kopin, Zach. "Convergent Corps: Line Officers, Staff Officers and the Modernization of the U.S. Navy." Naval Historical Foundation, NavyHistory.org, April 30, 2013. https://navyhistory.org/2013/04/convergent-corps-line-officers-staff-officers-modernization-us-navy/.

Kostin, Sergei, and Eric Raynaud. *Farewell: The Greatest Spy Story of the Twentieth Century*. Translated by Catherine Cauvin-Higgins, foreword by Richard V. Allen. Las Vegas: AmazonCrossing, 2011.

Kuzmarov, Jeremy. "The Improbable Militarist: Jimmy Carter, the Revolution in Military Affairs and Limits of the American Two-Party System." *Class, Race and Corporate Power* 6, no. 2 (November 10, 2018). https://doi.org/10.25148/CRCP.6.2.008311.

Lamb, Christopher J. "The *Mayaguez* Crisis, Mission Command, and Civil-Military Relations." 1st ed. Join History Office, Office of the Chairman of the Joint Chiefs of Staff, Washington, DC, 2018. https://www.jcs.mil/Portals/36/Documents/History/28270_MayaguezCrisis_web%20corrected.pdf?ver=2019-08-16-124241-780&timestamp=1565973771822.

Lambeth, Benjamin S. *The Transformation of American Air Power*. Cornell Studies in Security Affairs. Ithaca, NY: Cornell University Press, 2000.

Landolt, Richard Banks. "The Officer in Tactical Command and Tactical Data Information Exchange Systems (OTCIXS/TADIXS) and the Transition to the Military Strategic and Tactical Relay System (MILSTAR)." Master's thesis, Naval Postgraduate School, 1987. https://apps.dtic.mil/sti/tr/pdf/ADA181664.pdf.

Langer, Paul Fritz, and Joseph Jeremiah Zasloff. "Revolution in Laos: The North Vietnamese and the Pathet Lao." Memorandum RM-5935-ARPA, RAND Corporation, September 1969. https://www.rand.org/content/dam/rand/pubs/research_memoranda/2008/RM5935.pdf.

Laurie, Clayton D., and Michael J. Suk. *Leaders of the National Reconnaissance Office: Volume 1, 1962–1992; Directors, Deputy Directors, Staff Directors, Program Directors, Chiefs of Staff, Directorate and Office Managers*. 2nd rev. ed. Chantilly, VA: National Reconnaissance Office, Center for the Study of National Reconnaissance, 2019. https://www.nro.gov/Portals/65/documents/history/csnr/leaders/Leaders_of_NRO_Vol_I_July_2019_web.pdf?ver=2019-09-18-094920-410&timestamp=1568815046728.

Lavalle, A. J. C., ed. *The Tale of Two Bridges and The Battle for the Skies over North Vietnam*. USAF Southeast Asia Monograph Series, vol. 1, monographs 1 and 2. Washington, DC: Office of Air Force History, 1985.

Layton, Edwin T. *"And I Was There": Breaking the Secrets; Pearl Harbor and Midway.* With Roger Pineau and John Costello. Saybrook, CT: Konecky and Konecky, 2001.

Lee, Edward P., Robert T. Lundy, and Jerry A. Krill. "History of BGAAWC/FACT: Knitting the Battle Force for Air Defense." *Johns Hopkins APL Technical Digest* 23, nos. 2–3 (September 2002): 117–37. https://secwww.jhuapl.edu/techdigest/Content/techdigest/pdf/V23-N2-3/23-02-Lee.pdf.

Leese, Bryan H. "The Cold War Computer Arms Race." *Journal of Advanced Military Studies* 14, no. 2 (Fall 2023): 102–20. https://doi.org/10.21140/mcuj.20231402006.

———. "A Cold War–Education Approach for Today's Military." Unpublished manuscript. Last modified December 2024.

———. "C2W and Technology: The Story of OP-094 and the Navy's Attempt to Centralize Systems for Better Decision Making." Unpublished manuscript, last modified December 2023.

———. "The Evolution of U.S. Navy Operational Intelligence in the Cold War." PhD diss., King's College London, 2023.

———. "Naval Intelligence Professionals: Admiral Bobby R. Inman, 'Great Captain.'" Professional Articles. *Naval Intelligence Professionals Quarterly* (June 2016). https://www.navintpro.org/professional-articles/2016/06/15/admiral-bobby-r.-inman,-great-captain/ (paywall).

———. "NHHC Archive Research Strategy Meeting with Curtis Utz." Author's meeting notes, Naval History and Heritage Command, Washington, DC, April 20, 2018. Author's personal collection.

———. "Nobody Wants a Pacer! Reframe and Reassess the Fleet Intelligence Detachment Program Model." Naval Intelligence Professionals (website), April 19, 2016.

Lehman, John F. "Is Naval Aviation Culture Dead?" *Proceedings*, U.S. Naval Institute, 137, no. 9, 1.303 (September 2011). https://www.usni.org/magazines/proceedings/2011/september/naval-aviation-culture-dead.

———. *Oceans Ventured: Winning the Cold War at Sea.* 1st ed. New York: W. W. Norton, 2018.

Leighton, Richard M. *Strategy, Money, and the New Look, 1953–1956.* History of the Office of the Secretary of Defense vol. 3. Washington, DC: Historical Office, Office of the Secretary of Defense, 2001.

Leone, Dario. "The Story of the First, Ill Fated F-100 Super Sabre Combat Mission of the Vietnam War." *Aviation Geek Club* (blog), January 20, 2020. https://theaviationgeekclub.com/the-story-of-the-first-ill-fated-f-100-super-sabre-combat-mission-of-the-vietnam-war/.

———. "You Gotta Be Shitting Me! The Story of the First U.S. SAM-Hunters in Vietnam." *The Aviationist* (blog), March 13, 2014. https://theaviationist.com/2014/03/13/wild-weasel-f-100/.

Leuci, James L. "Navy Women in Ships: A Deployment to Equality, 1942–1982." U.S. Navy, Chief of Navy Reserve, Hampton Roads Naval Museum, Norfolk, VA, 2016. https://www.history.navy.mil/content/dam/museums/hrnm/Education/Women%20in%20Ships%201978%2020160207.pdf.

Levenbach, Ir. W. A. "Message Handling in a Military Environment." TNO report no. FEL-89-B260, TNO Physics and Electronics Laboratory, Netherlands Organization for Applied Science and Research, The Hague, September 18, 1989. https://apps.dtic.mil/sti/pdfs/ADA217929.pdf.

Li, Jin, Niko Matouschek, and Michael Powell. "Power Dynamics in Organizations." CSIO working paper no. 0139, Center for the Study of Industrial Organization, Kellogg School of Management, Northwestern University, Evanston, IL, December 2015. http://www.jin-li.org/uploads/1/1/4/5/114595093/7_li_power_dynamics_in_organizations_2015.pdf.

Loescher, Michael S. "Origins of Modern Naval Command and Control." In DiGirolamo, *Naval Command and Control*, 3–18.

Love, Robert William, Jr., ed. *The Chiefs of Naval Operations*. Annapolis, MD: Naval Institute Press, 1980.

Lowe, Jim. *The Green Door*. With the High Fives, phonograph recording. Hollywood, CA: Trinity Music, BMI, 1956. 2:11. Video archived online at https://www.youtube.com/watch?v=vle44kNHxDg.

Lowenthal, Mark M. *Intelligence: From Secrets to Policy*. 6th ed. Los Angeles: CQ Press, 2015.

MacKrell, Eileen F. "Network-centric Intelligence Works." *Proceedings*, U.S. Naval Institute, 129, no. 7, 1,205 (July 2003). https://www.usni.org/magazines/proceedings/2003/july/network-centric-intelligence-works.

Mahnken, Thomas G. *Uncovering Ways of War: U.S. Intelligence and Foreign Military Innovation, 1918–1941*. Ithaca, NY: Cornell University Press, 2009.

Maillefert, Christopher W. "Command and Control: A Contemporary Perspective." Advanced Research Project no. 062, Naval War College, Newport, RI, 1974. https://archive.org/details/DTIC_ADB001632.

Maneki, Sharon A. "Remembering the Lessons of the Vietnam War." *Cryptologic Quarterly* 23 (Spring/Summer 2004). National Security Agency Archive, https://www.nsa.gov/portals/75/documents/news-features/declassified-documents/cryptologic-quarterly/remembering_the_lessons.pdf.

Mansoor, Peter R., and Williamson Murray, eds. *The Culture of Military Organizations*. Cambridge: Cambridge University Press, 2019. https://www.cambridge.org/core/books/culture-of-military-organizations/67053E4FCE8B18077EFF8076D49992D6 (paywall).

Marks, Barry Alan. "The Idea of Propaganda in America." PhD diss., University of Minnesota, 1957. Archived online at https://www.proquest.com/docview/301928906/citation/E0310AB7450444B0PQ/1.

Marolda, Edward J. *The Approaching Storm: Conflict in Asia, 1945–1965*. The U.S. Navy and the Vietnam War. Washington, DC: Naval History and Heritage Command, Department of the Navy, 2009.

Marolda, Edward J., V. Zaikin, Mary Glantz, and David F. Winkler. "Conflict and Cooperation: The U.S. and Soviet Navies in the Cold War." Presentation at the Colloquium on Contemporary History 1989–1998, seminar 10, Naval History Center, Washington, DC, June 12, 1996. https://www.history.navy.mil/research/library/online-reading-room/title-list-alphabetically/c/conflict-coop-us-soviet-navies-cold-war.html.

Martinage, Robert. "Toward a New Offset Strategy: Exploiting U.S. Long-Term Advantages to Restore U.S. Global Power Projection Capability." Center for Strategic and Budgetary Assessments, CBSAonline.org, 2014. https://csbaonline.org/uploads/documents/Offset-Strategy-Web.pdf.

Maxwell, J. A. "1973 Naval Intelligence Training Conference." Report on conference held in Suitland, Maryland, September 11, 1973. Record group RG 24, A1-1022, box 26. National Archives and Records Administration, Archives II, College Park, MD.

MCARA: Marine Corps Aviation Reconnaissance Association. "MCARA Aircraft > F8U-1P/RF-8A Crusader." MCARA.us, 2010. https://www.mcara.us/F8U-1P_RF-8A.html.

McCone, John. "The Outlook for North Vietnam." Special National Intelligence Estimate SNIE 14.3-64, from the director of Central Intelligence, CIA, March 4, 1966. CIA FOIA Electronic Reading Room. https://www.cia.gov/readingroom/docs/CIA-RDP80R01720R000200010006-9.pdf.

McCormick, Gordon H. *The Soviet Presence in the Mediterranean*. Santa Monica, CA: RAND Corp., 1987. Available for download from https://www.rand.org/pubs/papers/P7388.html.

McCrea, Michael M., Karen N. Domabyl, and Alexander F. Parker. "The Offensive Navy since World War II: How Big and Why; A Brief Summary." Research memorandum. Center for Naval Analyses, Alexandria, VA, July 1989. Archived online at https://www.history.navy.mil/research/library/online-reading-room/title-list-alphabetically/o/the-offensive-navy-since-world-war-ii-how-big-and-why-a-brief-summary.html.

McFarland, Jim. "Cryptologic Support Group: (CSG) Rota, USN-726." Presentation, Operational Intelligence Learned Symposium, Spring Red Tie Luncheon, Naval Intelligence Professionals, Arlington, VA, April 29, 2016. Archived online at https://slideplayer.com/slide/10445420/.

McGill, Gerald A. "The Trawler Incident (1 March 1968)." *Operation Market Time* (blog), April 5, 2020. https://operationmarkettime.com/2020/04/05/the-trawler-incident-1-march-1968/.

McLachlan, Donald. *Room 39: A Study in Naval Intelligence*. New York: Atheneum, 1968. http://archive.org/details/room39studyinnav00mcla.

McQuilkin, William C. "Operation Sealords: A Front in a Frontless War; An Analysis of the Brown-Water Navy in Vietnam." Master's thesis, U.S. Army Command and General Staff College, 1996. https://apps.dtic.mil/sti/pdfs/ADA331787.pdf.

Mearsheimer, John J. *Conventional Deterrence*. Cornell Studies in Security Affairs Series. Ithaca, NY: Cornell University Press, 1983.

Meilinger, Phillip S. "10 Propositions Regarding Air Power." Air Force Histories and Museum Program. School of Advanced Airpower Studies, Maxwell Air Force Base, AL, 1995. https://media.defense.gov/2010/May/25/2001330281/-1/-1/0/AFD-100525-026.pdf.

Metrick, Andrew. "(Un)mind the Gap." *Proceedings*, U.S. Naval Institute, 145, no. 10, 1,400 (October 2019). https://www.usni.org/magazines/proceedings/2019/october/unmind-gap.

Middleton, Drew. "Role of U.S. Navy Base in Spain Expands as Soviet Fleet Grows." *New York Times*, May 14, 1972, p. 2. https://www.nytimes.com/1972/05/14/archives/role-of-us-navy-base-in-spain-expands-as-soviet-fleet-grows.html.

Milley, Mark. "Joint Maritime Operations." Joint Publication (JP) 3-32, Change 1, chairman, Joint Chiefs of Staff, September 20, 2021, U.S. Space Force and U.S. Department of the Air Force. https://irp.fas.org/doddir/dod/jp3_32.pdf.

Mitchell, John R. C. Command history 1976 of USS *Kennedy* (CV 67). From the commanding Officer to the Chief of Naval Operations, doc. ref. OPNAVINST 5750.12B, April 7, 1977. Naval History and Heritage Command.

Mobley, Richard A., and Edward J. Marolda. *Knowing the Enemy: Naval Intelligence in Southeast Asia*. U.S. government official ed. U.S. Navy and the Vietnam War. Washington, DC: Department of the Navy, 2015.

Mobley, Scott. *Progressives in Navy Blue: Maritime Strategy, American Empire, and the Transformation of U.S. Naval Identity, 1873–1898*. Studies in Naval History and Sea Power. Annapolis, MD: Naval Institute Press, 2018.

Molander, Roger C., Andrew Riddile, and Peter A. Wilson. "Strategic Information Warfare: A New Face of War." RAND Corp., Santa Monica, CA, 1996. https://www.rand.org/pubs/monograph_reports/MR661.html.

Morrison, Robert E. "Fleet Support Detachment, Da Nang, Republic of Vietnam (Det Bravo): Command History." Virginia Beach: Privately published, 2017. https://www.navycthistory.com/pdf/HistoryofDetBravoDaNang.pdf.

Morton, Tyler. "From Kites Through Cold War: The Evolution of United States Air Force Manned Airborne ISR." PhD diss., Air University, 2016. https://apps.dtic.mil/sti/pdfs/AD1030466.pdf.

Mosier, Richard. "Navy Information Warfare—What Is It?" *Center for International Maritime Security* (blog), September 13, 2016. https://cimsec.org/navy-information-warfare/.

M. Rosenblatt and Son. "USS *Saratoga*, Aircraft Carrier CV-60: Redacted Booklet of General Plans." Prepared for New York Naval Shipyard, Brooklyn, NY, June 24, 1957. Archived online at https://www.navsource.org/archives//02/0260bj.pdf.

Muir, Malcolm. *Black Shoes and Blue Water: Surface Warfare in the United States Navy, 1945–1975*. Repr. Honolulu: University Press of the Pacific, (1996) 2005.

Mukherjee, Avinandan, and Hongwei He. "Company Identity and Marketing: An Integrative Framework." *Journal of Marketing Theory and Practice* 16, no. 2 (Spring 2008): 111–25. https://www.jstor.org/stable/40470344 (paywall).

Museum of HP Calculators (website). "HP 9830A." Accessed May 23, 2019. https://www.hpmuseum.org/hp9830.htm.

Myers, Lowell R. Command history 1979 of USS *Kennedy* (CV 67). From the commanding officer to the Chief of Naval Operations, OPNAVINST, May 20, 1980. Naval History and Heritage Command.

Nalty, Bernard C. "The Air Force in Southeast Asia: Tactics and Techniques of Electronic Warfare; Electronic Countermeasures in the Air War Against North Vietnam, 1965–1973." Monograph. Office of Air Force History, Washington, DC, August 16, 1977. https://media.defense.gov/2011/Mar/23/2001330092/-1/-1/0/AFD-110323-034.pdf.

National Air and Space Museum. "Cutler-Hammer AIL 1540 Light Table." Smithsonian. Accessed March 15, 2020, https://airandspace.si.edu/collection-objects/cutler-hammer-ail-1540-light-table/nasm_A20050091000.

National Security Agency. "The National Security Agency and the EC-121 Shootdown." United States Cryptologic History, Special Series Crisis Collection vol. 3. [Fort Meade, MD]: Office of Archives and History, National Security Agency, 1989. https://media.defense.gov/2021/Jun/29/2002751426/-1/-1/0/THE%20NATIONAL%20SECURITY%20AGENCY%20AND%20THE%20EC-121%20SHOOTDOWN.PDF.

Naval Aviation News. "Editor's Corner: WAVE Maintenance Officers." (May 1970): 24. https://www.history.navy.mil/content/dam/nhhc/research/histories/naval-aviation/Naval%20Aviation%20News/1970/pdf/may70.pdf.

———. "New Orion Scheduled (EP-3E)." (July 1971). https://www.history.navy.mil/content/dam/nhhc/research/histories/naval-aviation/Naval%20Aviation%20News/1970/pdf/jul71.pdf.

———. "On Patrol with the Fleet Air Wings." (April 1970): 24–25. https://www.history.navy.mil/content/dam/nhhc/research/histories/naval-aviation/Naval%20Aviation%20News/1970/pdf/apr70.pdf.

———. "Tactical Aircraft Mission Planning System: Windows on the Future." (June 1995): 27–28. https://books.google.com/books?id=deiWwyjpQiQC&q=TAMPS#v=onepage&q=TAMPS&f=false.

———. "VP-5's Threefold Mission in Vietnam." (March 1968): 29. https://www.history.navy.mil/content/dam/nhhc/research/histories/naval-aviation/Naval%20Aviation%20News/1960/pdf/mar68.pdf.

Naval Historical Center. "Chief of Naval Operations." History.Navy.mil, June 28, 2006. Archived link https://web.archive.org/web/20071218005946/http://www.history.navy.mil/faqs/faq35-1.htm.

———. "The Office of Chief of Naval Operations." History.Navy.mil. Accessed July 27, 2018. https://www.history.navy.mil/browse-by-topic/people/chiefs-of-naval-operations/the-office1.html.

———. "US Navy Personnel Strength, 1775 to Present." History.Navy.mil, last updated July 27, 2020. https://www.history.navy.mil/research/library/online-reading-room/title-list-alphabetically/u/usn-personnel-strength.html.

Naval Intelligence Command. "Career Planning Information Guide for Intelligence Specialists Officers." Bureau of Naval Personnel, 1972. Personal papers of Rear Admiral Thomas A. Brooks, Arlington, VA.

———. "NAVINTCOM Fleet Intelligence Newsletter (FIN)-Change of Command." Commander, Naval Intelligence Command, July 1971. Personal papers of Vice Adm. Earl "Rex" Rectanus.

Naval Intelligence Professionals. "Information Warfare Community Changes Status: No Longer Restricted Line." News, NavIntPro.org, December 20, 2024. https://www.navintpro.org/news/2024/12/20/Change-in-Status-for-Information-Warfare-Community/.

Naval Intelligence Professionals Quarterly. "NMITC Dedication." (September 1986).

Neel, Spurgeon. *Medical Support, 1965–1970.* Vietnam Studies. Washington, DC: Department of the Army, 1973. 1991 reissue archived online at https://www.history.army.mil/html/books/090/90-16/index.html.

Nemfakos, Charles, Irv Blickstein, Aine Seitz McCarthy, and Jerry M. Sollinger. "The Perfect Storm: The Goldwater-Nichols Act and Its Effect on Navy Acquisition." Occasional paper. RAND Corporation, Santa Monica, CA, 2010. Archived online at https://www.rand.org/content/dam/rand/pubs/occasional_papers/2010/RAND_OP308.pdf.

New York Times. "Altitude Record Is Set by New Jet, Navy Says." December 16, 1960. https://timesmachine.nytimes.com/timesmachine/1960/12/16/99979553.html.

———. "Big Soviet Cruiser Sails into Atlantic." January 20, 1970, p. 8. https://www.nytimes.com/1970/01/20/archives/big-soviet-cruiser-sails-into-atlantic.html.

———. "Naval Operations Vice Chief Is Shifted After 4 Months." January 3, 1973. https://www.nytimes.com/1973/01/03/archives/naval-operations-vice-chief-is-shifted-after-4-months.html.

———. "Text of President Kennedy's Special Message to Congress on Defense Spending; Cutback in Bases Requested by President." March 29, 1961, p. 16. https://www.nytimes.com/1961/03/29/archives/text-of-president-kennedys-special-message-to-congress-on-defense.html.

———. "Vast Soviet Naval Exercise Raises Urgent Questions for West." *New York Times*, April 28, 1975. https://www.nytimes.com/1975/04/28/archives/vast-soviet-naval-exercise-raises-urgent-questions-for-west.html.

———. "Vietnam Bombing Evaluation by Institute for Defense Analyses." July 2, 1971, p. 10. https://www.nytimes.com/1971/07/02/archives/vietnam-bombing-evaluation-by-institute-for-defense-analyses.html.

———. "Vigilante Contract Is Let." August 18, 1960. https://www.nytimes.com/1960/08/18/archives/vigilante-contract-is-let.html (paywall).

———. "Vigilante Planes Ordered by Navy; $150-Million Will Be Spent for Electronic Aircraft." *New York Times*, April 5, 1967, p. 26. https://www.nytimes.com/1967/04/05/archives/vigilante-planes-ordered-by-nayy-150million-will-be-spent-for.html.

Nitze, Paul H. "Instructions for the Coordination and Control of Navy's Clandestine Intelligence Collection Program." Memorandum from the Secretary of the Navy, December 7, 1965. Archived online at https://nsarchive2.gwu.edu/NSAEBB/NSAEBB46/document1.pdf.

North American Rockwell. "NIPS Video Integration." Contract-proposal brochure, c. 1968. Nolan Leatherman Papers.

Northrop Grumman. "Understanding Voice Data Link Networking." Northrop-Grumman.com, December 2014. https://dl.icdst.org/pdfs/files/e90d37a9b93e2e607206320ea07d7ad2.pdf.

Notz, Frank P. *Some Thoughts for Naval Intelligence Officers*. Suitland, MD: Office of Naval Intelligence, 1988.

Office of Naval Intelligence. "Typical Career Assignment Pattern for Code 163X Officers." *Intelligence Officer (163X) Newsletter*, November 1957. Personal papers of Rear Admiral Thomas A. Brooks, Arlington, VA.

Olds, Robin. *Fighter Pilot: The Memoirs of Legendary Ace Robin Olds*. With Christina Olds and Ed Rasimus. 1st ed. New York: St. Martin's Press, 2010.

O'Malley, Dave. "The Zap Heard Round the World." *Vintage Wings of Canada/Les Ailes d'époque du Canada* (website), accessed June 27, 2020. https://www.vintagewings.ca/stories/the-zap-heard-round-the-world.

Omand, David. "Learning to Be Less Surprised by Surprise." Webinar presented at the Warning, Risk, and Resilience Lecture, King's College London, June 3, 2020.

O'Neil, William D., and Gene H. Porter. "What to Buy? The Role of Director of Defense Research and Engineering (DDR&E): Lessons from the 1970s." IDA paper P-4675, Institute for Defense Analysis, Alexandria, VA, January 2011. https://apps.dtic.mil/sti/pdfs/ADA549549.pdf.

Osburn, O. R. "CVA Integrated Operational Intelligence System." *NAESU Digest* (May 1969). Nolan Leatherman Papers.

Packard, Wyman H. *A Century of U.S. Naval Intelligence*. Washington, DC: Office of Naval Intelligence, Naval Historical Center, 1996. Archived online at https://archive.org/details/centuryofusnaval00wash.

Paine, Sally. "Who Lost the Vietnam War?" Lecture and discussion, NWC INS Lecture Series, Newport, RI, October 15, 2021. 58:00 mins. https://www.youtube.com/watch?v=tjXlvIBQmU0.

Palmer, Bruce, Jr. "US Intelligence and Vietnam." Special issue. *Studies in Intelligence*, Central Intelligence Agency (December 1984). https://documents.theblackvault.com/documents/vietnam/usvietnamintel.pdf.

Parks, W. Hays. "Rolling Thunder and the Law of War." *Air University Review* 33, no. 2 (January–February 1982): 2–23. https://www.airuniversity.af.edu/Portals/10/ASPJ/journals/1982_Vol33_No1-6/1982_Vol33_No2.pdf.

PCF45.com. "Sea Float: Ca Mau Peninsula, Cua Lon and Bo De Rivers." Accessed October 29, 2023. http://pcf45.com/sealords/seafloat/seafloat.html.

Peck, Charles R. "Engineering Duty Officers: The Dwindling Muster." *Proceedings*, U.S. Naval Institute, 91, no. 12, 754 (December 1965). https://www.usni.org/magazines/proceedings/1965/december/engineering-duty-officers-dwindling-muster.

Pedersen, Dan. *Topgun: An American Story*. 1st ed. New York: Hachette Books, 2019.

Pennington, Reina. "Behind the Green Door: Is There Intelligence in Fighters." *USAF Fighter Weapons Review*, (Summer/Fall 1983). Reprinted in *USAF Fighter Weapons Review*, "USAF Weapons School 50th Anniversary Issue" (Spring/Summer 1999).

Pennsylvania State University Advanced Research Lab, ed. "From the Sea to the Stars: A Chronicle of the U.S. Navy's Space and Space-Related Activities, 1944–2009." Revised and updated. Sponsored by Gary A. Federici. Naval History and Heritage Command, [Washington, DC], 2010. Archived online at https://www.history.navy.mil/content/dam/nhhc/browse-by-topic/exploration-and-innovation/navy-and-space-exploration/FromTheSeaToTheStars/FromTheSeaToTheStars%20-%202010ed.pdf.

Petersen, Michael B. "The Vietnam Cauldron: Defense Intelligence in the War for Southeast Asia." Defense Intelligence Historical Perspectives no. 2. Defense Intelligence Agency, Historical Research Division, Washington, DC, 2012. https://nsarchive2.gwu.edu/NSAEBB/NSAEBB534-DIA-Declassified-Sourcebook/documents/DIA-46.pdf.

Petersen, Phillip A. "Perceptions in the Cold War Theater Competition—The Soviet Northwestern TVD." The Potomac Foundation, Vienna, VA, November 18, 2014. https://www.esd.whs.mil/Portals/54/Documents/FOID/Reading%20Room/Litigation_Release/Litigation%20Release%20-%20The%20Northwestern

%20TVD%20in%20Soviet%20Operational%20Strategic%20Planning%20 %202014.pdf.

Pettitt, Robert B. "TAOs: To Fight the Ship." *Proceedings*, U.S. Naval Institute, 100, no. 2, 852 (February 1974). https://www.usni.org/magazines/proceedings/1974/february/taos-fight-ship.

Phillips, Chester C. "Battle Group Operations: War at Sea." *Johns Hopkins APL Technical Digest* 2, no. 4 (December 1981): 299–300. https://secwww.jhuapl.edu/techdigest/Content/techdigest/pdf/V02-N04/02-04-Phillips_Sea.pdf.

Pike, John. "CNO Project BEARTRAP." Intelligence Resource Program (website), Federation of American Scientists, last updated November 25, 1998. https://irp.fas.org/program/collect/beartrap.htm.

Polmar, Norman. "Norman's Corner: Analyzing Exercise Okean." Naval Historical Foundation, February 20, 2013. https://navyhistory.org/2013/02/normans-corner-analyzing-exercise-okean/.

Polmar, Norman, and Edward J. Marolda. *Naval Air War: The Rolling Thunder Campaign*. The U.S. Navy and the Vietnam War. Washington, DC: Naval History and Heritage Command, 2015.

Polmar, Norman, and Minoru Genda. *Aircraft Carriers: A History of Carrier Aviation and Its Influence on World Events*. 1st ed. Washington, DC: Potomac Books, 2006.

Porche, Isaac R., III, Bradley Wilson, Erin-Elizabeth Johnson, Shane Tierney, and Evan Saltzman. "Data Flood: Helping the Navy Address the Rising Tide of Sensor Information." RAND, Santa Monica, CA, May 1, 2014. Available for download from https://www.rand.org/pubs/research_reports/RR315.html.

Powell, Robert R. "Boom." *RA-5C Vigilante Units in Combat*. Osprey Combat Aircraft no. 51. Oxford: Osprey Publishing, 2004.

Powers, Bruce F. Interview conducted by Bob Sheldon and Mike Garrambone, Lake Barcroft, VA, May 13, 2015. Published Military Operations Research Society, Calhoun: Naval Postgraduate School Institutional Archive, Monterey, CA, February 21, 2016. https://calhoun.nps.edu/entities/publication/c1f9552d-6a3a-4d6a-a8c7-9c05cf490282.

P.O.W. Network. "Keirn, Richard Paul." Bios, accessed September 5, 2023. https://www.pownetwork.org/bios/k/k046.htm.

Prados, John. "Certainties, Doubts, and Imponderables: Levels of Analysis in the Military Balance." In Herman and Hughes, *Intelligence in the Cold War*, 24–36.

———. *Safe for Democracy: The Secret Wars of the CIA*. Chicago: Ivan R. Dee, 2006.

———. *The Soviet Estimate: U.S. Intelligence Analysis and Russian Military Strength*. New York: Dial Press, 1982.

Preddy, Raymond R., Roland E. Brandel, Paul J. Epperlein, Learmel Hursh, James R. Merikangas, and Everan C. Woodland. *USS Kitty Hawk (CVA 63) WestPac*

Cruise Book 1962–63. N.p.: n.p., n.d. Archived online at https://www.navysite.de/cruisebooks/cv63-63/index.html.

Press, Michael C. "Tactical Integrated Air Defense System." Master's thesis, U.S. Army Command and General Staff College, 1978. Available for download from https://www.hsdl.org/c/view?docid=722828.

Pressly, George B. "Creating FOSIF Rota." Presentation, Operational Intelligence Lessons Symposium, Spring Red Tie Luncheon, Naval Intelligence Professionals, Arlington, VA, April 29, 2016. https://navintpro.org/news/2016/05/15/red-tie-summary/.

Pribbenow, Merle L., II. *The Soviet-Vietnamese Intelligence Relationship During the Vietnam War: Cooperation and Conflict.* Cold War International History Project, working paper no. 73. Washington, DC: Woodrow Wilson International Center for Scholars, 2014. https://www.wilsoncenter.org/sites/default/files/media/documents/publication/CWIHP_Working_Paper_73_Soviet-Vietnamese_Intelligence_Relationship_Vietnam_War.pdf.

Proc, Jerry. "ADLIPS, LINK 11/14, CCS-280, CANEWS, CANEWS 2 and Other Systems." *Radio Communications and Signals Intelligence in the Royal Canadian Navy* (website), last updated September 19, 2024. http://jproc.ca/rrp/rrp2/1980s_adlips_link.html.

Rabinovich, Abraham. "From 'Futuristic Whimsy' to Naval Reality." *Naval History,* U.S. Naval Institute, 28, no. 3 (June 2014). https://www.usni.org/magazines/naval-history-magazine/2014/june/futuristic-whimsy-naval-reality.

———. "The Little-Known US-Soviet Confrontation During Yom Kippur War." The World from PRX, July 31, 2016. https://theworld.org/stories/2016/07/31/little-known-us-soviet-confrontation-during-yom-kippur-war.

Ravnitzky, Michael. "Consequential Words: Ship Mottos." *Proceedings,* U.S. Naval Institute, 146, no. 2, 1404 (February 2020). https://www.usni.org/magazines/proceedings/2020/february/consequential-words-ship-mottos.

Reade, David. *The Age of Orion: Lockheed P-3; An Illustrated History.* Schiffer Military/Aviation History. Atglen, PA: Schiffer, 1998.

Reckert, Clare M. "Major Companies Plan Big Mergers; North American Aviation in Consolidation Talks with Rockwell-Standard Corp." *New York Times,* March 22, 1967. https://www.nytimes.com/1967/03/22/archives/major-companies-plan-big-mergers-north-american-aviation-in.html.

Rectanus, Earl F. "Rex." Unpublished transcript of interview of Earl F. "Rex" Rectanus, conducted by Paul Stillwell, parts 1 and 2, November 19, 1982. Box 01, folder 11, Admiral Elmo R. Zumwalt Jr. Collection, Oral History Interviews, Vietnam Center and Sam Johnson Vietnam Archive, Texas Tech University, Lubbock, TX. Available for download from https://www.vietnam.ttu.edu/virtualarchive/items.php?item=6260111001.

Reddig, J. R. "The Creation of JIC-JAC." *Naval Intelligence Professionals Quarterly* (October 2001).

———. "The OSIS Culture: Intelligence Support to Naval Operations in the Cold War." Course paper, National War College, Washington, DC, February 2, 1998. J. R. Reddig Personal Papers.

Richardson, David C. *The Reminiscences of Vice Admiral David C. Richardson, U.S. Navy (Retired)*. Interview conducted by Paul Stillwell, 1992. Annapolis, MD: U.S. Naval Institute, 1998.

———. "Slides from Presentation on Attack Carrier Striking Forces, 1968, May 2." Record group RG-15 (Guest Lectures, Transcripts), box 39, folder 24 (Mixed Materials), U.S. Naval War College Archives, Newport, RI. https://usnwcarchives.org/repositories/2/archival_objects/24824.

Richelson, Jeffrey T. "Task Force 157: The US Navy's Secret Intelligence Service, 1966–77." *Intelligence and National Security* 11, no. 1 (January 1996): 106–45. https://doi.org/10.1080/02684529608432346 (paywall).

Rimson, I. J., W. E. Stahnke, and M. R. Demarest, eds. *USS Saratoga (CVA 60) Mediterranean Cruise Book 1971*. Norfolk, VA; San Diego, CA: Tiffany Publishing, n.d. Archived online at https://www.navysite.de/cruisebooks/cv60-71/index.html.

Roberts, Michael D. *The History of VP, VPB, VP(HL) and VP(AM) Squadrons*. Vol. 2 of *Dictionary of American Naval Aviation Squadrons*. Washington, DC: Naval Historical Center, 2000. https://www.history.navy.mil/research/histories/naval-aviation-history/dictionary-of-american-naval-aviation-squadrons-volume-2.html.

Rochlin, Gene I. Todd R. La Porte, and Karlene H. Roberts. "The Self-Designing High-Reliability Organization: Aircraft Carrier Flight Operations at Sea." *Naval War College Review* 40, no. 4 (Autumn 1987): 76–92. https://www.jstor.org/stable/44637690.

Rosen, Stephen Peter. "New Ways of War: Understanding Military Innovation." *International Security* 13, no. 1 (Summer 1988): 134–68. https://doi.org/10.2307/2538898 (paywall).

Rosenberg, David A. "Memorandum for OPINTEL Lessons Learned Symposium Panelists and Commentators; With History of Modern OPINTEL Chronology Enclosure." OPINTEL Lessons Learned Symposium, box 1 of 2, Office of Naval Intelligence Archive, Suitland, Maryland, June 8, 1998.

———. "The Origins of Overkill: Nuclear Weapons and American Strategy, 1945–1960." *International Security* 7, no. 4 (Spring 1983): 3–71. Archived online at https://ia600704.us.archive.org/view_archive.php?archive=/24/items/wikipedia-scholarly-sources-corpus/10.2307%252F2589218.zip&file=10.2307%252F2626731.pdf.

Rosenbloom, Seth, and Michelle J. Markus. "When Project and the Organizational Culture Clash." Paper presented at PMI Global Congress 2010, Project Management

Institute, Washington, DC, 2010. https://www.pmi.org/learning/library/project-organizational-culture-conflicts-resolve-6585.

Roughead, Gary. "NAVADMIN 058/10 Information Dominance Corps Warfare Insignia." From Chief of Naval Operations to NAVADMIN, U.S. Navy NAVADMIN Library, February 10, 2010. https://navynavadmin.wordpress.com/2010/02/19/information-dominance-corps-warfare-insignia/.

Ruiz Palmer, Diego A. "A Strategic Odyssey: Constancy of Purpose and Strategy-Making in NATO, 1949–2019." Strategy Series research paper no. 3. Research Division, NATO Defense College, Rome, Italy, June 2019. Available for download at http://www.ndc.nato.int/download/downloads.php?icode=598.

———. "Theatre Operations, High Commands and Large-Scale Exercises in Soviet and Russian Military Practice: Insights and Implications." Fellowship Monograph 12. Research Division, NATO Defense College, Rome, Italy, May 2018. https://www.ndc.nato.int/news/news.php?icode=1172.

Scarbro, Graham. "'Go Straight at 'Em!' Training and Operating with Mission Command." *Proceedings*, U.S. Naval Institute, 145, no. 5, 1,395 (May 2019). https://www.usni.org/magazines/proceedings/2019/may/go-straight-em-training-and-operating-mission-command.

Schein, Edgar H. *Organizational Culture and Leadership*. Hoboken, NJ: Wiley, 2010.

Schindler, John R. *A Dangerous Business: The U.S. Navy and National Reconnaissance During the Cold War*. Fort Meade, MD: Center for Cryptologic History, 2001.

Schulimson, Jack. *The Joint Chiefs of Staff and the War in Vietnam, 1960–1968, Part 1*. History of the Joint Chiefs of Staff series. Washington, DC: Office of Joint History, Office of the Chairman of the Joint Chiefs of Staff, 2011. https://www.jcs.mil/Portals/36/Documents/History/Vietnam/Vietnam_1960-1968_P001.pdf.

Schulz, Russell K. Command history 1975 of Patrol Squadron Seventeen (VP-17), from the Commanding Officer to the Chief of Naval Operations, February 27, 1976. Naval History and Heritage Command.

Schuster, Carl O. "The Rise of North Vietnam's Air Defenses." HistoryNet, July 27, 2016. https://www.historynet.com/13703647.htm.

Scott, Keith. "The Foghorn Leghorn Story." *Cartoon Research*, 2008. https://cartoonresearch.com/index.php/the-origin-of-foghorn-leghorn/.

Scott, Ridley, dir. *A Good Year*. Los Angeles: 20th Century Fox, 2006. 118 min.

Senge, Peter M. *The Fifth Discipline: The Art and Practice of the Learning Organization*. Rev. and updated. New York: Crown Business, 2006. First published Doubleday, 1990.

Seventh Air Force, U.S. Air Force. "Seventh Air Force In Country Tactical Air Operations Handbook (7AFP 55-1)." Headquarters Seventh Air Force, San Francisco, March 20, 1968. Archived online by the C-7A Caribou Association at http://www.c-7acaribou.com/history/7AF/7AFP_55-1.pdf.

Sheehan, Neil. "Order Didn't Get to USS Liberty; Pentagon Reports Message Directing Ship off Sinai to Move Arrived Late Ship 15.5 Miles Offshore." *New York Times*, June 29, 1967, p. 1. https://www.nytimes.com/1967/06/29/archives/order-didnt-get-to-uss-liberty-pentagon-reports-message-directing.html.

Sherman, Thomas R., ed. *USS America (CV 66) Mediterranean Cruise Book 1979*. No publication information available. https://www.navysite.de/cruisebooks/cv66-79/index.html.

Sherwood, John Darrell. "From Thanh Hoa to Sarajevo: The Odyssey of Admiral Leighton W. Smith." In *Nixon's Trident: Naval Power in Southeast Asia, 1968–1972*, U.S. Navy and the Vietnam War, 62–63. Washington, DC: Naval Historical Center, U.S. Department of the Navy, 2009. Archived online at https://archive.org/details/NixonsTrident/page/n67/mode/2up.

Showers, Donald M. "Commentary: VADM Rectanus on Former CIA Director Richard Helms's Book *A Look over My Shoulder* (Random House 2003)." *Naval Intelligence Professionals Quarterly* 19, no. 4 (December 2003).

Simpson, Charles M. Transcript of oral history of Charles M. Simpson, with comments by John McCarthy, interview 1, conducted by Ted Gittinger, May 5, 1984. LBJ Library Oral Histories, Lyndon Baines Johnson Library and Museum, Austin, TX. https://www.discoverlbj.org/item/oh-simpsonc-19840502-1-84-79.

Sims, Sean. "History of the Carrier Onboard Delivery (COD)." *The Hangardeck*, January 7, 2020. http://www.thehangardeck.com/news/2019/1/7/history-of-the-carrier-onboard-delivery-cod.

Sims, William Sowden, and Benjamin Armstrong. *21st Century Sims: Innovation, Education, and Leadership for the Modern Era*. Annapolis, MD: Naval Institute Press, 2015.

Small, William N. Transcript of oral history of Admiral William N. Small, U.S. Navy (Ret.), conducted by David F. Winkler, August 1997. Naval Historical Foundation, Washington, DC.

Smallwood, Jim, ed. *USS Ranger (CV 61) WestPac Cruise Book 1976*. N.p.: Josten's American Yearbooks, n.d. Archived online at https://www.navysite.de/cruisebooks/cv61-76/index.html.

Smith, Marvin M. "Pilot Retention in the Military: An Analysis of Alternative Bonus Plans." Staff working paper, Congressional Budget Office, U.S. Congress, [Washington, DC], June 1988. https://www.cbo.gov/sites/default/files/100th-congress-1987-1988/reports/doc09_1.pdf.

Socotra, Vic [James "J. R." Reddig]. "Air Intelligence." *DailySocotra* (blog), July 3, 2017. https://www.vicsocotra.com/wordpress/air-intelligence/.

———. "Big Smoke." *DailySocotra* (blog), February 4, 2013. https://www.vicsocotra.com/wordpress/big-smoke/.

———. "Illegal Alien." *DailySocotra* (blog), March 8, 2016. https://www.vicsocotra.com/wordpress/illegal-alien/.

———. "Operational Intelligence and the Creation of OSIS: VADM David C. Richardson and the Operator's Perspective on the Creation of the Ocean Surveillance Information System." *DailySocotra* (blog), June 14, 2008. https://www.vicsocotra.com/wordpress/operational-intelligence-and-the-creation-of-osis/.

———. "Point Loma: The Bull Ring." *DailySocotra* (blog), September 30, 2019. https://www.vicsocotra.com/wordpress/point-loma-the-bull-ring/.

Spencer, Richard V. "Officer Competitive Categories for the Active Duty List of the Navy and Marine Corps." SecNav Instruction (SECNAVINST) 1400.1C. Secretary of the Navy, U.S. Department of the Navy, April 5, 2019. https://www.secnav.navy.mil/doni/Directives/01000%20Military%20Personnel%20Support/01-400%20Promotion%20and%20Advancement%20Programs/1400.1C.pdf.

Spink, Tom, ed. *Pacific Patrol: A History of Patrol Aviation During the Cold War in the Pacific; A Collaboration*. [Seattle]: Kindle Publishing, 2020.

Spinney, Franklin C. "Chuck." "A Personal Remembrance: Black Jack Shanahan, VADM (USN Ret.)." POGO: Project On Government Oversight (website), October 30, 2013. https://www.pogo.org/analysis/personal-remembrance-black-jack-shanahan-vadm-usn-ret.

Spitzmiller, Ted S. *Century Series: The USAF Quest for Air Supremacy, 1950–1960; An Illustrated History*. Schiffer Military History. Atglen, PA: Schiffer Publishing, 2011. https://archive.org/details/centuryseriesusa0000spit/mode/2up.

Staats, Elmer B. "The Navy's Multimission Carrier Airwing: Can the Mission Be Accomplished with Fewer Resources?" Government Accountability Office Secret Report LCD-77-409. Comptroller General's Report to Congress, September 16, 1977. Unclassified version doc. LDC-77-451, published November 16, 1977. Archived online at https://www.gao.gov/assets/103996.pdf.

Stead, Michael. "Origins and Early Development of the Naval Intelligence Officer (1630) Designator." *Naval Intelligence Professionals Quarterly* (December 2004).

Steiner, Frederic E., and Thomas L. Schlosser, eds. *USS Constellation (CV 64) WestPac Cruise Book 1971–72 and Cruise Bravo Cruise Book*. N.p.: Pischel Yearbooks, n.d. Archived online at https://www.navysite.de/cruisebooks/cv64-71/index.html.

Stephan, Charles R. "Trawler!" *Proceedings*, U.S. Naval Institute, 94, no. 9, 787 (September 1968). https://www.usni.org/magazines/proceedings/1968/september/trawler.

Stephenson, Henry. "Masters or Jacks?" *Proceedings*, U.S. Naval Institute, 140, no. 10, 1,340 (October 2014). https://www.usni.org/magazines/proceedings/2014/october/masters-or-jacks.

———. "Navy Information Warfare: A Decade of Indulging a False Analogy." *Proceedings*, U.S. Naval Institute, 145, no. 1, 1,391 (January 2019). https://www.usni.org/magazines/proceedings/2019/january/navy-information-warfare-decade-indulging-false-analogy.

Stewart, Hank. "How the 1967 Fire on USS Forrestal Improved Future U.S. Navy Damage Control Readiness." *The Sextant* (blog), July 28, 2017. https://usnhistory.navylive.dodlive.mil/Recent/Article-View/Article/2686245/how-the-1967-fire-on-uss-forrestal-improved-future-us-navy-damage-control-readi/.

Stillion, John. "Trends in Air-to-Air Combat: Implications for Future Air Superiority." Center for Strategic and Budgetary Assessments, Washington, DC, 2015. https://csbaonline.org/uploads/documents/Air-to-Air-Report-.pdf.

Struble, Dan. "What Is Command and Control Warfare?" *Naval War College Review* 48, no. 3 (Summer 1995): 89–98. https://www.jstor.org/stable/44642810.

Swartz, Peter M. "Oral History of Captain Peter M. Swartz, USN (Ret.)." Conducted by Ryan Peeks and Justin Blanton, July 24, 2019. Transcribed and edited by Naval History and Heritage Command, U.S. Department of the Navy, Washington, DC, 2020. https://www.history.navy.mil/content/dam/nhhc/research/publications/publication-508-pdf/Swartz_Oral_History-508.pdf.

Tauer, John M., and Judith M. Harackiewicz. "Winning Isn't Everything: Competition, Achievement Orientation, and Intrinsic Motivation." *Journal of Experimental Social Psychology* 35, no. 3 (May 1999): 209–11. https://doi.org/10.1006/jesp.1999.1383 (paywall).

Taylor, Rufus. "The Security of Intelligence—an Oral History." Transcript of oral history of Vice Admiral Rufus L. Taylor, USN, circa 1985. Box 1 of 2, Manthorpe Archive, Office of Naval Intelligence, National Intelligence Maritime Center, Suitland, MD.

Thatcher, Margaret. "Speech at Kensington Town Hall ('Britain Awake') (The Iron Lady)." Chelsea, London, January 19, 1976. Margaret Thatcher Foundation, Speeches etc., https://www.margaretthatcher.org/document/102939.

Thomas, Patricia J. "The Relationship Between Navy Classification Test Scores and Final School Grades in 98 Class 'A' Schools." Research report SRR 72-22, Naval Personnel and Training Research Laboratory, San Diego, CA, April 1972. https://apps.dtic.mil/sti/tr/pdf/AD0741688.pdf.

Thompson, Roger. "Brown Shoes, Black Shoes, and Felt Slippers: Parochialism and the Evolution of the Post-war U.S. Navy." Research paper no. 5.95, Center for Naval Warfare Studies, Strategic Research Department, U.S. Naval War College, Newport, RI, September 11, 1995. https://apps.dtic.mil/sti/pdfs/ADA299970.pdf.

Thompson, Wayne. *To Hanoi and Back: The United States Air Force and North Vietnam, 1964–1973*. Washington, DC: Air Force History Office, 2000. https://web.archive.org/web/20151017014122/http://www.dtic.mil/dtic/tr/fulltext/u2/a439924.pdf.

Thomson, James R. "Navy-Style Officer Selection Boards Practice Ideal Management System." *Navy Management Review* 11, nos. 10–11 (November 1964).
Till, Geoffrey. *Seapower: A Guide for the Twenty-First Century*. 3rd ed. New York: Routledge, 2013.
Tomes, Robert. "The Cold War Offset Strategy: Origins and Relevance." Beyond Offset Special Series, *War on the Rocks*, November 6, 2014. https://warontherocks.com/2014/11/the-cold-war-offset-strategy-origins-and-relevance/.
Trevithick, Joseph. "Spies Helped the USAF Shoot Down a Third of North Vietnam's MiG-21s." *War Is Boring* (blog), December 30, 2014. https://medium.com/war-is-boring/spies-helped-the-usaf-shoot-down-a-third-of-north-vietnams-migs-ae81e42e50e7.
Tuthill, Don. "The Early Days of Naval Intelligence in Viet Nam." *Naval Intelligence Professionals Quarterly* (December 2003).
Tuttle, Jerry O. "A Brief History of JOTS." In DiGirolamo, *Naval Command and Control*, 119–22.
———. Command history 1977 of USS *Kennedy* (CV 67). From the commanding officer to the Chief of Naval Operations, March 22, 1978. Naval History and Heritage Command.
Turner, Stansfield. *Secrecy and Democracy: The CIA in Transition*. Boston: Houghton Mifflin, 1985.
Tyler, Brian J. "Intelligence and Design: Thinking About Operational Art." Drew Paper 14. Air University, Air Force Research Institute, Maxwell Air Force Base, AL, 2014. https://media.defense.gov/2017/Nov/21/2001847430/-1/-1/0/DP_0014_TYLER_INTELLIGENCE_DESIGN.PDF.
Unger, Miles. *Machiavelli: A Biography*. New York: Simon and Schuster, 2011. https://archive.org/details/machiavellibiogr0000unge/mode/2up.
U.S. Congress. 10 U.S.C. (Armed Forces), Subtitle C (Navy and Marine Corps), Part II (Personnel), Ch. 815 (Original Appointments), §8137 (Regular Navy). Enacted by act of Congress August 10, 1956, section repealed January 1, 2021. https://uscode.house.gov/view.xhtml?path=/prelim@title10/subtitleC&edition=prelim.
U.S. Congress, House Committee on Appropriations, Subcommittee of the Department of Defense. *Department of Defense Appropriations for 1979: Hearings Before a Subcommittee of the Committee on Appropriations, House of Representatives, Ninety-Fifth Congress, Second Session*. Washington, DC: U.S. Government Printing Office, 1978.
U.S. Congress, Joint Senate–House Armed Services Subcommittee on CVAN-70 Aircraft Carrier. *CVAN-70 Aircraft Carrier: Joint Hearings, Ninety-First Congress, Second Session . . .* Washington, DC: U.S. Government Printing Office, 1970.
U.S. Congress, Senate, Committee on Appropriations, Subcommittee on Department of Defense. *Department of Defense Appropriations for Fiscal Year 1981: Hearings*

Before a Subcommittee on Appropriations, United States Senate, Ninety-Sixth Congress, Second Session, part iv, *Procurement/R. D. T. & E. (Pages 1–948), Department of Defense, Department of the Navy*. Washington, DC: U.S. Government Printing Office, 1980, https://www.google.com/books/edition/Department_of_Defense_Appropriations_for/4hje_az-aJMC?q=Congressional+testimony+AN/USQ-81(V)&gbpv=1#f=false.

U.S. Congress, Senate, Committee on Armed Services. *Hearings on Military Posture and H.R. 11500 (H.R. 12438), Department of Defense Authorization for Appropriations for Fiscal Year 1977; Before the Committee on Armed Services, House of Representatives, Ninety-Fourth Congress, Second Session*. Washington, DC: U.S. Government Printing Office, 1976.

U.S. Department of the Air Force. "AFSC 14NX Intelligence Officer: Career Field Education and Training Plan." CFETP 14NX, in 2 parts, February 13, 2013.

U.S. Department of the Army. "Information Operations." Field Manual no. (FM) 100-6, Headquarters, Washington, DC, August 27, 1996. Archived online at https://archive.org/details/fm-100-6-information-operations-1996/mode/2up.

U.S. Department of Defense. "Defense Procurement: Air Force." *Defense Industry Bulletin* 2, nos. 1, 2, 7, 8, and 10 (1966), archived online at https://babel.hathitrust.org/cgi/pt?id=ucl.c2790783&view=1up&seq=1.

——. "Defense Procurement: Air Force." *Defense Industry Bulletin* 3, nos. 8, 11, and 12 (1967), archived online at https://babel.hathitrust.org/cgi/pt?id=ucl.c2790784&view=1up&seq=1.

——. "Defense Procurement: Air Force." *Defense Industry Bulletin* 4, no. 9 (1968), archived online at https://archive.org/details/defenseindustryb4119wash.

——. "Defense Procurement: Air Force." *Defense Industry Bulletin* 5, nos. 2 and 8 (1969), archived online at https://archive.org/details/defenseindustryb4119wash.

——. "Defense Procurement: Air Force." Defense Industry Bulletin 6, no. 8 (August 1970), archived online at https://babel.hathitrust.org/cgi/pt?id=ucl.c2790787&view=1up&seq=1.

U.S. Department of the Navy. "Department of the Navy Justification of Estimates for Fiscal Year 1983: Submitted to Congress February 1982; Procurement Book 1 of 2, Aircraft Procurement." Budget report, govt. accession no. AD A114941, Navy Aircraft Procurement and Weapons Procurement, Department of the Navy, February 1982. https://apps.dtic.mil/sti/pdfs/ADA114941.pdf.

——. *The Integrated Operational Intelligence System: Electronic Intelligence Station*." N.p.: Audio Productions, 1967. U.S. Navy Training Film no. MN-100005f, 27:36. National Archives identifier 330-dvic-920, archival resource key ark:/13960/t7jr0gd3w. Archived online at https://archive.org/details/330-dvic-920.

——. *The Integrated Operational Intelligence System: Photo Interpretation Station*. N.p.: Audio Productions, 1967. U.S. Navy Training Film no. MN-100005e,

24:36. National Archives identifiers 330-dvic-914, archival resource key ark:/13960/t3vvl4x9g. Archived online at https://archive.org/details/330-dvic-914.

———. *The Integrated Operational Intelligence System: Reconnaissance Mission Planning and Intelligence Data Flow.* N.p.: Audio Productions, 1967. U.S. Navy Training Film no. MN-100005c, 19:18. National Archives identifier 330-dvic-915, archival resource key ark:/13960/t3sv73510. Archived online at https://archive.org/details/330-dvic-915.

U.S. Department of the Navy, Naval Historical Center. "CAPT Manthorpe Archive at: The US Navy's Operations on Inland Waters." Government Printing Office, Washington, DC, [1969] 2006. https://www.history.navy.mil/research/library/online-reading-room/title-list-alphabetically/r/riverine-warfare-us-navys-operations-inland-waters.html.

U.S. Department of the Navy, Office of the Chief of Naval Operations. "Naval Aeronautical Organization for Fiscal Year 1970; Promulgation Of." OPNAV notice 05400, Washington, DC, July 1969. Naval History and Heritage Command, https://www.history.navy.mil/content/dam/nhhc/research/histories/naval-aviation/Naval%20Aeronautical%20Organization/1968-1977/jul1969.pdf.

U.S. General Accounting Office. "DOD's Budget Status: Fiscal Years 1990–94 Budget Reduction Decisions Still Pending." NSIAD-90-125BR, February 22, 1990. https://www.gao.gov/products/nsiad-90-125br.

———. "Navy Command and Control: Data Fusion Needs and Capabilities for Battle Group Commanders." Briefing report to the chairman of the Legislation and National Security Subcommittee, Committee on Government Operations, House of Representatives, GAO/NSIAD-90-69BR, March 1990. https://www.gao.gov/pdf/product/77739.

U.S. National Archives. "The Adventures of CORTDIV 11." *The NDC Blog*, June 18, 2019. https://declassification.blogs.archives.gov/2019/06/18/the-adventures-of-cortdiv-11/.

U.S. Navy. "Command History, Naval Air Forces Atlantic." Commander, Naval Air Force Atlantic (AIRLANT) (website), accessed March 13, 2021. https://www.airlant.usff.navy.mil/Organization/Carrier-Air-Wings/Carrier-Air-Wing-CVW-8/Command-History/.

———. "Navy Strategy for Achieving Information Dominance 2013–2017: Optimizing Navy's Primacy in the Maritime and Information Domains." Office of the Deputy Chief of Naval Operations for Information Dominance, Washington, DC, 2011. https://archive.org/details/DTIC_ADA571217/.

U.S. Navy Patrol Squadrons (website). "Operation Market Time History." VP/VPB Summary Page, VPNavy.org, accessed November 5, 2023. https://www.vpnavy.org/vp_operation_market_time.html.

U.S. Navy Recruiting Command. *Combat Scholar.* N.p.: John J. Hennessy Motion Pictures, 1975. Film.

U.S. Navy Research Development Test and Evaluation. "Exhibit R-2, RDT&E Budget Item Justification." Appropriation/budget activity report, February 2007. Archived online at https://www.dacis.com/budget/budget_pdf/FY08/RDTE/N/0603254N.pdf.

U.S. Senate, Committee on Armed Services. *Hearings Before the Committee on Armed Services, United States Senate, Ninety-Fourth Congress, First Session, on S. 920: Fiscal Year 1976 and July–September 1976 Transition Period Authorization for Military Procurement, Research and Development, and Active Duty, Selected Reserve, and Civilian Personnel Strengths.* Washington, DC: U.S. Government Printing Office, February 1975. Archived online at https://babel.hathitrust.org/cgi/pt?id=mdp.39015076083842&seq=1.

U.S. Senate, Committee on Finance. *The Trade Reform Act of 1973: Hearings; Ninety-Third Congress, Second Session, on H.R. 10710.* 6 vols. Washington, DC: U.S. Government Printing Office, 1974. https://www.congress.gov/bill/93rd-congress/house-bill/10710#:~:text=10710%20%2D%20An%20Act%20to%20promote,93rd%20Congress%20(1973%2D1974).

Valki, László, ed. *Changing Threat Perceptions and Military Doctrines.* New York: St. Martin's Press, 1992.

Vandergriff, Donald E. "How the Germans Defined Auftragstaktik: What Mission Command Is—and—Is Not." *Small Wars Journal*, June 21, 2018. https://archive.smallwarsjournal.com/jrnl/art/how-germans-defined-auftragstaktik-what-mission-command-and-not.

Van Staaveren, Jacob. *Gradual Failure: The Air War over North Vietnam, 1965–1966.* Washington, DC: Air Force History and Museums Program, United States Air Force, 2002. https://media.defense.gov/2010/May/26/2001330292/-1/-1/0/GradualFailure.pdf.

Van Tol, Jan M. "Military Innovation and Carrier Aviation—an Analysis." *Joint Force Quarterly* (Autumn/Winter 1997–1998): 97–108. https://ndupress.ndu.edu/portals/68/Documents/jfq/jfq-17.pdf.

Vego, Milan N. *Joint Operational Warfare: Theory and Practice.* Newport, RI: U.S. Naval War College, 2009.

———. *Major Fleet-versus-Fleet Operations in the Pacific War, 1941–1945.* 2nd ed. Naval War College Historical Monograph Series no. 22. Newport, RI: Naval War College Press, 2016.

———. *Operational Warfare at Sea: Theory and Practice.* 2nd ed. CASS Naval Policy and History Series. London: Routledge, Taylor and Francis Group, 2017.

———. "RECCE-Strike Complexes in Soviet Theory and Practice." Soviet Army Studies Office, U.S. Combined Arms Center, Fort Leavenworth, KS, June 1990. https://apps.dtic.mil/sti/tr/pdf/ADA231900.pdf.

Vice Chief of Naval Operations, Office of the Chief of Naval Operations, U.S. Department of the Navy. "Debrief of SECDEF Meeting on Program Package #6, Saturday 9 September 1961." Box 19 (Memoranda for the Record 1961), OP-09 (Vice Chief of Naval Operations), Organizational Records: The Office of the Chief of Naval Operations 1946–2000, Archives Branch, Naval History and Heritage Command, Washington, DC.

Vietnam War Commemoration. "Week of February 19, 2023: Week of February 19–February 25, 2023; American Special Forces Adviser Killed During Rescue, February 19, 1965." VietnamWar50th.com. Accessed October 28, 2023, https://www.vietnamwar50th.com/education/week_of_february_19_2023/.

Vinson, John E., and Peter B. Decker. "Bad Things Happen When You Take a War Littorally (A Tale of Two NILOs)." *Naval Intelligence Professionals Quarterly* (January 2007).

VIP Club. "24-Bit Computers, Chapter 51." VIPClubMN.org, last updated August 25, 2024. shttps://vipclubmn.org/CP24bit.html.

Vlaun, Brian. "Selling Schweinfurt: Targeting, Assessment, and Marketing in the Air Campaign Against Germany." PhD diss., Air University, 2017. https://apps.dtic.mil/sti/tr/pdf/AD1042098.pdf.

Wallace, Randall, dir. *We Were Soldiers.* Los Angeles: Paramount Pictures, 2002. Film, 138 mins.

Warner, Michael. "The Collapse of Intelligence Support for Air Power, 1944–52: Two Steps Backward." *Studies in Intelligence* 49, no. 3 (2005). https://www.cia.gov/resources/csi/static/collapse-intel-support-air-power.pdf.

———. "Reading the Riot Act: The Schlesinger Report, 1971." *Intelligence and National Security* 24, no. 3 (June 2009): 387–417. https://doi.org/10.1080/02684520903036974 (paywall).

Wellman, David A. *A Chip in the Curtain: Computer Technology in the Soviet Union.* Washington, DC: National Defense University Press, 1989.

Westerfield, H. Bradford. "Inside Ivory Bunkers: CIA Analysts Resist Managers' 'Pandering'; Part II." *International Journal of Intelligence and CounterIntelligence* 10, no. 1 (March 1997): 19–54. https://doi.org/10.1080/08850609708435332 (paywall).

Whyte, William H. *The Organization Man.* Foreword by Joseph Nocera. Philadelphia: University of Pennsylvania Press, 2002. Originally published Simon and Schuster, 1956.

Winkler, David F. *Cold War at Sea: High-Seas Confrontation Between the United States and the Soviet Union.* Annapolis, MD: Naval Institute Press, 2000.

Wyatt, Richard L. "Supporting the Naval Outer Air Battle." In DiGirolamo, *Naval Command and Control,* 96–105. Originally published under the same title in *Signal* 41, no. 1 (September 1986): 19–28, and archived online at https://

books.google.com/books?id=3hgLeKnH5ooC&pg=PA19#v=onepage&q&f=false.

Wylie, J. C. *Military Strategy: A General Theory of Power Control*. Annapolis, MD: Naval Institute Press, 2014.

———. "Why a Sailor Thinks like a Sailor." *Proceedings*, U.S. Naval Institute, 83, no. 8 (August 1957): 811–17. https://www.usni.org/magazines/proceedings/1957/august/why-sailor-thinks-sailor.

Yardley, Roland J., Peter Schirmer, and Harry J. Thie. "OPNAV N14 Quick Reference: Officer Manpower and Personnel Governance in the U.S. Navy; Law, Policy, and Practice, Technical Report." Primer, with Samantha J. Merck. National Defense Research Institute, RAND Corporation, Santa Monica, CA, 2005. https://www.rand.org/content/dam/rand/pubs/technical_reports/2005/RAND_TR264.pdf.

Zachary, Wayne W. "Decision Aids for Naval Air ASW." Technical report 1366-A. Analytics, Willow Grove, PA, March 15, 1980. https://apps.dtic.mil/sti/tr/pdf/ADA085134.pdf.

Zajonc, Robert B. "Attitudinal Effects of Mere Exposure." *Journal of Personality and Social Psychology* 9, no. 2 (part 2) (June 1968): 1–27. https://psycnet.apa.org/doiLanding?doi=10.1037%2Fh0025848.

Zimmerman, S. Rebecca, Kimberly Jackson, Natasha Lander, Colin Roberts, Dan Madden, and Rebeca Orrie. "Movement and Maneuver: Culture and the Competition for Influence Among the U.S. Military Services." RAND Corporation, Santa Monica, CA, 2019. https://www.rand.org/content/dam/rand/pubs/research_reports/RR2200/RR2270/RAND_RR2270.pdf.

Zumwalt, Elmo R., Jr. *On Watch: A Memoir*. New York: Quadrangle/New York Times Book Co., 1976.

———. "Project Sixty: Memorandum for All Flag Officers (and Marine General Officers)." OP-00 (CNO), September 16, 1970, Office of the Chief of Naval Operations, U.S. Department of the Navy, Washington, DC. Document, item no. 6230911006, box 09, folder 11, Admiral Elmo R. Zumwalt Jr. Collection: General Subject Files, Vietnam Center and Sam Johnson Vietnam Archive, Texas Tech University, Lubbock, TX. Available for download from https://vva.vietnam.ttu.edu/repositories/2/digital_objects/404169.

Zurcher, Louis A., Jr. "The Sailor Aboard Ship: A Study of Role Behavior in a Total Institution." *Social Forces* 43, no. 3 (March 1965): 389–400. https://doi.org/10.2307/2574769 (paywall).

INDEX

9TV, 54–55, 223–25, 239
7th Air Force (7th AF), 54–55, 58–59
12MC, ship's internal communication system, classified, 224, 238, 246
35-mm, camera, handheld, 29, 190

A Century of U.S. Naval Intelligence (Packard). *See* Packard, Wyman.
A-1H Skyraider, 100
A-4 Skyhawk, 25, 53, 75, 96, 369
A-6 Intruder, 53
A-7 Corsair, 53, 77
achievement motivation, high (HAM), low (LAM) 25, 150, 173, 175, 272
ACINT, acoustic intelligence, 71, 133–34, 139, 144, 152. *See also* P-3
Adak, Alaska, 128–29, 131–32, 137
adaptation. *See* organizational culture
advanced tactical support base (ATSB), *See* Sealords, 112–13
advanced technology panel (ATP), 261, 282–83. *See also* Small, William
Aegis combat system, 209, 216, 364n26
Aeschbach, Kelly, 293
AFAITC, Air Force's technical training center, 149–50, 194–95, 237, 239. *See also* NMITC
AGI, Soviet Navy *Vishnya*-Class intelligence collection trawlers (AGIs), 44, 190
AGM-12 Bullpup, 74
AGM-45 Shrike, 46
AGM-62 Walleye II, 77
AGM-78 ARM, Standard, 46
AIM-7E Sparrow, 62–63, 65, 325n7
AIM-9 Sidewinder, 63

air intelligence office. *See* shipboard intelligence organization, IOIC
air intelligence officer (AI), Navy; before 1350–1630 merger, 5, 24–25, 59, 69, 85, 86, 94, 101, 116, 277, 299; after merger (1610), 55–56, 64, 88, 93, 121, 129, 131–46, 150–51, 246. *See also* intelligence officer (Navy)
air strike outcome calculator (ASOC), 240
air strike timing decision aid (ASTDA), 240
air target materials program (ATMP), 279
airborne naval tactical data system (ATDS or ANTDS), 126, 182
aircraft carrier air group's senior air intelligence Officer (CAGAI), 55, 57, 72, 246, 270–71, 275, 290
aircraft carrier, organization (intelligence). *See* shipboard intelligence organization.
aircraft carrier division (CARDIV), 87–88
aircraft carrier group (CARGRU), 243–45, 253
aircraft carrier intelligence center (CVIV, also called Intel Center and IOIC). *See* Shipboard Intelligence Organization
aircraft systems support center (ASSC), 23, 25. *See also* RA-5C and shipboard intelligence organization (IOIC)
alert-5, aircraft readiness status, 191–92, 197, 224, 360n38
America, 30, 153, 181, 223–25, 229, 235–36
AN/APX-81 Combat Tree, 67

431

AN/AYA-1, computer, 23–24. *See also* RA-5C
AN/GYK-9, computer, 220, 368n15. *See also* Ironhorse
AN/USQ-20, computer. *See* NTDS
AN/UYK-1, computer, 27–28, 220. *See also* IOIC
anti-aircraft Artillery (AAA), 33, 37–39, 42, 45–46, 55, 57–58, 61–62, 69. *See also* IADS
anti-submarine Classification and Analysis Center (ASCAC), 181, 188
anti-submarine warfare (ASW), 116, 123–25, 131, 143, 145–46, 180–81, 184, 188, 196, 199, 219. *See also* P-3 and ASCAC
AQA-1 Jezebel, sonobuoy, 127–28. *See also* P-3
Arab-Israeli wars, (1967 and 1973), 155, 170–71, 198, 204, 208–9. *See also* IADS
Arctic Sea, 120
Arnold, 136. *See also* Pony Express
Assault Breaker, project, 206
Ault Report, air-to-air missile review, 1968), 63, 64, 326
automated sata processing (ADP), 28–30, 215
aviation culture, Navy, identity, 121, 178, 187, 277–78, 281, 299–300. *See also* organizational culture, collectivism

B-52 Stratofortress, 44
Barents Sea, 120, 125, 200
Barnett, Roger, 10
basic encyclopedia of targets, 72, 240
basic test battery (BTB), 91
bastions, Soviet Navy, xii, 125, 259
battle group antiair warfare coordination (BGAAWC), 209. *See also* Aegis
battleship admirals (Navy), 4, 9–12, 276
BearTrap program, 143–44, 149. *See also* P-3
beyond visible range (BVR) fight, 62–63, 67. *See also* OTH

Big Smoke, yacht. *See* TF-157
billet restructuring (for organizational change), 294, 301, 303
Bird Dog, Cessna 160 aircraft, 112–13. *See also* NILO
blockade, close and distant, 2, 96–97, 100, 115, 120–21, 124, 140, 144, 151. *See also* Market Time
Bolo, Operation, 65–67. *See also* Olds
Boyd, John, 208, 287
Branch, Ted N., 291. *See also* Information Warfare Community
Bray, William R., 291
Brooks, Thomas, A., xviii, 87–88, 114, 166, 210, 212–13, 252, 257–58, 263, 266, 273, 281–82, 285
Bureau of Air, Navy (BuAir), 82
Burke, Arleigh, 9, 12–3
Bush, G. H. W., xv–xvi

C-130 Hercules, 50, 149
C-2 Greyhound (carrier on board delivery), 59
command and control (C2), 38–39, 62, 69, 129, 187–88, 200, 205, 208–10, 217, 219, 225, 233–34, 275
command, control, and communications (C3), 141, 146, 165, 167, 169, 171, 175, 199, 216, 219
command and control warfare (C2W, 217, 287
Cambodia. *See* Sihanoukville
card of the day, 56–57
Carl Vinson, 247
Carter, Jimmy, President, 206
catapult (Cat), aircraft carrier, 191–92
Cebrowski, Arthur K, 288, 290. *See also* network-centric warfare
Center for Naval Analyses (CNA), 185, 259, 261
centralization. *See* organizational culture
CIA, central intelligence organization, 1, 41, 49–50, 99, 109–10, 163, 242, 249, 253–54, 259

Channell, Norm "Ralph," 87–88, 99–100, 104, 105–6
charts, paper: use of, 55–56, 73, 223, 235; maintenance of, 240–41
China, People's Republic of, 40–43, 203–4, 207
Chisholm, Donald, 267–72, 274
Clarey, Bernard A., 198
Classic Bullseye, ELINT system (shore), 168, 229
Classic Outboard, ELINT system (ship), 226, 229
Classic Wizard, ELINT system (space), 226, 229, 282
Claud Jones-Class, Modified Destroyer, 136–37
coastal surveillance centers (CSC), 101, 118. *See also* Market Time
cohesion, organizational, 90, 274. *See also* organizational culture, centralization
Combat Air Patrol (CAP), 53, 61
combat information center (CIC), 70, 183, 187–89, 222, 224–25, 234–35, 238, 246, 267, 273, 282
Combs Board, personnel system review, 86
COMINT, communications intelligence, 103, 108, 138–42, 161, 193, 220. *See also* SIGINT
Command Support Systems (OP-094), 216–19, 227. *See also* Zumwalt and Harlfinger
Commander in Chief, Pacific, (CINCPAC), 107, 196, 198
common intelligence plot (CIP), picture, 211, 219, 222–25, 231, 232, 246. *See also* ECLIPS
common operational plot (COP), picture, 219, 222, 232, 246, 282. *See also* CIP and Tuttle, Jerry
communication security (COMSEC), 104, 149
Compartmented Mode Processing System (CMPS), 240–41

Complex adaptive systems, 269, 297
Constellation, 181
coordination without hierarchy, organizational, 380, 381. *See also* Chisholm
competition (great powers), xviii, 40–41, 123, 144, 157, 264, 290, 303
Coronado, 242
Cothron, Tony L., 236, 369
Cracknell, William, 116, 117, 129, 145, 180
Cramer, Michael RADM, USN, 258, 287
Credibility, part of intelligence officer identity, 108–9, 111, 250, 252–56, 260, 275, 292. *See also* organization culture, identity
cruise book, ship or squadron, 20, 82, 92, 145, 184
cruiser-destroyer group (CRUDESGRU), 24, 243, 244, 245, 253
cryptology, 146, 149, 216
cryptologic direct support element (CDSE), 139, 275
Cryptologic Technician (CT), enlisted, 140, 168, 189, 193, 195
Cryptology Officer (1610), Navy (special duty), 3, 161, 167, 193
CSG, cryptologic security group, *See* OSIS, FOSIF Rota
Cuban missile crisis (1962), 13, 21, 40, 124, 126
culture. *See* organizational culture
CWC, composite warfare commander concept: use of, 210–11, 225, 232, 237, 245; officer in tactical command (OTC), 210–11, 234, 245
cyclic operations, aircraft carrier, 53, 188

Da Nang, Vietnam, 33, 61, 69–70, 105, 108, 118, 220–22. *See also* IronHorse and 'four trawlers'
daily intelligence summary (DISUM), 25, 55
decentralization. *See* organizational culture

434 INDEX

Decker, Peter B., 112. *See also* NILO
Defense Intelligence Agency (DIA), 41, 49, 56, 60, 68, 71, 73, 85, 103, 109–10, 133, 161, 166, 232, 279
Defense Intelligence School (DIS), renamed the National Intelligence University, 257
Defense Research and Engineering (DDR&E), 48
Defense Special Missile and Astronautics Center (DEFSMAC), 137. *See also* Pony Express
defense special security Communications System (DSSCS), 103
Delta-class (SSBN), SNS, 96, 126, 133
Democratic Republic of Vietnam (DRV), or North Vietnam, 19, 35, 38–50, 57, 60–61, 63, 65–72, 76–77, 96–97, 100, 104, 111–13, 118, 141
depth and breadth debate, intelligence Officer career, 278–80. *See also* intelligence officer (14N), USAF
DESOTO (DeHaven special operations off TsingtaO) missions, 35
detailing, officer (Navy), 87, 149, 252, 258
Director of Naval Intelligence (DNI), 5, 99, 104, 114–15, 162, 216, 233, 249–52, 257–58, 260, 285, 287, 301
discovery-learning, 78
District Intelligence Offices (DIO), 104–5. *See also* Naval Investigative Service Offices (NISO)
doctrine, military, 108, 181, 204–5, 261, 269, 272–73, 287–88, 291, 296
Donald, Miskill, 128, 144. *See also* VP-50
Duffle Bag, unattended ground sensor, Vietnam War, 112. *See also* NILO
Durr, Donald G., 188, 192–93, 196
Duval, Thomas, 163. *See also* TF-157

E-2 Hawkeye, 182, 189, 191–92, 224
EA-3B/AD-3 Skywarrior, 25, 68, 139, 165
EA-6B Prowler (EW), 241
EB-66 Destroyer, 37, 47

EC-121 Warning Star, 44, 68, 141
Eisenhower, Dwight D., 12, 34
Eisenhower, Dwight D. (Ike), 232, 234–35, 242, 244–46
electronic intelligence (ELINT), 22, 30, 44, 49–50, 69, 71, 139–40, 168, 193–94, 226, 282. *See also* SIGINT
electronic warfare (EW), 44–45, 47, 76, 138, 143, 159, 181, 188, 216, 218, 236, 287
embargo policy (computers), 206–8
embedding change. *See* organizational culture
enhanced calculator link processing system (ECLIPS): development and use of, 212–15, 223–24, 226, 232–33, 235–38, 247, 282; HP 9830A computer use in, 212. *See also* shipboard intelligence organization (SupPlot)
Enterprise, 82–83, 94, 193, 236, 254
EP-3E Aries, 139, 140, 142, 226
Equal Rights Amendment, 147
Essex-class, 24, 94
every-analyst-a-warning-analys (EAAWA), 157
evolution. *See* organizational culture
evolvability. *See* organizational culture
expeditionary plot (ExPlot), amphibious warships, 247
extended surface plot (ESP), early COP, 189, 219. *See also* Outlaw project

F-100 Super Sabre, 33–35, 46,
F-105 Thunderchief, 37, 46, 62–63
F-14 Tomcat, 180, 201, 224, 261
F-4 Phantom, 25, 37, 53, 63, 66, 96, 191–92
F-8D Crusader, 33, 36, 51, 61, 63
Falklands War (1982), 287
Fan Song radar, 37, 45–46. *See also* AS-2
Firebee, Model 120 (drone), 49–50, 60. *See also* TECINT
First World War (WWI), 4, 11–12, 125
flag command centers (FCC), 219, 368. *See also* Outlaw program

Fleet Air Intelligence Center, Atlantic's (FAITCLANT), later called Fleet Intelligence Training Center (FITCLANT), 116, 239. *See also* NMITC
Fleet Air Reconnaissance Squadron (VQ-1), 68, 132, 139–40, 142
Fleet Air Reconnaissance Squadron (VQ-2), 138, 142, 149, 163, 165
Fleet Command Support Centers (FCSC), 367. *See also* Outlaw program,
Fleet Electronic Warfare Support Group (FEWSG), 143
fleet imagery support terminals (FIST), 242
Fleet Intelligence Center Facility Pacific (FICPACFAC), 56, 74. *See also* Richardson, David
Fleet Intelligence Center Pacific (FICPAC), 56, 72
fleet satellite communication system (FLTSATCOM), 225, 227
Fleet Weather Center (FWC), Europe, 163. *See also* FOSIF Rota
Fobair, Roscoe, 37
Ford, David (*The Admiral's Advantage*), 71, 287
foreign instrument signals intelligence (FISINT), 136. *See also* SIGINT,
Forrestal, 19, 24–25, 53, 82–83, 89, 92, 94–96, 193, 224, 235–36. *See also* Ore
Fort Meade, Maryland (NSA), 68, 85, 140, 161, 167, 222, 260
four trawlers incident (Vietnam war), 118–19. *See also* Point Welcome
FOSIC, Fleet Ocean Surveillance Information Center. *See* OSIS
FOSIF, Fleet Ocean Surveillance Information Facility. *See* OSIS
fragmentary order (FRAGO), 54
Friedman, Norman (Network-Centric Warfare), 159, 204, 218

Frog, FOSIF, 179. *See also* organizational culture, collectivism

Game Warden, operation, Vietnam war, 100, 102, 104–5, 145, 152.
Gapfiller, satellite communications system, 226
Gentry, John A. (*Warning Intelligence*), 156–57
Gerras, Stephen J. (Culture and Military Organizations), 8, 89
Giacchino, Louis, 161
Gilday, Michael M., 293
Goldwater-Nichols National Defense Reform Act (1986), 284–85
Goodman, Michael S., 156–57
Gordon, Joseph S. (*Warning Intelligence*), 156–57
Gorshkov, Sergey, Soviet Navy, 122
Grabo, Cynthia M. (*Anticipating Surprise*), 155–56, 158. *See also* intelligence, warning
Graf, Jack (KIA, Vietnam, 1969), 113–14. *See also* NILO
Greenert, Jonathan, 293
Greenland-Iceland-United Kingdom (GIUK) Gap, 120, 189, 227
ground control intercept (GCI), 39, 45, 62, 66–67, 70, 194, 223, 327
GRU, Glavnoye razvedyvatel'noye upravleniye, 44
Gulf of Tonkin Resolution, 35
Gulf War, operation (Desert Shield-Desert Storm), 285–86

halo effect, 89. *See also* organizational culture
HAM. *See* achievement motivation
Hammock, project, 69–70, 221. *See also* IronHorse
Handel, Michael, 17, 265–66, 379, 380, 431
Harlfinger, Fredrick, 162–63, 216–18, 281. *See also* Command Support Systems

Harris, Gail, 149
Hartford, Robin W., xix, 11, 27, 52, 58, 91
Haver, Rich, 260
Hayward, Thomas, 201, 260–61
Helms, Richard M. (CIA director), 110
high-frequency direction finding (HFDF), 164, 168, 220–21, 226, 229
Ho Chi Minh Trail, 97
Hofstede, Geert, (Global Leadership and Organizational Behavior Effectiveness), 8
Holloway, James L. III, 94, 148–49, 250–51, 257
Hone, Thomas (Power and Change and History of the Office of the Chief of Naval Operations), xvii, xix, 20, 260
Hone, Trent (*Learning War*), 10, 14, 78, 260, 267–68, 298
Hoyt Vandenberg, 136–37. *See also* Pony Express
HP 9830A, computer. *See* ECLIPS
HUMINT, human intelligence, 104–6, 108–9, 112–13, 115, 152, 163, 278–79. *See also* TF-157

identification friend or foe (IFF), 67, 79. *See also* Combat Tree
identity. *See* organizational culture
imagery (Photo/imagery) intelligence (IMINT), 20–23, 25, 309, 47–48, 50–53, 58–59, 64, 68, 71, 74, 77, 82–84, 108–9, 129, 131–32, 140, 161–63, 165, 190–91, 194, 204, 241–42, 278–79, 283, 290. *See also* shipboard intelligence organization, MSI
Independence, 22, 82, 83, 158, 179, 235
Indochina (French colony, today Socialist Republic of Vietnam (SRV)), 13, 34, 43, 204
Information Dominance Corps (IDC): creation, 289–91; information dominance warfare officer (IDWO) warfare insignia, 289

Information Warfare Community (IWC), replaced IDC, 291–96
IWCmdr, 291–92, 294–96. *See also* information warfare community
Inman, Bobby R., 173, 249–60, 281, 300–301
Inman's touch, talent management, 250–53, 256–58, 260, 281, 300, 377n27
innovation, 10, 41, 88, 138, 144, 264–68, 272, 274–76, 280–81, 296, 298, 300, 302. *See also* organizational culture
institutionalization, 31, 81, 94, 258, 280
integrated air defense system (IADS): in Vietnam war, 36–46, 48, 57, 59, 61, 67–69, 73, 76, 78–79. *See also* TECINT and SA-2
institutionalize, 15, 31, 81, 94, 244, 258, 280. *See also* IOIC
intelligence community (IC), U.S., 39–41, 49, 59, 67, 71, 109, 132, 155, 157, 160, 168, 186, 207, 249, 259, 270, 287. *See also* CIA and DIA
intelligence officer (14N), USAF, 278–80
intelligence officer (Navy): aviation (1350), 19, 24–25, 59, 82, 85–88, 94–95, 101, 114, 116, 121, 145, 270, 277, 289, 299; line subspecialists; 2–5, 85, 99, 102–3, 114, 133, 148–49, 167, 177; meger of 1350 into 1630, 86, 94, 116, 121, 289; special duty (1630), 2–5, 59, 84–85, 87, 94, 99, 100–5, 108–9, 113–14, 116, 120–21, 133, 140, 145, 148–49, 152, 159, 161, 163, 167, 172, 176–77, 188, 190, 194, 223, 250–2, 270, 278, 280, 286–87, 289–90, 296, 299–301
intelligence, warning, 155–67, 169–72, 179, 183–86, 191–93, 196–98, 211, 224, 232, 237, 246, 258, 276, 283, 299. *See also* LRA problem
intelligence Detachments (FID), 290, 385
integrated operational intelligence center (IOIC): brief/debrief, 31, 55–57, 129, 131, 135, 188–89 (*see also*

Mitran); darkroom, 26, 51, 58, 190 (*see also* Hartford, Robin); Electronic Evaluation (EE), 55–56, 236 (*see also* PECM); Electronic Data Processing (EDP), 27–29, 58; importance of, 14, 36, 64, 80, 82–83, 89, 90, 92–95, 129, 188, 220, 236, 241, 267, 272, 276, 280, 297 (*see also* CVIC, shipboard intelligence organization); installation and maintenance of, 24–26, 28–30, 34, 83–84; mission planning, 19, 24, 51, 54–55, 57, 59, 72–73, 90, 95, 129, 134, 189, 238–42, 258; multi-sensor interpretation (MSI), 88, 235 (*see also* SCV). *See also* shipboard intelligence organization

intercontinental ballistic missile (ICBM), 136

IOIC Supervisor, 57, 83–84, 89, 92. *See also* Ship's Intelligence Officer

IOIS, integrated operational intelligence system, 19–20, 23, 26, 81. *See also* RA-5C

Iron Hand operations, 45–47, 73

IronHorse system, 70–71, 79, 220–22, 228,

IS, Intelligence Specialist (enlisted), 133, 168, 190, 195, 224, 236, 238–39, 244

IWCmdr, information operations warfare commander, 291–92, 294–96. *See also* IDC/IWC

Jacoby, Lowell "Jake" E., 5, 80, 186, 195, 197, 233, 246, 258, 282–83, 285–86. *See also* JICPAC

John F. Kennedy, 145, 220, 224, 232

Johnson, Lyndon B., President, 35–36, 45, 71, 309

Joint Analysis Center (JAC) at RAF Molesworth, UK, 286

Joint Intelligence Center, Pacific (JICPAC), 286

Joint Personnel Recovery Center (JPRC), 114

Joint Reconnaissance Center (JRC), 49, 68

JOTS, joint operations tactical system, 232, 246, 282. *See also* Tuttle, Jerry

KA-74 Hycon camera, 131. *See also* RA-5C

Kamchatka, Russia, 133, 136

Kamiseya, Japan, 166. *See also* FOSIF

KB-18A, camera. *See* RA-5C and P-3

Keirn, Richard, 37, 60

Keith Board, personnel system review (1959), 84

Kennedy, John F. President, 17

Kentian vs. Kendall/Gatesian intelligence school debates, 253–54

KGB, Komitet gosudarstvennoy bezopasnosti, 43–44

Khrushchev, Nikita, First Secretary, Soviet Union, 43

Kidd, Jr., Isaac C., 198, 201

Kitty Hawk, 25, 33–35, 82–83, 88, 94, 181, 188, 193, 219, 224, 236

Klusmann, Charles, 33, 36

Komer, Robert, 35

Korean War, 1, 3, 6, 9, 12, 14, 103, 140–41, 277, 279

Kuehn, John, 11

LAM. *See* achievement motivation

Lambert, Andrew, xix

Lao, Pathet Communist (see Laos), 33, 36

Laos, People's Democratic Republic, 33–5, 45

Lasko, Paul G., 234, 238, 242, 244

learning, 78–79, 265, 267, 301

learning organizations, 47, 74, 78–79, 83, 95, 138, 150, 152, 186, 192, 195, 197, 263–64, 266–67, 276, 281, 295, 302. *See also* Hone Trent

Leatherman, Nolan H., 241. *See also* RA-5C

Lehman, John F., former Secretary of the Navy, 200–1, 261–62

Liberty, 141, 153–55, 159, 165
line officer, unrestricted (URL): aviation and its culture, 3– 4, 11–13, 62, 87, 93, 125, 148, 150, 177–79, 244, 270–71, 276–77, 280–81, 299, 300–1; aviation intelligence (1350), 2–5, 19, 24–25, 59, 68, 82, 85–88, 94–95, 101, 116, 121, 145, 270, 277, 289, 293, 299; submarine, 3, 11, 13, 17, 87, 217, 244, 293, 299; subspecilist intelligence (*see also* intelligence officer (Navy)); surface line, 4, 11, 13, 161, 213, 244, 276, 277, 299. *See also* battleship admirals and SWO
line officer, restricted (RL or special duty): cryptologic (1610). *See* cryptologic officer; intelligence (1630). *See* intelligence officer (Navy)
Linebacker I and II, operation (Vietnam), 64, 198
Link 11, data link, 126, 182
Link 14, data link, 212–15, 219, 223, 226. *See also* ECLIPS
Litsinger, Nelson H., 84, 88, 93, 102, 168–70, 174–77, 179, 186, 189, 196–97, 227, 234–38, 242, 244, 245–46
little brother syndrome, 196–98, 283–84, 360n36. *See also* OSIS
Little Rock, 160, 162–63, 165
Long Arm, project. *See* Firebee
loosely coupled system, 269–70 *See also* decentralization
Lowenthal, Mark, 253
long-range aviation (LRA) problem, Soviet, 183–84, 186–87, 190–93. *See also* intelligence, warning
Lyons Jr., Aloysius James, 165, 199–201, 261. *See also* Ocean Venture

MacKrell, Eileen F., 289
Maddox, 35, 317n4
magnetic tape units (MTU), *See also* IOIC, 27–28
Mahan, Alfred Thayer, 122
Mansoor, Peter R. (*The Culture of Military Organizations*). *See* organizational culture
Marine Corps tactical data system (MTDS), 221. *See also* IronHorse
maritime patrol (MARPAT), 121, 125
maritime patrol and reconnaissance aircraft (MPRA). *See also* P-2 and P-3
maritime patrol and reconnaissance forces (MPRF), 115, 120–21, 125, 128, 143, 147, 149. *See also* blockading
Maritime Strategy, U.S. Navy, xvii, 15, 201, 260–61, 283
Market Time, operation (Vietnam war), 100–2, 104–7, 117–21, 126, 128, 152. *See also* blockade
Marocchi, John, 279
Mayaguez, SS, 203–4
McDonald, David L., 84, 86. *See also* Combs Board
McFarland, James, 170. *See also* FOSIF ROtA
McNamara, Robert (SecDef), 17, 34, 37, 40–41, 48–49, 72–73
Mekong River delta, 96–97, 99–100, 106, 110–11, 301
Midway, 94, 179, 242
Midway Atoll, U.S. territory, 2, 135, 136, 137, 155, 179. *See also* P-3
MiG, aircraft: general use of, 39, 62, 67, 69; Fagot (15), 42, 61; Fresco (17), 42, 61; Farmer (19), 42, 37; Fishbed (21), 42, 65–66. *See also* Bolo
military assistance advisory group (MAAG), 34, 35, 99–100
Military Assistance Command, Vietnam (MACV), 100, 103, 105
military culture, 331. *See also* Wong
miniature transparencies (MITRAN), *See also* IOIC, 72
Miramar, Naval Air Station (California), 63–64. *See also* TopGun
Miskill, Donald, 128, 144. *See also* P-3

missile defense: anti-ballistic (ABM), 41; ballistic (BMD), 41
mixed wing, aircraft carrier, 124, 180–82
Mk-32 (Zunni), 96. *See also Forrestal*
Moffett Field, Alameda, California, 117, 128, 150, 281, 301. *See also* VP-50
Moffett, William, 281, 301
Monkey Mountain, Da Nang, Vietnam, 69
Moorer, Thomas, 77, 162–63, 184–85
Moskva, SNS, 125, 164–65
Mount Whitney, 210, 212–14, 283
multiple independent reentry vehicles (MIRV), 135
Murphy, Daniel, 171

N2, staff intelligence officer, 26, 87, 99, 102, 104–5, 107, 109, 114, 116, 135, 142–43, 145, 161, 196, 210, 212, 234, 238, 242–46, 251–52, 270–71, 275, 282, 285, 289–92. *See also* intelligence officer (Navy)
national intelligence estimate (NIE), 39–41
National Reconnaissance Office (NRO), 217
National SIGINT Operations Center (NSOC), 141, 167
National War College, 199, 239
NATO, 41, 159, 189, 201, 205–6, 208–9, 212, 247, 282
Naval Advisory Group (NAG), 102–3, 105
Naval Air and Strike Warfare Center (NASWC) at Fallon, Nevada, 290
Naval Air Observers (NAO), 117
Naval Flight Officer (NFO), 116
Naval Forces, Vietnam (NAVFORV), 105, 107, 112, 114–15, 166, 302. *See also* Zumwalt
Naval Information Forces (NAVIFOR), 293, 296
Naval Intelligence Liaison Officer (NILO), Vietnam war, 26, 105–6, 110, 112–15, 301, 391. *See also* Graff, John

Naval Intelligence Processing System Support Activity (NIPSSA), 28
Naval Investigative Service Offices (NISO), 105, 114–15, 301
Naval Ocean Surveillance Information Center (NOSIC), 166. *See also* OSIS
Naval Photographic Interpretation Center (NPIC), 29
Naval Postgraduate School, 239
Naval Reconnaissance and Technical Support Center (NRTSC), 26, 28, 29, 60, 96, 102. *See also* IOIC
Naval Scientific and Technical Intelligence Center (NAVSTIC), 48, 60, 134
Naval Security Group (NSG), 136, 139–41, 143, 146, 161, 163–65, 167–68, 176, 189, 192–93, 195. *See also* OSIS
Naval Surface Forces Atlantic (SURFLANT), 214–15
Naval Tactical Data System (NTDS): Aegis, connection with, 208–9; AN/USQ-20, computer, 28–30, 56, 220; IronHorse connection, 220–21 (*see also* IronHorse); with Link 11, 126; with Link 14, 213–14 (*see also* ECLIPS); Outlaw program connection, 229, 234–35; Surveillance and operating picture, 182–83, 188–89; as Redcrown, 70. *See also* COP
Naval War College, 4, 145, 199, 232, 239, 261, 265, 267, 280, 293
Navy and Marine Corps Intelligence TrainingCcenter (NMITC), 195, 199. *See also* AFAITC
Navy Field Operational Intelligence Office (NFOIO), 30, 85, 161, 166–67, 260. *See also* OSIS
Navy rating and Enlisted Code (NEC), 91, 238–39
Network-centric Warfare, xvii, 159, 208, 288–89, 295. *See also* Cebrowski, Arthur

New Look national security policy, 12–13
Nimitz-class (CVN), 94, 185, 234–36, 244, 247
NIPS, naval intelligence processing system, 29–30, 168, 194–95, 239–40, 242
Nixon, Richard, President, 198, 254
Noble, Richard A., 195, 237
Noll, Frank, 100
Norfolk, Virginia, 166, 179, 196, 197, 222–23, 227, 239, 283. *See also* OSIS
North American Aviation/Rockwell (NAA, NAR), 26–27, 83. *See also* RA-5C and shipboard intelligence organization (IOIC)
Northern Wedding, exercise. *See* Oceans Venture
Notz, F. P., 255
NSA, National Security Agency, 68–69, 104, 136, 139–41, 146, 166, 170–71, 220, 222, 260. *See also* FOSIF Rota
nuclear (atomic) weapons, 6, 12, 17, 34, 120, 205, 259, 278–79. *See also* SIOP

ocean surveillance information system (OSIS): 'afloat', 204, 213, 215, 233, 235, 237–39, 246–47, 282–87; creation and use, 14, 77, 95, 115, 124, 146–47, 152, 159, 164, 166, 172, 178–80, 185–90, 192, 194, 254, 266–67, 269, 275–76, 297–98, 300–1; competition between big and little brother, 195–98; support to Outlaw project, 216, 218–20, 222, 225, 227–28 (*see also* Outlaw project (Shark)); FOSIC, 166, 176, 179, 187, 196–97, 222–23, 227, 283, 286; FOSIF Rota, 146, 163–72, 174–79, 185, 191–92, 195, 197–99, 226–27, 235, 237–38 (*see also* Richardson, David); NOSIC, 166; SIGINT (CSG) support of, 136, 139, 140, 141, 143, 146, 161, 163–68, 170–71, 176, 190, 192. *See also* NSG

Ocean Venture, exercise: activities, 200–1, 232, 261–62, 355, 361; Northern Wedding, exercise, 201, 361n1. *See also* Tuttle, Jerry and Lehman, John
Office of Naval Intelligence (ONI), 4, 19, 28–29, 56, 72, 85, 134, 259, 260, 273, 290
officer in tactical command (OTC), *See* CWC
officer in tactical command information exchange system datalink (OTCIXS), 227, 232
Ogarkov, Nikolai V., 205–6
Okean, Soviet exercises (1970 & 1975), 132, 166
Olds, Robin, 66. *See also* Bolo
Omand, David Sir, 158. *See also* warning intelligence
OP, Photographic division, *See* shipboard intelligence organization
operational intelligence, Navy Opintel: function of, xv, xvi, 4–6, 14–15, 64, 77; air warfare support, character of, 59, 71, 83, 85–88, 92, 95–96, 102, 104, 108, 114–16, 120–21, 129, 131, 142, 144–46, 151–52; evolution mechanisms of, 263–71, 274–77, 280–81; identity of, 249–52, 254, 256, 259, 297–303; ocean surveillance support, character of, 158, 160–63, 166, 170–74, 177, 179, 180; outer air battle support, character, 183–84, 186–87, 190–92, 194–99; post-Cold War, character of; 282–84, 286, 289, 290, 296; tactical support, character of, 204–5, 210–13, 215, 220–23, 233–34, 236–41, 243–47
operational reporting (OPREP-3), 57
operational security (OPSEC), 104
OpNav N2/N6, 290, 291, 385. *See also* IWC
OpNav, Navy operation and planning staff, 20, 26, 149, 199, 214, 216
OpsComm, operations communication circuit, 26, 186, 197, 222, 223,

230, 235, 373. *See also* shipboard intelligence organization
Ore, William "Rock" E., 19, 24, 83, 86, 89, 92, 96
organizational change (informal and formal). *See* organizational culture, evolution
organizational culture: description of, 7–8 (*see also* Schein); centralization & decentralization of 9, 129, 161, 166, 264, 266, 268–69, 271, 274–76, 278, 285, 287, 291–92, 298, 300–3 (*see also* OSIS); change (informal and formal), 7, 9, 14–15, 17, 37, 78, 80–81, 83, 144, 147, 150–51, 187, 198, 233, 243, 265, 272–74, 289, 296–97, 300–3 (*see also* IOIC and IWC); collectivism (in-group) 8, 15, 90–92, 95, 152, 177 (*see also* patches and zaps); competition (promotion), xii, xviii, 7, 9, 11, 172–79, 192, 254, 271, 298, 299 (*see also* FOSIF Rota); embedding change, 118, 192, 249; evolvability of, 144, 234, 263–66, 268, 270, 276, 296, 298, 301–2; evolution of, 9–11, 13–15, 36, 53, 79, 90, 115, 125, 159, 172, 180, 183, 191, 233–34, 249, 263, 266–70, 276, 296–99, 301–3 (*see also* Hone, Trent); identity within, 8, 69–70, 76, 78, 90, 92, 152, 179, 191, 234, 247, 250, 254, 265, 276–77, 299 (*see also* Inman); exceptionalism within, 90, 92, 179 (*see also* IOIC); military specific, 6–8 (*see also* Wong); performance orientation, 8, 15, 59, 83, 87–88, 90, 95, 114, 152, 179, 186, 188, 192, 197, 236, 247, 258, 277, 299 (*see also* LRA problem); power distance, 8, 89, 90, 243, 270; reinforcing change, 92, 151, 173, 179, 192, 249 (*see also* Inman); regarding achievement motivation, 25, 26, 150, 173, 174, 175, 271; reinforcing change of, 8, 249; revolution of, 7, 320, 342, 172, 309, 317, 354, 362, 364–65

organizational learning, 78, 79, 265, 267, 301. *See also* organizational culture
OS, Cryptologic division, *See* shipboard intelligence organization
OTH-T Gold (Rainform message), 226–27
over-the-horizon-targeting (OTH-T), 26, 205, 209, 218; SOSUS, underwater surveillance and ASW, 124, 127, 131, 134, 143, 144, 146, 220–21, 226–27, 231, 238n19
Outlaw programs: Outlaw project, 199, 219, 222, 225, 231, 276; Hawk, 219–20, 222, 224–25, 232; Outlaw Shark, 14, 219, 220–23, 225–33, 237, 247, 282, 297. *See also* Wessman
outer air battle. *See* operational intelligence
OZ, Intelligence division. *See* shipboard intelligence organization

P-2V Neptune, 100, 116–18
P-3 Orion, 116–17, 121, 123, 125–27, 129, 131, 137–38, 140, 142–44, 149. *See also* Market Time and blockade
PARPRO, 140–42. *See also* P-3
passive electronic countermeasures (PECM) 23–24, 28. *See also* IOIC
patches, 91–93, 178. *See also* organizational culture, collectivism,
patrol plane commander (PPC), P-3, 131
PB4Y-2 Privateer, 138
PDP 11/18, computer, Digital Equipment Corporation, 169, 353n69. *See also* FOSIF Rota
Pearl Harbor, Hawaii, 2, 12, 137, 166, 241
Pedersen, Dan, 64. *See also* TopGun
Perras, Wayne, 30
Petropavlovsk, Russia, 132
PH, photographers mate, 2, 26, 51–52, 91, 131
Philippines, Republic of, 2, 33, 56, 68, 74, 117, 138
Photographic Intelligenceman (PT), 55, 84, 91, 168, 194

Pierce Arrow, operation, 35–36, 42
Plain of Jars, Laos, 33, 35
plot, intelligence (picture warfare), 31, 70, 85, 102, 109, 168, 170, 189, 204, 210–15, 220, 223–27, 230, 235, 247, 282. *See also* shipboard intelligence organization, SupPlot
Point Welcome. *See* Four Trawlers
Polaris missile, 13, 17, 280
politicization, intelligence, 253–54
Pony Express, mission, 135–37. *See also* P-3
power distance. *See* organizational culture
Powers, Bruce F., 40, 185, 357,
Pressly, George, 163. *See also* FOSIF Rota
prototype ocean surveillance terminal (POST), 222, 246, 282, 382
prototype OSIS terminal (POST), 222, 246, 282
Pueblo, 141, 155
Pyle, Robert, 114

RA-5C Vigilante: cameras, 22–23, 58, 131; development and use of, 20–23, 51, 68, 77, 131, 188, 280; electronic collection, *See* passive electronic countermeasures. *See also* IOIS
Radar Homing and Warning (RHAW), 46–47
Radar Intercept Officers (RIO), 64
Radar, Electronic Warfare, Sonar (REWSON) Project, Naval Electronics Systems Command, 159, 218
Rainform message format, 132, 143, 170, 190, 214, 219, 223, 226
Ranger 25, EP-3E, 226–27. *See also* Outlaw Shark
Ranger, 181, 184
RC-130 Silver Dawn (COMINT), 65
Reagan, Ronald, President, 200, 205, 260–61
Rectanus, Earl, 105–10, 115, 166, 217, 281, 302. *See also* NILO

Redcrown. *See* NTDS
Reddig, James (aka Vic Socotra), 174–76, 178–79, 242, 287
reinforcing change, *See* organizational culture
revolution. *See* organizational culture
RF-8 Crusader, reconnaissance, 33, 36, 51, 61, 63–64
Richardson, David C., 73–74, 76–77, 95, 154–55, 159–63, 165, 198–99, 273, 281. *See also* FOSIF Rota Richardson, John M., 293
Rickover, Hyman G., 13
Rocky and Bullwinkle Show, 92. *See also* organizational culture, collectivism
Rolling Thunder, operation. 36, 38–40, 42, 45, 53, 59, 63–64, 70–73, 77, 273
Rondeau, Ann E., 133, 145–46, 149–51
Rosenberg, David (*The Admiral's Advantage*), 71, 286
Rota Naval Air Station, Spain. *See* OSIS, FOSIF Rota
rules of engagement (ROE), 62, 73

SA-2 Guideline, 23, 37–38, 40, 42, 45–47, 49–51, 60, 68, 73. *See also* TECINT
SA-5 Gammon, 41
S-2 Tracker, 59, 181
S-3 Viking, 180–81, 188
Saigon, RVN, 36, 77, 96, 99, 102–3, 105, 111, 117
Sanctuary, 148
Saratoga, 19, 56, 58, 82–83, 92, 181, 189, 191, 195–97
Schein, Edgar H., *See* organizational culture
Schlesinger Report, 249, 302
Sea Float, 111. *See also* Sealords
SEAD, suppression of enemy air defenses, 44–45, 47, 51
SEALORDS, Southeast Asia lake, ocean, river, and delta strategy (Vietnam war), 100, 104, 107–12, 145, 152. *See also* Zumwalt

INDEX

second world war (WWII), 84
Senge, Peter M., 296
servant ethos, 263–66, 269, 291–92, 298–302. *See also* organizational culture, identity
SH-3 Sea King, 180
Shapiro, Sumner, 260, 281
SheShark, (Hargan, Laurel), 230. *See also* Outlaw programs
ship alteration (ShipAlt), 25, 234–35. *See also* IOIC
ship's or senior intel officer (SIO), 89, 191–92, 196, 238, 243–46, 252, 270–71, 275, 290, 292. *See also* IOIC
ship's signals exploitation space SSES, (replaced SupRad), 189, 192–94, 196, 222, 235, 241–43, 245–46, 271. *See also* shipboard intelligence organization, OS division
shipboard intelligence organization: air intelligence office (before IOIC), 19, 24, 89, 90; CVIC (renaming of IOIC), 54, 179–80, 182, 187–92, 194, 215, 235–36, 240, 242–43, 245–46, 271, 301; IOIC, OP division, 82–83, 89, 188; OS division (cryptology, SSES), 186, 189–90, 192–94, 196, 222, 235, 241–46, 271, 301; OW division, 181, 356; OX division, 181, 356; OZ division (intelligence), 11, 54, 83, 89, 188, 236, 290, 301, 333; SupPlot (supplemental plot, part of OZ div), 220, 222–25, 228–29, 232–39, 242–47, 267, 269, 271, 276, 282, 284, 287, 289–90, 297, 301
Shoes, color, brown (aviation officer) or black (surface officer), 85–86; intelligence officers, 88. *See also* organizational culture, collectivism
Showers, Donald, 99, 104
signals intelligence (SIGINT), xviii, 43, 45, 48, 58, 67–71, 100, 102, 107–9, 121, 129, 135–36, 138–41, 152, 161, 163, 167–68, 171, 186, 193–96, 204, 228, 237, 278–79, 283. *See also* Shipboard intelligence organization, spaces and divisions (OS div)
signals warfare coordinator (SIWAC), 245
Sigonella, naval air station, Sicily, 125
Sihanoukville, Cambodia, 109–10, 117, 203. *See also* Sunshine Park
Sims, William, 280
single integrated operational plan (SIOP), 13, 24, 280
Sixth Fleet, Mediterranean Sea, xv, 77, 95, 138, 154–55, 159–71, 184–85, 189, 198, 245, 257, 275. *See also* FOSIF Rota
Smetlivy, RFN, xv
SNOOPIE, ship's nautical or otherwise photographic intelligence exploitation, 190. *See also* 35-mm handheld camera
Socotra, Vic. *See* Reddig, James
sonar array sensor systems, towed (SURTASS), 124
sonobuoy (SSQ-26, SSQ-35, SSQ-53) , 128, 132–33
Soriano, Joseph R., 83
sound surveillance system (SOSUS), 124, 127, 131, 134, 143–44, 146
Sourbeer, E. R., 161
South China Sea, 21, 34, 44, 115, 120
Soviet missile range instrumentation ships (SMRIS), 136–37. *See also* Pony Express
Soviet Navy; operations, descriptions of, 44, 82, 87, 117, 120, 122–5, 131–33, 135–36, 143, 146, 155, 164, 166, 181, 184, 186, 190, 196, 224, 283
Soviet Naval strategy debate, 14, 248, 250, 259–61
Soviet Union (USSR): Bloc, xi, 39, 164, 199, 206–7; equipment, military provided, 23, 36–37, 41, 43, 46, 48, 61, 136; Sino, split from, 40, 43; strategy of, xii, 1, 12, 40, 204–7, 207, 209, 248, 259

special compartmented information (SCI), 68–69, 80, 99, 102–3, 114, 134–35, 140, 142–43, 146, 160–62, 165, 175, 186, 194, 196, 198, 204–5, 215, 220, 224, 228–29, 235, 243–44
special compartmented information facility (SCIF), 102–3, 135, 205, 233
special electronic search project (SESP), 138
special intelligence (SI), 5, 6, 160, 170, 186, 222, 233
SS-N-18 Stingray submarine launch (SLBM), 120, 135
SS-N-2 Styx anti-ship cruise missile, 23, 356n33
SS-N-25, Switchblade, anti-ship cruise missile, xv
SSO, special security officer, 103, 161
SSSC, surface, subsurface surveillance coordination, 147, 182, 188–90
Stephenson, Henry, 291
stereometric comparison viewers (SCV), see also IOIC, 26–28, 58, 83–84
Strategic Air Command (SAC), Air Force, 68
Strategic Arms Limitation Talks (SALT), 136
Strategic Studies Group (SSG), 261
Studeman, William O., 257–58, 301
Submarines: operation of, 6, 109, 280; Soviet activities of, 120, 122–23, 132–33, 135, 151; tracking of, 123–29, 131–33, 135, 143, 144–46, 152, 169, 176, 181, 185–86, 225, 226, 228. See also BearTrap
Submarine Group-8, Naples, Italy, 226–27, 230. See also Outlaw program, Shark
Sunshine Park, operation, human intelligence network, 109, 338. See also TF-157
supplemental plot (SupPlot). See shipboard intelligence organization
supplemental radio (SupRad), replaced by SSES, 189

Surface Forces Atlantic (SURFLANT), 214–15
surface-to-air Firing (SAFIRE), 57
surface-to-Air-Missiles (SAM), 23, 30–31, 37–39, 41–42, 45–46, 47–48, 51, 55, 57–58, 62, 69, 73, 113. See also SA-2
Surface Warfare Officer (SWO): creation of 243–44. See also cruiser-destroyer group
Swartz, Peter M., 199–200, 259

tactical action officer (TAO), 187, 234, 246. See also CWC
tactical air control center-north sector (TACC-NS), 69
tactical analysis plot (TAP), early-SupPlot, 235–38, 244–46
tactical automated mission planning system (TAMPS), 241
tactical coordinator (TACCO), 117, 126, 128, 131–32, 135, 140
tactical data information exchange system-broadcast (TADIXS-B), 231
tactical exploitation of national capabilities (TENCAP), 42, 44–45, 48–50, 59–60, 67–68, 71, 136. See also IADS
tactical intelligence broadcast (TACINTEL), 228, 246
tactical receive equipment (TRE) and related applications (TRAP) broadcasts, 231. See also Outlaw projects, Shark
tactical support center (TSC), 129, 131–33, 135, 146, 150. See maritime patrol and reconnaissance forces
TADIXS, tactical data information exchange subsystem datalink, 231–32. See also Outlaw project
talent keyhole (TK) imagery, 162
talent management, 64, 250–53, 256–58, 260, 281, 300. See also Inman
Taylor, Rufus, 99, 104, 387n2
Teamwork, NATO exercise, 212, 282

technical intelligence (TECINT), 27, 42, 44–45, 48–50, 59–60, 67–68, 71, 136. *See also* SA-2

Technical Intelligence Center (TIC), ONI, 48. *See also* TECINT

TENCAP, tactical exploitation of national capabilities, 199, 350n29. *See also* OSIS

Terlizzi, Thomas P., 235, 238, 242

Tet Offensive (Vietnam war), 100, 118

TF 157, Naval Field Operations Support Group (NFOSG), 105, 108–9, 163–64. *See also* Sunshine Park.

TFCC, tactical flag command center (shipboard), 219–20, 222, 224–25, 228, 2332–5, 242, 247, 282. *See also* shipboard intelligence organization, SupPlot

Thanh Hoa bridge, Vietnam, 37, 61–62, 71, 74–77, 79. *See also* Richardson, David C.

Thatcher, Margaret, Prime Minister, 205, 362, 451

Theater Strategic Operations (TSO), Soviet military strategy, 205–6, 362n9

Thompson, Dale, P., 131–35, 141–43, 145–46, 149. *See also* VP-50

Tolle, Robert J., xix, 22, 159–60, 349, 350, 351, 352, 391

Tomahawk cruise missile: anti-ship (TASCM/TASM), 22–21, 209, 220, 222, 225, 231, 241 (*see also* Outlaw project (Shark)); land attack missile (BGM-109), 241

Tonkli, Mario, 56, 92, 195

TopGun (Top Gun), strike fighter weapons school, 64. *See also* Ault report

Training Command, Atlantic Fleet (TraLant), 81

Trawler, used by DRV weapons smuggling, 99–100, 118–19. *See also* four trawler incident

TU-16 Badger, 185, 283

TU-22 Backfire, 283

TU-95/TU-142 Bear, 184, 185, 191–92, 196–97, 201, 223–24, 238, 357. *See also* LRA

Tuthill, Don CDR, USN, 103

Tuttle, Jerry O., 232, 234, 242. *See also* JOTS

"two squares of linoleum," concept, 210–11, 225, 232, 234. *See also* Brooks

U.S. Air Force Intelligence Officer, 14Nx, 278–79

U.S. and U.S.S.R. Prevention of Incidents on the High Seas (INCSEA) agreement, 122–23

U.S. Navy Bureau of Personnel BuPers), 251, 257

U-2 Dragon Lady, 37, 40

United Kingdom (UK), 207

USQ-81(V), computer, part of Common Weapons Control System (CWCS), 228, 231. *See also* Outlaw programs, Shark

U-Tapao, Thailand, Royal Thai Airbase, 117

Utz, Curtis (History of the Office of the Chief of Naval Operations), xvii

VA, fixed wing, attack squadron, Navy, 73, 75

Valley Forge, 2

Vego, Milan N., Professor, 78, 122, 272, 295

Versamat film processing (Kodak). 51–52, *See also* IOIC

VF, fixed wing, fighter squadron, Navy, 33, 64, 93, 128

Vice-Chief of Naval Operations (VCNO), 34, 217, 251

Viet Cong (National Liberation Front of South Vietnam), Vietnam war, 71–72, 96–97, 99–100, 105, 109, 111–12, 114, 118–19, 152

Vietnam War: causes of 13, 34–35; escalation of, 13, 33, 35–36, 60; China,

involvement in, 36, 40, 42–43; Soviet involvement in, 40–42, 44. *See also* GRU
Vietnam, Republic of: Navy of (VNN), 99, 119; as South Vietnam, 43, 69, 96–97, 102, 105, 116–17, 121. *See also* Vietnam war
Vinson, John E., 112–13. *See also* NILO
Visual Observation (VISOB) posts, 39, 44. *See also* IADS
Vladivostok, Russia, 132
VP, fixed wing, patrol squadron (MPRA): creation of, 116, 118–20; VP-5 Mad Foxes, 125–26; VP-50, Blue Dragons, 118–19, 128, 131, 134, 137, 141–43, 145–47, 149–51
VQ, fixed wing, reconnaissance (SIGINT) squadron (MPRA): VQ-1 World Watchers, 68, 132, 139–40, 144; VQ-2 Sandeman, 138, 142, 149, 163, 165

Wang Laboratories word processor, 169, 353n353. *See also* FOSIF Rota
Warrington, 165
warrior vs engineer debate, 10–11, 276, 302
Warsaw Pact (Treaty of Friendship, Cooperation and Mutual Assistance), 212, 227, 247, 285
Watkins, James, 257, 261
Weisner, Maurice, 249, 251–52, 375n3. *See also* Inman
Wessman, Lynn G., 225–26, 228, 230. *See also* Outlaw programs
White, Robert, 114. *See also* Graff, John
Whyte, William H. (*Organizational Man*), 173–75
Wild Weasel, operations, 45–47, 321n11. *See also* SA-2
Willoz, Clifford P., 213–14. *See also* ECLIPS
Wimex. *See* Worldwide Military Command and Control System
Wilson, Thomas R., 88, 124
Winkler, David (*Cold War at Sea*), xix, 122
Women Accepted for Volunteer Emergency Service (WAVES), 148
Wong, Leonard (Culture and Military Organizations), 8, 89
Wood, Sidney, 140. *See also* VQ-1
Worldwide Military Command and Control System (WWMCCS), 216, 218–19, 368
Wylie, J. C., 8, 122

Yankee Station (Vietnam war), 55, 73, 96
Yeoman (YN), 2, 168, 194–95, 236

Z-Grams, 147. *See also* Zumwalt
Zumwalt, Elmo R., Jr., 107, 147, 180, 214, 216–17, 244, 260, 293
Zaps (zapping), 178–79. *See also* organizational culture, collectivism

ABOUT THE AUTHOR

CAPT. BRYAN H. LEESE, USN (RET.) was a career naval intelligence officer with extensive experience in operational intelligence, including key roles supporting ground-combat operations and tours at sea, including as the (head of intelligence) of the *Bataan* Amphibious Ready Group and the *George H. W. Bush* Carrier Strike Group.. He has held senior positions across the intelligence community, most notably as Chair, Defense Intelligence Department at the National Intelligence University, and as Branch Chief, Transregional and then North/West Africa in J2 (Joint Intelligence) Africa Command, during the 2011 crisis in Libya. Before joining the Joint Forces Staff College in September 2023, Dr. Leese served on the faculty of the U.S. Naval War College's Joint Military Operations Department. He holds a PhD in war studies from King's College London and lives in Chesapeake, Virginia, with his wife, Elizabeth.

THE NAVAL INSTITUTE PRESS is the book-publishing arm of the U.S. Naval Institute, a private, nonprofit, membership society for sea service professionals and others who share an interest in naval and maritime affairs. Established in 1873 at the U.S. Naval Academy in Annapolis, Maryland, where its offices remain today, the Naval Institute has members worldwide.

Members of the Naval Institute support the education programs of the society and receive the influential monthly magazine *Proceedings* or the colorful bimonthly magazine *Naval History* and discounts on fine nautical prints and on ship and aircraft photos. They also have access to the transcripts of the Institute's Oral History Program and get discounted admission to any of the Institute-sponsored seminars offered around the country.

The Naval Institute's book-publishing program, begun in 1898 with basic guides to naval practices, has broadened its scope to include books of more general interest. Now the Naval Institute Press publishes about seventy titles each year, ranging from how-to books on boating and navigation to battle histories, biographies, ship and aircraft guides, and novels. Institute members receive significant discounts on the Press' more than eight hundred books in print.

Full-time students are eligible for special half-price membership rates. Life memberships are also available.

For more information about Naval Institute Press books that are currently available, visit www.usni.org/press/books. To learn about joining the U.S. Naval Institute, please write to:

Member Services
U.S. NAVAL INSTITUTE
291 Wood Road
Annapolis, MD 21402-5034
Telephone: (800) 233-8764
Fax: (410) 571-1703
Web address: www.usni.org